TOKYO GHOUL:re

This is the last page.
TOKYO GHOUL:re reads right to left.

CHILDREN OF THE WHALES

In this postapocalyptic fantasy, a sea of sand swallows everything but the past.

In an endless sea of sand drifts the Mud Whale, a floating island city of clay and magic. In its chambers a small community clings to survival, cut off from its own history by the shadows of the past.

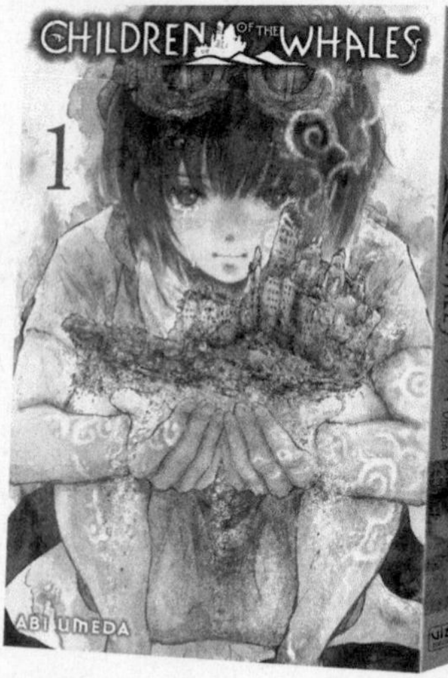
CHILDREN OF THE WHALES
1
ABI UMEDA

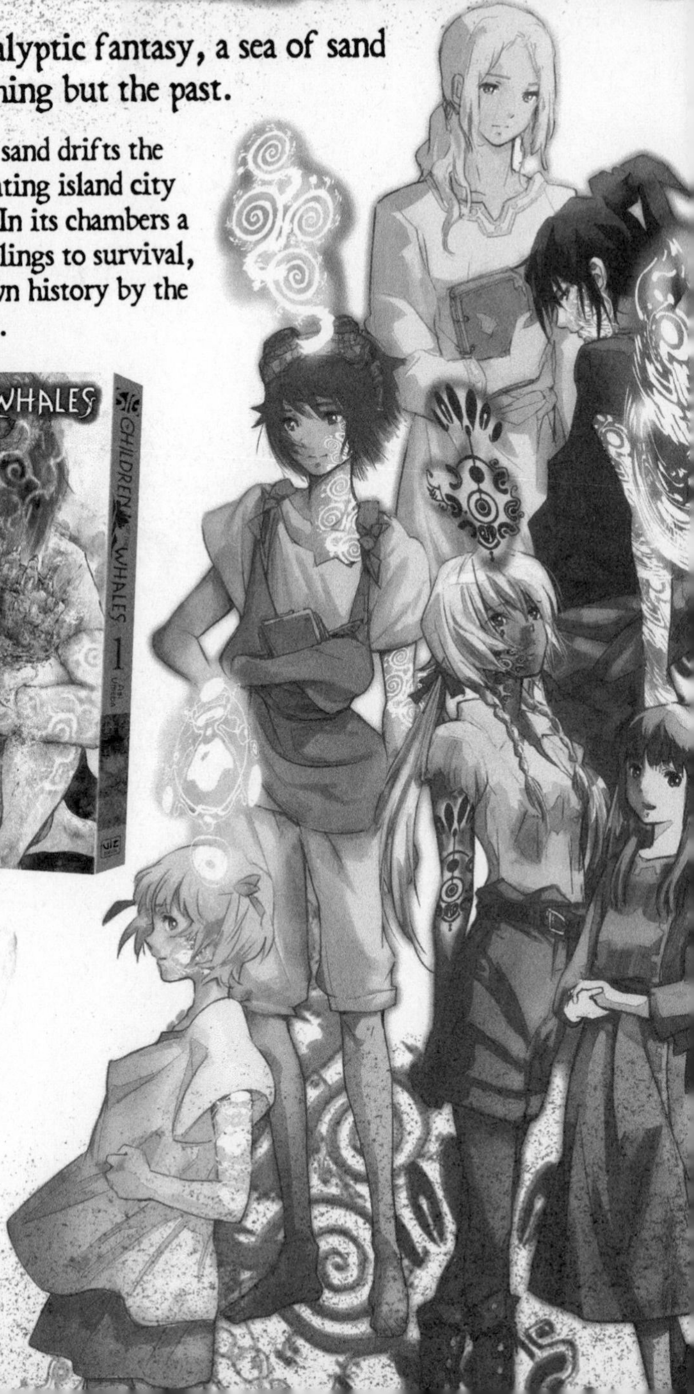

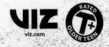

en me the last time any book disturbed you. When you give up, buy Uzumaki.
– Warren Ellis

UZUMAKI

Story and Art by **JUNJI ITO**

SPIRALS... THIS TOWN IS CONTAMINATED WITH SPIRALS...

Kurouzu-cho, a small fogbound town on the coast of Japan, is cursed. According to Shuichi Saito, the withdrawn boyfriend of teenager Kirie Goshima, their town is haunted not by a person or being but by a pattern: uzumaki, the spiral, the hypnotic secret shape of the world. It manifests itself in everything from seashells and whirlpools in water to the spiral marks on people's bodies, the insane obsessions of Shuichi's father and the voice from the cochlea in our inner ear. As the madness spreads, the inhabitants of Kurouzu-cho are pulled ever deeper into a whirlpool from which there is no return!

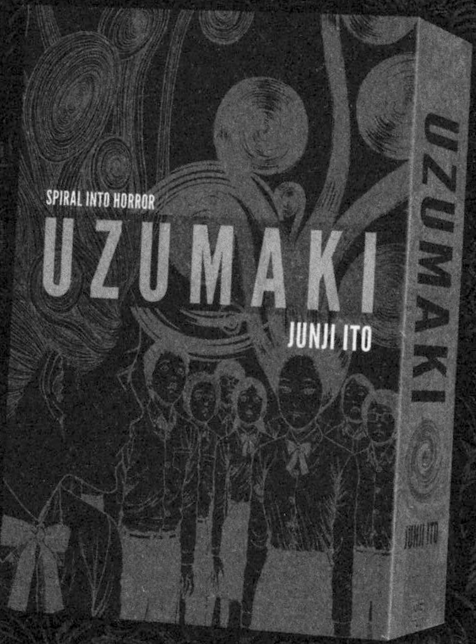

SPIRAL INTO HORROR
UZUMAKI
JUNJI ITO

UZUMAKI
JUNJI ITO

A masterpiece of horror manga, now available in a DELUXE HARDCOVER EDITION!

VIZ SIGNATURE

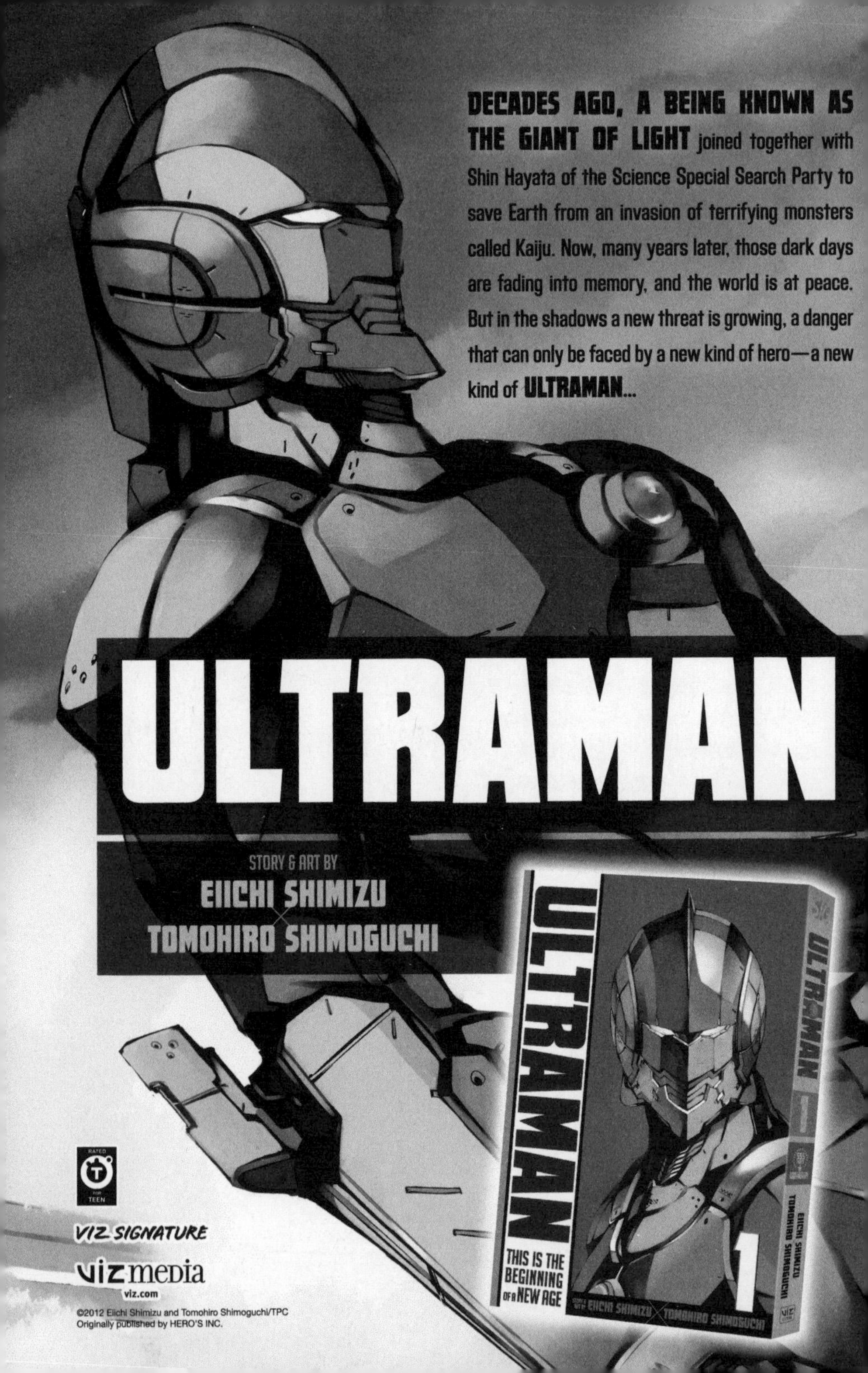
DECADES AGO, A BEING KNOWN AS THE GIANT OF LIGHT joined together with Shin Hayata of the Science Special Search Party to save Earth from an invasion of terrifying monsters called Kaiju. Now, many years later, those dark days are fading into memory, and the world is at peace. But in the shadows a new threat is growing, a danger that can only be faced by a new kind of hero—a new kind of ULTRAMAN...
ULTRAMAN
STORY & ART BY
EIICHI SHIMIZU × TOMOHIRO SHIMOGUCHI
ULTRAMAN
THIS IS THE BEGINNING OF A NEW AGE
1
RATED T FOR TEEN
VIZ SIGNATURE
viz media
viz.com
©2012 Eiichi Shimizu and Tomohiro Shimoguchi/TPC
Originally published by HERO'S INC.

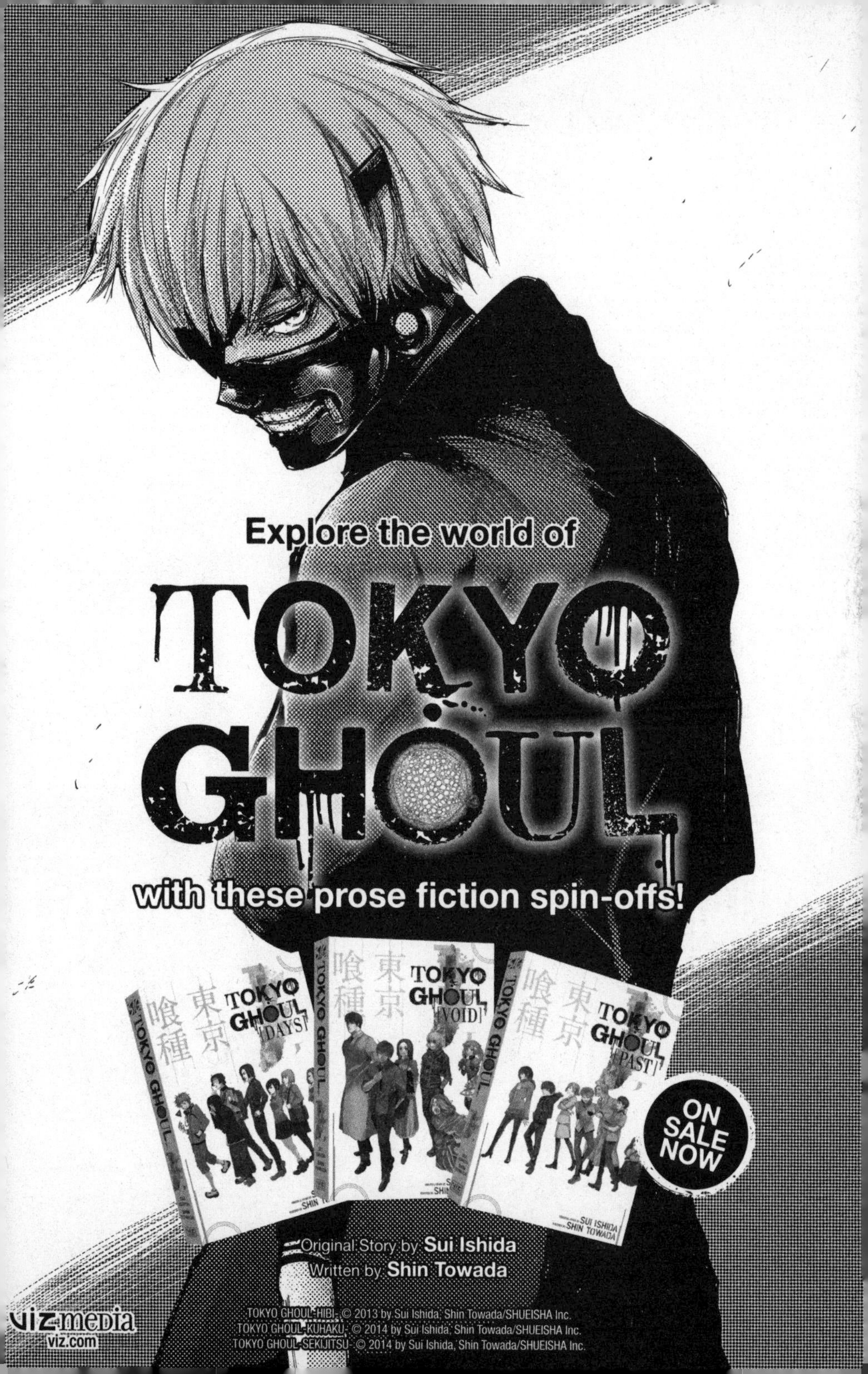
Explore the world of
TOKYO GHOUL
with these prose fiction spin-offs!
TOKYO GHOUL [DAYS]
TOKYO GHOUL [VOID]
TOKYO GHOUL [PAST]
ON SALE NOW
Original Story by Sui Ishida
Written by Shin Towada
viz media
viz.com
TOKYO GHOUL-HIBI- © 2013 by Sui Ishida, Shin Towada/SHUEISHA Inc.
TOKYO GHOUL-KUHAKU- © 2014 by Sui Ishida, Shin Towada/SHUEISHA Inc.
TOKYO GHOUL-SEKIJITSU- © 2014 by Sui Ishida, Shin Towada/SHUEISHA Inc.

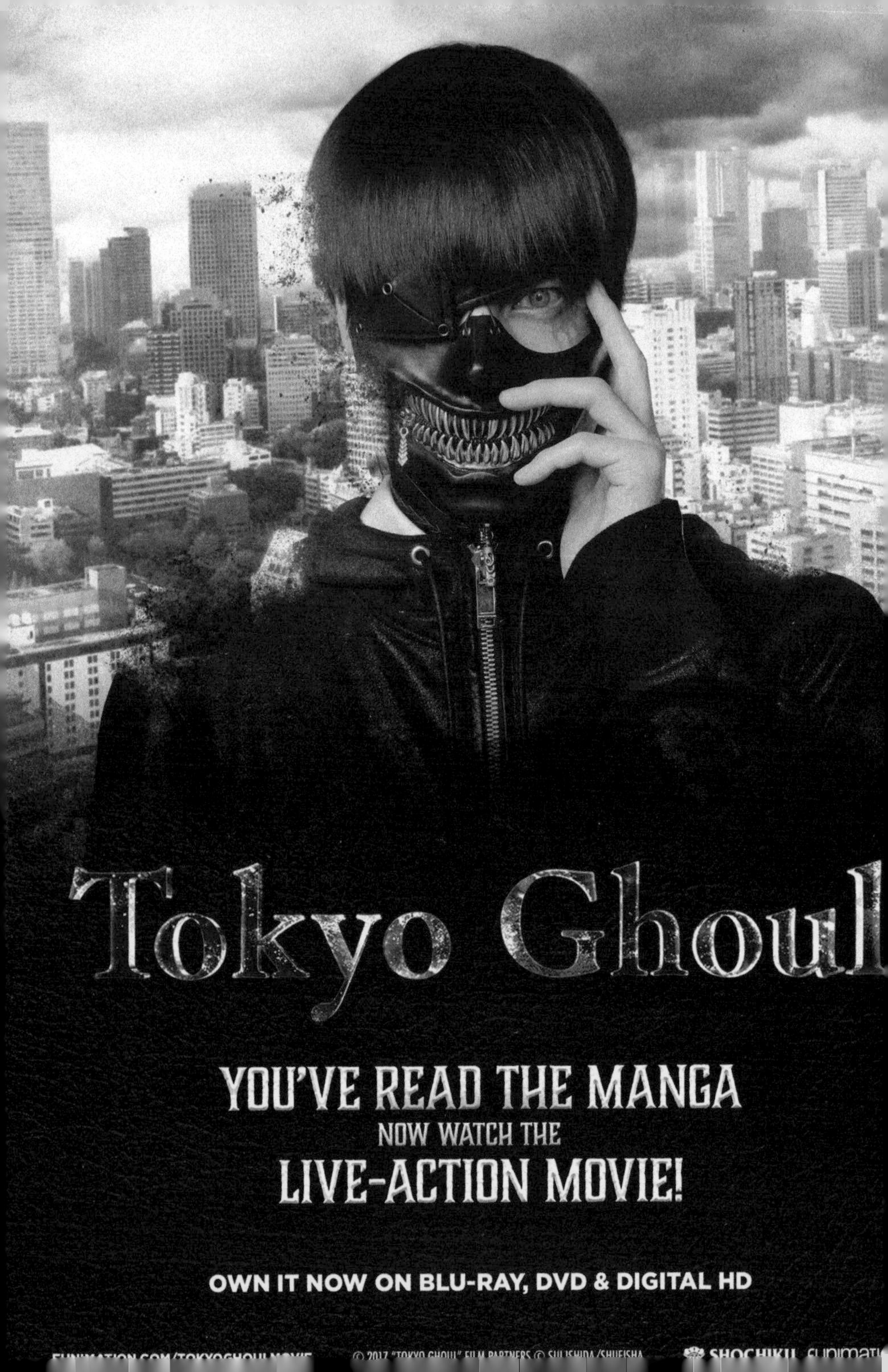
Tokyo Ghoul
YOU'VE READ THE MANGA
NOW WATCH THE
LIVE-ACTION MOVIE!
OWN IT NOW ON BLU-RAY, DVD & DIGITAL HD

CCG Ghoul Investigators

Tokyo Ghoul :re

The CCG is the only organization in the world that investigates and solves Ghoul-related crimes. Founded by the Washu Family, the CCG developed and evolved Quinques, a type of weapon derived from Ghouls' Kagune. Quinx, an advanced, next-generation technology where humans are implanted with Quinques, is currently under development.

Mado Squad

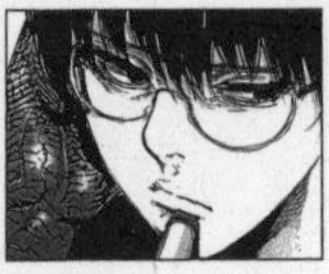

● Haise Sasaki
佐々木琲世

Assistant Special Investigator
Investigating the Aogiri Tree with Furuta after resigning from his duty as mentor of the Qs Squad. Still subject to criticism in the CCG for being a half-Ghoul.

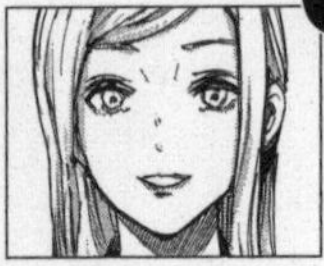

● Akira Mado
真戸 暁

Assistant Special Investigator
Mentors Haise. Takes after her father. Determined to eradicate Ghouls. Investigating the Aogiri Tree. Concerned about Fueguchi.

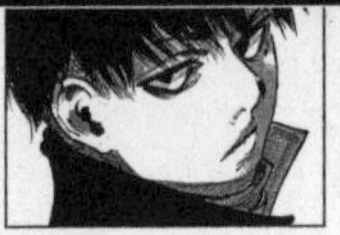

● Kuki Urie
瓜江久生

Rank 1 Investigator
Former Quinx Squad Leader. The most talented fighter in the squad. His father, a special investigator, was killed by a Ghoul. Urie seeks to avenge his death. Demonstrating leadership after the death of Shirazu Ginshi.

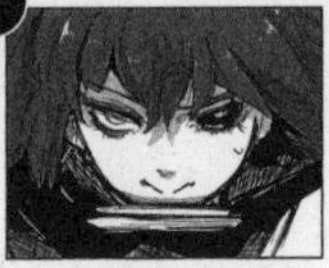

● Saiko Yonebayashi
米林才子

Rank 2 Investigator
Supporting Urie as deputy squad leader while playing with her subordinates. By far the most suitable Quinx Procedure candidate, but very bad at time management and a sucker for games and snacks.

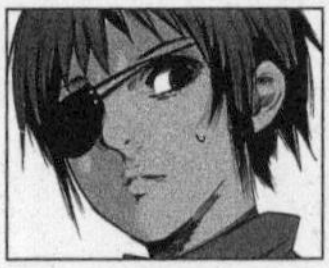

● Toru Mutsuki
六月 透

Rank 1 Investigator
Both parents were killed by a Ghoul and he decided to become a Ghoul investigator. Assigned female at birth, he transitioned after the Quinx procedure. Skilled with knives. Providing support for various squads.

Qs (Quinx): Investigators implanted with Quinques. They all live together in a house called the Chateau under Urie's new mentorship.

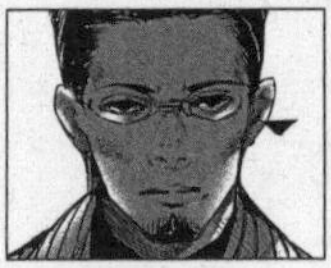

● Matsuri Washu
和修 政

Special Investitgator
Yoshitoki's son. A Washu supremacist and skeptical of the Quinxes. Brought down the Rosewald family in Germany.

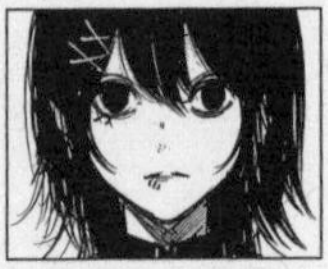

● Juzo Suzuya
鈴屋什造

Special Investigator
Promoted to special investigator at 22, a feat previously only accomplished by Kisho Arima. A maverick who fights with knives hidden in his prosthetic leg.

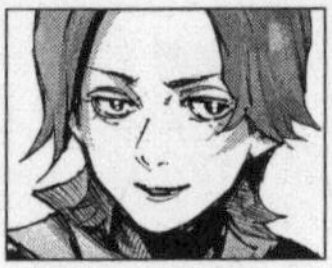

● Toma Higemaru
髯丸トウマ

Rank 3 Investigator
Discovered his Quinx aptitude before enrolling in the academy. Looks up to Urie. Comes from a wealthy family.

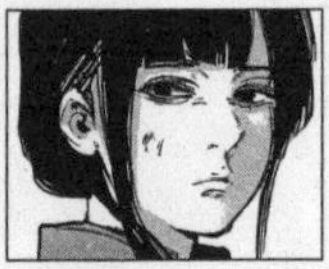

● Ching-li Hsiao
小静麗

Rank 1 Investigator
From Hakubi Garden like Hairu Ihei. Skilled in hand-to-hand combat. Came to Japan from Taiwan as a child.

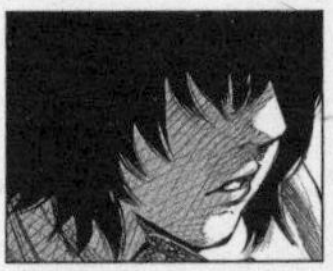

● Shinsanpei Aura
安浦晋三平

Rank 2 Investigator
Nephew of Special Investigator Kiyoko Aura. Unlike his aunt, who graduated at the top of her class, his grades were not great.

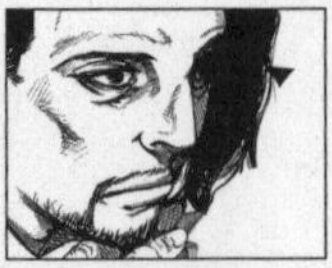

● Yoshitoki Washu
和修吉時

CCG Bureau Chief
Supervisor of the Quinx project. A member of the CCG's founding family, but he still has an approachable side.

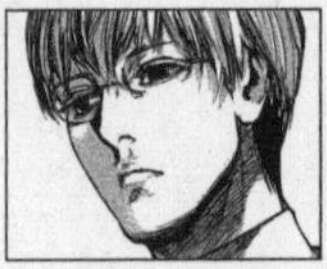

● Kisho Arima
有馬貴将

Special Investigator
An undefeated investigator respected by many at the CCG.

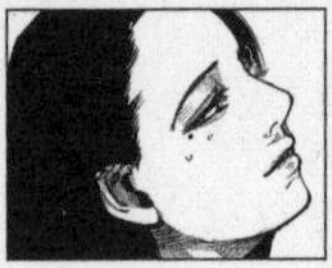

● Nimura Furuta
旧多二福

Rank 1 Investigator
Former subordinate of the late Shiki Kijima. Has many secrets.

Mysterious Organization V

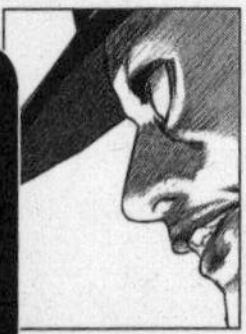

● Kaiko
芥子

Unknown

Tokyo Ghoul :re

T ● K Y ● G H ● U L

Tokyo Ghoul :re ● Ghouls

They appear human, but have a unique predation organ called Kagune and can only survive by feeding on human flesh. They are the nemesis of humanity. Besides human flesh, the only other thing they can ingest is coffee. Ghouls can only be wounded by a Kagune or a Quinque made from a Kagune. One of the most prominent Ghoul factions is the Aogiri Tree, a hostile organization that is increasing its strength.

The Aogiri Tree

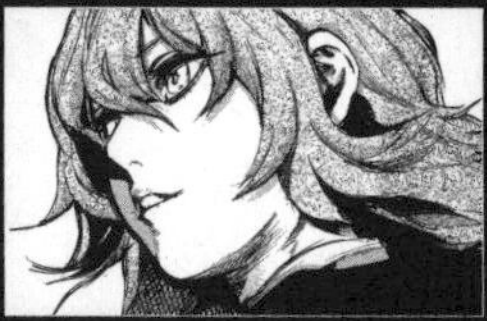

Eto/Sen Takatsuki
エト／高槻泉
Founder of the Aogiri Tree. Also a reknown author with many fans. Revealed herself as a Ghoul after announcing her final novel.

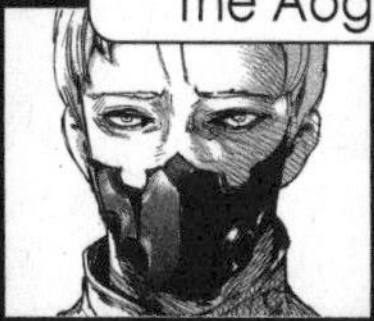

Tatara
タタラ
A leading member of the Aogiri Tree. Related to the former head of the Chi Shé Lián. A Chinese Ghoul.

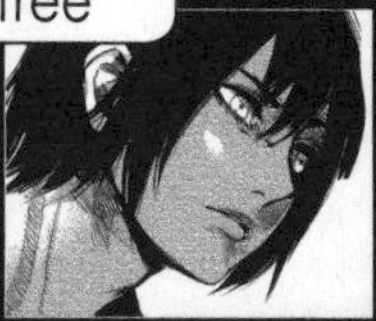

Ayato
アヤト
A leading member of the Aogiri Tree. A Rate SS Ghoul known as the Rabbit.

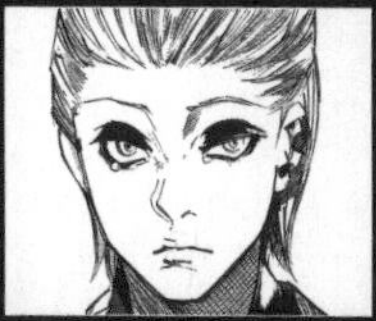

Naki
ナキ
Member of the Aogiri Tree. Current leader of the White Suits. A Rate S, but frequently loses control.

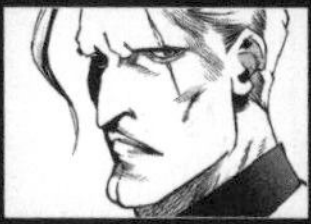

Shosei
承正
Member of the Aogiri Tree and the White Suits. Joined after being beaten by Naki during Jason's leadership.

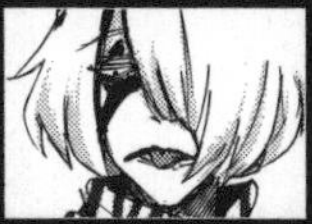

Hohguro
ホオグロ
Member of the Aogiri Tree and the White Suits. Joined after tying with Shosei.

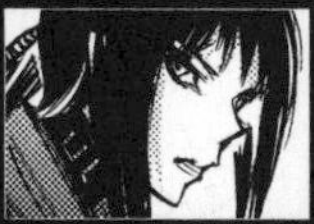

The Grave Robber
墓盗り
Member of the Aogiri Tree. Protégé of the Bin Brothers. Somehow has experience using a Quinque.

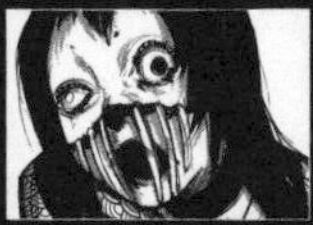

Shikorae
死堪
Member of the Aogiri Tree. Was detained in Cochlea, but escaped after the Aogiri assault on the complex.

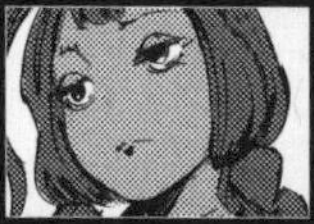

Miza
ミザ
Member of the Aogiri Tree. Controlled the 18th Ward as the head of the Blades. A.K.A. Triple Blade.

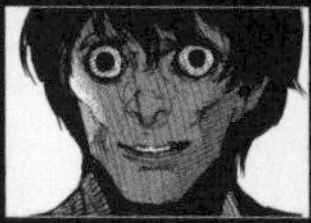

Torso (Karao Saeki)
トルソー(冴木空男)
Abused his position as a taxi driver to prey on women with scars. Obsessed with Toru Mutsuki.

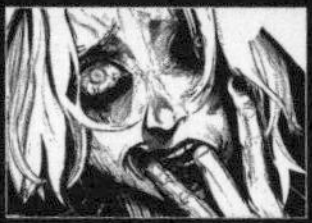

The Owl
オウル
The current incarnation of Ghoul Investigator Seido Takizawa after Professor Kano implanted him with a Kakuho. Overwhelmingly powerful.

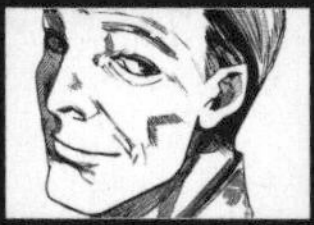

Professor Kano
嘉納教授
Medical examiner for the Aogiri Tree. Researching transplanting Kakuho into humans to create artificial half-Ghouls.

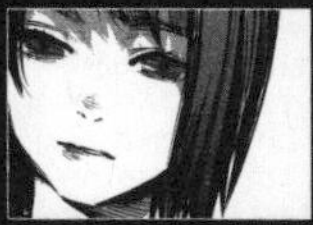

Hinami Fueguchi
フエグチヒナミ
Member of the Aogiri Tree. Captured by Haise Sasaki during Operation Auction Sweep and sent to Cochlea. Awaiting disposal.

Café:re

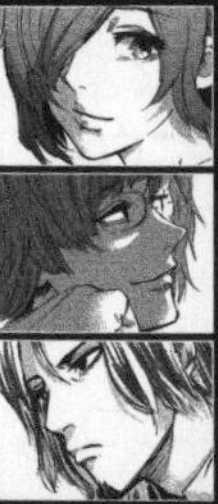

So far in :re

T ● K Y ● G H ● U L

The Quinx Project was implemented to develop investigators to surpass Kisho Arima in order to combat the growing strength of Ghoul organizations. Haise Sasaki and the four Qs who fight using Ghoul abilities were recognized for their role in the Tsukiyama family eradication operation and assigned to individual cases. The CCG discovered the Aogiri's stronghold, Rushima. Meanwhile, Haise discovered that the novelist Sen Takatsuki was the One-Eyed Owl after singlehandedly defeating her, and began questioning her editor, Shiono. At the same time, Sen Takatsuki revealed that she was a Ghoul during the press conference for her final novel. The rift between humans, Ghouls and the CCG grows ever deeper...

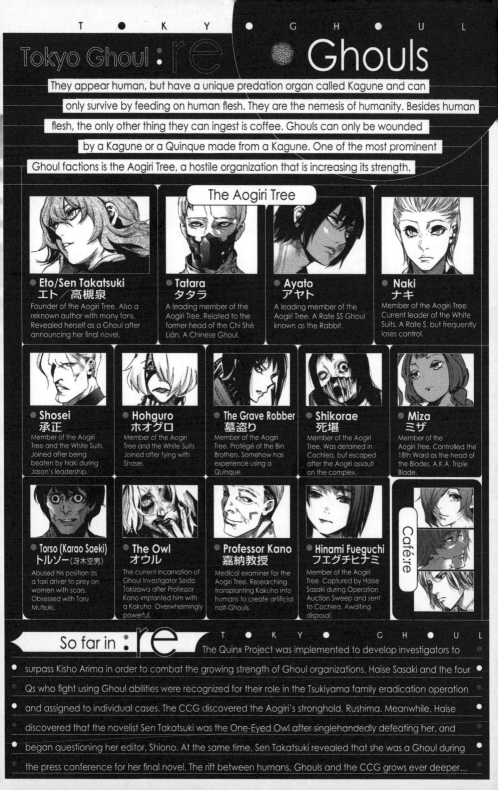

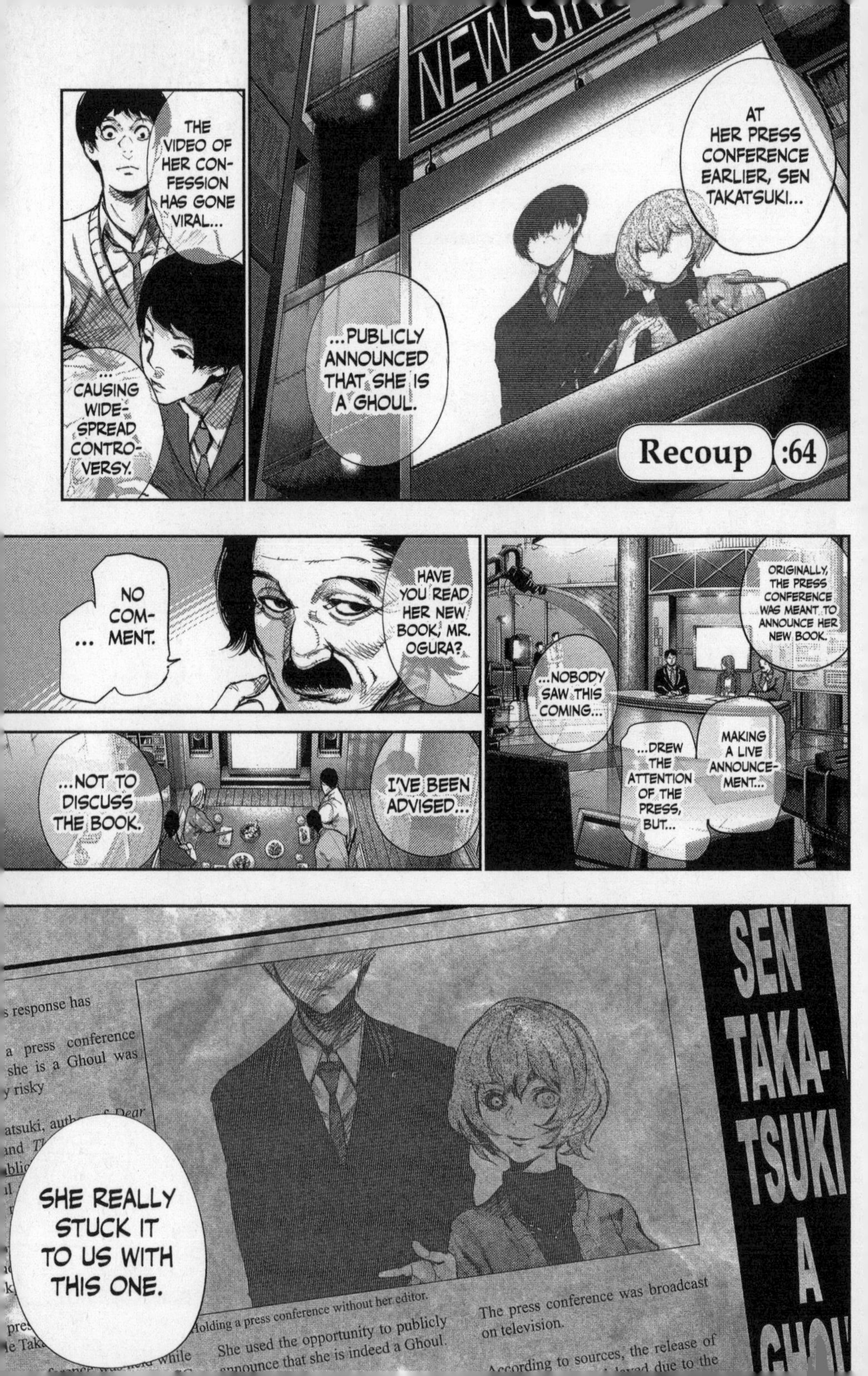

NEW
AT HER PRESS CONFERENCE EARLIER, SEN TAKATSUKI...
...PUBLICLY ANNOUNCED THAT SHE IS A GHOUL.
Recoup :64
THE VIDEO OF HER CONFESSION HAS GONE VIRAL...
...CAUSING WIDESPREAD CONTROVERSY.
ORIGINALLY, THE PRESS CONFERENCE WAS MEANT TO ANNOUNCE HER NEW BOOK.
MAKING A LIVE ANNOUNCEMENT...
...DREW THE ATTENTION OF THE PRESS, BUT...
...NOBODY SAW THIS COMING...
HAVE YOU READ HER NEW BOOK, MR. OGURA?
... NO COMMENT.
I'VE BEEN ADVISED...
...NOT TO DISCUSS THE BOOK.
SEN TAKA-TSUKI A
Holding a press conference without her editor.
She used the opportunity to publicly announce that she is indeed a Ghoul.
The press conference was broadcast on television.
SHE REALLY STUCK IT TO US WITH THIS ONE.

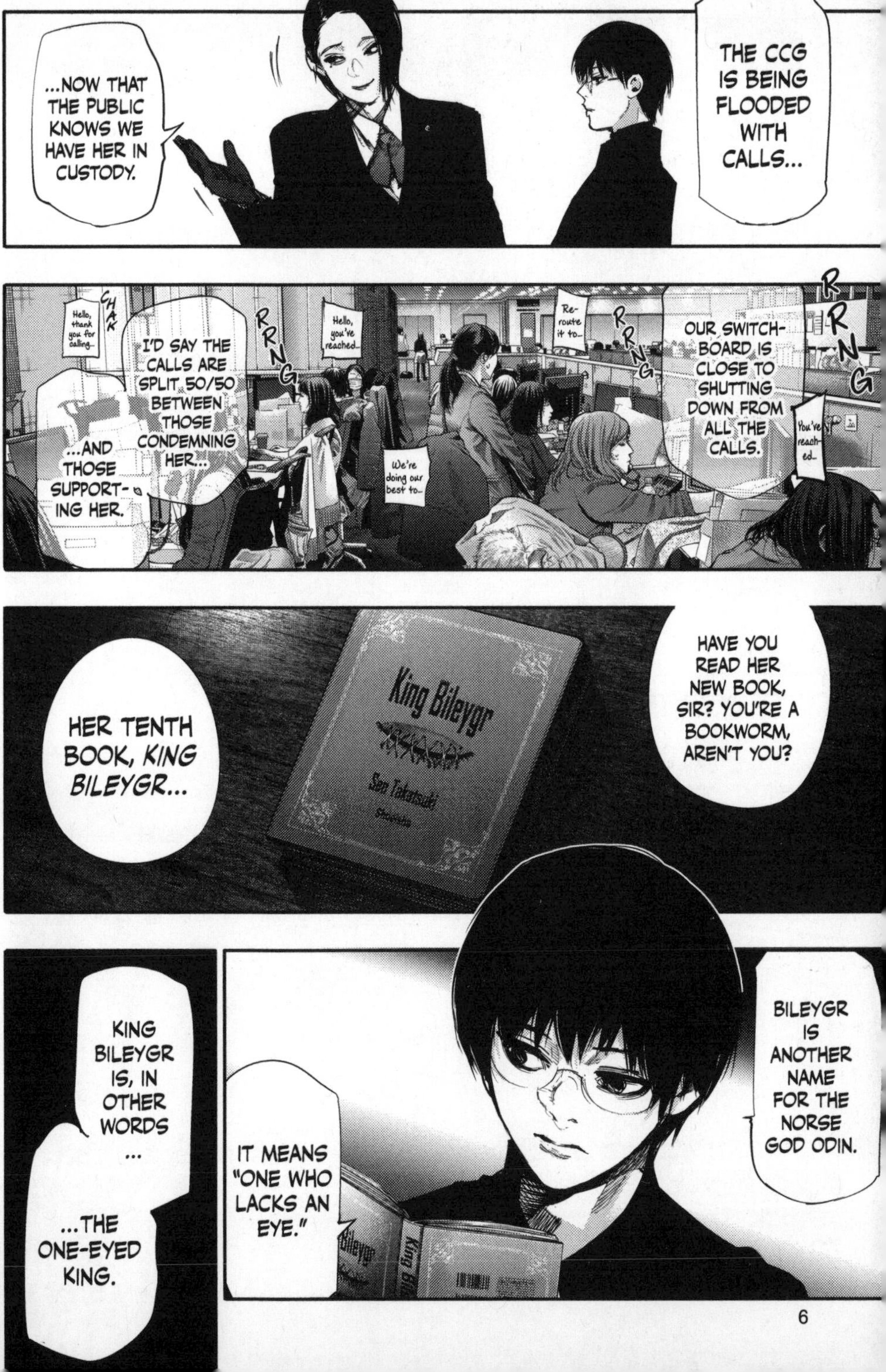
THE CCG IS BEING FLOODED WITH CALLS...
...NOW THAT THE PUBLIC KNOWS WE HAVE HER IN CUSTODY.
RRNG
OUR SWITCH-BOARD IS CLOSE TO SHUTTING DOWN FROM ALL THE CALLS.
You've reach-ed...
RRNG
Re-route it to...
We're doing our best to...
RRNG
Hello, you've reached...
I'D SAY THE CALLS ARE SPLIT 50/50 BETWEEN THOSE CONDEMNING HER...
...AND THOSE SUPPORT-ING HER.
Hello, thank you for calling...
CHAK
HAVE YOU READ HER NEW BOOK, SIR? YOU'RE A BOOKWORM, AREN'T YOU?
King Bileygr
Sen Takatsuki
HER TENTH BOOK, *KING BILEYGR*...
BILEYGR IS ANOTHER NAME FOR THE NORSE GOD ODIN.
IT MEANS "ONE WHO LACKS AN EYE."
KING BILEYGR IS, IN OTHER WORDS ...
...THE ONE-EYED KING.

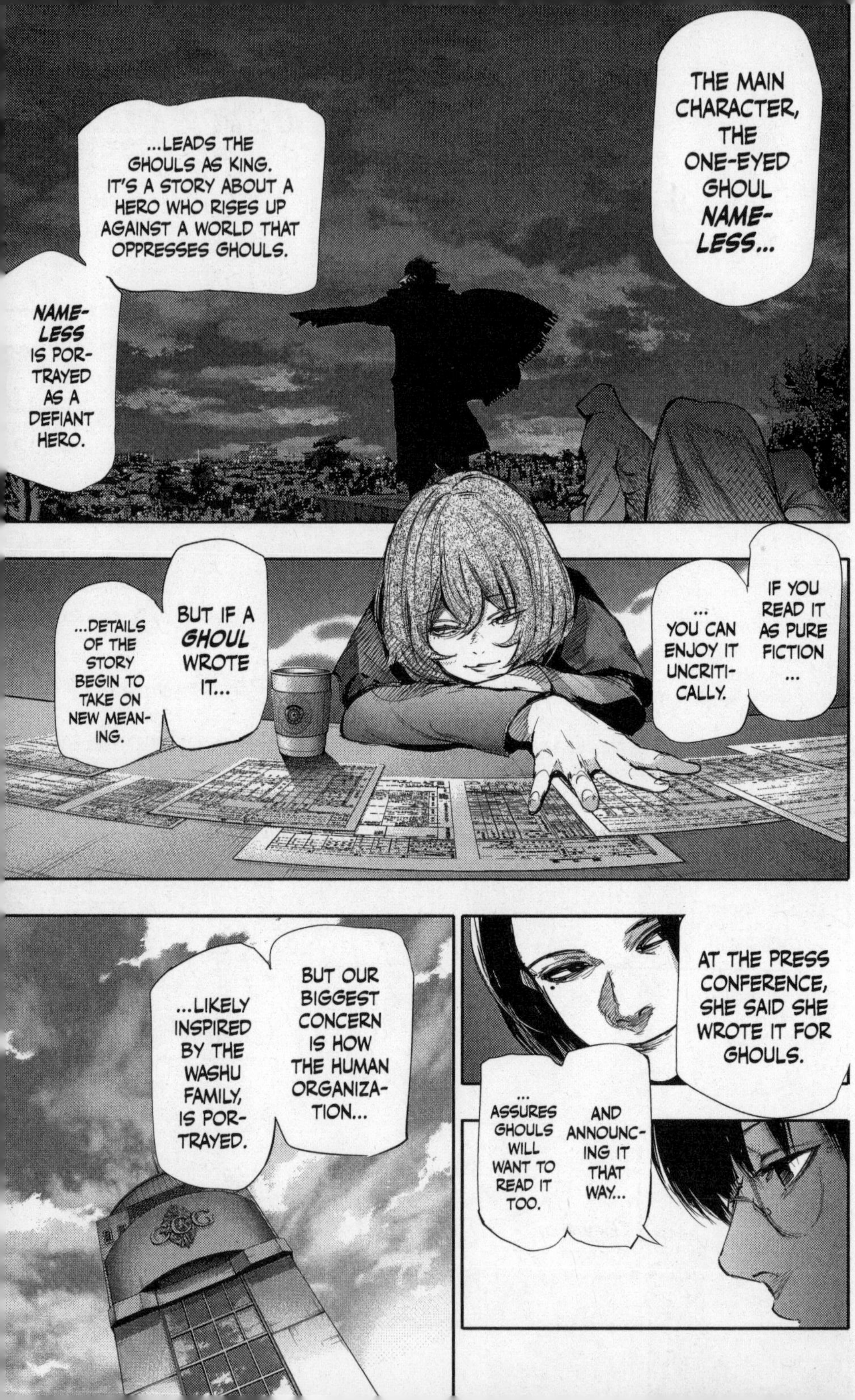
THE MAIN CHARACTER, THE ONE-EYED GHOUL *NAMELESS*...
...LEADS THE GHOULS AS KING. IT'S A STORY ABOUT A HERO WHO RISES UP AGAINST A WORLD THAT OPPRESSES GHOULS.
NAMELESS IS PORTRAYED AS A DEFIANT HERO.
IF YOU READ IT AS PURE FICTION...
...YOU CAN ENJOY IT UNCRITICALLY.
BUT IF A *GHOUL* WROTE IT...
...DETAILS OF THE STORY BEGIN TO TAKE ON NEW MEANING.
AT THE PRESS CONFERENCE, SHE SAID SHE WROTE IT FOR GHOULS.
AND ANNOUNCING IT THAT WAY...
...ASSURES GHOULS WILL WANT TO READ IT TOO.
BUT OUR BIGGEST CONCERN IS HOW THE HUMAN ORGANIZATION...
...LIKELY INSPIRED BY THE WASHU FAMILY, IS PORTRAYED.
CCG

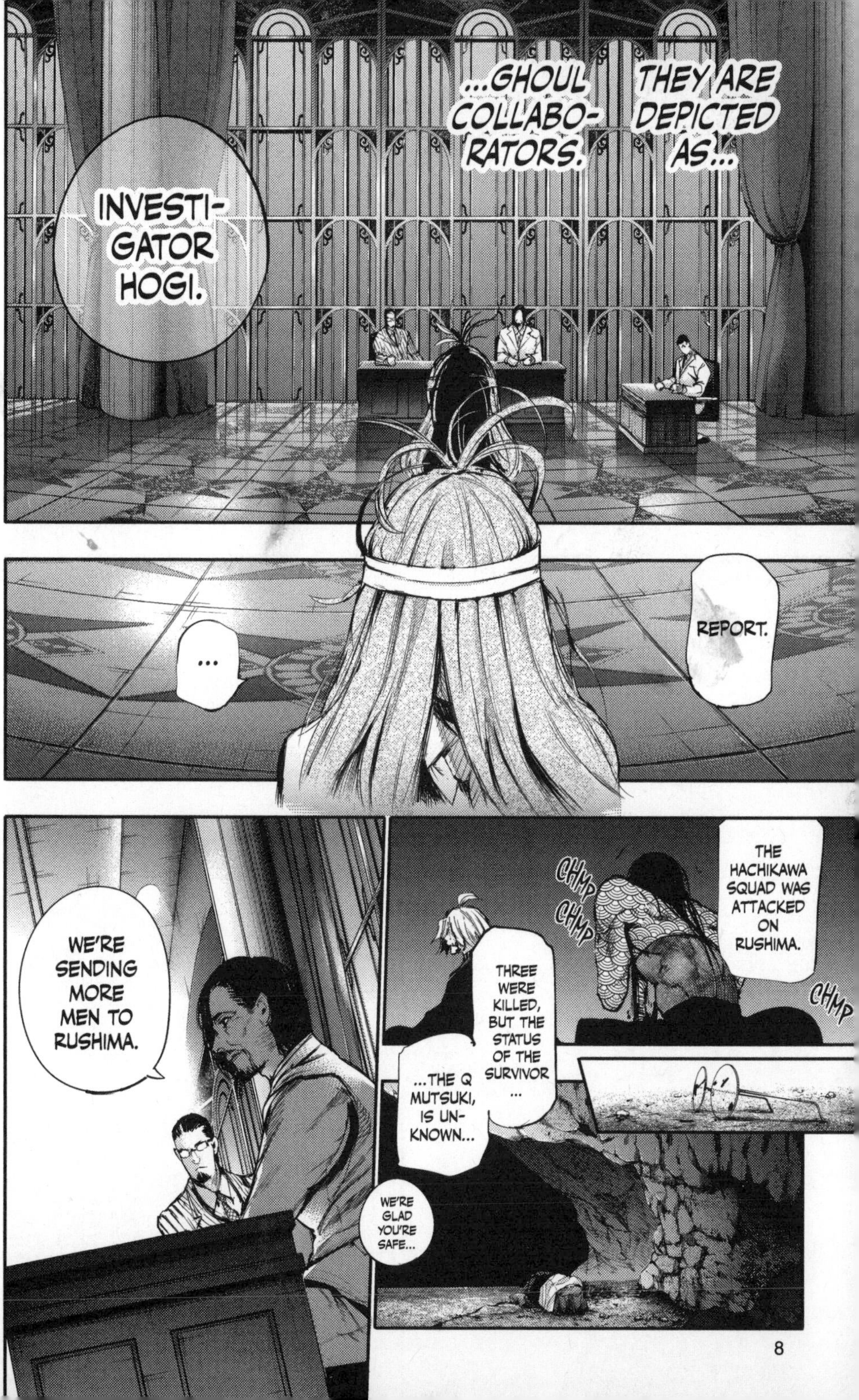
THEY ARE DEPICTED AS...
...GHOUL COLLABO-RATORS.
INVESTI-GATOR HOGI.
REPORT.
...
THE HACHIKAWA SQUAD WAS ATTACKED ON RUSHIMA.
CHMP
CHMP
CHMP
THREE WERE KILLED, BUT THE STATUS OF THE SURVIVOR ...
...THE Q MUTSUKI, IS UN-KNOWN...
WE'RE GLAD YOU'RE SAFE...
WE'RE SENDING MORE MEN TO RUSHIMA.

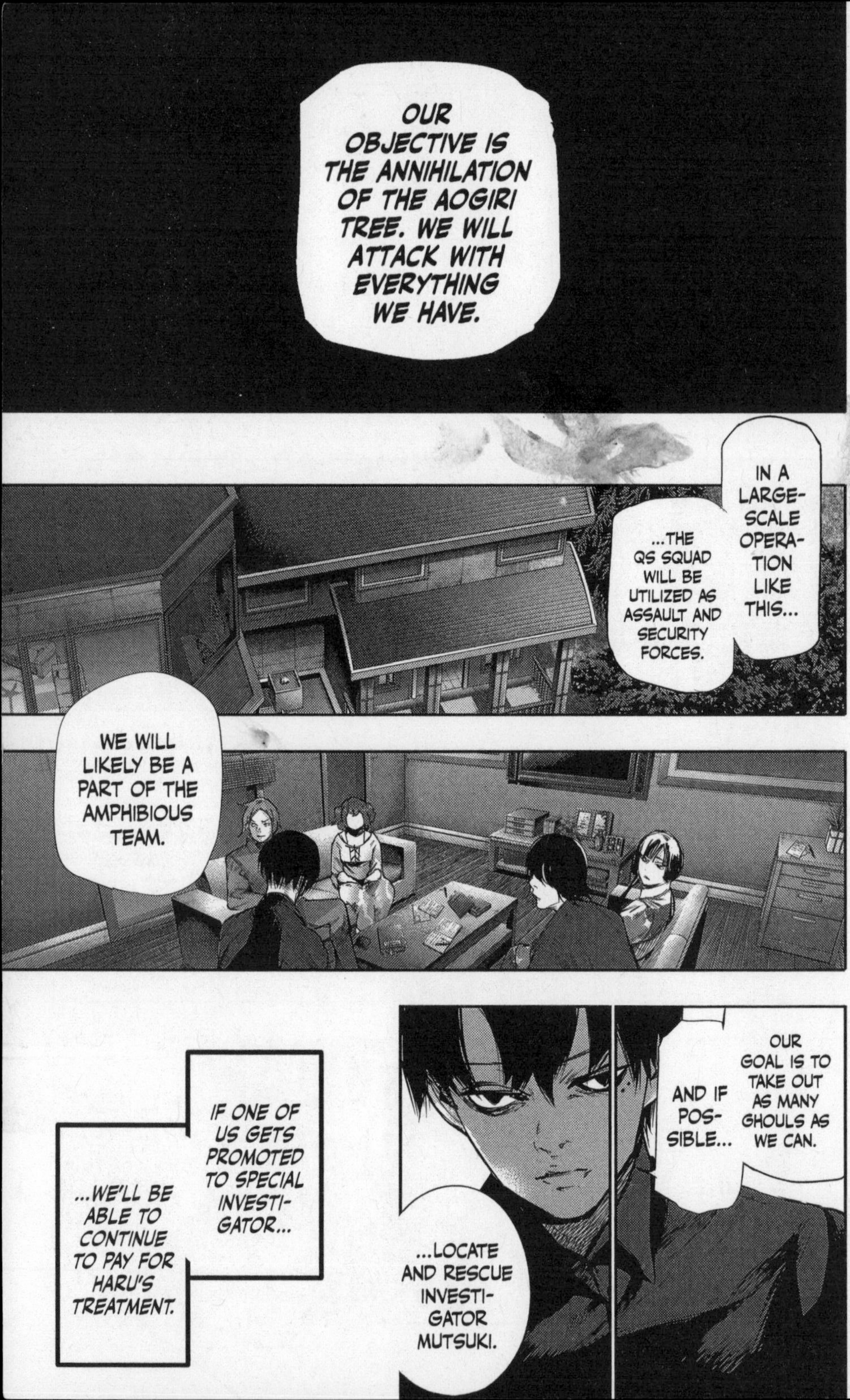
OUR OBJECTIVE IS THE ANNIHILATION OF THE AOGIRI TREE. WE WILL ATTACK WITH EVERYTHING WE HAVE.
IN A LARGE-SCALE OPERATION LIKE THIS...
...THE QS SQUAD WILL BE UTILIZED AS ASSAULT AND SECURITY FORCES.
WE WILL LIKELY BE A PART OF THE AMPHIBIOUS TEAM.
OUR GOAL IS TO TAKE OUT AS MANY GHOULS AS WE CAN.
AND IF POSSIBLE...
...LOCATE AND RESCUE INVESTIGATOR MUTSUKI.
IF ONE OF US GETS PROMOTED TO SPECIAL INVESTIGATOR...
...WE'LL BE ABLE TO CONTINUE TO PAY FOR HARU'S TREATMENT.

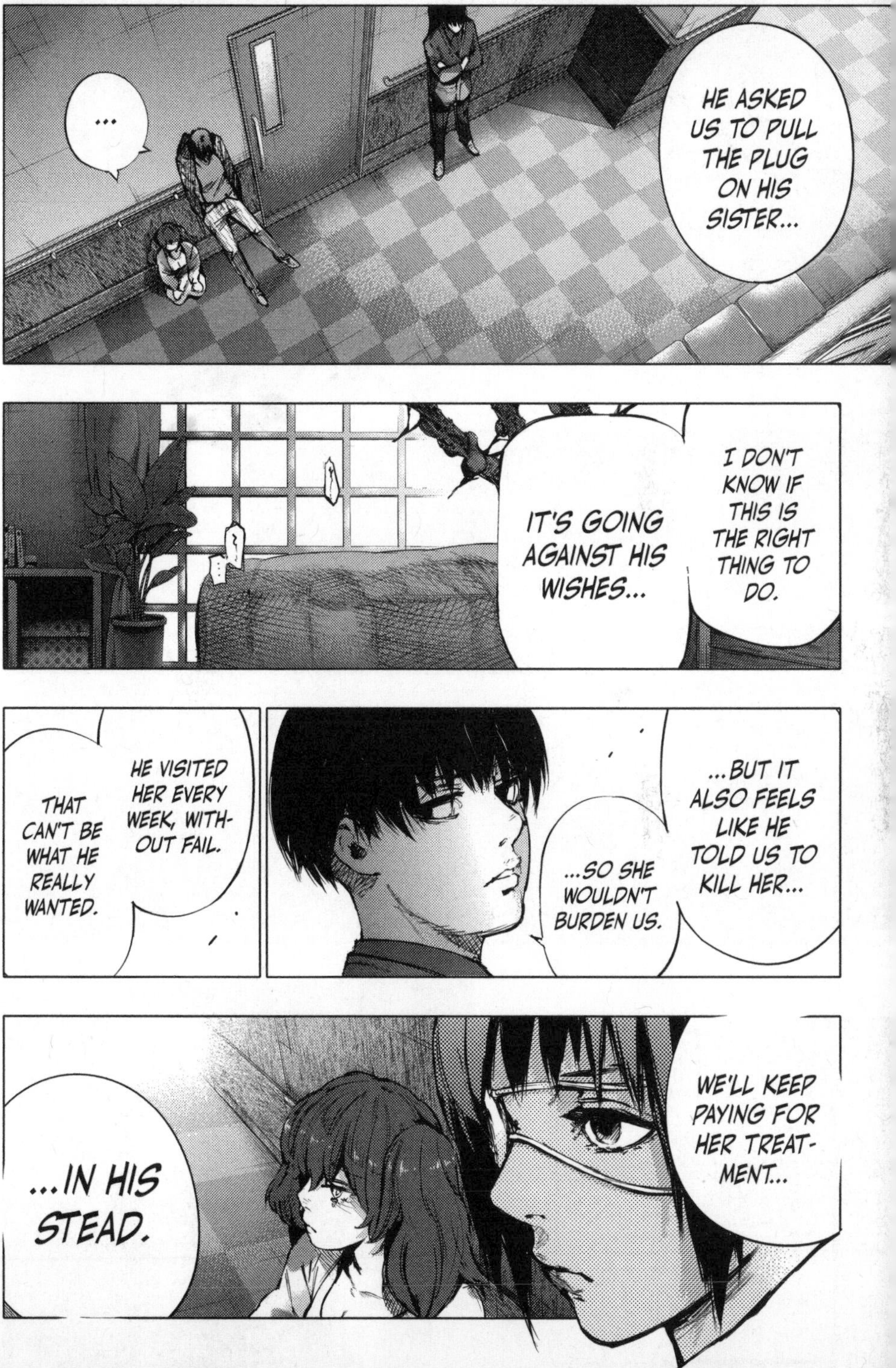
HE ASKED US TO PULL THE PLUG ON HIS SISTER...
...
I DON'T KNOW IF THIS IS THE RIGHT THING TO DO.
IT'S GOING AGAINST HIS WISHES...
...BUT IT ALSO FEELS LIKE HE TOLD US TO KILL HER...
...SO SHE WOULDN'T BURDEN US.
HE VISITED HER EVERY WEEK, WITH-OUT FAIL.
THAT CAN'T BE WHAT HE REALLY WANTED.
WE'LL KEEP PAYING FOR HER TREAT-MENT...
...IN HIS STEAD.

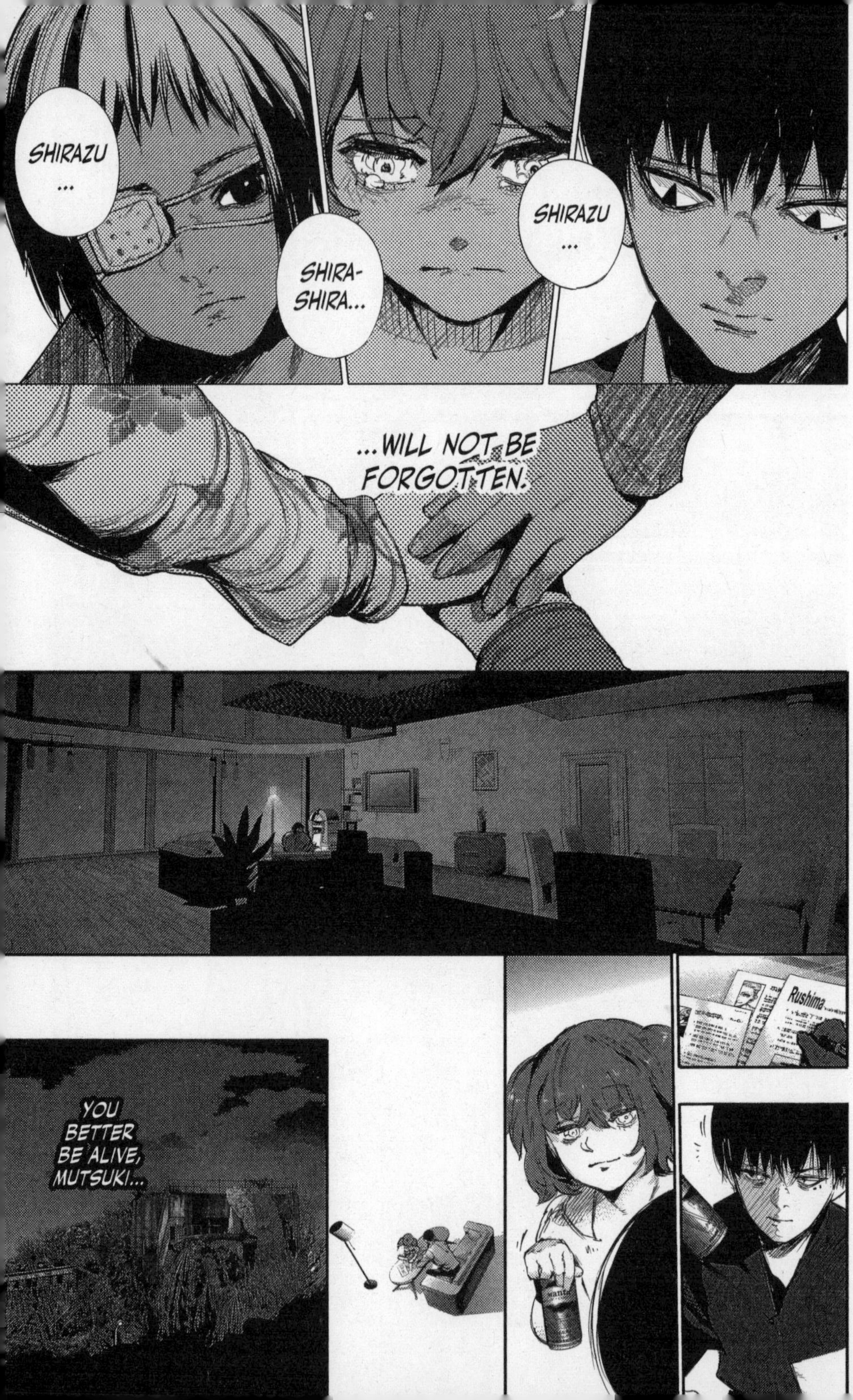
SHIRAZU ...
SHIRA-SHIRA...
SHIRAZU ...
...WILL NOT BE FORGOTTEN.
Rushima
YOU BETTER BE ALIVE, MUTSUKI...

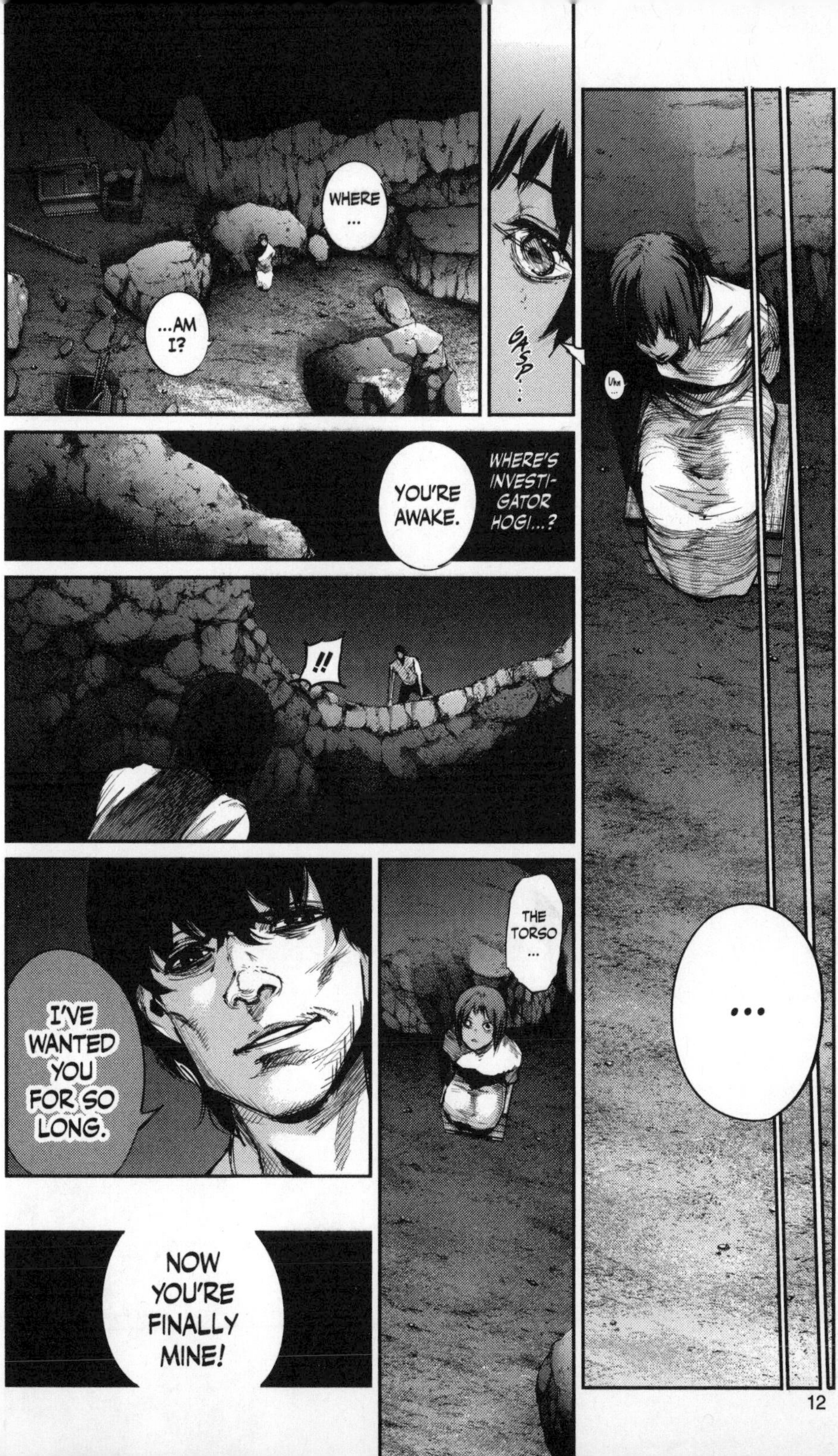
Uhn ...
...
GASP...
WHERE ...
...AM I?
WHERE'S INVESTI-GATOR HOGI...?
YOU'RE AWAKE.
!!
THE TORSO ...
I'VE WANTED YOU FOR SO LONG.
NOW YOU'RE FINALLY MINE!

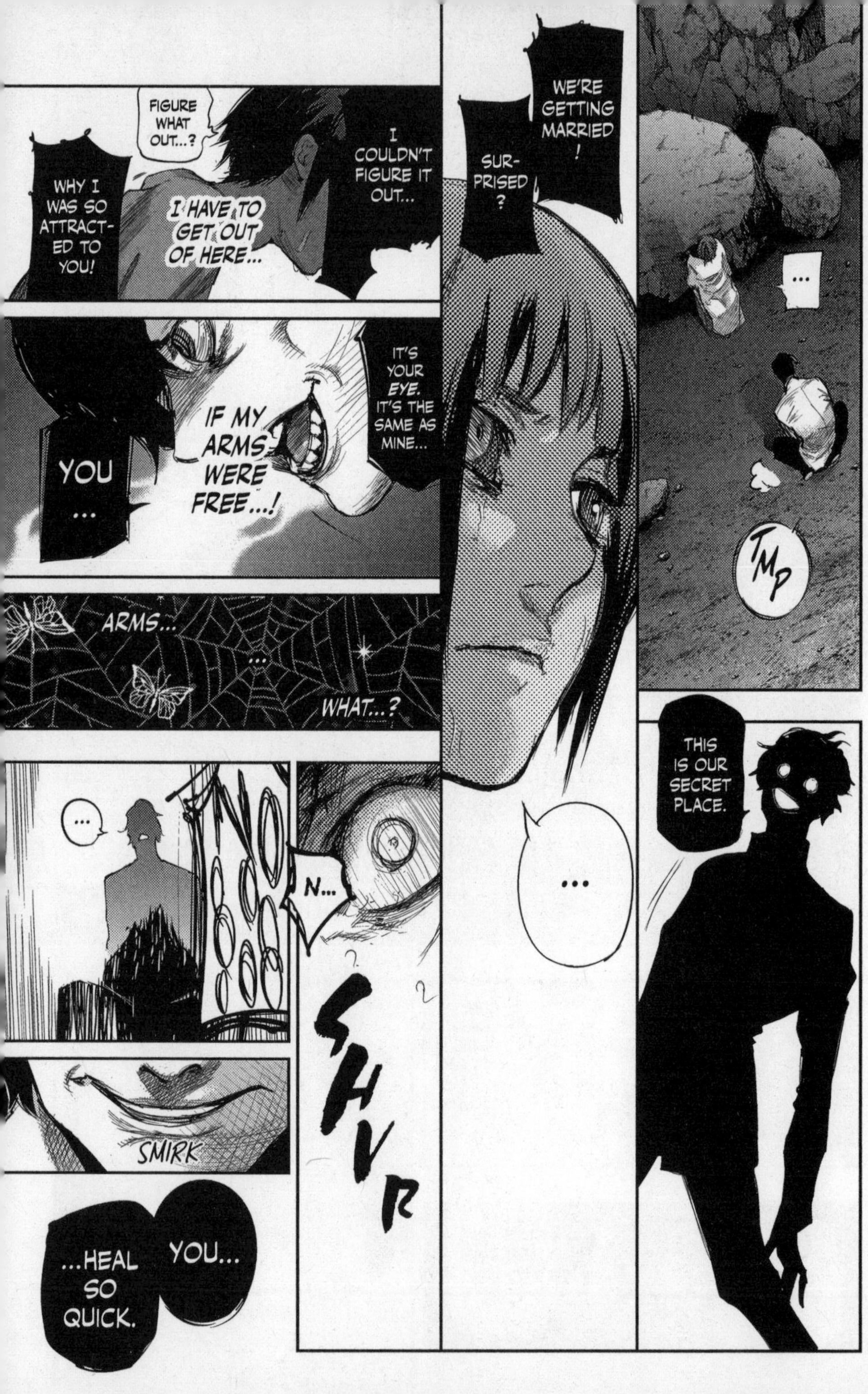
...
TMP
WE'RE GETTING MARRIED!
SUR-PRISED?
I COULDN'T FIGURE IT OUT...
FIGURE WHAT OUT...?
WHY I WAS SO ATTRACT-ED TO YOU!
I HAVE TO GET OUT OF HERE...
IT'S YOUR *EYE.* IT'S THE SAME AS MINE...
IF MY ARMS WERE FREE...!
YOU ...
ARMS...
...
WHAT...?
THIS IS OUR SECRET PLACE.
...
N...
SHVR
...
SMIRK
YOU...
...HEAL SO QUICK.

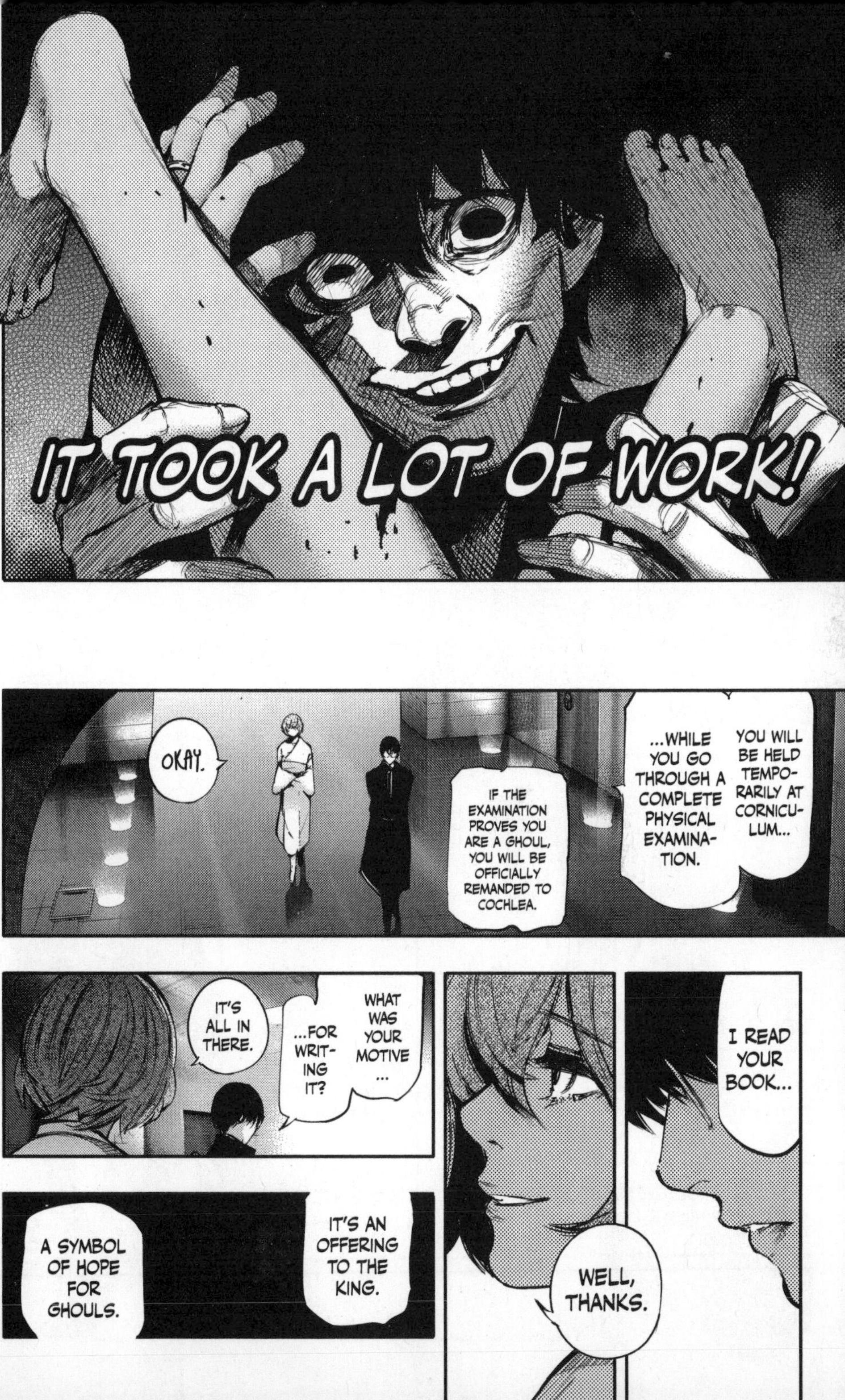
IT TOOK A LOT OF WORK!
YOU WILL BE HELD TEMPORARILY AT CORNICULUM...
...WHILE YOU GO THROUGH A COMPLETE PHYSICAL EXAMINATION.
IF THE EXAMINATION PROVES YOU ARE A GHOUL, YOU WILL BE OFFICIALLY REMANDED TO COCHLEA.
OKAY.
I READ YOUR BOOK...
WELL, THANKS.
WHAT WAS YOUR MOTIVE ...
...FOR WRITING IT?
IT'S ALL IN THERE.
IT'S AN OFFERING TO THE KING.
A SYMBOL OF HOPE FOR GHOULS.

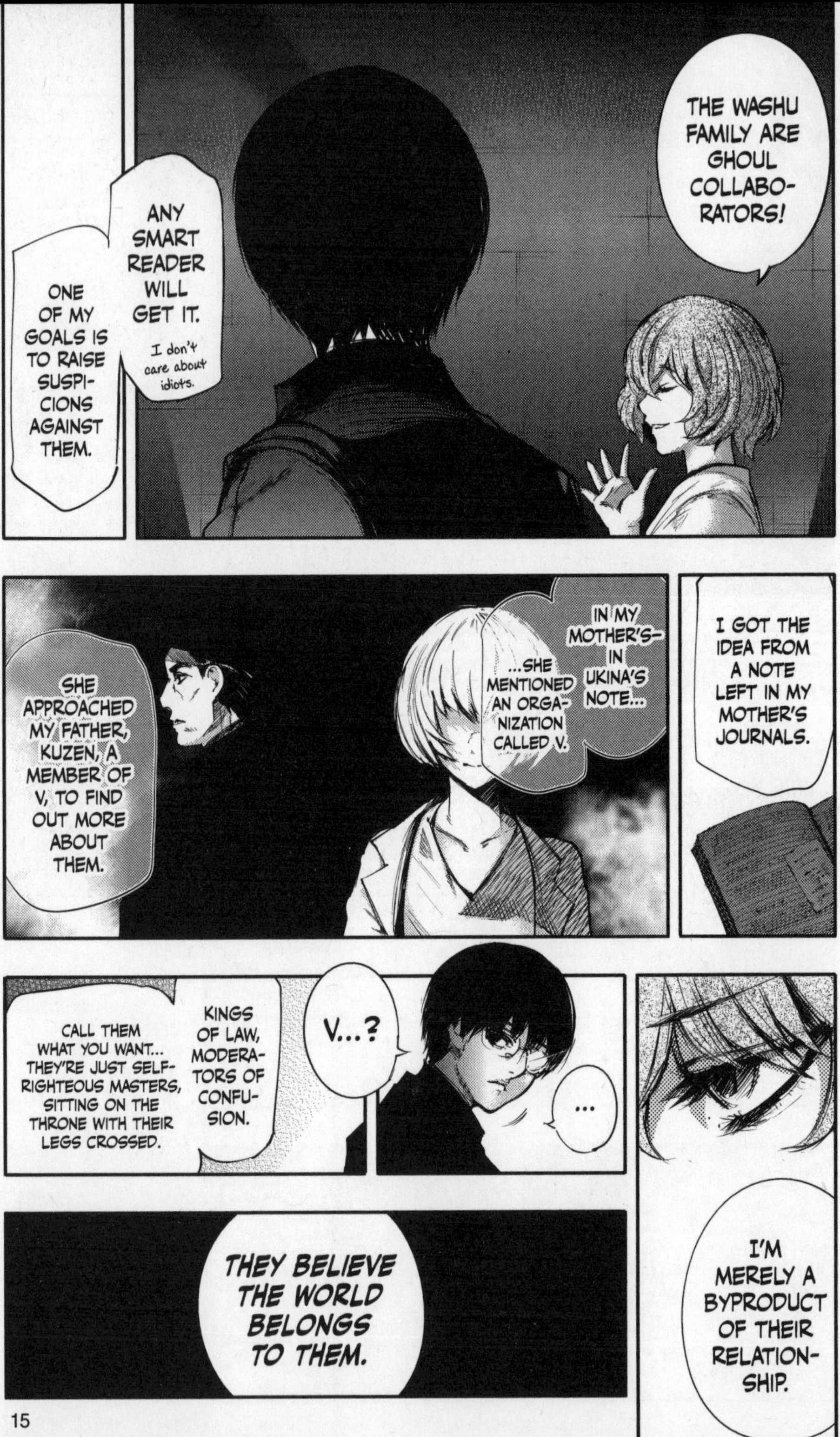

THE WASHU FAMILY ARE GHOUL COLLABORATORS!
ANY SMART READER WILL GET IT.
I don't care about idiots.
ONE OF MY GOALS IS TO RAISE SUSPICIONS AGAINST THEM.
I GOT THE IDEA FROM A NOTE LEFT IN MY MOTHER'S JOURNALS.
IN MY MOTHER'S—IN UKINA'S NOTE...
...SHE MENTIONED AN ORGANIZATION CALLED V.
SHE APPROACHED MY FATHER, KUZEN, A MEMBER OF V, TO FIND OUT MORE ABOUT THEM.
I'M MERELY A BYPRODUCT OF THEIR RELATIONSHIP.
V...?
...
KINGS OF LAW, MODERATORS OF CONFUSION.
CALL THEM WHAT YOU WANT... THEY'RE JUST SELF-RIGHTEOUS MASTERS, SITTING ON THE THRONE WITH THEIR LEGS CROSSED.
THEY BELIEVE THE WORLD BELONGS TO THEM.

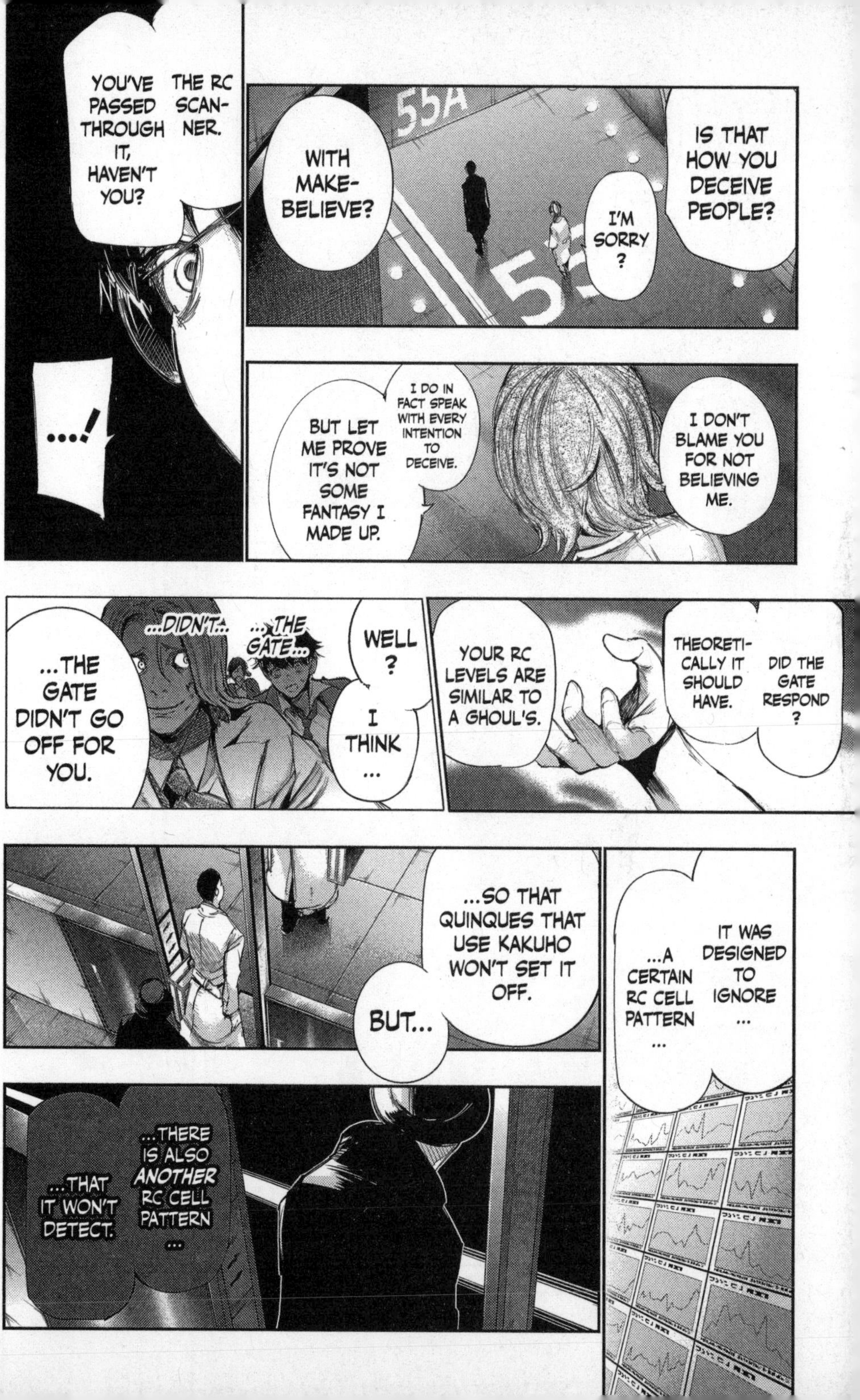
IS THAT HOW YOU DECEIVE PEOPLE?
I'M SORRY ?
WITH MAKE-BELIEVE?
55A
I DON'T BLAME YOU FOR NOT BELIEVING ME.
I DO IN FACT SPEAK WITH EVERY INTENTION TO DECEIVE.
BUT LET ME PROVE IT'S NOT SOME FANTASY I MADE UP.
THE RC SCANNER.
YOU'VE PASSED THROUGH IT, HAVEN'T YOU?
...!
DID THE GATE RESPOND ?
THEORETICALLY IT SHOULD HAVE.
YOUR RC LEVELS ARE SIMILAR TO A GHOUL'S.
WELL ?
I THINK ...
...THE GATE...
...DIDN'T...
...THE GATE DIDN'T GO OFF FOR YOU.
IT WAS DESIGNED TO IGNORE ...
...A CERTAIN RC CELL PATTERN ...
...SO THAT QUINQUES THAT USE KAKUHO WON'T SET IT OFF.
BUT...
...THERE IS ALSO ANOTHER RC CELL PATTERN ...
...THAT IT WON'T DETECT.

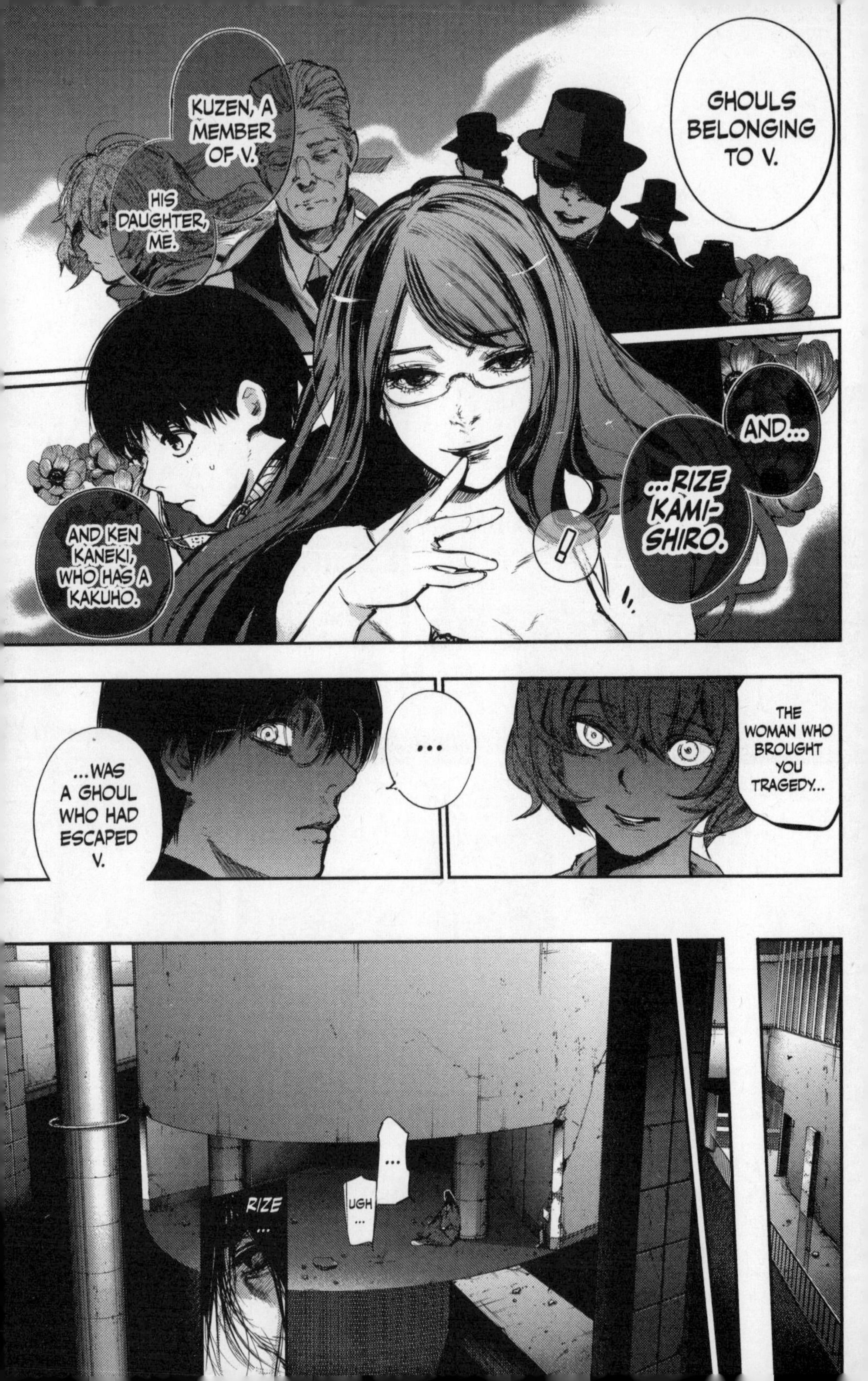
GHOULS BELONGING TO V.
KUZEN, A MEMBER OF V.
HIS DAUGHTER, ME.
AND...
...RIZE KAMI-SHIRO.
!
AND KEN KANEKI, WHO HAS A KAKUHO.
THE WOMAN WHO BROUGHT YOU TRAGEDY...
...
...WAS A GHOUL WHO HAD ESCAPED V.
...
UGH ...
RIZE ...

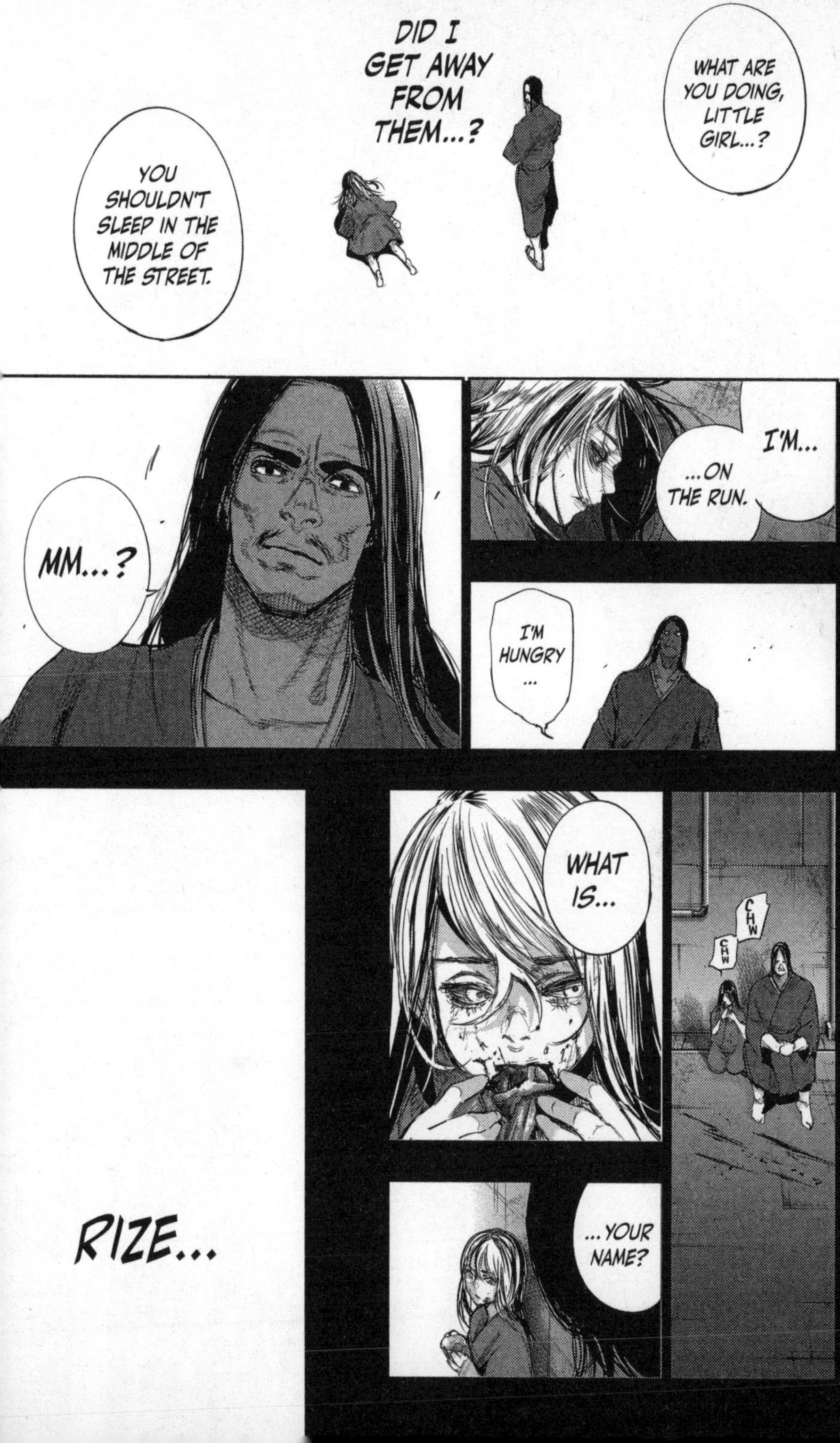
WHAT ARE YOU DOING, LITTLE GIRL...?
DID I GET AWAY FROM THEM...?
YOU SHOULDN'T SLEEP IN THE MIDDLE OF THE STREET.
I'M...
...ON THE RUN.
I'M HUNGRY ...
MM...?
CHW
CHW
WHAT IS...
...YOUR NAME?
RIZE...

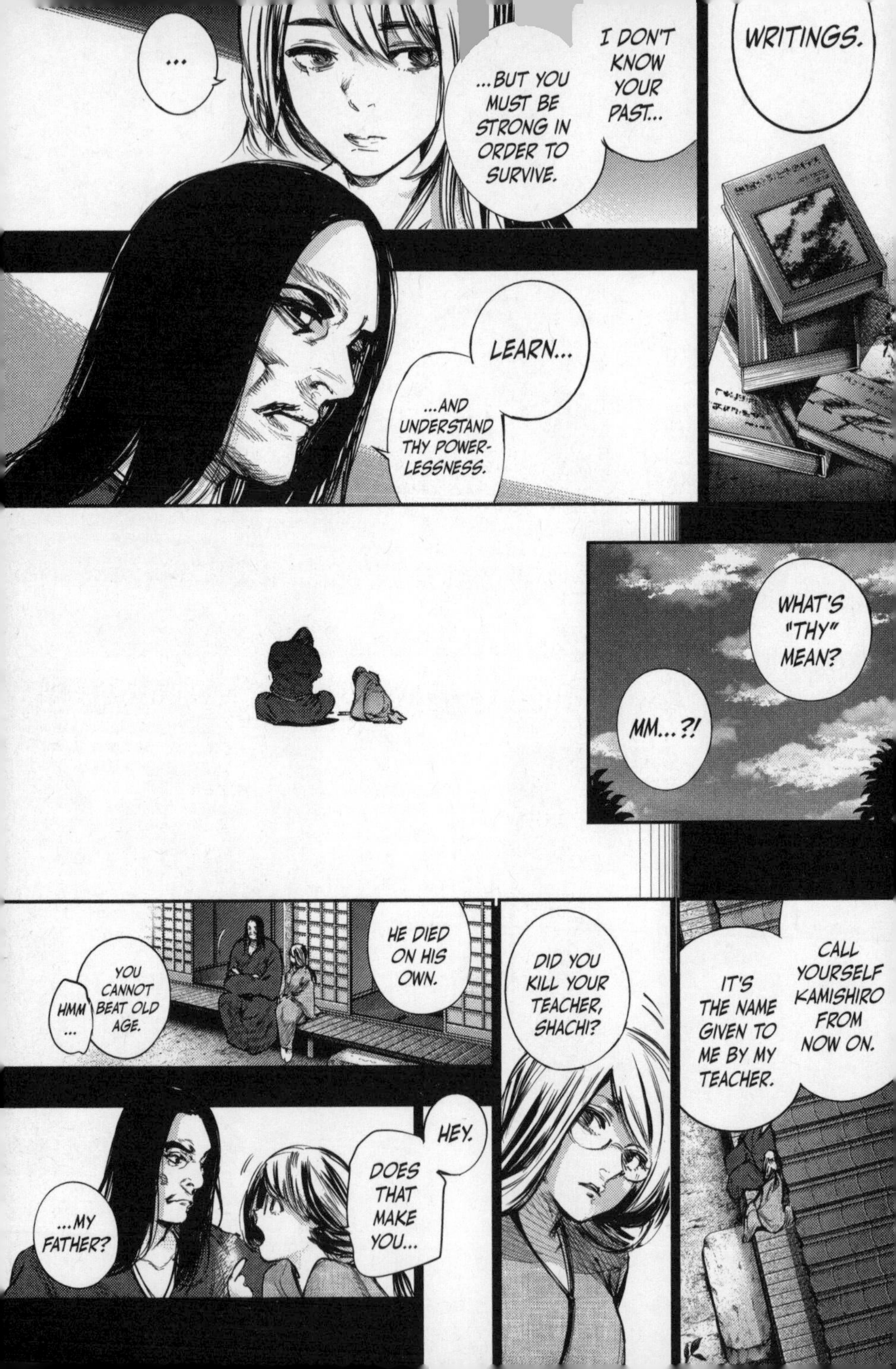
WRITINGS.
I DON'T KNOW YOUR PAST...
...BUT YOU MUST BE STRONG IN ORDER TO SURVIVE.
...
LEARN...
...AND UNDERSTAND THY POWER-LESSNESS.
WHAT'S "THY" MEAN?
MM...?!
CALL YOURSELF KAMISHIRO FROM NOW ON.
IT'S THE NAME GIVEN TO ME BY MY TEACHER.
DID YOU KILL YOUR TEACHER, SHACHI?
HE DIED ON HIS OWN.
YOU CANNOT BEAT OLD AGE.
HMM...
HEY.
DOES THAT MAKE YOU...
...MY FATHER?

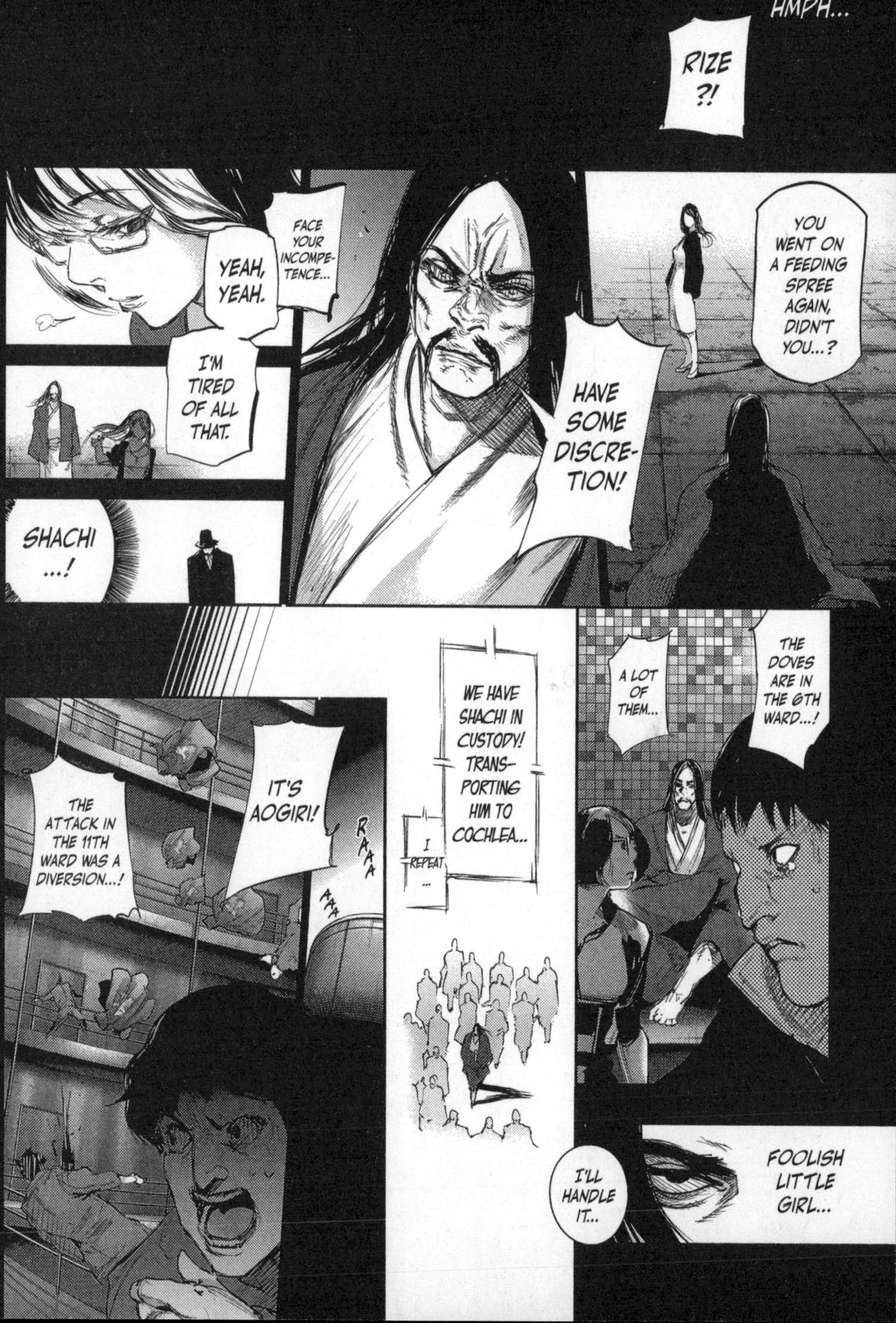
HMPH...
RIZE ?!
YOU WENT ON A FEEDING SPREE AGAIN, DIDN'T YOU...?
HAVE SOME DISCRETION!
FACE YOUR INCOMPETENCE...
YEAH, YEAH.
I'M TIRED OF ALL THAT.
SHACHI ...!
THE DOVES ARE IN THE 6TH WARD...!
A LOT OF THEM...
FOOLISH LITTLE GIRL...
I'LL HANDLE IT...
WE HAVE SHACHI IN CUSTODY! TRANSPORTING HIM TO COCHLEA...
I REPEAT...
IT'S AOGIRI!
THE ATTACK IN THE 11TH WARD WAS A DIVERSION...!
RAAA
AAA

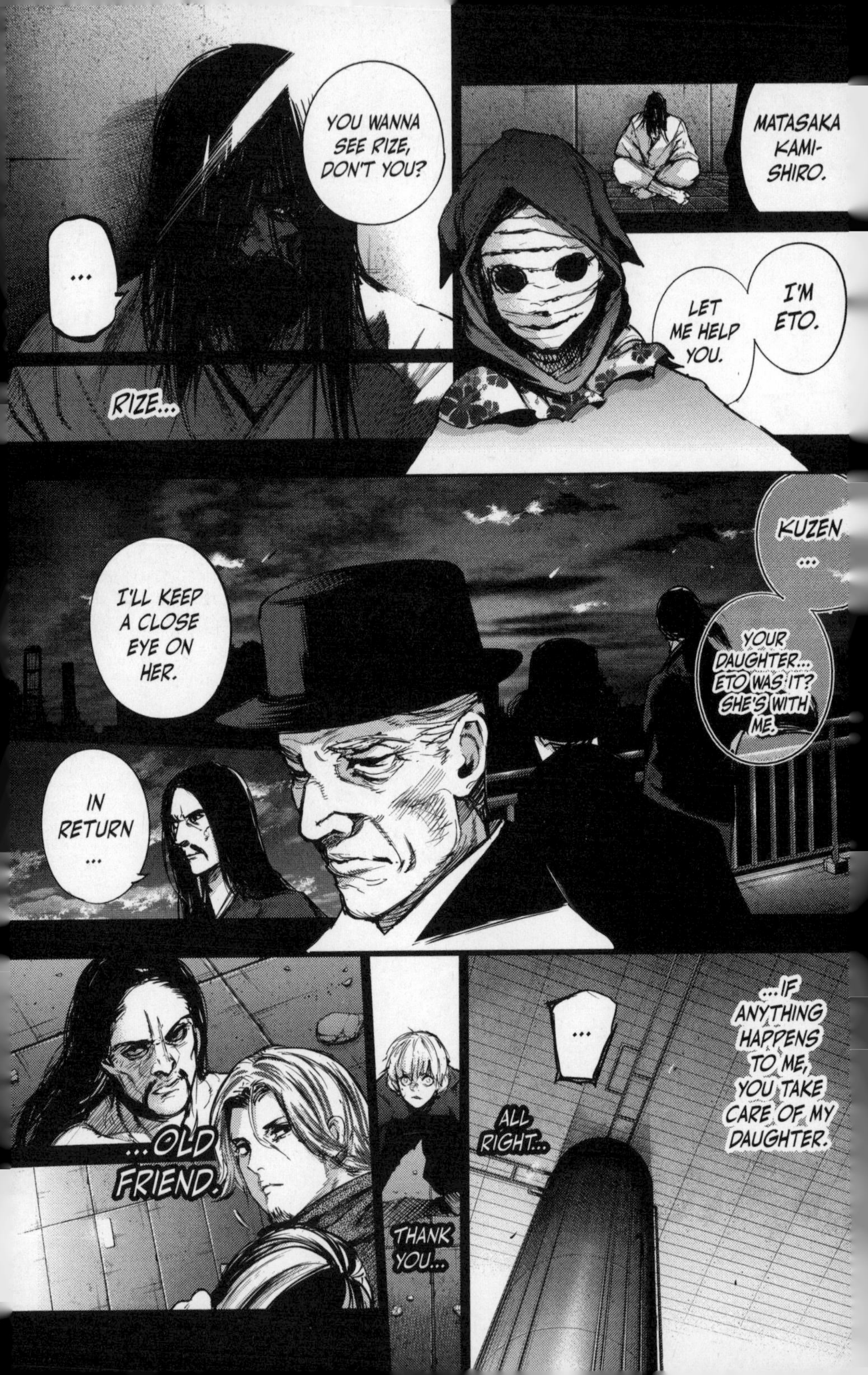
MATASAKA KAMI-SHIRO.
I'M ETO.
LET ME HELP YOU.
YOU WANNA SEE RIZE, DON'T YOU?
...
RIZE...
KUZEN ...
YOUR DAUGHTER... ETO WAS IT? SHE'S WITH ME.
I'LL KEEP A CLOSE EYE ON HER.
IN RETURN ...
...IF ANYTHING HAPPENS TO ME, YOU TAKE CARE OF MY DAUGHTER.
...
ALL RIGHT...
THANK YOU...
...OLD FRIEND.

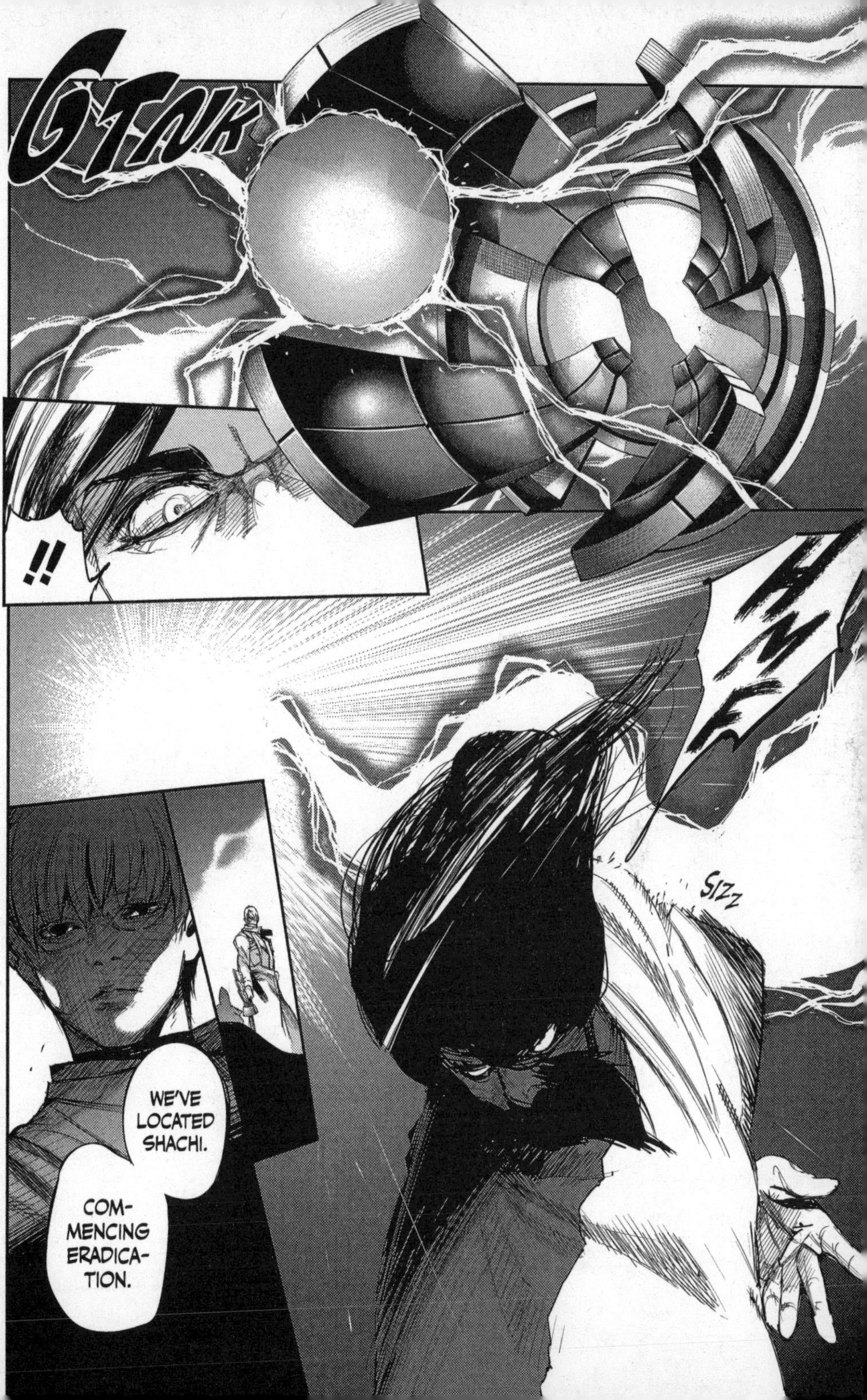
GTAK
!!
HMF
SIZZ
WE'VE LOCATED SHACHI.
COM-MENCING ERADICA-TION.

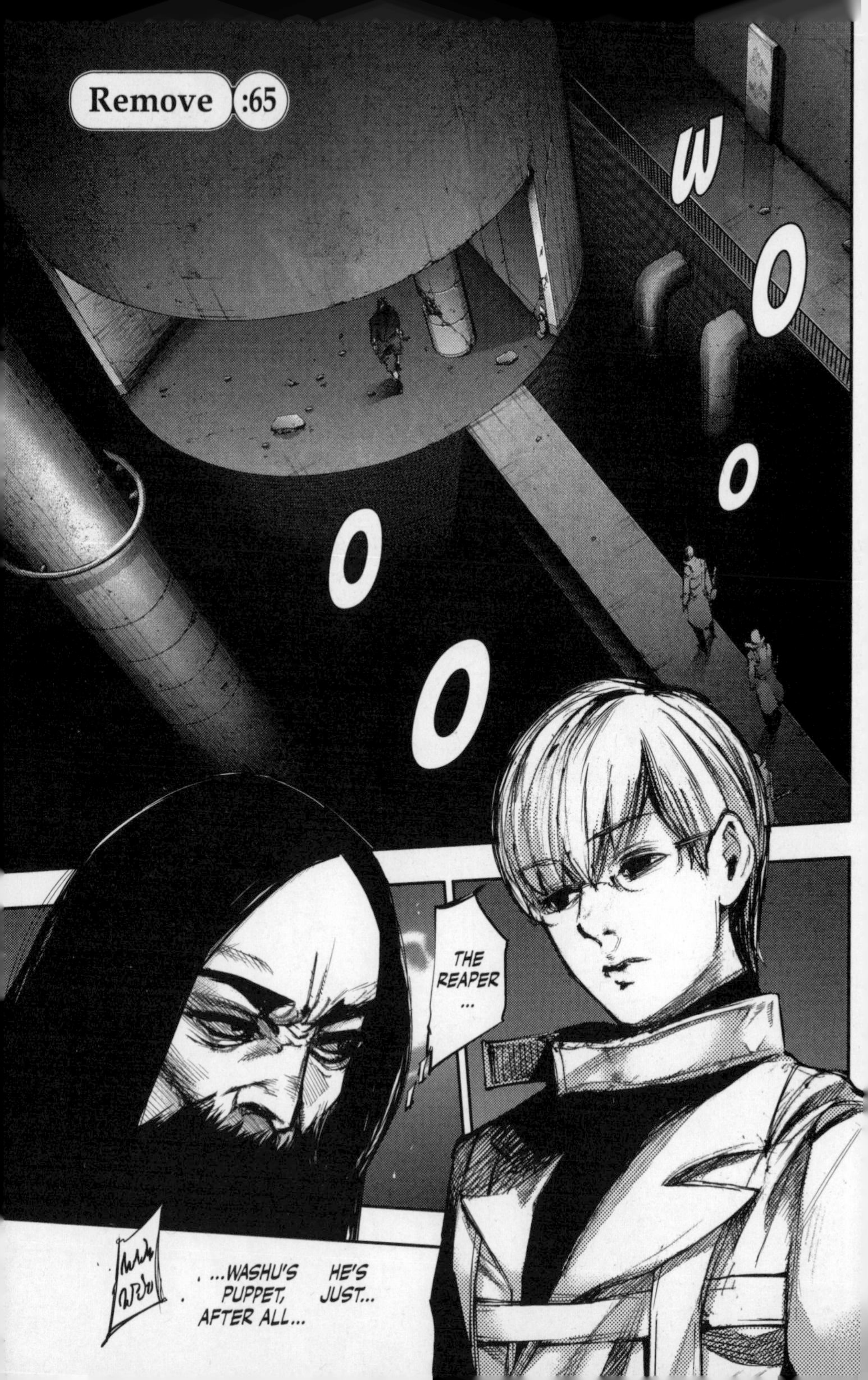
Remove :65
WOOOO
THE REAPER ...
HE'S JUST...
...WASHU'S PUPPET, AFTER ALL...

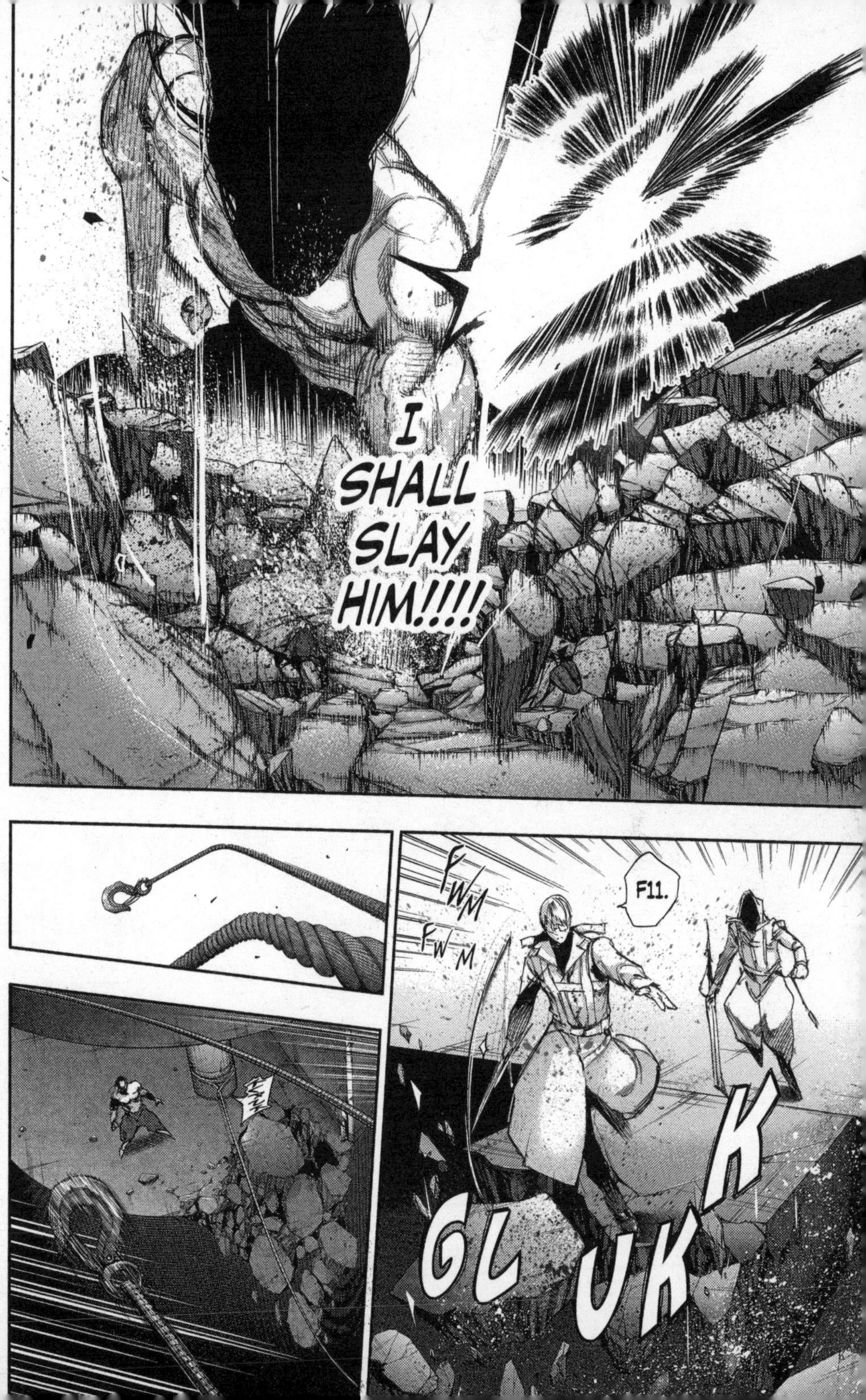
I SHALL SLAY HIM!!!!
FWM FWM
F11.
GLUKK

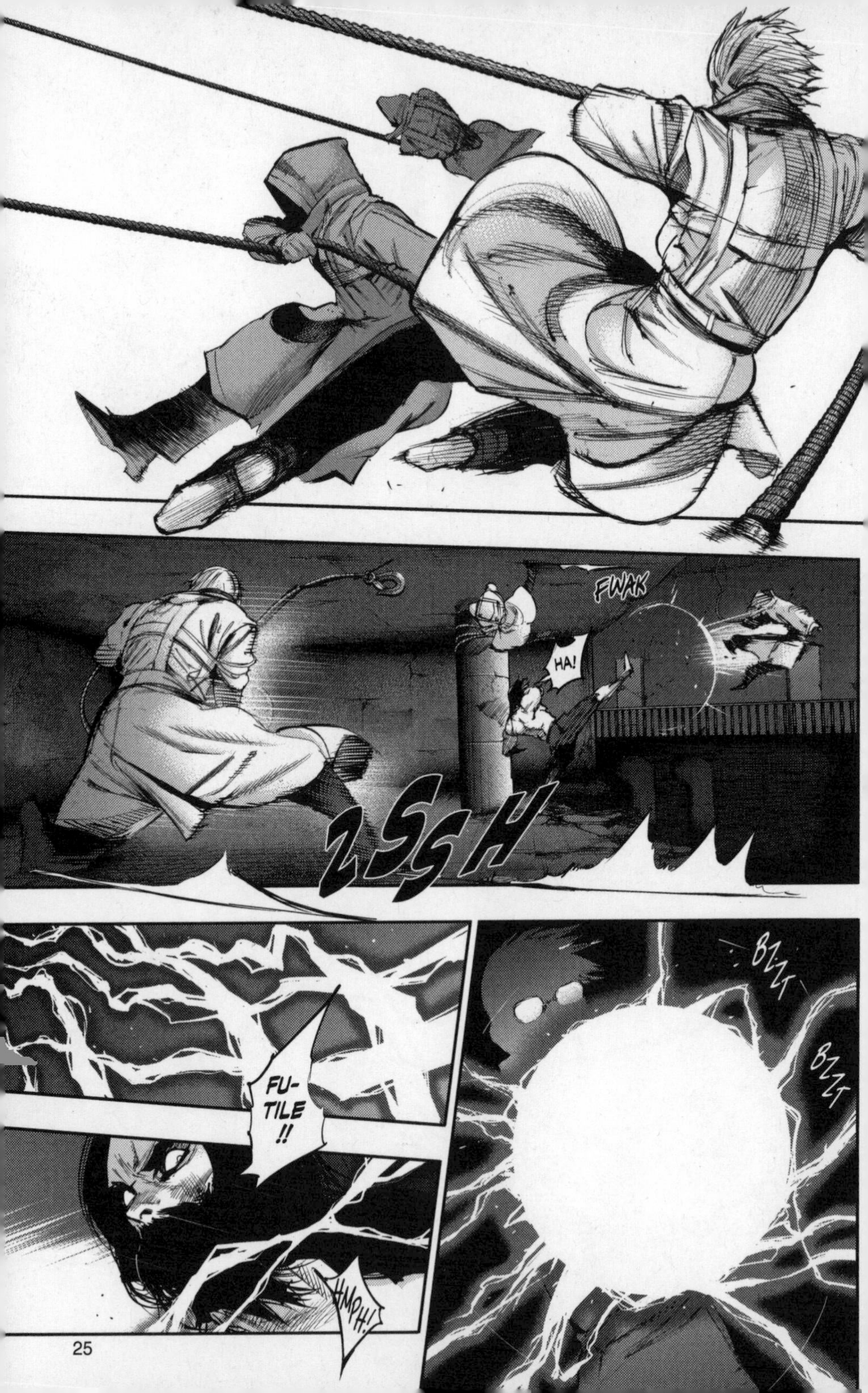
FWAK
HA!
ZSSH
BZZT
BZZT
FU-TILE!!
HMPH!

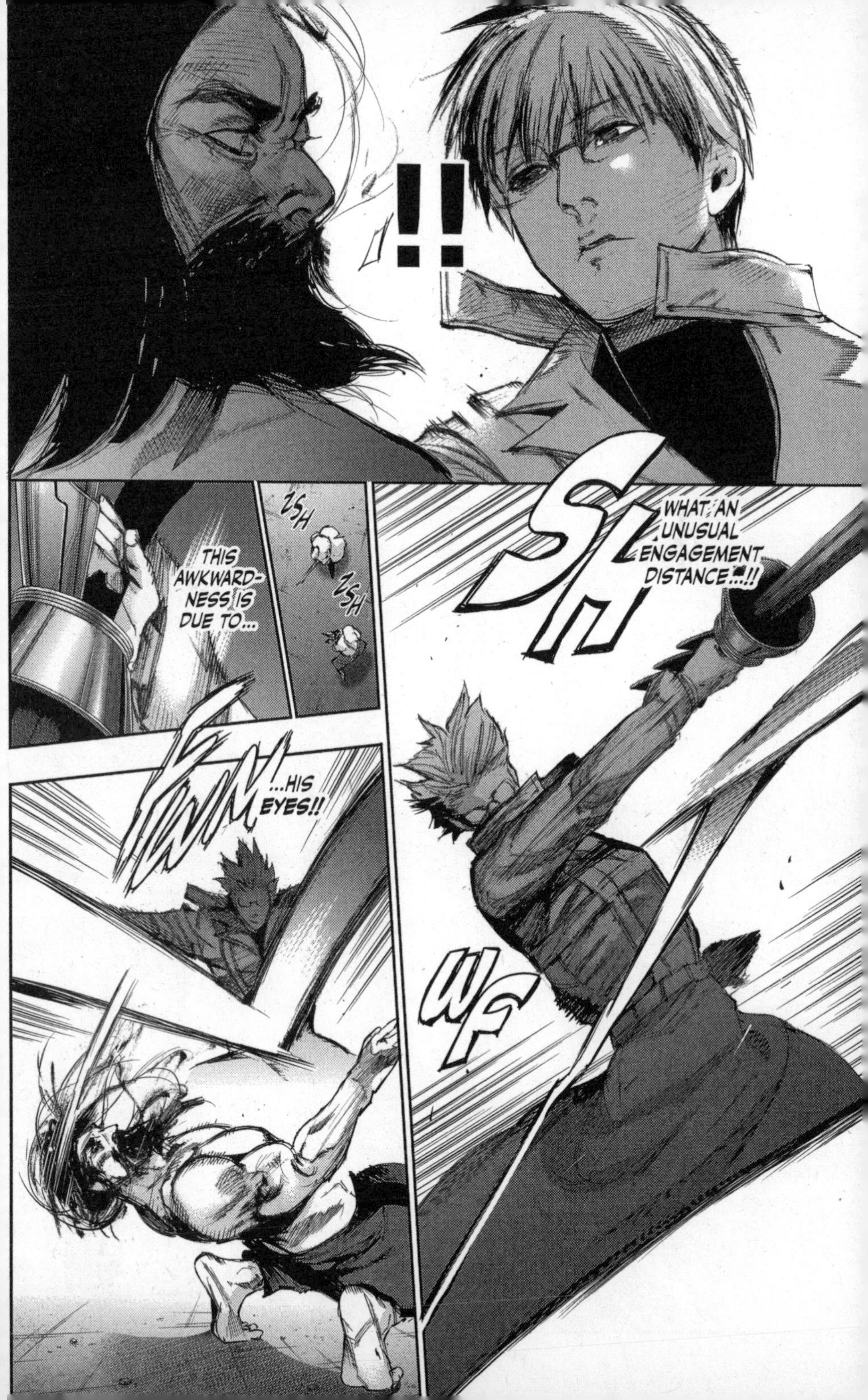
!!
WHAT AN UNUSUAL ENGAGEMENT DISTANCE...!!
ZSH
ZSH
THIS AWKWARDNESS IS DUE TO...
...HIS EYES!!

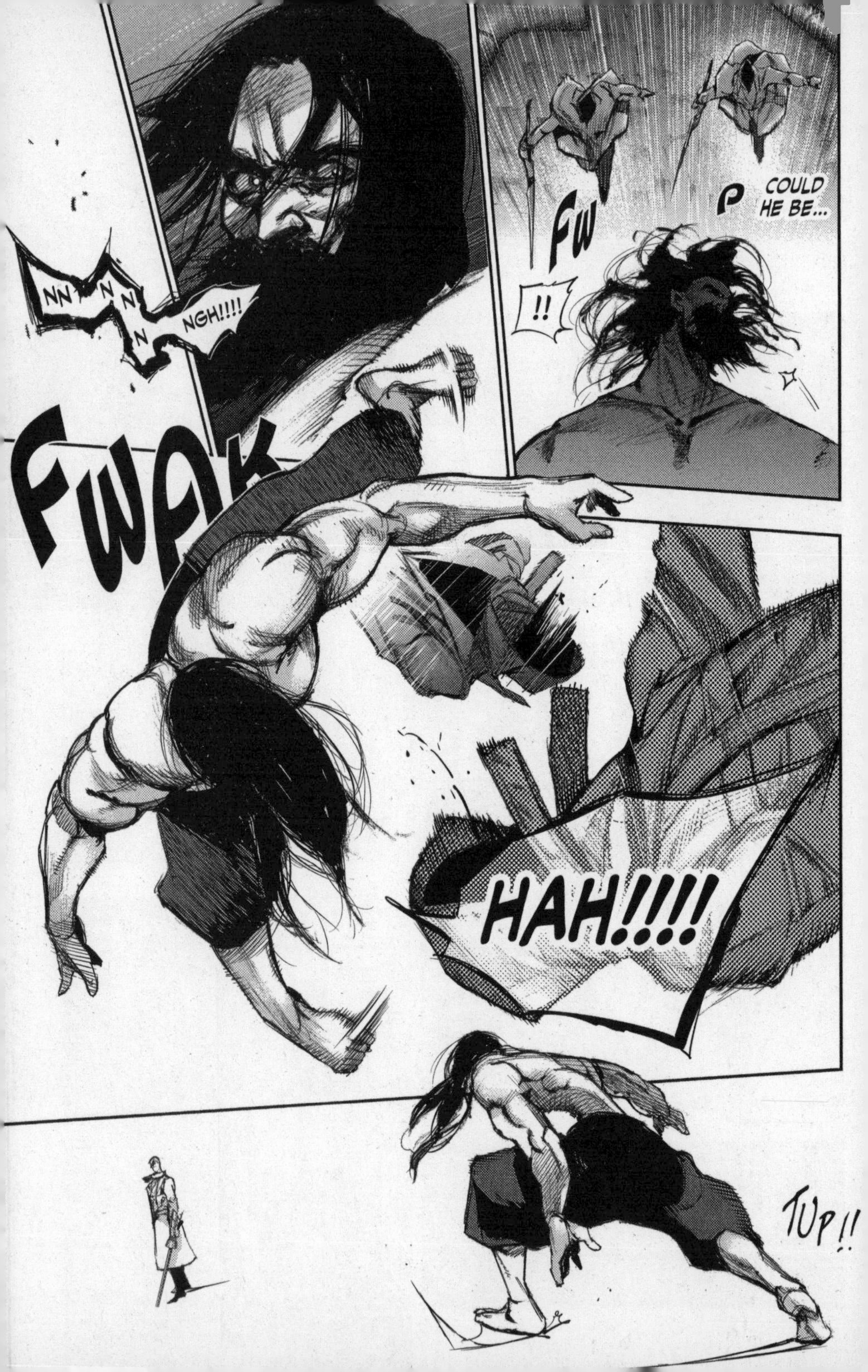

COULD HE BE...
FW
!!
NN N N N NGH!!!!
FWAK
HAH!!!!!
TUP!!

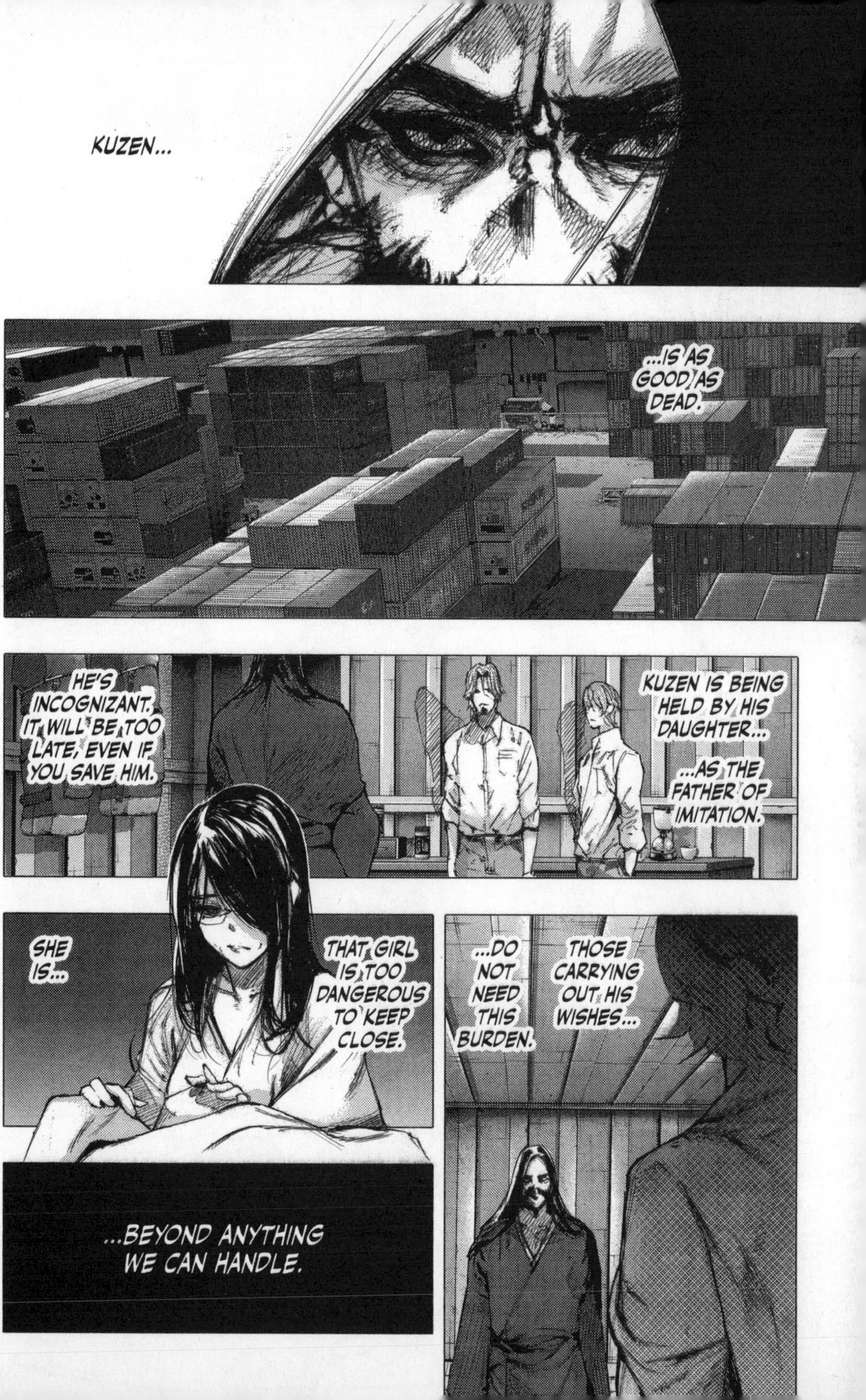
KUZEN...
...IS AS GOOD AS DEAD.
KUZEN IS BEING HELD BY HIS DAUGHTER...
...AS THE FATHER OF IMITATION.
HE'S INCOGNIZANT. IT WILL BE TOO LATE, EVEN IF YOU SAVE HIM.
THOSE CARRYING OUT HIS WISHES...
...DO NOT NEED THIS BURDEN.
THAT GIRL IS TOO DANGEROUS TO KEEP CLOSE.
SHE IS...
...BEYOND ANYTHING WE CAN HANDLE.

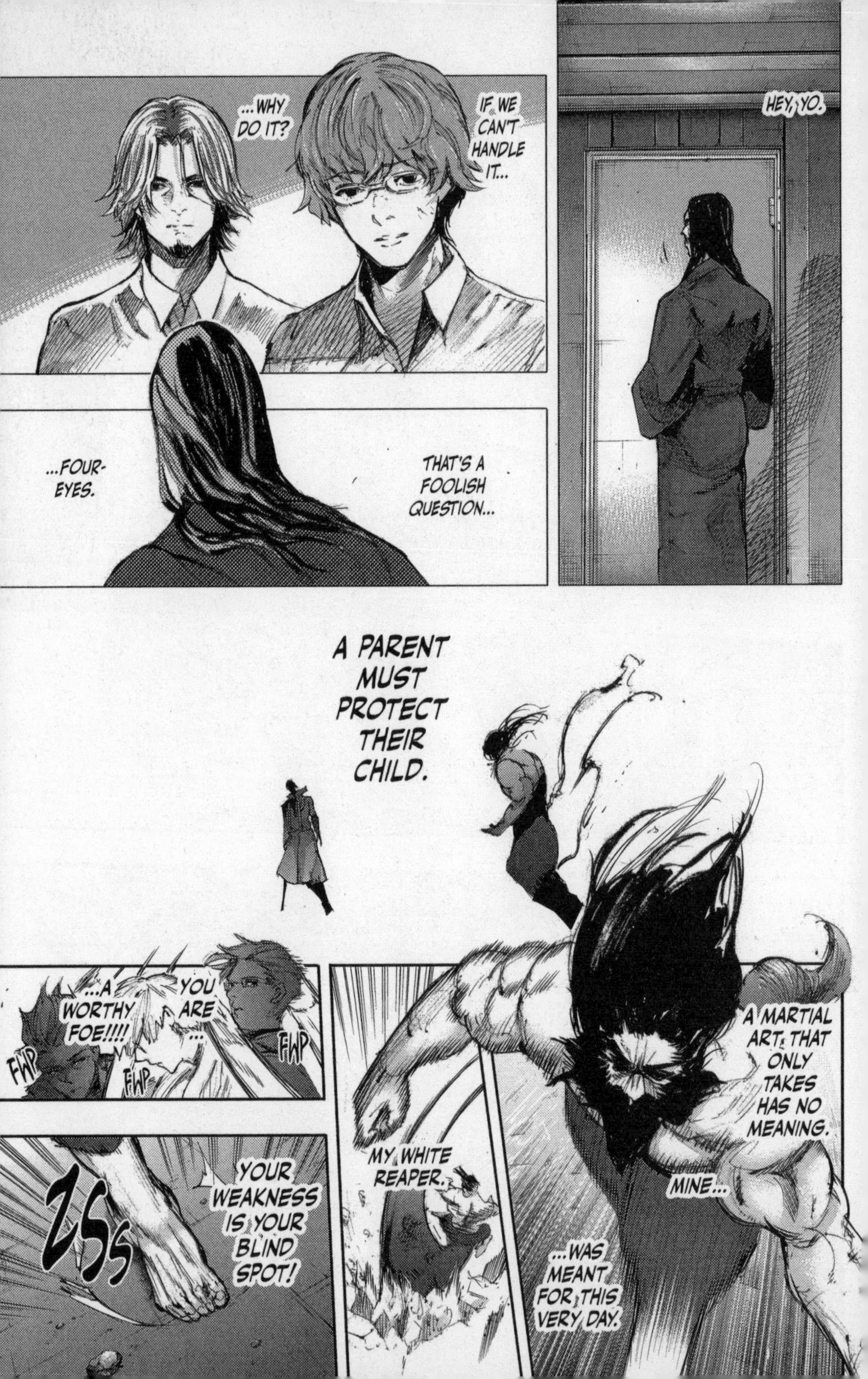
HEY, YO.
IF WE CAN'T HANDLE IT...
...WHY DO IT?
THAT'S A FOOLISH QUESTION...
...FOUR-EYES.
A PARENT MUST PROTECT THEIR CHILD.
A MARTIAL ART THAT ONLY TAKES HAS NO MEANING.
MINE...
MY WHITE REAPER.
...WAS MEANT FOR THIS VERY DAY.
FWP
YOU ARE ...
...A WORTHY FOE!!!!
FWP
FWP
YOUR WEAKNESS IS YOUR BLIND SPOT!
ZSS

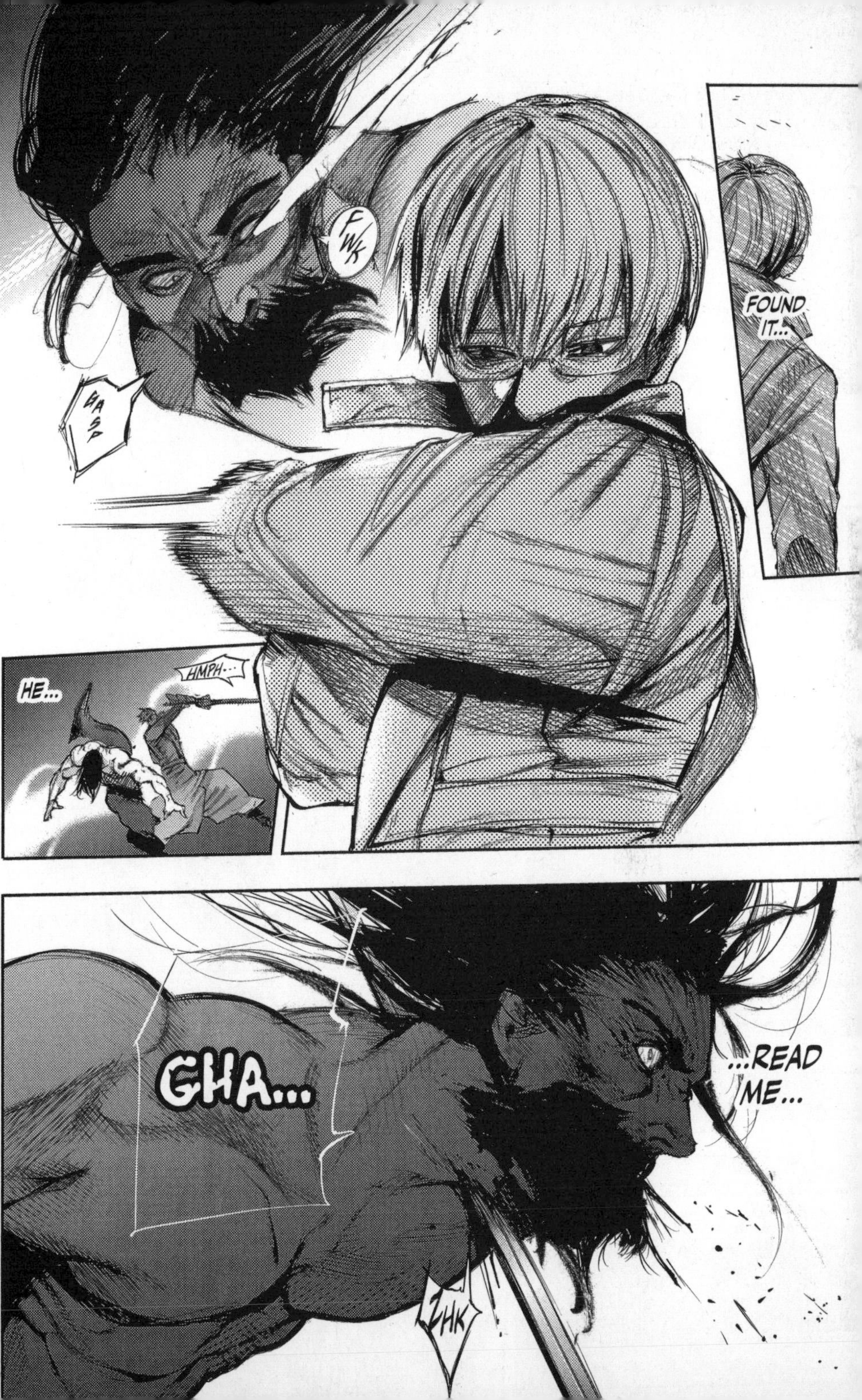
FOUND IT...
FWK
GASP
HMPH...
HE...
...READ ME...
GHA...
ZHK

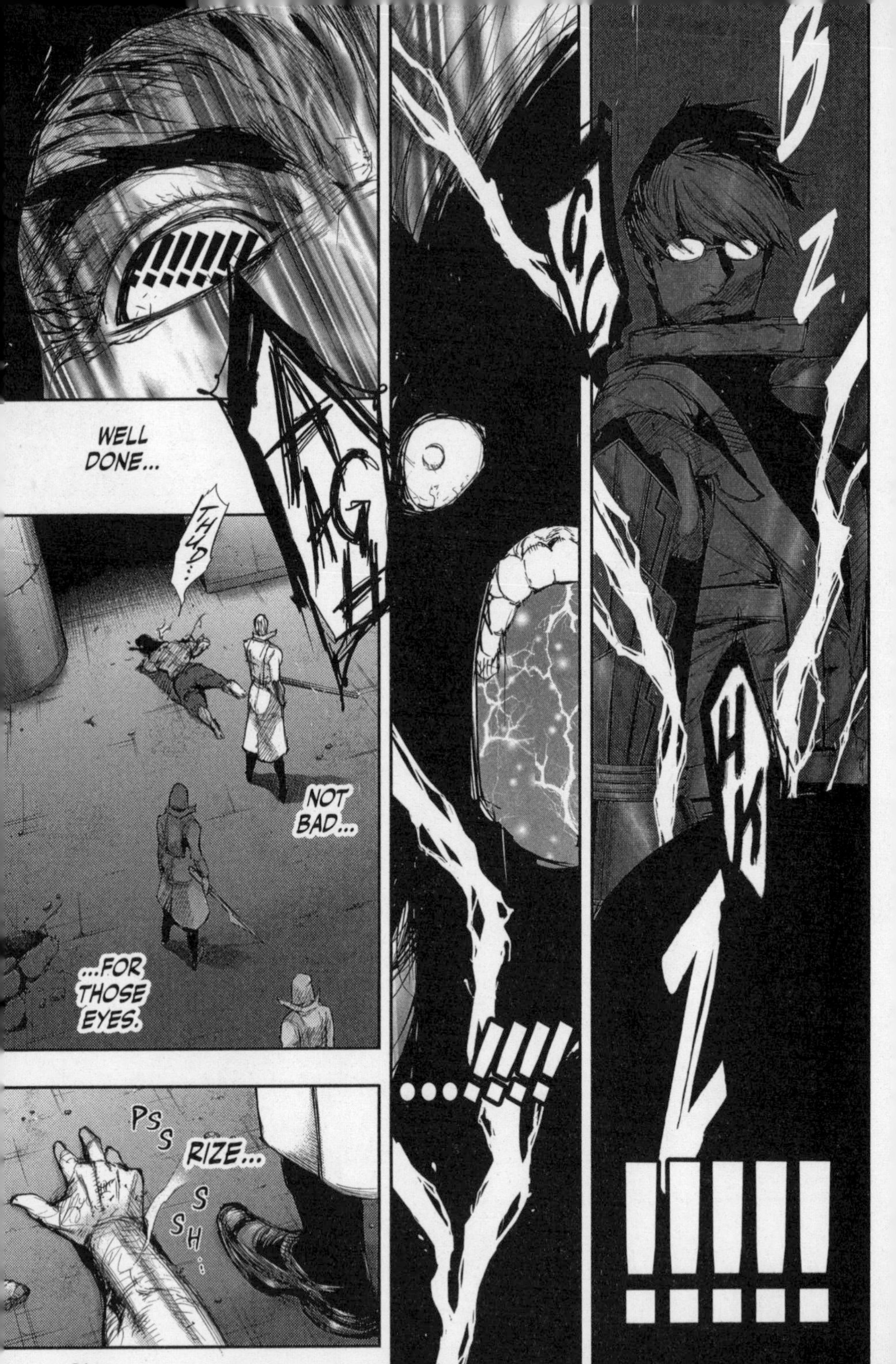
!!!!!
....!!!!
!!!!!
AGH
WELL DONE...
THUD...
NOT BAD...
...FOR THOSE EYES.
PSS
RIZE...
SSH..

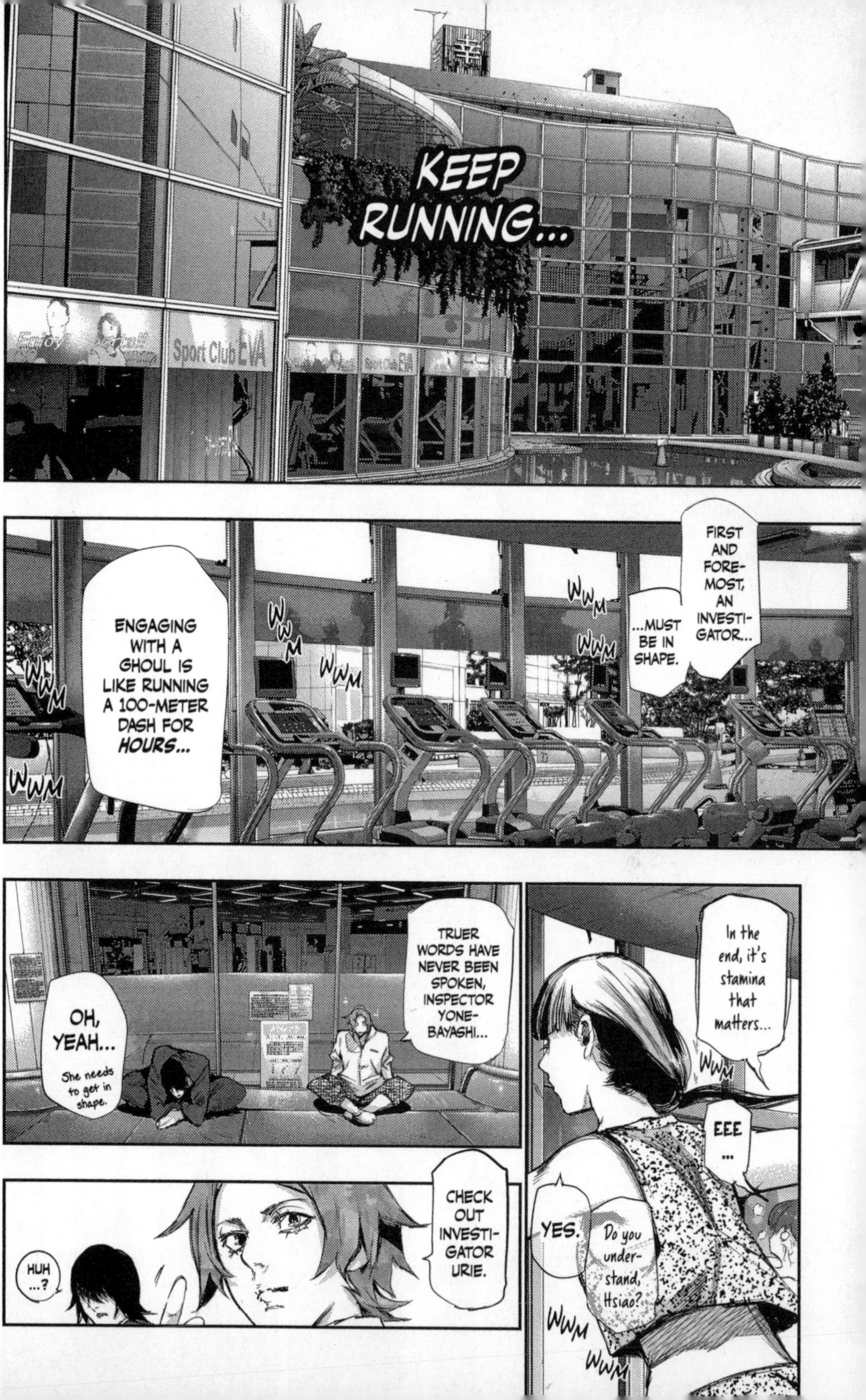
KEEP RUNNING...
Sport Club EVA
Sport Club EVA
FIRST AND FOREMOST, AN INVESTIGATOR...
...MUST BE IN SHAPE.
WWM
WWM
WWM
WWM
ENGAGING WITH A GHOUL IS LIKE RUNNING A 100-METER DASH FOR HOURS...
WWM
WWM
In the end, it's stamina that matters...
WWM
EEE...
YES.
Do you understand, Hsiao?
WWM
WWM
TRUER WORDS HAVE NEVER BEEN SPOKEN, INSPECTOR YONEBAYASHI...
OH, YEAH...
She needs to get in shape.
CHECK OUT INVESTIGATOR URIE.
HUH...?

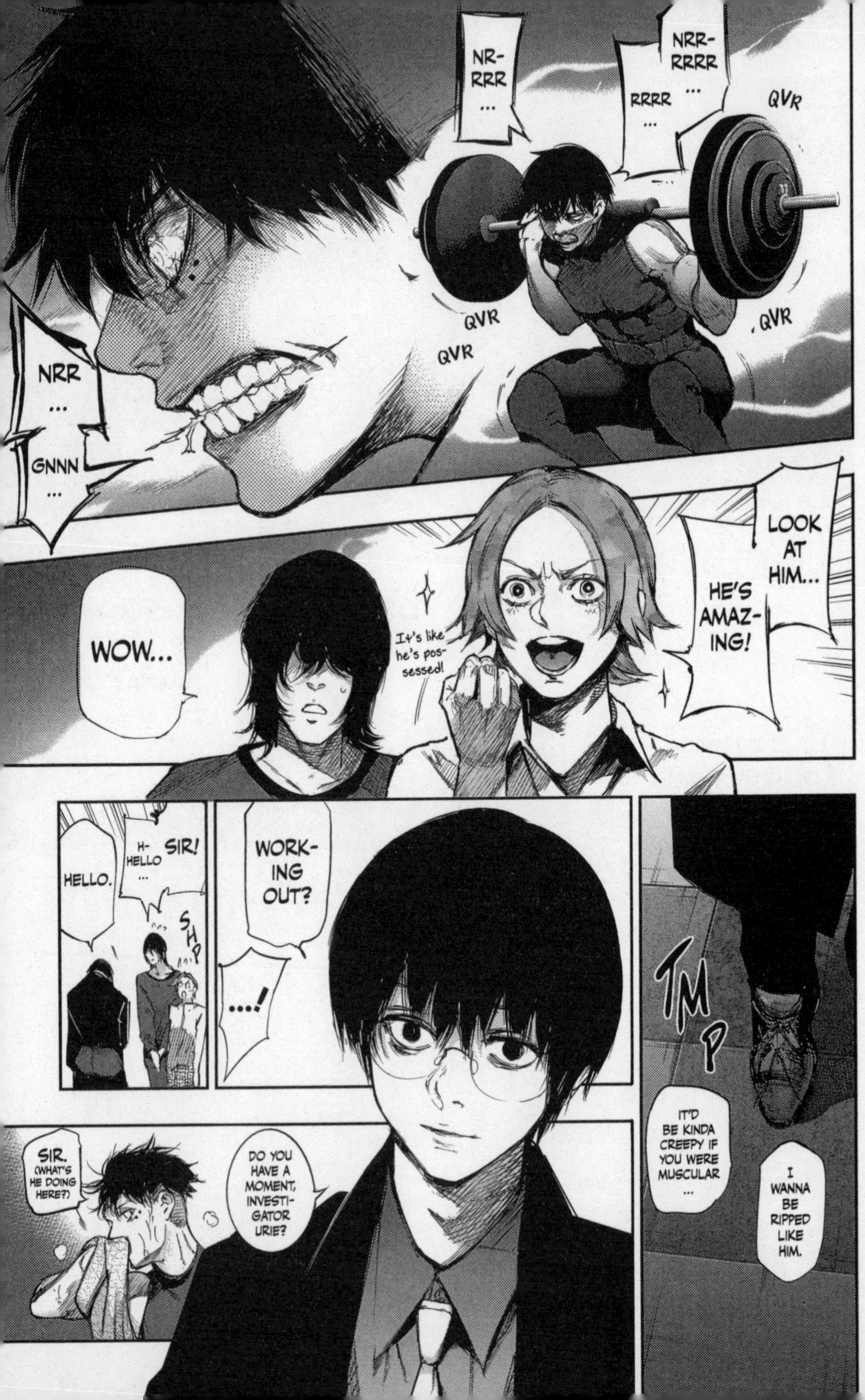
NRR-RRRR...
RRRR...
QVR
NR-RRR...
QVR
QVR
QVR
NRR...
GNNN...
LOOK AT HIM... HE'S AMAZING!
It's like he's possessed!
WOW...
TMP
I WANNA BE RIPPED LIKE HIM.
IT'D BE KINDA CREEPY IF YOU WERE MUSCULAR...
WORKING-ING OUT?
...!
SIR!
H-HELLO...
HELLO.
SHP
DO YOU HAVE A MOMENT, INVESTIGATOR URIE?
SIR. (WHAT'S HE DOING HERE?)

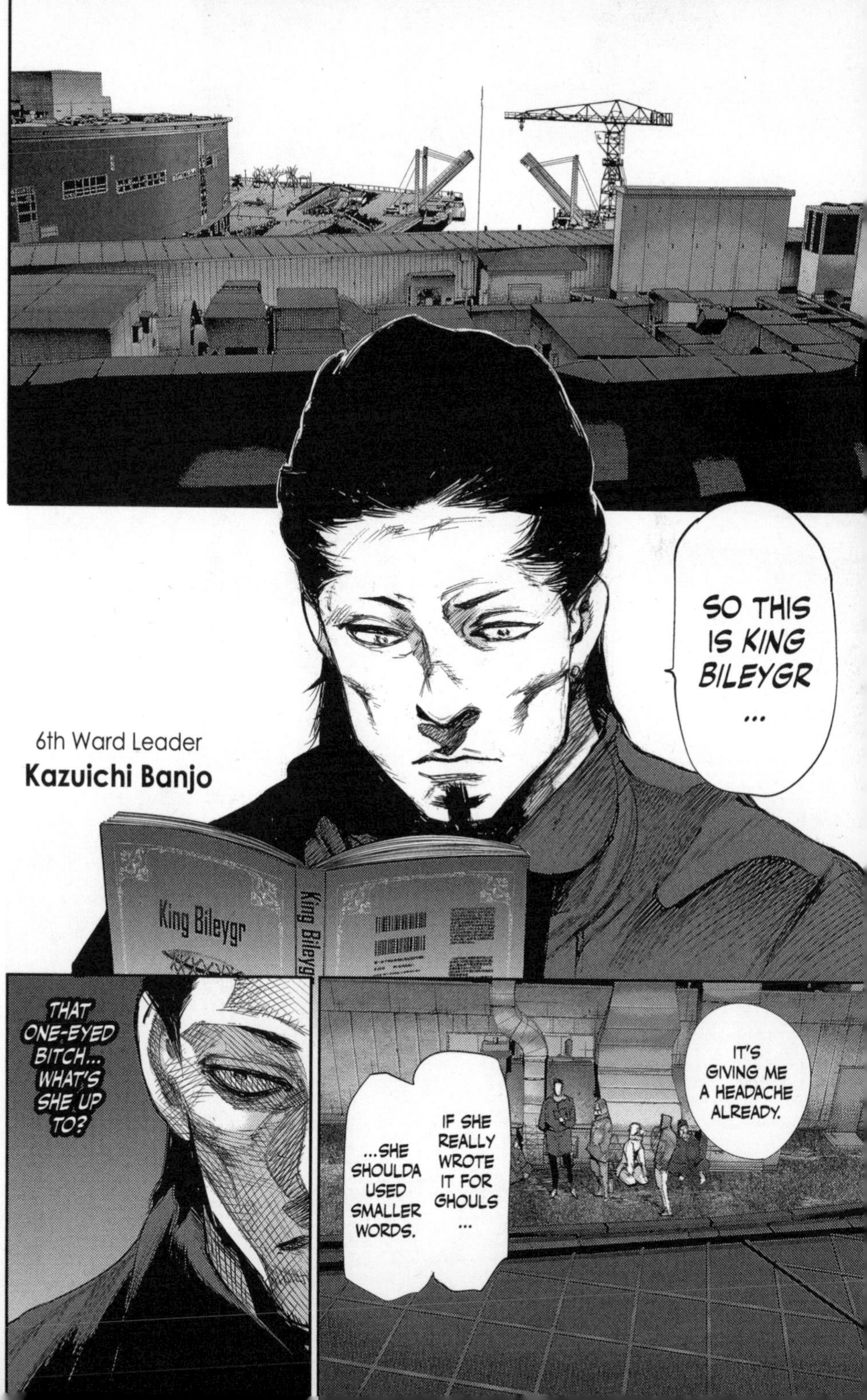
SO THIS IS KING BILEYGR ...
6th Ward Leader
Kazuichi Banjo
King Bileygr
IT'S GIVING ME A HEADACHE ALREADY.
IF SHE REALLY WROTE IT FOR GHOULS ...
...SHE SHOULDA USED SMALLER WORDS.
THAT ONE-EYED BITCH... WHAT'S SHE UP TO?

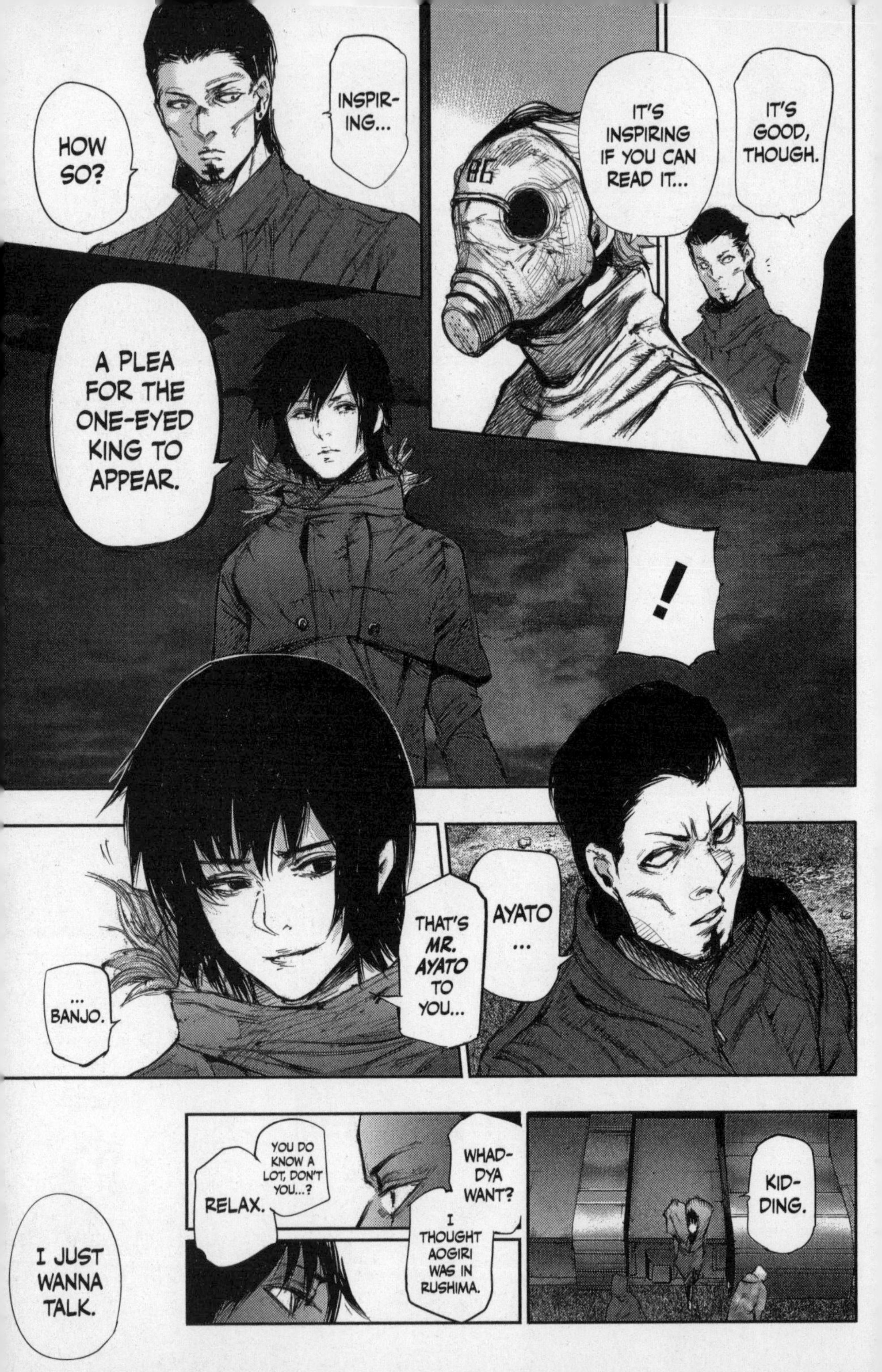
IT'S GOOD, THOUGH.
IT'S INSPIRING IF YOU CAN READ IT...
INSPIRING...
HOW SO?
A PLEA FOR THE ONE-EYED KING TO APPEAR.
!
AYATO...
THAT'S *MR. AYATO* TO YOU...
... BANJO.
KIDDING.
WHADDYA WANT?
I THOUGHT AOGIRI WAS IN RUSHIMA.
YOU DO KNOW A LOT, DON'T YOU...?
RELAX.
I JUST WANNA TALK.

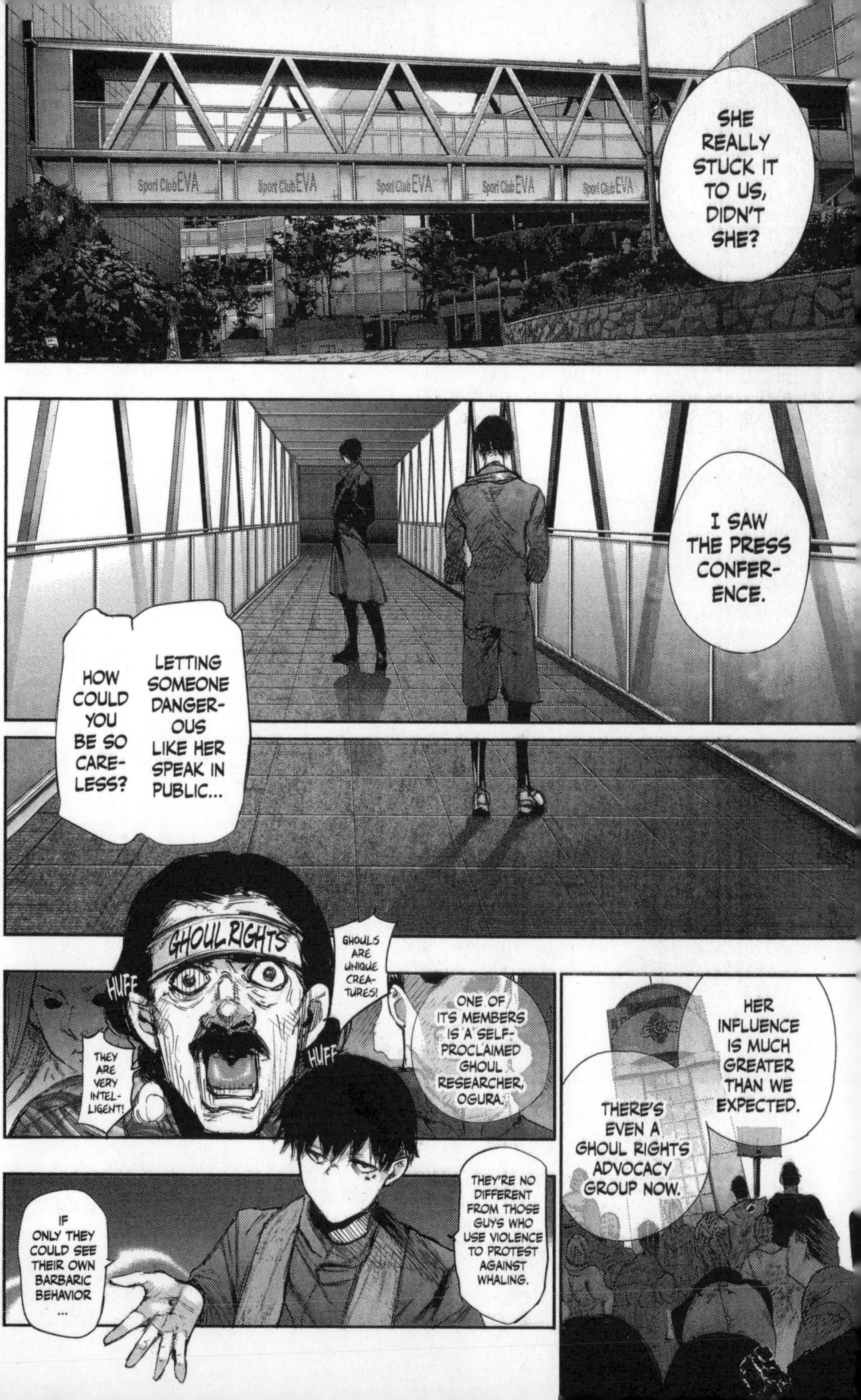
Sport Club EVA
SHE REALLY STUCK IT TO US, DIDN'T SHE?
I SAW THE PRESS CONFERENCE.
LETTING SOMEONE DANGEROUS LIKE HER SPEAK IN PUBLIC...
HOW COULD YOU BE SO CARELESS?
HER INFLUENCE IS MUCH GREATER THAN WE EXPECTED.
THERE'S EVEN A GHOUL RIGHTS ADVOCACY GROUP NOW.
GHOUL RIGHTS
GHOULS ARE UNIQUE CREATURES!
ONE OF ITS MEMBERS IS A SELF-PROCLAIMED GHOUL RESEARCHER, OGURA.
HUFF
HUFF
THEY ARE VERY INTELLIGENT!
THEY'RE NO DIFFERENT FROM THOSE GUYS WHO USE VIOLENCE TO PROTEST AGAINST WHALING.
IF ONLY THEY COULD SEE THEIR OWN BARBARIC BEHAVIOR...

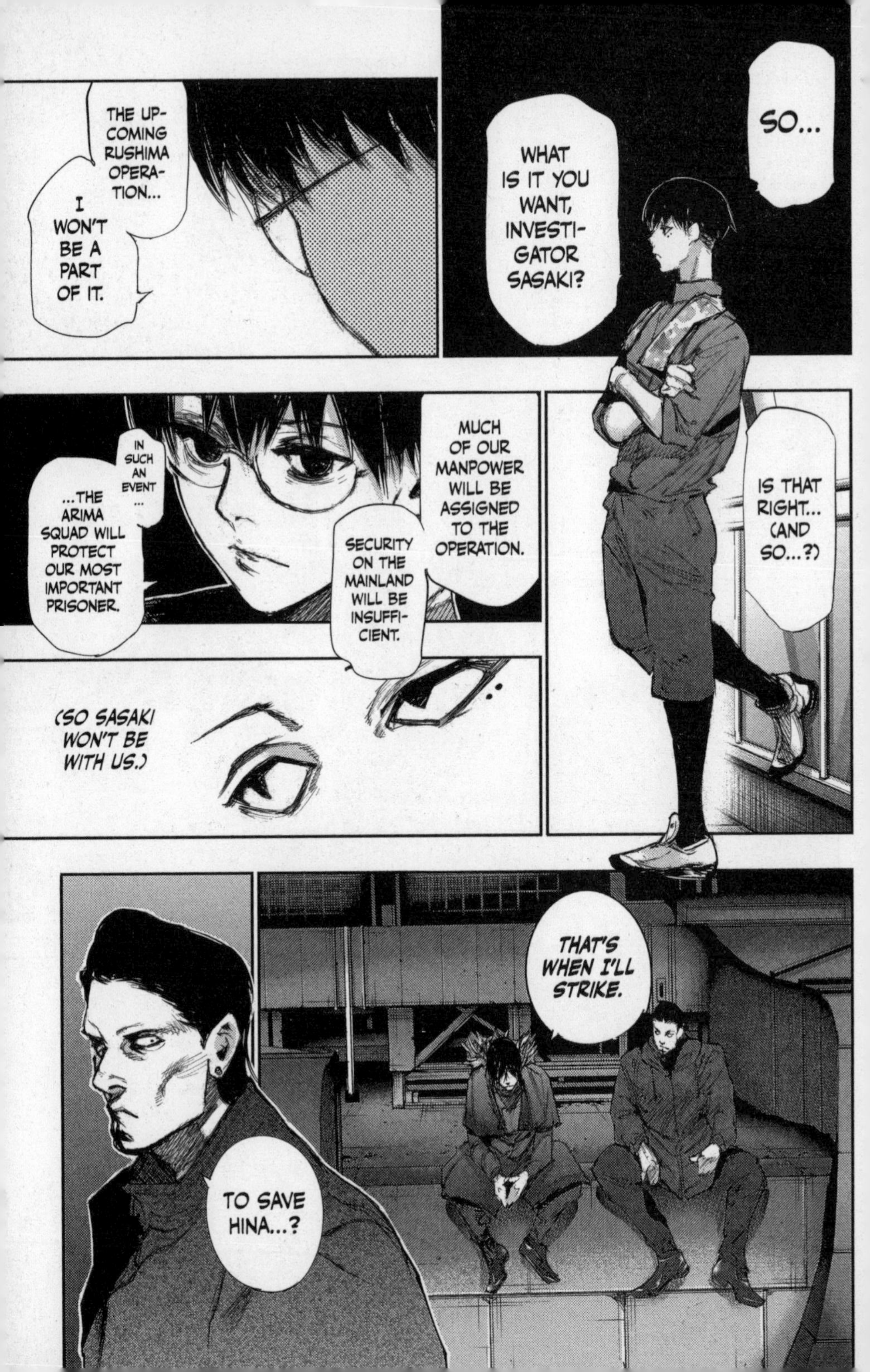
SO...
WHAT IS IT YOU WANT, INVESTIGATOR SASAKI?
THE UPCOMING RUSHIMA OPERATION...
I WON'T BE A PART OF IT.
IS THAT RIGHT... (AND SO...?)
MUCH OF OUR MANPOWER WILL BE ASSIGNED TO THE OPERATION.
SECURITY ON THE MAINLAND WILL BE INSUFFICIENT.
IN SUCH AN EVENT...
...THE ARIMA SQUAD WILL PROTECT OUR MOST IMPORTANT PRISONER.
(SO SASAKI WON'T BE WITH US.)
THAT'S WHEN I'LL STRIKE.
TO SAVE HINA...?

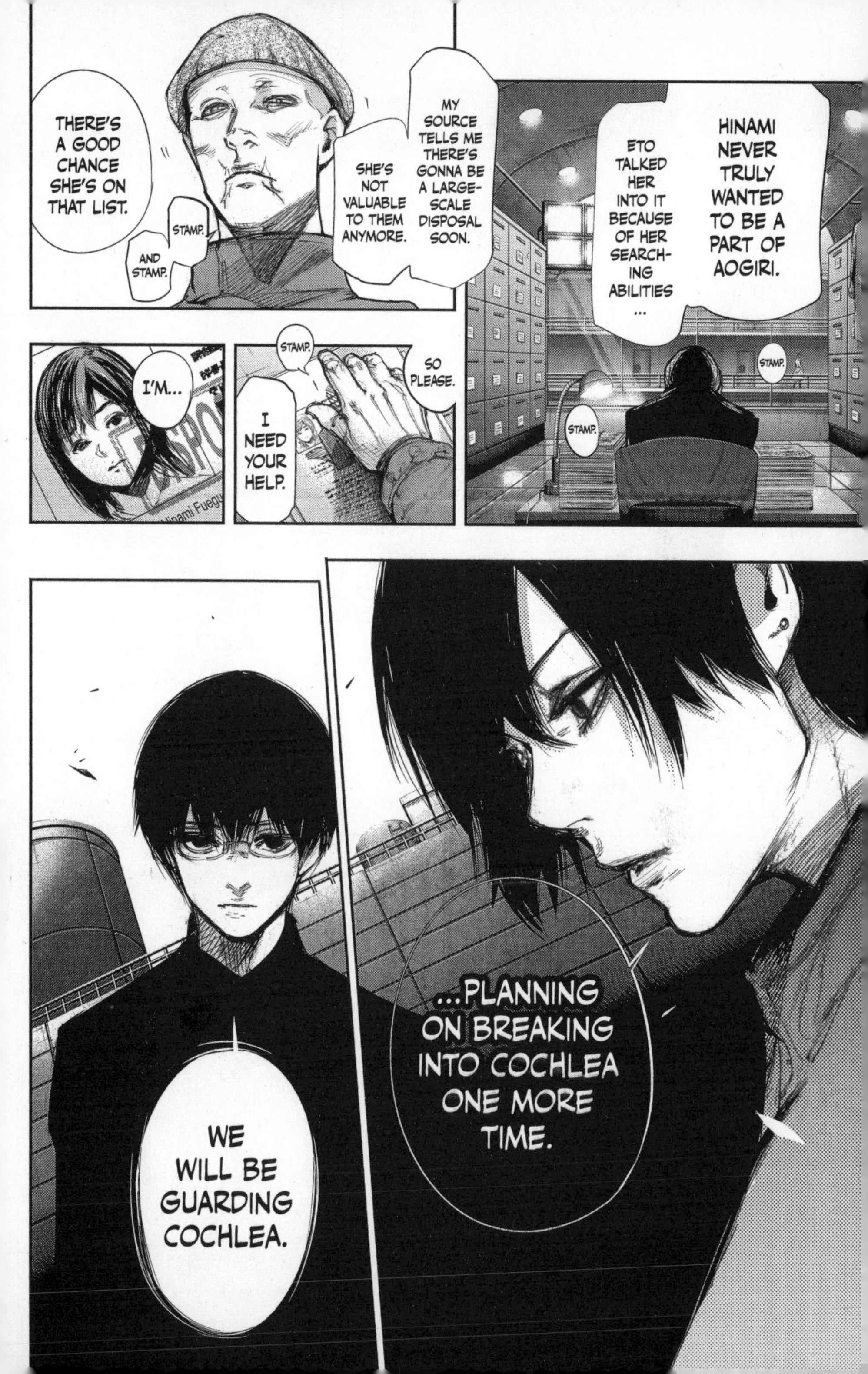
HINAMI NEVER TRULY WANTED TO BE A PART OF AOGIRI.
ETO TALKED HER INTO IT BECAUSE OF HER SEARCHING ABILITIES ...
STAMP.
STAMP.
MY SOURCE TELLS ME THERE'S GONNA BE A LARGE-SCALE DISPOSAL SOON.
SHE'S NOT VALUABLE TO THEM ANYMORE.
THERE'S A GOOD CHANCE SHE'S ON THAT LIST.
STAMP.
AND STAMP.
SO PLEASE.
STAMP.
I NEED YOUR HELP.
I'M...
...PLANNING ON BREAKING INTO COCHLEA ONE MORE TIME.
WE WILL BE GUARDING COCHLEA.

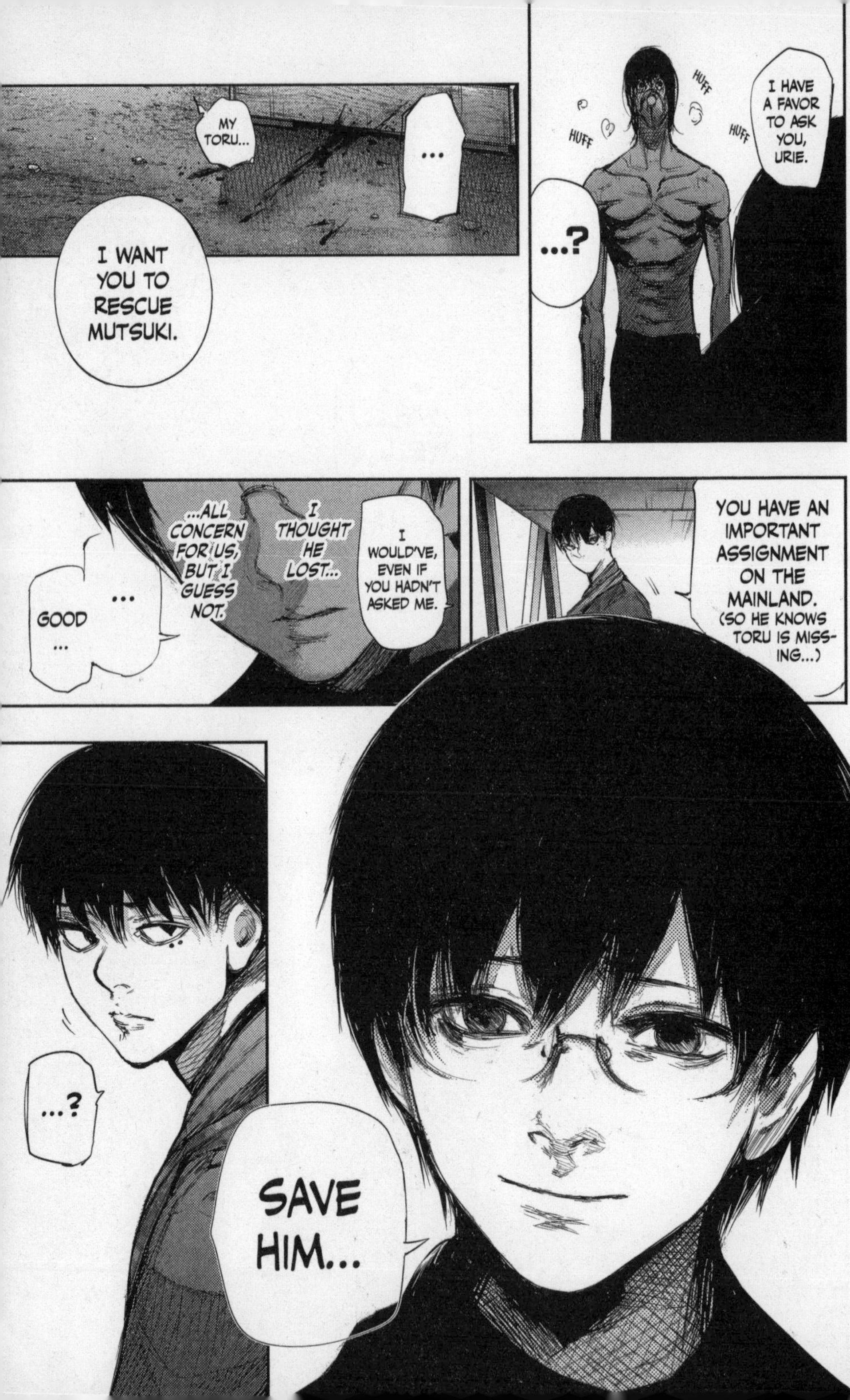
I HAVE A FAVOR TO ASK YOU, URIE.
HUFF
HUFF
HUFF
...?
MY TORU...
...
I WANT YOU TO RESCUE MUTSUKI.
YOU HAVE AN IMPORTANT ASSIGNMENT ON THE MAINLAND.
(SO HE KNOWS TORU IS MISSING...)
I WOULD'VE, EVEN IF YOU HADN'T ASKED ME.
I THOUGHT HE LOST...
...ALL CONCERN FOR US, BUT I GUESS NOT.
... GOOD ...
SAVE HIM...
...?

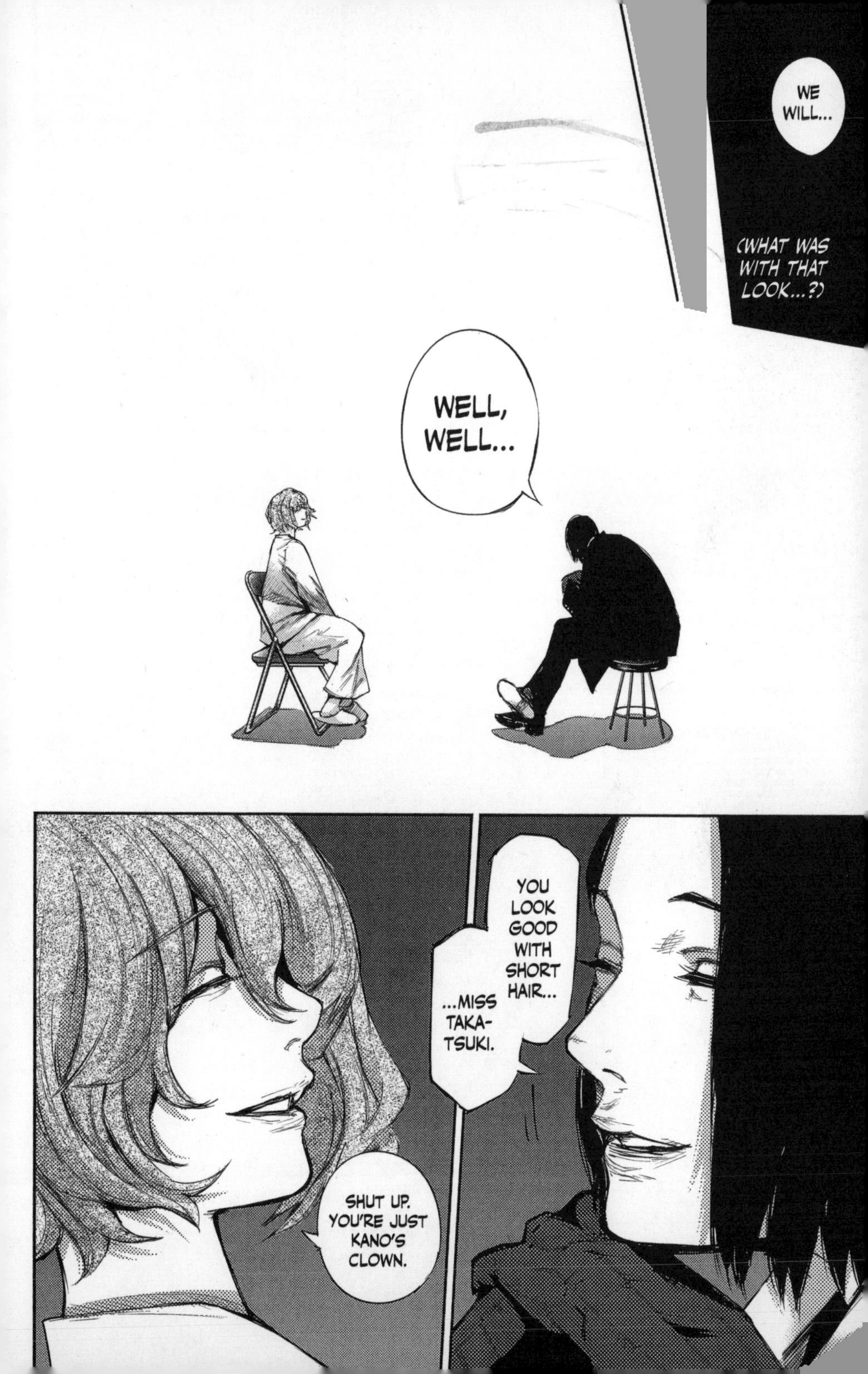
WE WILL...
(WHAT WAS WITH THAT LOOK...?)
WELL, WELL...
YOU LOOK GOOD WITH SHORT HAIR...
...MISS TAKA-TSUKI.
SHUT UP. YOU'RE JUST KANO'S CLOWN.

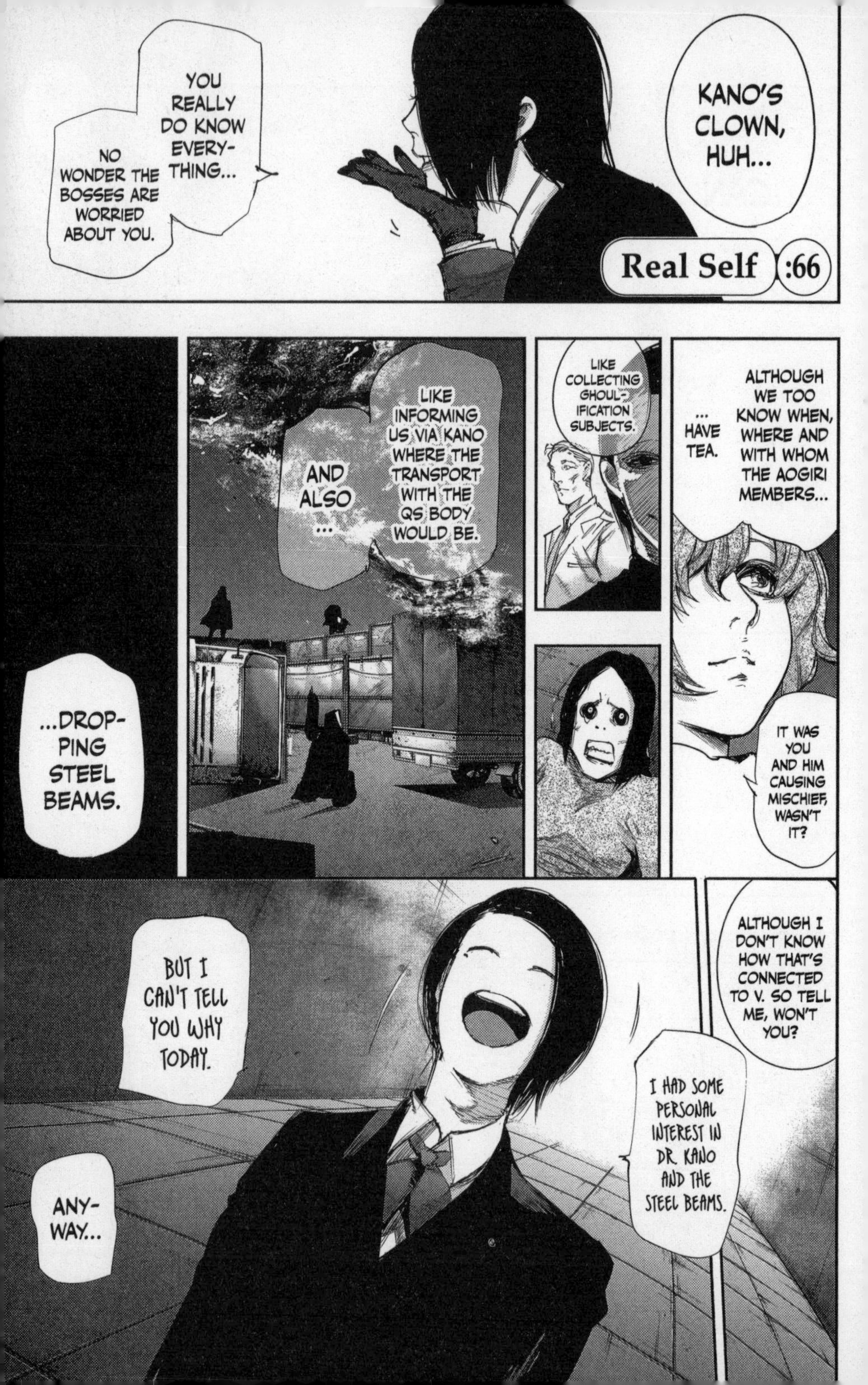
KANO'S CLOWN, HUH...
Real Self :66
YOU REALLY DO KNOW EVERY-THING...
NO WONDER THE BOSSES ARE WORRIED ABOUT YOU.
ALTHOUGH WE TOO KNOW WHEN, WHERE AND WITH WHOM THE AOGIRI MEMBERS...
... HAVE TEA.
IT WAS YOU AND HIM CAUSING MISCHIEF, WASN'T IT?
LIKE COLLECTING GHOUL-IFICATION SUBJECTS.
LIKE INFORMING US VIA KANO WHERE THE TRANSPORT WITH THE QS BODY WOULD BE.
AND ALSO ...
...DROP-PING STEEL BEAMS.
ALTHOUGH I DON'T KNOW HOW THAT'S CONNECTED TO V. SO TELL ME, WON'T YOU?
I HAD SOME PERSONAL INTEREST IN DR. KANO AND THE STEEL BEAMS.
BUT I CAN'T TELL YOU WHY TODAY.
ANY-WAY...

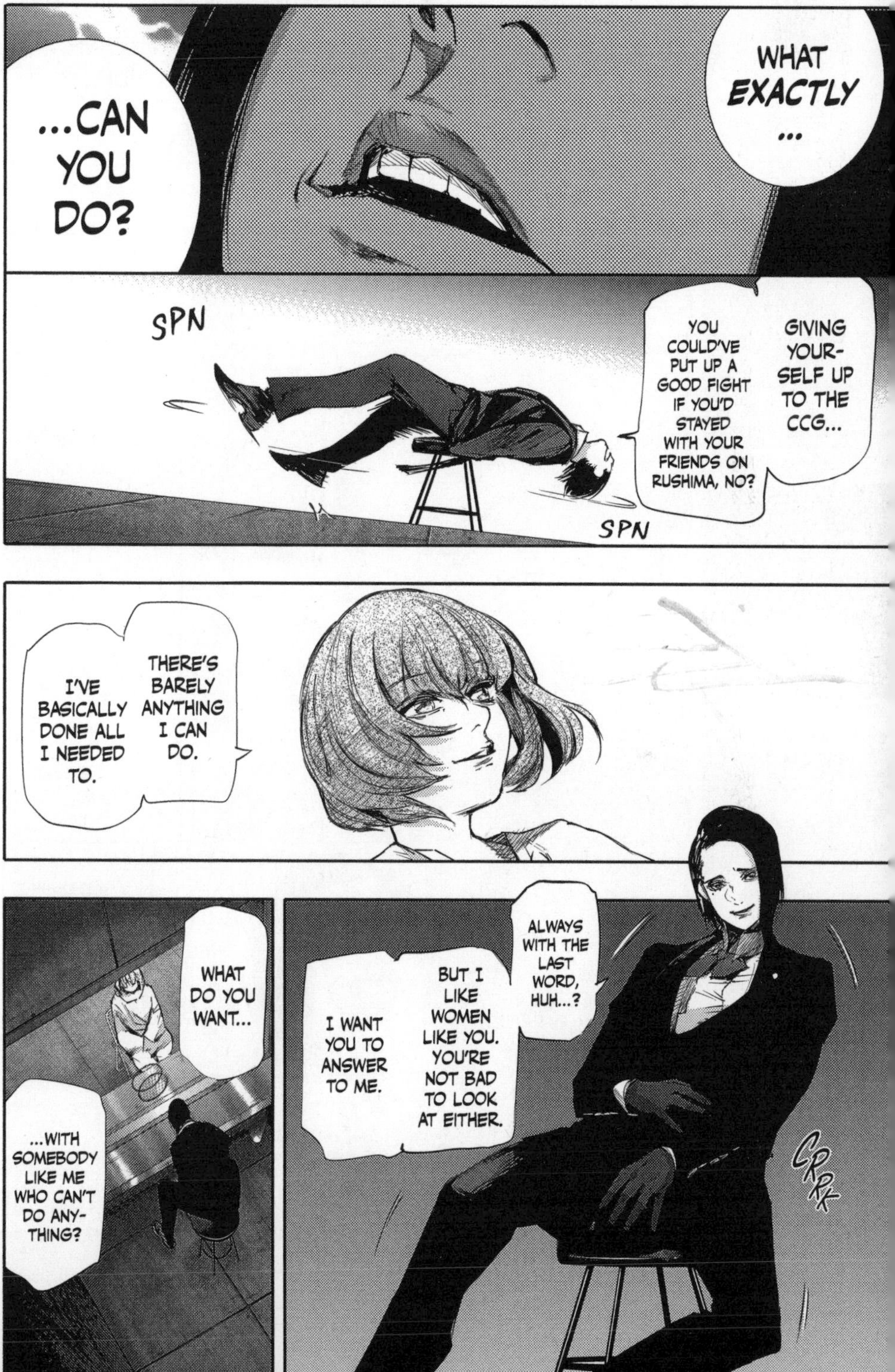
WHAT EXACTLY ...
...CAN YOU DO?
GIVING YOURSELF UP TO THE CCG...
YOU COULD'VE PUT UP A GOOD FIGHT IF YOU'D STAYED WITH YOUR FRIENDS ON RUSHIMA, NO?
SPN
SPN
THERE'S BARELY ANYTHING I CAN DO.
I'VE BASICALLY DONE ALL I NEEDED TO.
ALWAYS WITH THE LAST WORD, HUH...?
BUT I LIKE WOMEN LIKE YOU. YOU'RE NOT BAD TO LOOK AT EITHER.
I WANT YOU TO ANSWER TO ME.
CRRK
WHAT DO YOU WANT...
...WITH SOMEBODY LIKE ME WHO CAN'T DO ANYTHING?

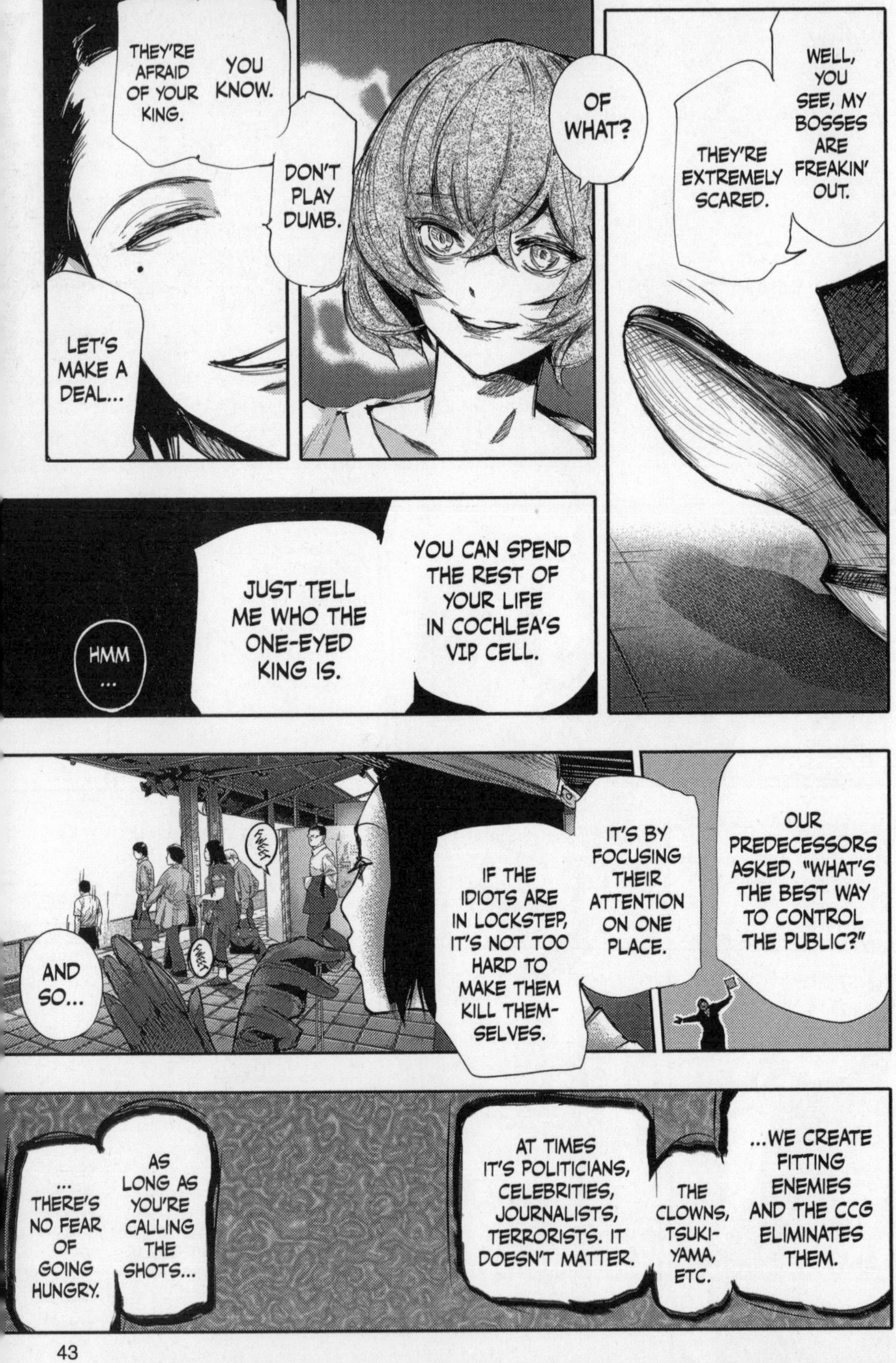
WELL, YOU SEE, MY BOSSES ARE FREAKIN' OUT.
THEY'RE EXTREMELY SCARED.
OF WHAT?
YOU KNOW.
THEY'RE AFRAID OF YOUR KING.
DON'T PLAY DUMB.
LET'S MAKE A DEAL...
YOU CAN SPEND THE REST OF YOUR LIFE IN COCHLEA'S VIP CELL.
JUST TELL ME WHO THE ONE-EYED KING IS.
HMM ...
OUR PREDECESSORS ASKED, "WHAT'S THE BEST WAY TO CONTROL THE PUBLIC?"
IT'S BY FOCUSING THEIR ATTENTION ON ONE PLACE.
IF THE IDIOTS ARE IN LOCKSTEP, IT'S NOT TOO HARD TO MAKE THEM KILL THEM-SELVES.
AND SO...
...WE CREATE FITTING ENEMIES AND THE CCG ELIMINATES THEM.
THE CLOWNS, TSUKI-YAMA, ETC.
AT TIMES IT'S POLITICIANS, CELEBRITIES, JOURNALISTS, TERRORISTS. IT DOESN'T MATTER.
AS LONG AS YOU'RE CALLING THE SHOTS...
... THERE'S NO FEAR OF GOING HUNGRY.

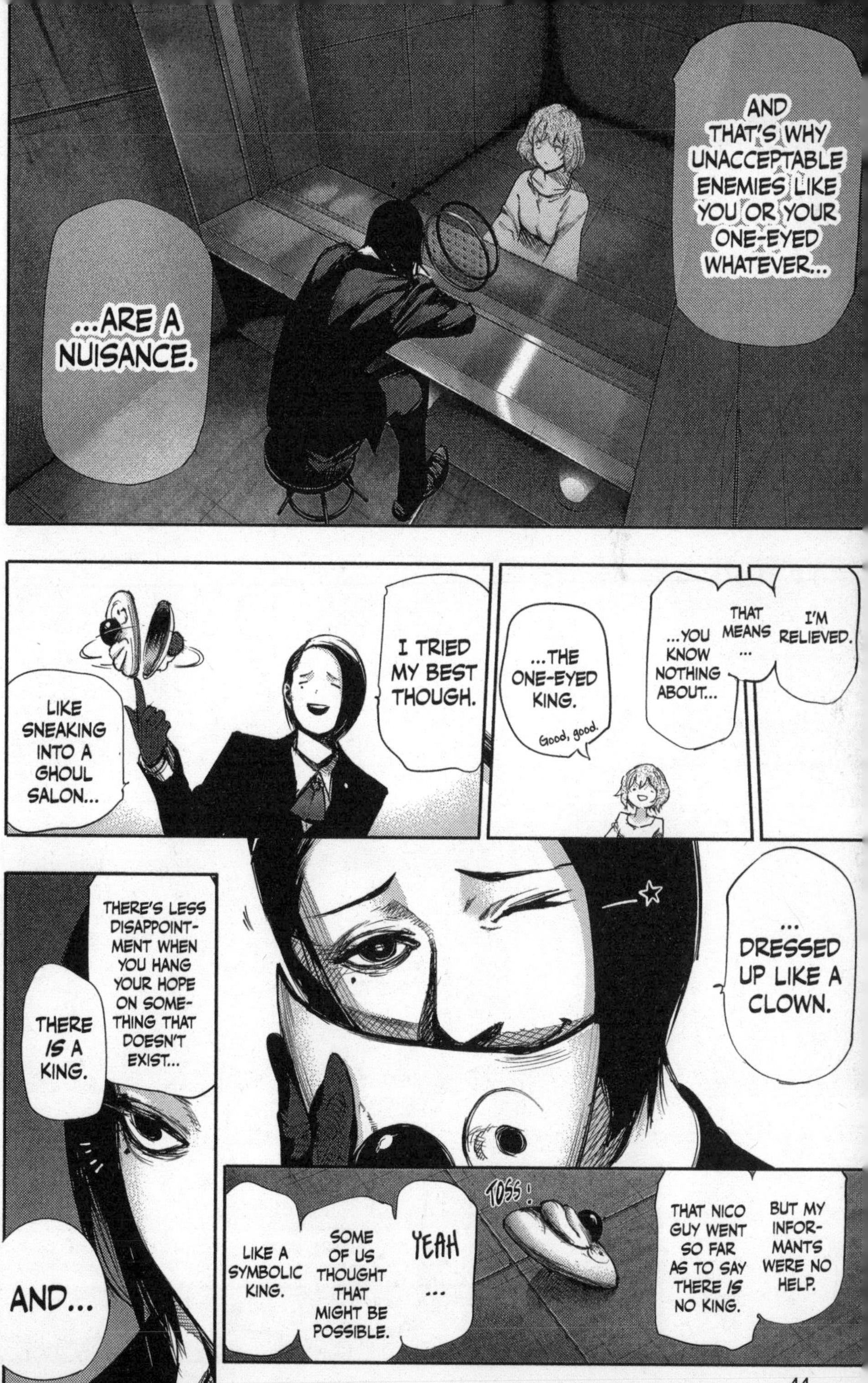
AND THAT'S WHY UNACCEPTABLE ENEMIES LIKE YOU OR YOUR ONE-EYED WHATEVER...
...ARE A NUISANCE.
I'M RELIEVED.
THAT MEANS ...
...YOU KNOW NOTHING ABOUT...
...THE ONE-EYED KING.
Good, good.
I TRIED MY BEST THOUGH.
LIKE SNEAKING INTO A GHOUL SALON...
... DRESSED UP LIKE A CLOWN.
BUT MY INFORMANTS WERE NO HELP.
THAT NICO GUY WENT SO FAR AS TO SAY THERE *IS* NO KING.
TOSS!
YEAH ...
SOME OF US THOUGHT THAT MIGHT BE POSSIBLE.
LIKE A SYMBOLIC KING.
THERE'S LESS DISAPPOINTMENT WHEN YOU HANG YOUR HOPE ON SOMETHING THAT DOESN'T EXIST...
THERE *IS* A KING.
AND...

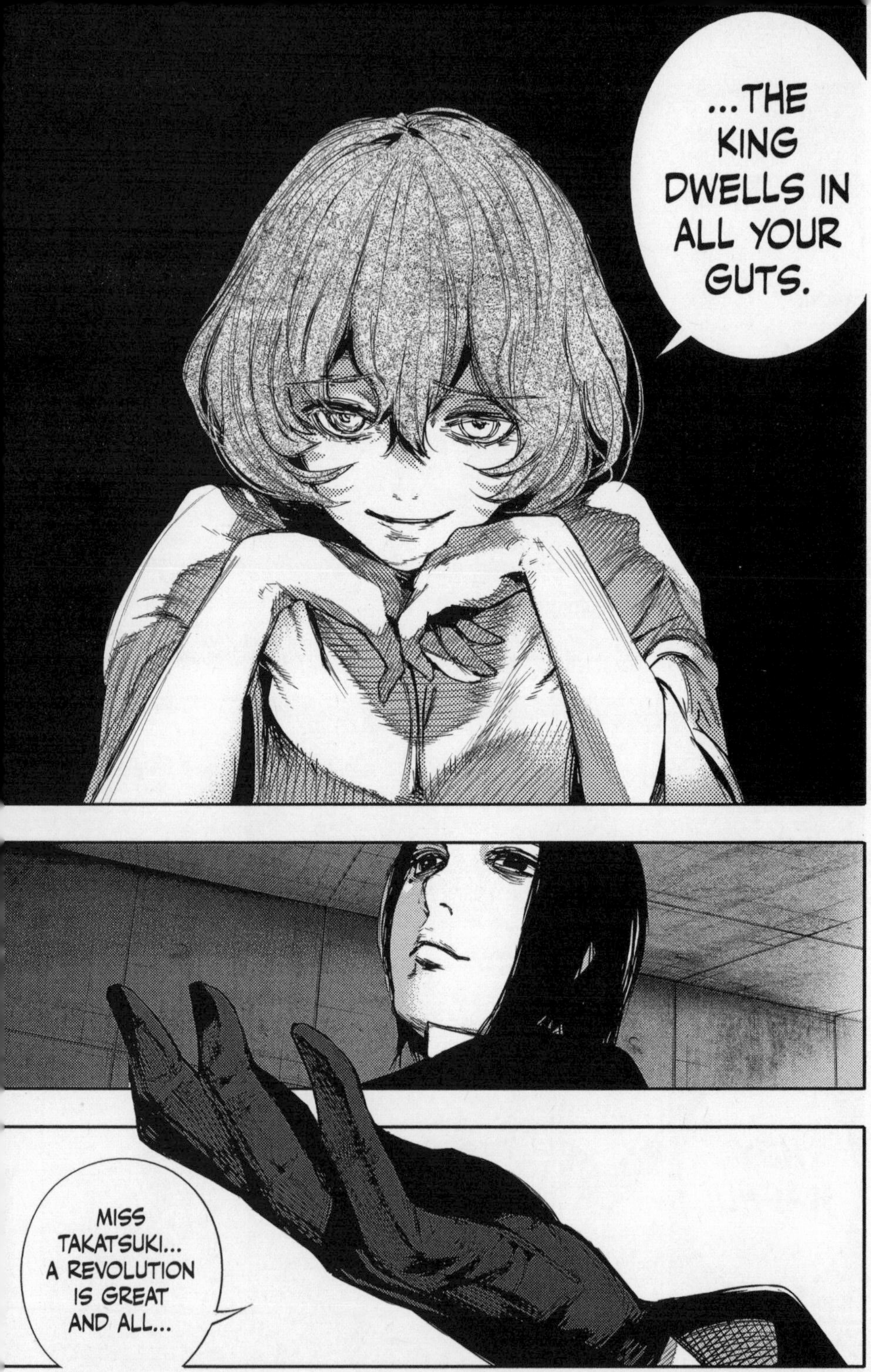
...THE KING DWELLS IN ALL YOUR GUTS.
MISS TAKATSUKI... A REVOLUTION IS GREAT AND ALL...

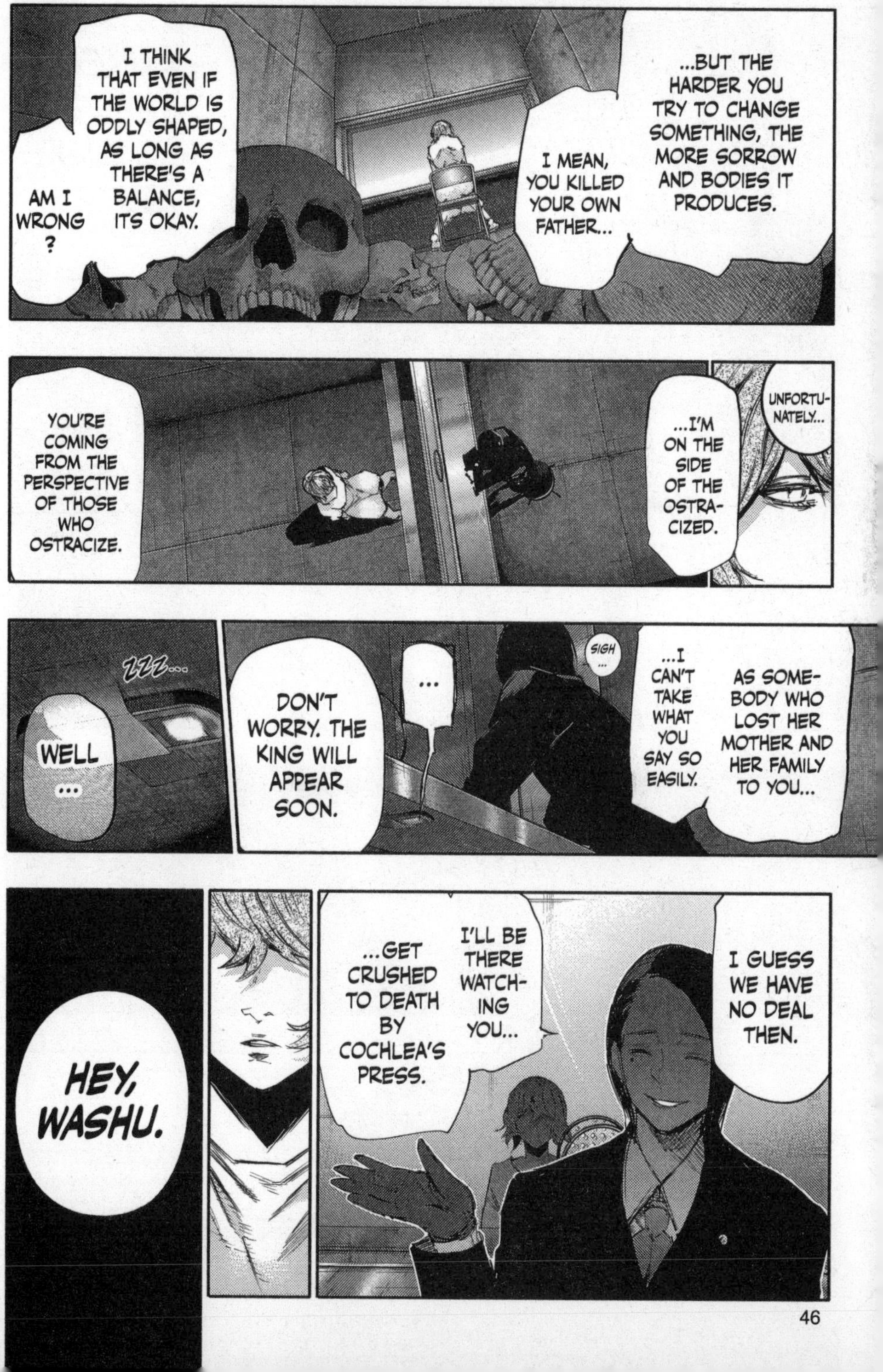
...BUT THE HARDER YOU TRY TO CHANGE SOMETHING, THE MORE SORROW AND BODIES IT PRODUCES.
I MEAN, YOU KILLED YOUR OWN FATHER...
I THINK THAT EVEN IF THE WORLD IS ODDLY SHAPED, AS LONG AS THERE'S A BALANCE, ITS OKAY.
AM I WRONG?
UNFORTUNATELY...
...I'M ON THE SIDE OF THE OSTRACIZED.
YOU'RE COMING FROM THE PERSPECTIVE OF THOSE WHO OSTRACIZE.
AS SOMEBODY WHO LOST HER MOTHER AND HER FAMILY TO YOU...
...I CAN'T TAKE WHAT YOU SAY SO EASILY.
SIGH...
...
DON'T WORRY. THE KING WILL APPEAR SOON.
ZZZ...
WELL...
I GUESS WE HAVE NO DEAL THEN.
I'LL BE THERE WATCHING YOU...
...GET CRUSHED TO DEATH BY COCHLEA'S PRESS.
HEY, WASHU.

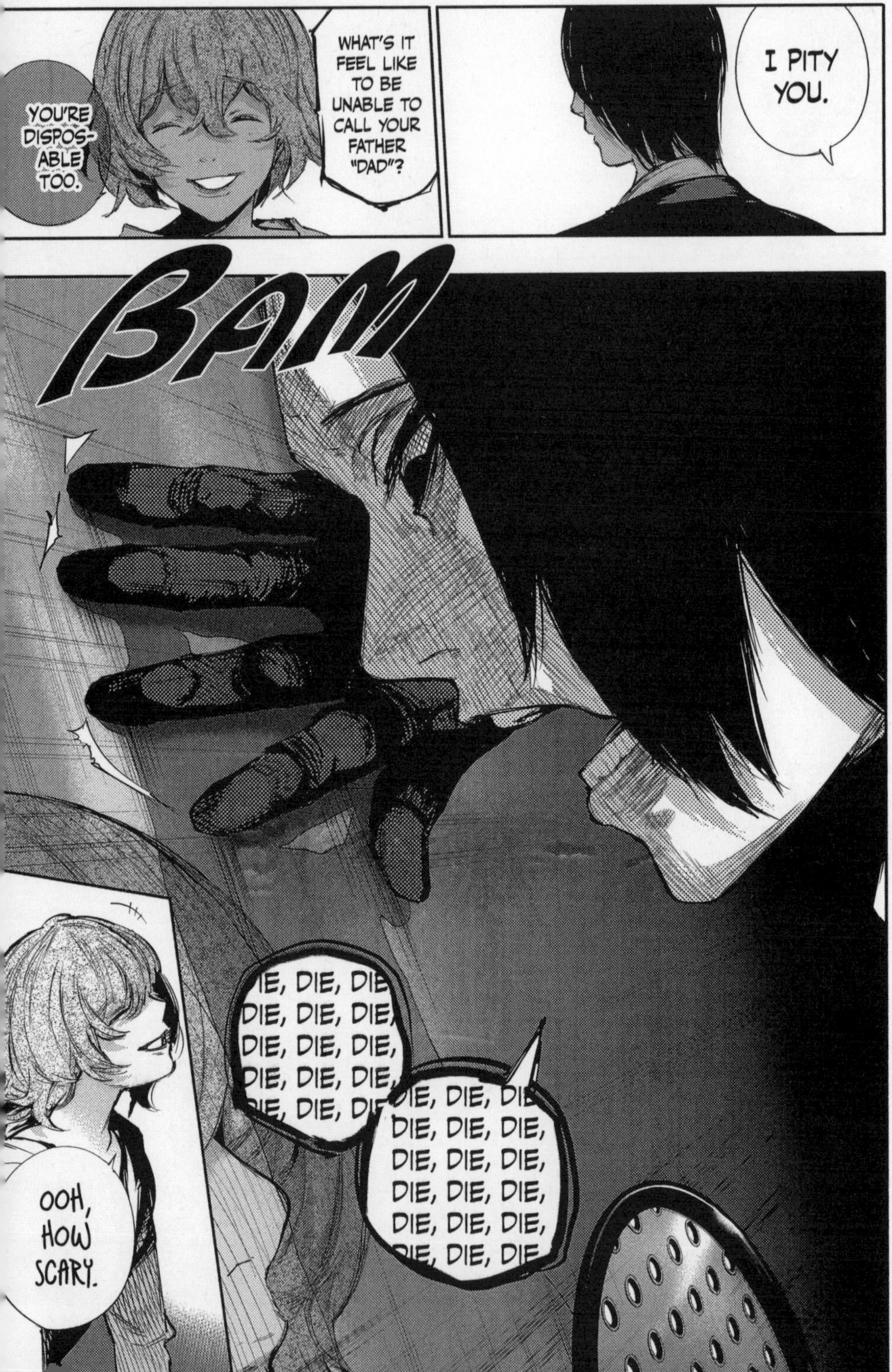
I PITY YOU.
WHAT'S IT FEEL LIKE TO BE UNABLE TO CALL YOUR FATHER "DAD"?
YOU'RE DISPOS-ABLE TOO.
BAM
DIE, DIE, DIE, DIE, DIE, DIE, DIE, DIE, DIE, DIE, DIE, DIE, DIE, DIE, DIE
DIE, DIE, DIE, DIE, DIE, DIE, DIE, DIE, DIE, DIE, DIE, DIE, DIE, DIE, DIE, DIE, DIE, DIE, DIE, DIE, DIE
OOH, HOW SCARY.

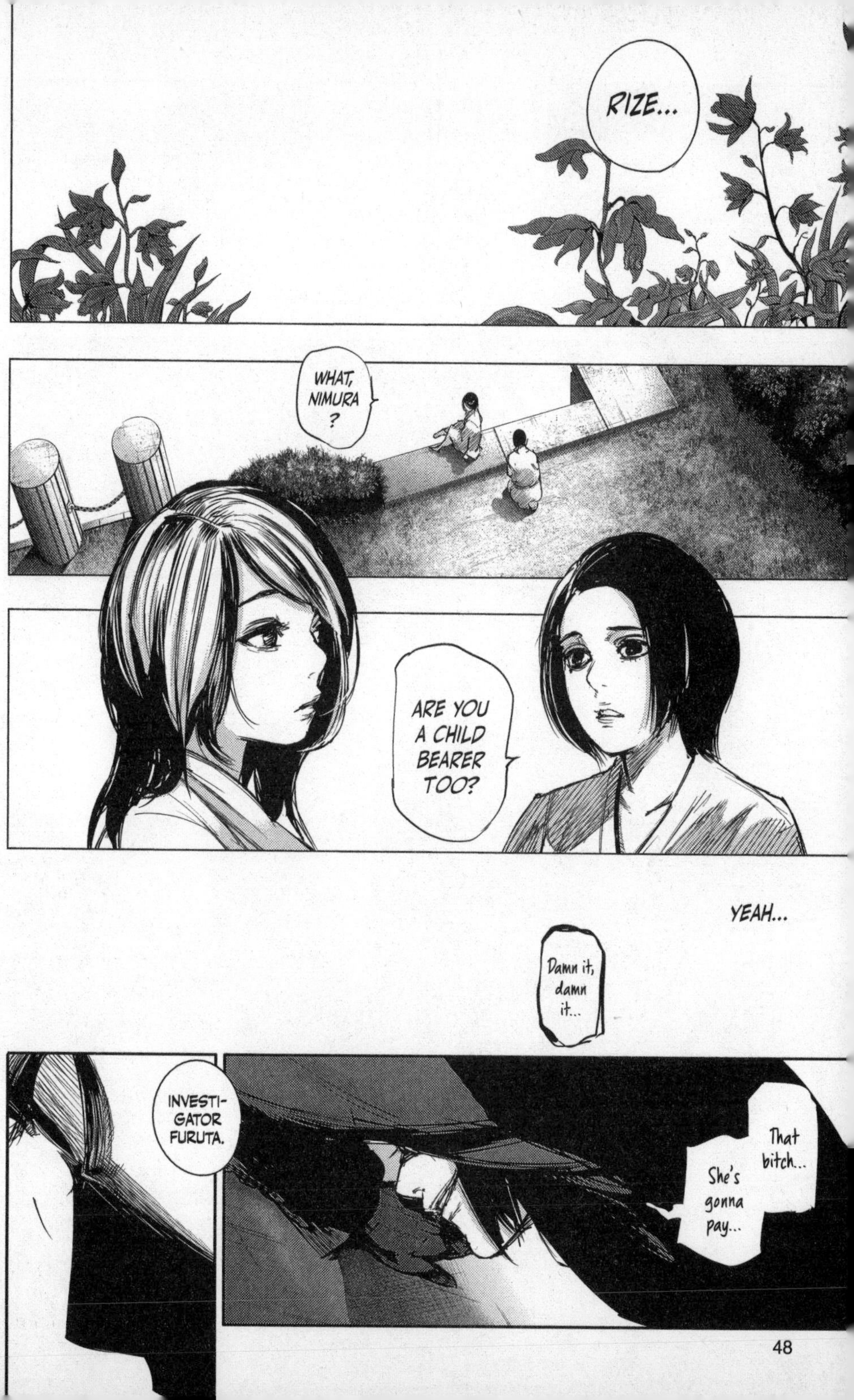
RIZE...
WHAT, NIMURA?
ARE YOU A CHILD BEARER TOO?
YEAH...
Damn it, damn it...
That bitch...
She's gonna pay...
INVESTI-GATOR FURUTA.

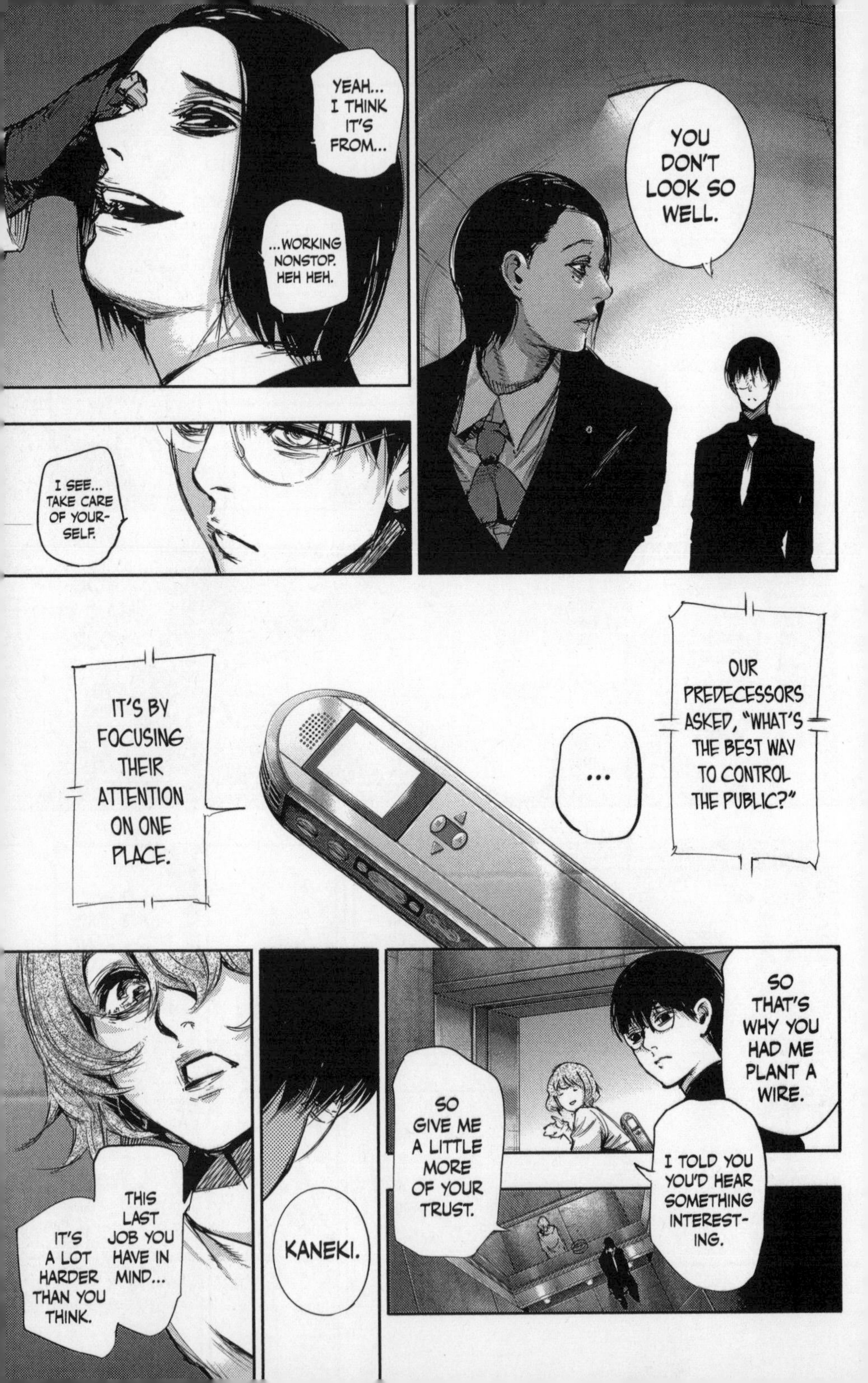
YOU DON'T LOOK SO WELL.
YEAH... I THINK IT'S FROM...
...WORKING NONSTOP. HEH HEH.
I SEE... TAKE CARE OF YOUR-SELF.
OUR PREDECESSORS ASKED, "WHAT'S THE BEST WAY TO CONTROL THE PUBLIC?"
...
IT'S BY FOCUSING THEIR ATTENTION ON ONE PLACE.
SO THAT'S WHY YOU HAD ME PLANT A WIRE.
I TOLD YOU YOU'D HEAR SOMETHING INTEREST-ING.
SO GIVE ME A LITTLE MORE OF YOUR TRUST.
KANEKI.
THIS LAST JOB YOU HAVE IN MIND...
IT'S A LOT HARDER THAN YOU THINK.

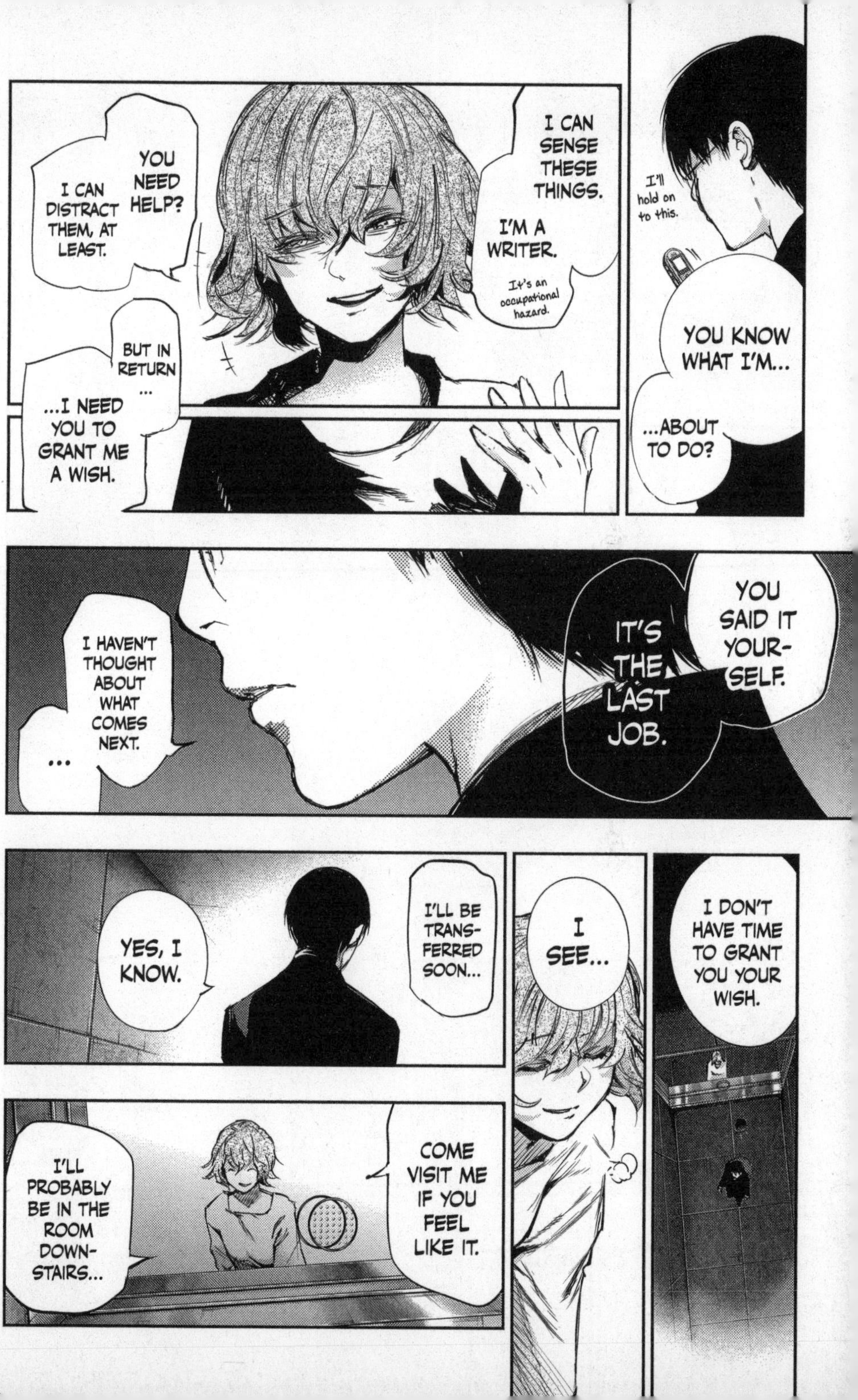
I'll hold on to this.
YOU KNOW WHAT I'M...
...ABOUT TO DO?
I CAN SENSE THESE THINGS.
I'M A WRITER.
It's an occupational hazard.
YOU NEED HELP?
I CAN DISTRACT THEM, AT LEAST.
BUT IN RETURN...
...I NEED YOU TO GRANT ME A WISH.
YOU SAID IT YOUR-SELF.
IT'S THE LAST JOB.
I HAVEN'T THOUGHT ABOUT WHAT COMES NEXT.
...
I DON'T HAVE TIME TO GRANT YOU YOUR WISH.
I SEE...
I'LL BE TRANS-FERRED SOON...
YES, I KNOW.
COME VISIT ME IF YOU FEEL LIKE IT.
I'LL PROBABLY BE IN THE ROOM DOWN-STAIRS...

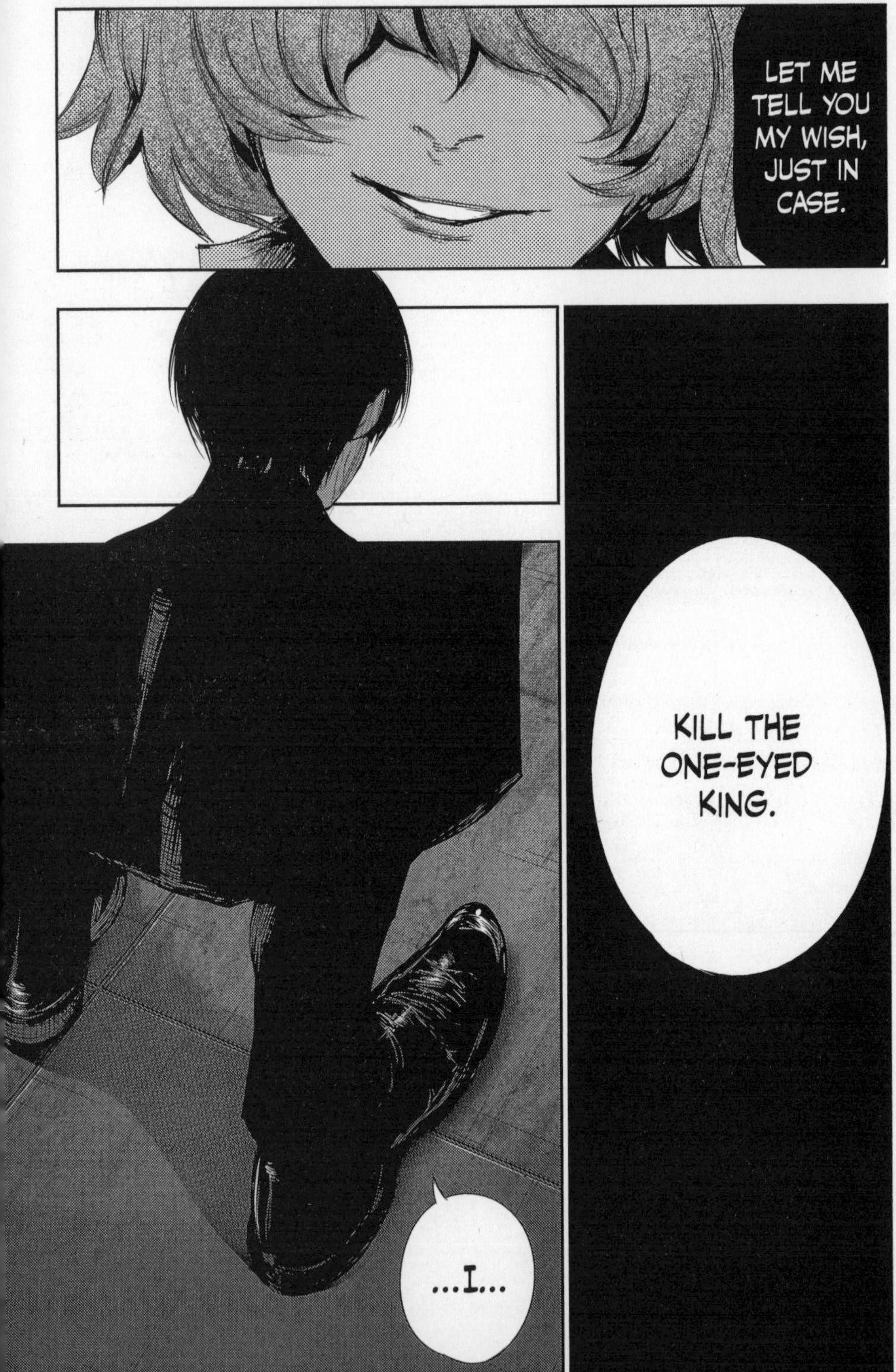
LET ME TELL YOU MY WISH, JUST IN CASE.
KILL THE ONE-EYED KING.
...I...

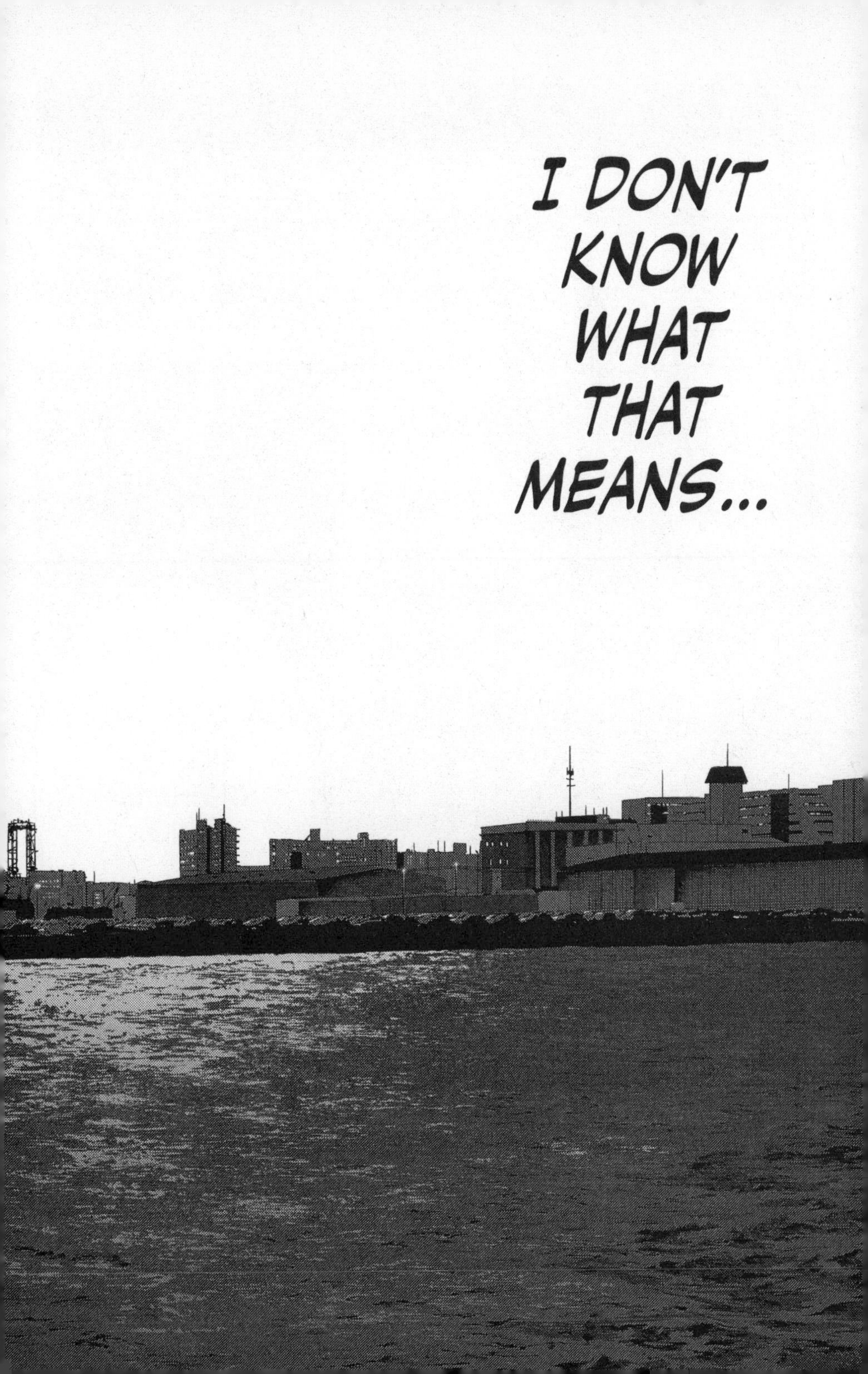
I DON'T KNOW WHAT THAT MEANS...

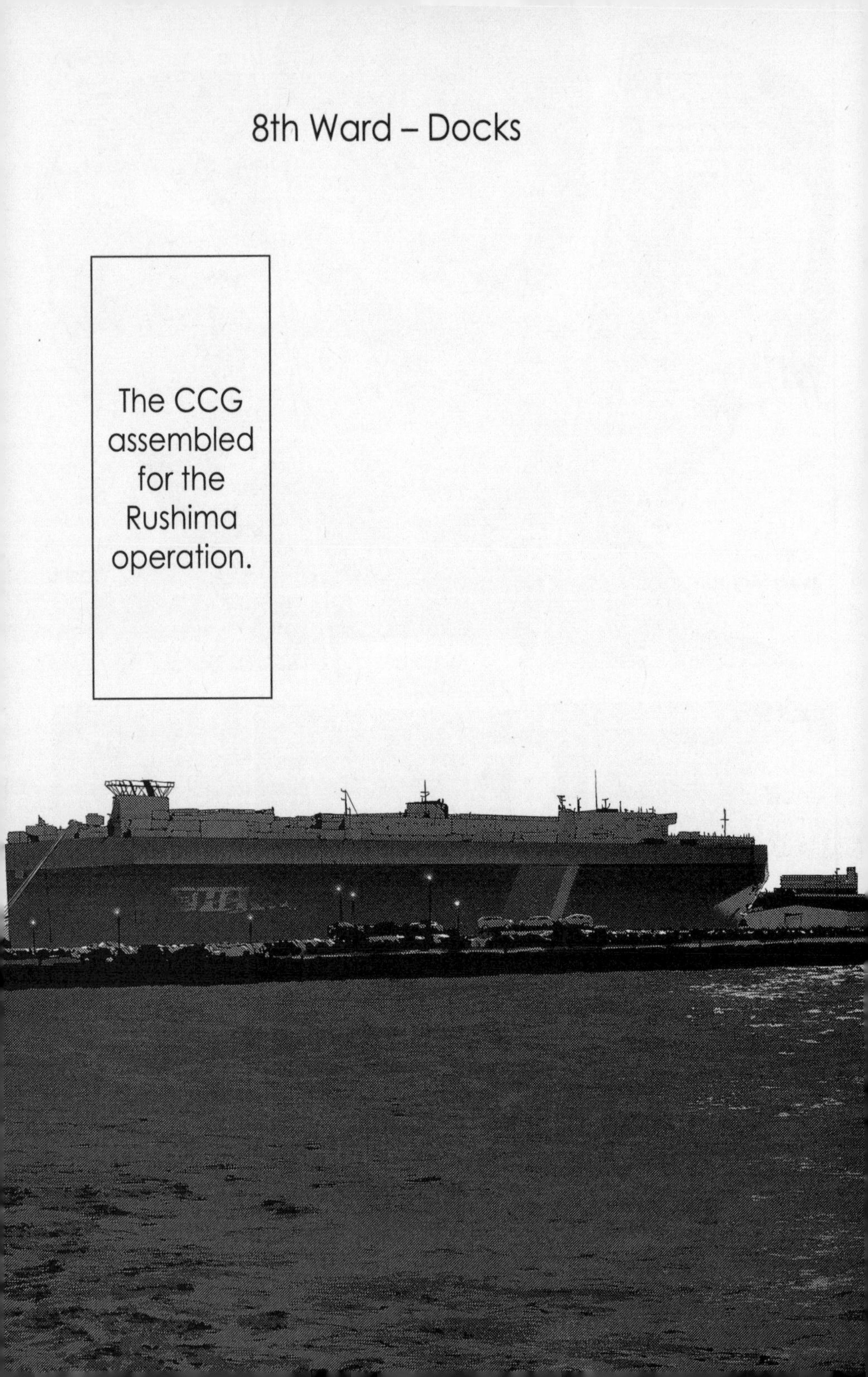
8th Ward – Docks
The CCG assembled for the Rushima operation.

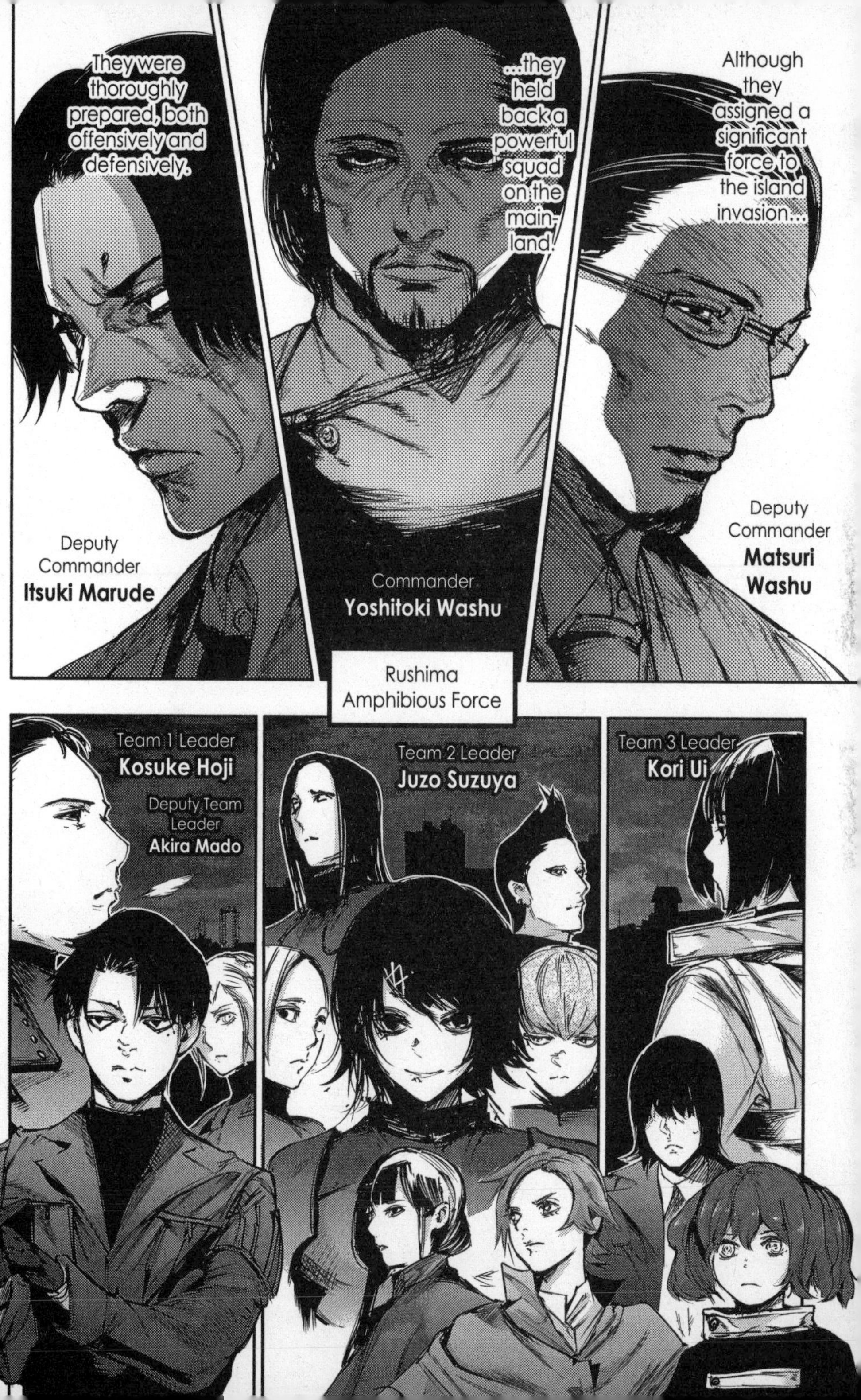
Although they assigned a significant force to the island invasion...
Deputy Commander Matsuri Washu
...they held back a powerful squad on the mainland.
Commander Yoshitoki Washu
They were thoroughly prepared, both offensively and defensively.
Deputy Commander Itsuki Marude
Rushima Amphibious Force
Team 3 Leader Kori Ui
Team 2 Leader Juzo Suzuya
Team 1 Leader Kosuke Hoji
Deputy Team Leader Akira Mado

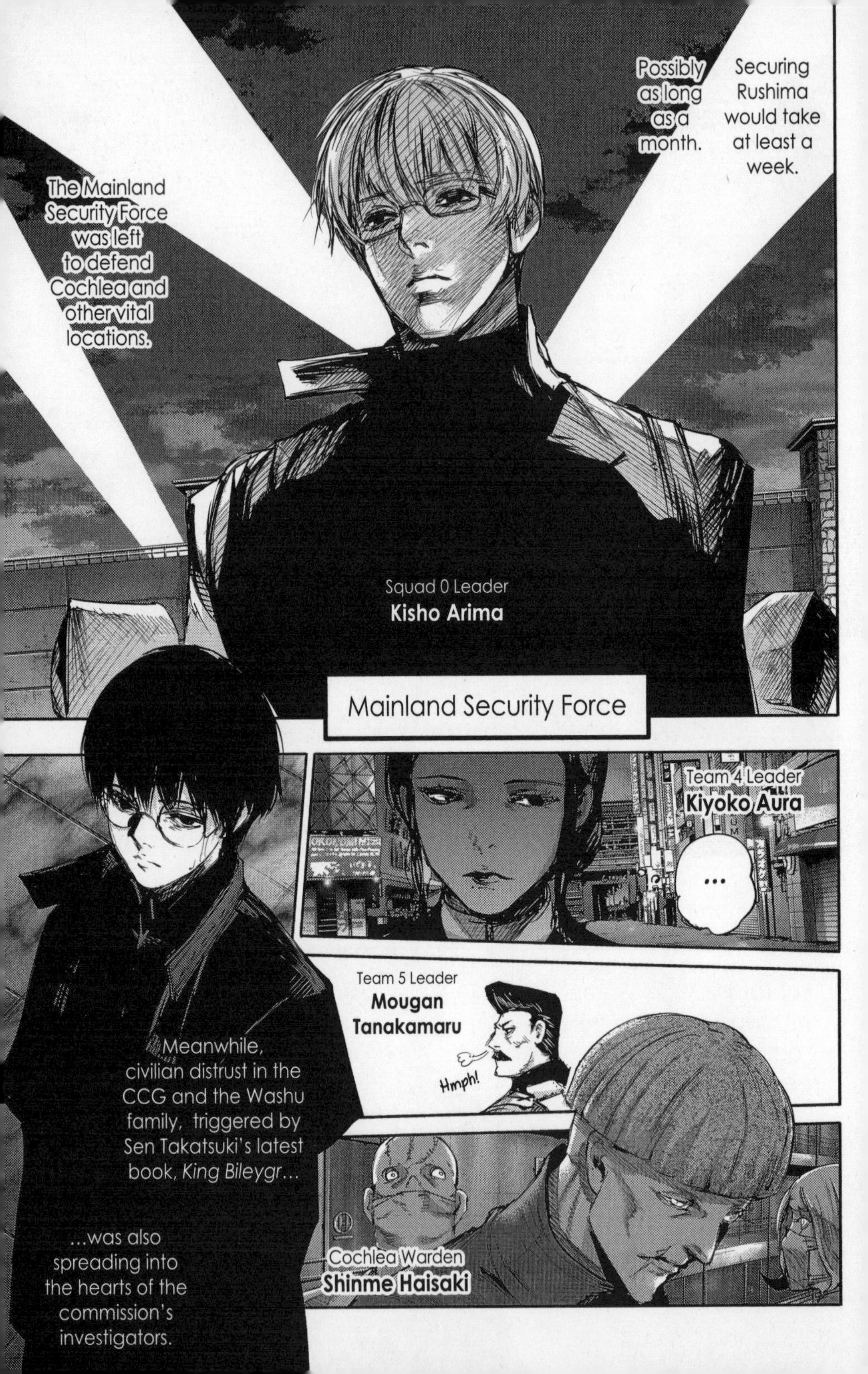
Securing Rushima would take at least a week.
Possibly as long as a month.
The Mainland Security Force was left to defend Cochlea and other vital locations.
Squad 0 Leader
Kisho Arima
Mainland Security Force
Team 4 Leader
Kiyoko Aura
...
Team 5 Leader
Mougan Tanakamaru
Hmph!
Cochlea Warden
Shinme Haisaki
Meanwhile, civilian distrust in the CCG and the Washu family, triggered by Sen Takatsuki's latest book, *King Bileygr*...
...was also spreading into the hearts of the commission's investigators.

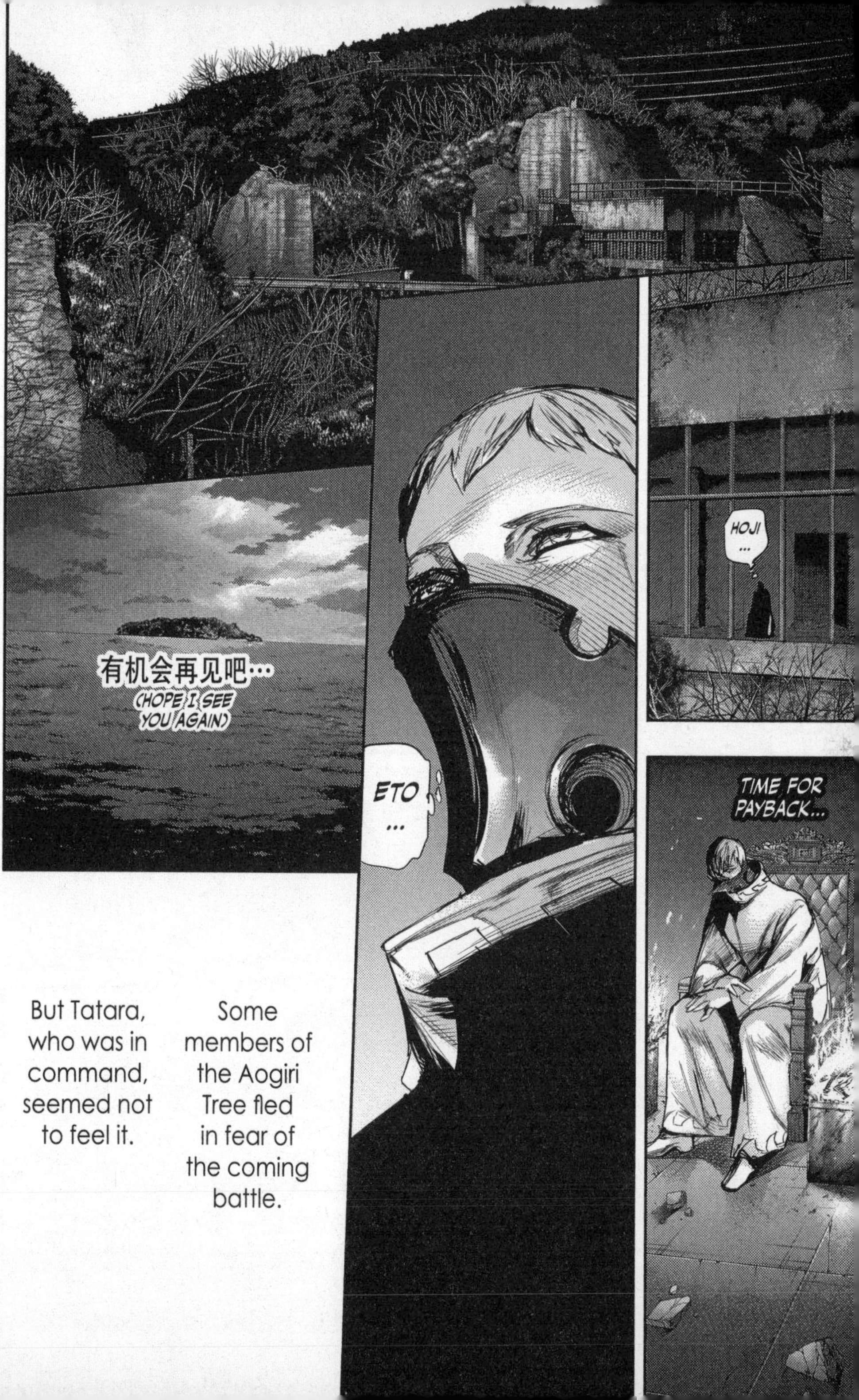
HOJI ...
TIME FOR PAYBACK...
ETO ...
有机会再见吧…
(HOPE I SEE YOU AGAIN)
Some members of the Aogiri Tree fled in fear of the coming battle.
But Tatara, who was in command, seemed not to feel it.

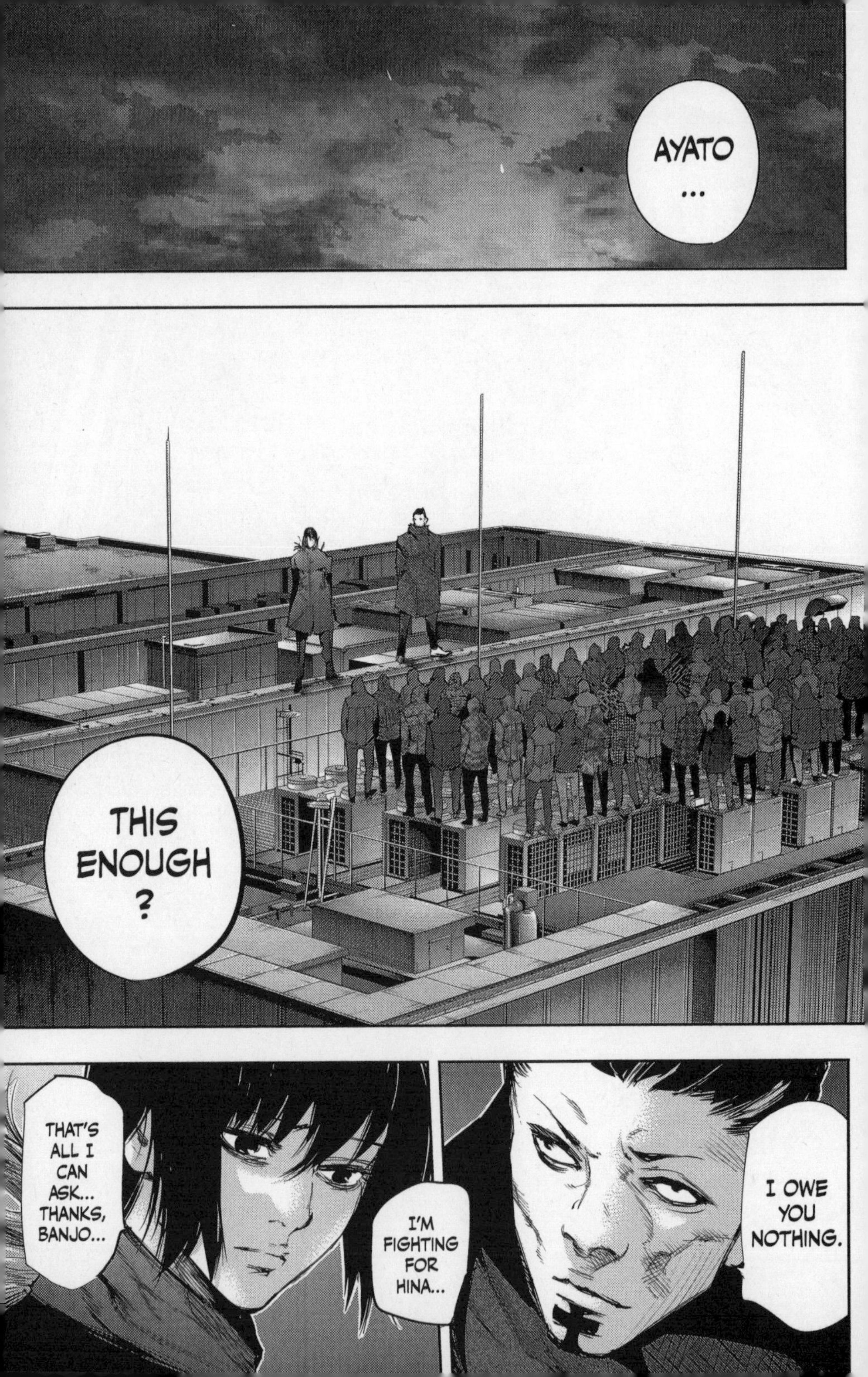
AYATO ...
THIS ENOUGH ?
I OWE YOU NOTHING.
I'M FIGHTING FOR HINA...
THAT'S ALL I CAN ASK... THANKS, BANJO...

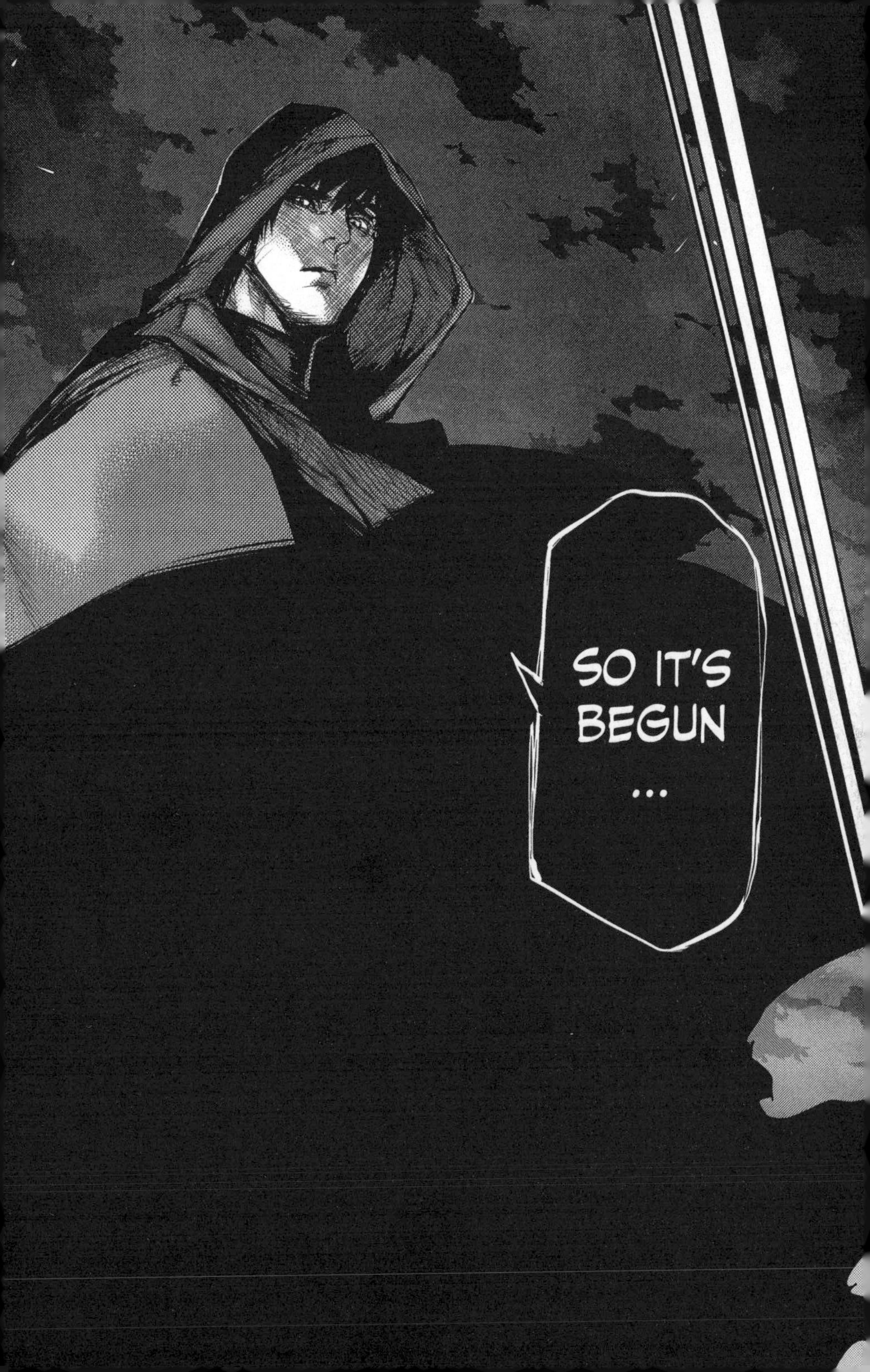
SO IT'S BEGUN ...

"BORING, ISN'T IT INVESTIGATOR SASAKI?"
"NO."

"ARE YOU THIRSTY?"
"I'M FINE."

"I KNOW I COULD USE A CUP OF COFFEE."
"..."

"WHADDAYA SAY WE PLAY A GAME AND THE LOSER GETS THE COFFEE?"
"..."

"HOW ABOUT A CCG WORD CHAIN GAME? ANYTHING THAT HAS TO DO WITH INVESTIGATORS OR GHOULS IS OKAY! IF YOU END WITH AN 'N' YOU LOSE!"
"..."

"I'LL START. FURUTA.☆ 'TA'!"
"..."

"TANAKAMARU MOUGAN. I LOSE."

"C'MON..."
"... *(SIGH)*. TAKE HIRAKO."

"THAT'S KINDA UNFAIR. KO... COCHLEA!"
"AKIRA MADO."

"DO... DO... DONATO!"
"TOMA HIGEMARU."

"IS THAT SOME KINDA MARTIAL ARTS MOVE?"
"RU..."

"RU?"
"YES, RU. HAVE ONE?"

"...NO."
"I'LL TAKE MINE BLACK, THANK YOU."

"YOU'RE SO CHILDISH, INVESTIGATOR SASAKI!"

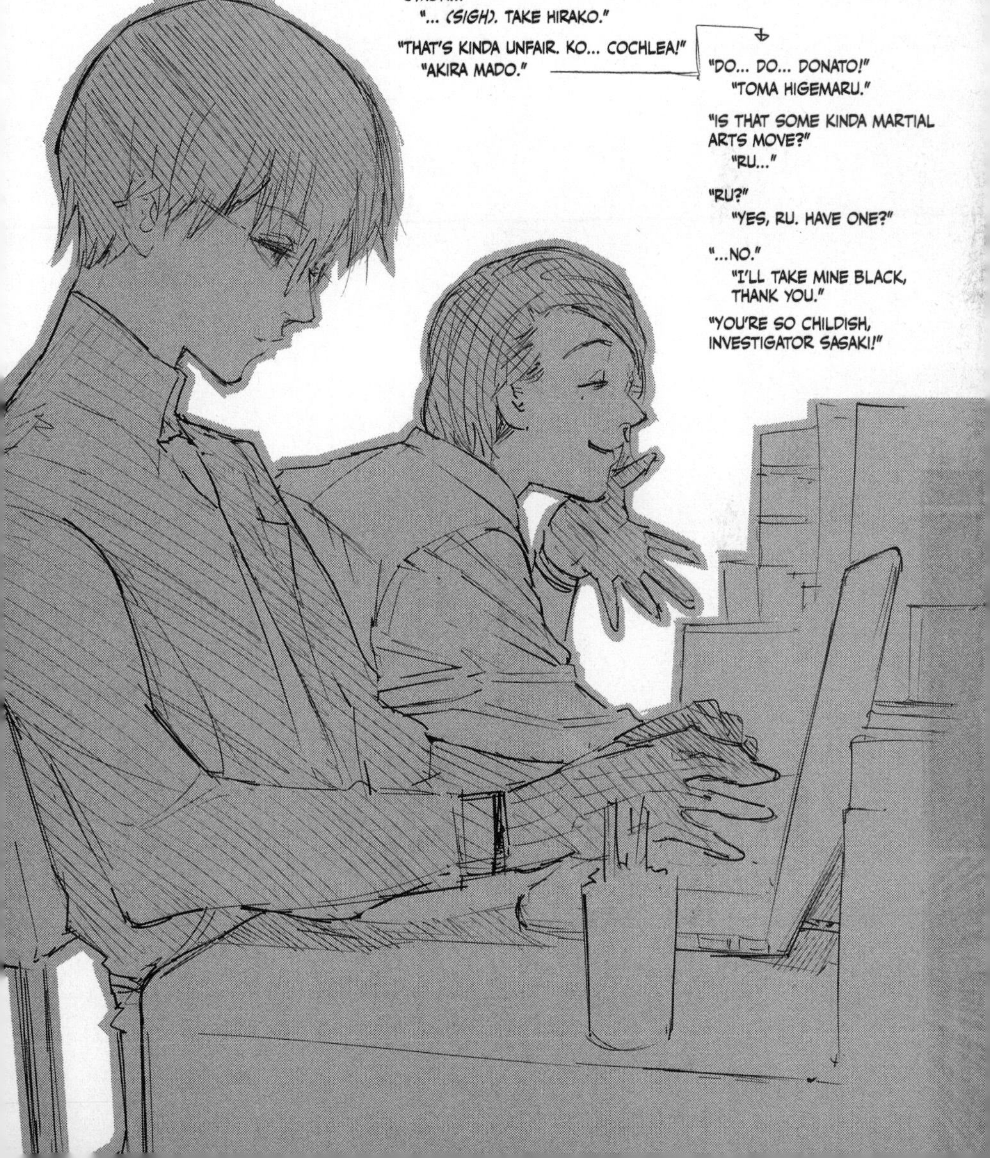

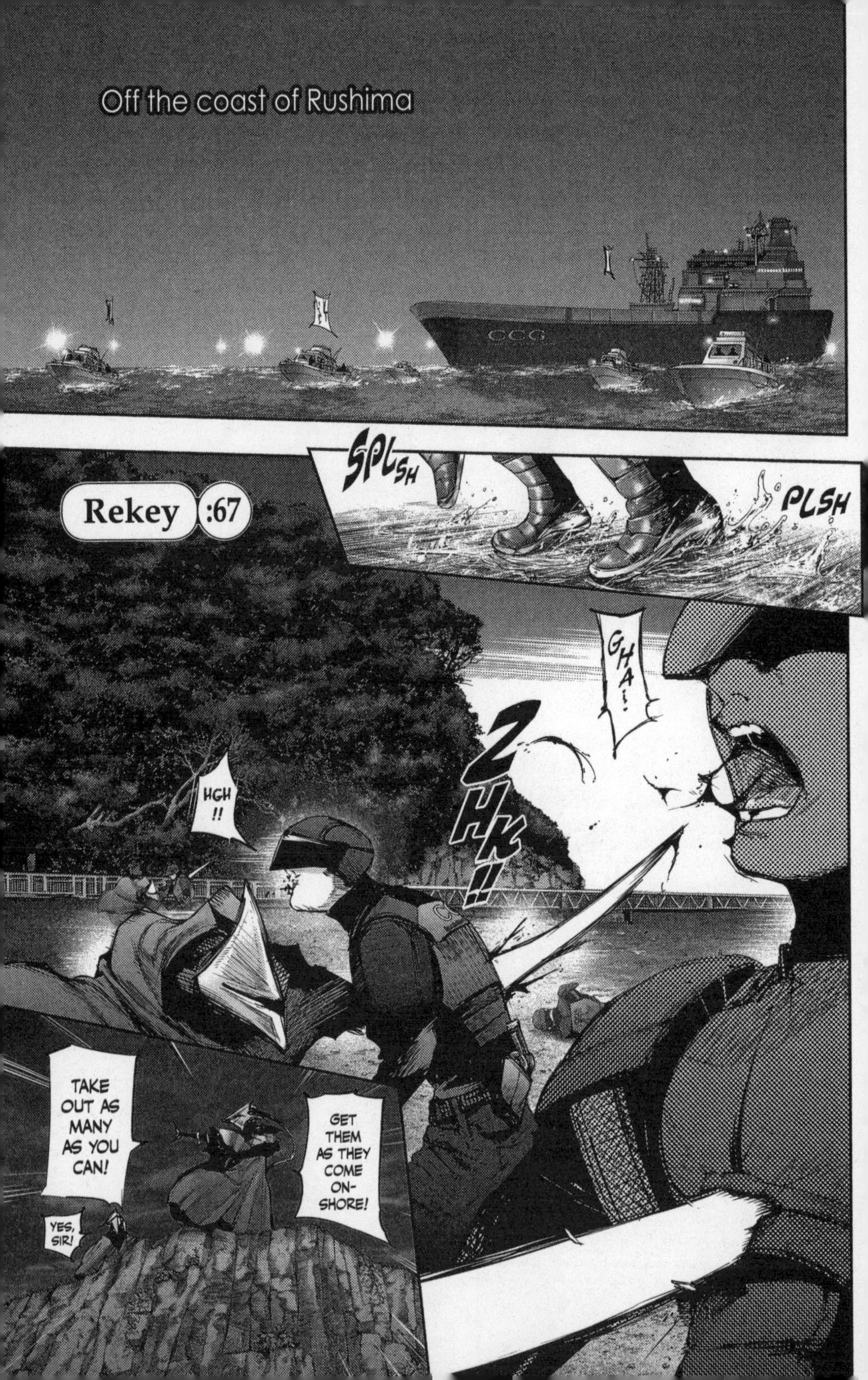
Off the coast of Rushima
SPLSH
PLSH
Rekey :67
GHA!
ZHK!!
HGH!!
GET THEM AS THEY COME ON-SHORE!
TAKE OUT AS MANY AS YOU CAN!
YES, SIR!

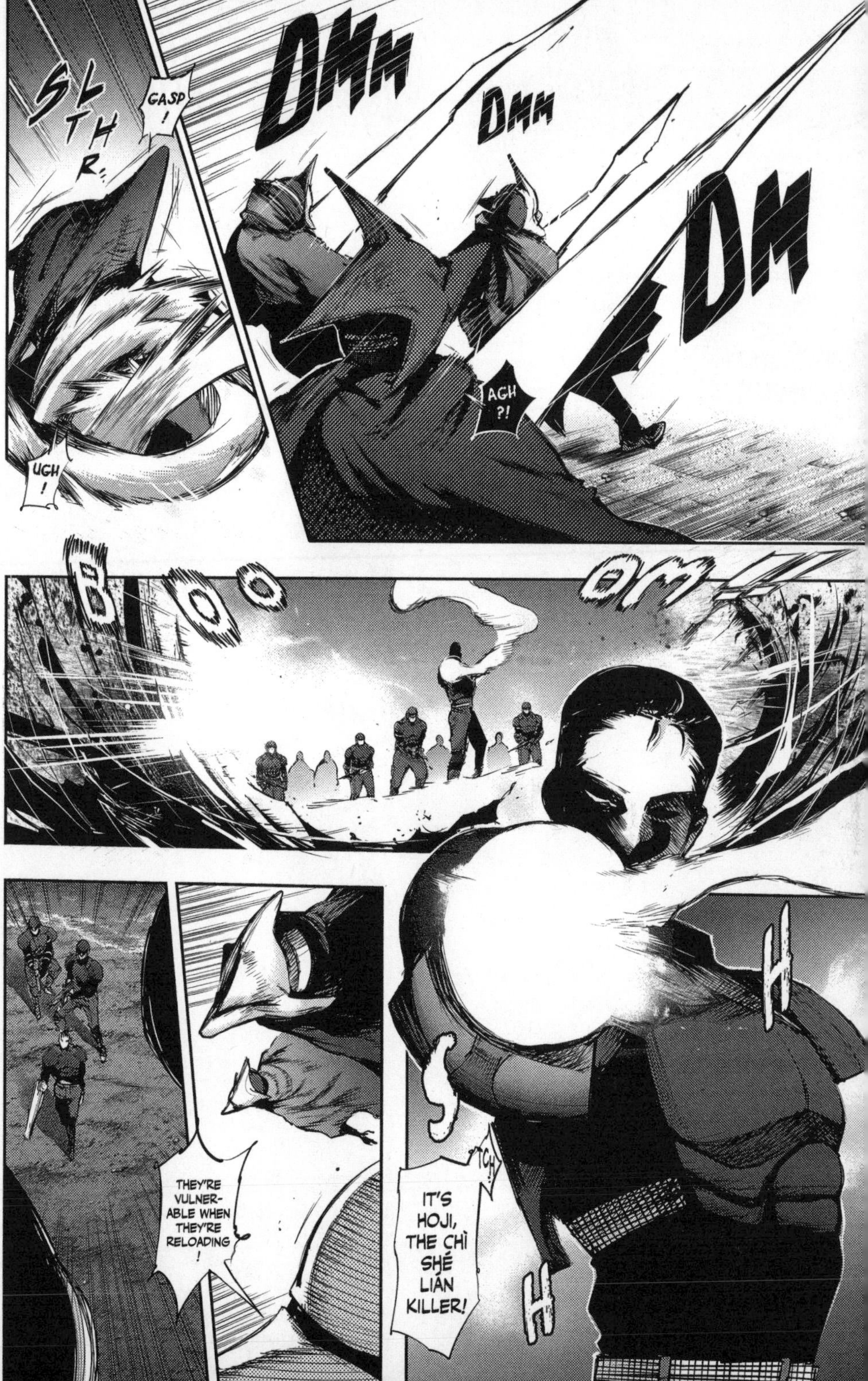
DMM
DMM
DM
AGH ?!
SLTHR
GASP!
UGH!
BOOOM
TCH
IT'S HOJI, THE CHÌ SHÉ LIÁN KILLER!
HH
THEY'RE VULNER-ABLE WHEN THEY'RE RELOADING!

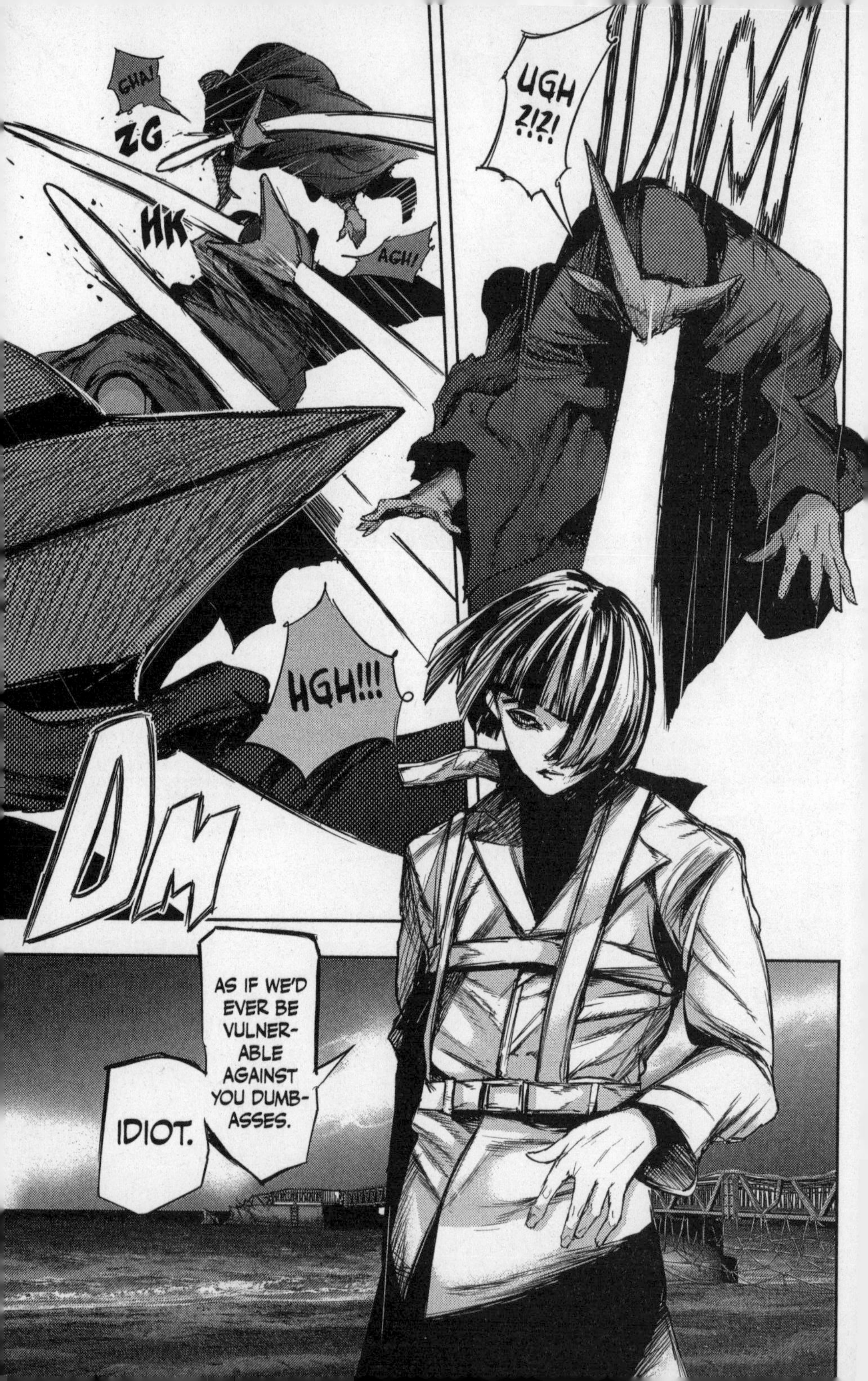
UGH ?!?!
DM
GHA!
ZG
HK
AGH!
HGH!!!
DM
AS IF WE'D EVER BE VULNER-ABLE AGAINST YOU DUMB-ASSES.
IDIOT.

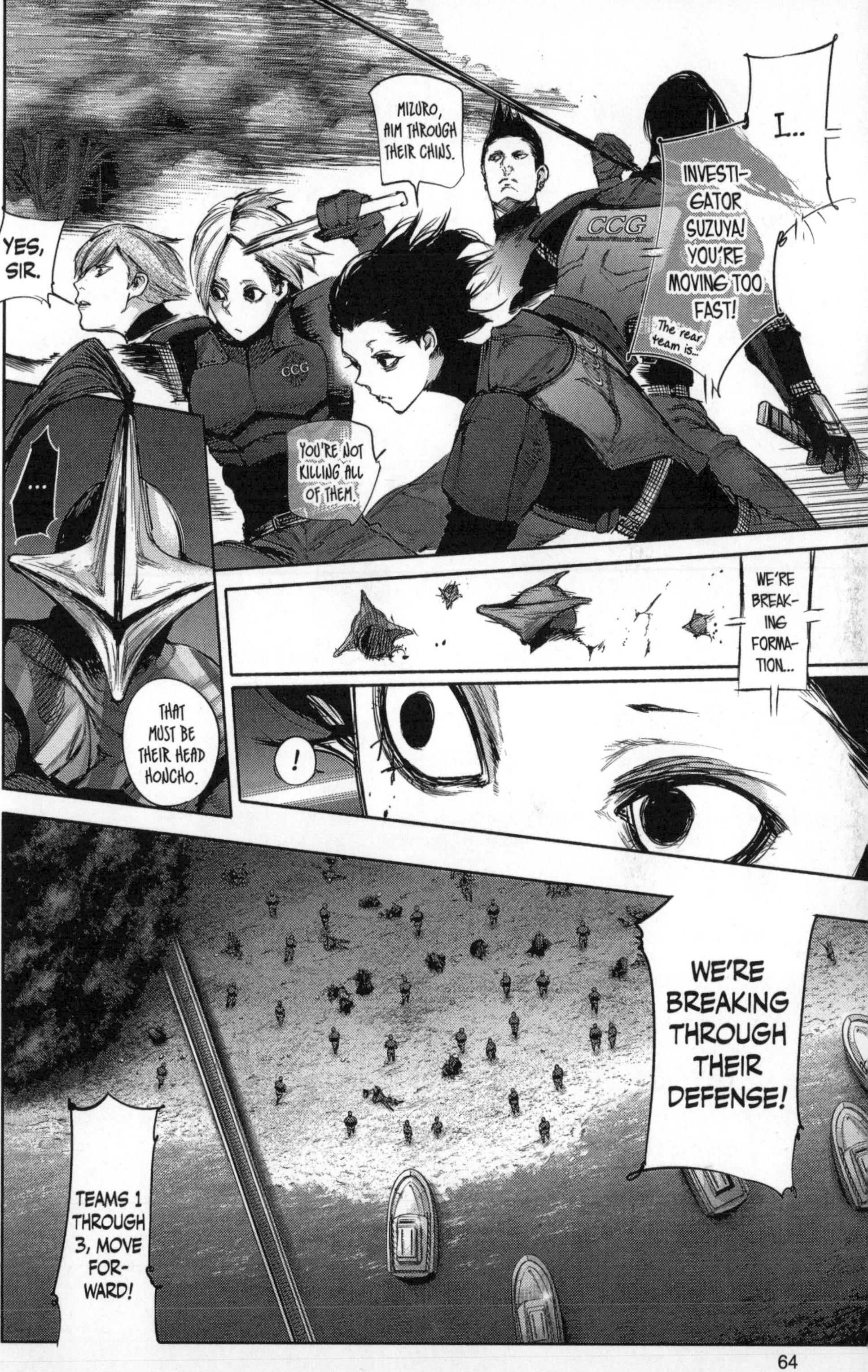
I...
INVESTIGATOR SUZUYA! YOU'RE MOVING TOO FAST!
The rear team is...
MIZURO, AIM THROUGH THEIR CHINS.
YES, SIR.
YOU'RE NOT KILLING ALL OF THEM.
WE'RE BREAKING FORMATION...
!
...
THAT MUST BE THEIR HEAD HONCHO.
WE'RE BREAKING THROUGH THEIR DEFENSE!
TEAMS 1 THROUGH 3, MOVE FORWARD!

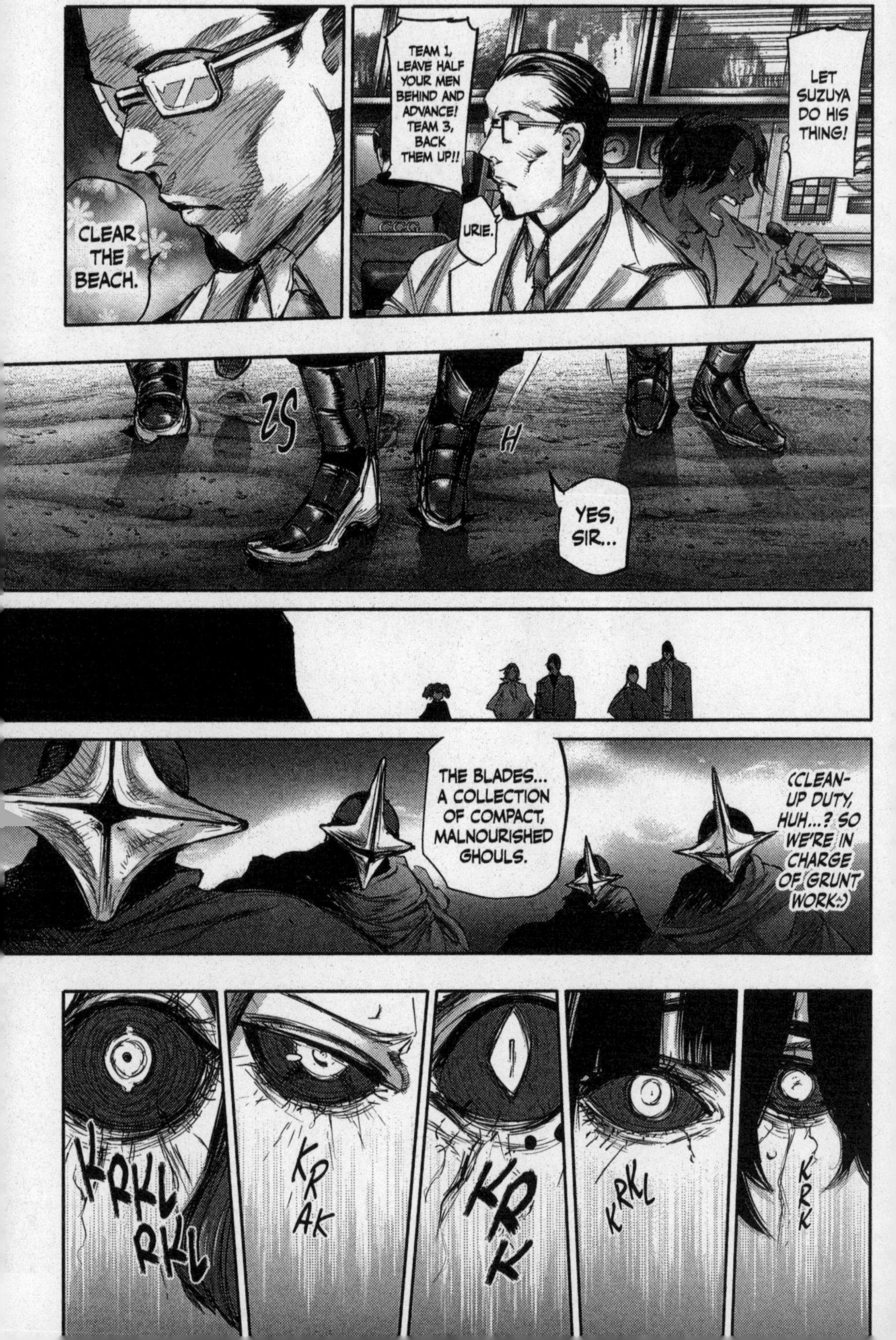
LET SUZUYA DO HIS THING!
TEAM 1, LEAVE HALF YOUR MEN BEHIND AND ADVANCE! TEAM 3, BACK THEM UP!!
URIE.
CLEAR THE BEACH.
YES, SIR...
H
ZS
(CLEAN-UP DUTY, HUH...? SO WE'RE IN CHARGE OF GRUNT WORK:)
THE BLADES... A COLLECTION OF COMPACT, MALNOURISHED GHOULS.
KRK
KRKL
KRKK
KRAK
KRKL RKL

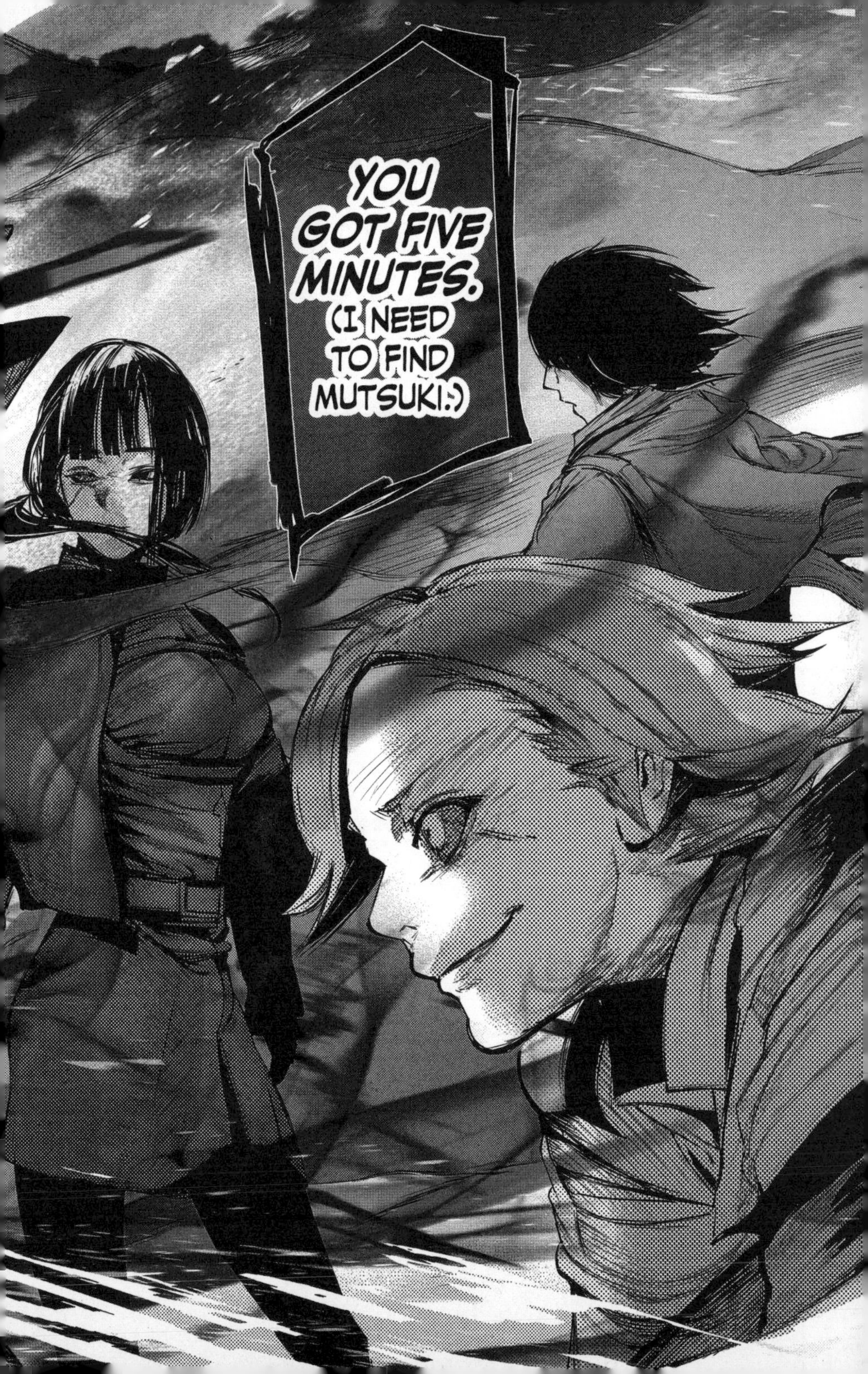
YOU GOT FIVE MINUTES.
(I NEED TO FIND MUTSUKI.)

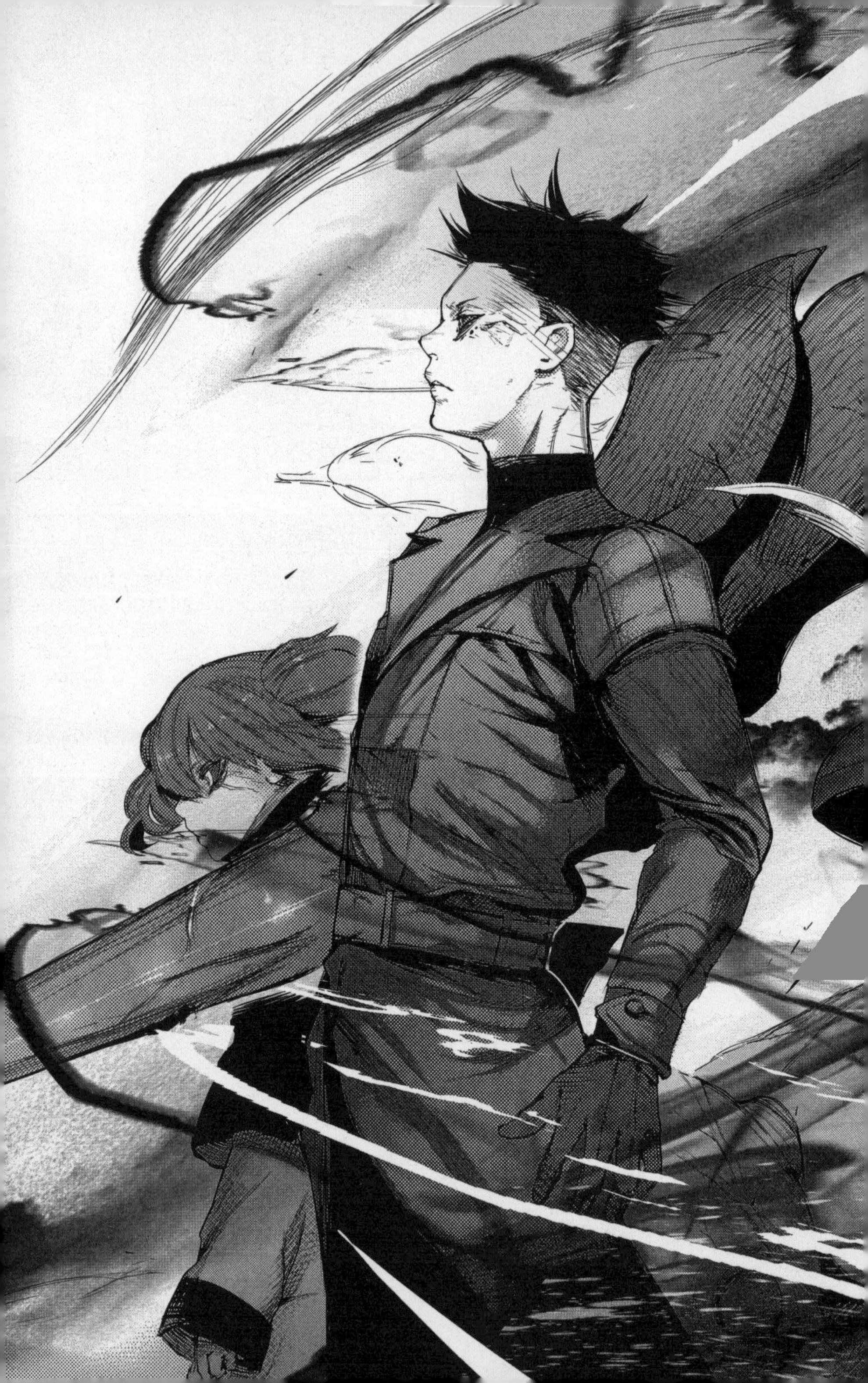

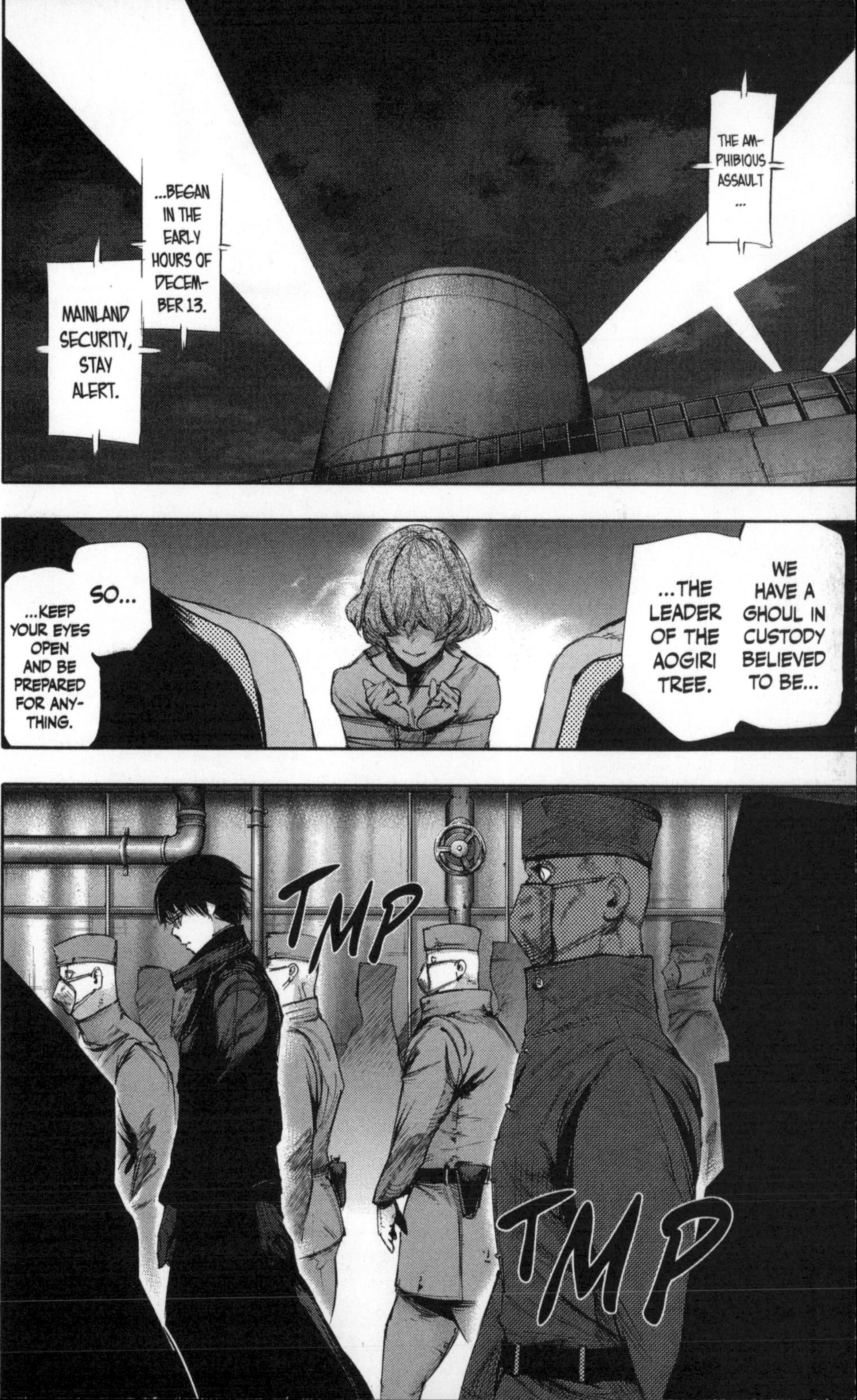
THE AM-PHIBIOUS ASSAULT ...
...BEGAN IN THE EARLY HOURS OF DECEM-BER 13.
MAINLAND SECURITY, STAY ALERT.
WE HAVE A GHOUL IN CUSTODY BELIEVED TO BE...
...THE LEADER OF THE AOGIRI TREE.
SO...
...KEEP YOUR EYES OPEN AND BE PREPARED FOR ANY-THING.
TMP
TMP

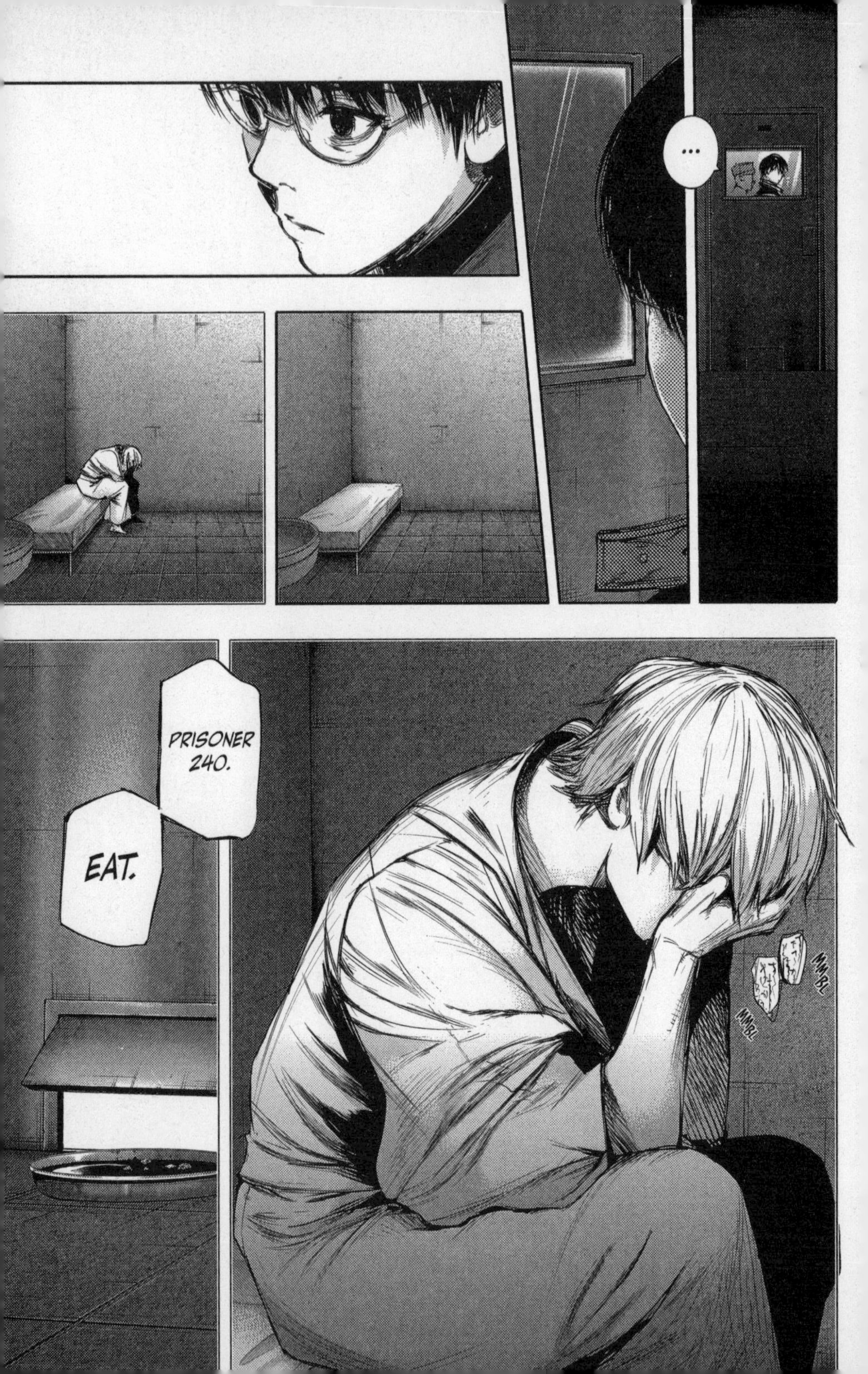
...
MMBL
MMBL
PRISONER 240.
EAT.

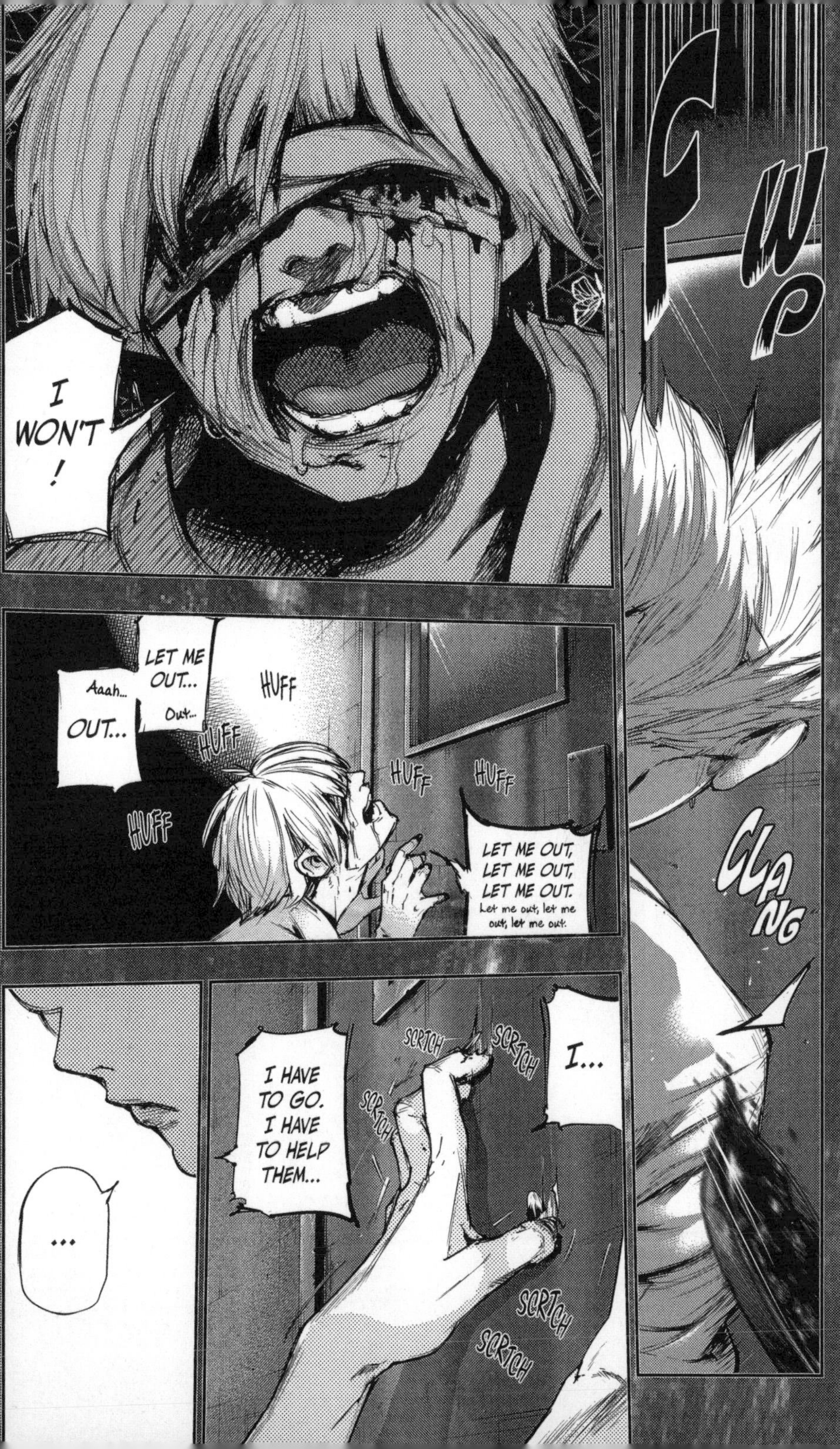
FWP
CLANG
I WON'T!
HUFF
LET ME OUT... Out...
Aaah... OUT...
HUFF
HUFF
HUFF
LET ME OUT, LET ME OUT, LET ME OUT. Let me out, let me out, let me out.
HUFF
I...
SCRITCH
SCRITCH
SCRITCH
I HAVE TO GO. I HAVE TO HELP THEM...
SCRITCH
SCRITCH
...

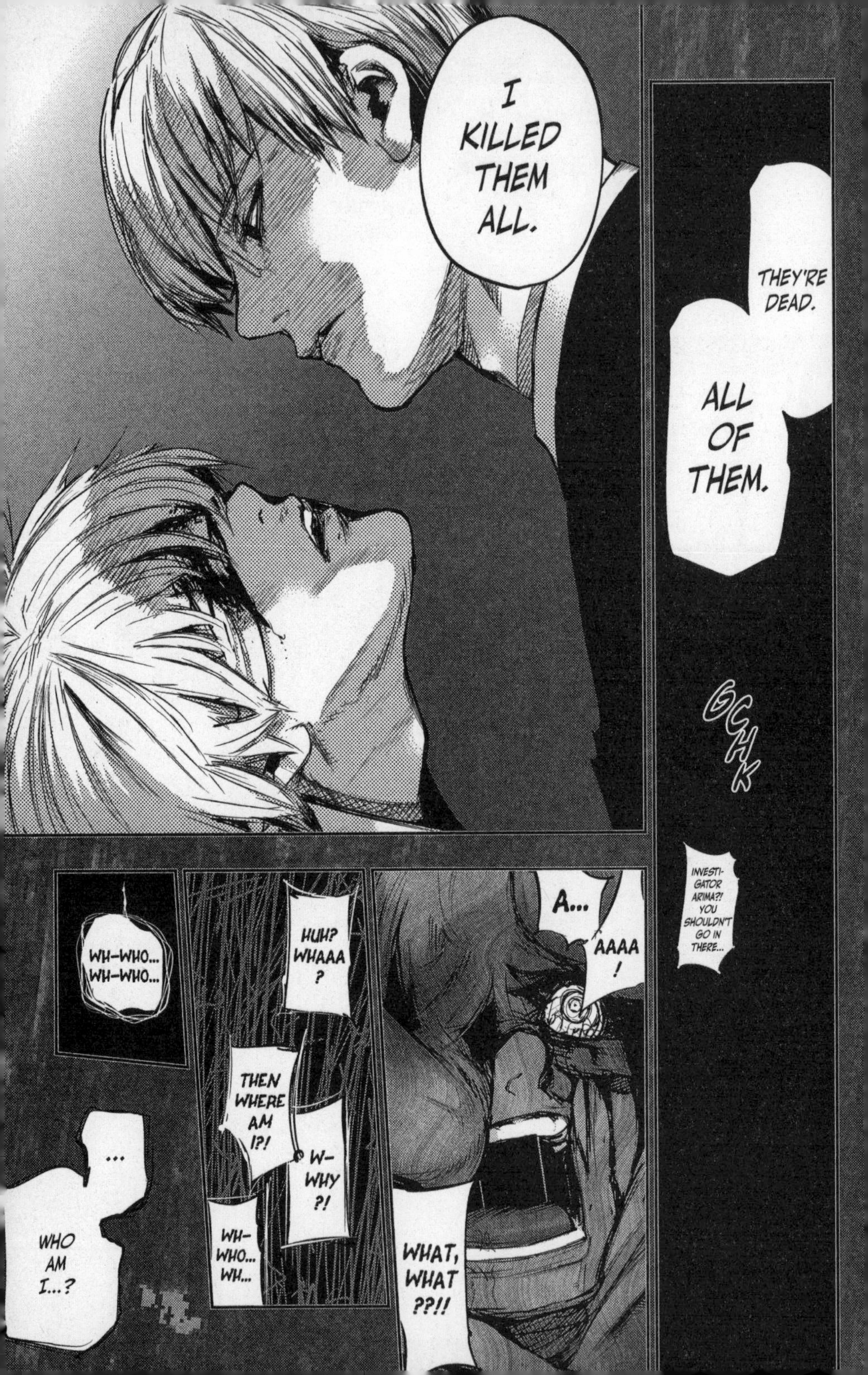
THEY'RE DEAD.
ALL OF THEM.
GCHK
INVESTI-GATOR ARIMA?! YOU SHOULDN'T GO IN THERE...
I KILLED THEM ALL.
A...
AAAA!
WHAT, WHAT ??!!
HUH? WHAAA?
THEN WHERE AM I?!
W-WHY?!
WH-WHO... WH...
WH-WHO... WH-WHO...
...
WHO AM I...?

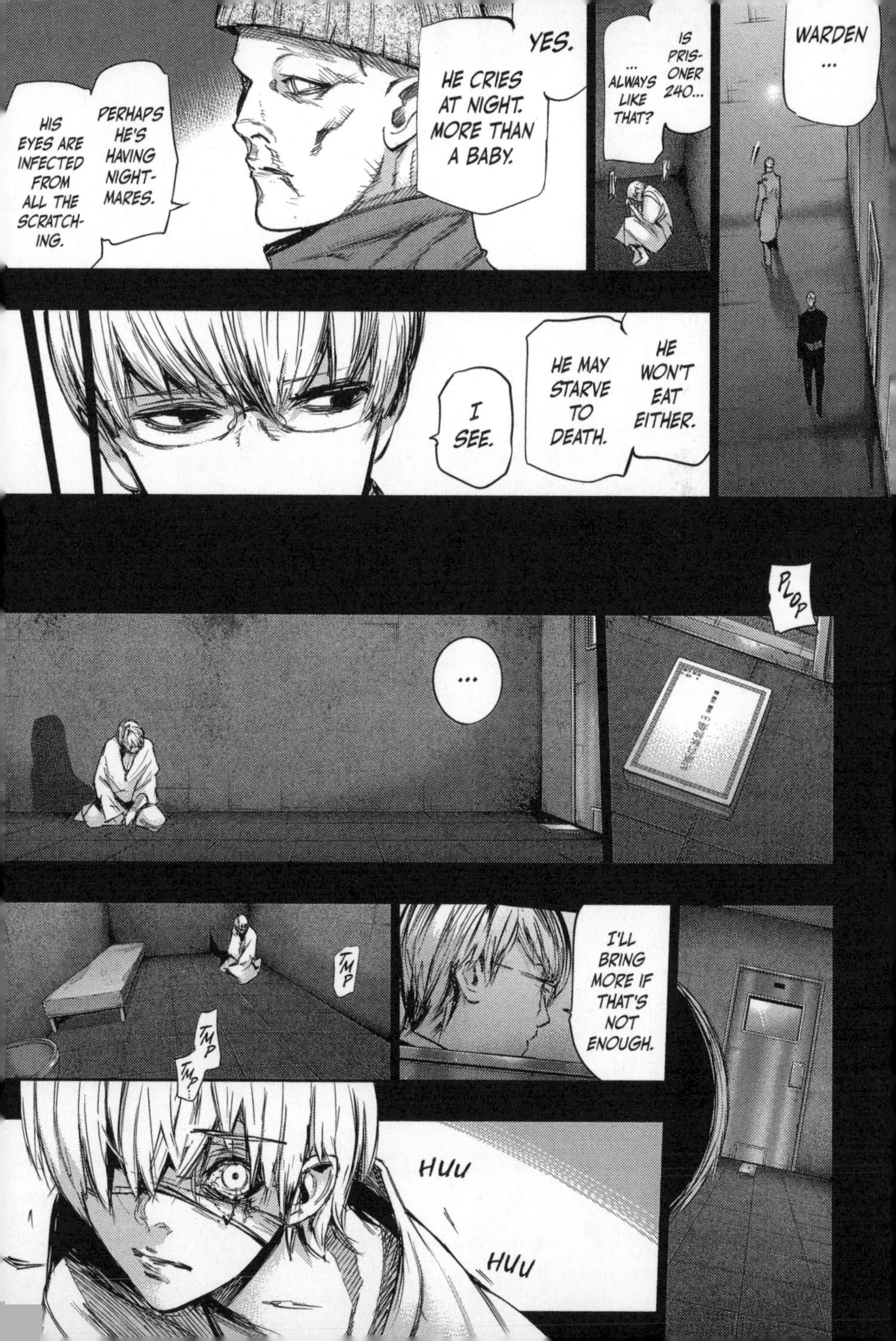
WARDEN ...
IS PRISONER 240...
... ALWAYS LIKE THAT?
YES.
HE CRIES AT NIGHT. MORE THAN A BABY.
PERHAPS HE'S HAVING NIGHTMARES.
HIS EYES ARE INFECTED FROM ALL THE SCRATCHING.
HE WON'T EAT EITHER.
HE MAY STARVE TO DEATH.
I SEE.
PLOP
...
I'LL BRING MORE IF THAT'S NOT ENOUGH.
TMP
TMP
TMP
HUU
HUU

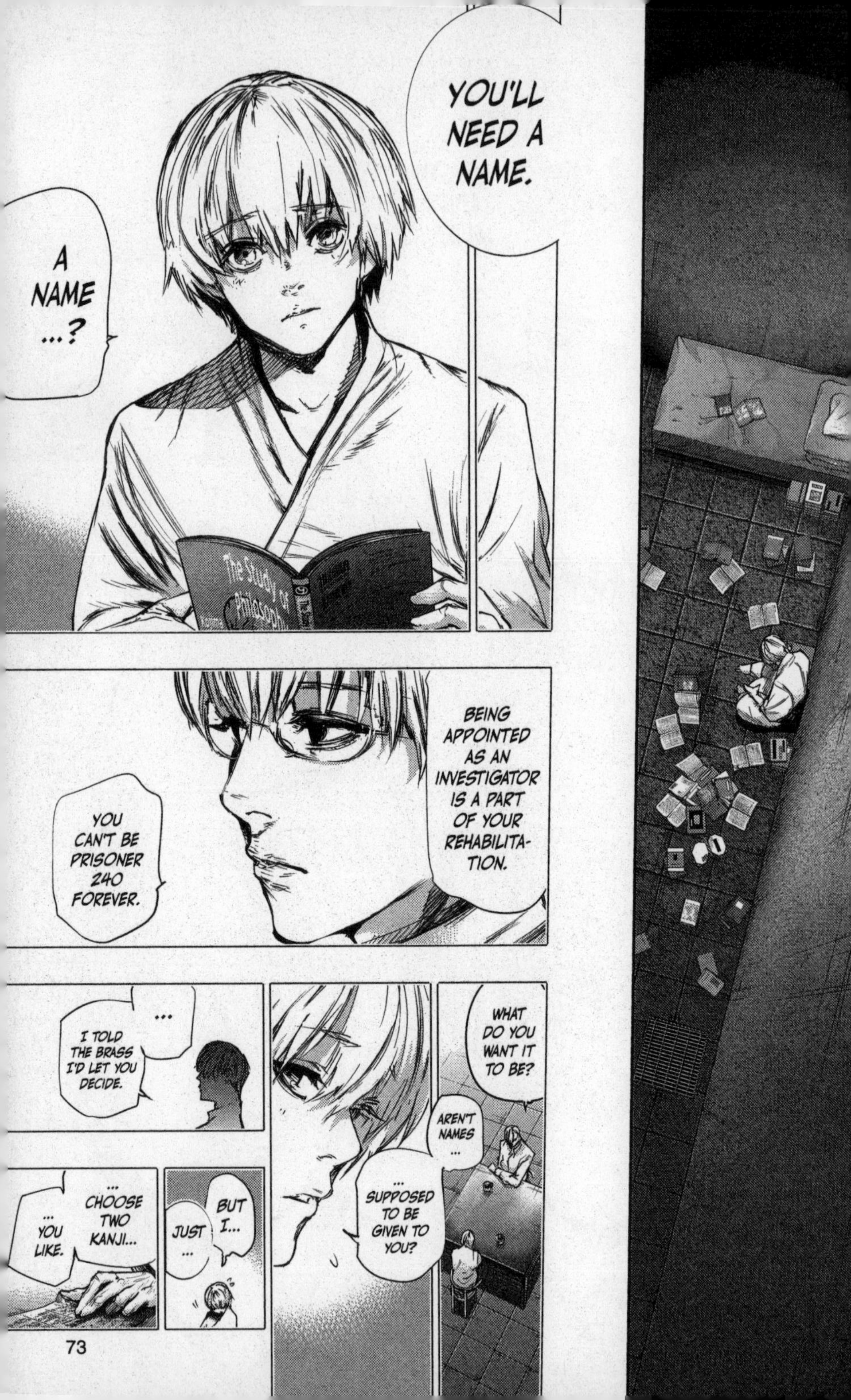
YOU'LL NEED A NAME.
A NAME ...?
BEING APPOINTED AS AN INVESTIGATOR IS A PART OF YOUR REHABILITATION.
YOU CAN'T BE PRISONER 240 FOREVER.
WHAT DO YOU WANT IT TO BE?
AREN'T NAMES ...
... SUPPOSED TO BE GIVEN TO YOU?
...
I TOLD THE BRASS I'D LET YOU DECIDE.
BUT I...
JUST ...
... CHOOSE TWO KANJI...
... YOU LIKE.

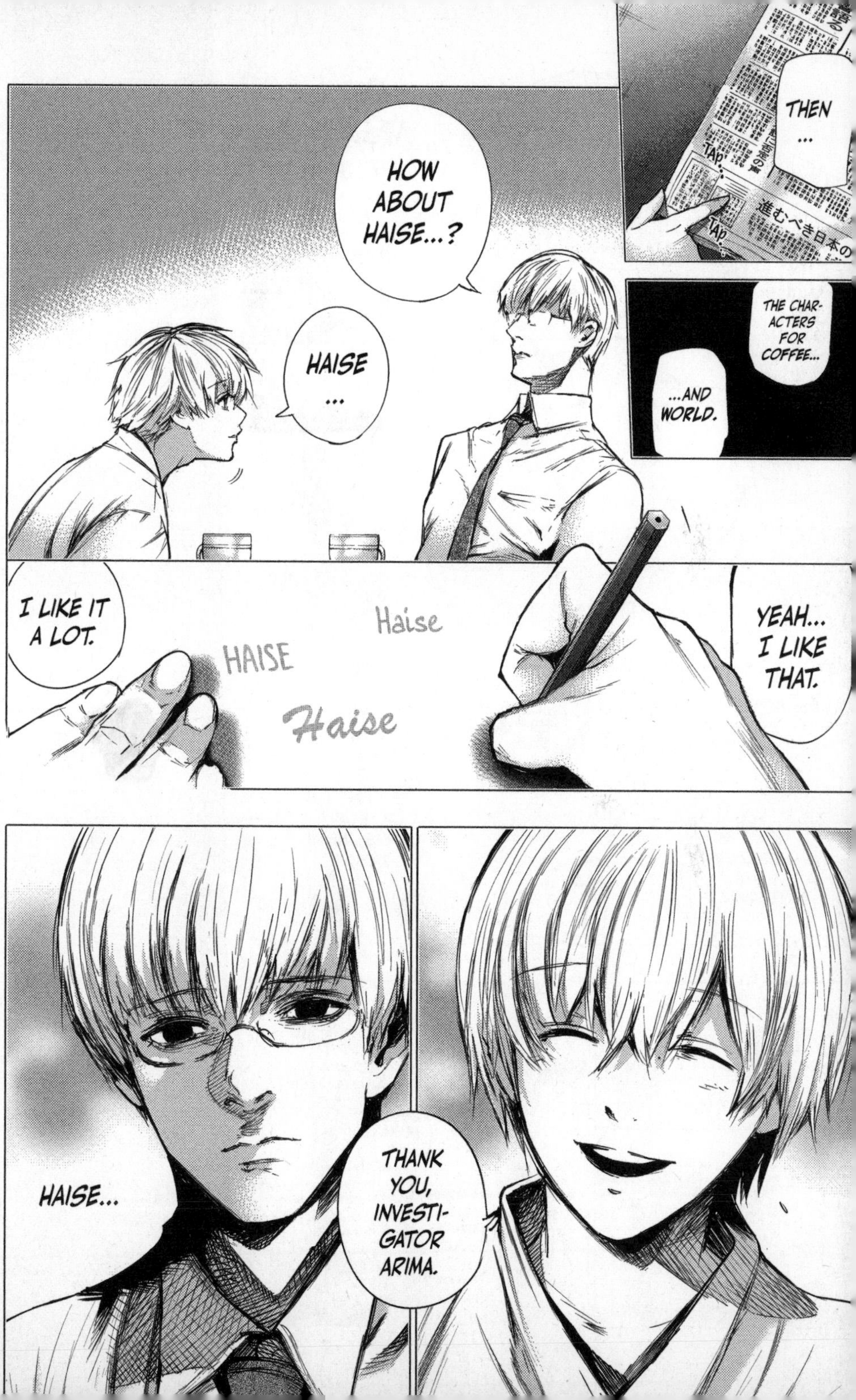
THEN ...
TAp
TAp
進むべき日本の
THE CHAR-ACTERS FOR COFFEE...
...AND WORLD.
HOW ABOUT HAISE...?
HAISE ...
YEAH... I LIKE THAT.
Haise
HAISE
Haise
I LIKE IT A LOT.
THANK YOU, INVESTI-GATOR ARIMA.
HAISE...

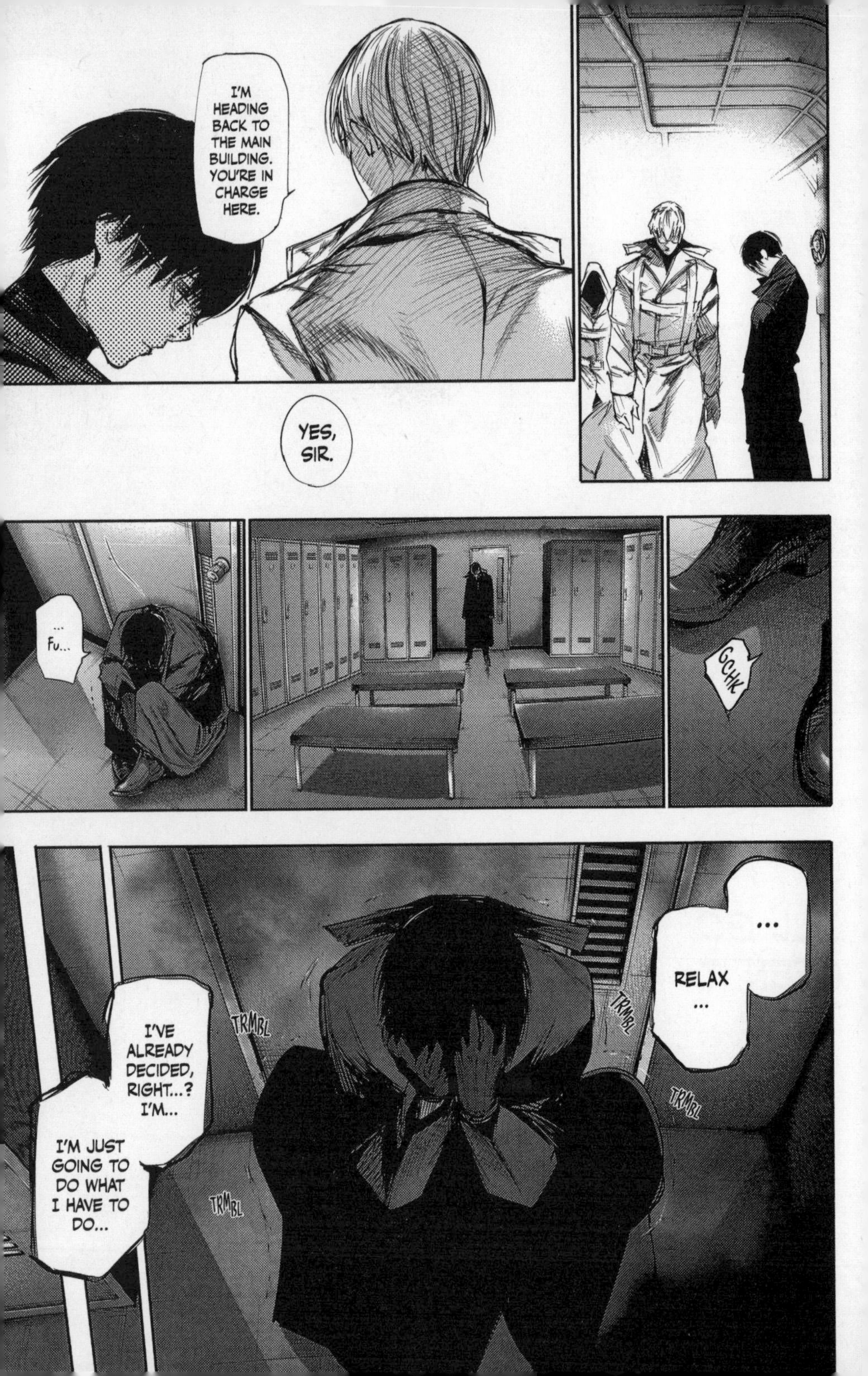
I'M HEADING BACK TO THE MAIN BUILDING. YOU'RE IN CHARGE HERE.
YES, SIR.
GCHK
... Fu...
... RELAX ...
TRMBL
TRMBL
TRMBL
I'VE ALREADY DECIDED, RIGHT...? I'M...
TRMBL
I'M JUST GOING TO DO WHAT I HAVE TO DO...

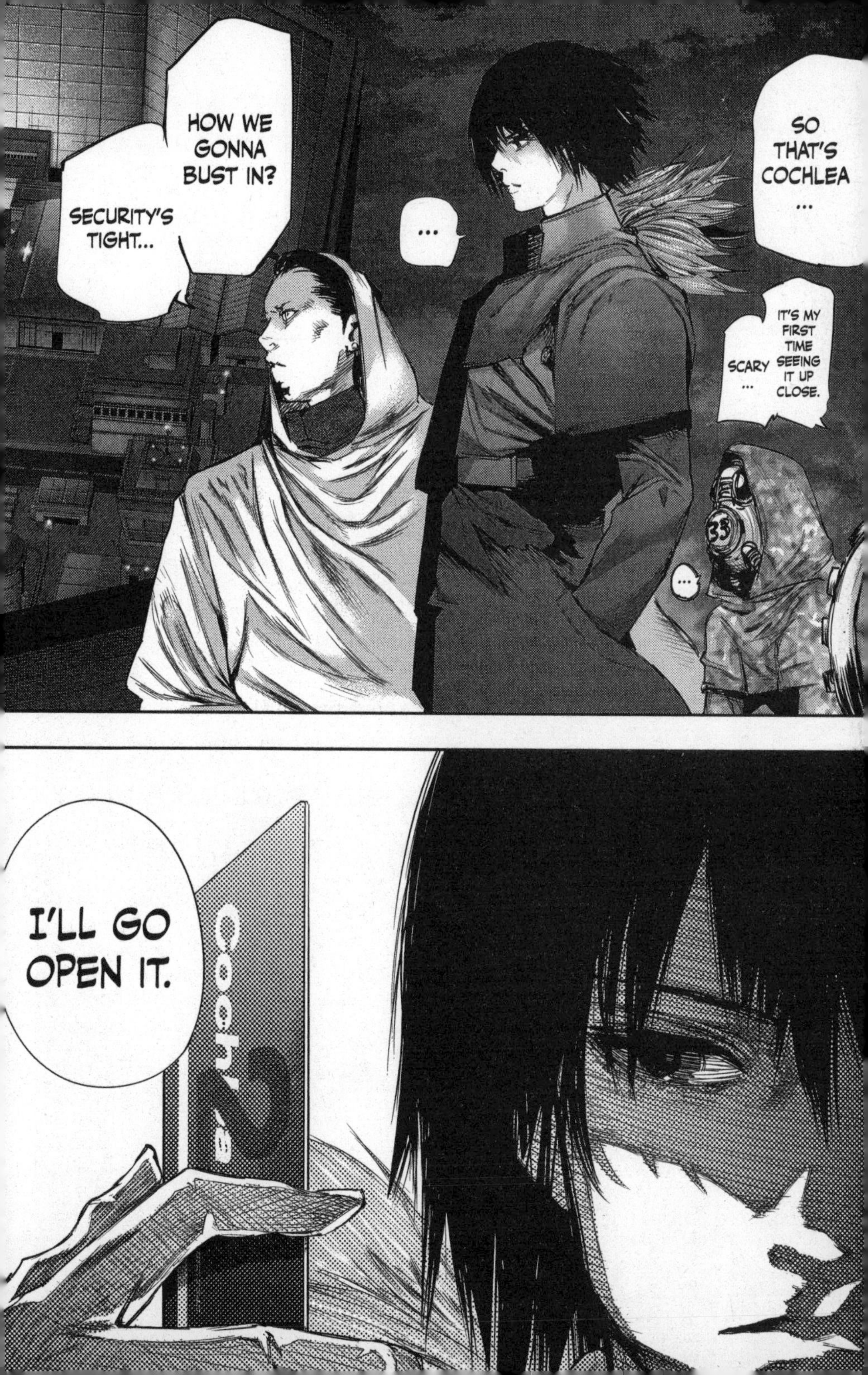
SO THAT'S COCHLEA ...
IT'S MY FIRST TIME SEEING IT UP CLOSE.
SCARY ...
...
...
HOW WE GONNA BUST IN?
SECURITY'S TIGHT...
I'LL GO OPEN IT.

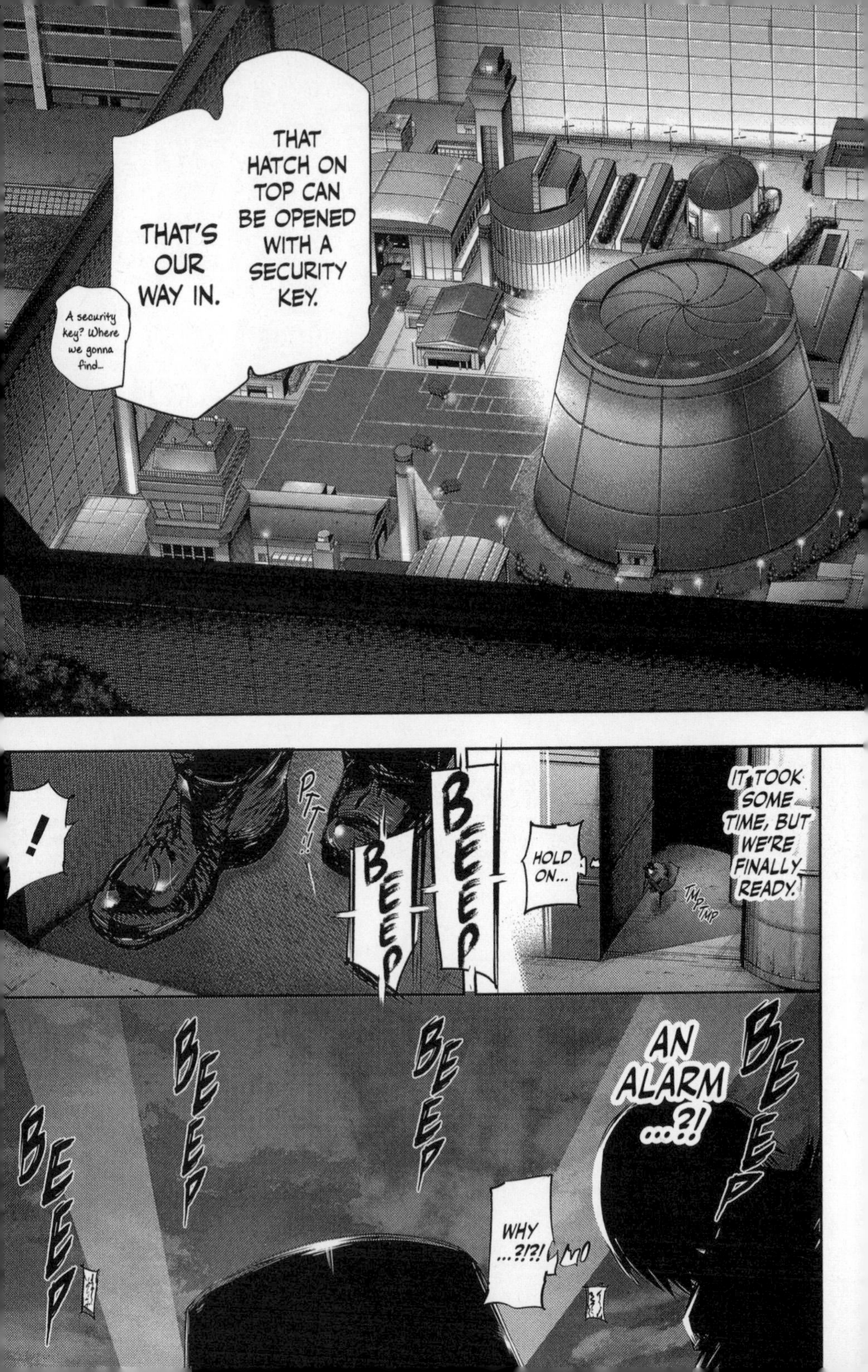
THAT HATCH ON TOP CAN BE OPENED WITH A SECURITY KEY.
THAT'S OUR WAY IN.
A security key? Where we gonna find...
IT TOOK SOME TIME, BUT WE'RE FINALLY READY.
TMP TMP
HOLD ON...
BEEP
BEEP
PTT!!
!
BEEP
AN ALARM ...?!
BEEP
WHY ...?!?!
BEEP

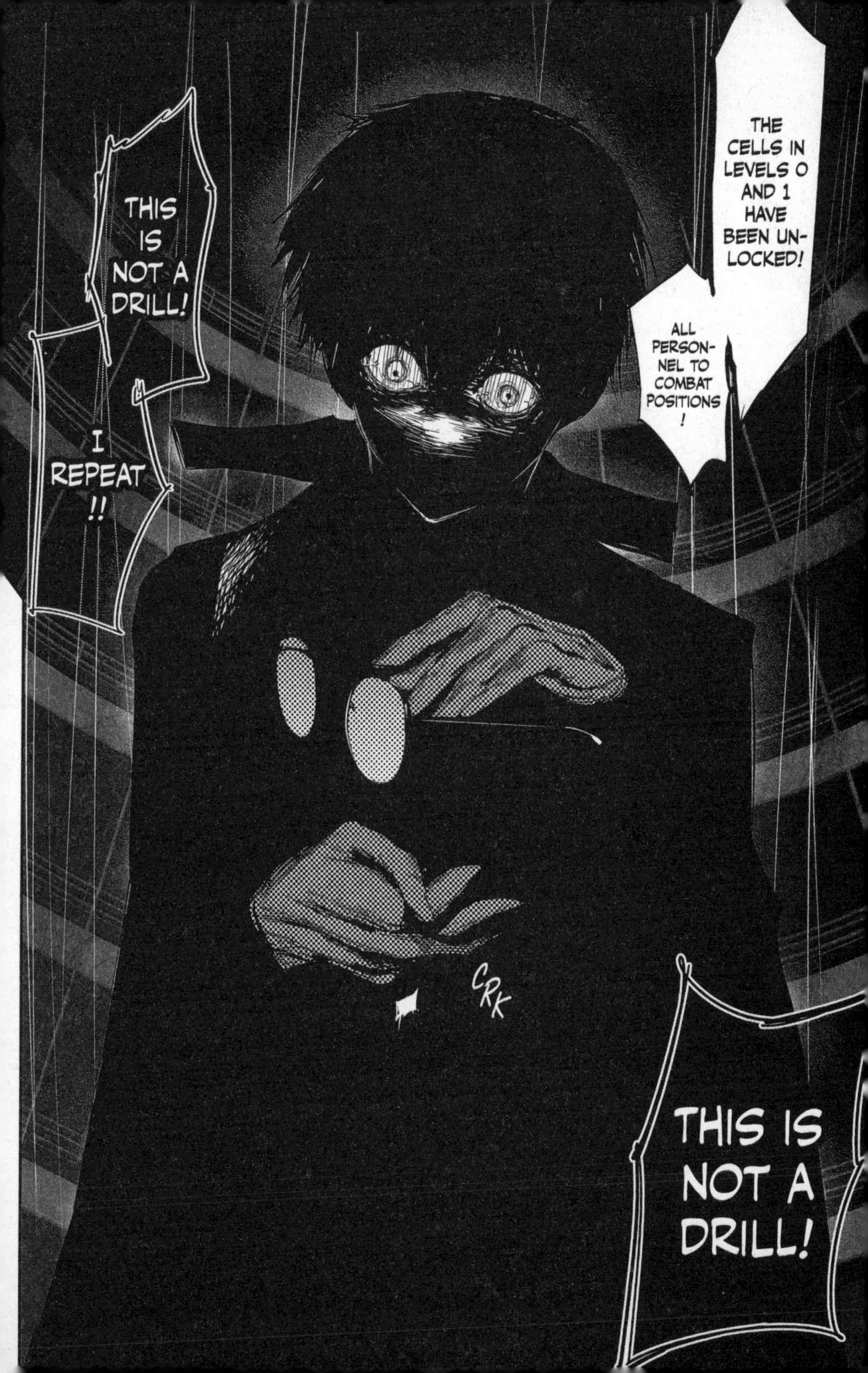
THE CELLS IN LEVELS 0 AND 1 HAVE BEEN UN-LOCKED!
ALL PERSON-NEL TO COMBAT POSITIONS!
THIS IS NOT A DRILL!
I REPEAT!!
CRK
THIS IS NOT A DRILL!

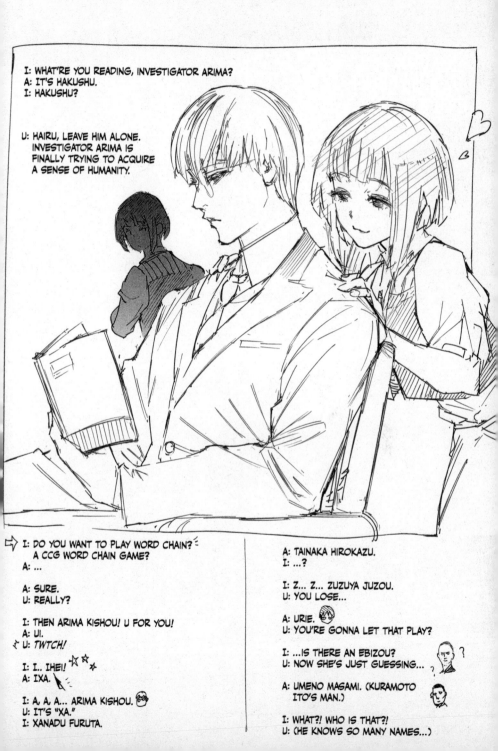

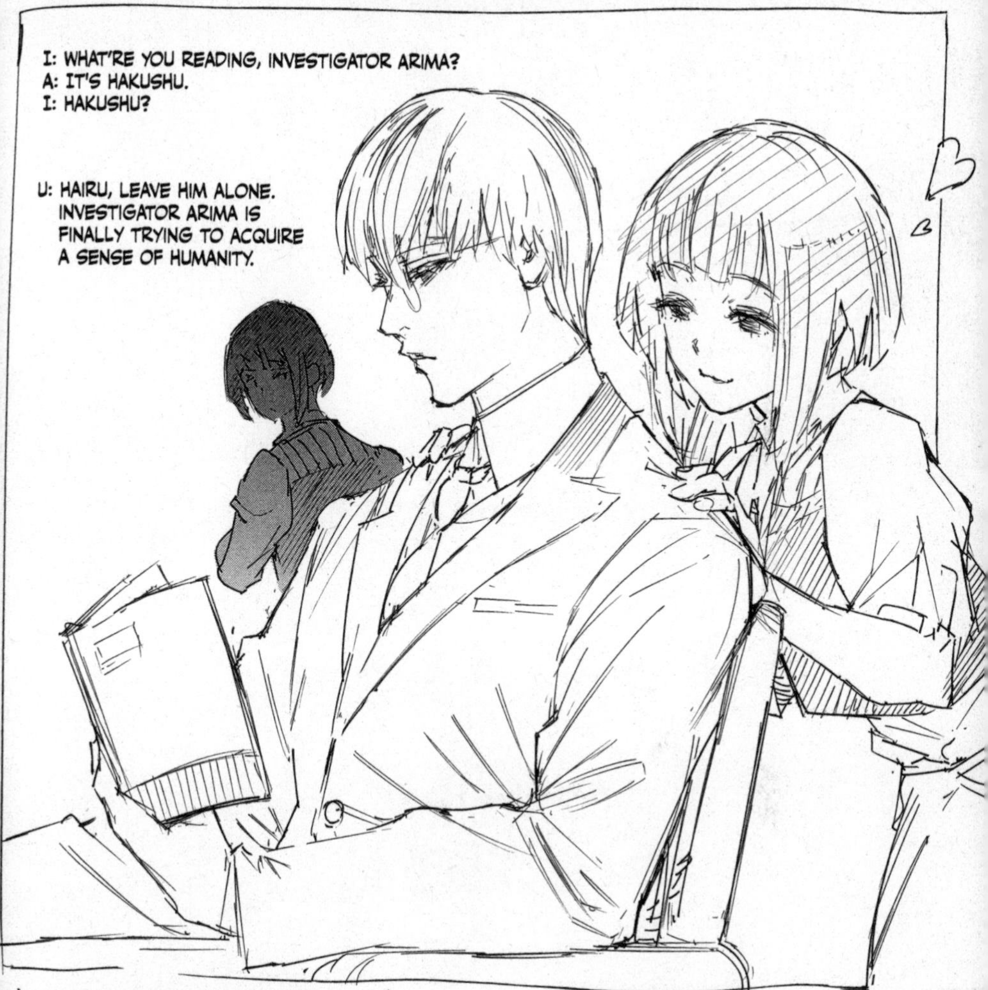
I: WHAT'RE YOU READING, INVESTIGATOR ARIMA?
A: IT'S HAKUSHU.
I: HAKUSHU?
U: HAIRU, LEAVE HIM ALONE. INVESTIGATOR ARIMA IS FINALLY TRYING TO ACQUIRE A SENSE OF HUMANITY.

I: DO YOU WANT TO PLAY WORD CHAIN? A CCG WORD CHAIN GAME?
A: ...

A: SURE.
U: REALLY?

I: THEN ARIMA KISHOU! U FOR YOU!
A: UI.
U: *TWTCH!*

I: I.. IHEI!
A: IXA.

I: A, A, A... ARIMA KISHOU.
U: IT'S "XA."
I: XANADU FURUTA.

A: TAINAKA HIROKAZU.
I: ...?

I: Z... Z... ZUZUYA JUZOU.
U: YOU LOSE...

A: URIE.
U: YOU'RE GONNA LET THAT PLAY?

I: ...IS THERE AN EBIZOU?
U: NOW SHE'S JUST GUESSING...

A: UMENO MASAMI. (KURAMOTO ITO'S MAN.)

I: WHAT?! WHO IS THAT?!
U: (HE KNOWS SO MANY NAMES...)

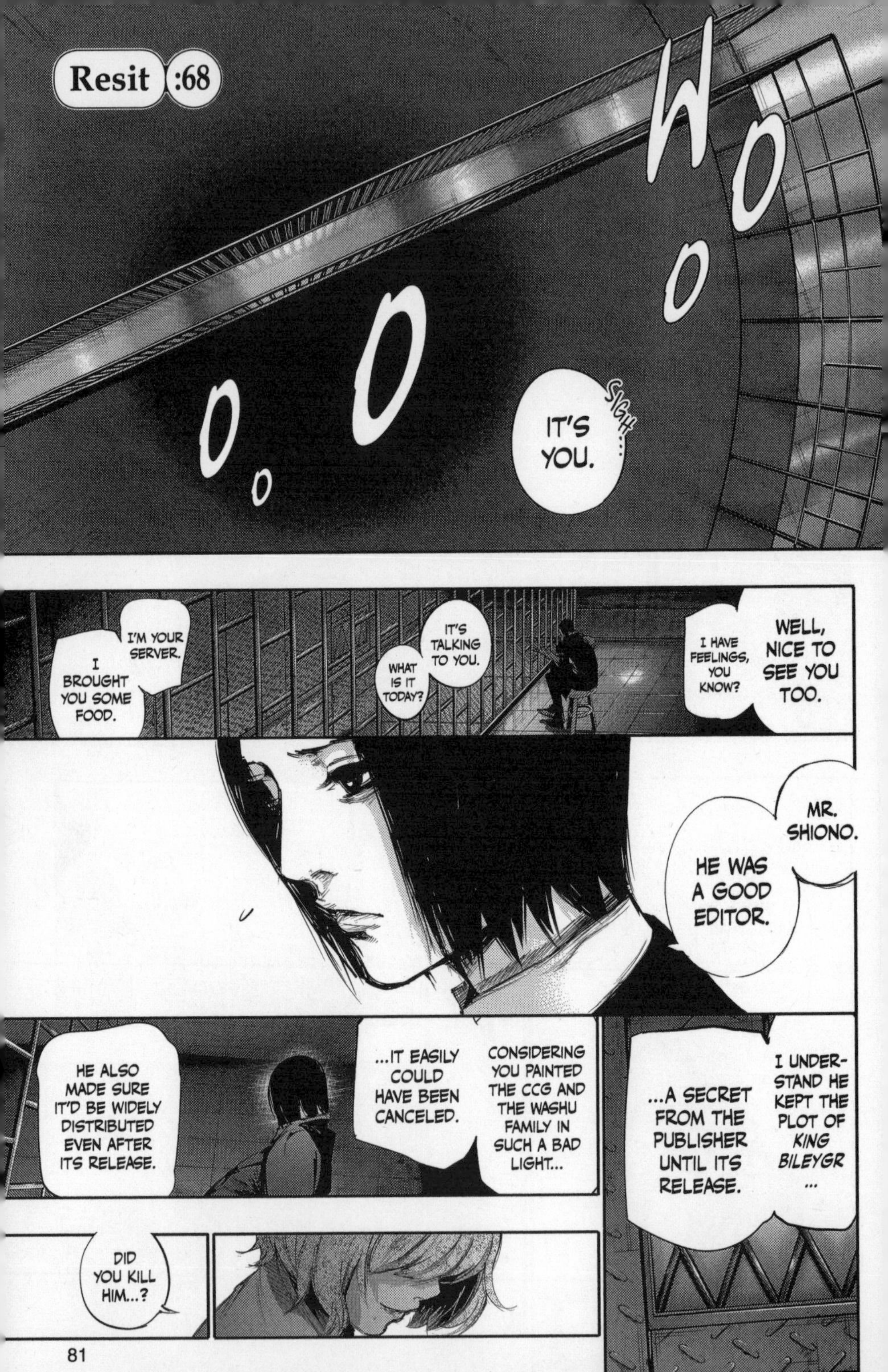
Resit :68
WOOOOO
SIGH...
IT'S YOU.
WELL, NICE TO SEE YOU TOO.
I HAVE FEELINGS, YOU KNOW?
IT'S TALKING TO YOU.
WHAT IS IT TODAY?
I'M YOUR SERVER.
I BROUGHT YOU SOME FOOD.
MR. SHIONO.
HE WAS A GOOD EDITOR.
I UNDER-STAND HE KEPT THE PLOT OF *KING BILEYGR*...
...A SECRET FROM THE PUBLISHER UNTIL ITS RELEASE.
CONSIDERING YOU PAINTED THE CCG AND THE WASHU FAMILY IN SUCH A BAD LIGHT...
...IT EASILY COULD HAVE BEEN CANCELED.
HE ALSO MADE SURE IT'D BE WIDELY DISTRIBUTED EVEN AFTER ITS RELEASE.
DID YOU KILL HIM...?

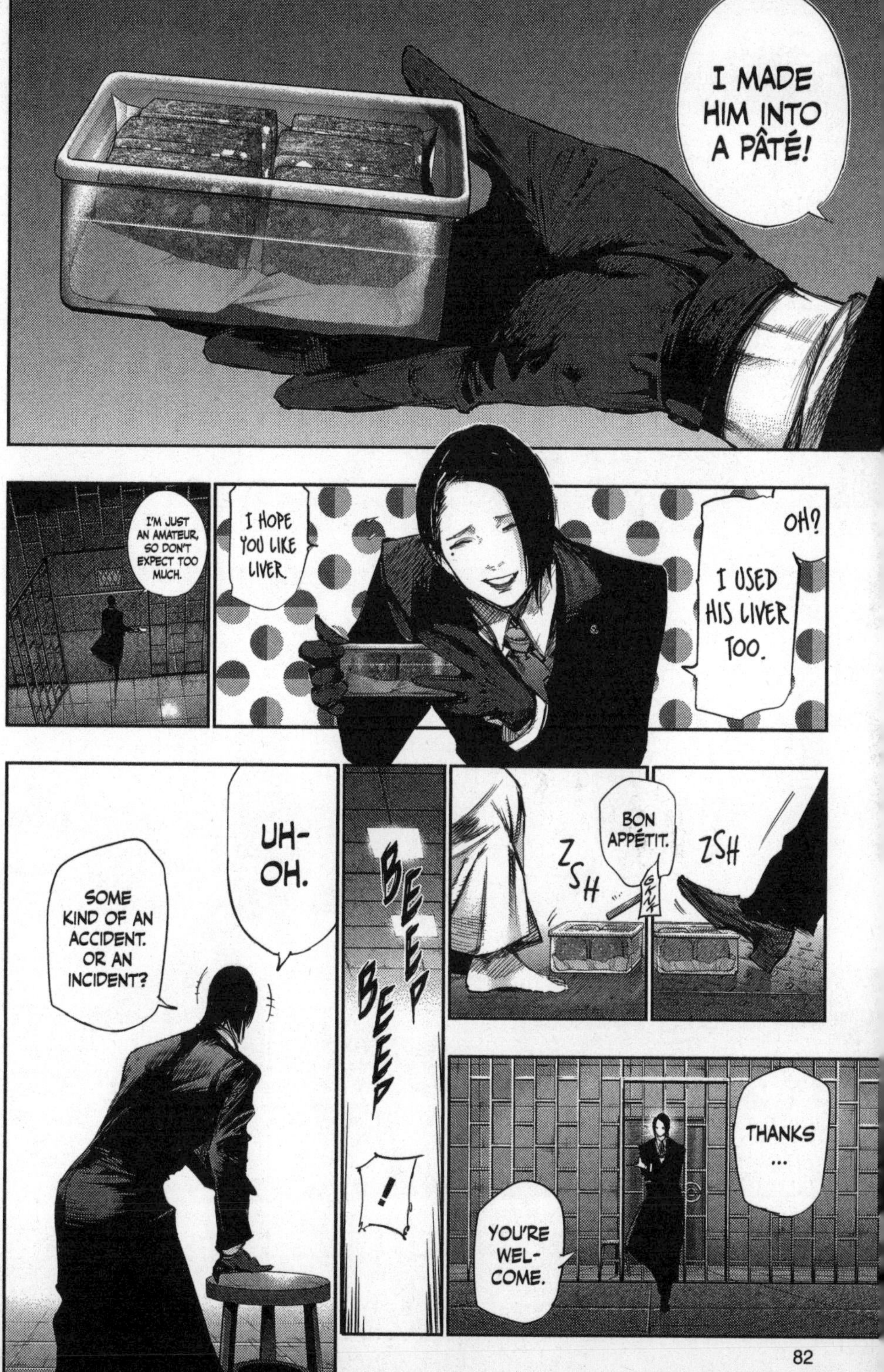

I MADE HIM INTO A PÂTÉ!
OH?
I USED HIS LIVER TOO.
I HOPE YOU LIKE LIVER.
I'M JUST AN AMATEUR, SO DON'T EXPECT TOO MUCH.
ZSH
BON APPÉTIT.
ZSH
THANKS ...
YOU'RE WEL-COME.
BEEP BEEP
!
UH-OH.
SOME KIND OF AN ACCIDENT. OR AN INCIDENT?

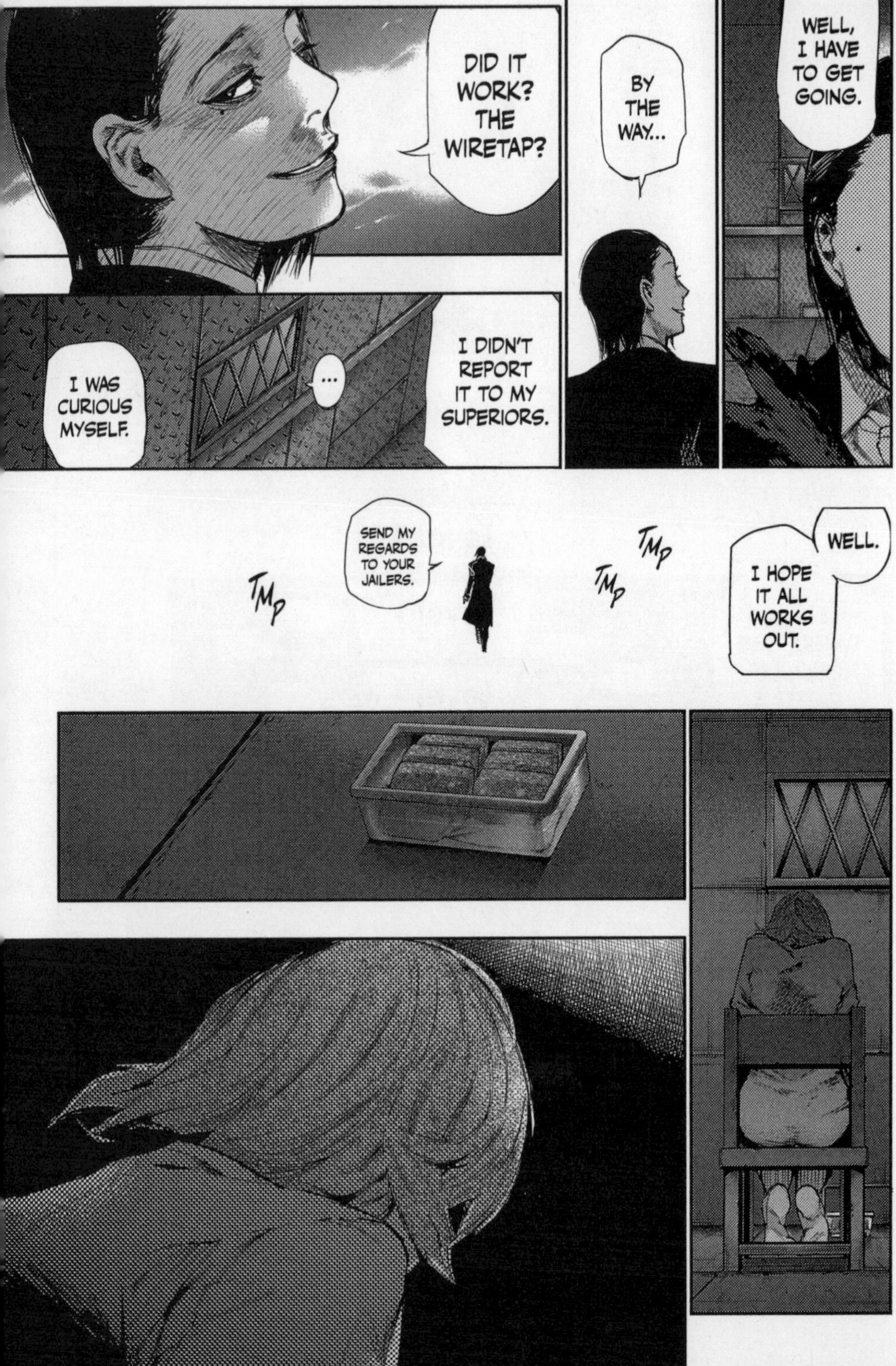
WELL, I HAVE TO GET GOING.
BY THE WAY...
DID IT WORK? THE WIRETAP?
I DIDN'T REPORT IT TO MY SUPERIORS.
...
I WAS CURIOUS MYSELF.
WELL.
I HOPE IT ALL WORKS OUT.
TMP
TMP
SEND MY REGARDS TO YOUR JAILERS.
TMP

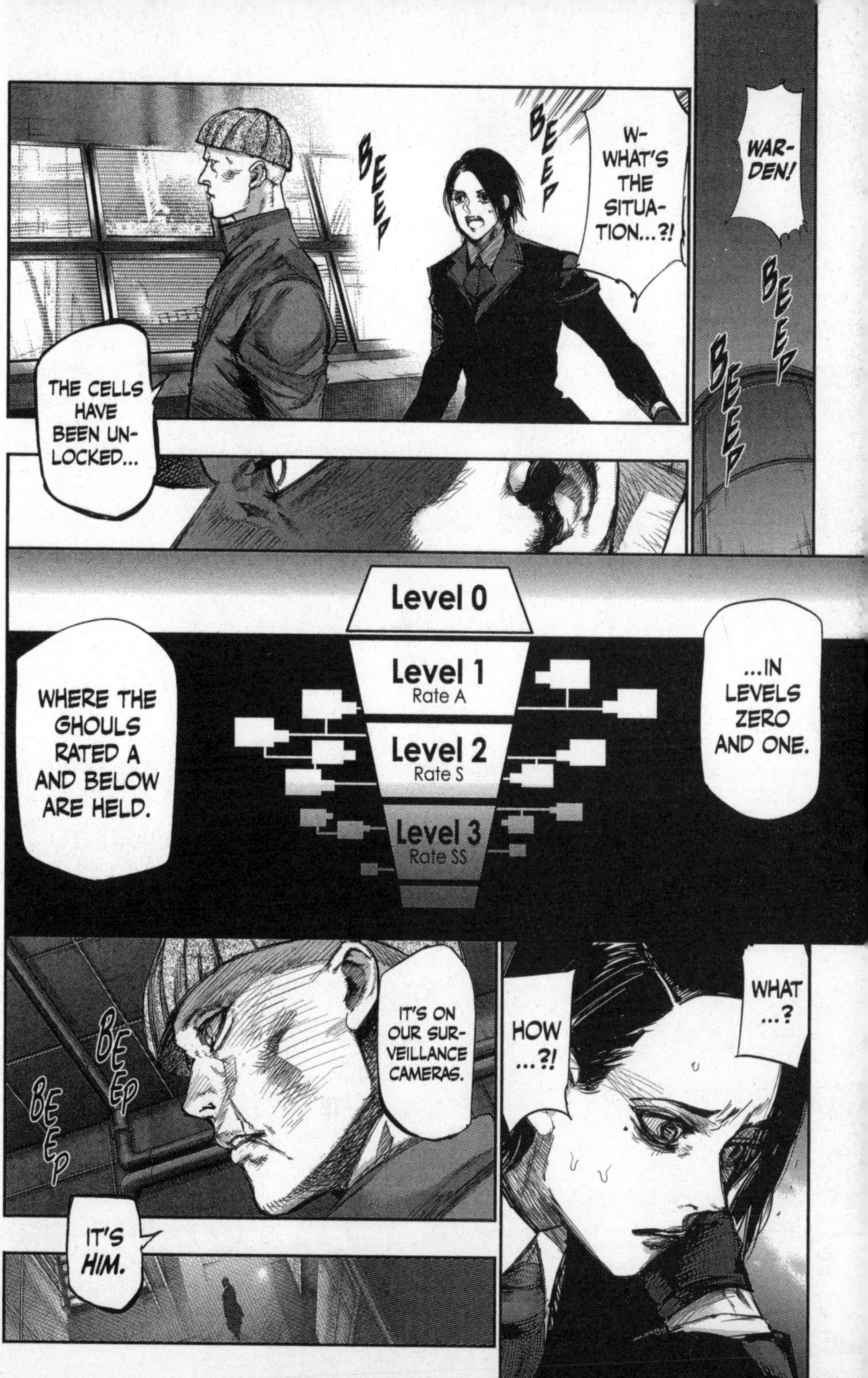
WAR-DEN!
BEEP
BEEP
BEEP
BEEP
W-WHAT'S THE SITUA-TION...?!
BEEP
THE CELLS HAVE BEEN UN-LOCKED...
...IN LEVELS ZERO AND ONE.
Level 0
Level 1
Rate A
Level 2
Rate S
Level 3
Rate SS
WHERE THE GHOULS RATED A AND BELOW ARE HELD.
WHAT...?
HOW...?!
IT'S ON OUR SUR-VEILLANCE CAMERAS.
BEEP
BEEP
IT'S HIM.

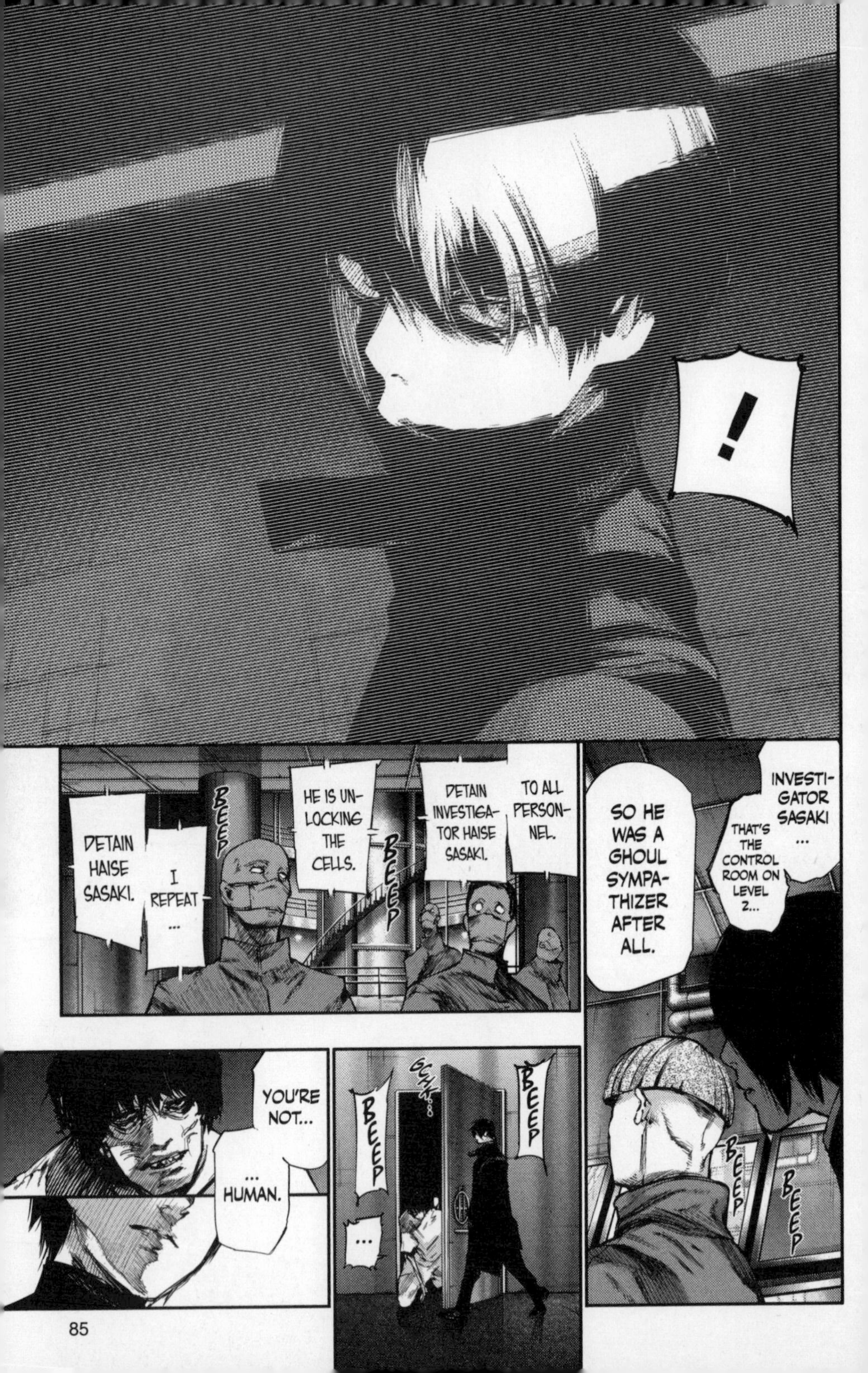
!
INVESTIGATOR SASAKI...
THAT'S THE CONTROL ROOM ON LEVEL 2...
SO HE WAS A GHOUL SYMPATHIZER AFTER ALL.
BEEP
BEEP
TO ALL PERSONNEL.
DETAIN INVESTIGATOR HAISE SASAKI.
BEEP
HE IS UNLOCKING THE CELLS.
BEEP
I REPEAT...
DETAIN HAISE SASAKI.
BEEP
BEEP
GCHK...
BEEP
...
YOU'RE NOT...
...HUMAN.

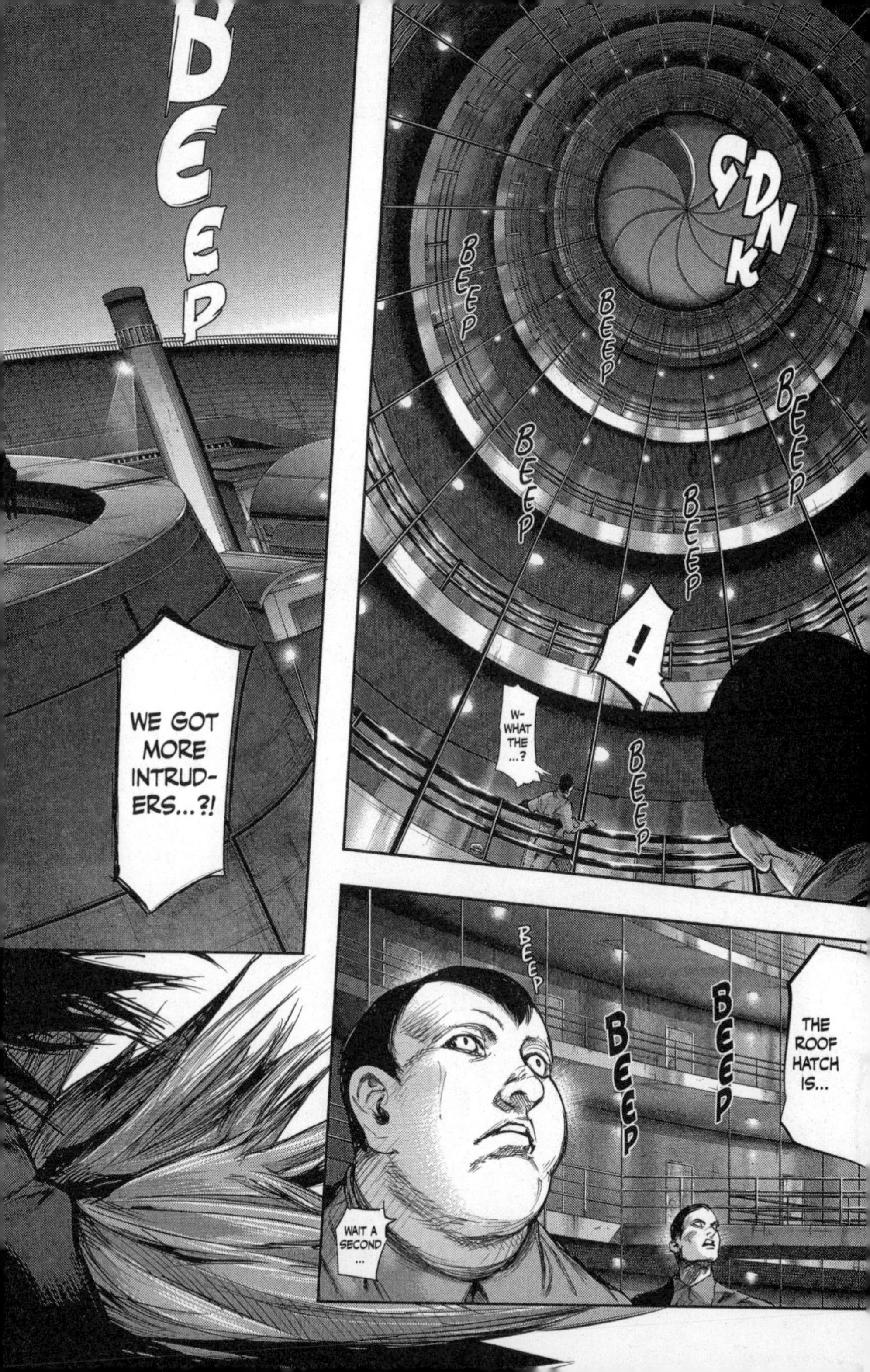
GDNK
BEEP
BEEEP
BEEP
BEEEP
BEEEP
!
W-WHAT THE ...?
BEEEP
BEEP
BEEP
BEEEP
THE ROOF HATCH IS...
WAIT A SECOND ...
BEEEP
WE GOT MORE INTRUDERS...?!

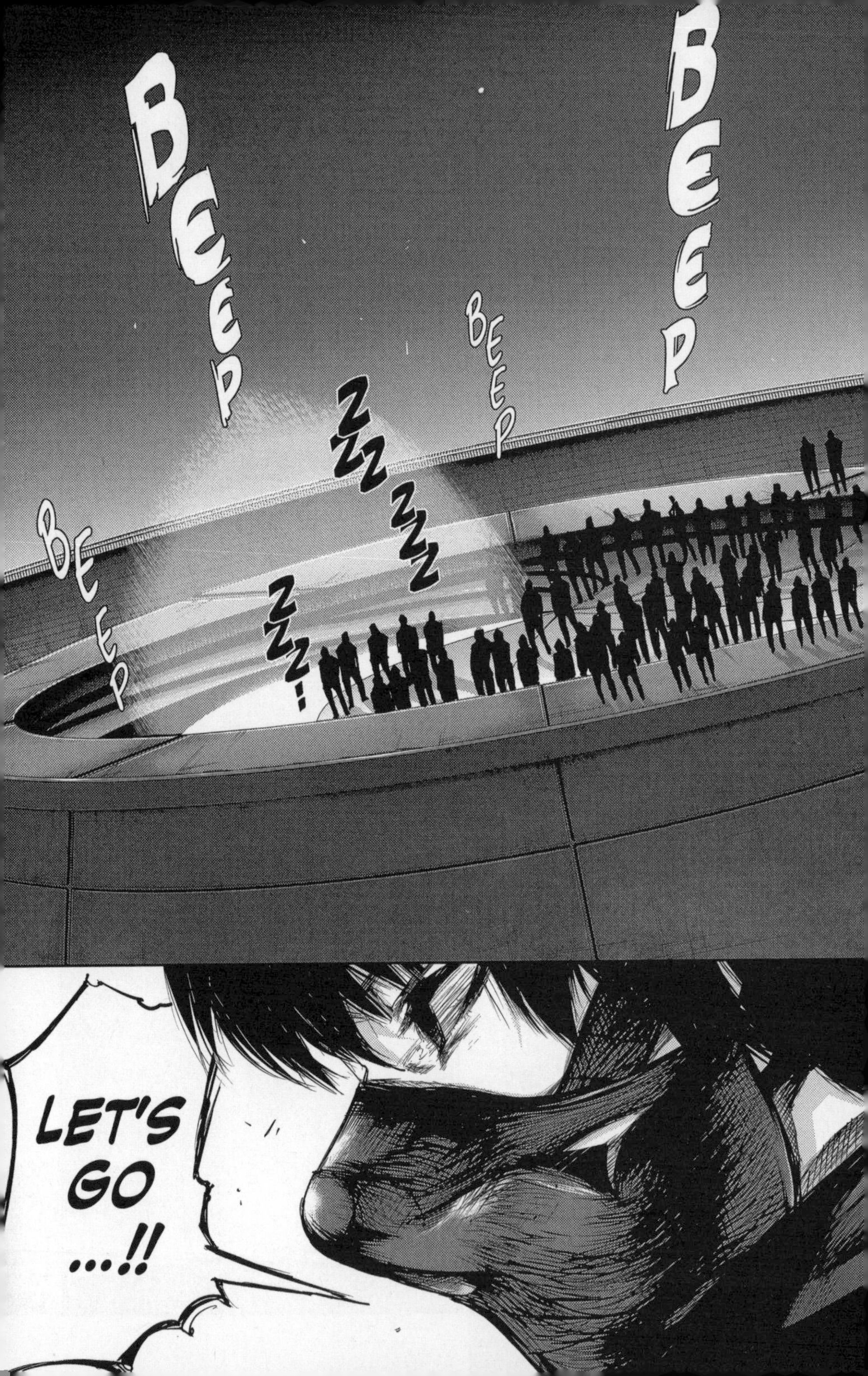

BEEP
BEEP
BEEP
BEEP
LET'S GO ...!!

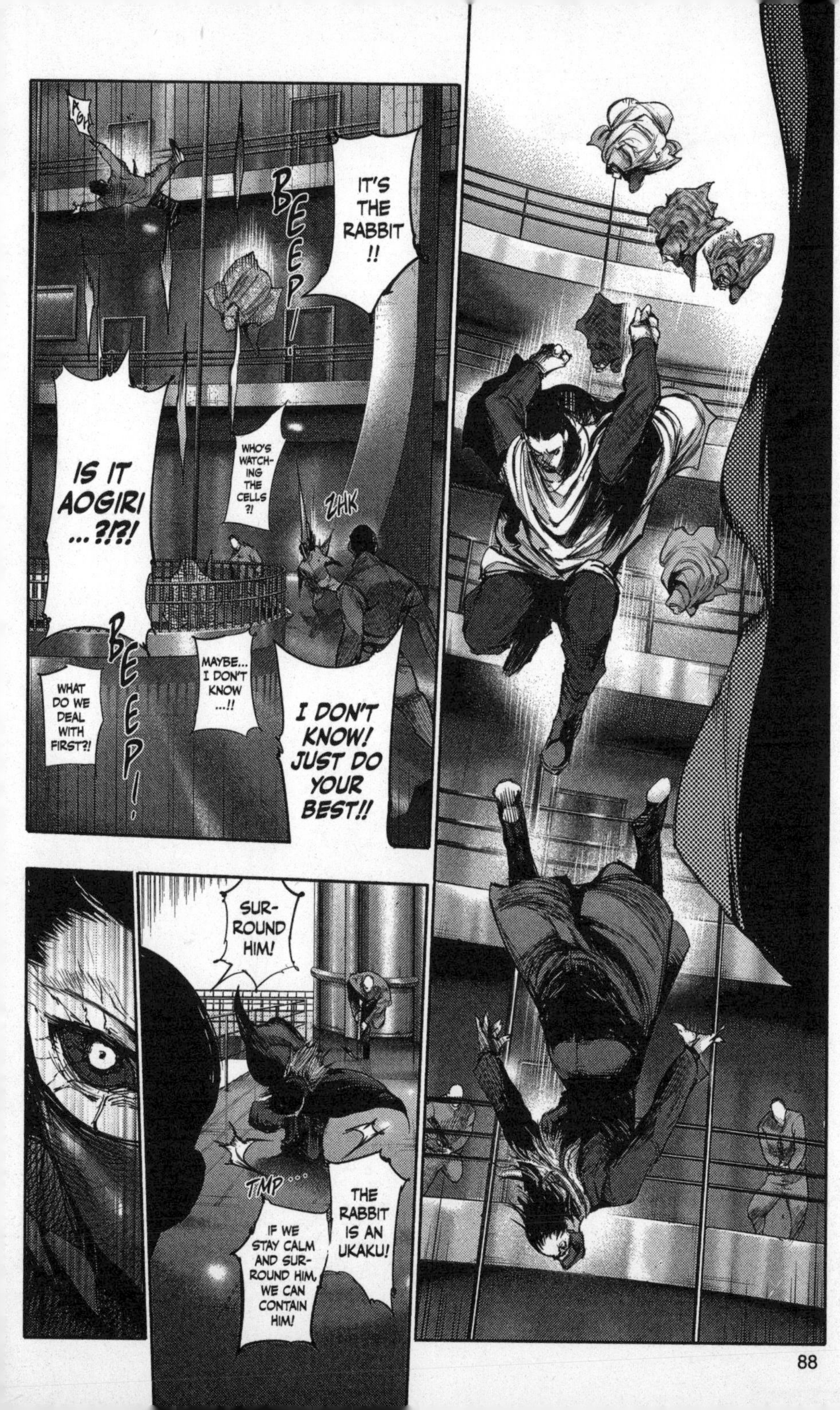
AGH
IT'S THE RABBIT!!
BEEP!
WHO'S WATCHING THE CELLS?!
IS IT AOGIRI...?!?!
ZHK
MAYBE... I DON'T KNOW...!!
I DON'T KNOW! JUST DO YOUR BEST!!
WHAT DO WE DEAL WITH FIRST?!
BEEP!
SUR-ROUND HIM!
TMP...
THE RABBIT IS AN UKAKU!
IF WE STAY CALM AND SUR-ROUND HIM, WE CAN CONTAIN HIM!

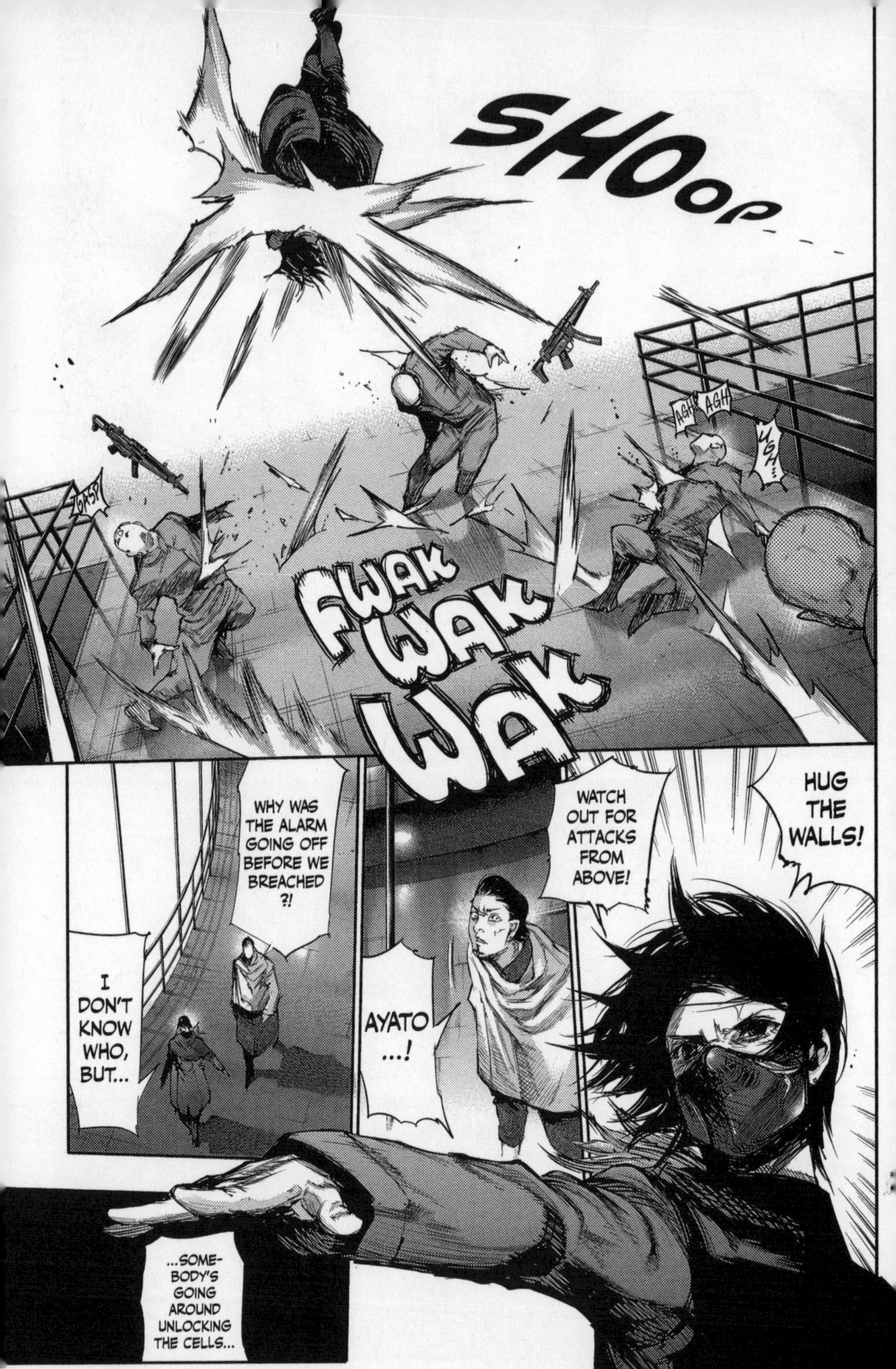
SHOOP
AGH! AGH
UGH...
GASP!
FWAK WAK WAK
HUG THE WALLS!
WATCH OUT FOR ATTACKS FROM ABOVE!
AYATO ...!
WHY WAS THE ALARM GOING OFF BEFORE WE BREACHED ?!
I DON'T KNOW WHO, BUT...
...SOME-BODY'S GOING AROUND UNLOCKING THE CELLS...

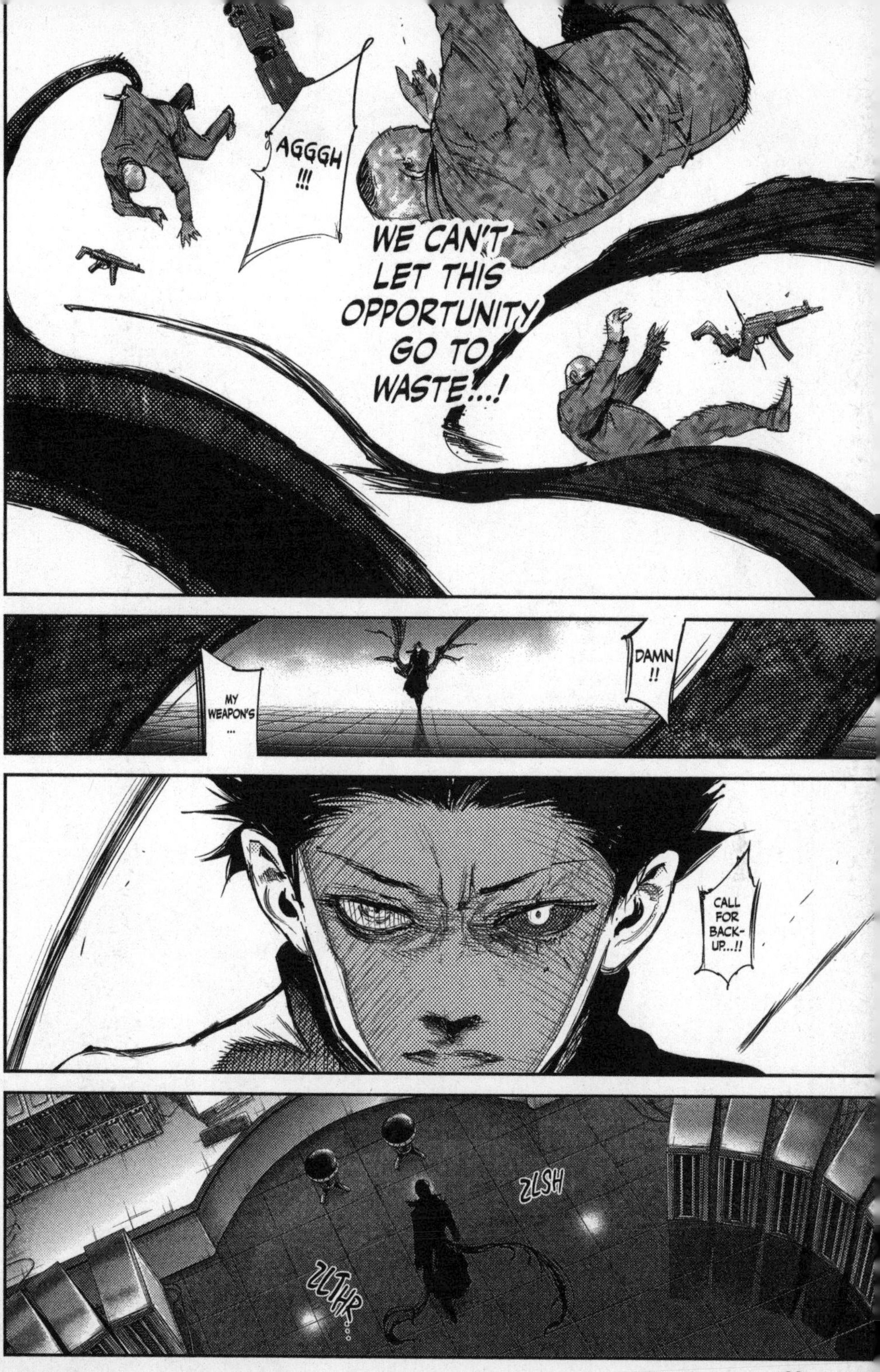
AGGGH !!!
WE CAN'T LET THIS OPPORTUNITY GO TO WASTE...!
DAMN !!
MY WEAPON'S ...
CALL FOR BACK-UP...!!
ZLSH
ZLTHR...

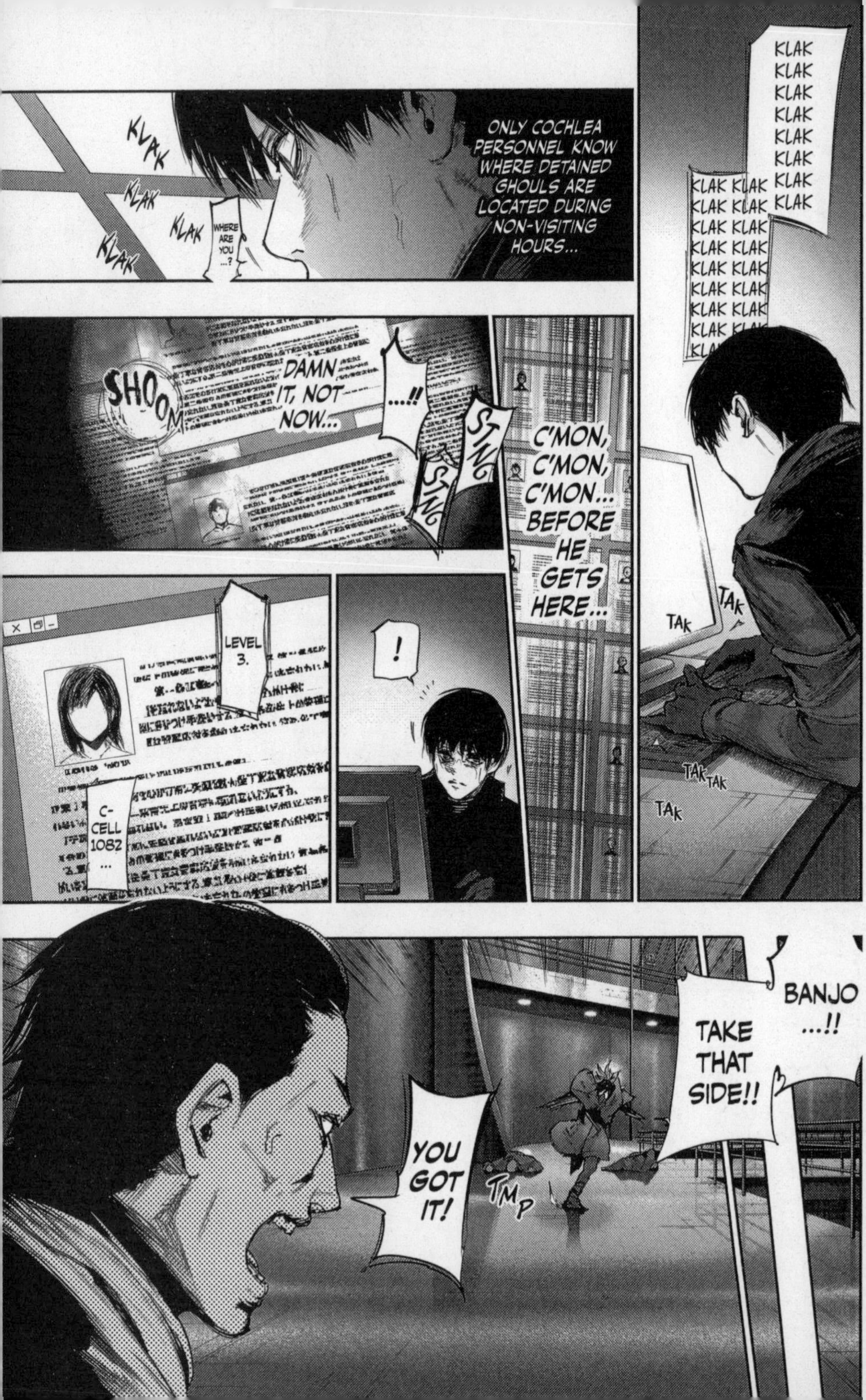
KLAK KLAK KLAK KLAK KLAK KLAK KLAK KLAK
KLAK KLAK KLAK KLAK KLAK KLAK KLAK KLAK KLAK KLAK KLAK KLAK KLAK KLAK KLAK KLAK KLAK KLAK KLAK
TAK
TAK
TAK TAK
TAK
ONLY COCHLEA PERSONNEL KNOW WHERE DETAINED GHOULS ARE LOCATED DURING NON-VISITING HOURS...
WHERE ARE YOU ...?
KLAK
KLAK
KLAK
KLAK
C'MON, C'MON, C'MON... BEFORE HE GETS HERE...
...!!
STING
STING
DAMN IT, NOT NOW...
SHOOM
!
LEVEL 3.
C-CELL 1082 ...
BANJO ...!!
TAKE THAT SIDE!!
YOU GOT IT!
TMP

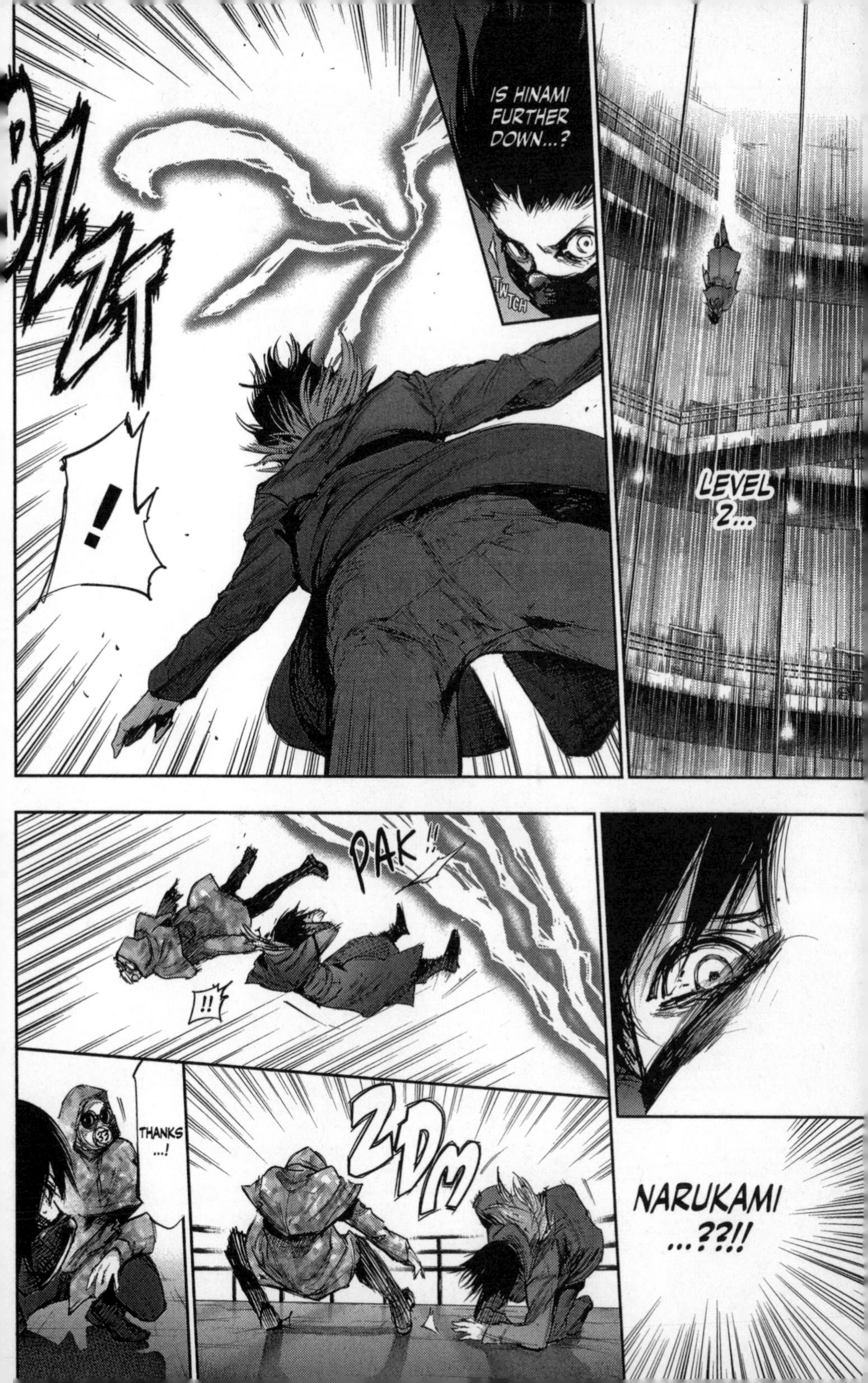
LEVEL 2...
IS HINAMI FURTHER DOWN...?
TWTCH
!
PAK!!
!!
NARUKAMI ...??!!
ZDM
THANKS ...!

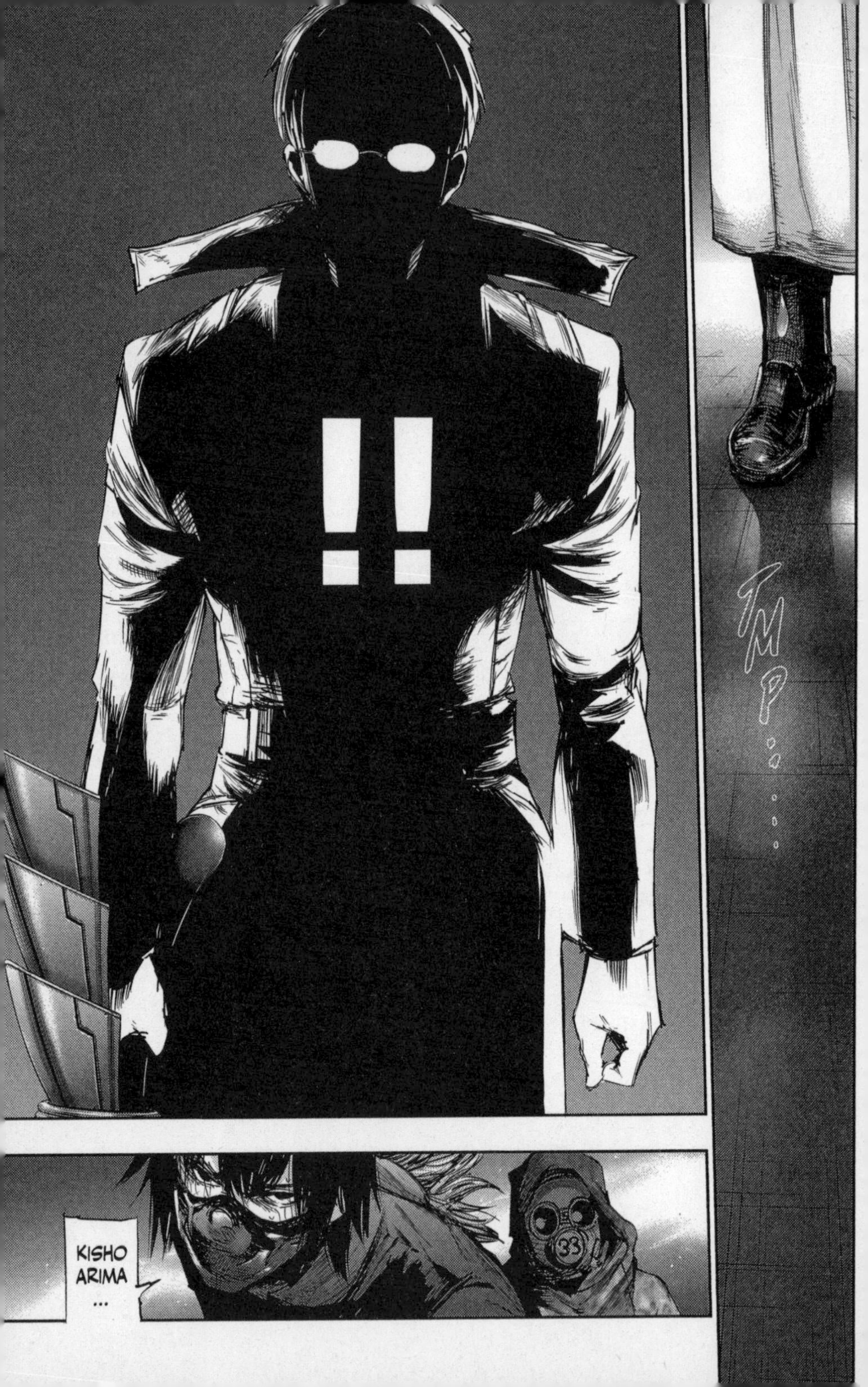
TMP...
!!
KISHO ARIMA
...

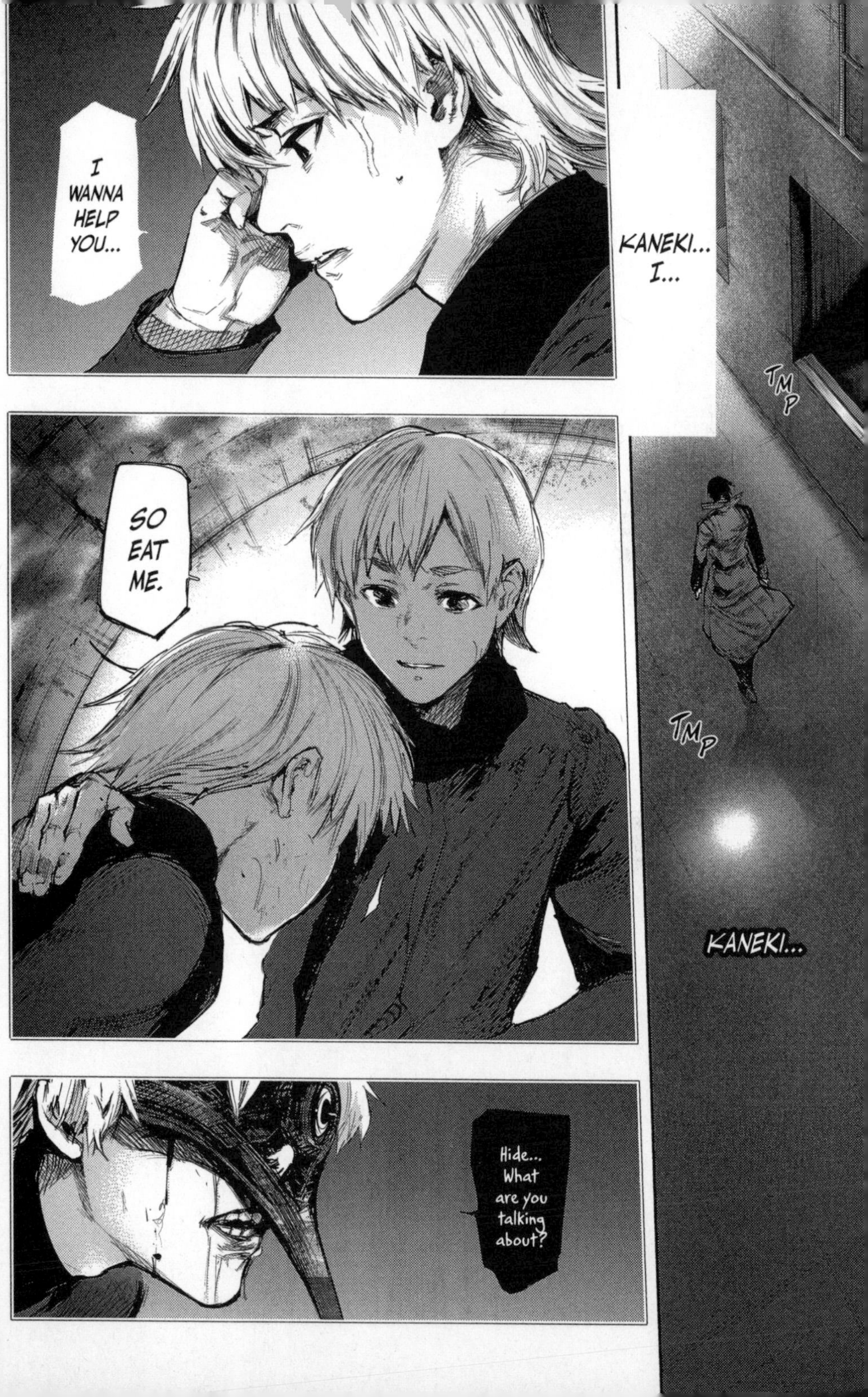
KANEKI... I...
TMP
TMP
KANEKI...
I WANNA HELP YOU...
SO EAT ME.
Hide... What are you talking about?

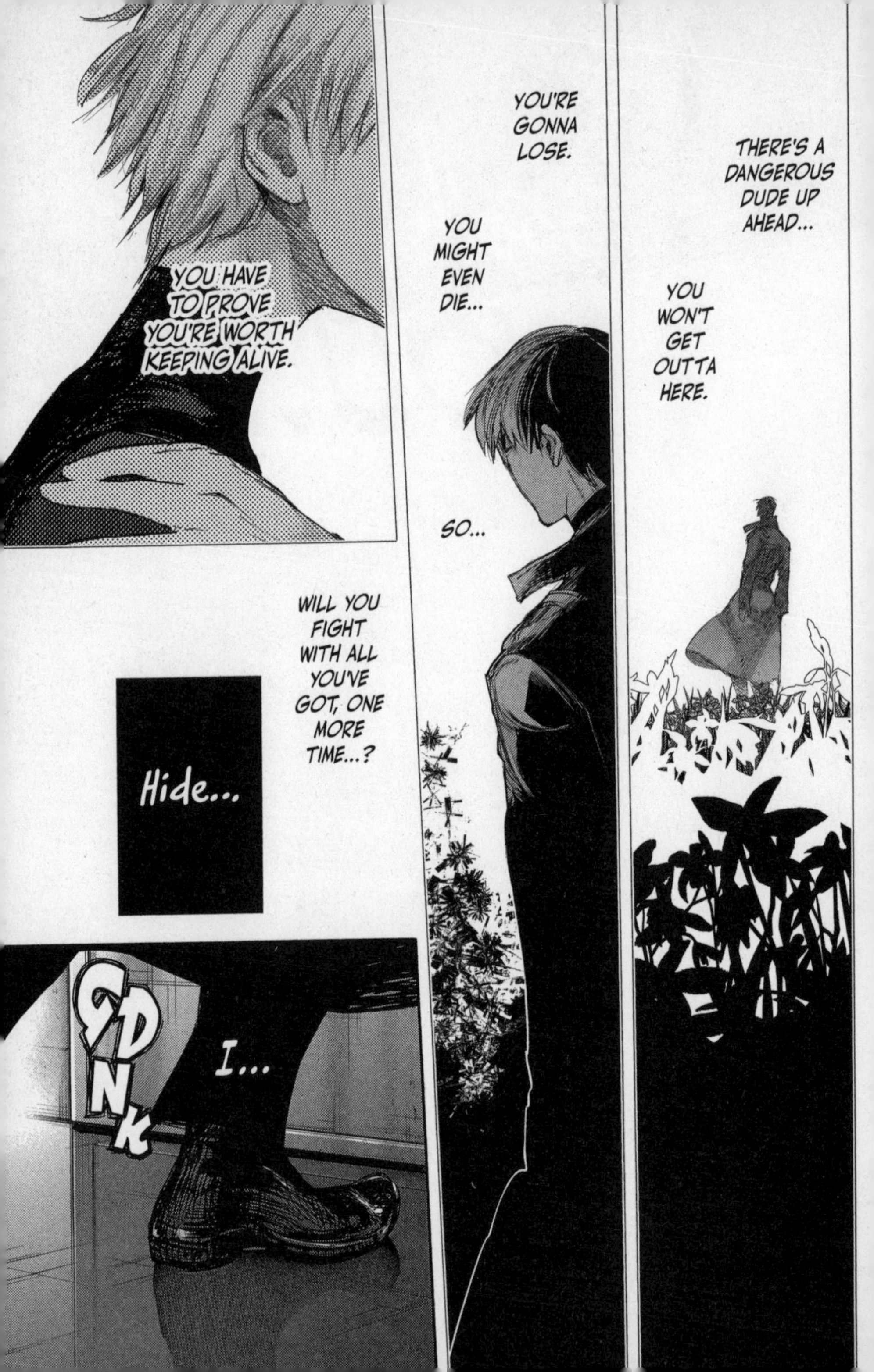

THERE'S A DANGEROUS DUDE UP AHEAD...
YOU WON'T GET OUTTA HERE.
YOU'RE GONNA LOSE.
YOU MIGHT EVEN DIE...
SO...
YOU HAVE TO PROVE YOU'RE WORTH KEEPING ALIVE.
WILL YOU FIGHT WITH ALL YOU'VE GOT, ONE MORE TIME...?
Hide...
I...
GDNK

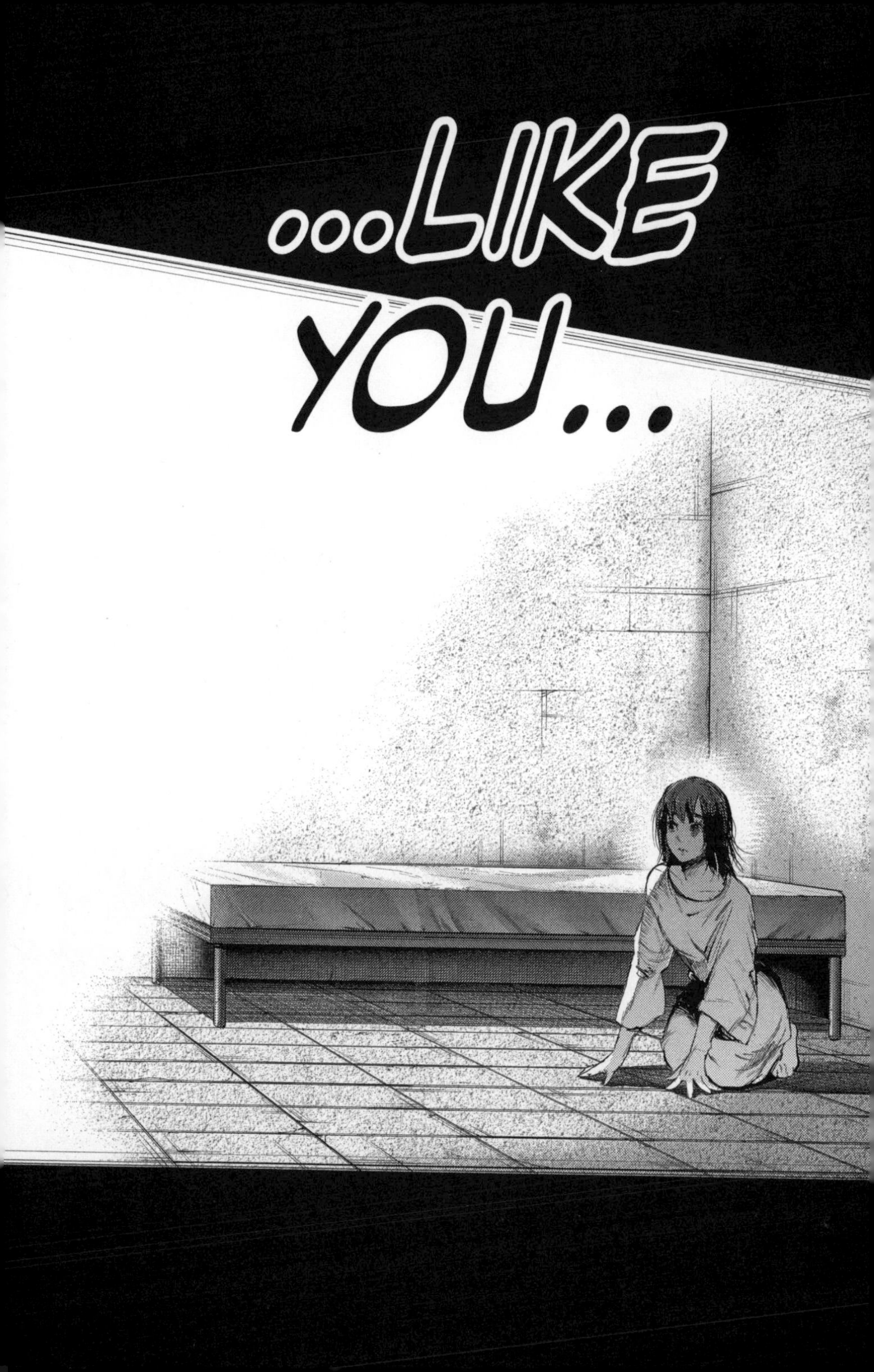
...LIKE
YOU...

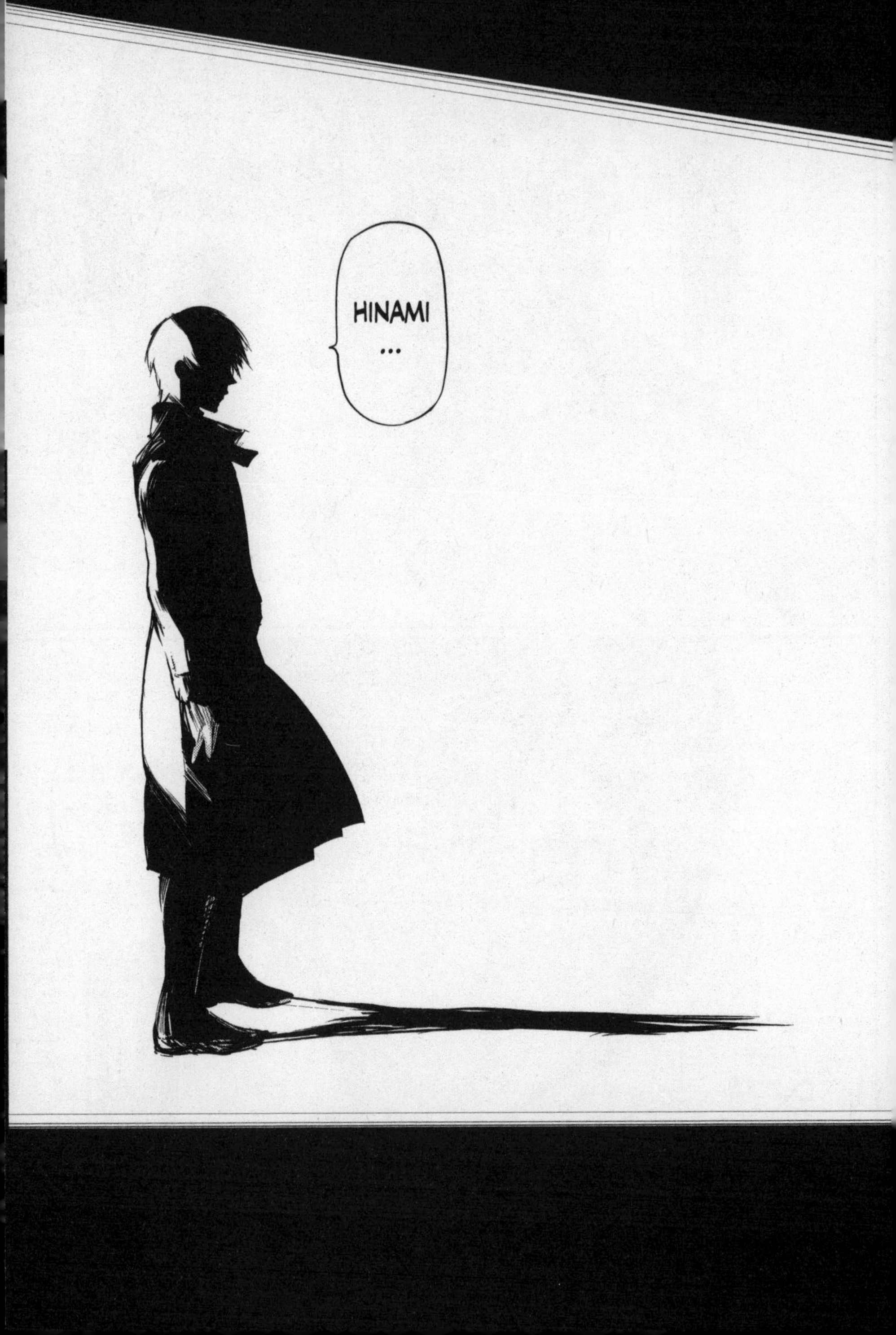
HINAMI ...

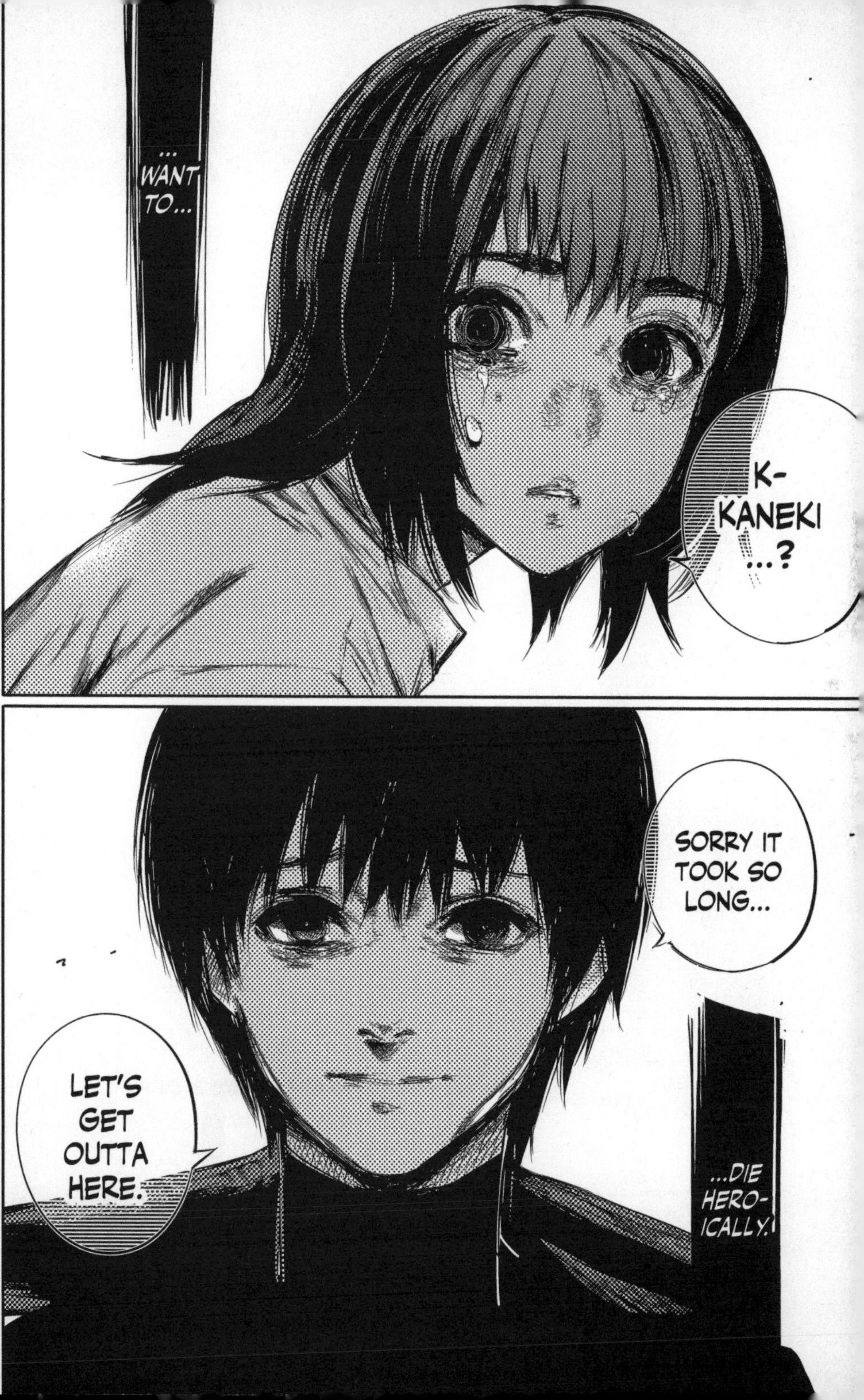
K-KANEKI ...?
...WANT TO...
SORRY IT TOOK SO LONG...
...DIE HEROICALLY!
LET'S GET OUTTA HERE.

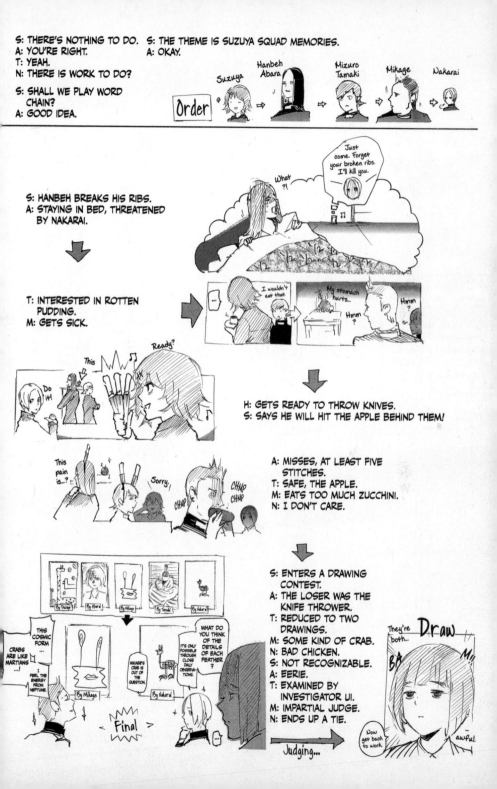

S: THERE'S NOTHING TO DO.
A: YOU'RE RIGHT.
T: YEAH.
N: THERE IS WORK TO DO?

S: SHALL WE PLAY WORD CHAIN?
A: GOOD IDEA.

S: THE THEME IS SUZUYA SQUAD MEMORIES.
A: OKAY.

Order
Suzuya
Hanbeh Abara
Mizuro Tamaki
Mikage
Nakarai

S: HANBEH BREAKS HIS RIBS.
A: STAYING IN BED, THREATENED BY NAKARAI.

Just come. Forget your broken ribs. I'll kill you.
What ?!

T: INTERESTED IN ROTTEN PUDDING.
M: GETS SICK.

...
I wouldn't eat that.
My stomach hurts...
Hmm ?
Hmm ?

Ready?
This
Do it!

H: GETS READY TO THROW KNIVES.
S: SAYS HE WILL HIT THE APPLE BEHIND THEM!

CHMP CHMP
CHMP
Sorry.
This pain is...?

A: MISSES, AT LEAST FIVE STITCHES.
T: SAFE, THE APPLE.
M: EATS TOO MUCH ZUCCHINI.
N: I DON'T CARE.

By Suzuya
By Abara
By Mikage
By Tamaki
By Nakarai
WHAT DO YOU THINK OF THE DETAILS OF EACH FEATHER?
IT'S ONLY POSSIBLE THROUGH CLOSE DAILY OBSERVATIONS.
MIKAGE'S CRAB IS OUT OF THE QUESTION.
By Nakarai
...
THIS COSMIC FORM...
CRABS ARE LIKE MARTIANS...!
I FEEL THE ENERGY FROM NEPTUNE.
By Mikage
Final

S: ENTERS A DRAWING CONTEST.
A: THE LOSER WAS THE KNIFE THROWER.
T: REDUCED TO TWO DRAWINGS.
M: SOME KIND OF CRAB.
N: BAD CHICKEN.
S: NOT RECOGNIZABLE.
A: EERIE.
T: EXAMINED BY INVESTIGATOR UI.
M: IMPARTIAL JUDGE.
N: ENDS UP A TIE.

Judging...

Draw
They're both...
BAM!!
...awful.
Now get back to work.

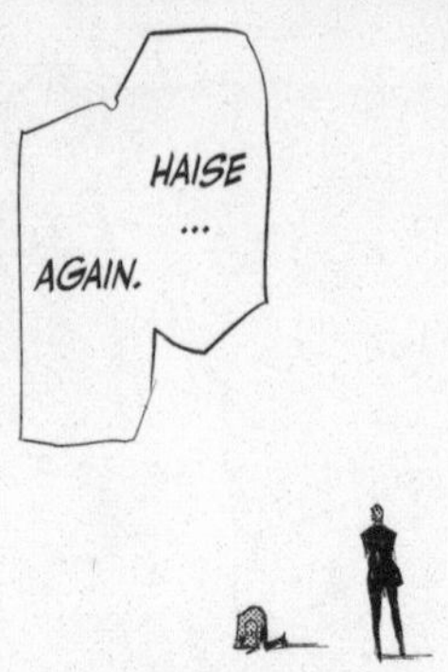
HAISE ... AGAIN.

Relock :69

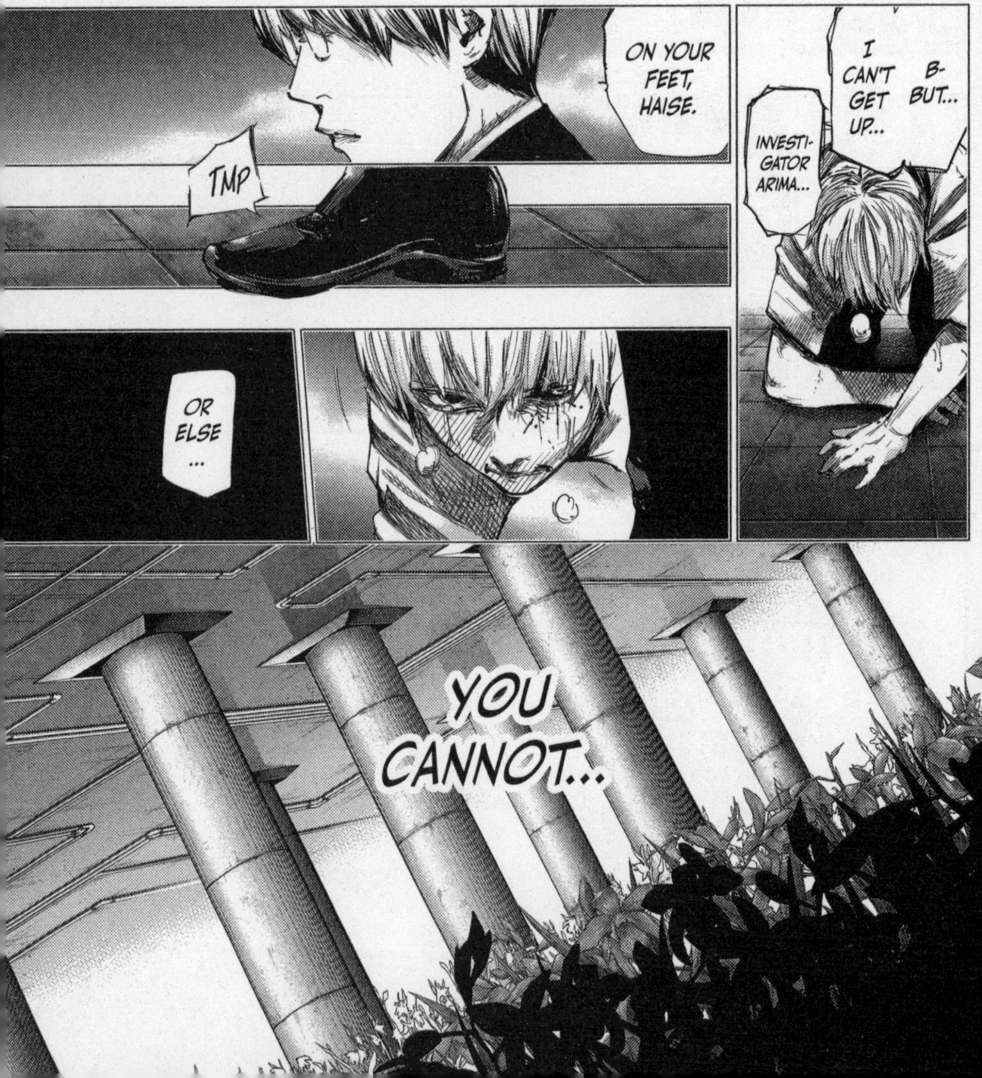
B-BUT...
I CAN'T GET UP...
INVESTI-GATOR ARIMA...
ON YOUR FEET, HAISE.
TMP
OR ELSE ...
YOU CANNOT...

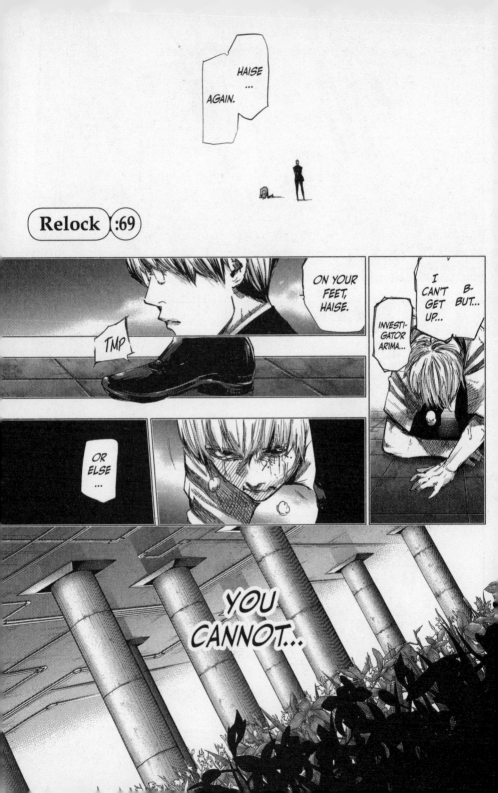

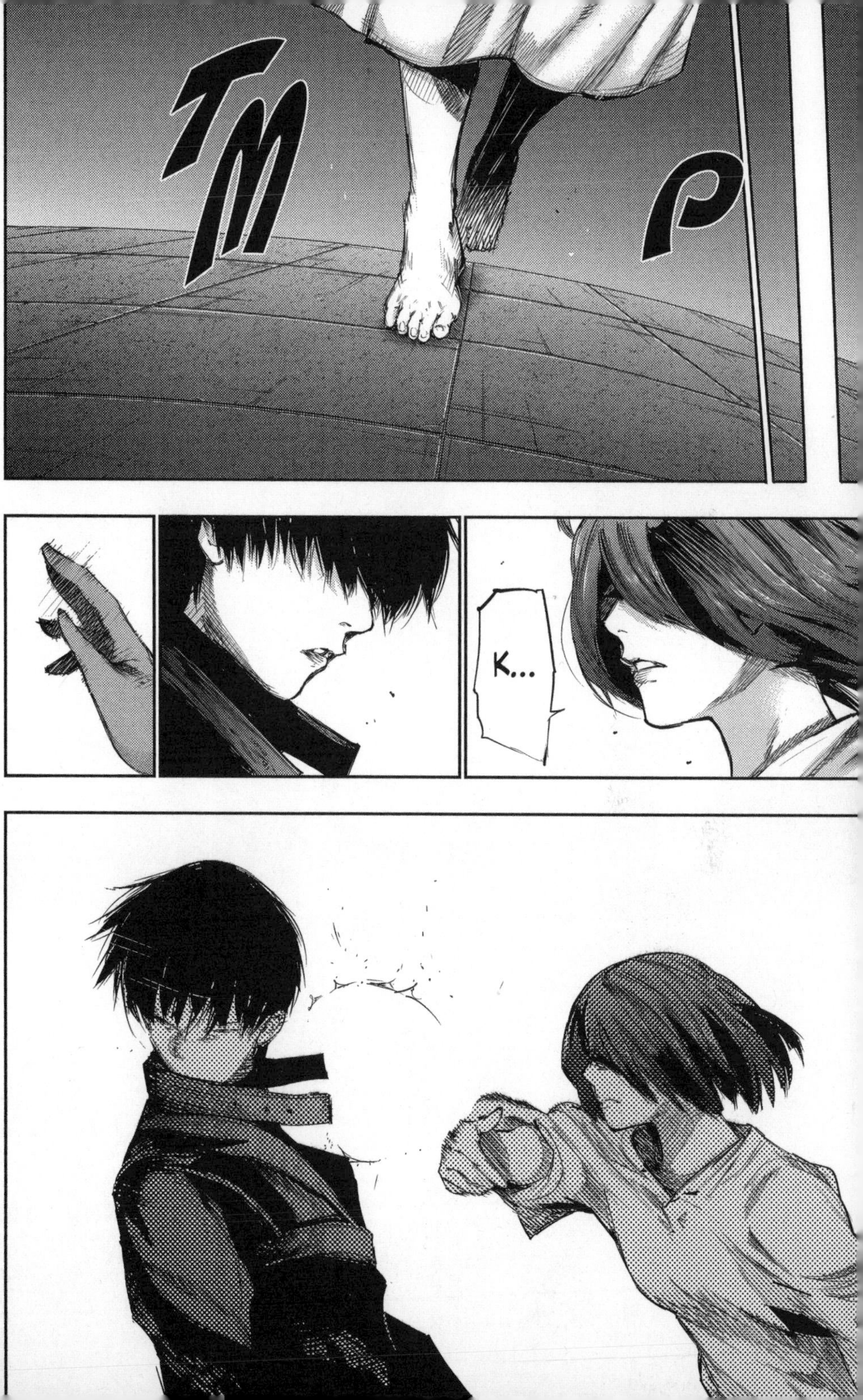
TMP
K...

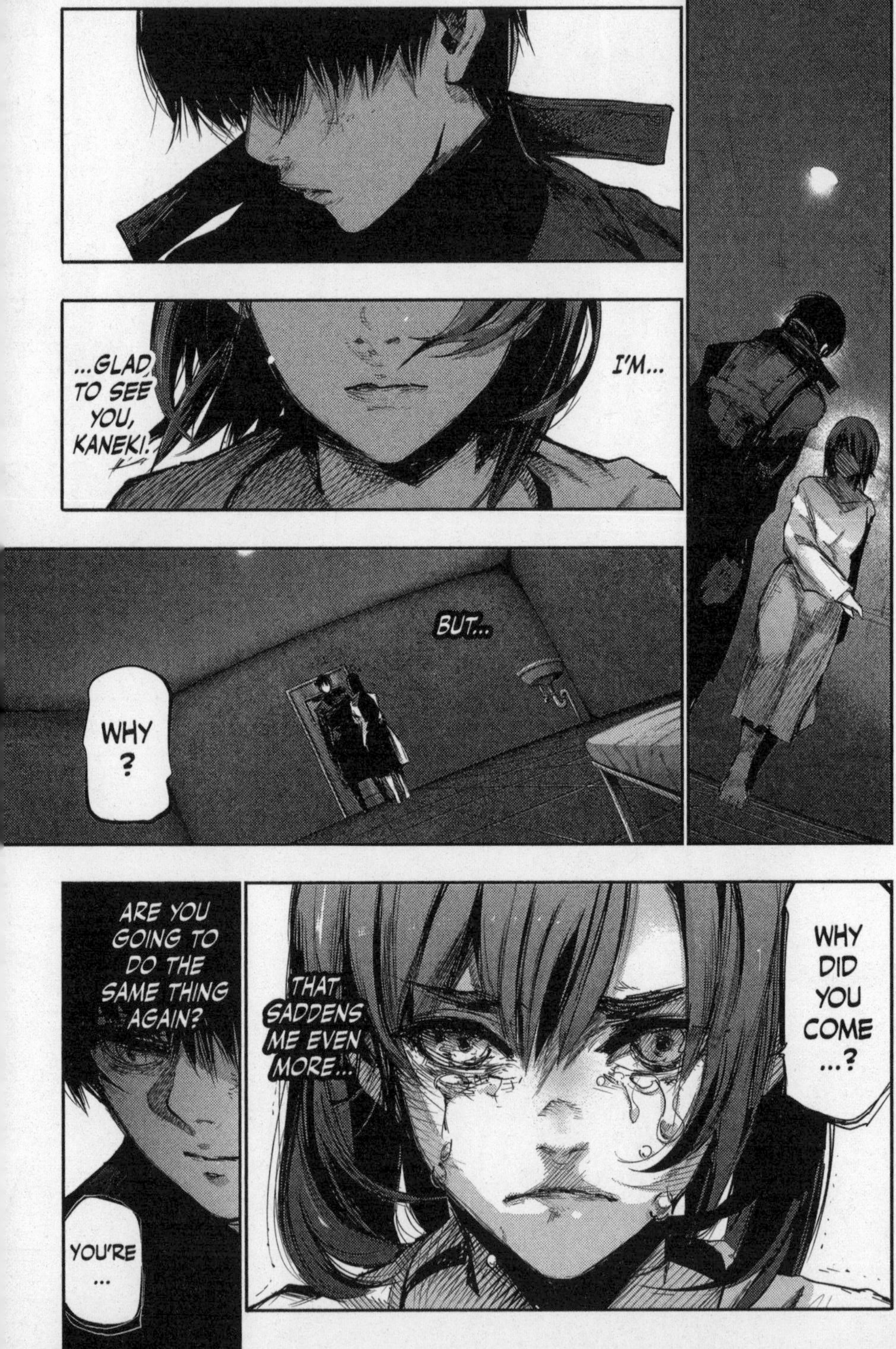
I'M...
...GLAD TO SEE YOU, KANEKI.
BUT...
WHY?
WHY DID YOU COME...?
THAT SADDENS ME EVEN MORE...
ARE YOU GOING TO DO THE SAME THING AGAIN?
YOU'RE...

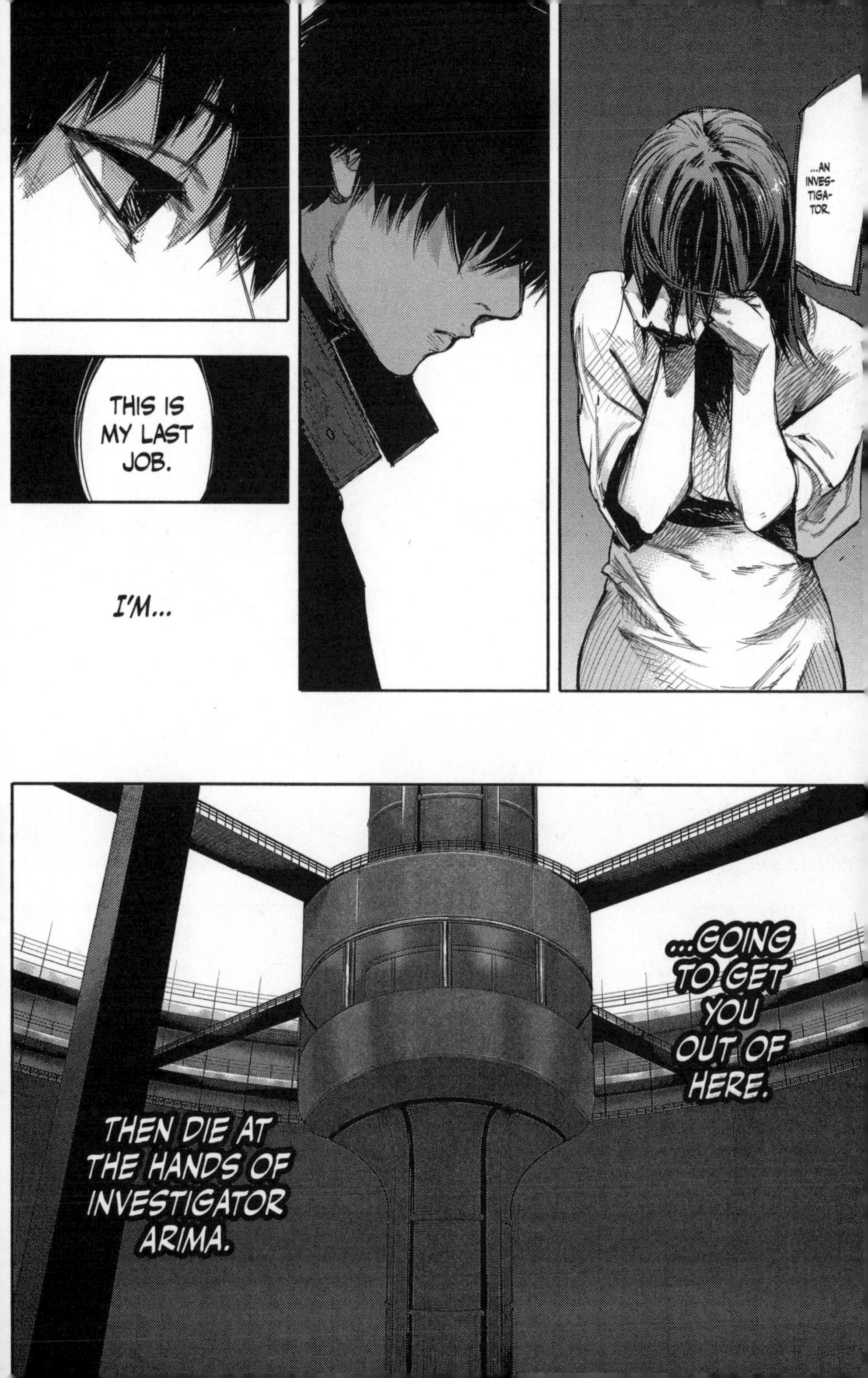
...AN INVESTIGATOR.
THIS IS MY LAST JOB.
I'M...
...GOING TO GET YOU OUT OF HERE.
THEN DIE AT THE HANDS OF INVESTIGATOR ARIMA.

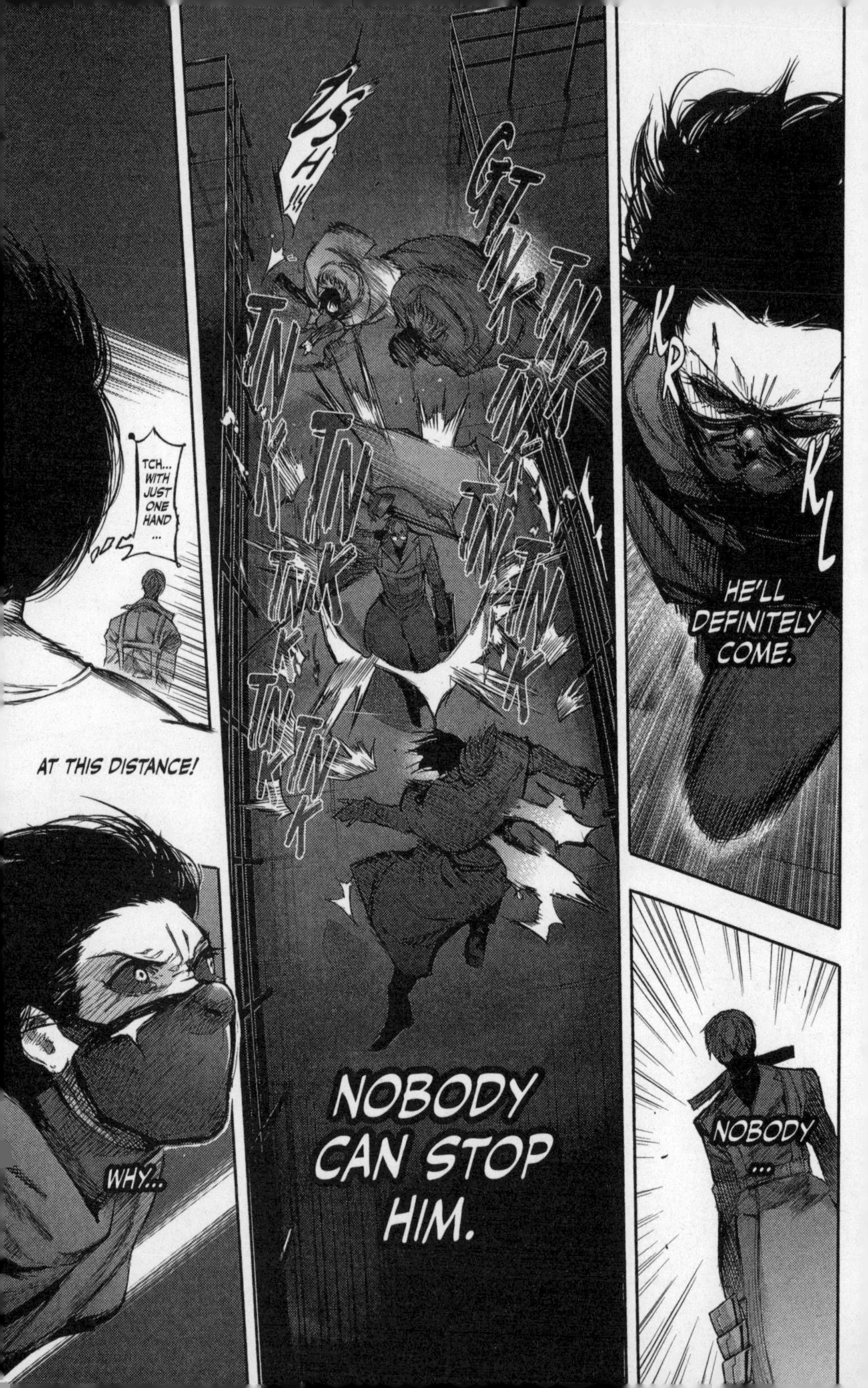
KRKL
HE'LL DEFINITELY COME.
NOBODY...
ZSH!!
GTINK TINK
TINK TINK
NOBODY CAN STOP HIM.
TCH... WITH JUST ONE HAND...
AT THIS DISTANCE!
WHY...

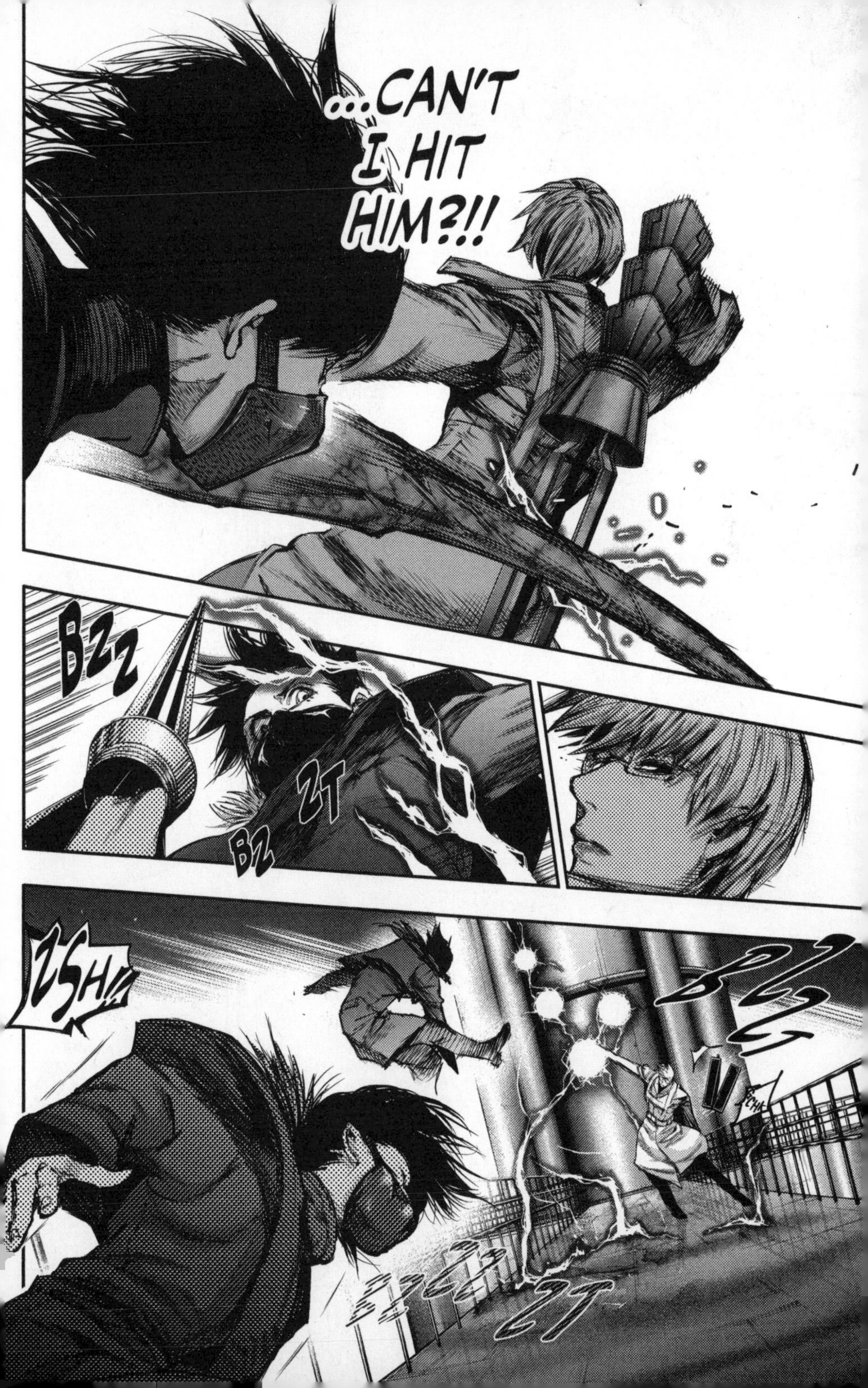
...CAN'T I HIT HIM?!!
BZZ
BZ ZT
ZSH!!

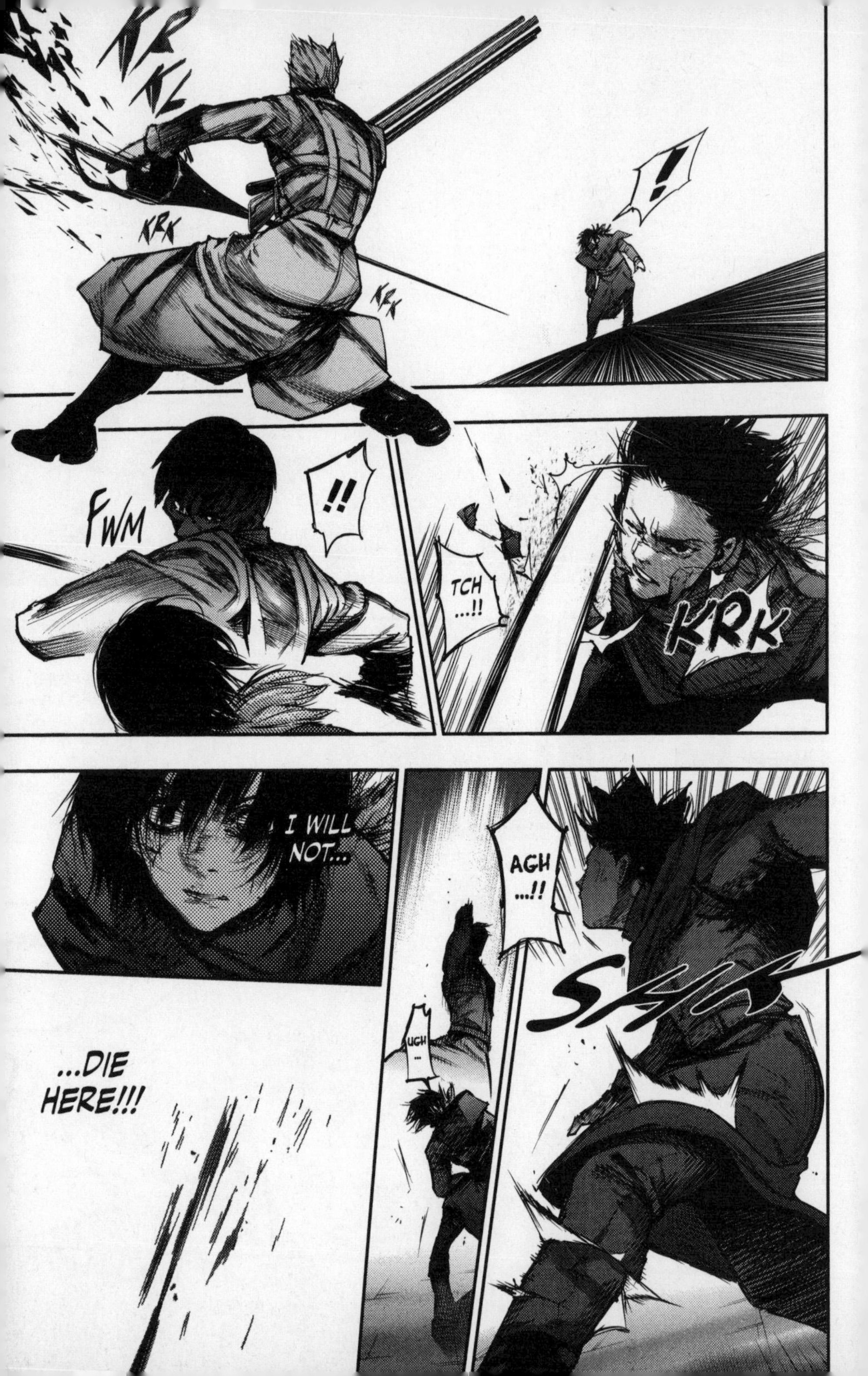
!
KRK
KRK
KRK
TCH ...!!
!!
FWM
AGH ...!!
UGH ...
I WILL NOT...
...DIE HERE!!!

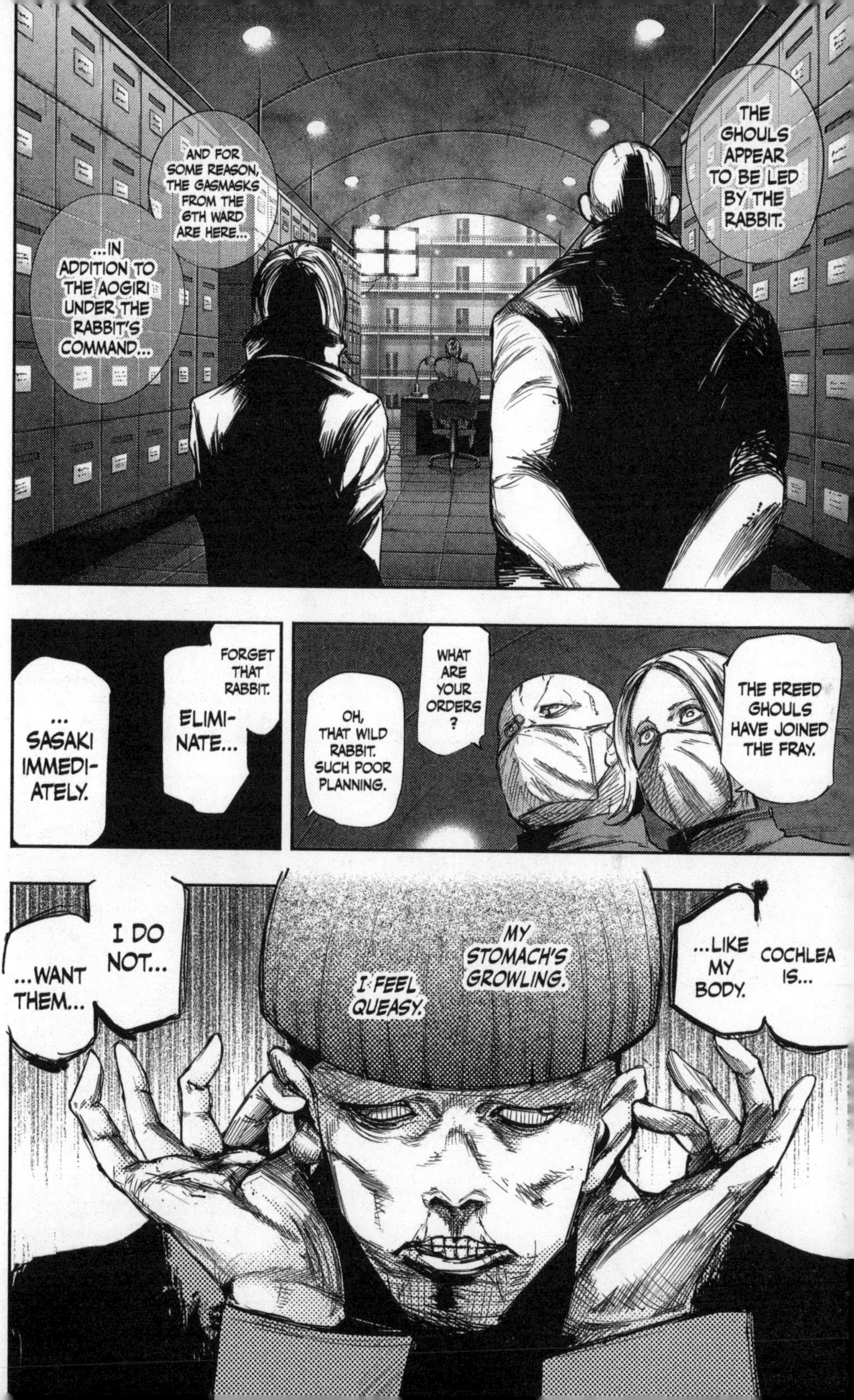
THE GHOULS APPEAR TO BE LED BY THE RABBIT.
AND FOR SOME REASON, THE GASMASKS FROM THE 6TH WARD ARE HERE...
...IN ADDITION TO THE AOGIRI UNDER THE RABBIT'S COMMAND...
THE FREED GHOULS HAVE JOINED THE FRAY.
WHAT ARE YOUR ORDERS?
OH, THAT WILD RABBIT. SUCH POOR PLANNING.
FORGET THAT RABBIT.
ELIMINATE...
...SASAKI IMMEDIATELY.
COCHLEA IS...
...LIKE MY BODY.
MY STOMACH'S GROWLING.
I FEEL QUEASY.
I DO NOT...
...WANT THEM...

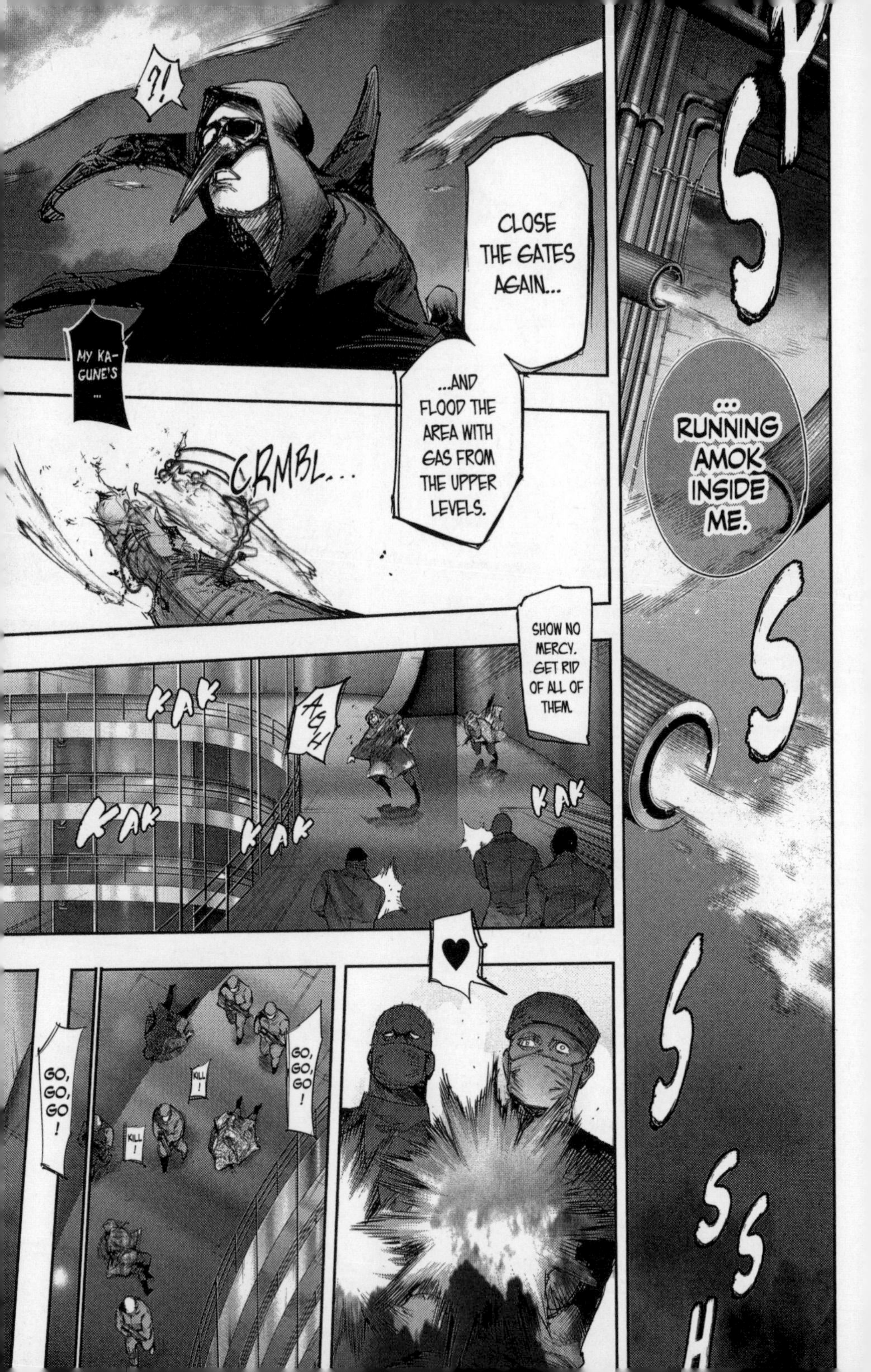

...RUNNING AMOK INSIDE ME.
?!
CLOSE THE GATES AGAIN...
MY KA-GUNE'S ...
...AND FLOOD THE AREA WITH GAS FROM THE UPPER LEVELS.
CRMBL...
SHOW NO MERCY. GET RID OF ALL OF THEM.
AGH
KAK
KAK
KAK
KAK
♥
GO, GO, GO!
KILL!
KILL!
GO, GO, GO!

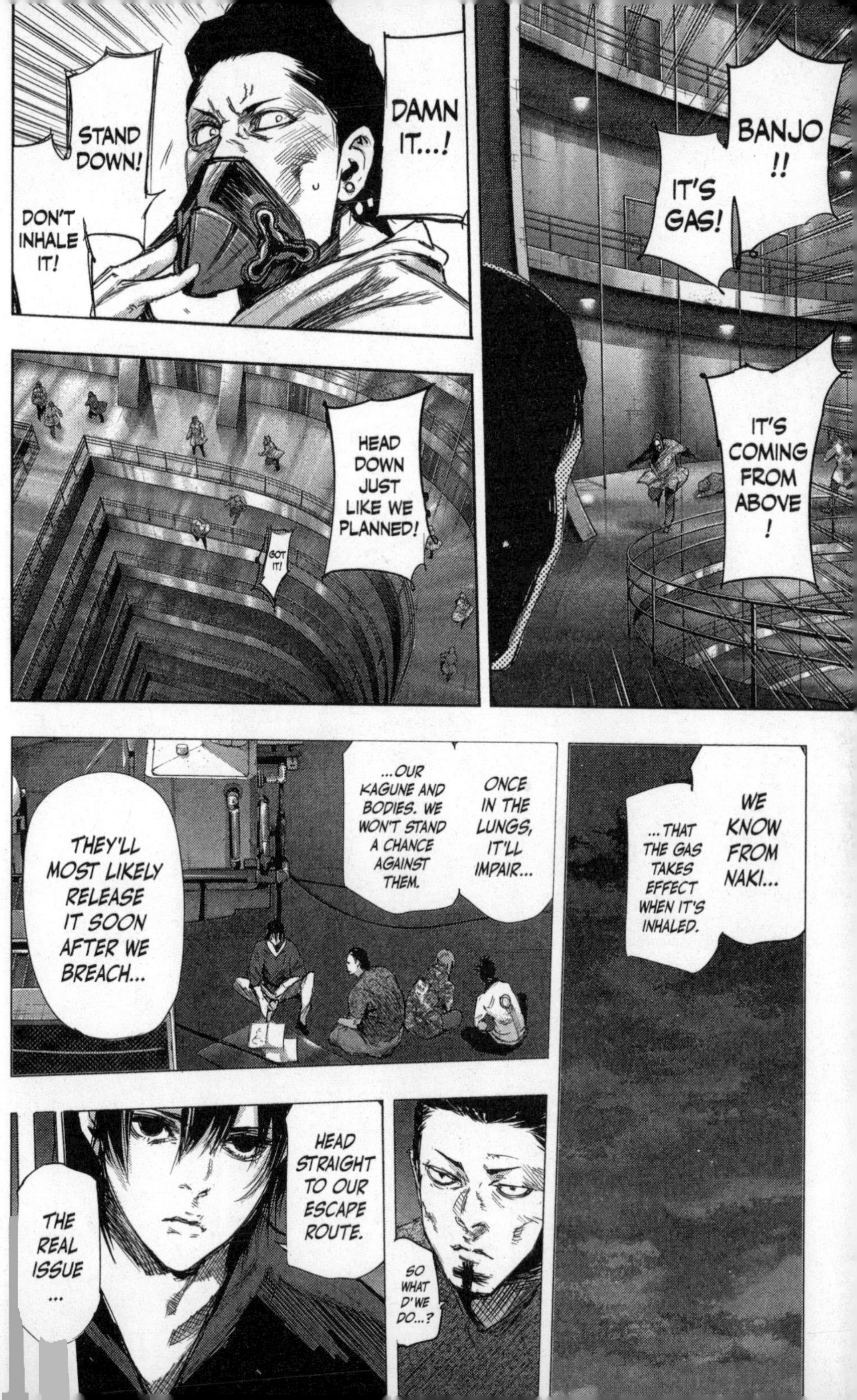
BANJO!!
IT'S GAS!
IT'S COMING FROM ABOVE!
DAMN IT...!
STAND DOWN!
DON'T INHALE IT!
HEAD DOWN JUST LIKE WE PLANNED!
GOT IT!
WE KNOW FROM NAKI...
...THAT THE GAS TAKES EFFECT WHEN IT'S INHALED.
ONCE IN THE LUNGS, IT'LL IMPAIR...
...OUR KAGUNE AND BODIES. WE WON'T STAND A CHANCE AGAINST THEM.
THEY'LL MOST LIKELY RELEASE IT SOON AFTER WE BREACH...
SO WHAT D'WE DO...?
HEAD STRAIGHT TO OUR ESCAPE ROUTE.
THE REAL ISSUE ...

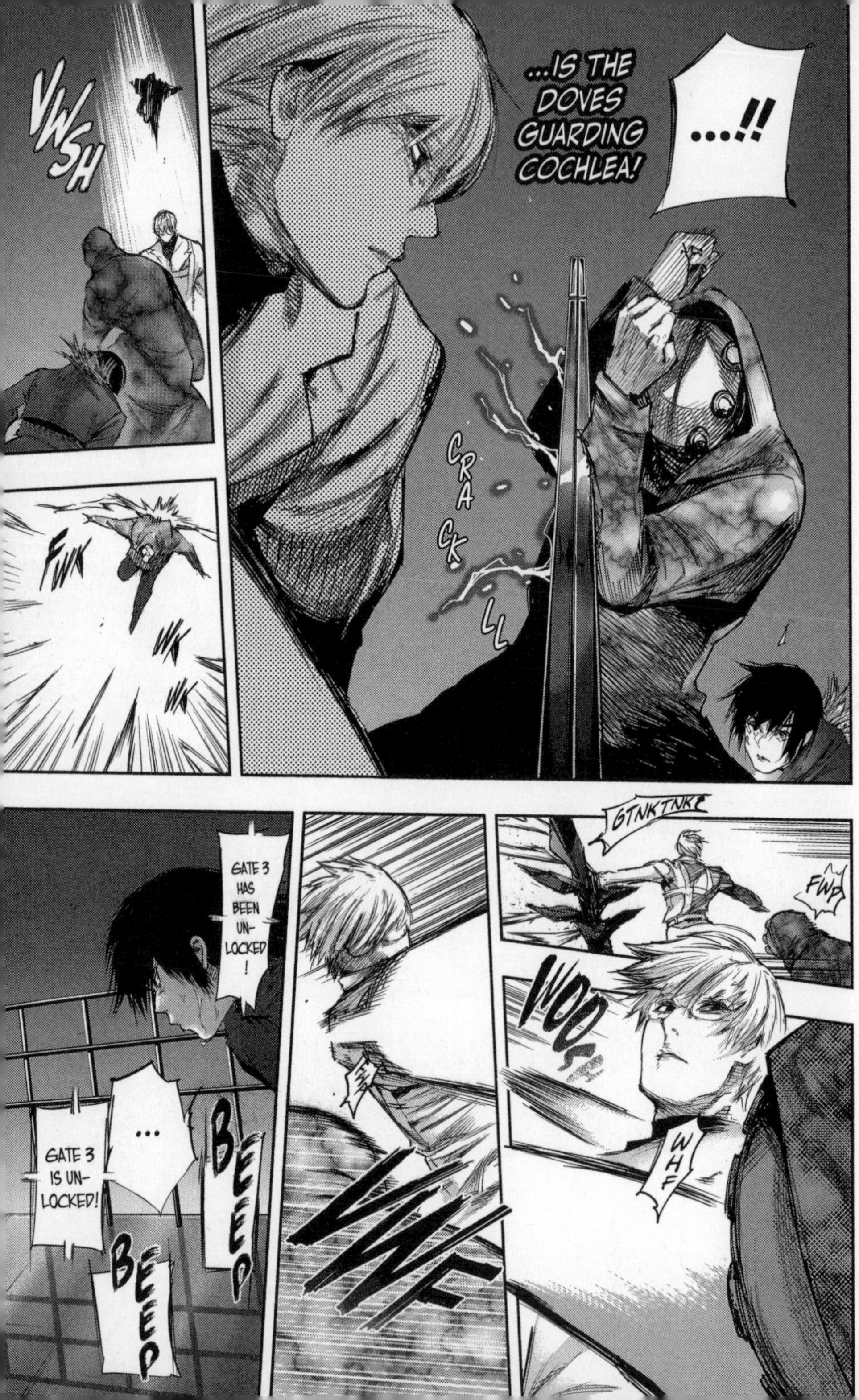
...IS THE DOVES GUARDING COCHLEA!
...!!
CRACK
VWSH
FWK
WK
WK
GTNKTNK
FWP
WOOS
WHF
VWF
GATE 3 HAS BEEN UN-LOCKED!
...
GATE 3 IS UN-LOCKED!
BEEEP
BEEEP

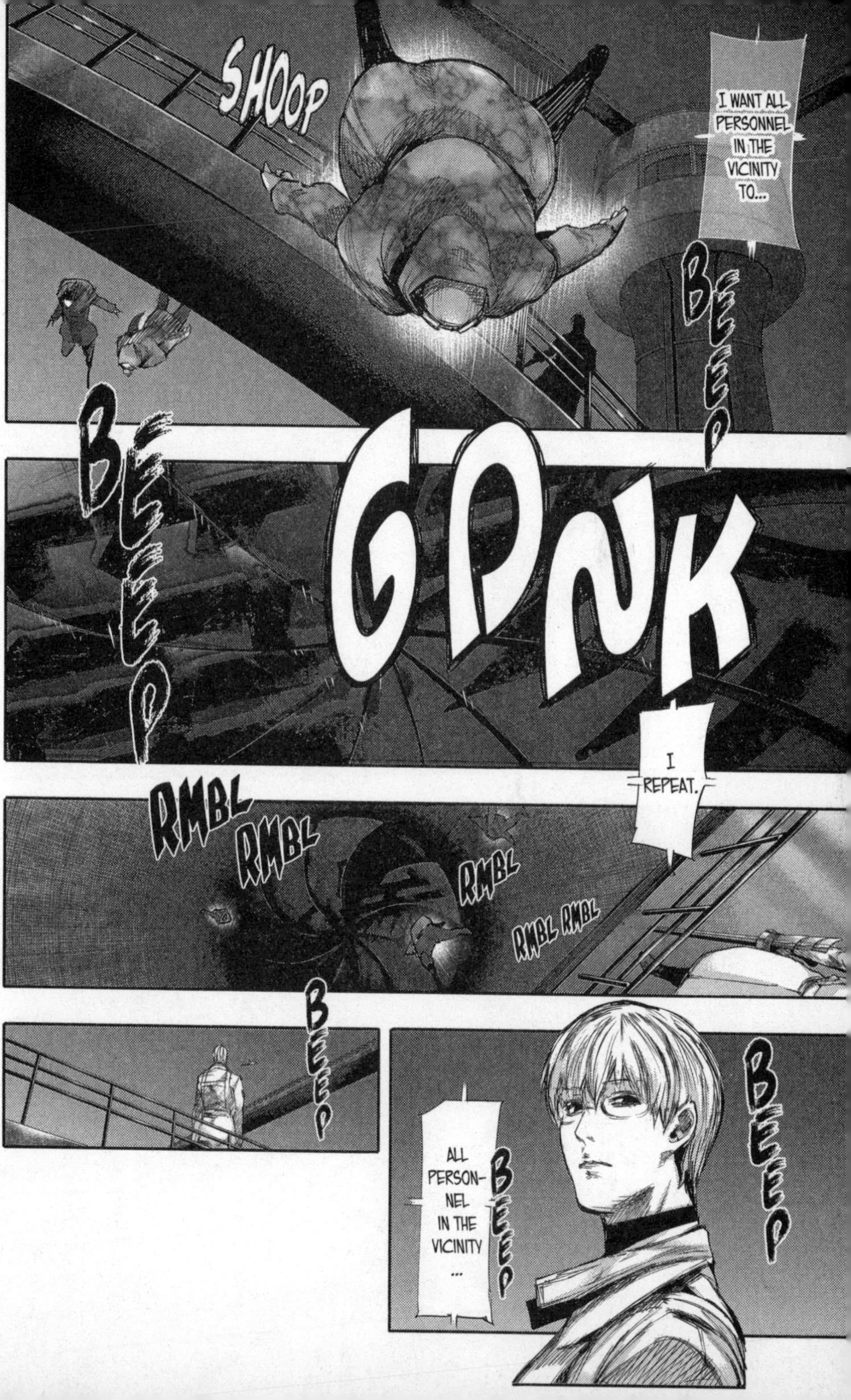
I WANT ALL PERSONNEL IN THE VICINITY TO...
BEEP
SHOOP
BEEEP
GONK
I REPEAT.
RMBL RMBL
RMBL
RMBL RMBL
BEEEP
ALL PERSON-NEL IN THE VICINITY ...
BEEEP
BEEP

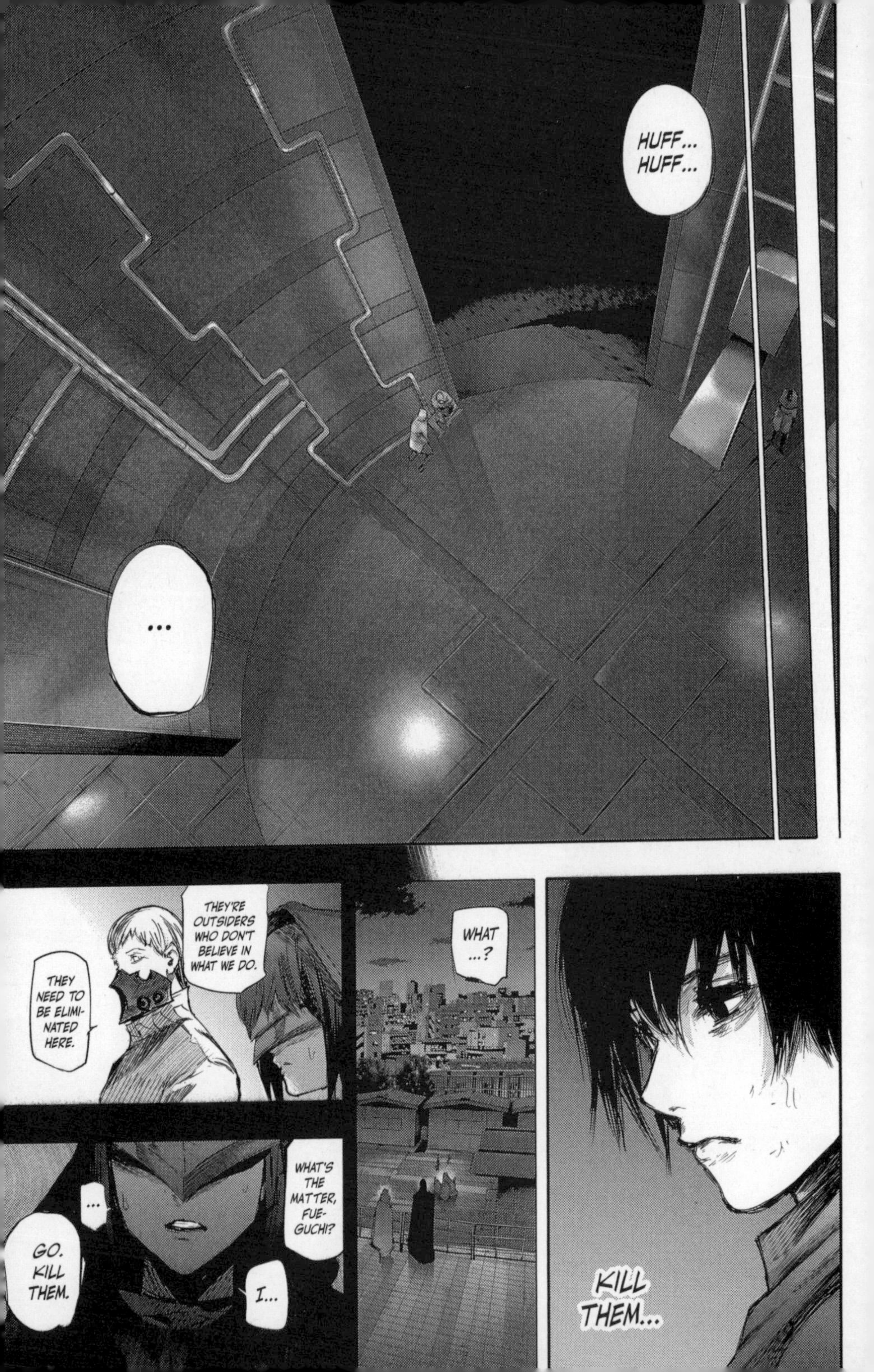
HUFF... HUFF...
...
KILL THEM...
WHAT ...?
THEY'RE OUTSIDERS WHO DON'T BELIEVE IN WHAT WE DO.
THEY NEED TO BE ELIMINATED HERE.
WHAT'S THE MATTER, FUE-GUCHI?
...
I...
GO. KILL THEM.

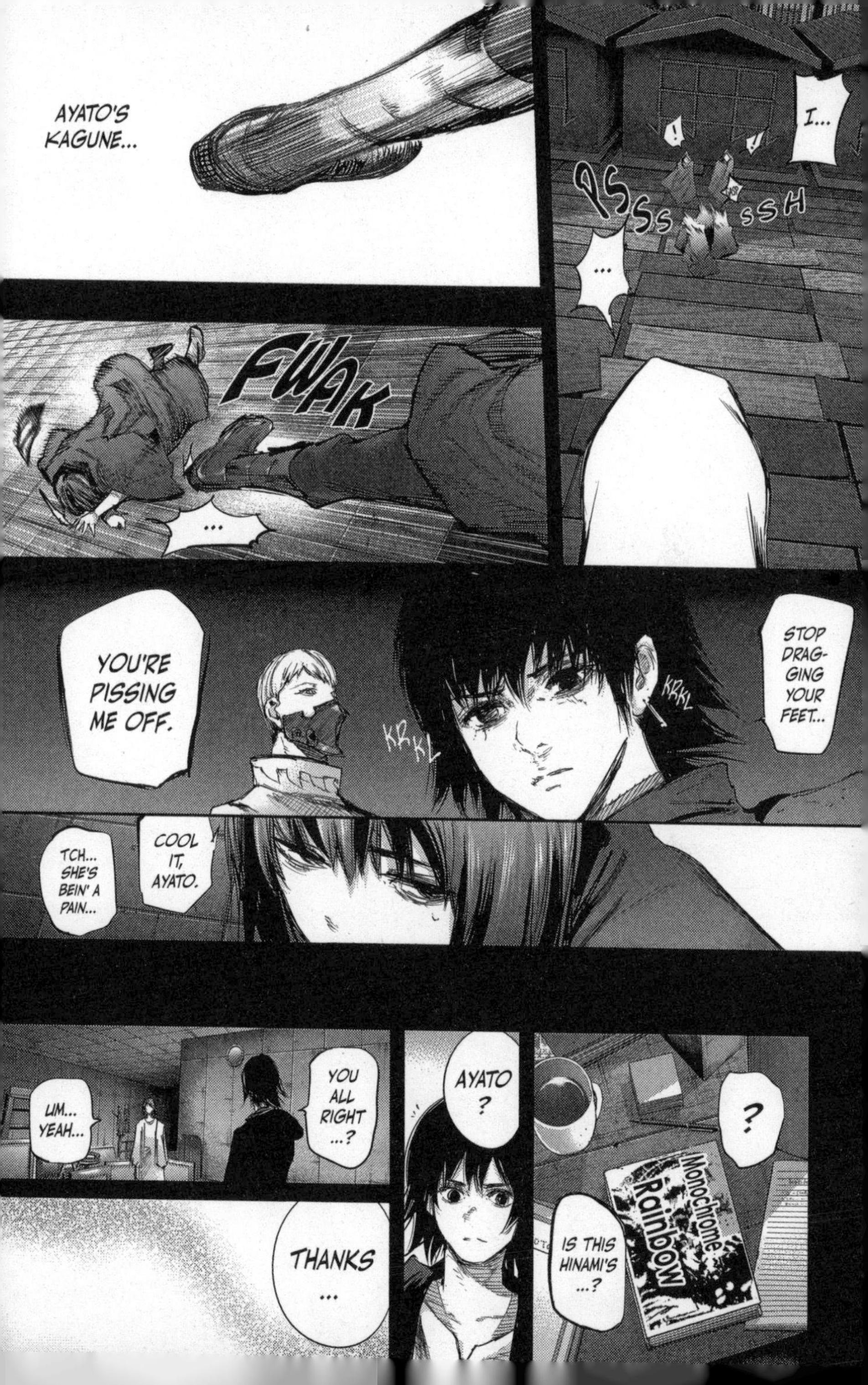
I...
!
!
PSSSSSSH
...
AYATO'S KAGUNE...
FWAK
...
STOP DRAG-GING YOUR FEET...
KRKL
KRKL
YOU'RE PISSING ME OFF.
COOL IT, AYATO.
TCH... SHE'S BEIN' A PAIN...
?
IS THIS HINAMI'S ...?
Monochrome Rainbow
AYATO ?
YOU ALL RIGHT ...?
UM... YEAH...
THANKS ...

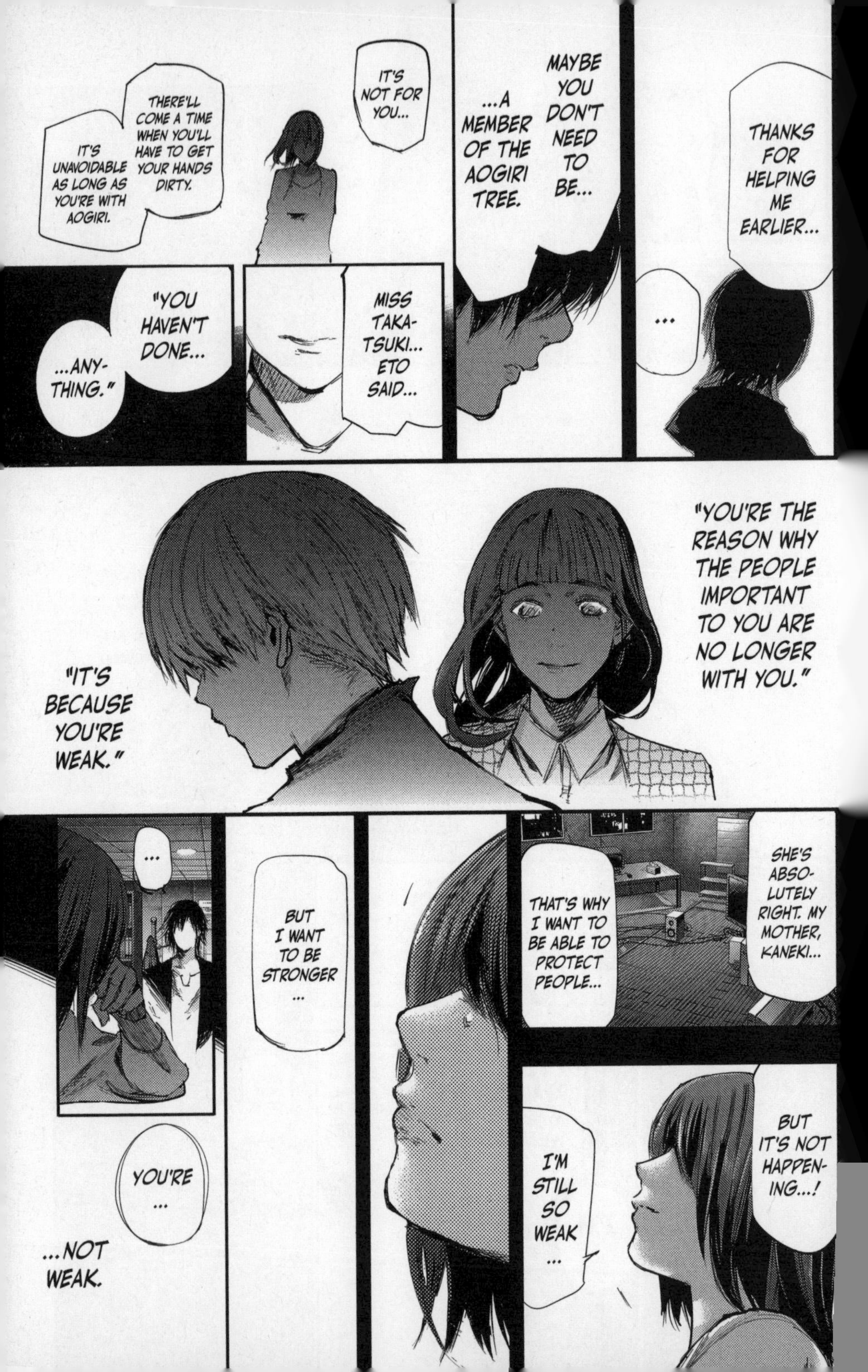
THANKS FOR HELPING ME EARLIER...
MAYBE YOU DON'T NEED TO BE...
...A MEMBER OF THE AOGIRI TREE.
IT'S NOT FOR YOU...
THERE'LL COME A TIME WHEN YOU'LL HAVE TO GET YOUR HANDS DIRTY.
IT'S UNAVOIDABLE AS LONG AS YOU'RE WITH AOGIRI.
...
MISS TAKA-TSUKI... ETO SAID...
"YOU HAVEN'T DONE...
...ANY-THING."
"YOU'RE THE REASON WHY THE PEOPLE IMPORTANT TO YOU ARE NO LONGER WITH YOU."
"IT'S BECAUSE YOU'RE WEAK."
SHE'S ABSO-LUTELY RIGHT. MY MOTHER, KANEKI...
THAT'S WHY I WANT TO BE ABLE TO PROTECT PEOPLE...
BUT IT'S NOT HAPPEN-ING...!
I'M STILL SO WEAK...
BUT I WANT TO BE STRONGER...
...
YOU'RE...
...NOT WEAK.

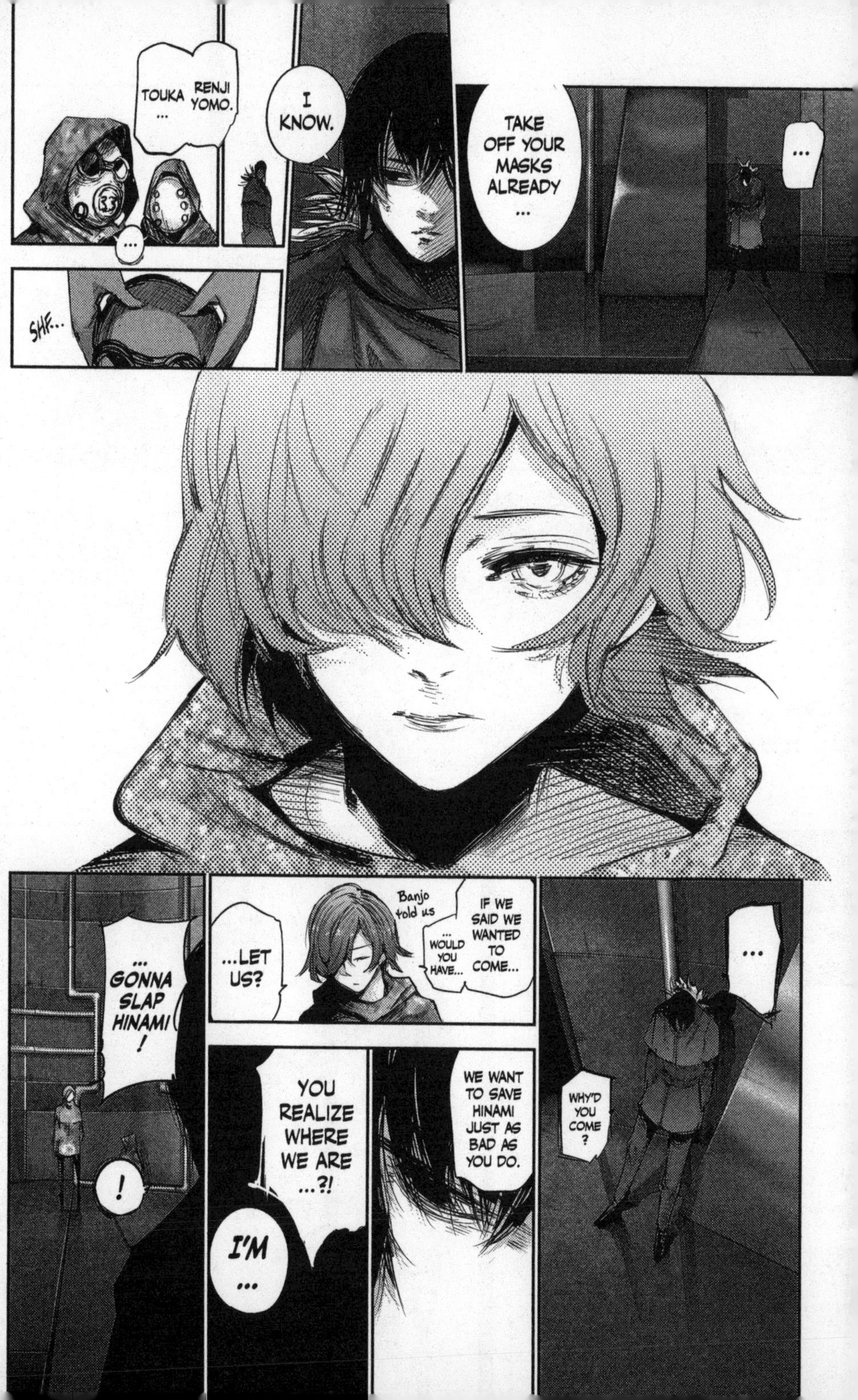
...
TAKE OFF YOUR MASKS ALREADY ...
I KNOW.
RENJI YOMO.
TOUKA ...
...
SHF...
...
WHY'D YOU COME?
IF WE SAID WE WANTED TO COME...
... WOULD YOU HAVE...
Banjo told us
...LET US?
WE WANT TO SAVE HINAMI JUST AS BAD AS YOU DO.
YOU REALIZE WHERE WE ARE ...?!
I'M ...
... GONNA SLAP HINAMI!
!

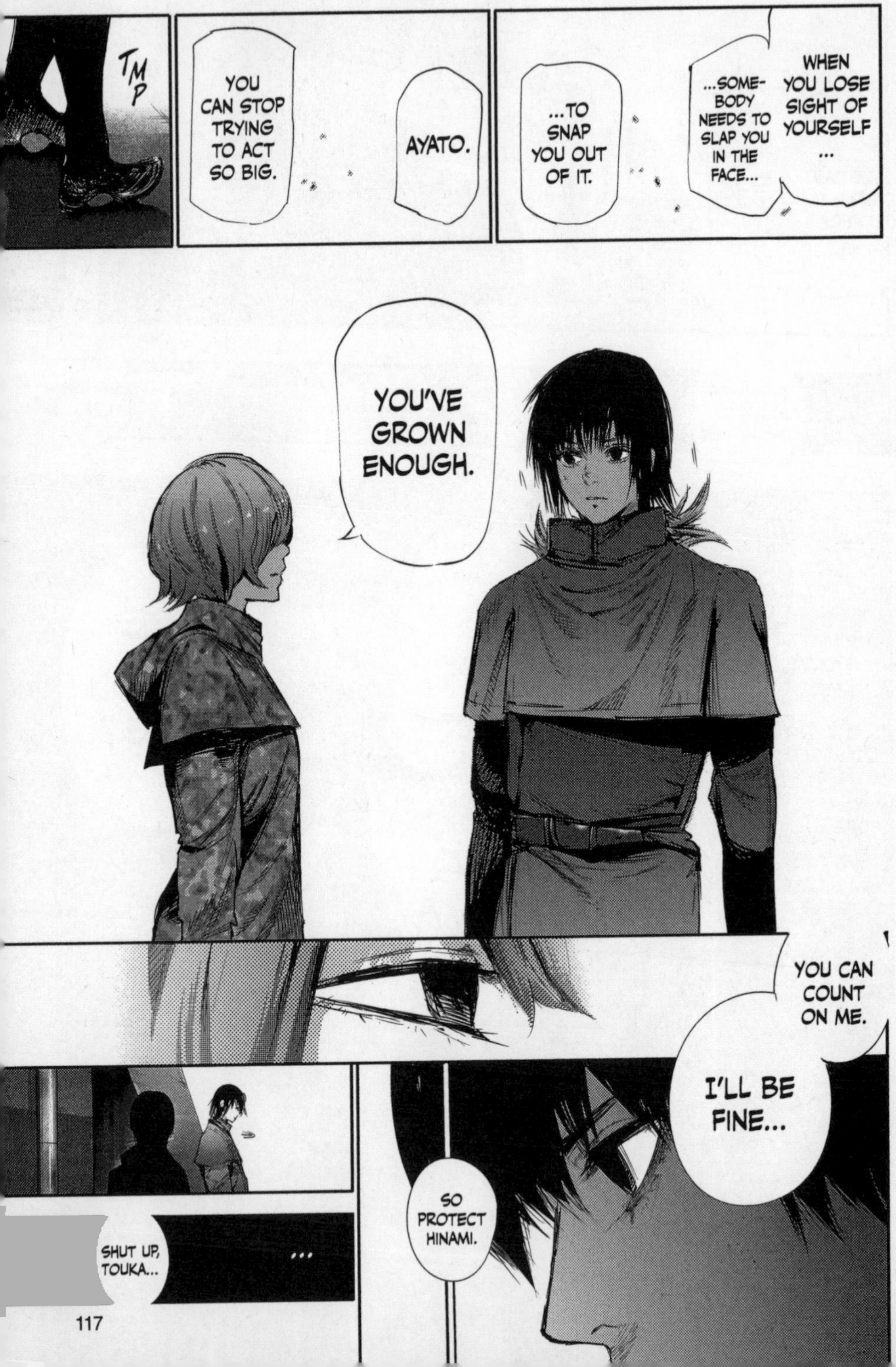
WHEN YOU LOSE SIGHT OF YOURSELF ...
...SOME-BODY NEEDS TO SLAP YOU IN THE FACE...
...TO SNAP YOU OUT OF IT.
AYATO.
YOU CAN STOP TRYING TO ACT SO BIG.
TMP
YOU'VE GROWN ENOUGH.
YOU CAN COUNT ON ME.
I'LL BE FINE...
SO PROTECT HINAMI.
...
SHUT UP, TOUKA...

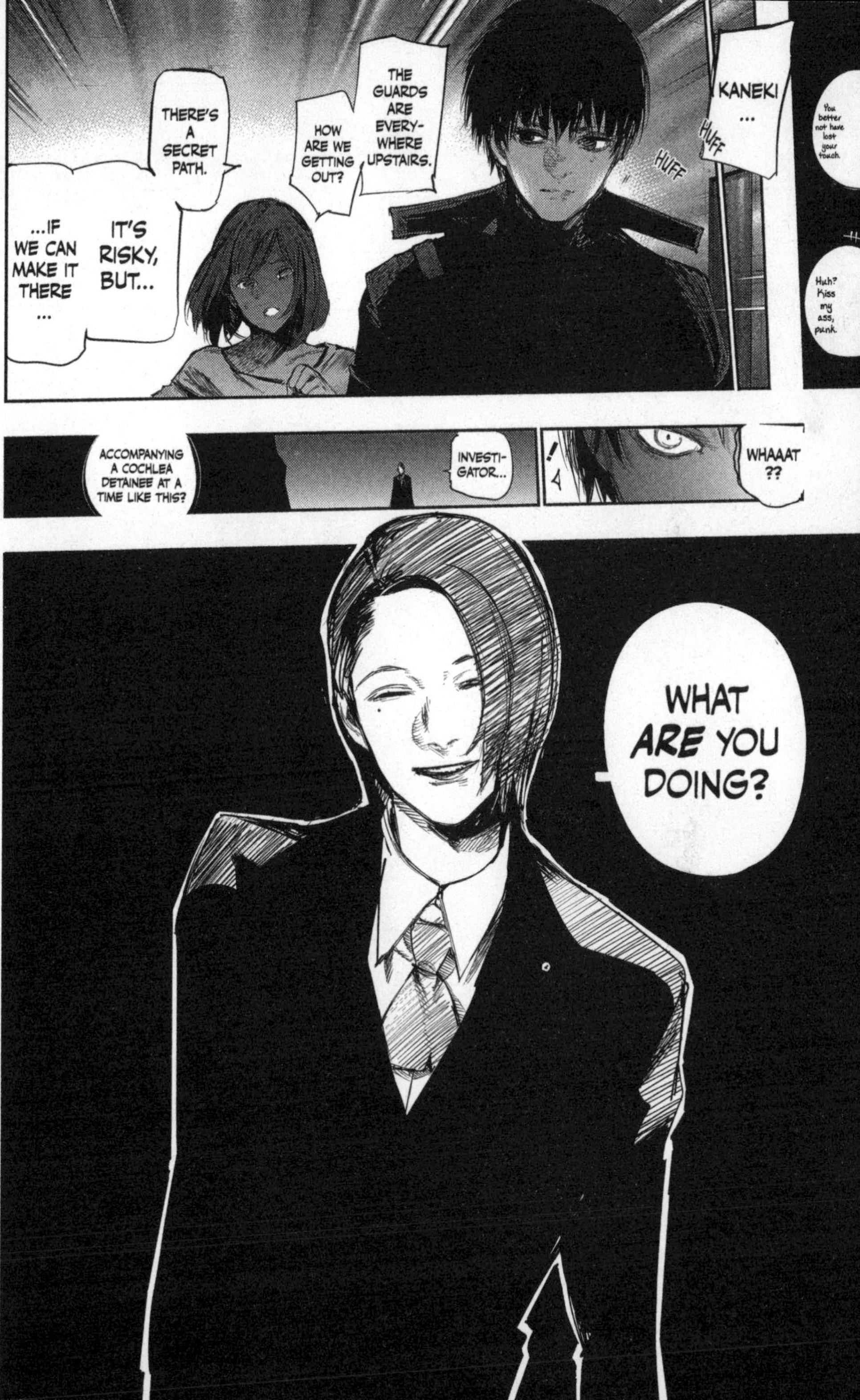
You better not have lost your touch.
Huh? Kiss my ass, punk.
KANEKI ...
HUFF
HUFF
THE GUARDS ARE EVERY-WHERE UPSTAIRS.
HOW ARE WE GETTING OUT?
THERE'S A SECRET PATH.
IT'S RISKY, BUT...
...IF WE CAN MAKE IT THERE ...
WHAAAT ??
INVESTI-GATOR...
ACCOMPANYING A COCHLEA DETAINEE AT A TIME LIKE THIS?
WHAT *ARE* YOU DOING?

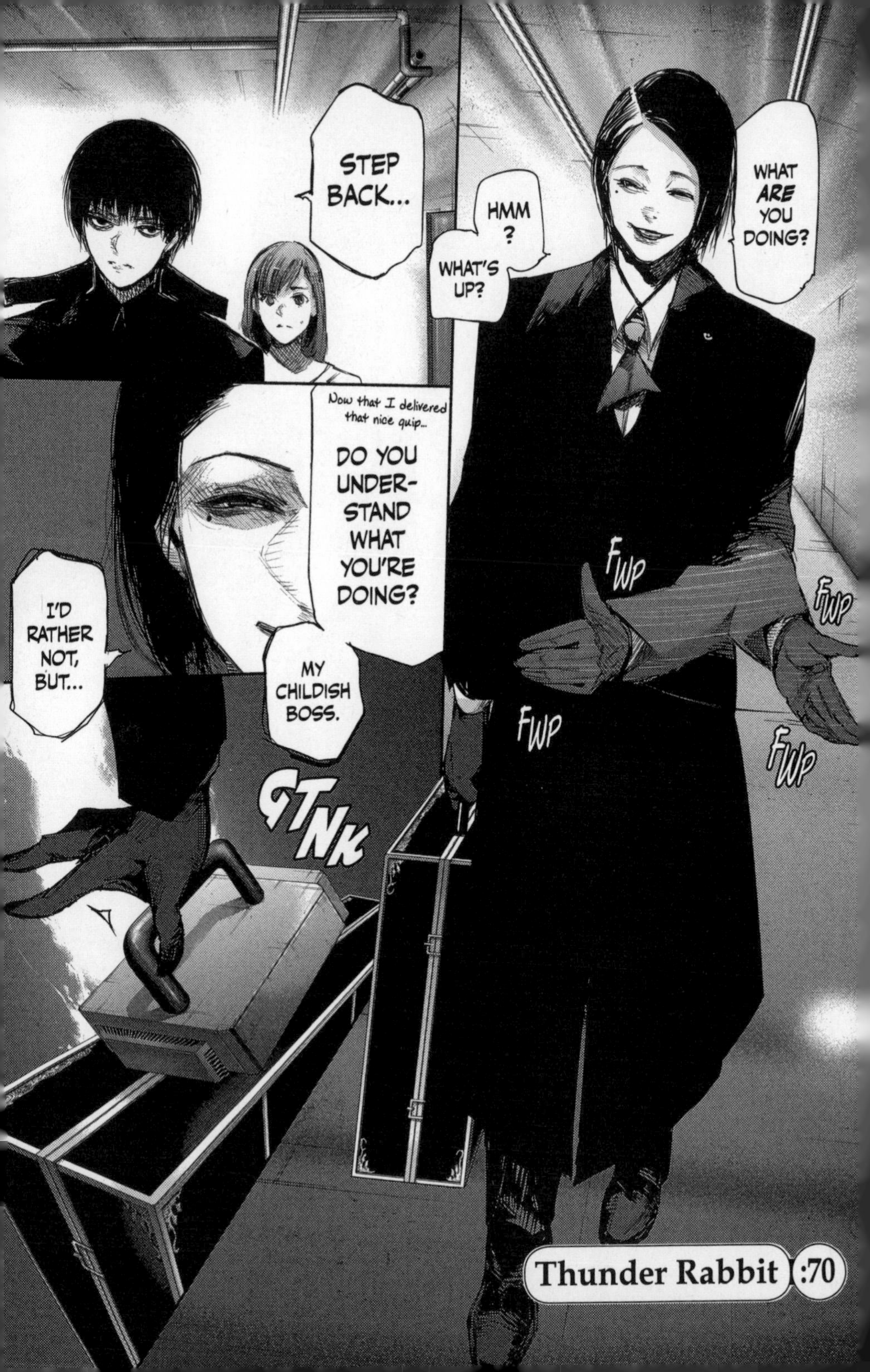
WHAT ARE YOU DOING?
HMM?
WHAT'S UP?
FWP
FWP
FWP
FWP
STEP BACK...
Now that I delivered that nice quip...
DO YOU UNDER-STAND WHAT YOU'RE DOING?
MY CHILDISH BOSS.
I'D RATHER NOT, BUT...
GTNK
Thunder Rabbit :70

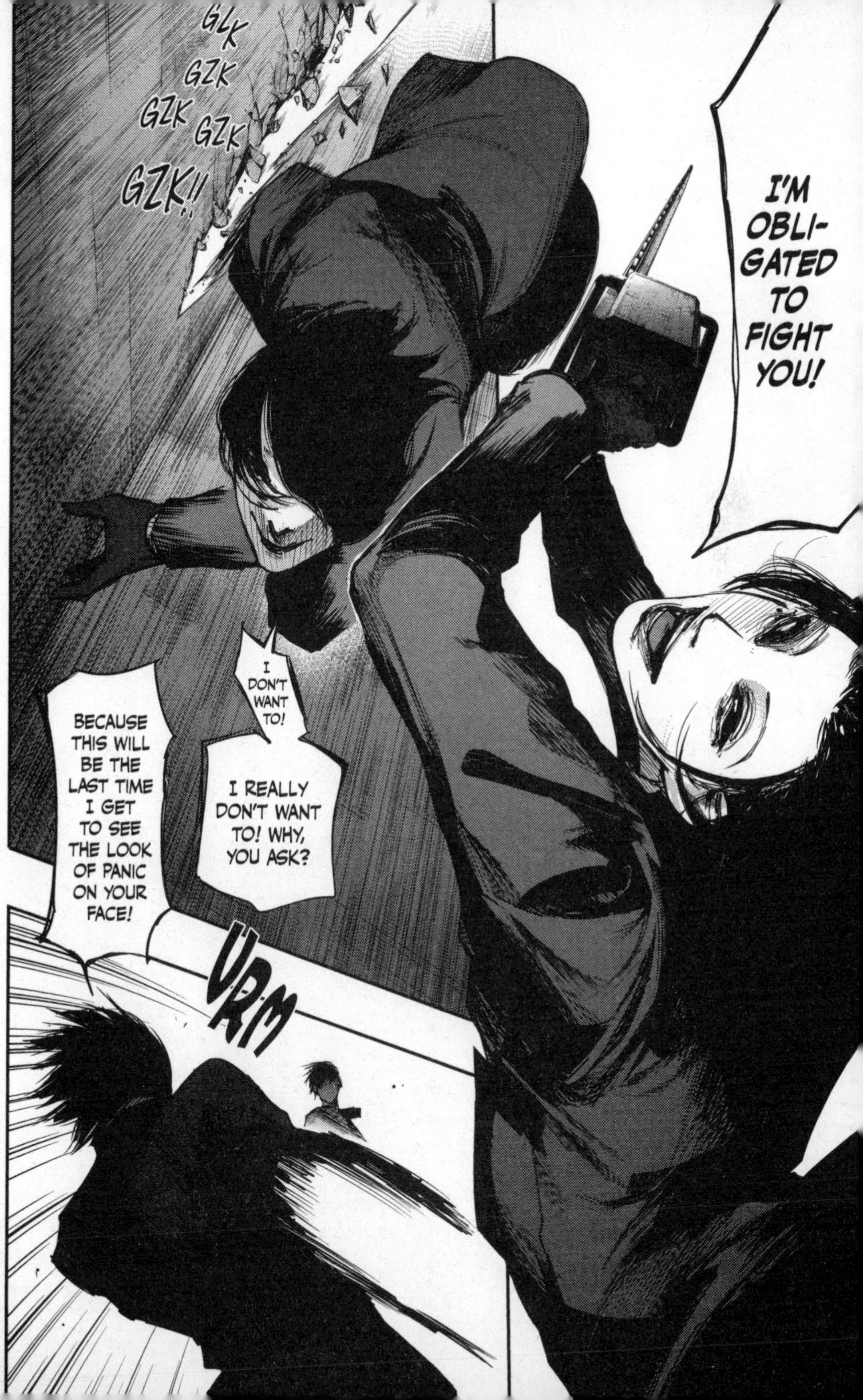
I'M OBLIGATED TO FIGHT YOU!
GZK GZK GZK GZK GZK!!
I DON'T WANT TO!
I REALLY DON'T WANT TO! WHY, YOU ASK?
BECAUSE THIS WILL BE THE LAST TIME I GET TO SEE THE LOOK OF PANIC ON YOUR FACE!
VRM

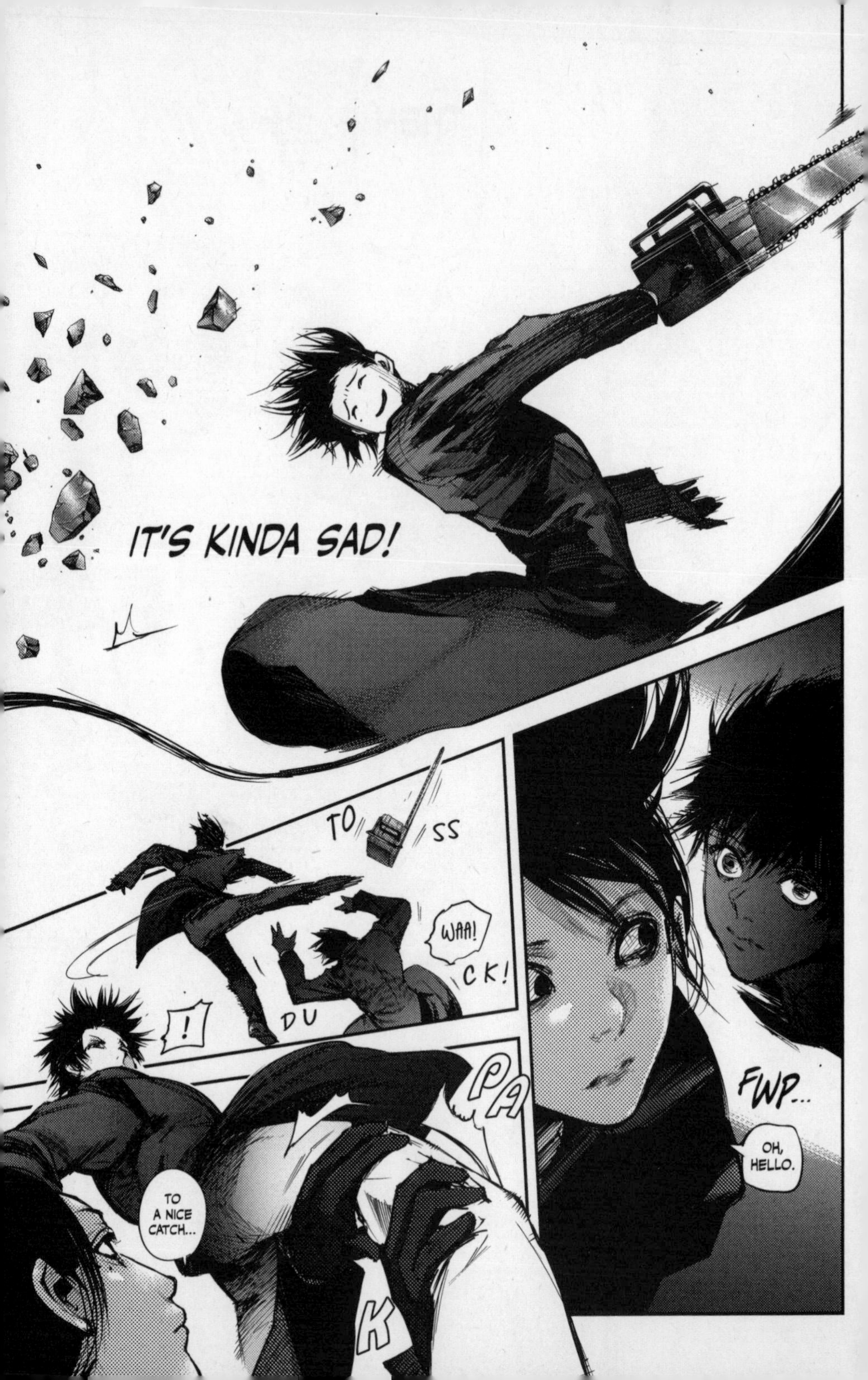
IT'S KINDA SAD!
FWP...
OH, HELLO.
TO SS
WAA!
CK!
DU
!
PA
TO A NICE CATCH...
K

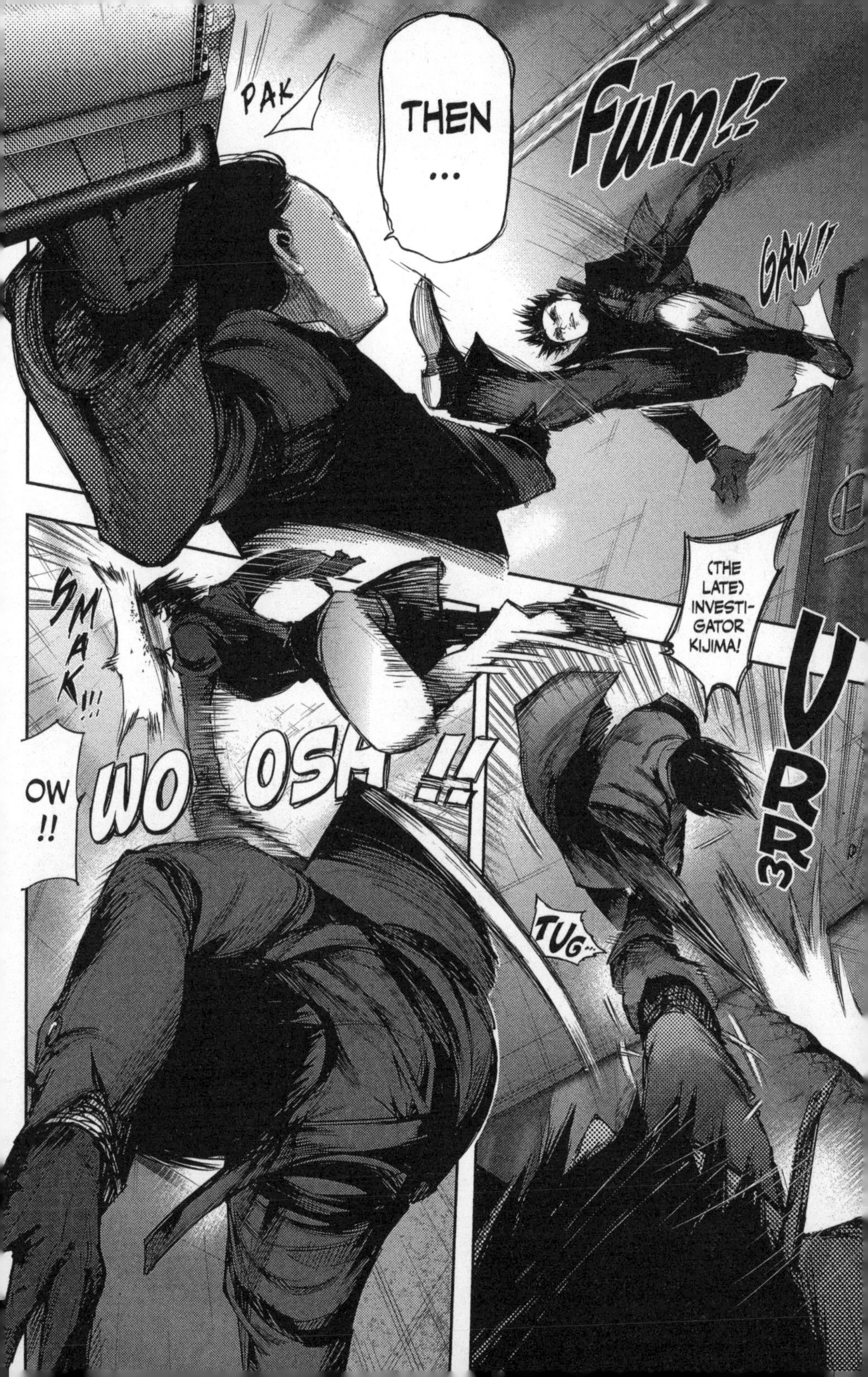
FWM!!
GAK!!
THEN ...
PAK
(THE LATE) INVESTIGATOR KIJIMA!
VRRM
TUG...
SMAK!!!
WO OSH !!
OW !!

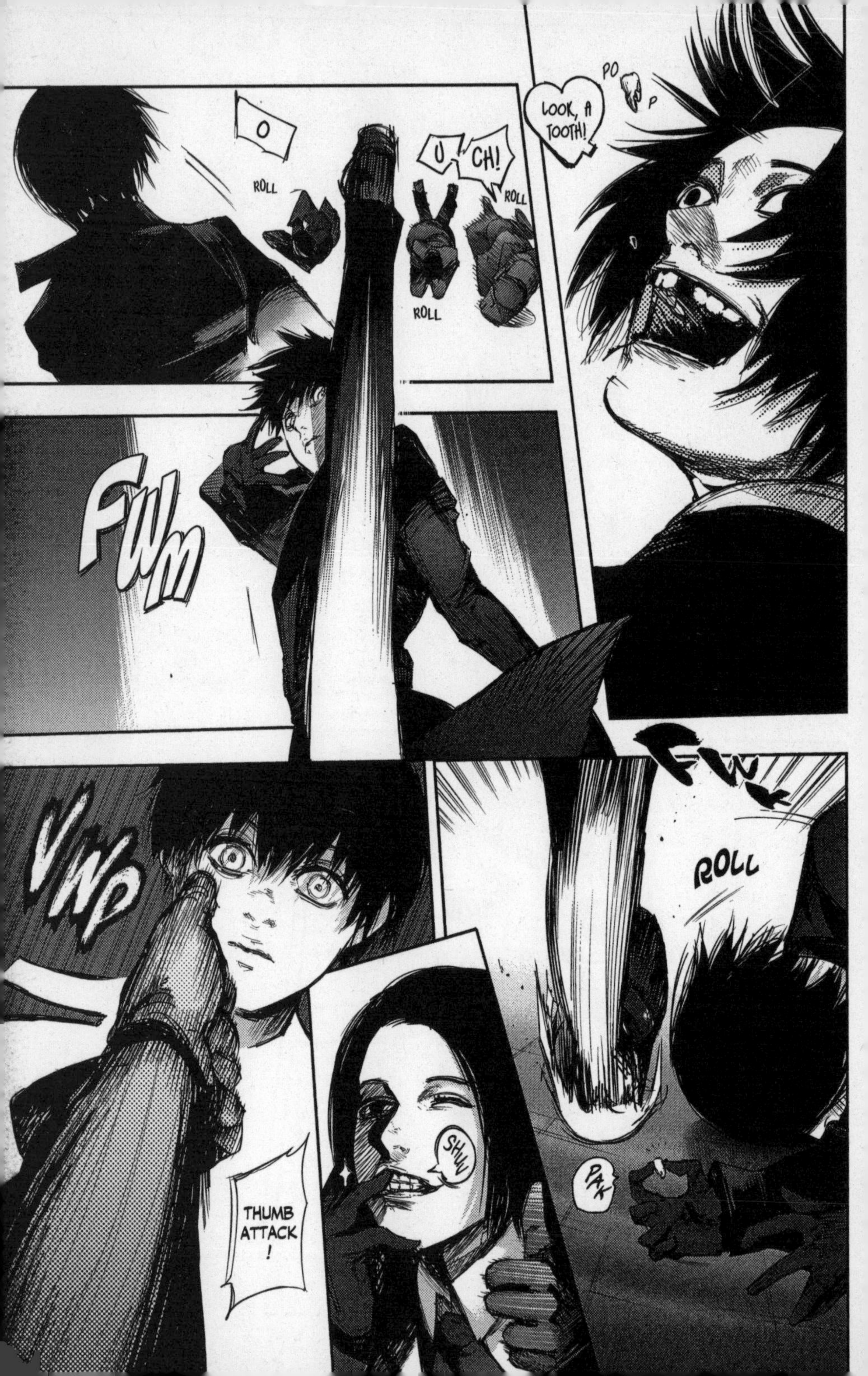
PO P
LOOK, A TOOTH!
O
ROLL
U CH!
ROLL
ROLL
FWM
ROLL
PAK
THUMB ATTACK !
SHW

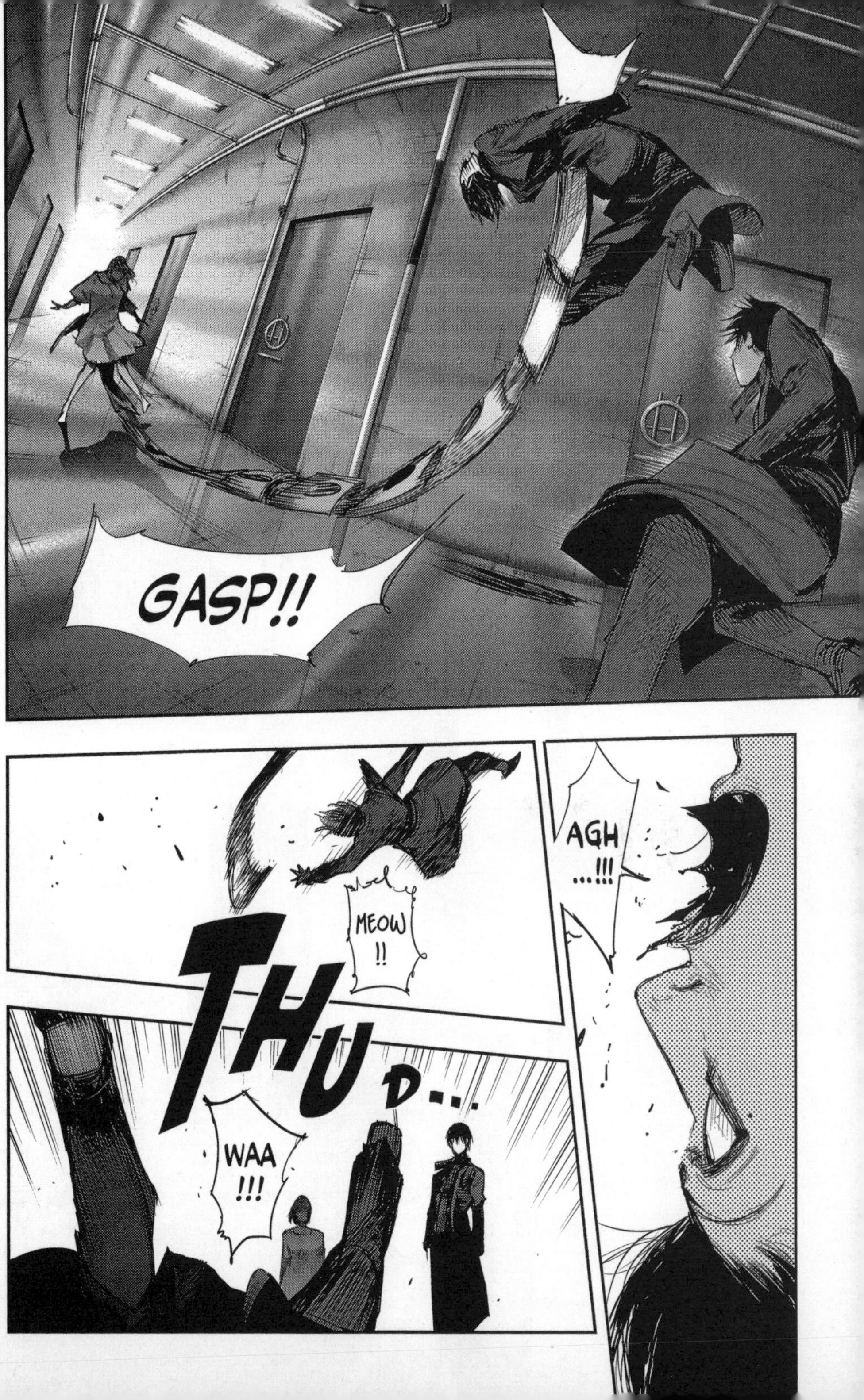
GASP!!
AGH ...!!!
MEOW !!
THUD...
WAA !!!

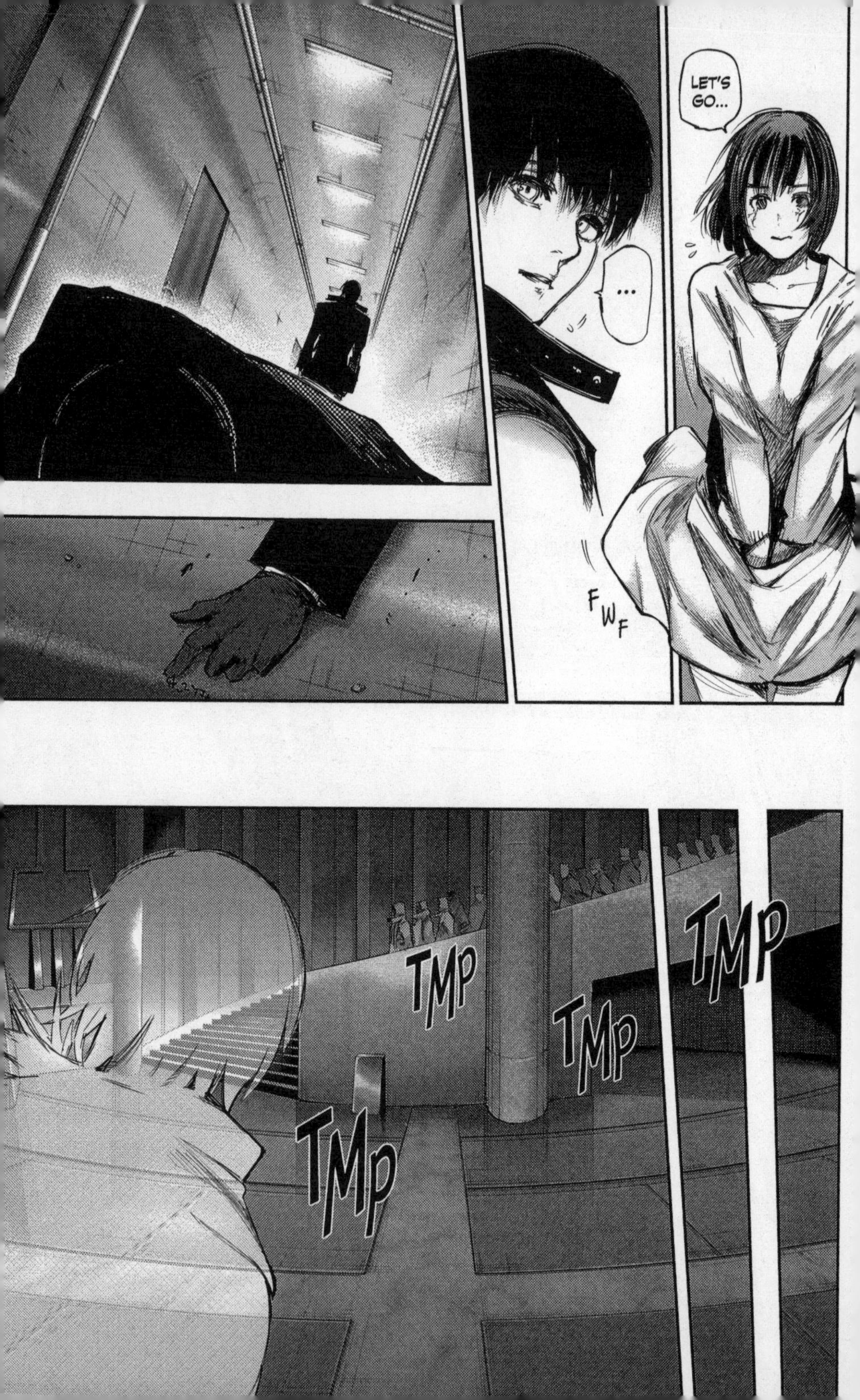
LET'S GO...
...
FWF
TMP
TMP
TMP
TMP

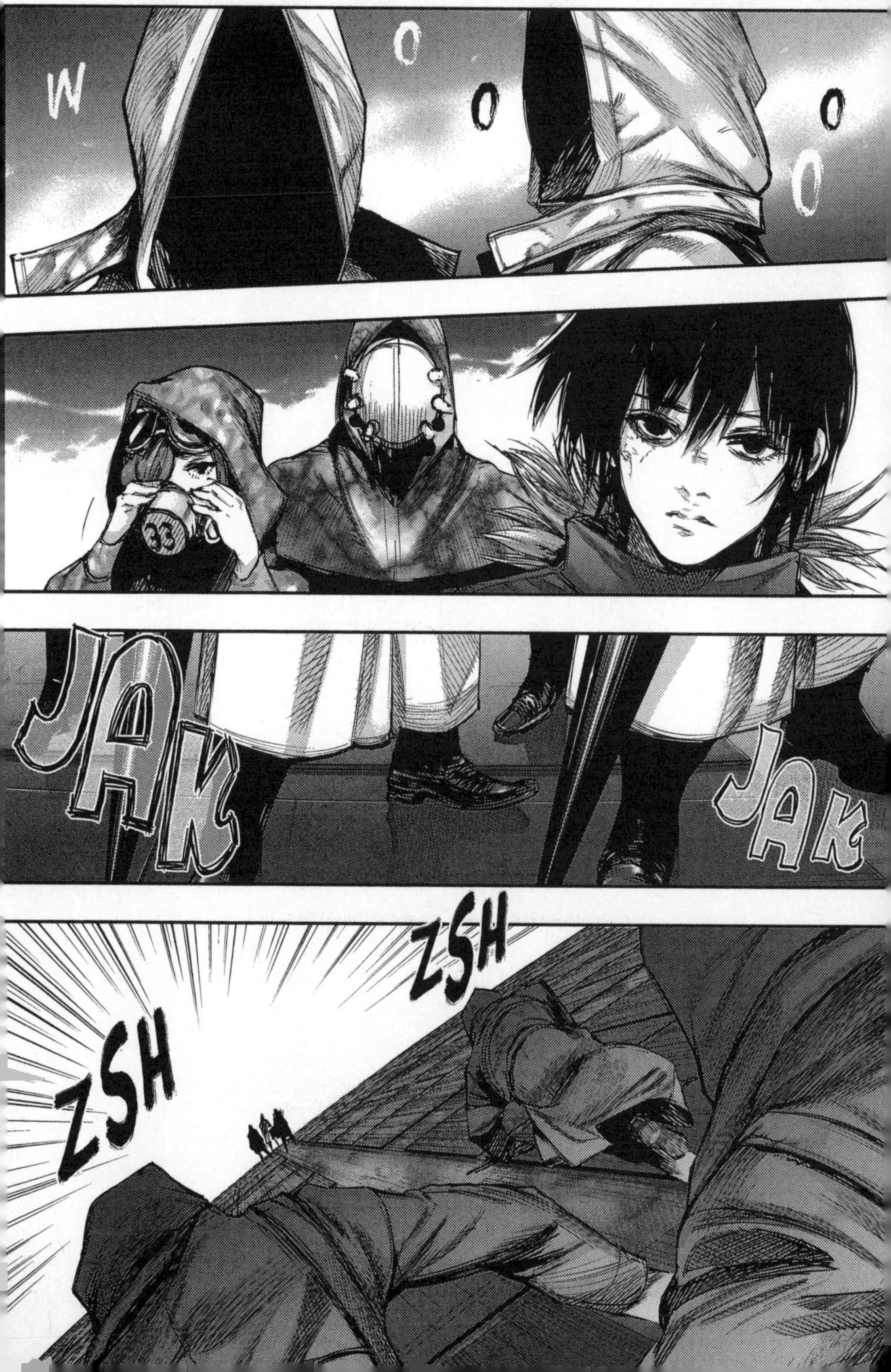
WOOOO
JAK
JAK
ZSH
ZSH

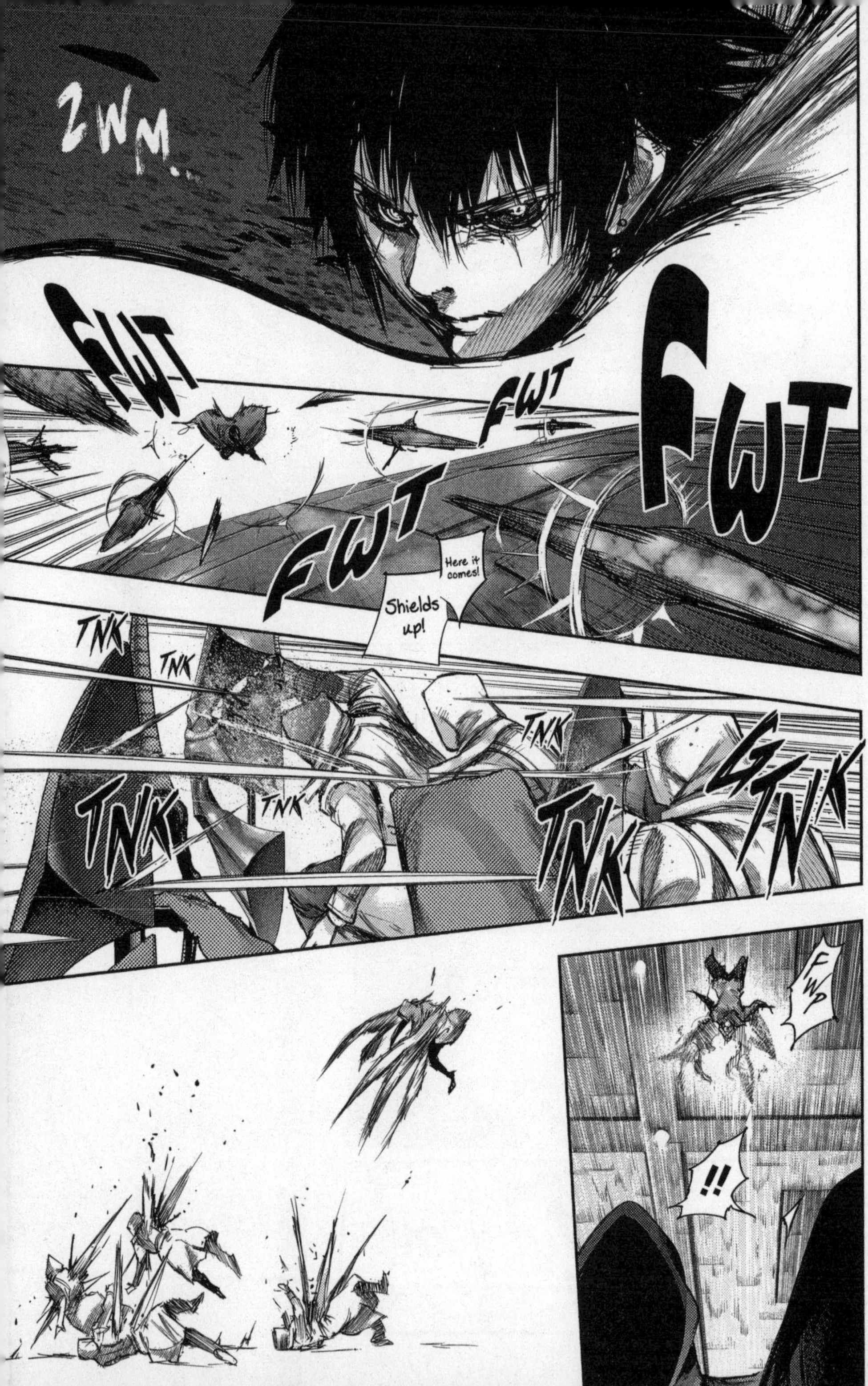
ZWM...
FWT
FWT
FWT
FWT
Here it comes!
Shields up!
TNK
TNK
GTNK
TNK
TNK
TNK
TNK
FWP
!!

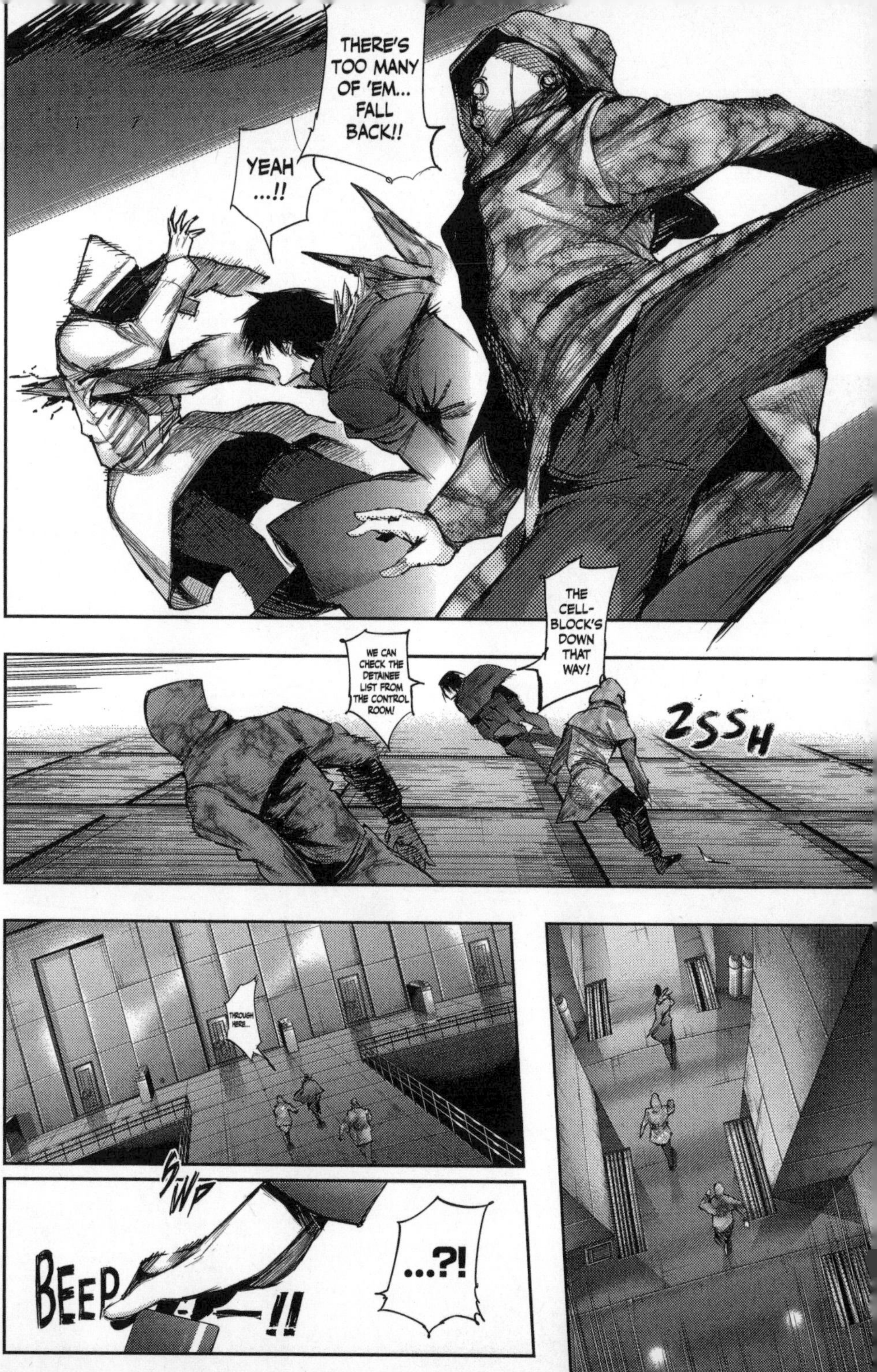
THERE'S TOO MANY OF 'EM... FALL BACK!!
YEAH ...!!
THE CELL-BLOCK'S DOWN THAT WAY!
WE CAN CHECK THE DETAINEE LIST FROM THE CONTROL ROOM!
ZSSH
THROUGH HERE...
SWP
...?!
BEEP—!!

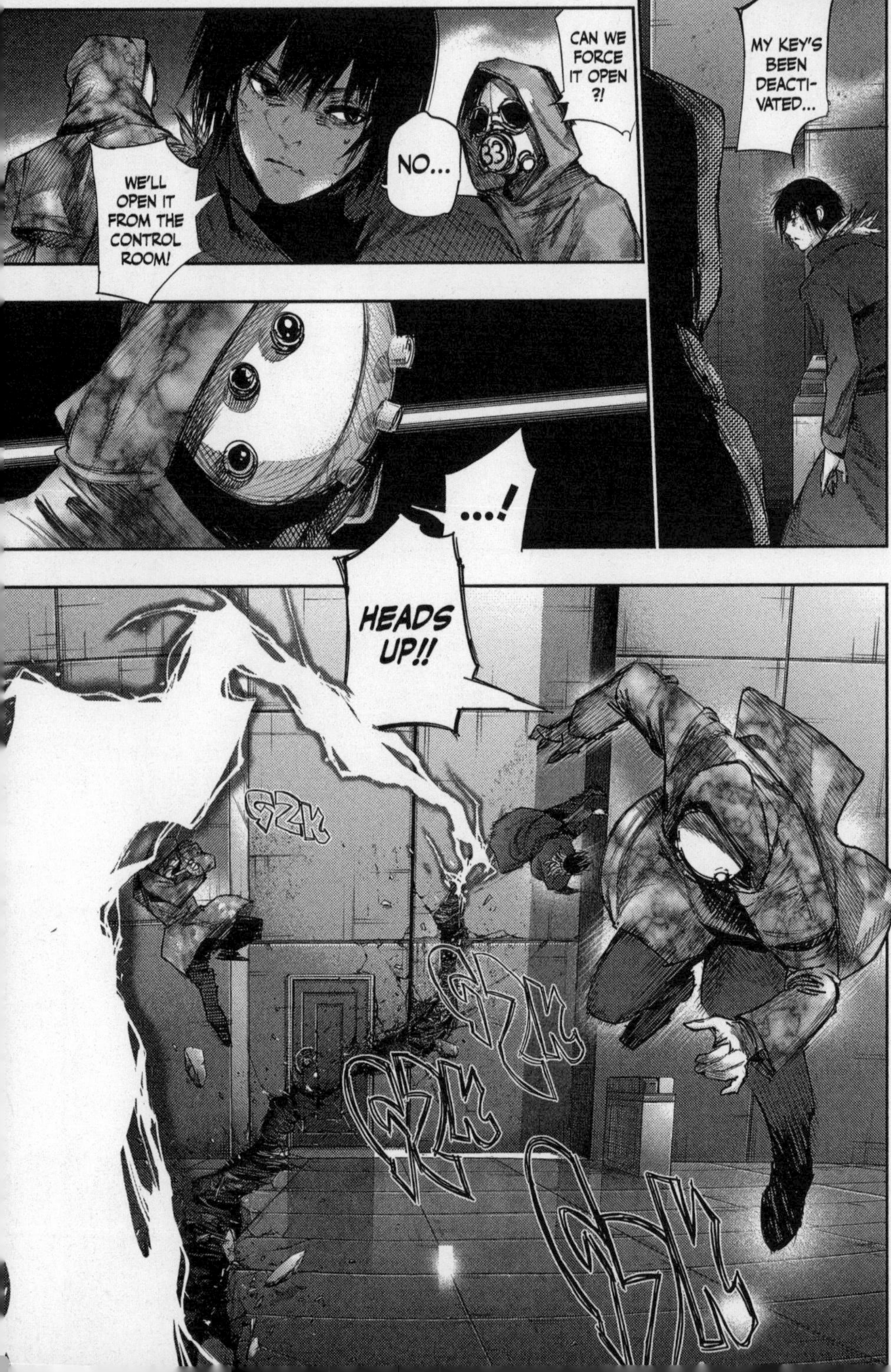
MY KEY'S BEEN DEACTI-VATED...
CAN WE FORCE IT OPEN ?!
NO...
WE'LL OPEN IT FROM THE CONTROL ROOM!
...!
HEADS UP!!
GZK
GZK
GZK
GZK

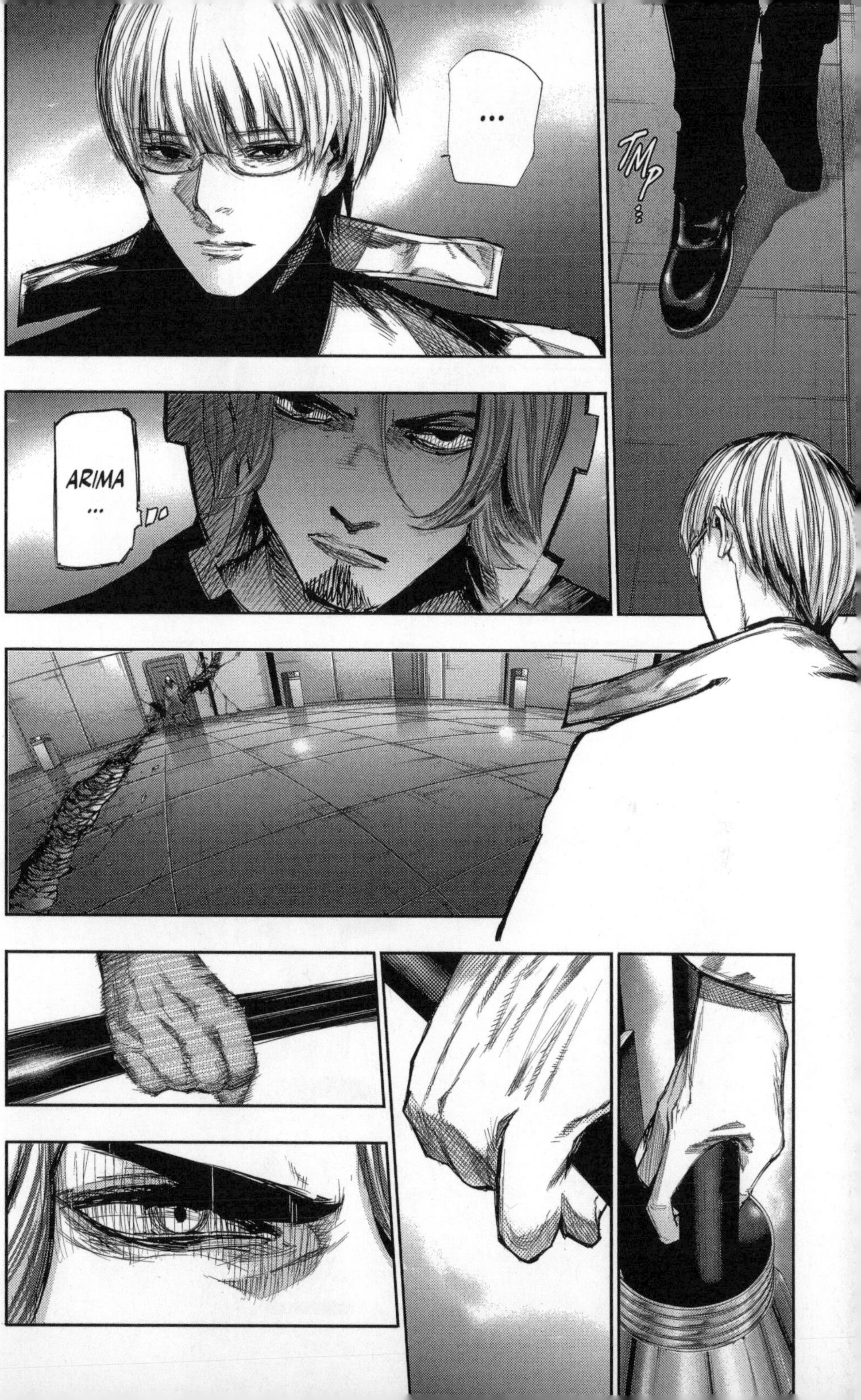
TMP ...
...
ARIMA ...

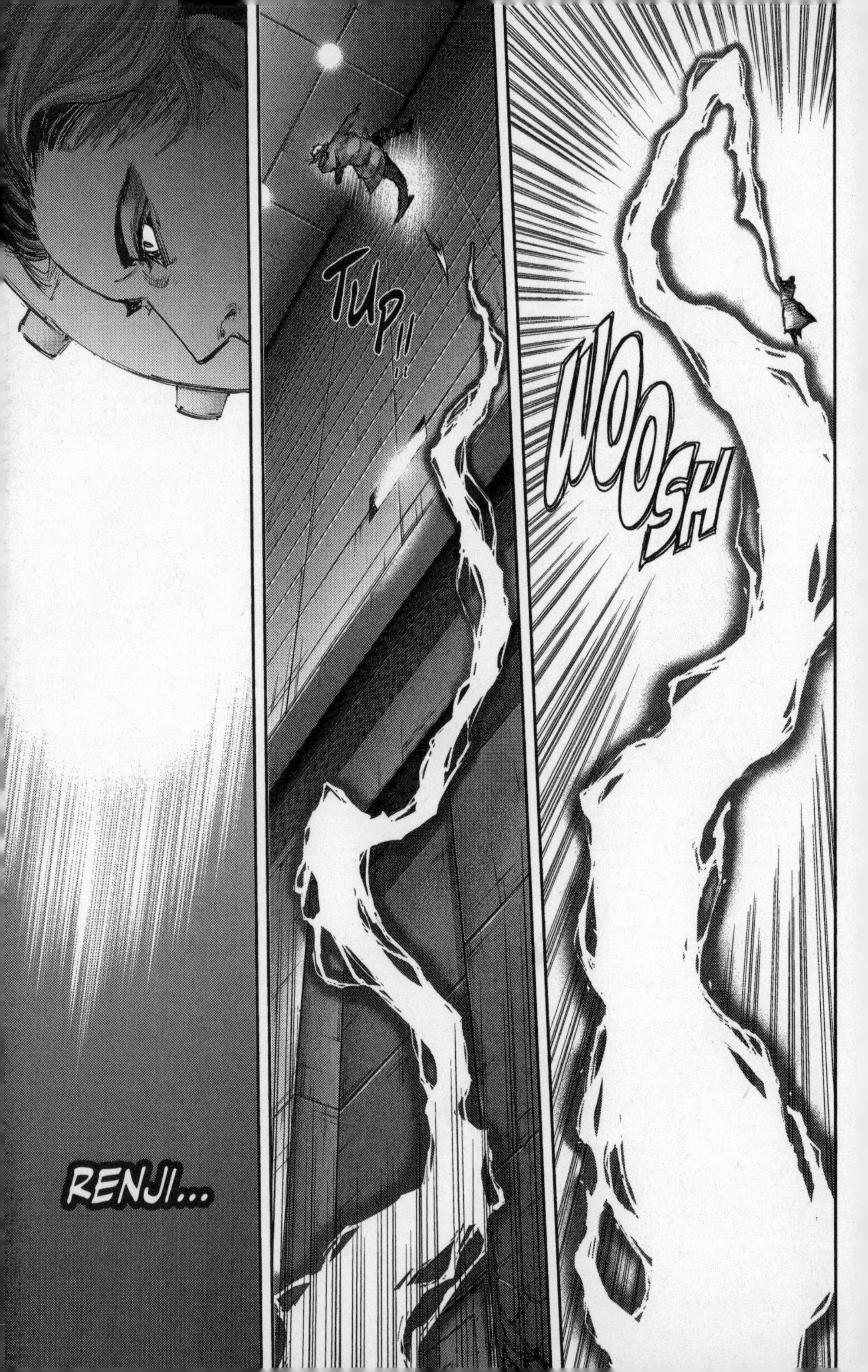
WOOOSH
TUP!!
RENJI...

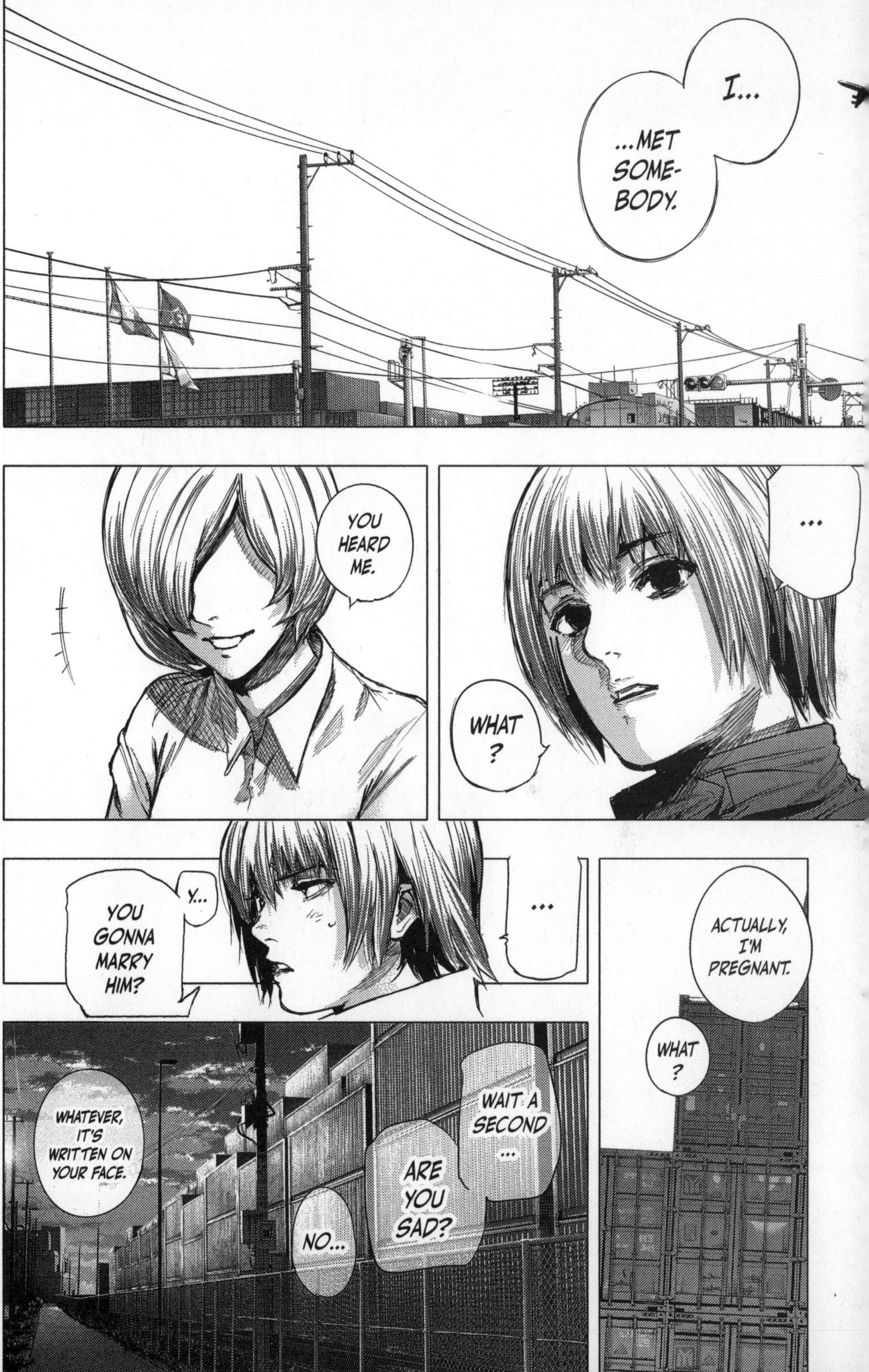
I...
...MET SOMEBODY.
...
WHAT ?
YOU HEARD ME.
ACTUALLY, I'M PREGNANT.
WHAT ?
...
Y...
YOU GONNA MARRY HIM?
WAIT A SECOND ...
ARE YOU SAD?
NO...
WHATEVER, IT'S WRITTEN ON YOUR FACE.

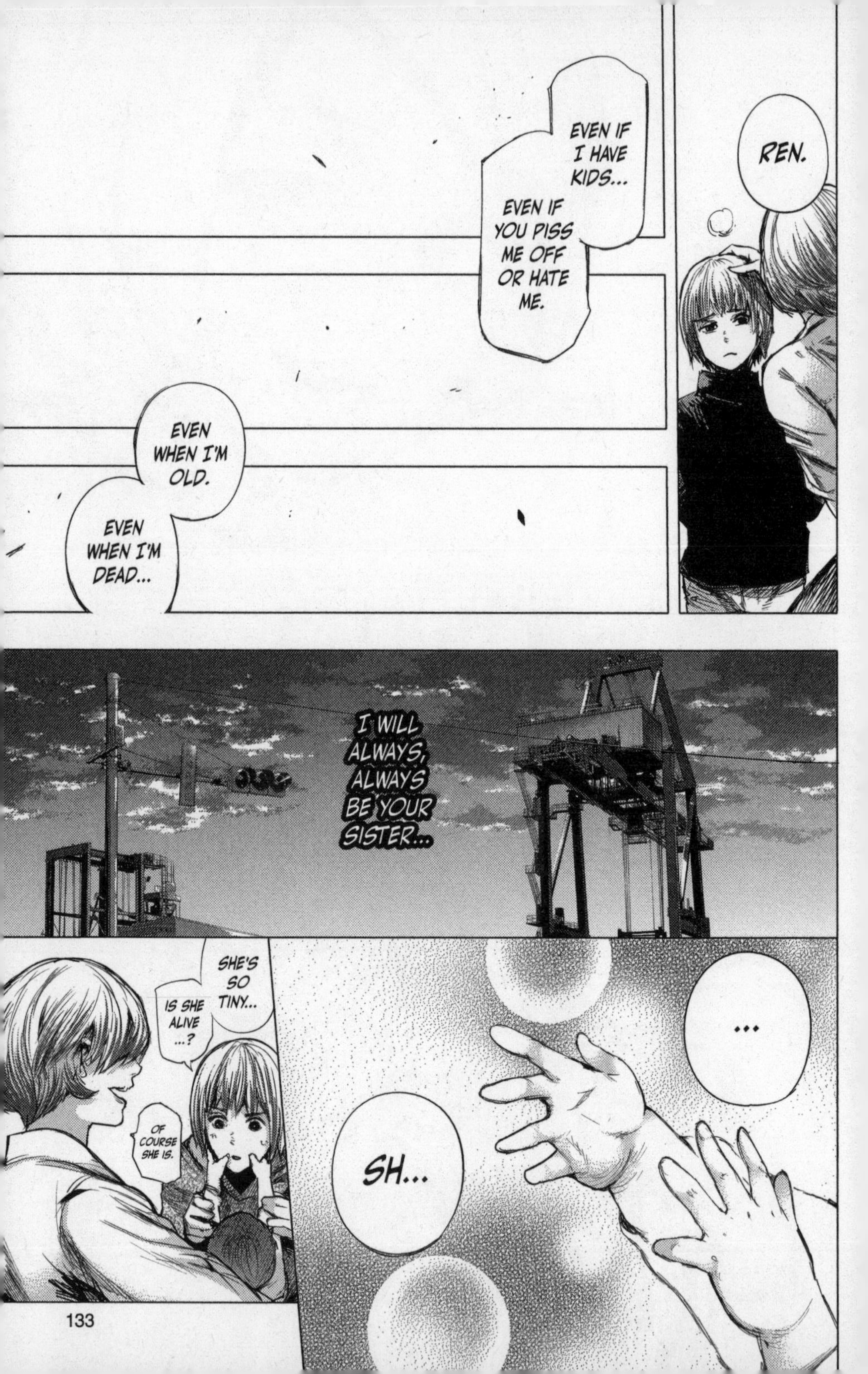
REN.
EVEN IF I HAVE KIDS...
EVEN IF YOU PISS ME OFF OR HATE ME.
EVEN WHEN I'M OLD.
EVEN WHEN I'M DEAD...
I WILL ALWAYS, ALWAYS BE YOUR SISTER...
...
SH...
SHE'S SO TINY...
IS SHE ALIVE ...?
OF COURSE SHE IS.

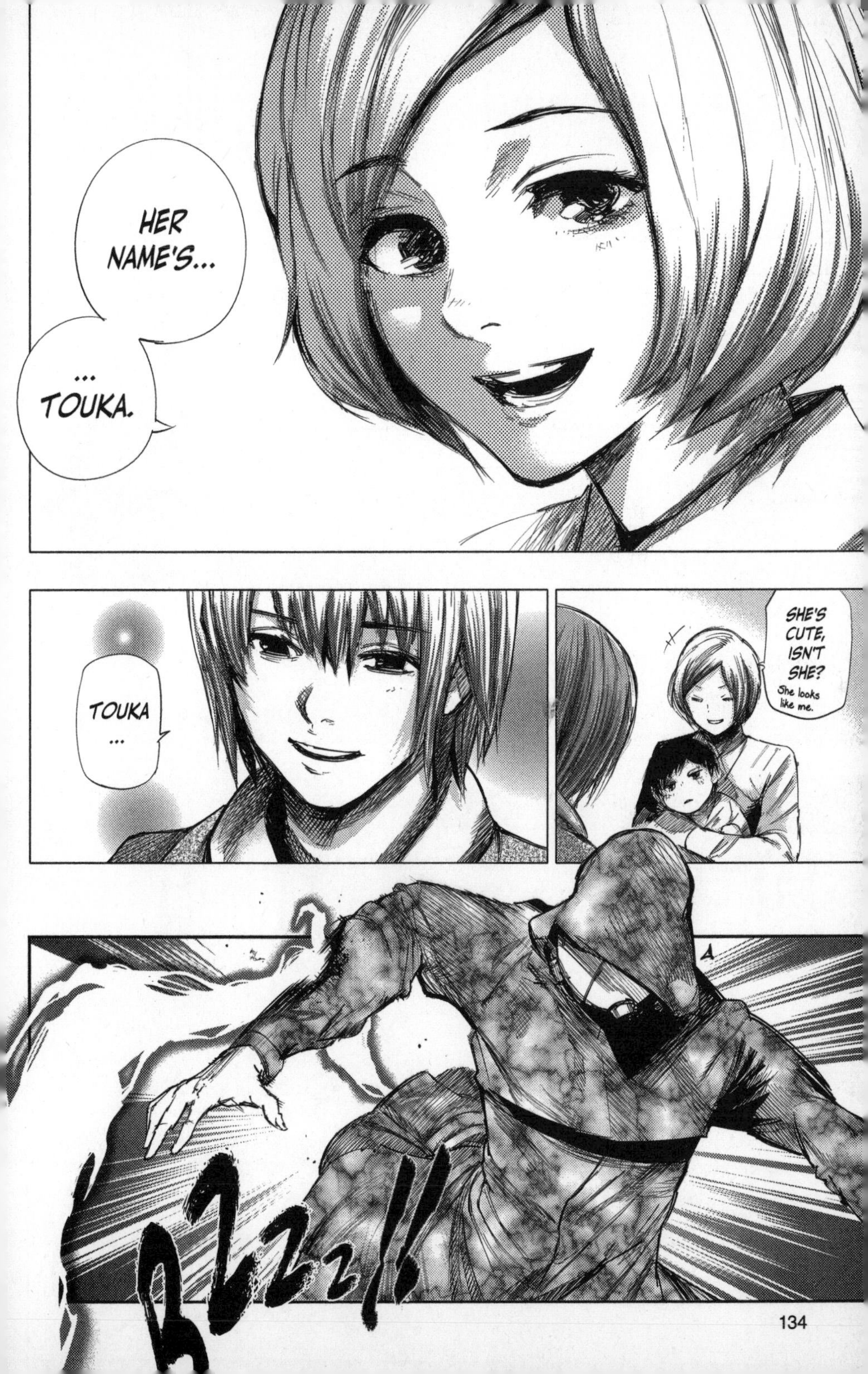
HER NAME'S...
...TOUKA.
SHE'S CUTE, ISN'T SHE?
She looks like me.
TOUKA...
BZZZ!!

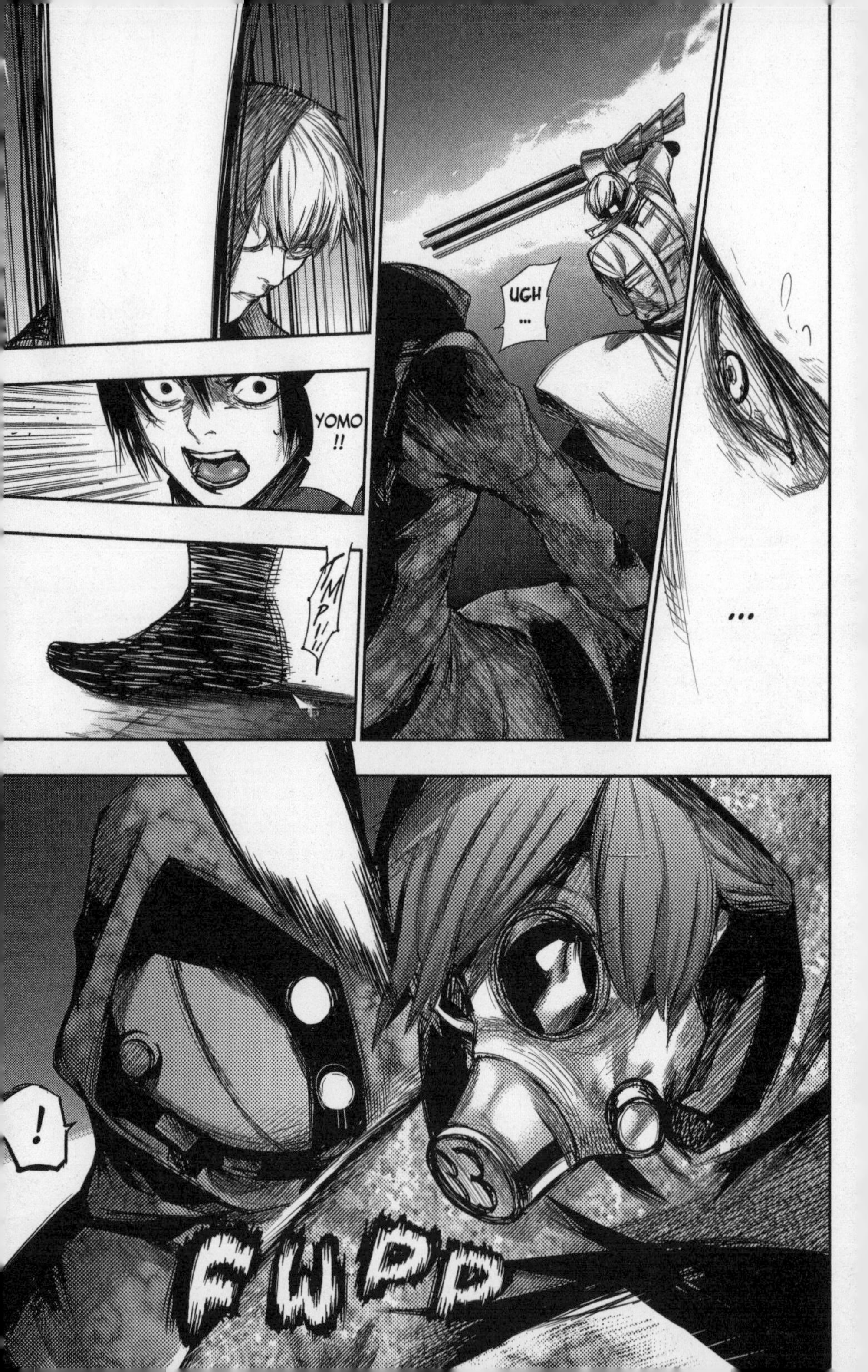
!..?
...
UGH ...
YOMO !!
TMP!!
!
FWPP

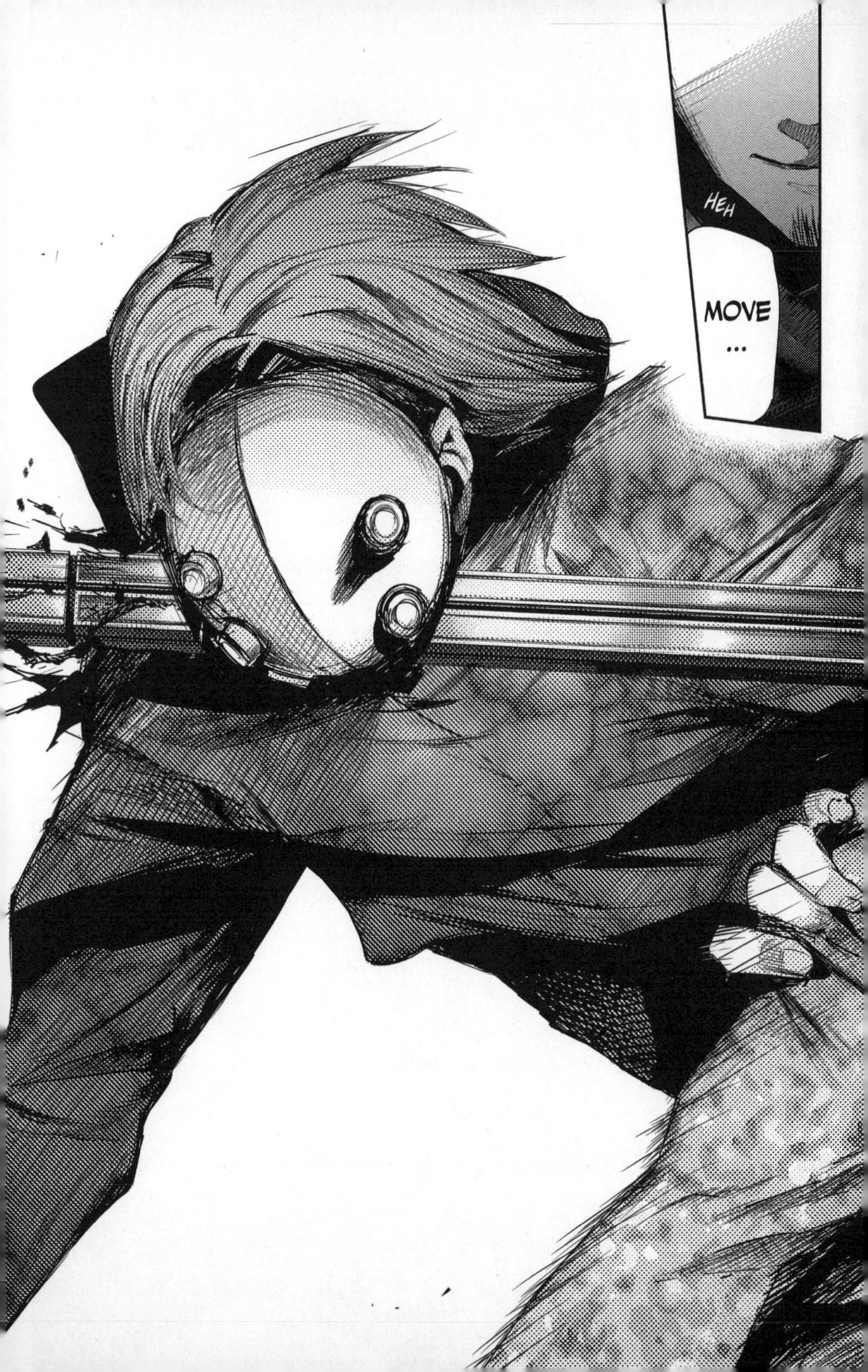
HEH
MOVE
...

Revoke :71

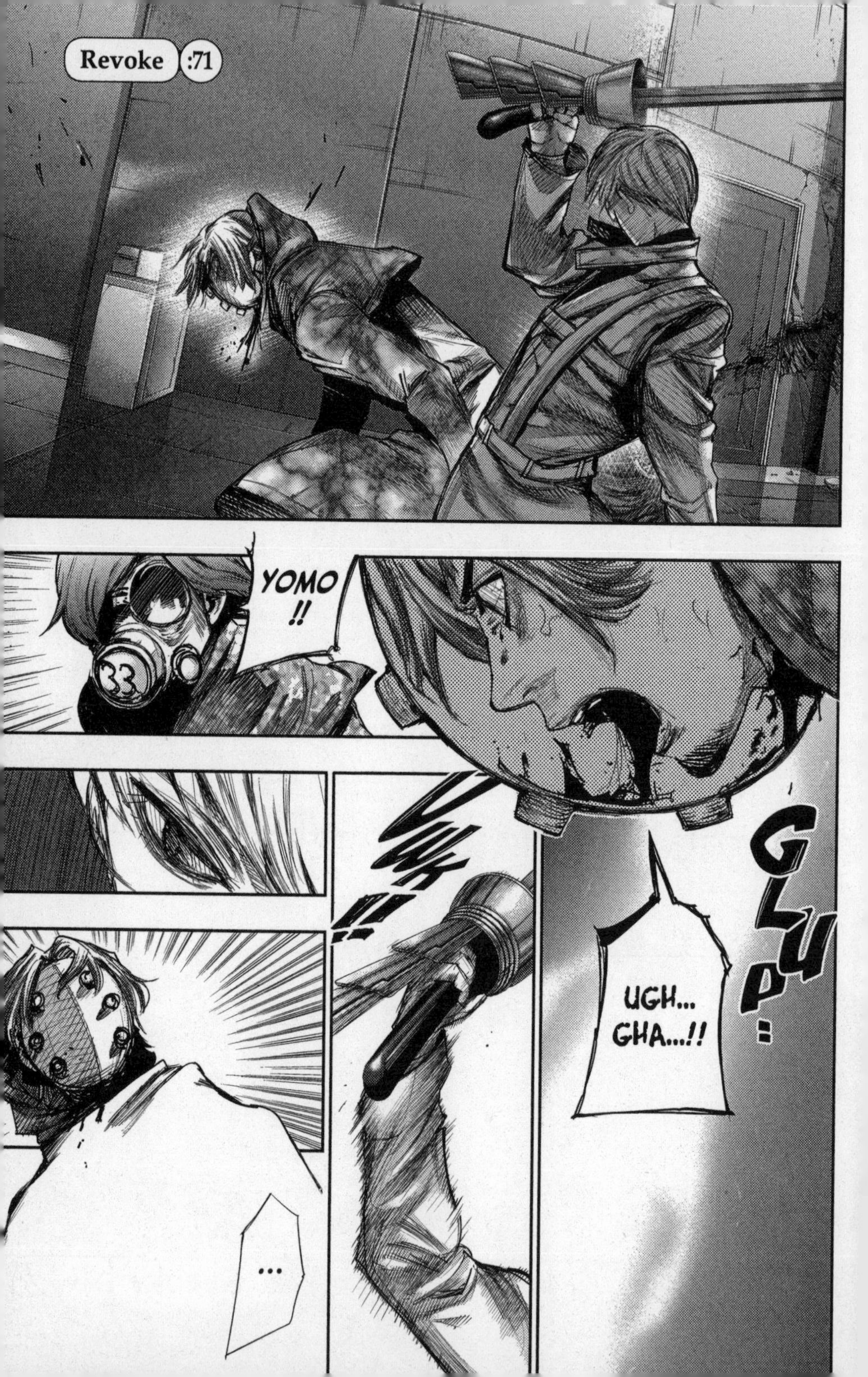
YOMO!!
GLUP!
UGH... GHA...!!
UWK!!
...

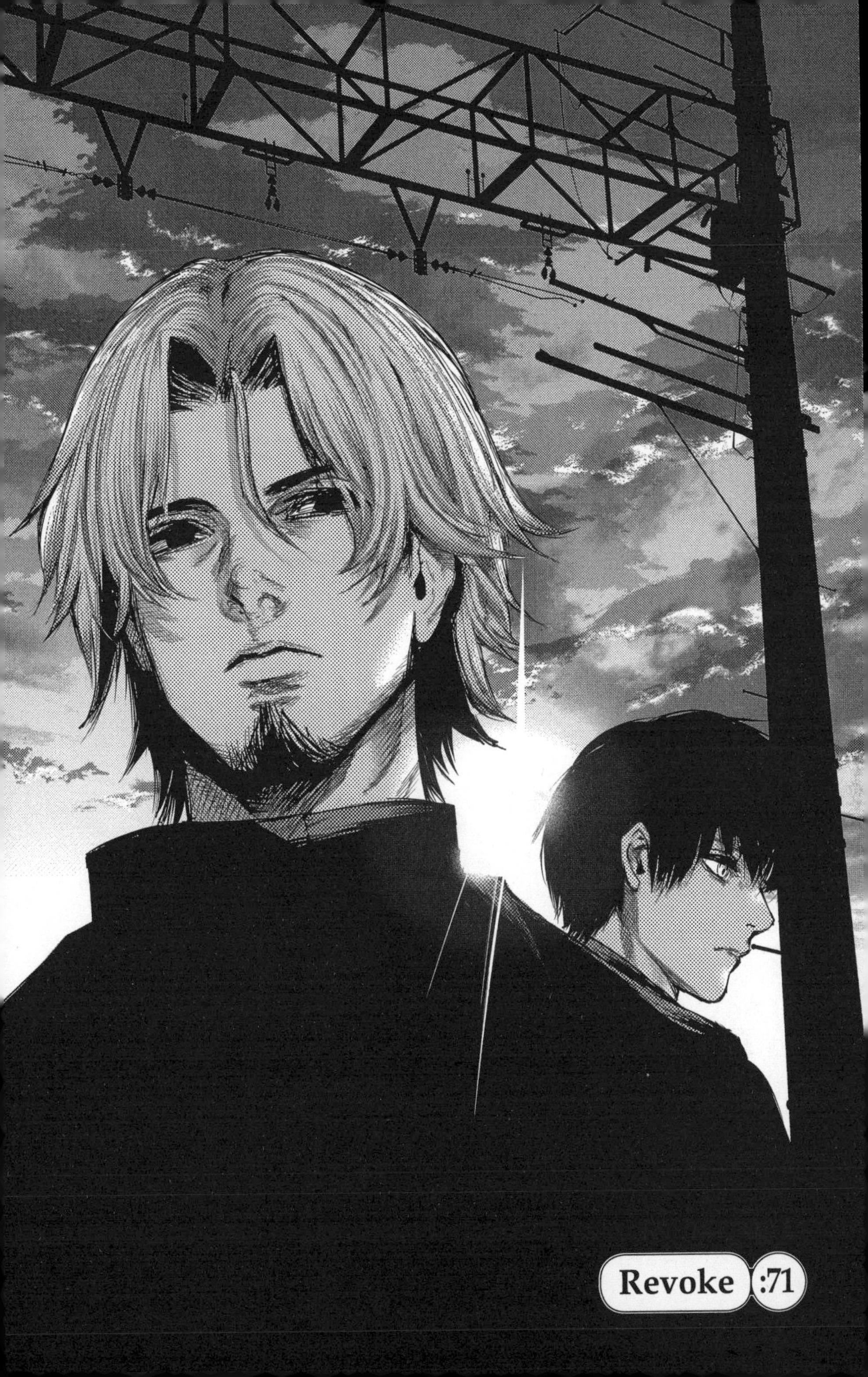
Revoke :71

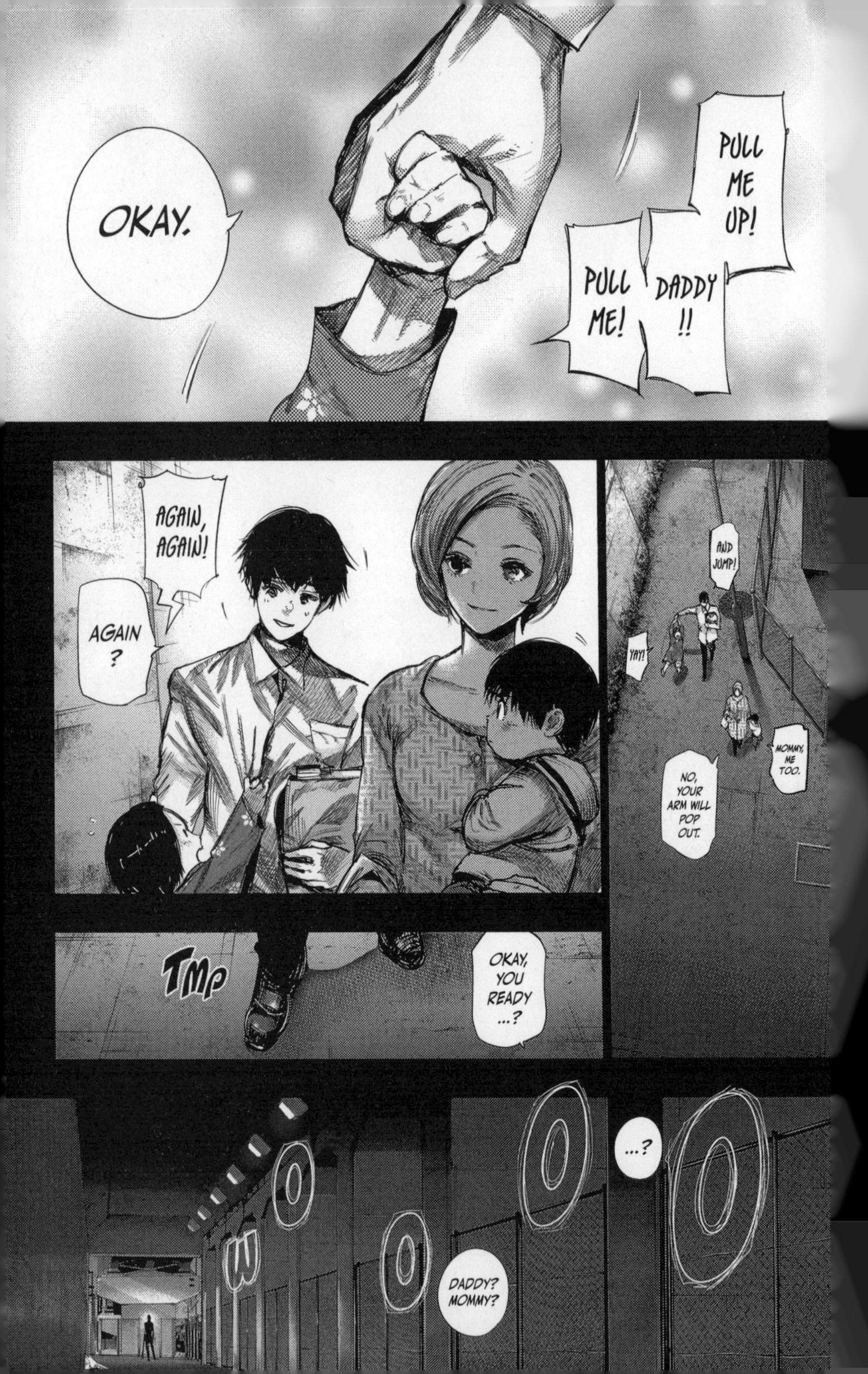
PULL ME UP!
DADDY !!
PULL ME!
OKAY.
AND JUMP!
YAY!
MOMMY, ME TOO.
NO, YOUR ARM WILL POP OUT.
AGAIN, AGAIN!
AGAIN ?
OKAY, YOU READY ...?
TMP
...?
DADDY? MOMMY?

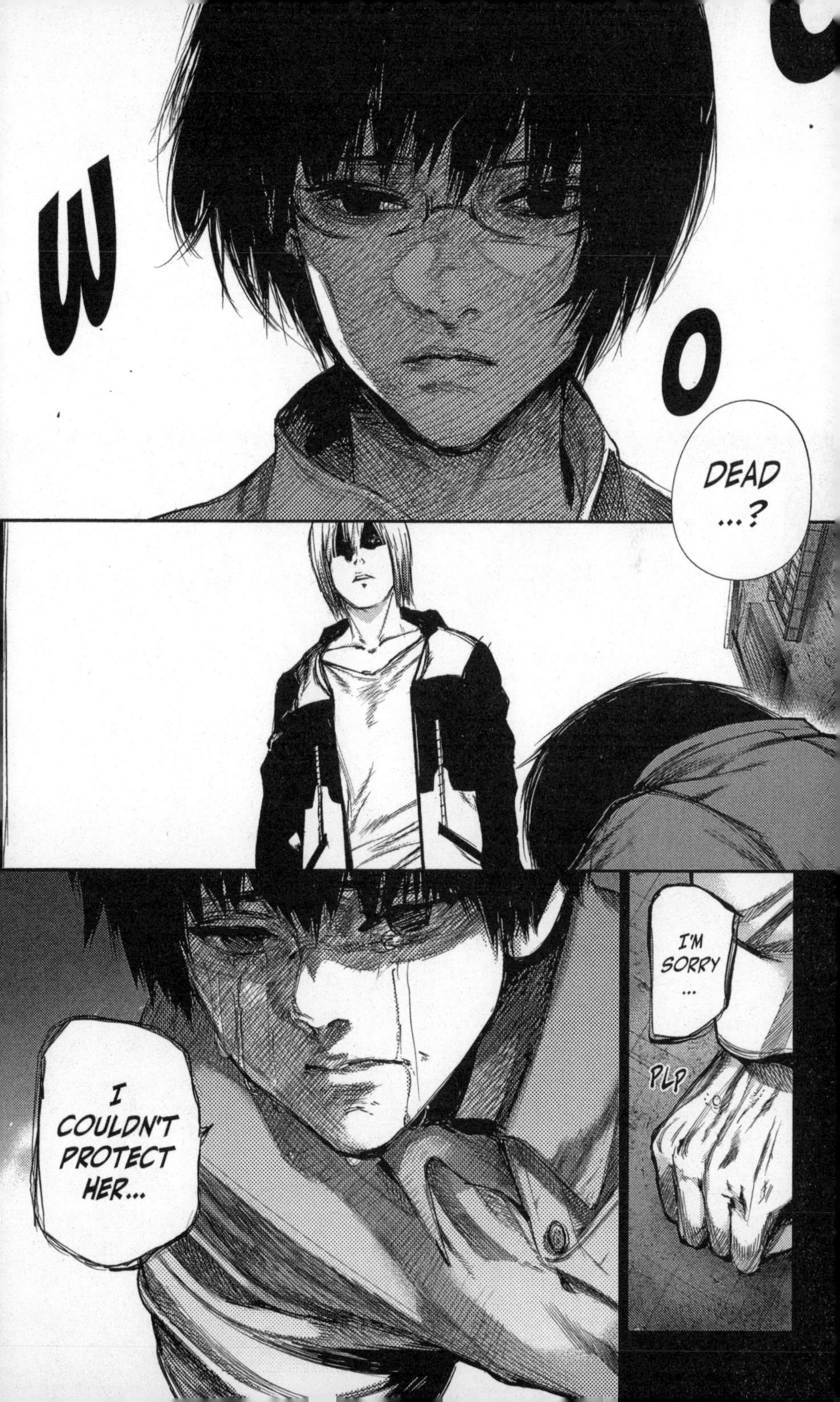
DEAD ...?
I'M SORRY ...
PLP
I COULDN'T PROTECT HER...

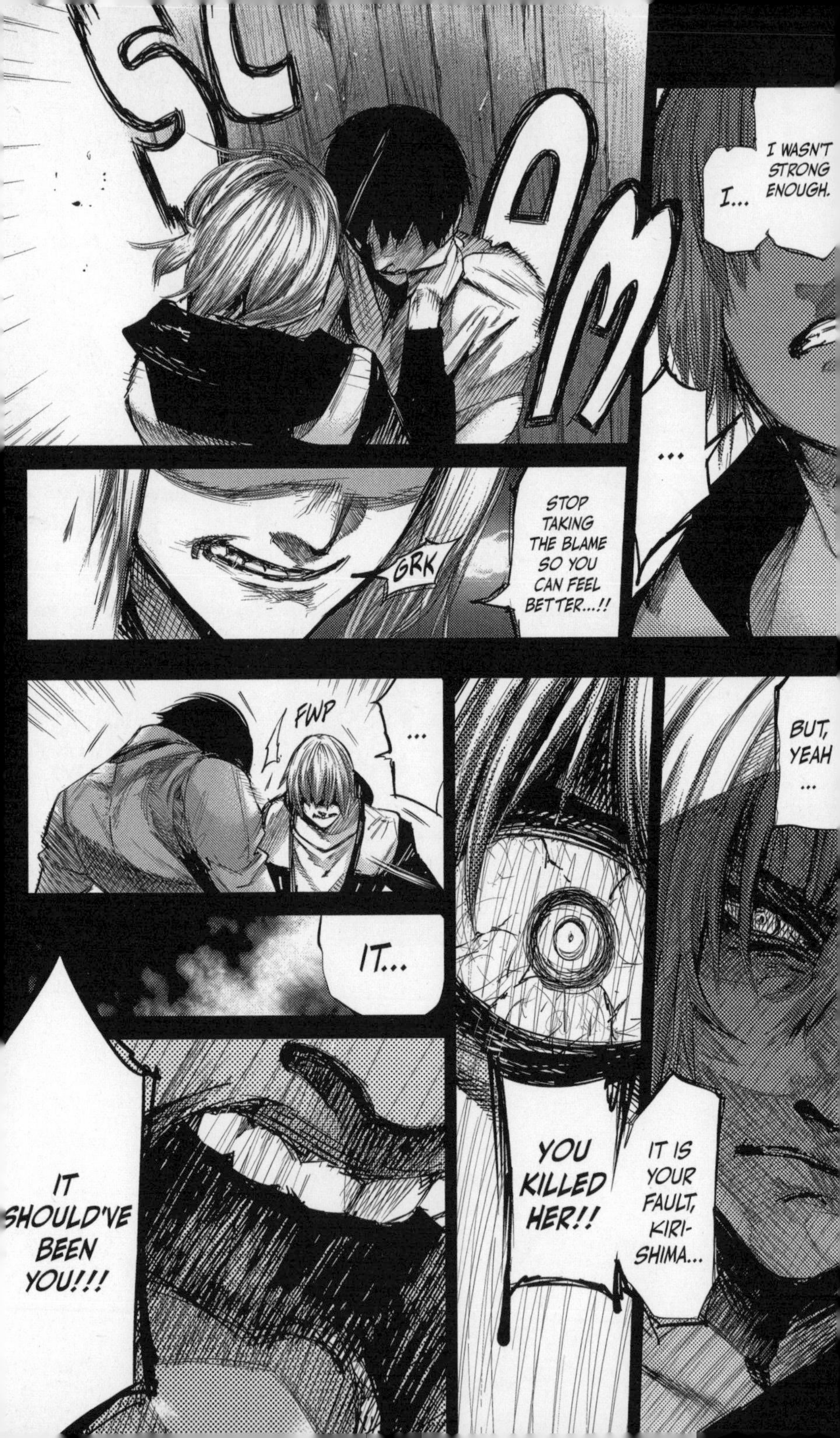
I WASN'T STRONG ENOUGH.
I...
...
SLAM
STOP TAKING THE BLAME SO YOU CAN FEEL BETTER...!!
GRK
BUT, YEAH ...
IT IS YOUR FAULT, KIRI-SHIMA...
YOU KILLED HER!!
...
FWP
IT...
IT SHOULD'VE BEEN YOU!!!

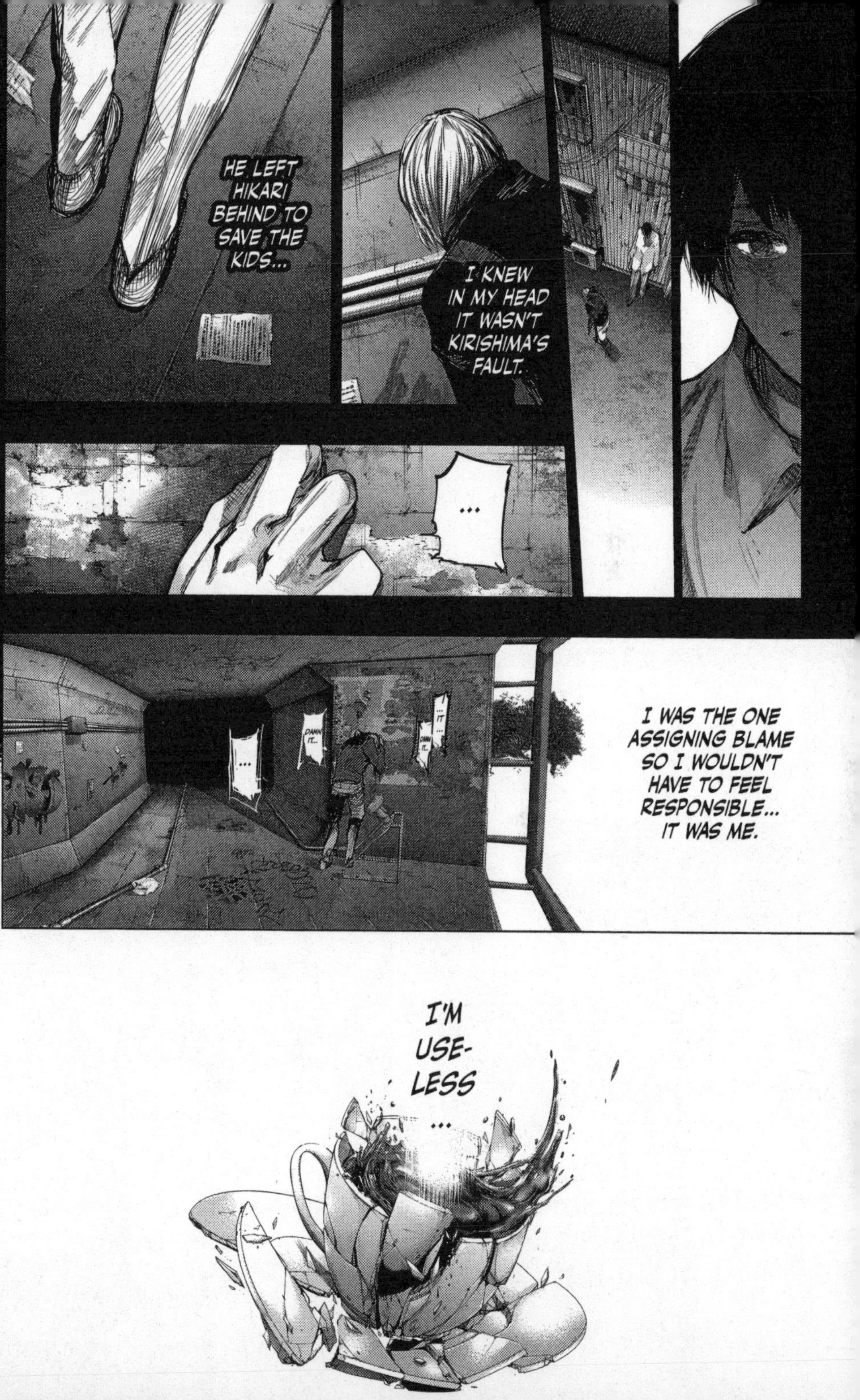
I KNEW IN MY HEAD IT WASN'T KIRISHIMA'S FAULT.
HE LEFT HIKARI BEHIND TO SAVE THE KIDS...
...
I WAS THE ONE ASSIGNING BLAME SO I WOULDN'T HAVE TO FEEL RESPONSIBLE... IT WAS ME.
... IT
DAMN IT...
DAMN IT...
...
I'M USE-LESS
...

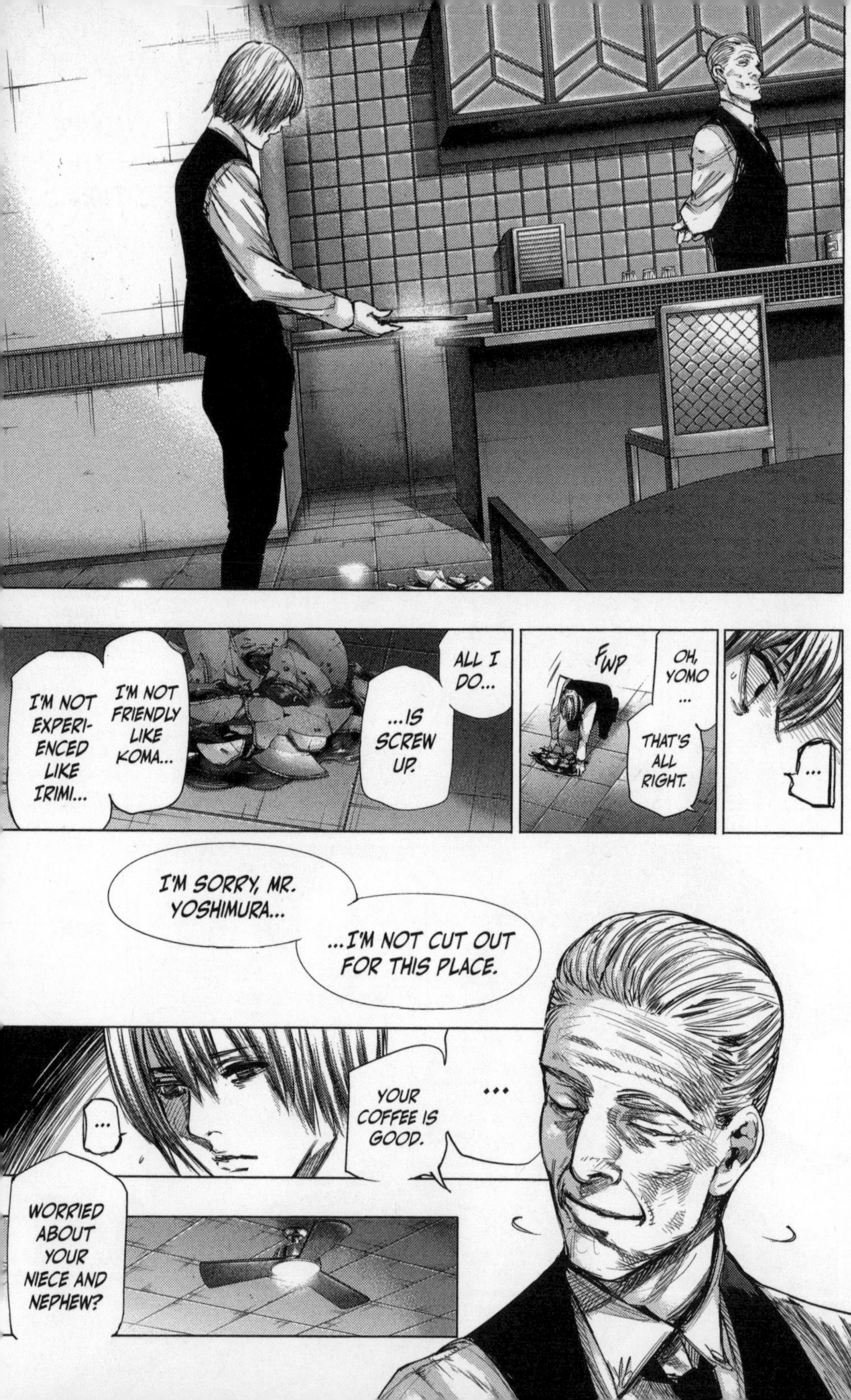
...
OH, YOMO ... THAT'S ALL RIGHT.
FWP
ALL I DO...
...IS SCREW UP.
I'M NOT FRIENDLY LIKE KOMA...
I'M NOT EXPERI-ENCED LIKE IRIMI...
I'M SORRY, MR. YOSHIMURA...
...I'M NOT CUT OUT FOR THIS PLACE.
...
YOUR COFFEE IS GOOD.
...
WORRIED ABOUT YOUR NIECE AND NEPHEW?

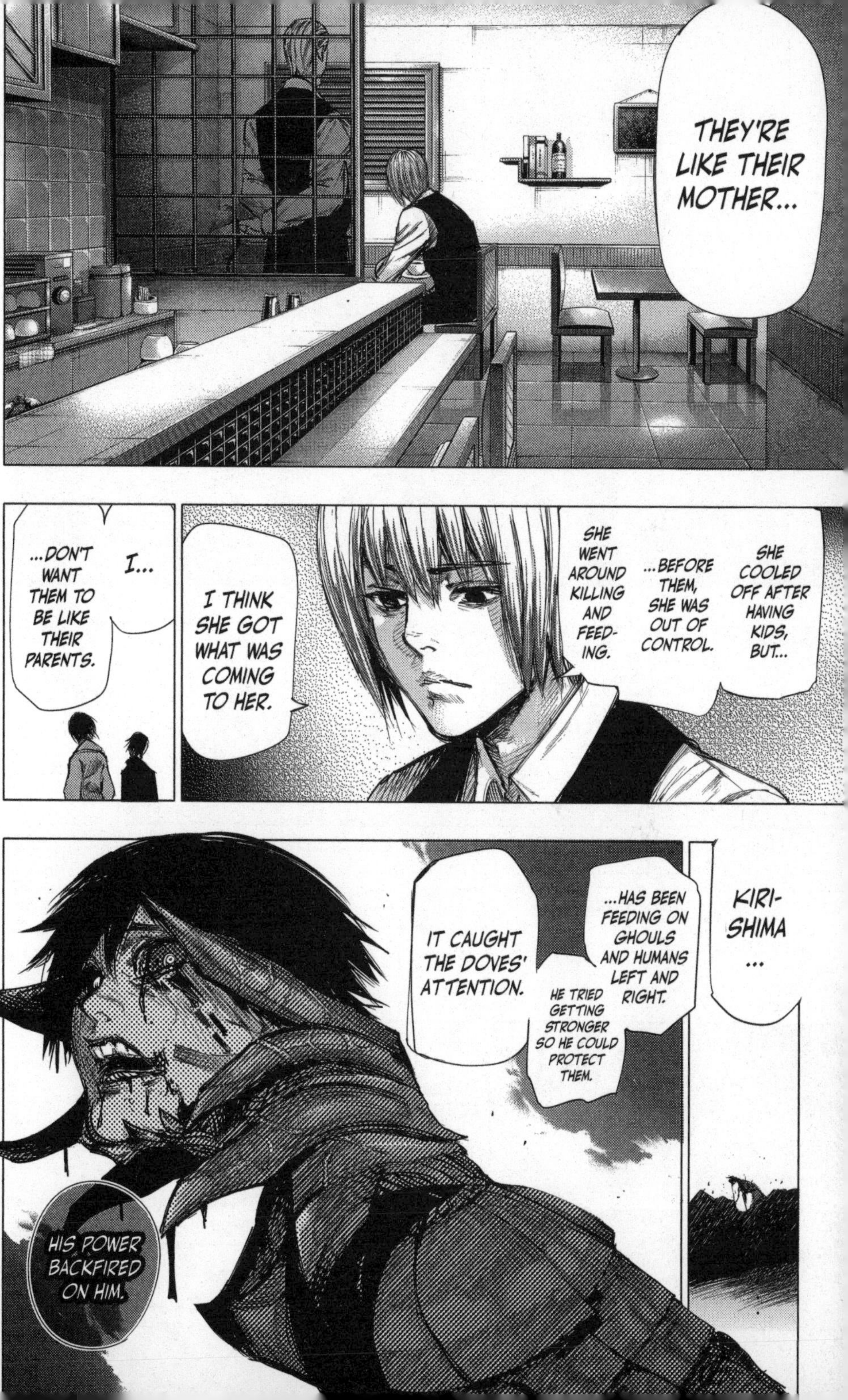
THEY'RE LIKE THEIR MOTHER...
SHE COOLED OFF AFTER HAVING KIDS, BUT...
...BEFORE THEM, SHE WAS OUT OF CONTROL.
SHE WENT AROUND KILLING AND FEEDING.
I THINK SHE GOT WHAT WAS COMING TO HER.
I...
...DON'T WANT THEM TO BE LIKE THEIR PARENTS.
KIRISHIMA...
...HAS BEEN FEEDING ON GHOULS AND HUMANS LEFT AND RIGHT.
HE TRIED GETTING STRONGER SO HE COULD PROTECT THEM.
IT CAUGHT THE DOVES' ATTENTION.
HIS POWER BACKFIRED ON HIM.

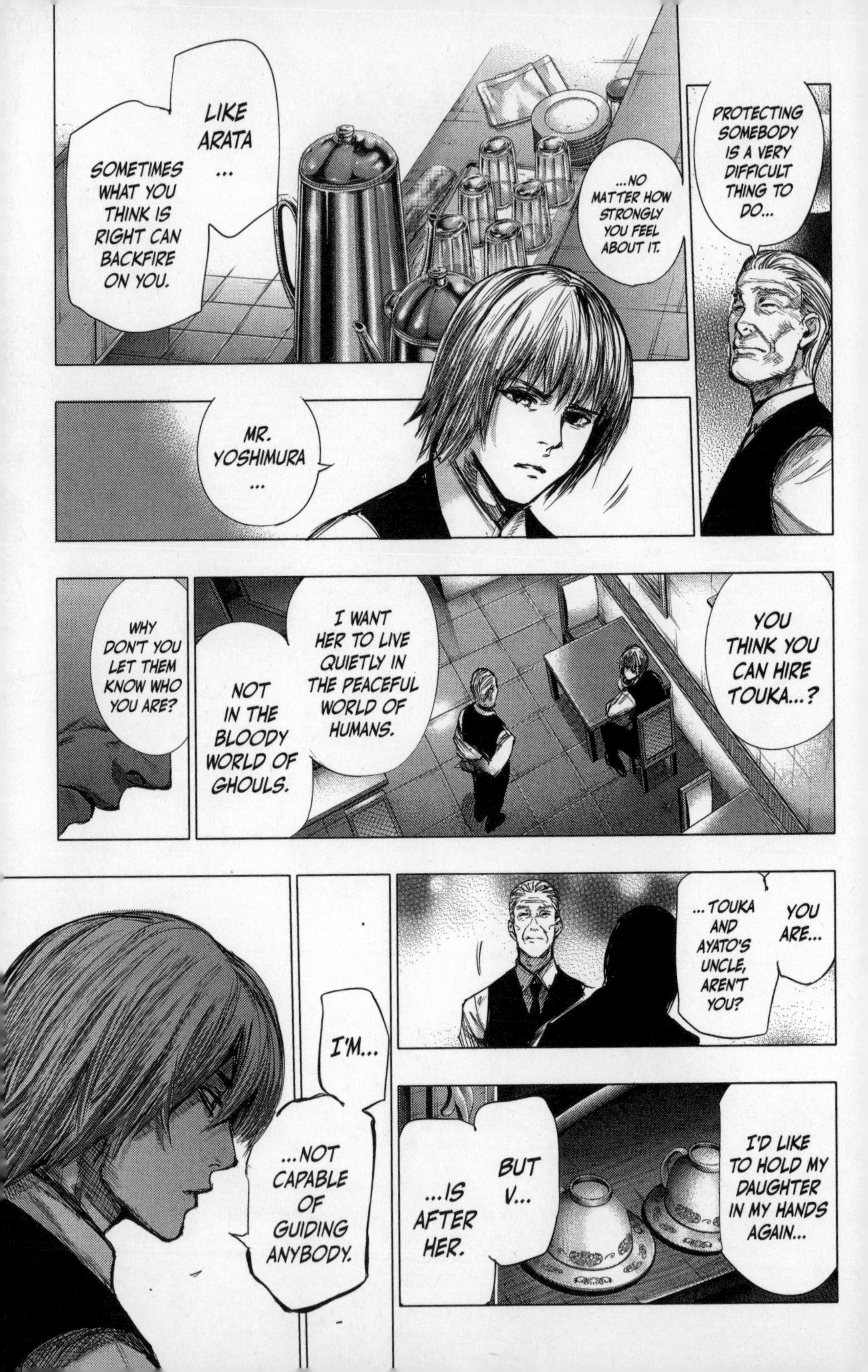
PROTECTING SOMEBODY IS A VERY DIFFICULT THING TO DO...
...NO MATTER HOW STRONGLY YOU FEEL ABOUT IT.
LIKE ARATA ...
SOMETIMES WHAT YOU THINK IS RIGHT CAN BACKFIRE ON YOU.
MR. YOSHIMURA ...
YOU THINK YOU CAN HIRE TOUKA...?
I WANT HER TO LIVE QUIETLY IN THE PEACEFUL WORLD OF HUMANS.
NOT IN THE BLOODY WORLD OF GHOULS.
WHY DON'T YOU LET THEM KNOW WHO YOU ARE?
YOU ARE...
...TOUKA AND AYATO'S UNCLE, AREN'T YOU?
I'D LIKE TO HOLD MY DAUGHTER IN MY HANDS AGAIN...
BUT V...
...IS AFTER HER.
I'M...
...NOT CAPABLE OF GUIDING ANYBODY.

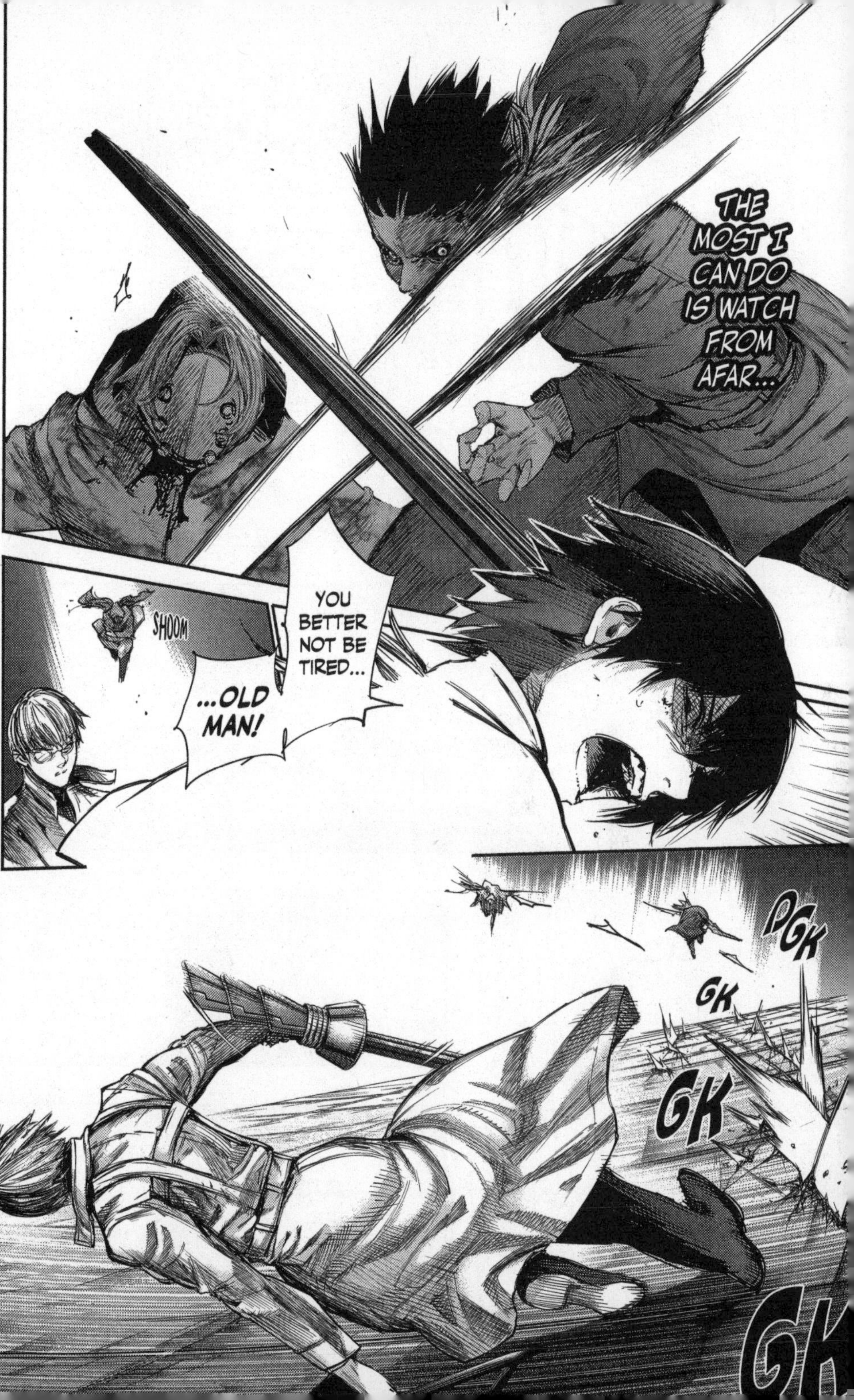
THE MOST I CAN DO IS WATCH FROM AFAR...
YOU BETTER NOT BE TIRED...
...OLD MAN!
SHOOM
DGK
GK
GK
GK

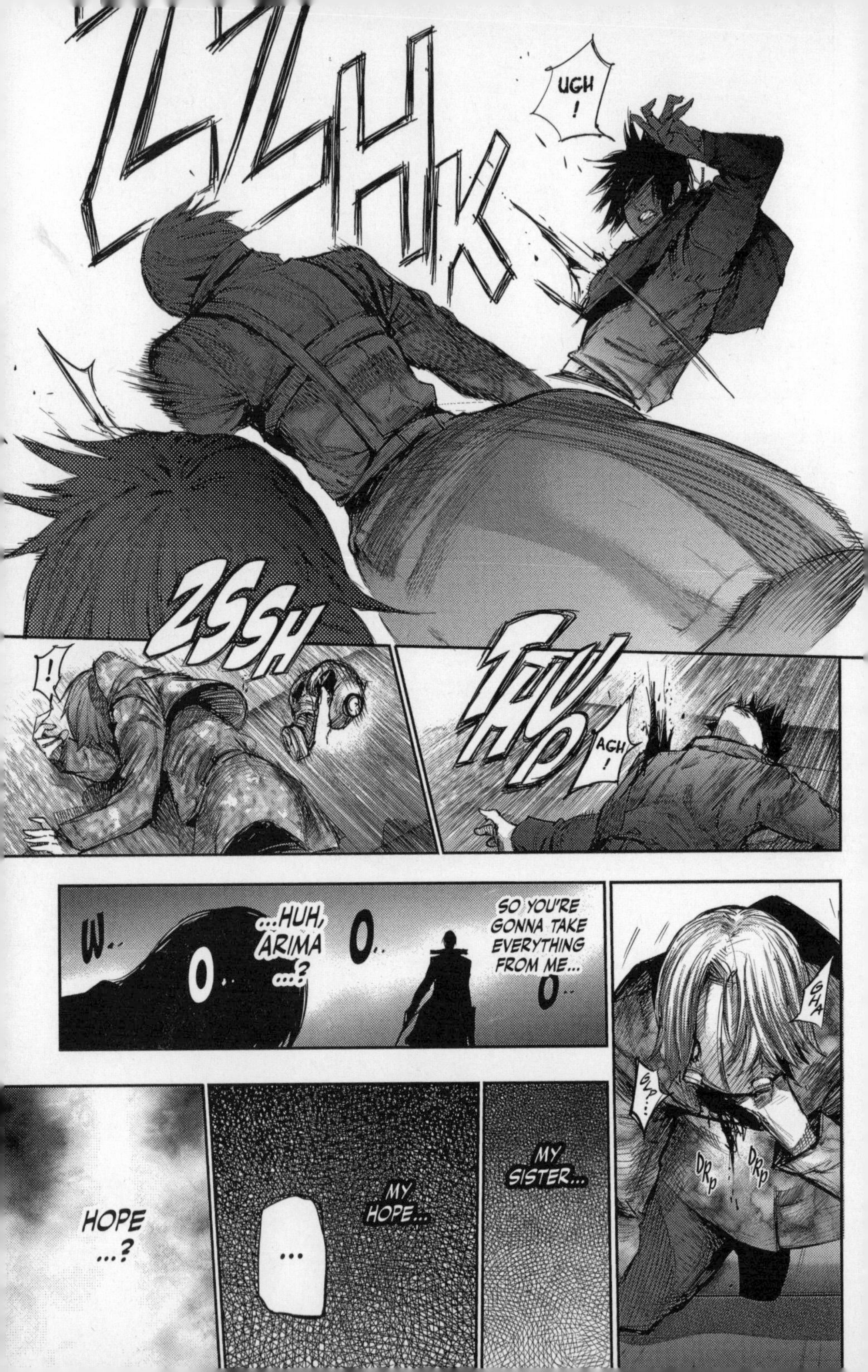
ZZSHK
UGH!
THUD
AGH!
ZSSH
!
GHA
GLP...
DRP
DRP
SO YOU'RE GONNA TAKE EVERYTHING FROM ME...
O..
O..
...HUH, ARIMA ...?
O..
W..
MY SISTER...
MY HOPE...
...
HOPE ...?

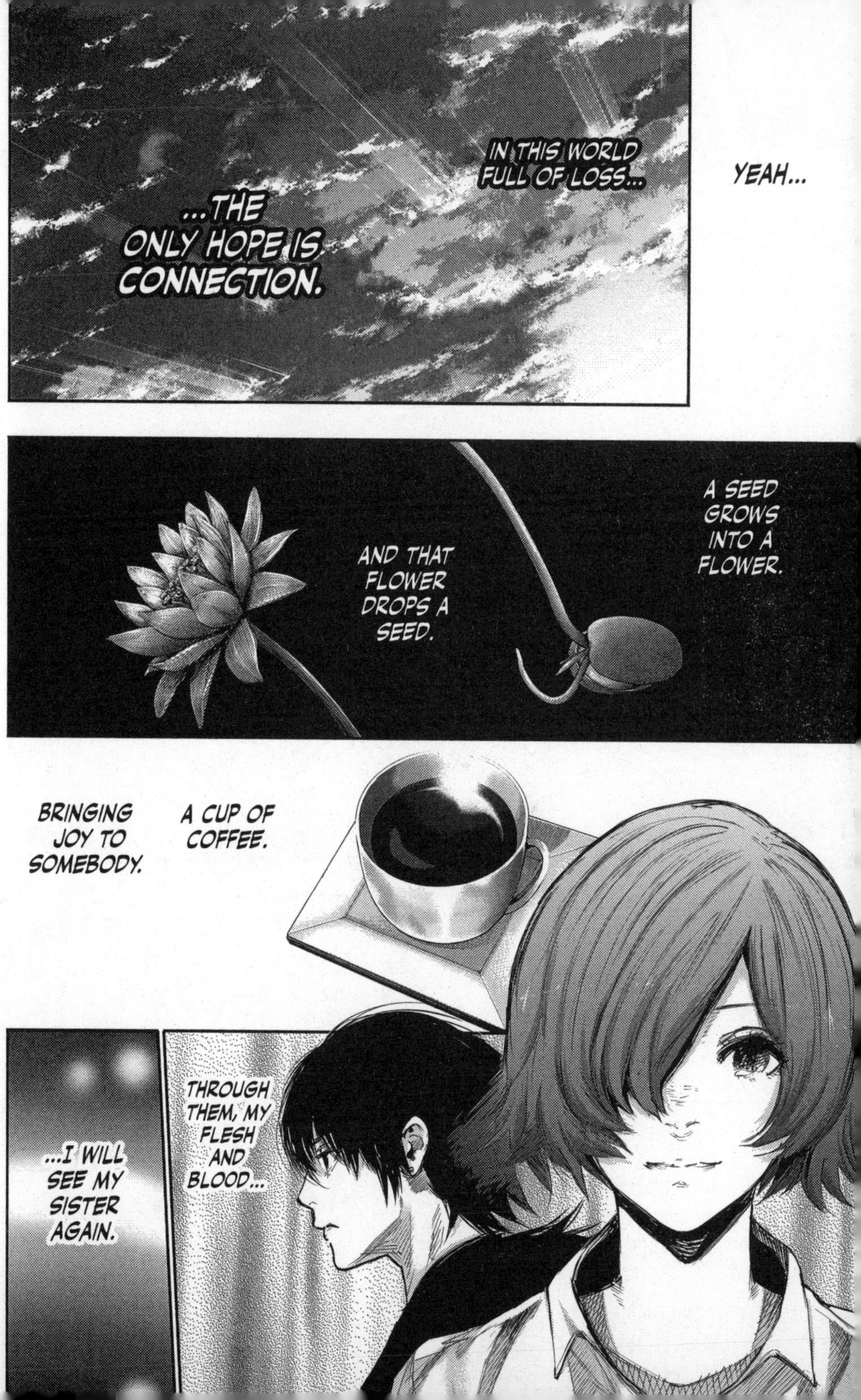
YEAH...
IN THIS WORLD FULL OF LOSS...
...THE ONLY HOPE IS CONNECTION.
A SEED GROWS INTO A FLOWER.
AND THAT FLOWER DROPS A SEED.
A CUP OF COFFEE.
BRINGING JOY TO SOMEBODY.
THROUGH THEM, MY FLESH AND BLOOD...
...I WILL SEE MY SISTER AGAIN.

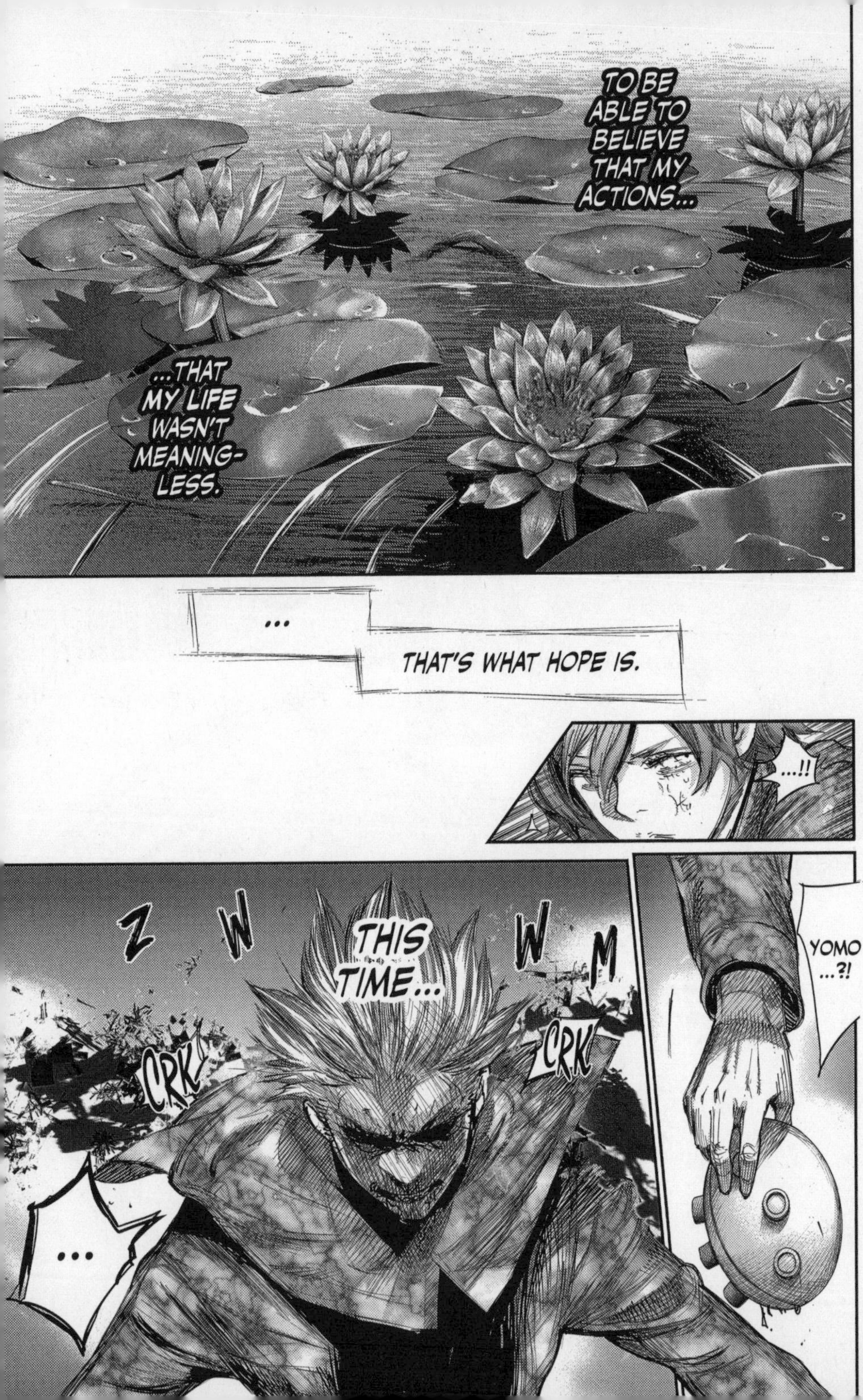
TO BE ABLE TO BELIEVE THAT MY ACTIONS...
...THAT MY LIFE WASN'T MEANING-LESS.
...
THAT'S WHAT HOPE IS.
...!!
YOMO ...?!
ZWWM
THIS TIME...
CRK
CRK
...

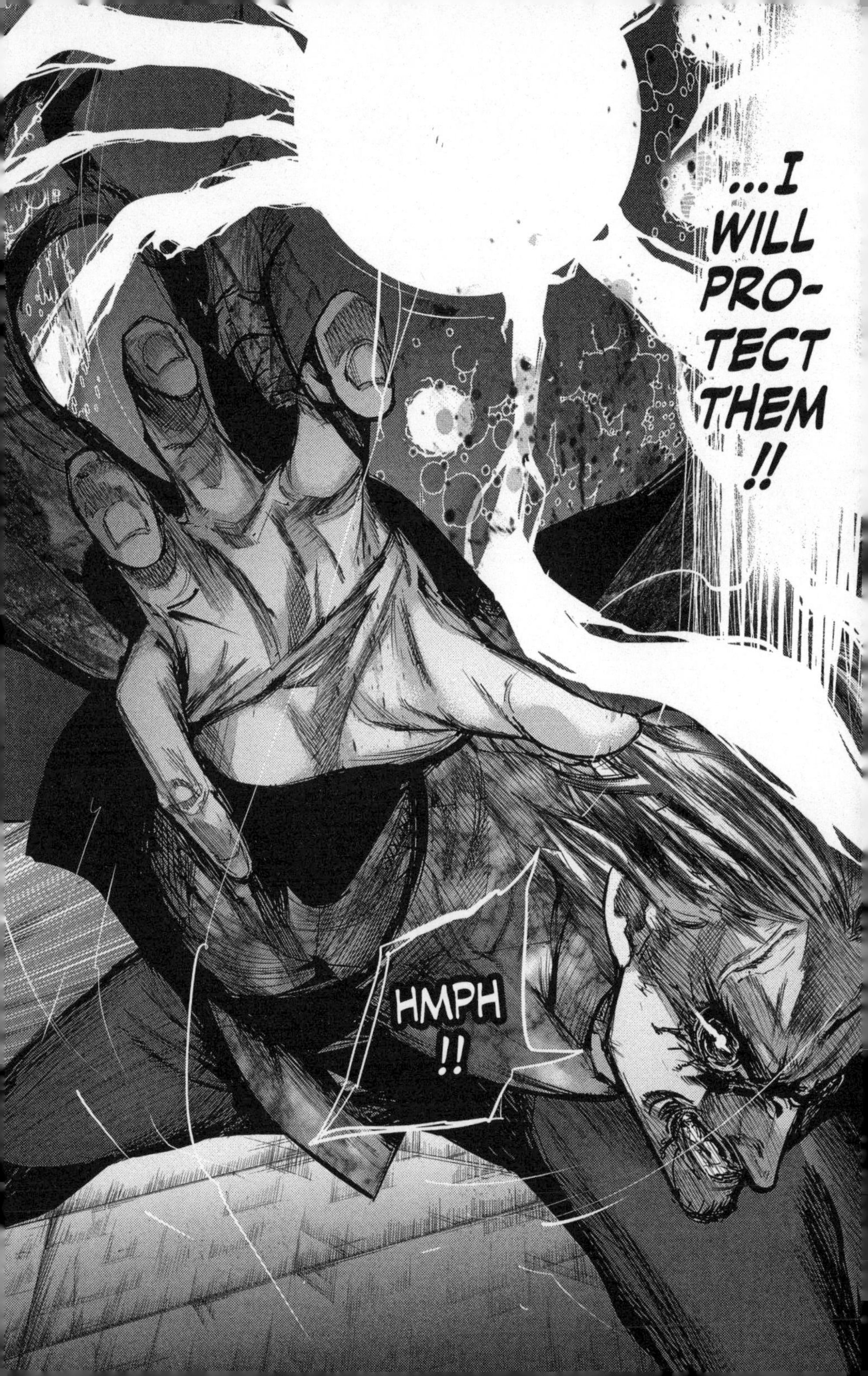
...I WILL PRO- TECT THEM !!
HMPH !!

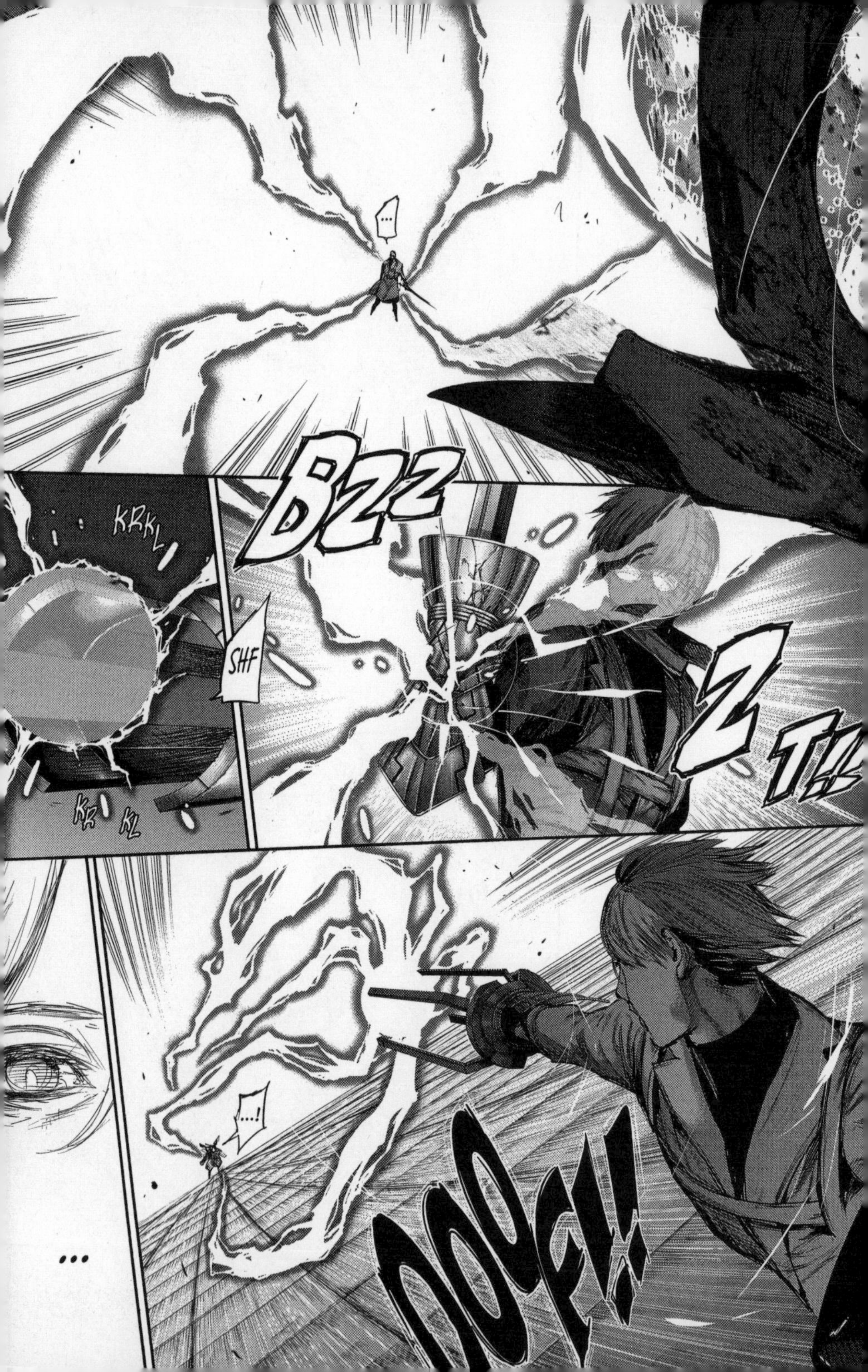
...
BZZ
Z
SHF
KRKL
KR KL
DOOF!!
...!
...

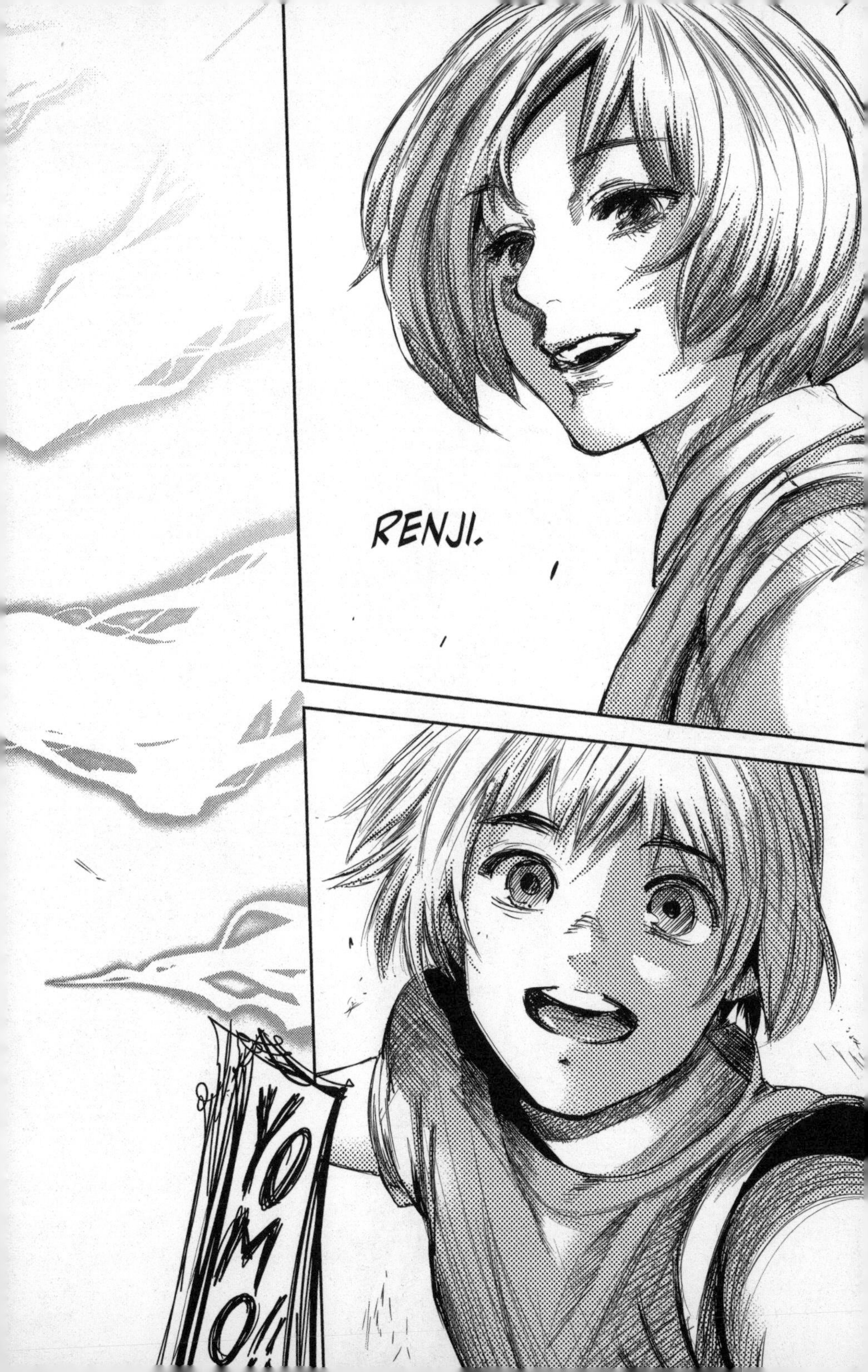
RENJI.
YOMO!!

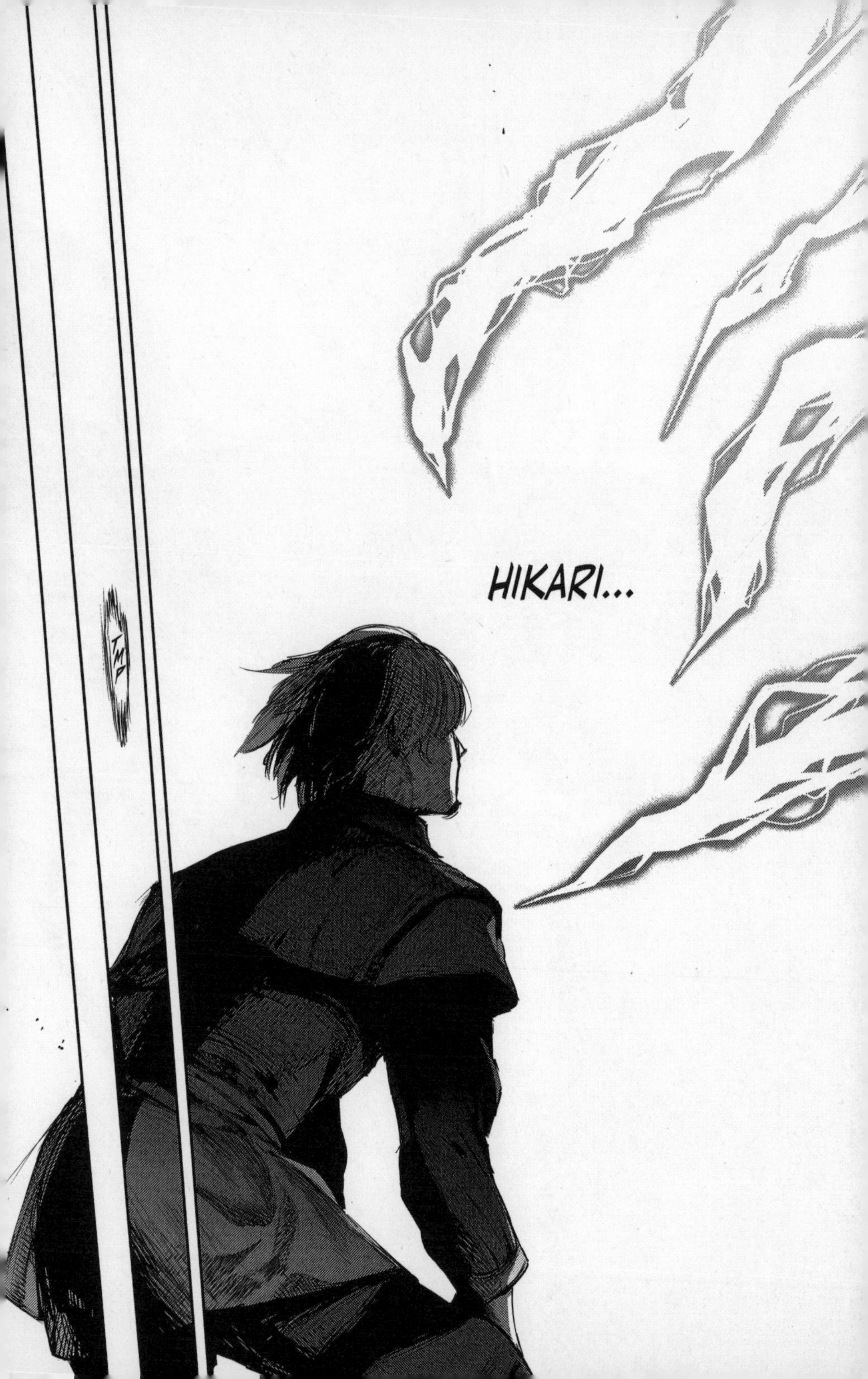
HIKARI...
TMP

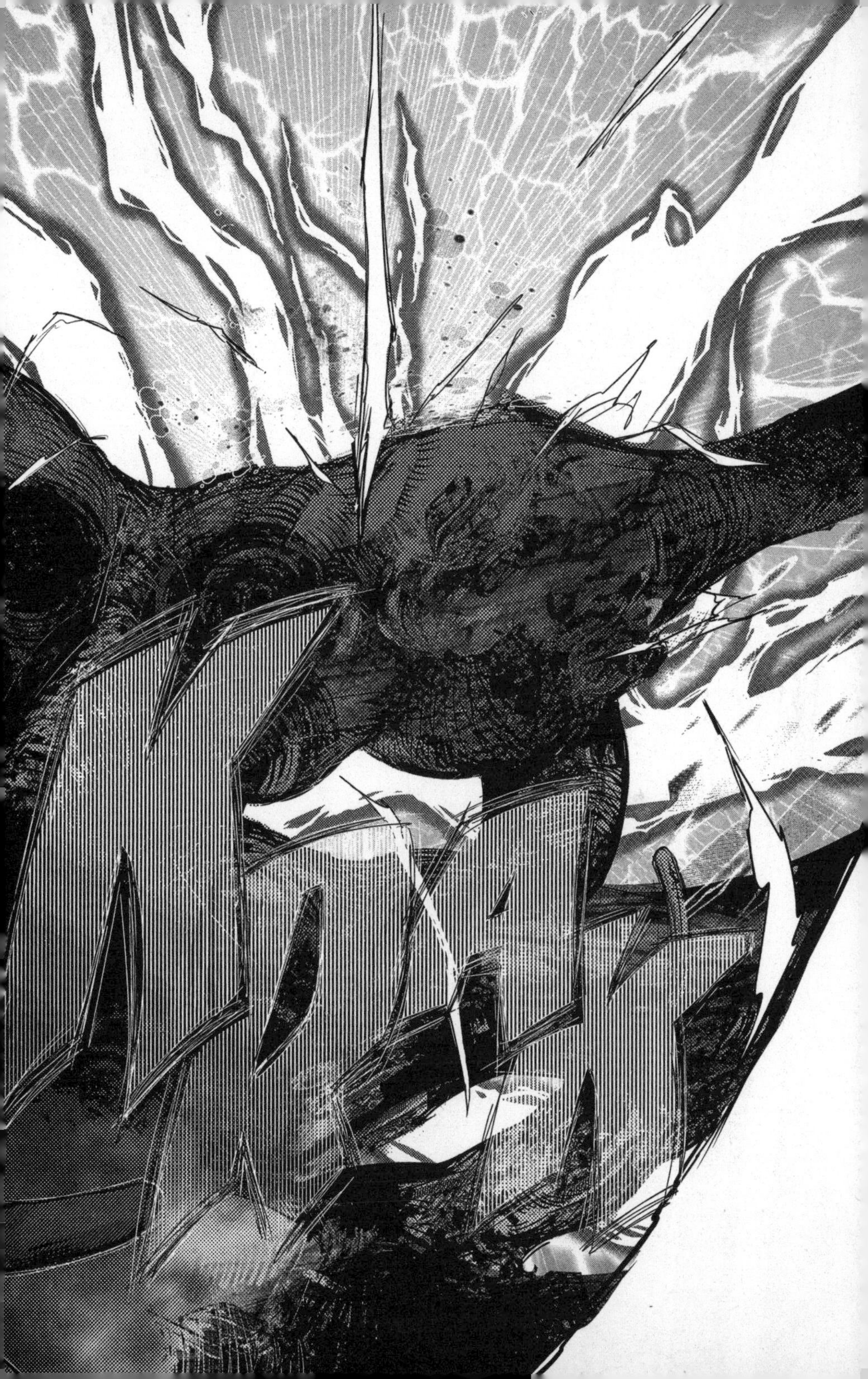

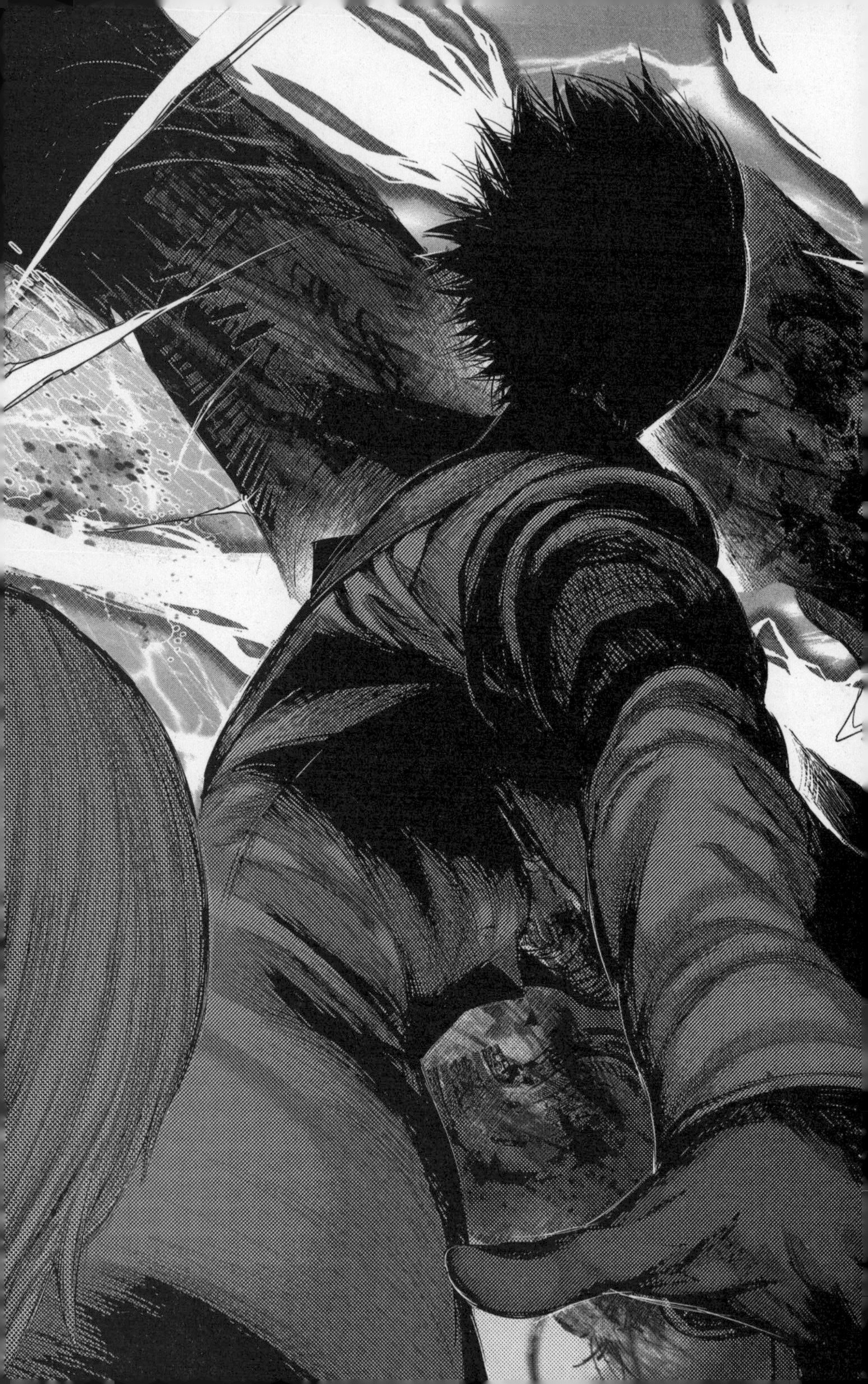

"IT'S BEEN A WHILE, MUTSUKI."

"HAVEN'T BEEN BACK TO THE CHATEAU LATELY. HOW'S EVERYONE DOING?"
"..."

"WANNA PLAY WORD CHAIN?"

"HUH? WHY...? OKAY, SURE..."

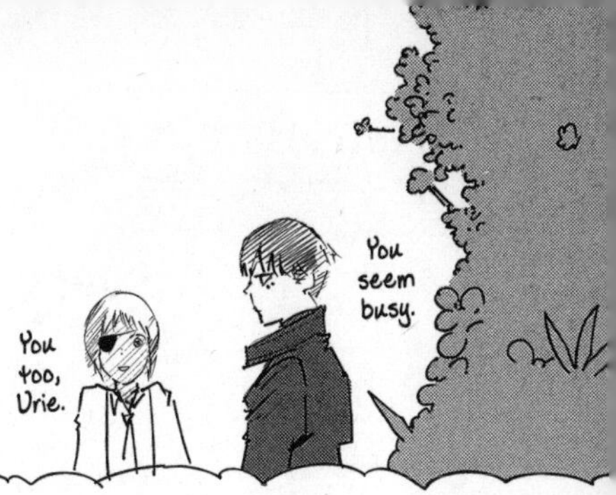
You seem busy.
You too, Urie.

"***CHAIN.*** (YOU LOST WEIGHT, MUTSUKI...)"
"***NECTAR.***"
"***RICE.*** (HOPE THEY'RE NOT OVERWORKING YOU.)"
"***ELEPHANT.***"

"***THANKSGIVING.*** (IT'S POSSIBLE. THE SUZUYA SQUAD IS KNOWN TO BE ASSIGNED TO ROUGH WARDS...)"
"***GARLIC.***"

"***CHOCOLATE.*** (HANG IN THERE... YEAH, BY EATING CHOCOLATE...)"

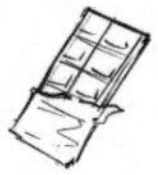

"***ERASER.***"
"***RECORD-KEEPER.*** (LET ME KNOW IF I CAN HELP! I CAN BE A RECORD KEEPER...)"

"***RAP.***"
"***PARTY.*** (IT DOESN'T HAVE TO BE WORK-RELATED... I CAN HOST A PARTY...)"

"***YACHTS.***"
"***SAUSAGE.*** (A REAL EXTRAVAGANT PARTY. WE CAN HAVE A SPREAD OF SAUSAGES...)"

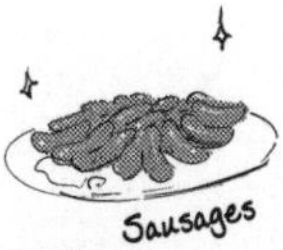
Sausages

"***SHOES.***"
"***SANDWICH.*** (AND SANDWICHES TOO... YOU LIKE THEM, RIGHT? WE'LL HAVE A PARTY! I PROMISE...)"

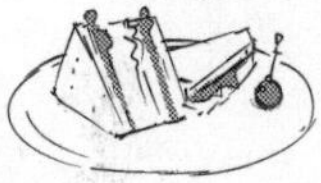

"***HERTZ.***"
"***ZUCCHINI.*** (I'VE BEEN THINKING IF THERE WAS ANYTHING I COULD DO FOR YOU...)"

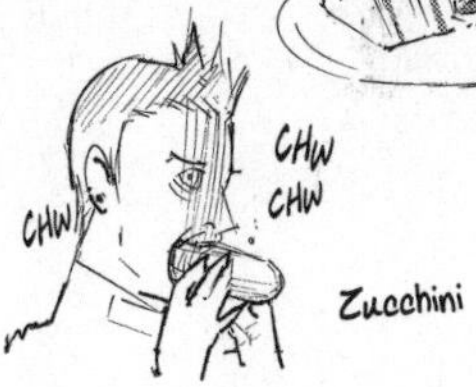
CHW
CHW
CHW
Zucchini

"***IDIOM.***"
"***MEDICAL CHECKUP.*** (YEAH, LIKE A MEDICAL CHECKUP... YOU WANNA GET ONE?)"

"***PSYCHOLOGIST.***"
"***TAKEOMI KUROIWA.*** (KUROIWA GOT ONE THE OTHER DAY.)"

"***APPLE.***"
"***EGGPLANT.*** (HOPE THEY DON'T FIND SOMETHING... SOMETHING BAD...)"

"***THUMBSCREW.***"
"***WHAT IF THEY FIND SOMETHING.*** (WHAT IF SOMETHING'S WRONG...?)"

"WHY A SENTENCE ALL OF SUDDEN, URIE?"
"MM...? OH, SORRY. I WAS THINKING ABOUT SOMETHING ELSE. (I SAID WHAT I WAS THINKING OUT LOUD...)"

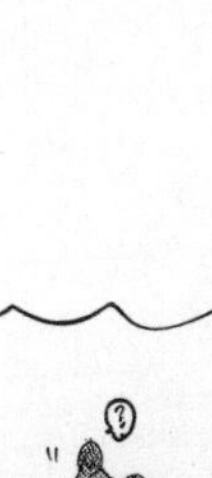

Retransmit :72

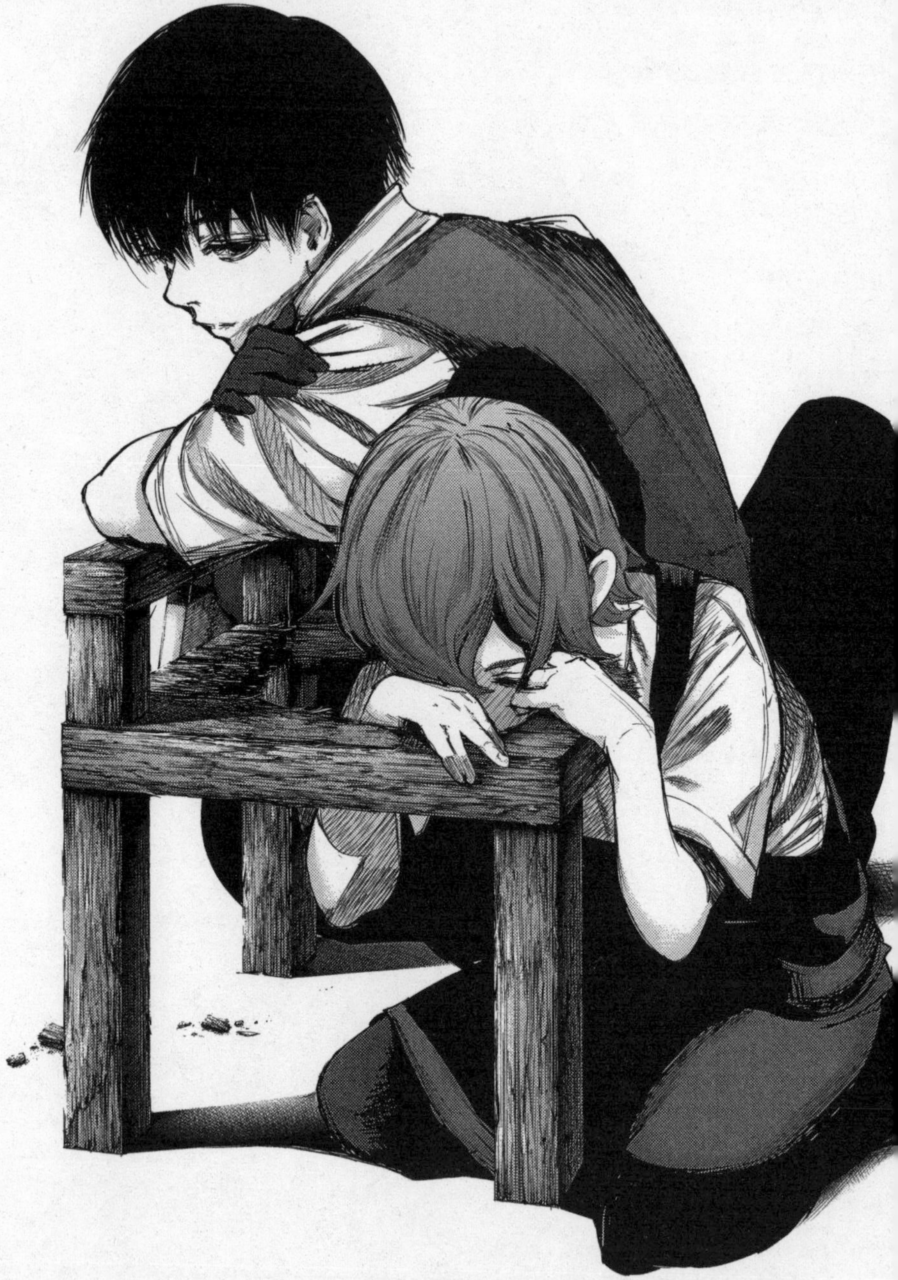

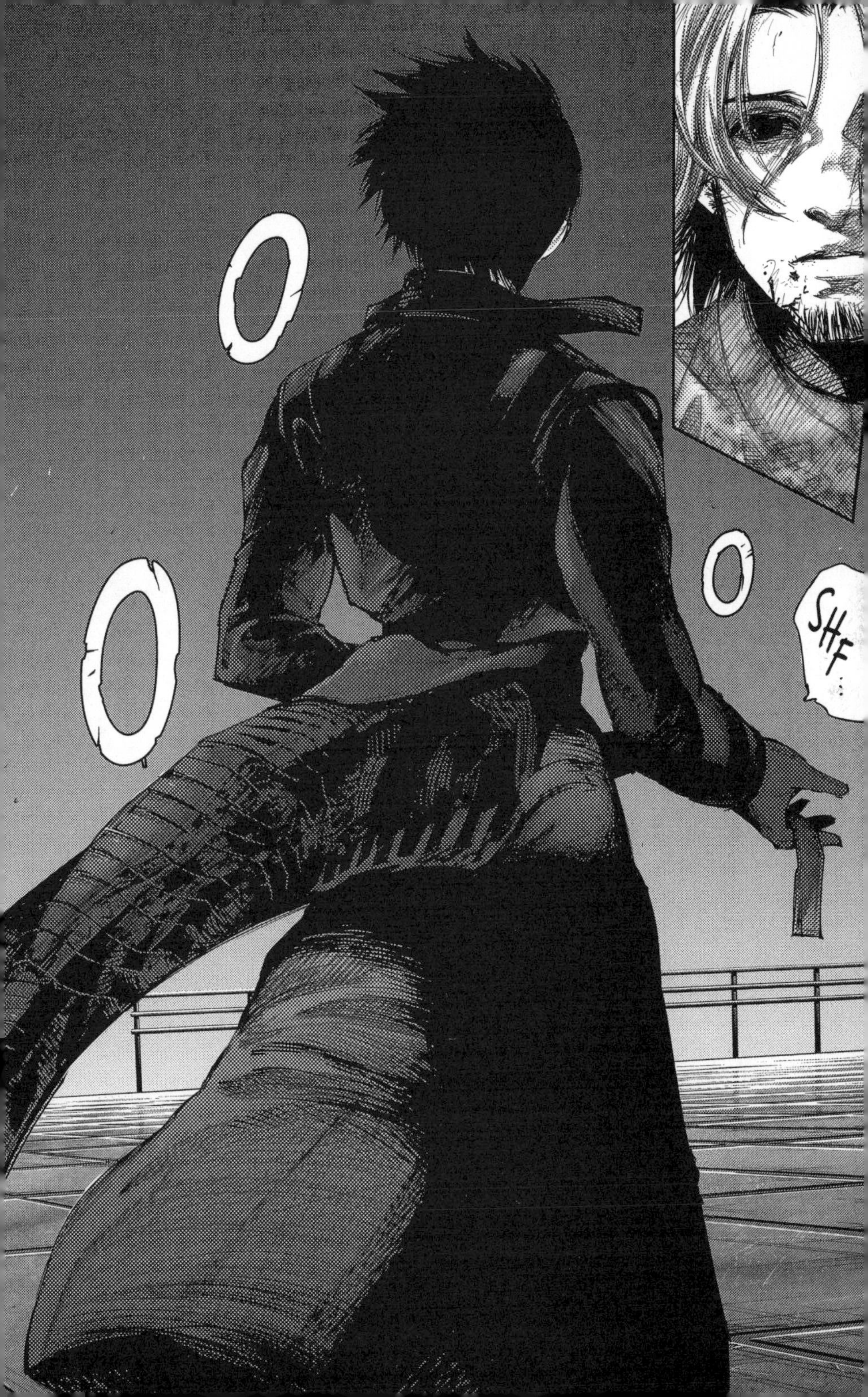
SHF

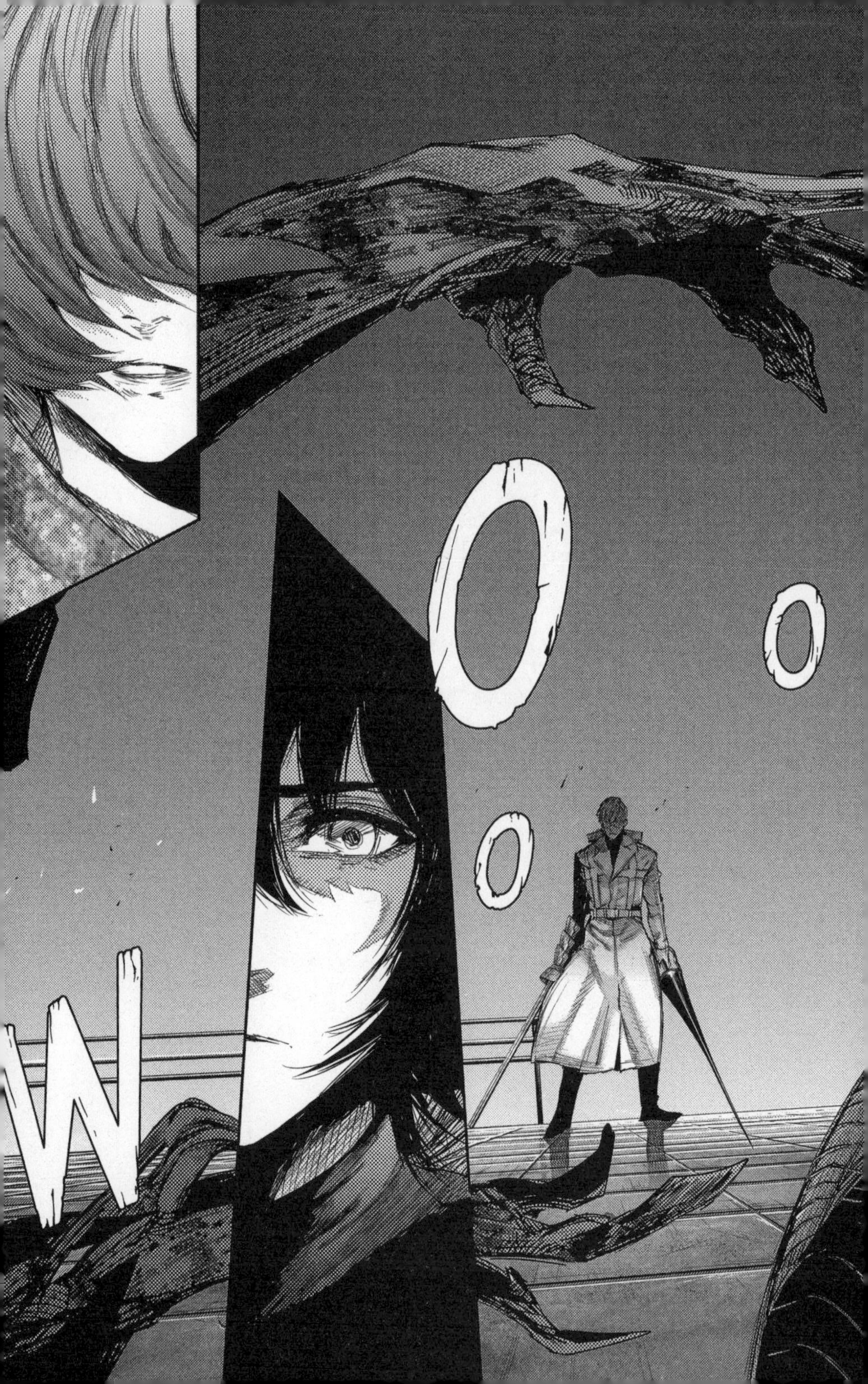
WOOO

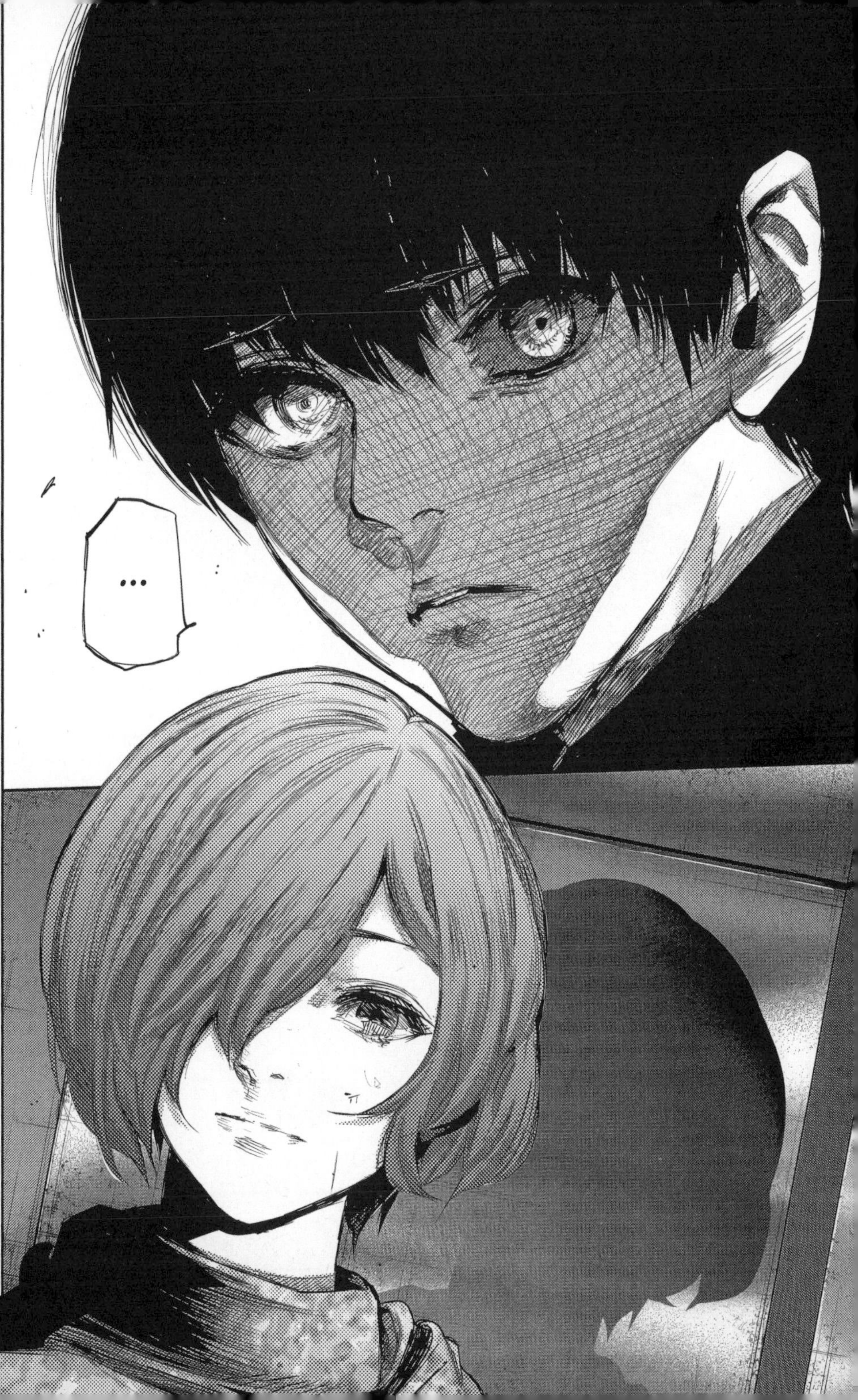
...

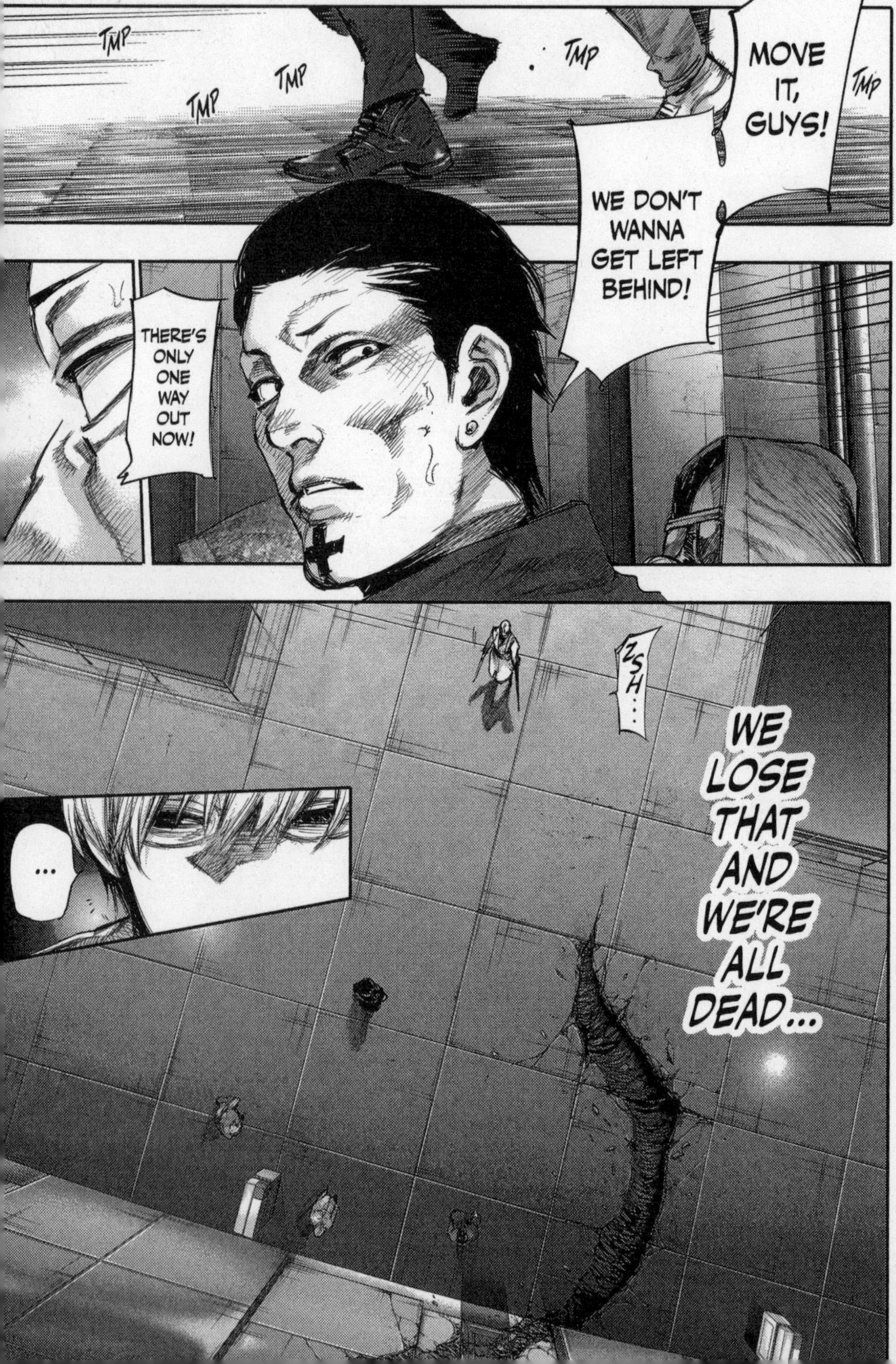
MOVE IT, GUYS!
TMP
TMP
TMP
TMP
TMP
WE DON'T WANNA GET LEFT BEHIND!
THERE'S ONLY ONE WAY OUT NOW!
ZSH...
WE LOSE THAT AND WE'RE ALL DEAD...
...

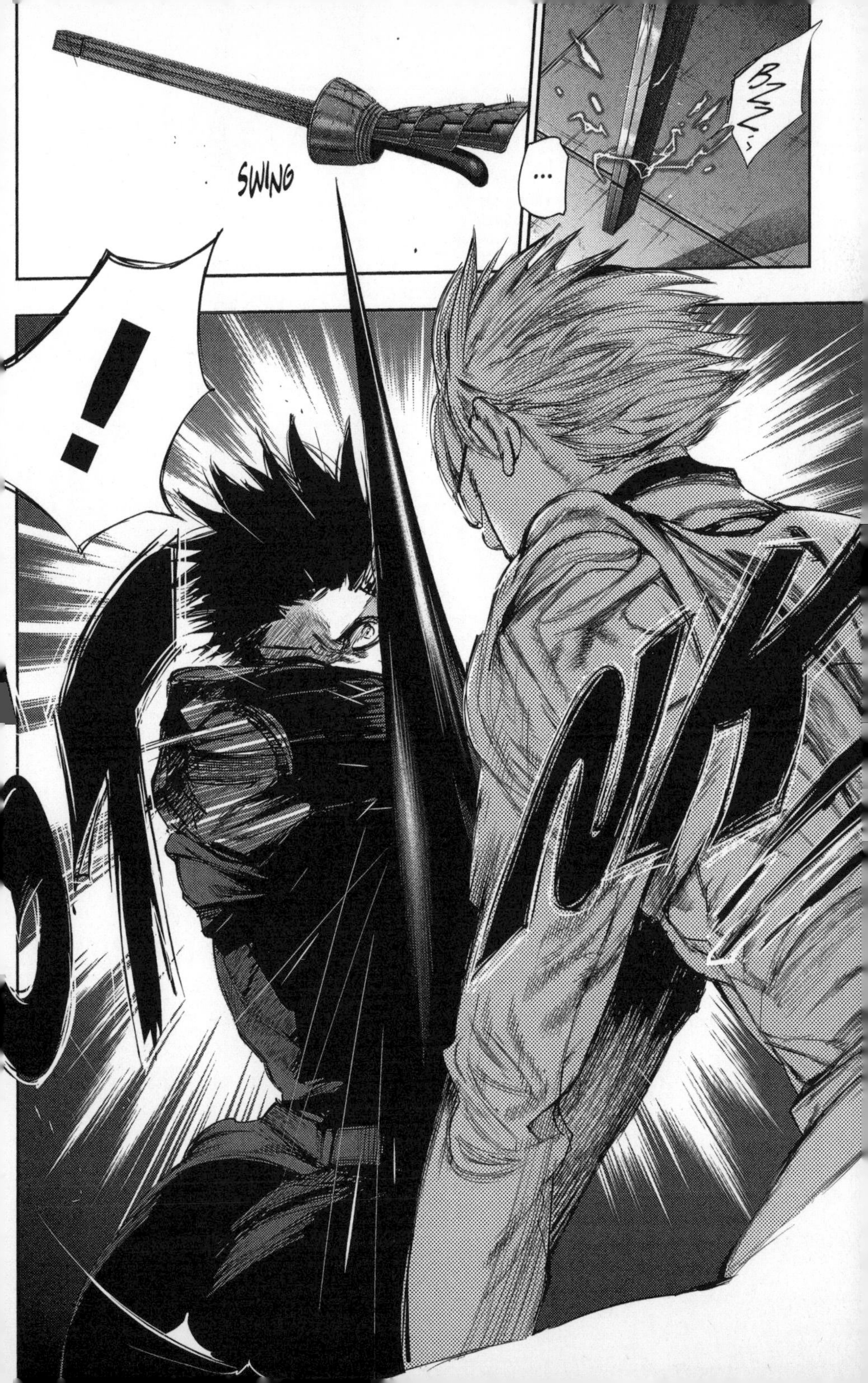

...
SWING
!

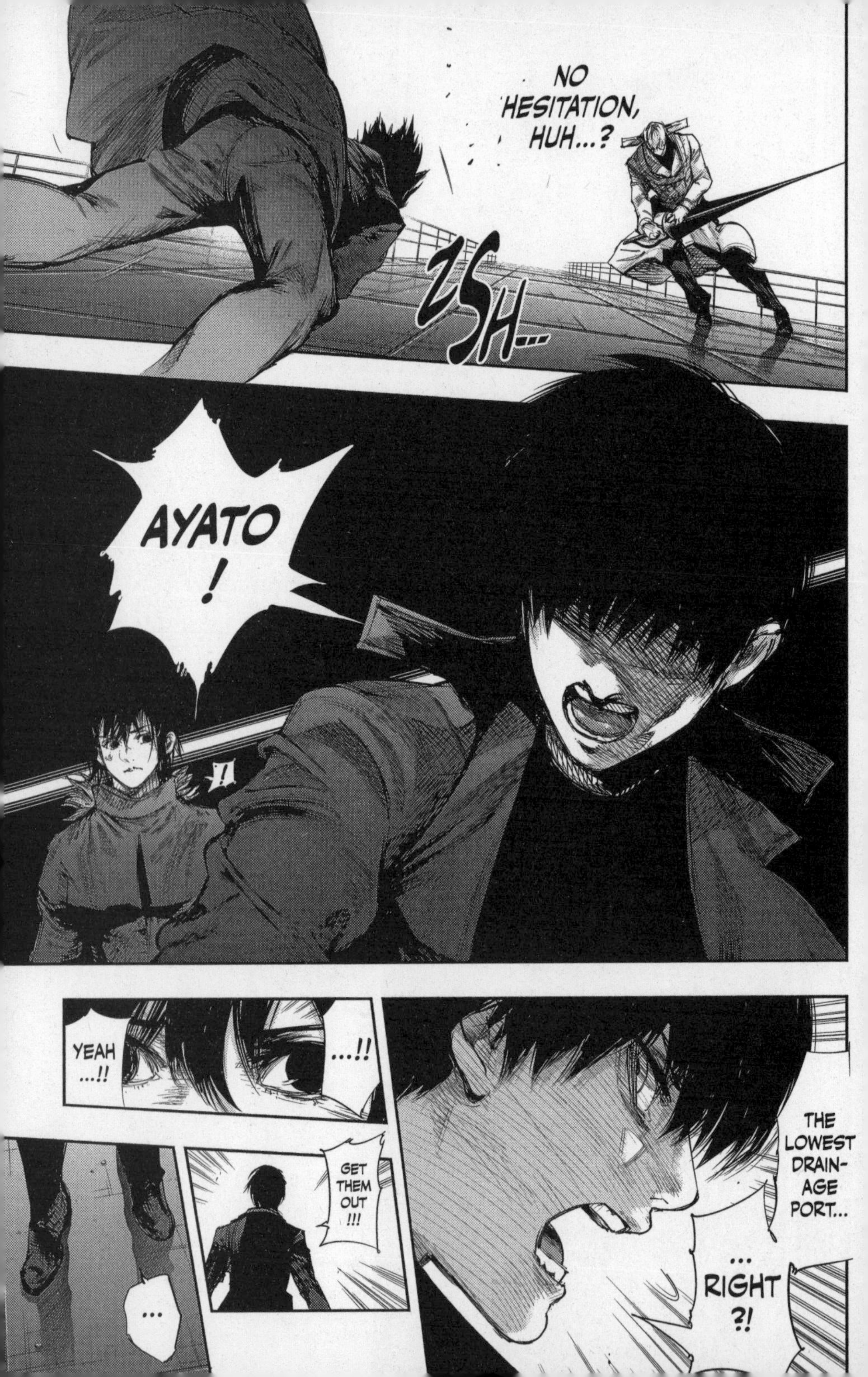
NO HESITATION, HUH...?
ZSH...
AYATO !
!
THE LOWEST DRAINAGE PORT...
...RIGHT ?!
...!!
YEAH ...!!
GET THEM OUT !!!
...

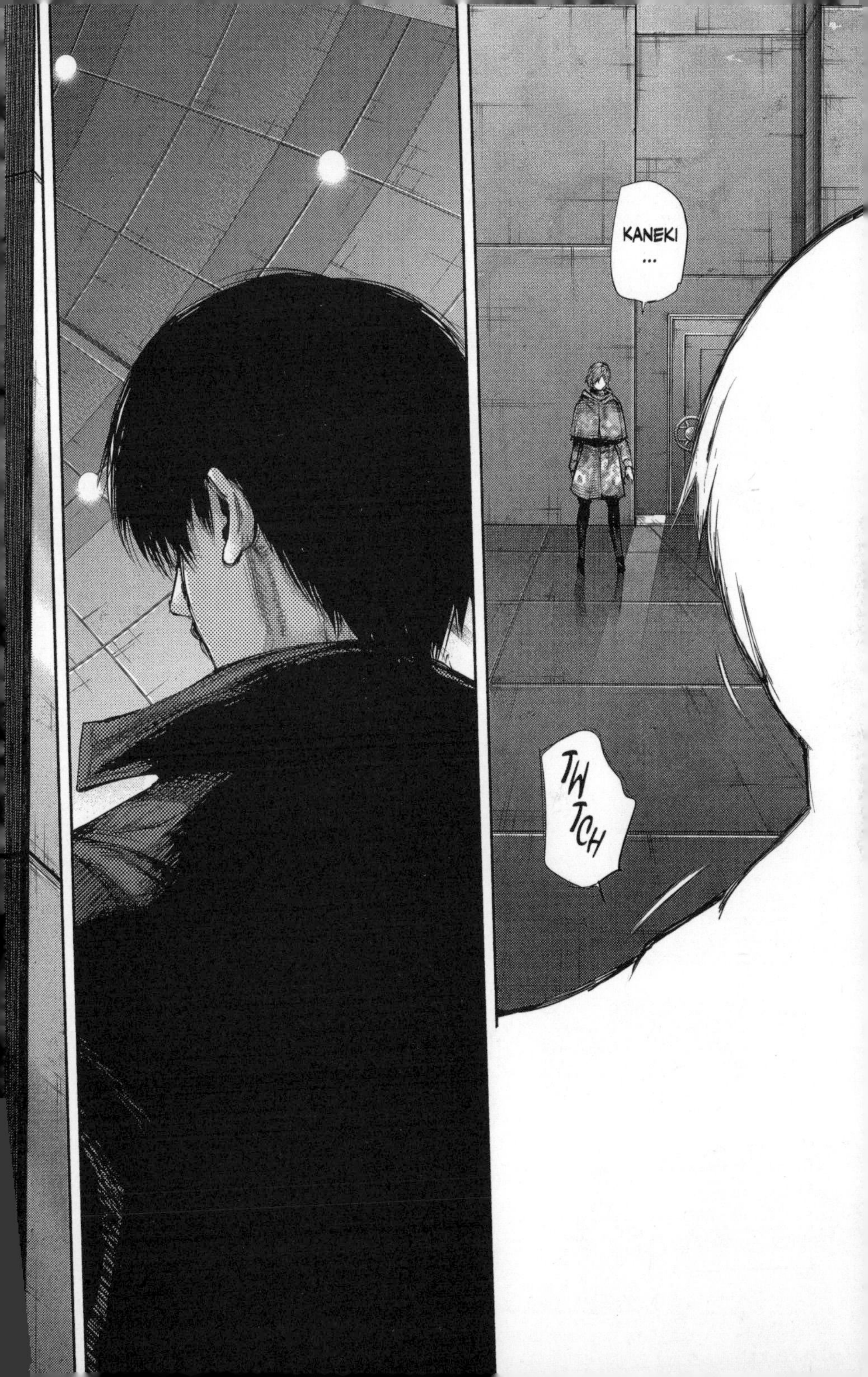
KANEKI ...
TWITCH

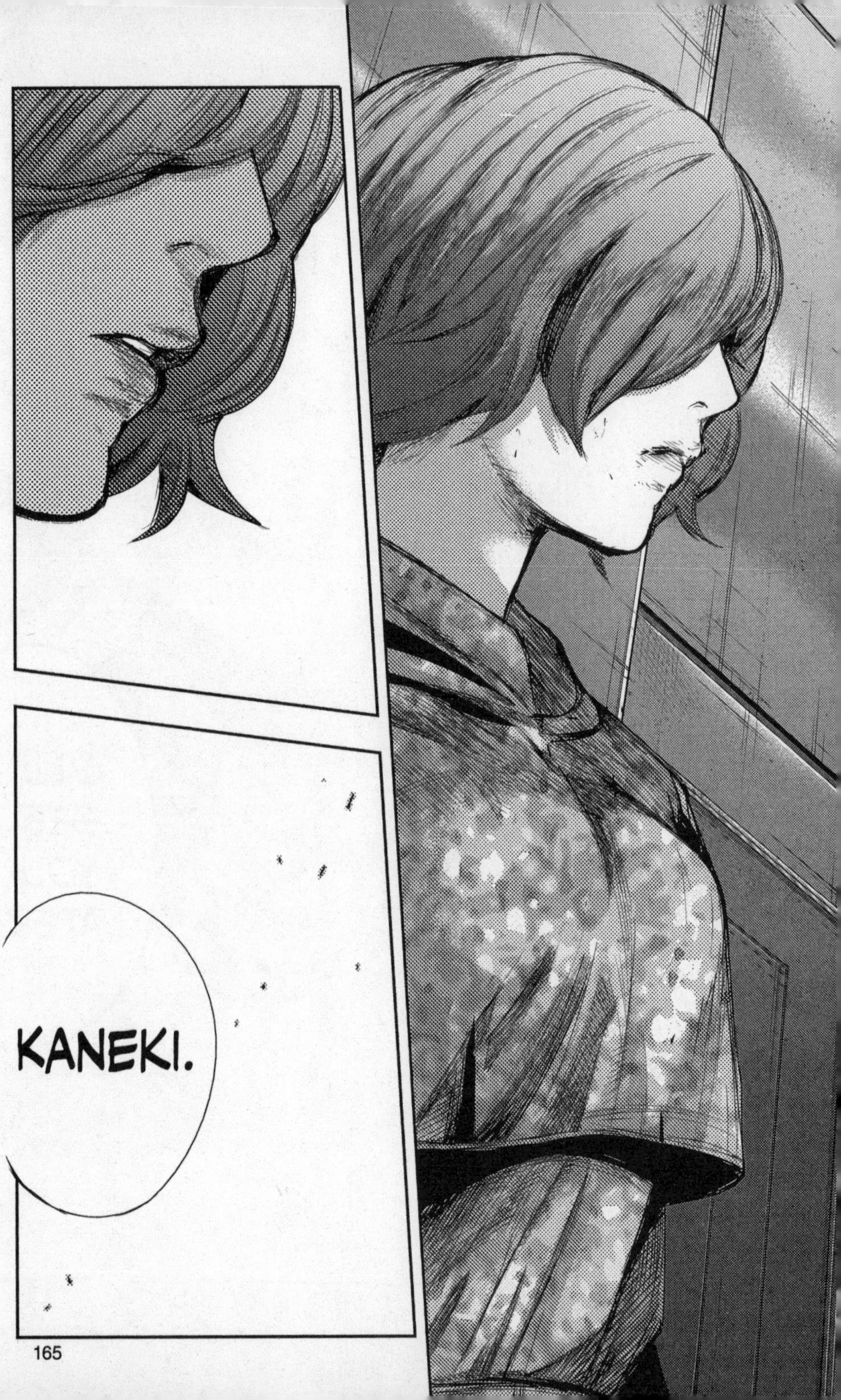
KANEKI.

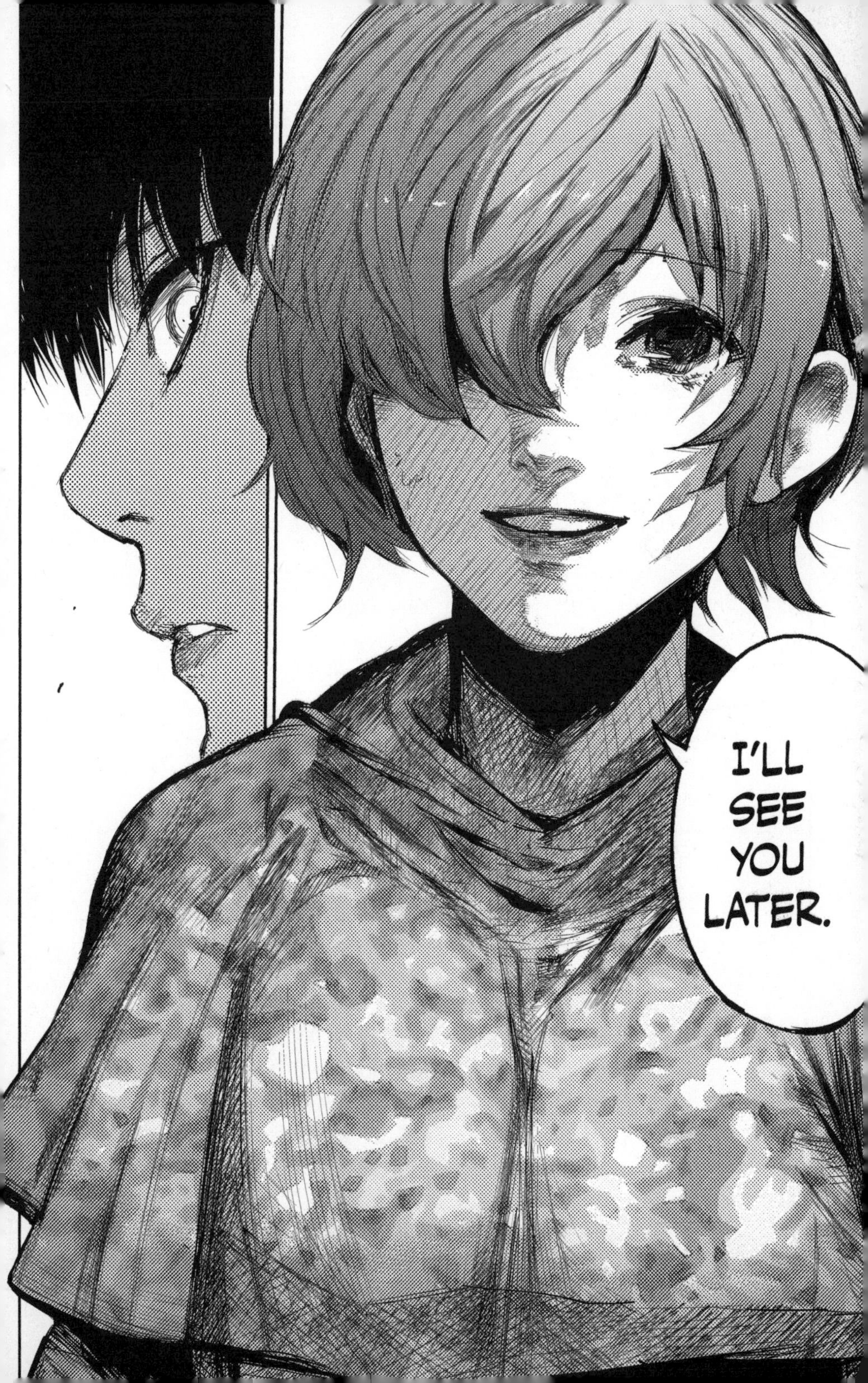
I'LL SEE YOU LATER.

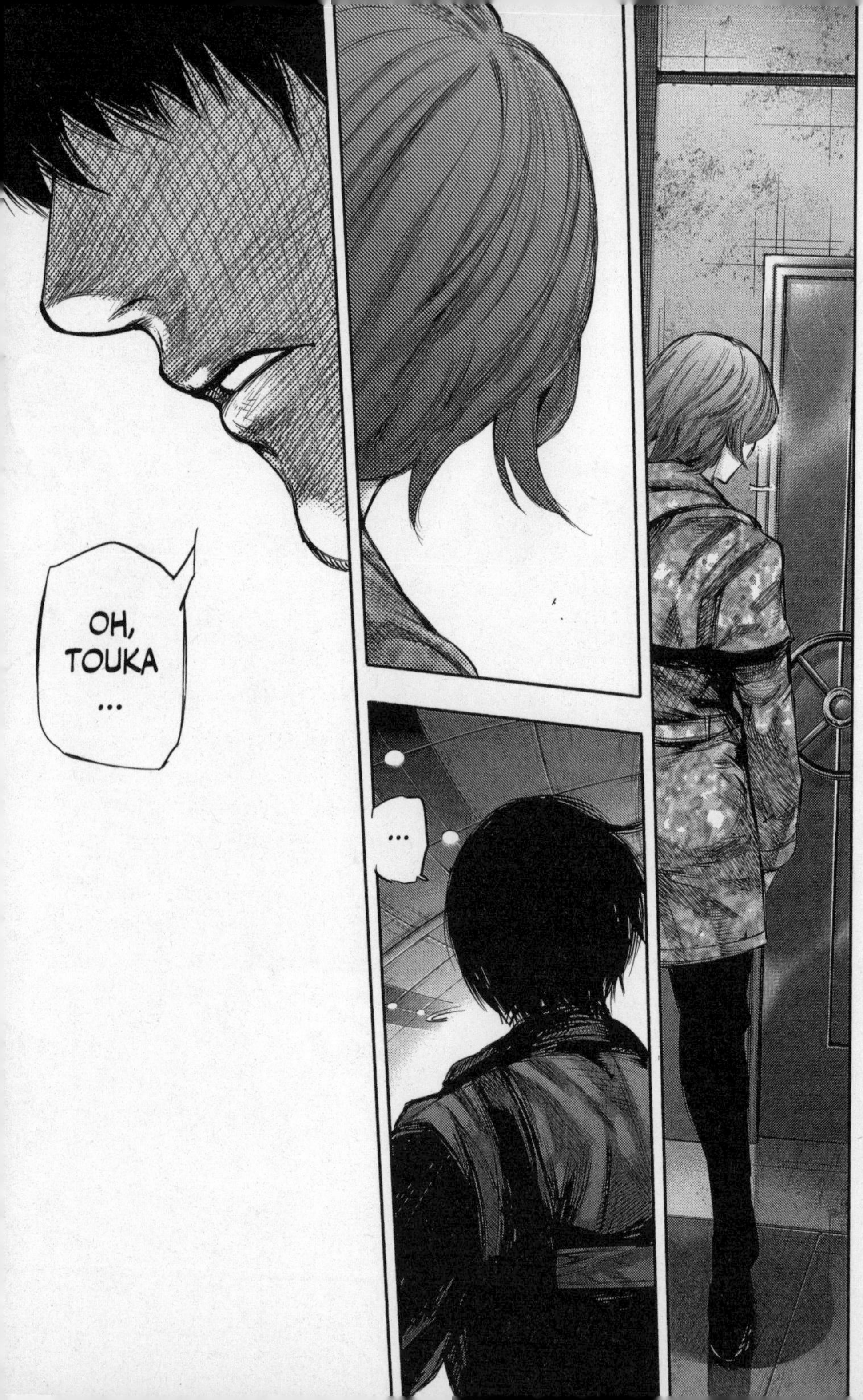
...
OH, TOUKA ...

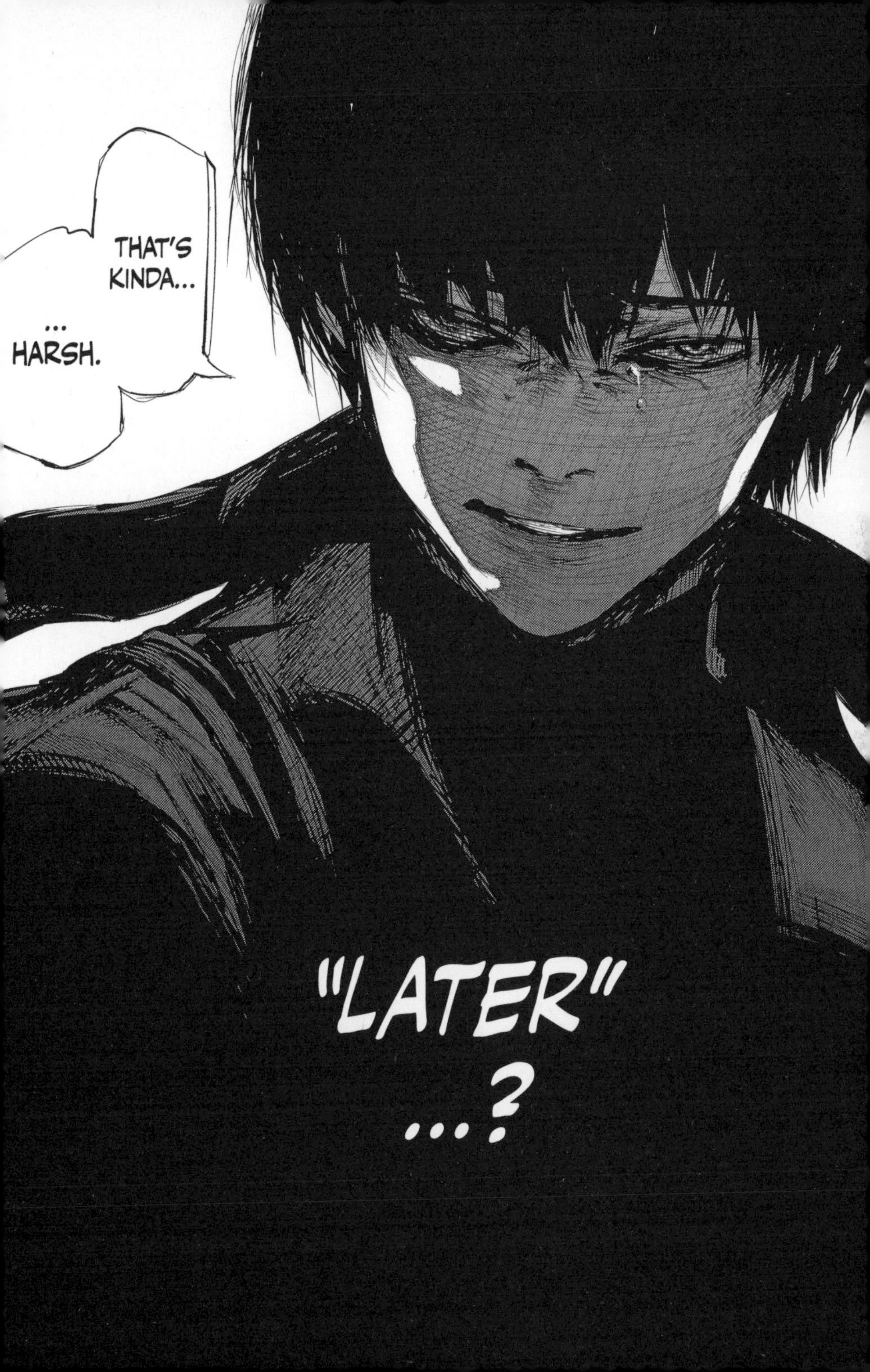
THAT'S KINDA... ... HARSH.
"LATER" ...?

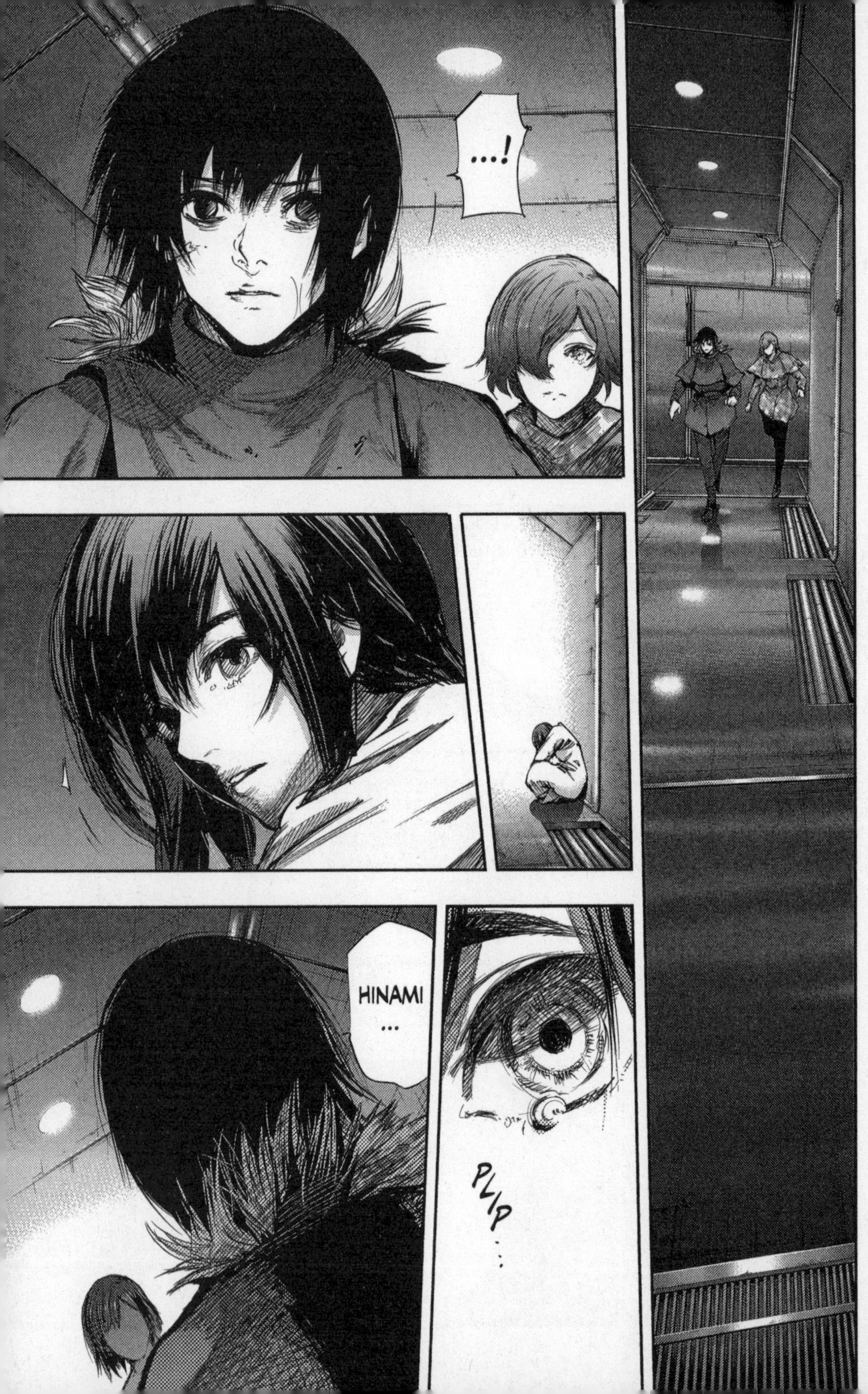
...!
HINAMI ...
PLIP ...

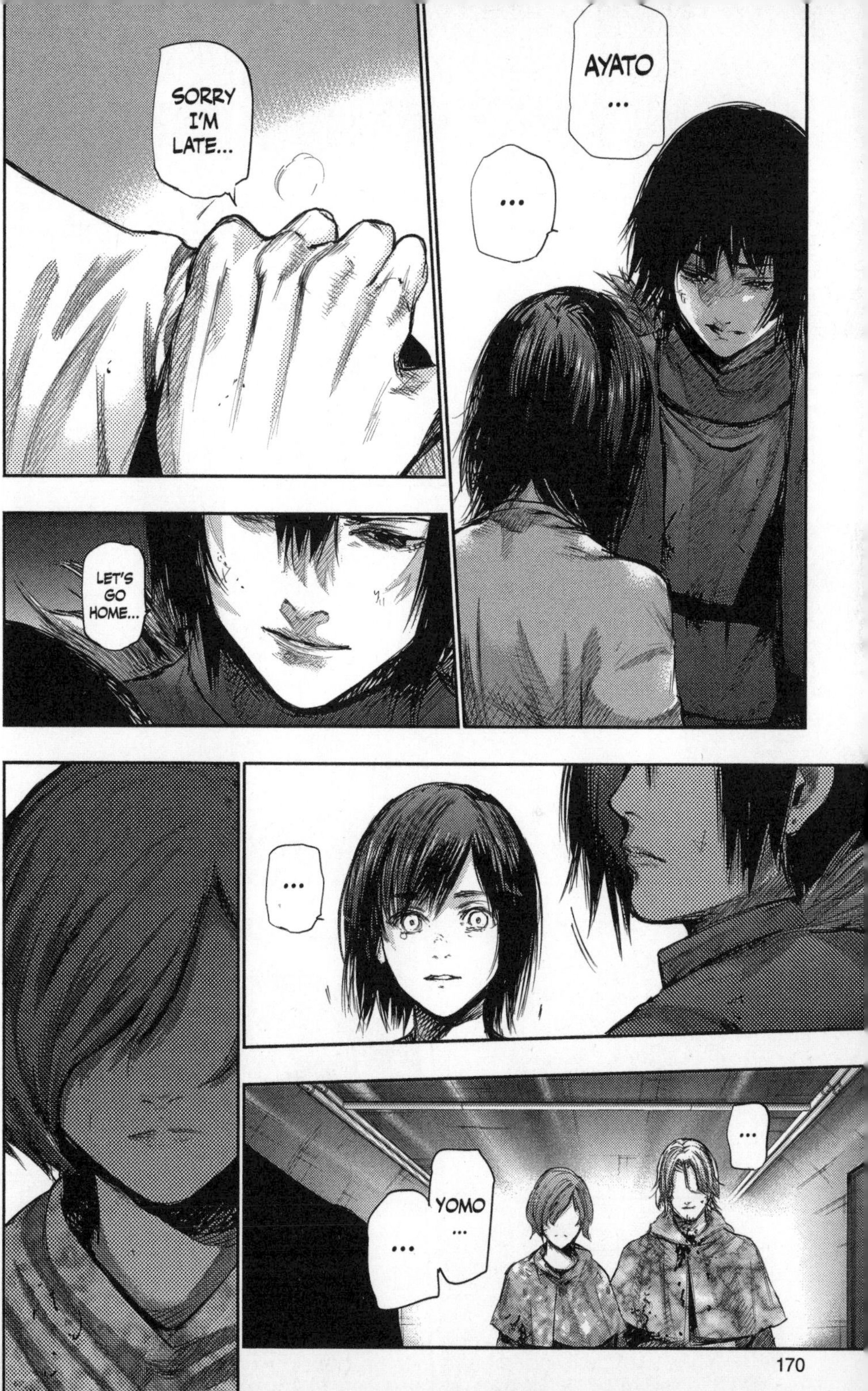
AYATO ...
...
SORRY I'M LATE...
LET'S GO HOME...
...
...
YOMO ...
...

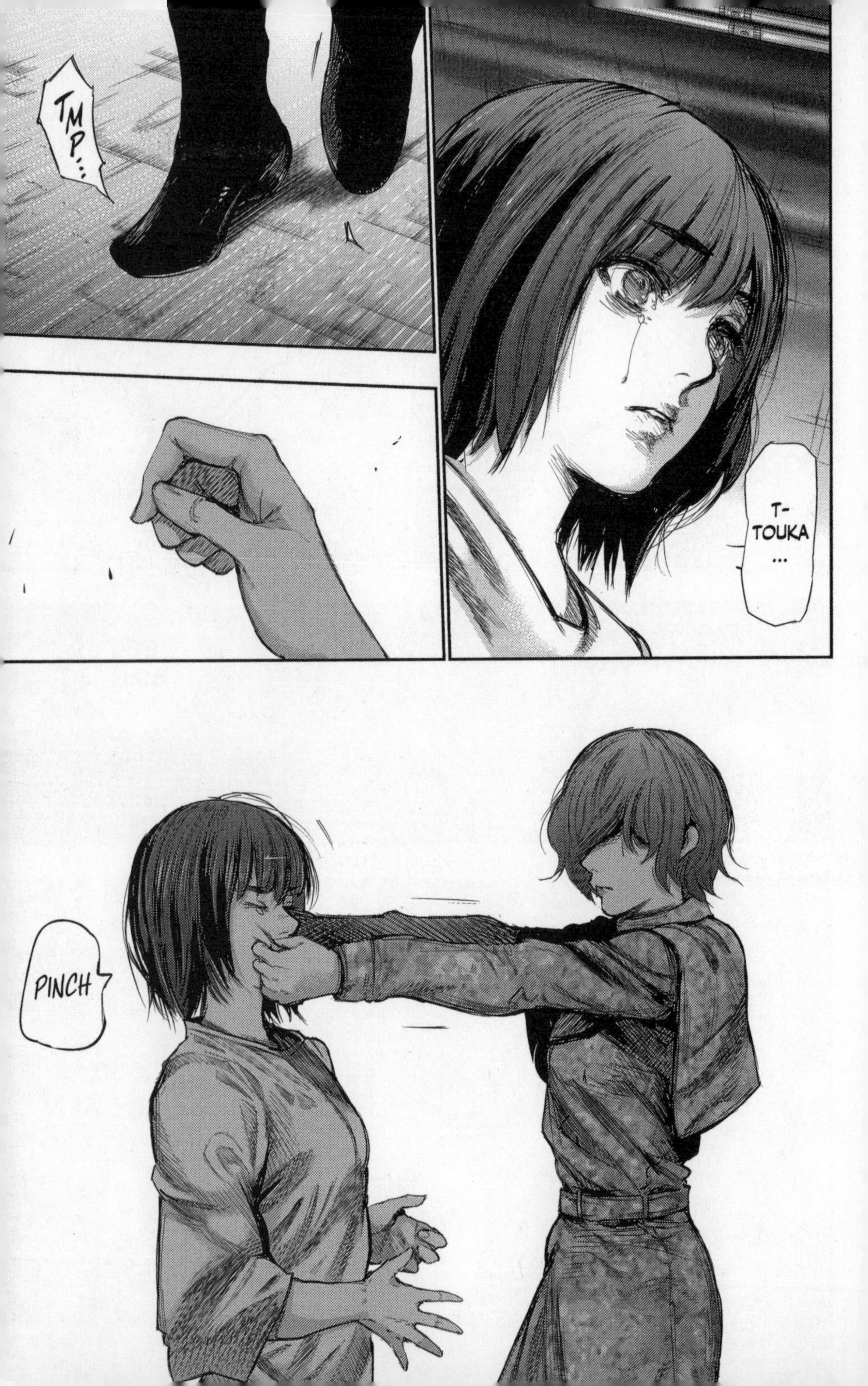
T-TOUKA...
TMP...
PINCH

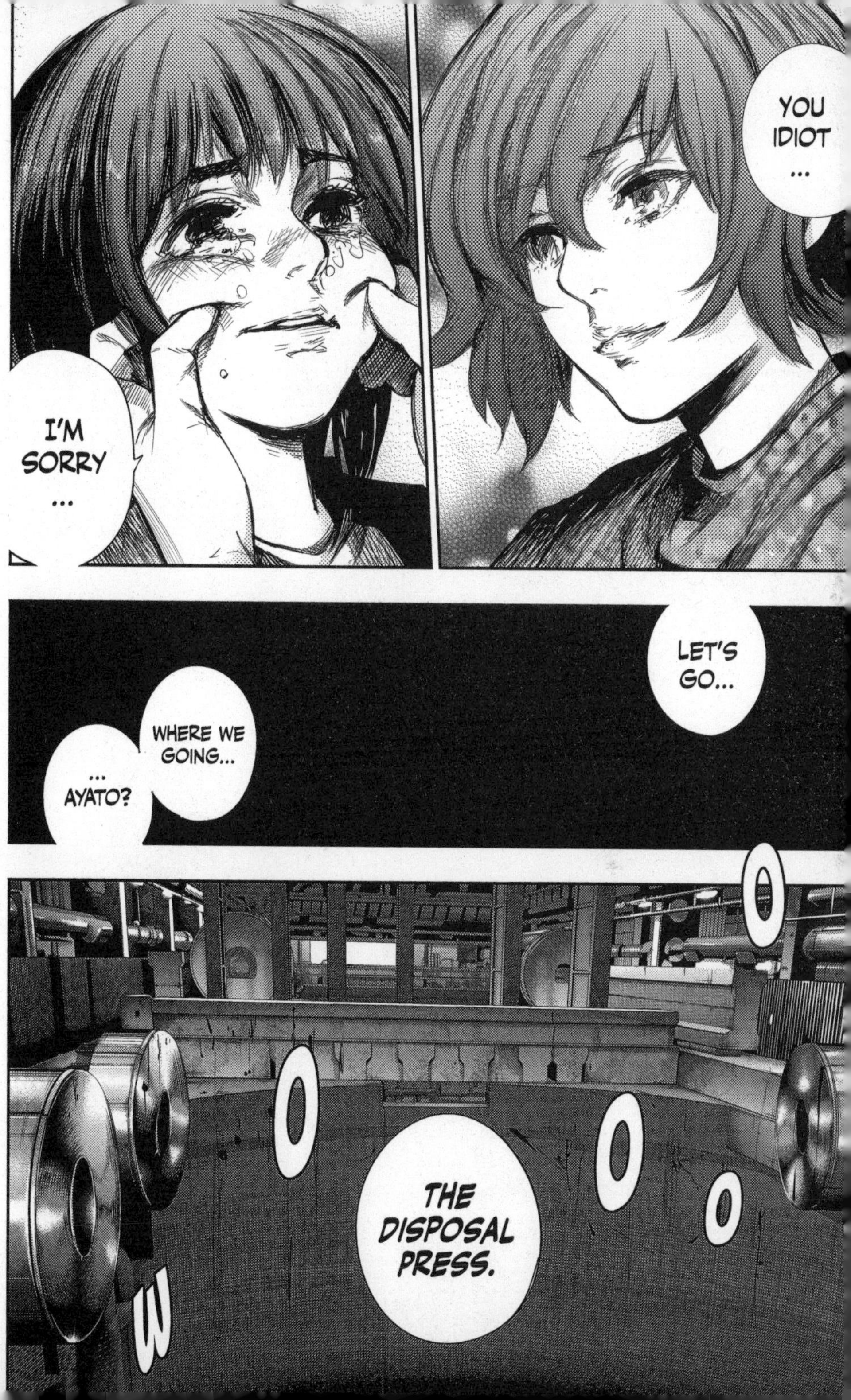
YOU IDIOT ...
I'M SORRY ...
LET'S GO...
WHERE WE GOING...
... AYATO?
THE DISPOSAL PRESS.

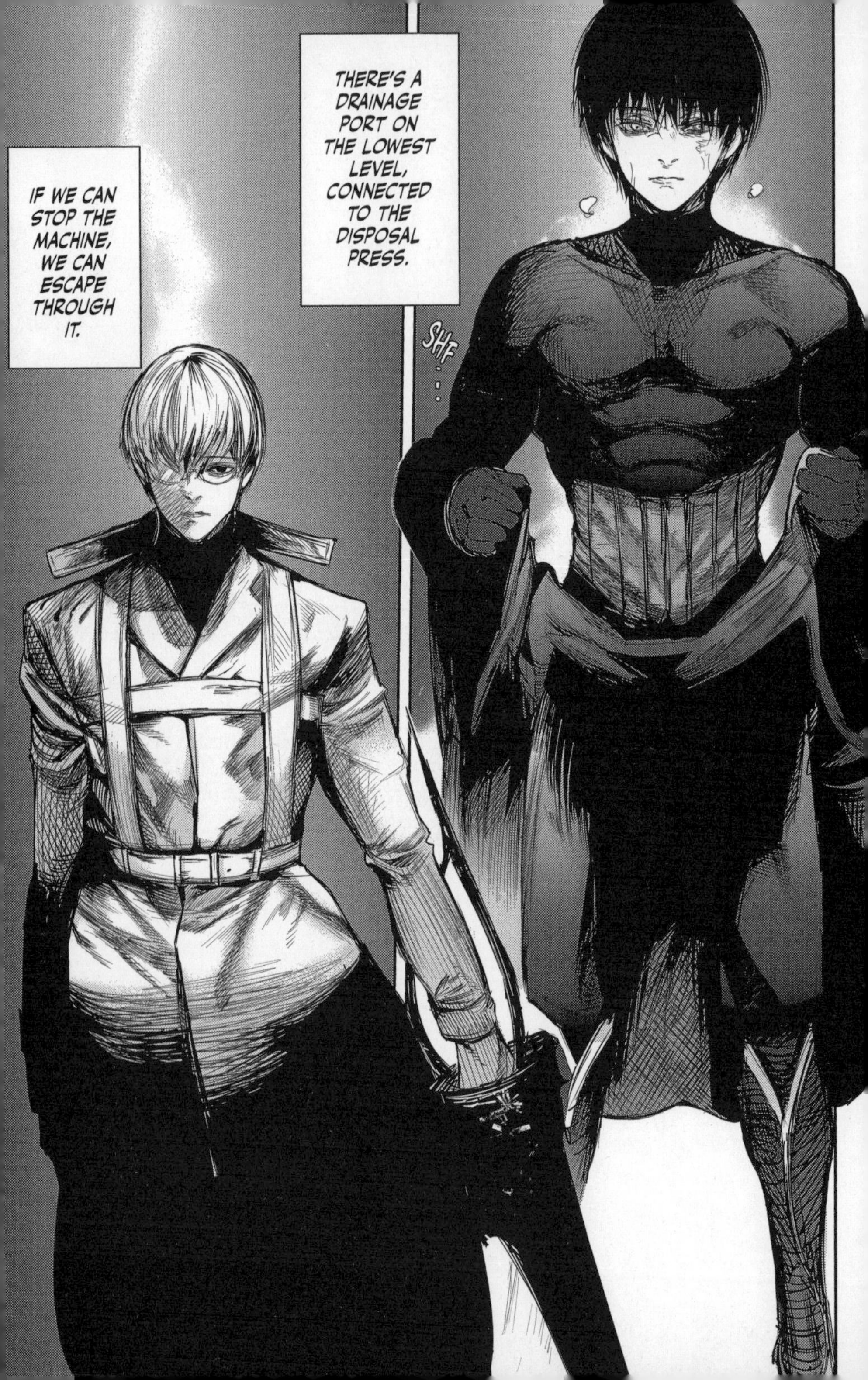
THERE'S A DRAINAGE PORT ON THE LOWEST LEVEL, CONNECTED TO THE DISPOSAL PRESS.
SHF
IF WE CAN STOP THE MACHINE, WE CAN ESCAPE THROUGH IT.

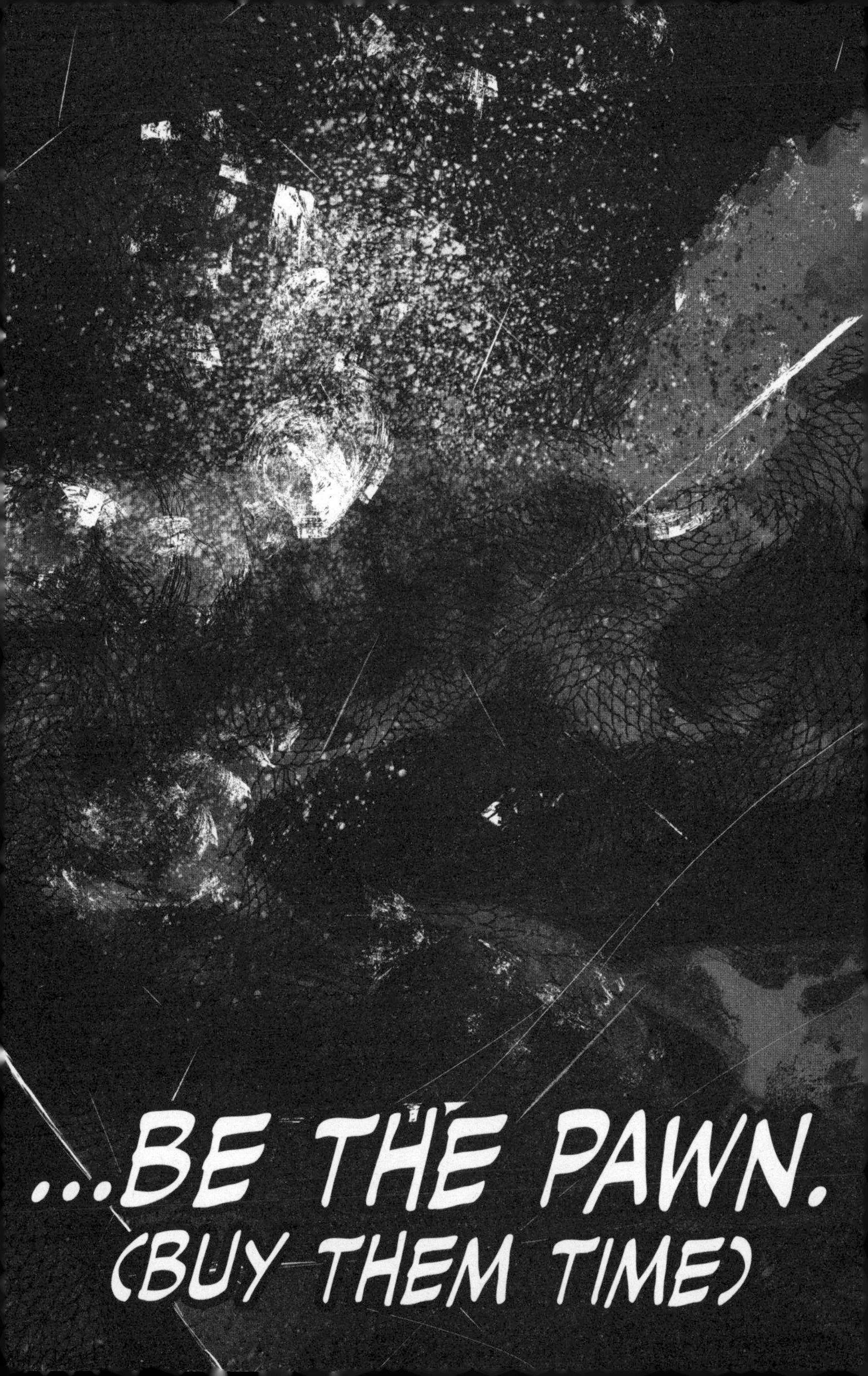
...BE THE PAWN.
(BUY THEM TIME)

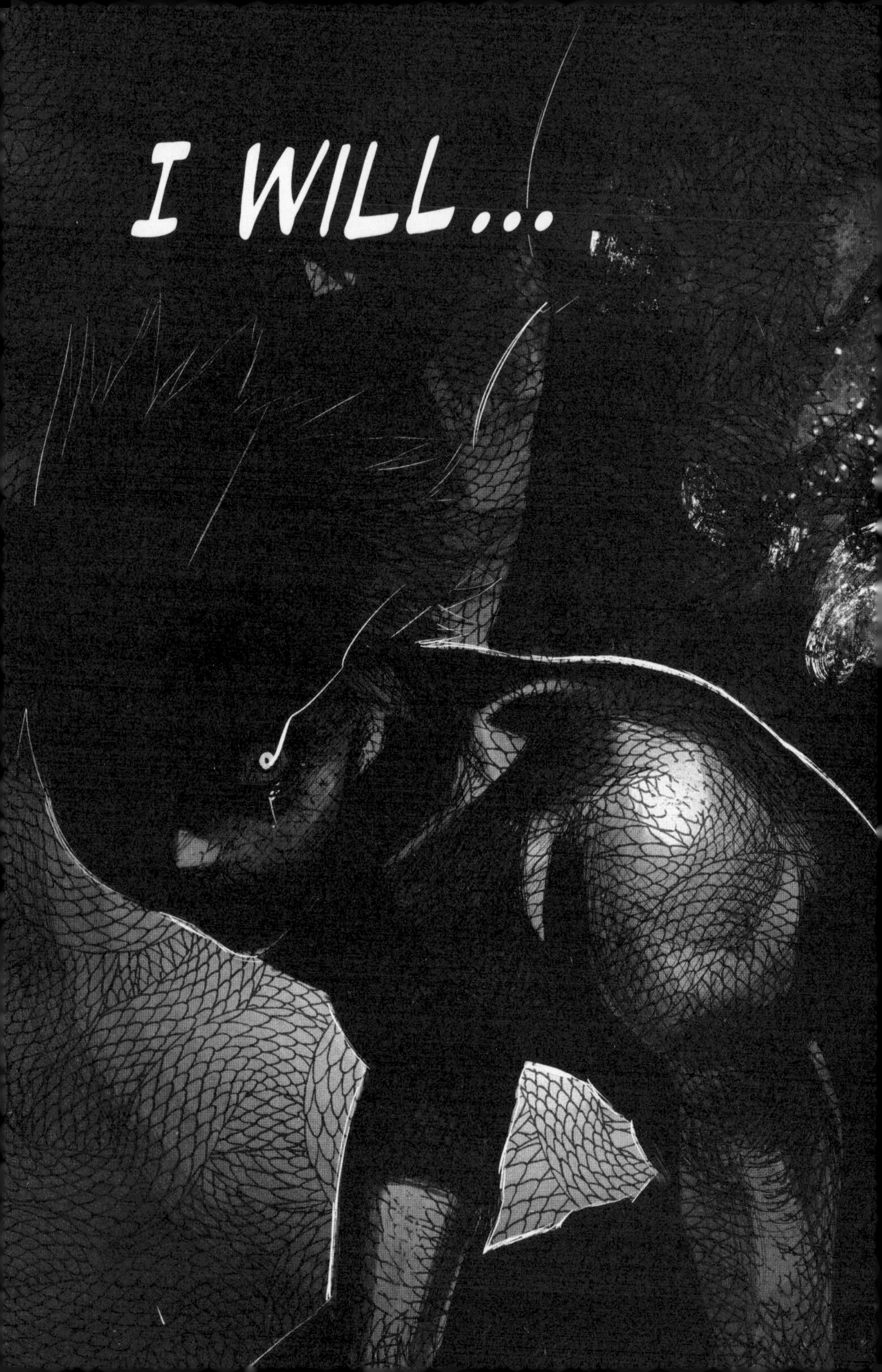
I WILL...

S: THERE'S NOTHING TO DO. URI'S NOT HERE EITHER.

S: YO, YOU GUYS.

A: HUH...?
T: WHAT CAN WE DO FOR YOU, MA'AM?

S: PLAY A GAME TO KILL TIME.
A: OKAY...
T: I KNOW! WORD CHAIN, RIGHT?!

S: NO, THE "SAY NICE THINGS ABOUT SAIKO GAME!"
A: SAY NICE THINGS...?
T: INTERESTING... LET'S PLAY!

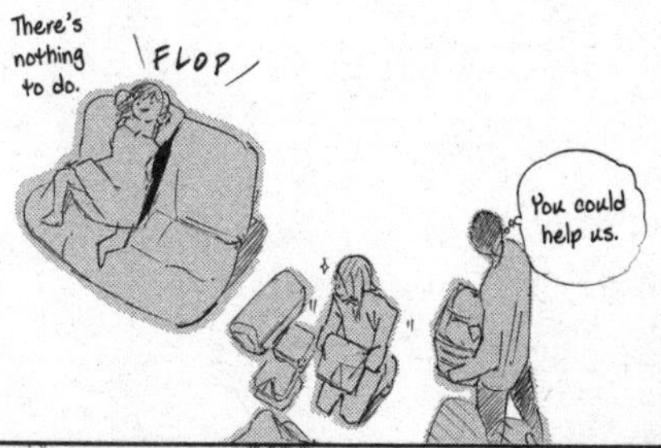
There's nothing to do.
FLOP
You could help us.

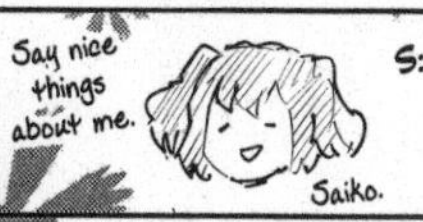
Say nice things about me.
Saiko.

S: THE RULES OF SAY NICE THINGS ABOUT SAIKO ARE SIMPLE.
1. TAKE TURNS SAYING NICE THINGS ABOUT THE MASTER. WHOEVER HESITATES, LOSES.
2. IF SAIKO (MASTER) BLUSHES, THE MASTER LOSES.

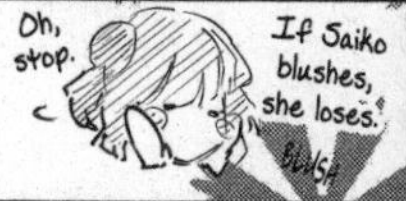
Oh, stop.
If Saiko blushes, she loses.
BLUSH

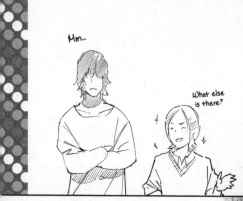

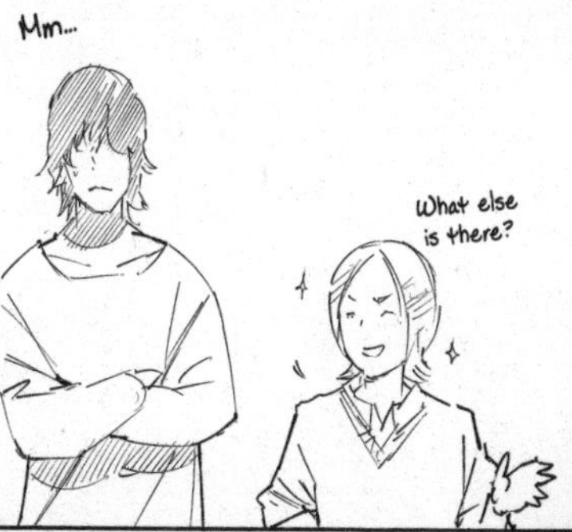
Mm...
What else is there?

A: SHOULD I START...? UM, ***"ACTUALLY QUITE CARING."***
S: YUP.
T: ***STRONG!***

A: MM... ***"SHE'S THE LIFE OF THE PARTY."***
T: ***"IS A CALMING INFLUENCE!"***
S: FOR SURE, FOR SURE.

A: ***"SOMETIMES COOKS."*** (NO COMMENT ON THE TASTE.)
T: ***HAS A SEXY BODY!***
S: OH, YOU PERV!!

A: UM... ***"SHE'S SMALL SO DOESN'T TAKE UP MUCH SPACE."***
S: MM...? OK.
T: ***"HER BEAUTY!"***
S: NICE ONE, HIGE!!

A: MM... ***"DOESN'T MIND IF THE ROOM IS DIRTY."***
S: MM...?
T: ***"LOVABLE LIKE A MASCOT!"***
S: YUP, YUP. THAT'S WHAT I WANNA HEAR.

A: UM... "GOOD AT VIDEO GAMES."
S: YEAH, I GUESS... THAT'S PRETTY OBVIOUS.
T: "CAN EAT NONSTOP!"
S: ...

A: "HAS LOTS OF STRANGE DOLLS..." MAYBE?
T: "CAN SLEEP FOREVER!"
A: "SLOW RUNNER."NO, THAT'S NOT IT. UM...
T: "SHE'S CELIBATE!!"
A: UH... UM...

S: **WHAT THE HELL, GUYS?!!!**

A/T: **EEEK...!!**

S: **C'MON! SAY NICE THINGS ABOUT ME!!!**

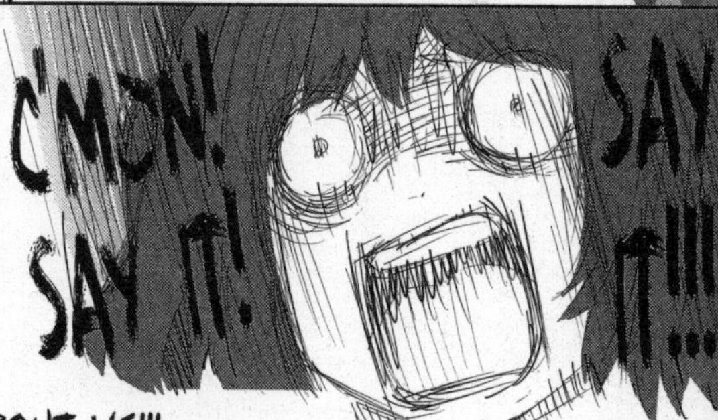
SAY IT!!!
C'MON! SAY IT!

U: WHAT ARE YOU DOING, YONEBAYASHI? (I HEARD YOU FROM OUTSIDE.)
S: YOU SEE, URIBO... THESE GUYS WON'T SAY NICE THINGS ABOUT ME.
U: OKAY...?

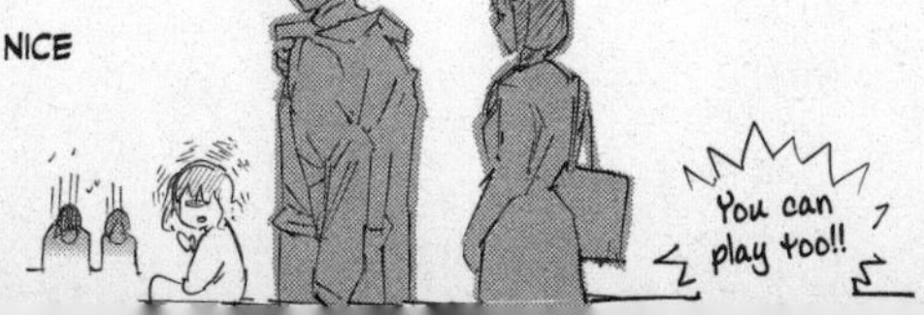
You can play too!!

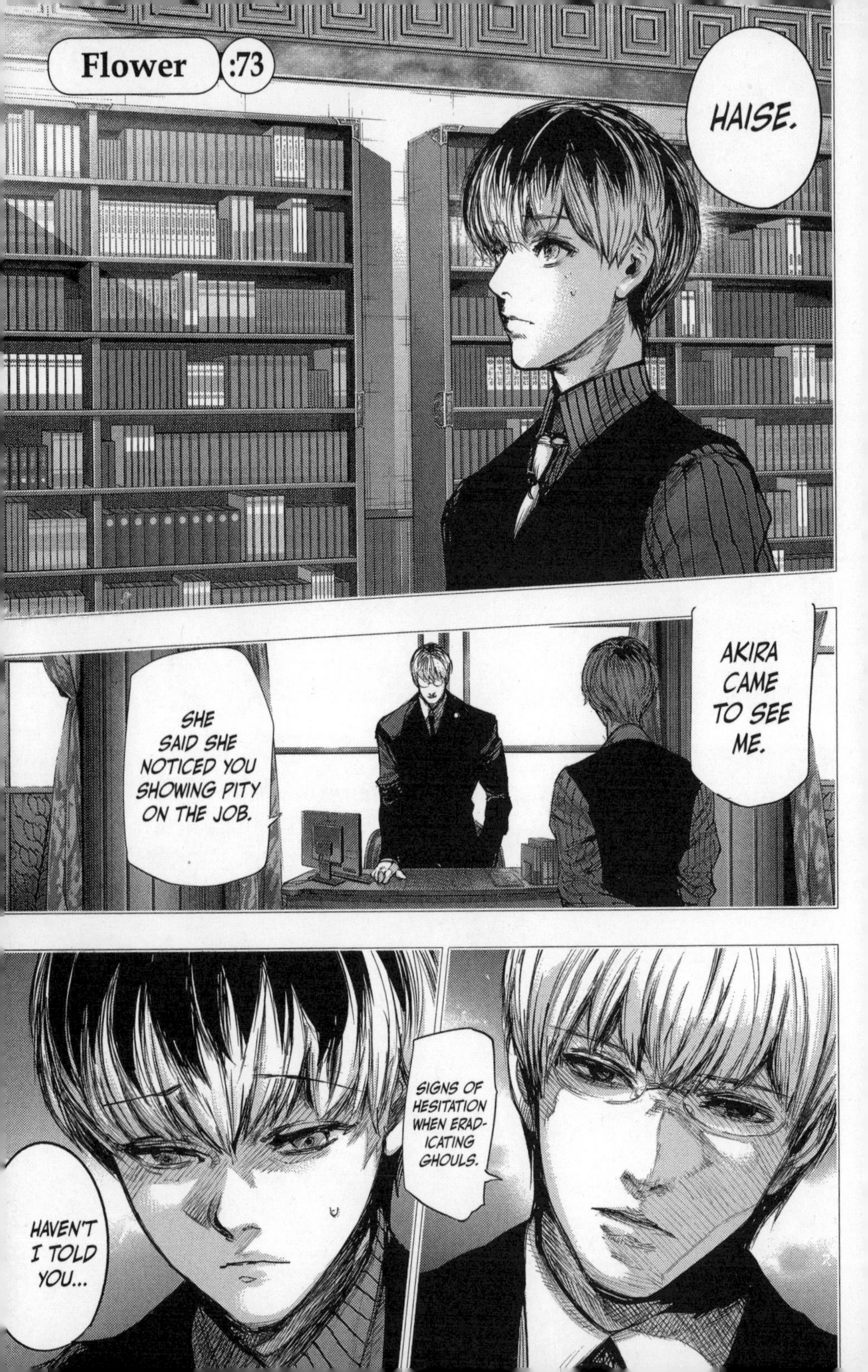
Flower :73
HAISE.
AKIRA CAME TO SEE ME.
SHE SAID SHE NOTICED YOU SHOWING PITY ON THE JOB.
SIGNS OF HESITATION WHEN ERAD-ICATING GHOULS.
HAVEN'T I TOLD YOU...

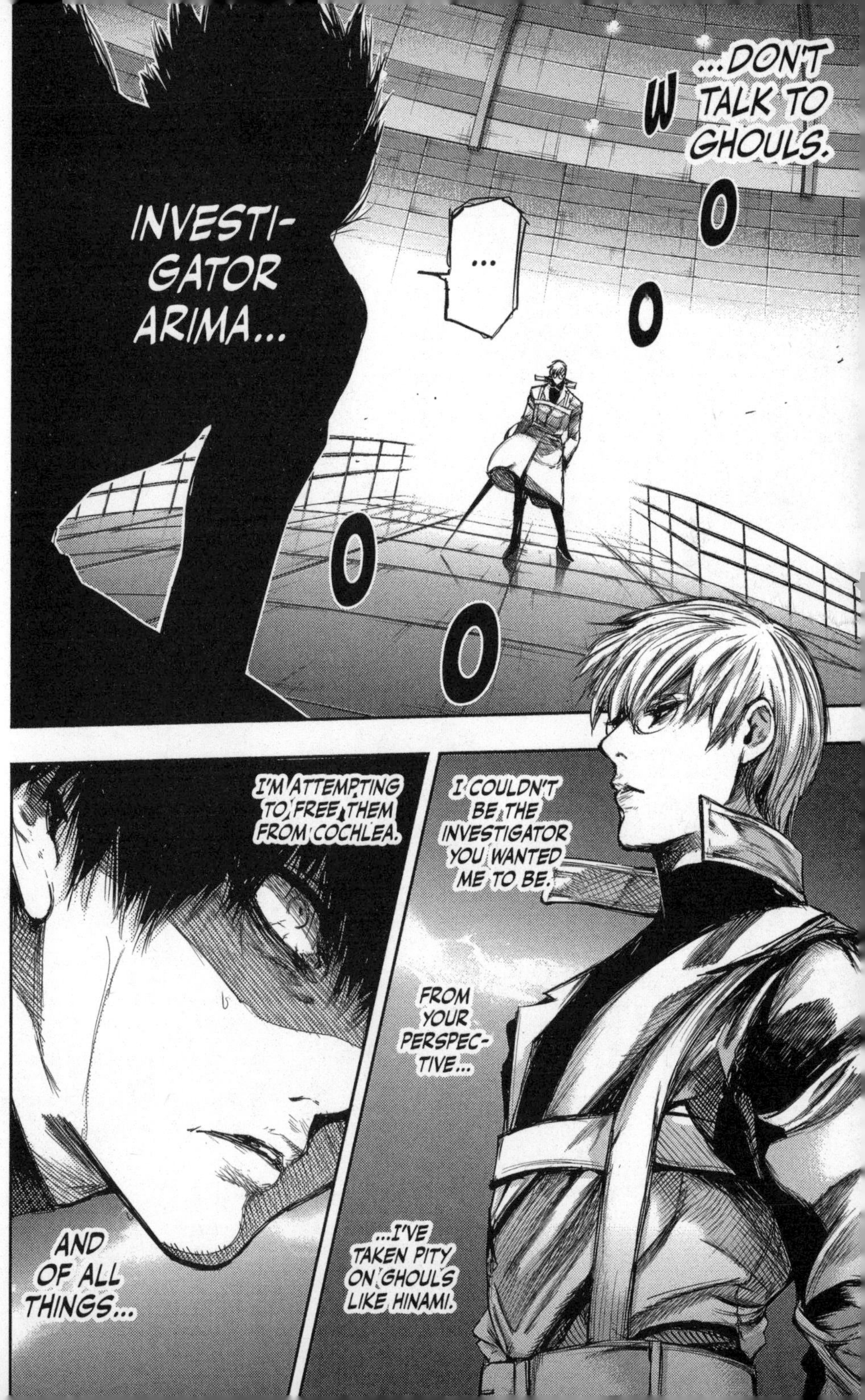
...DON'T TALK TO GHOULS.
WOOOO
...
INVESTI-GATOR ARIMA...
I COULDN'T BE THE INVESTIGATOR YOU WANTED ME TO BE.
FROM YOUR PERSPEC-TIVE...
...I'VE TAKEN PITY ON GHOULS LIKE HINAMI.
I'M ATTEMPTING TO FREE THEM FROM COCHLEA.
AND OF ALL THINGS...

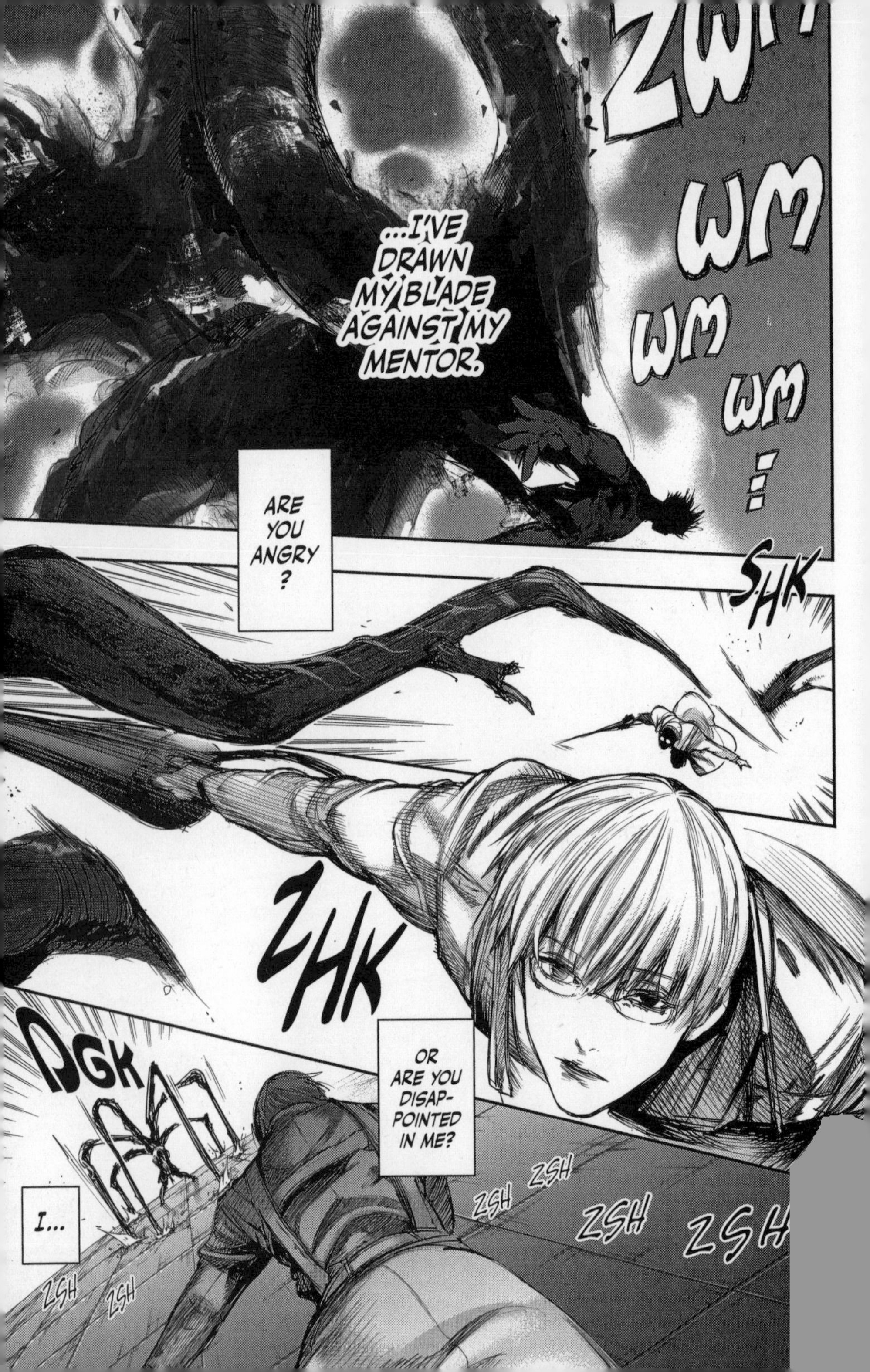
ZWM
WM
WM
WM
...I'VE DRAWN MY BLADE AGAINST MY MENTOR.
ARE YOU ANGRY?
SHK
ZHK
OR ARE YOU DISAP-POINTED IN ME?
ZSH ZSH ZSH ZSH
AGK
I...
ZSH ZSH

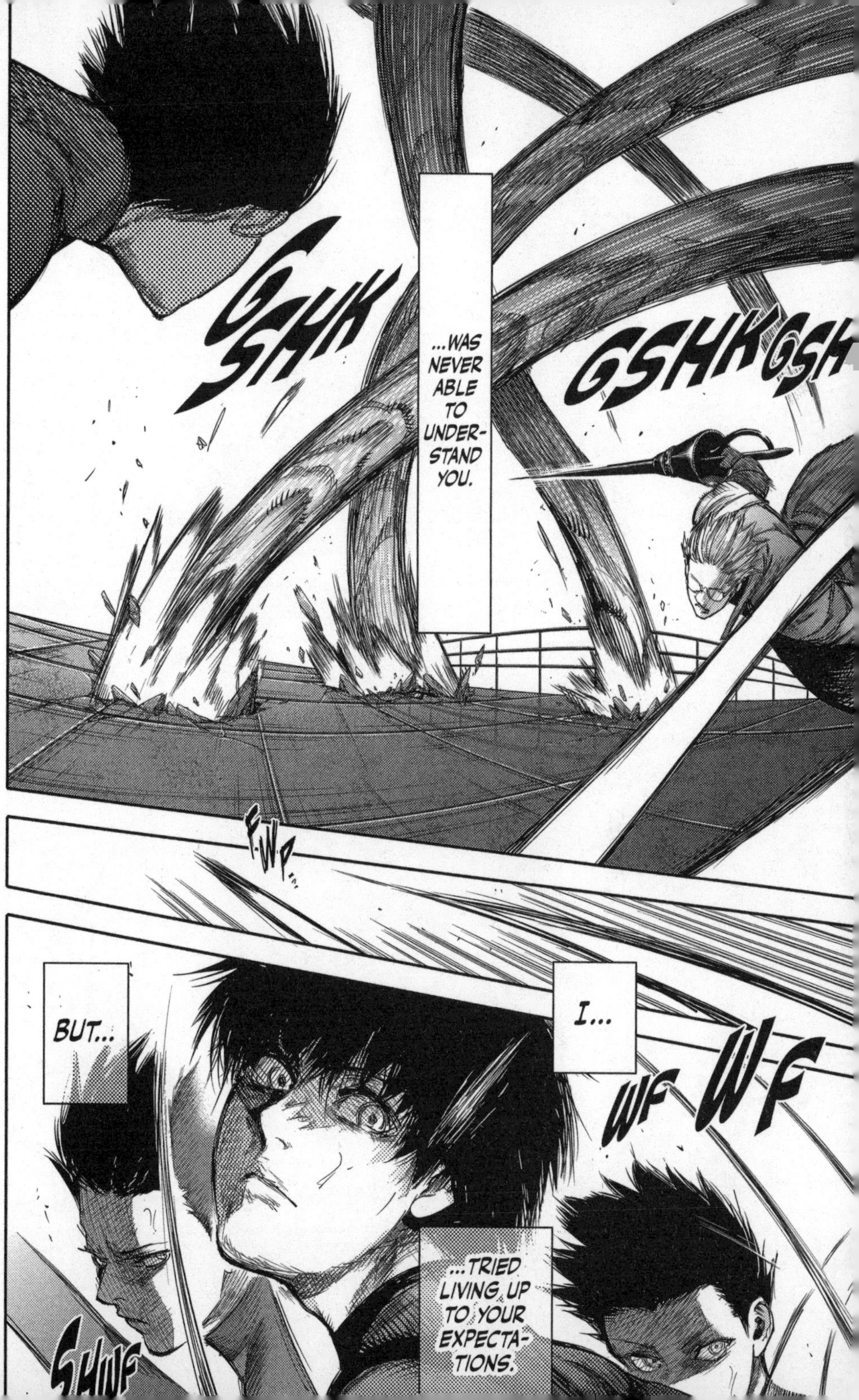
GSHKGSH
...WAS NEVER ABLE TO UNDER-STAND YOU.
GSHK
FWP...
I...
WF WF
BUT...
...TRIED LIVING UP TO YOUR EXPECTA-TIONS.

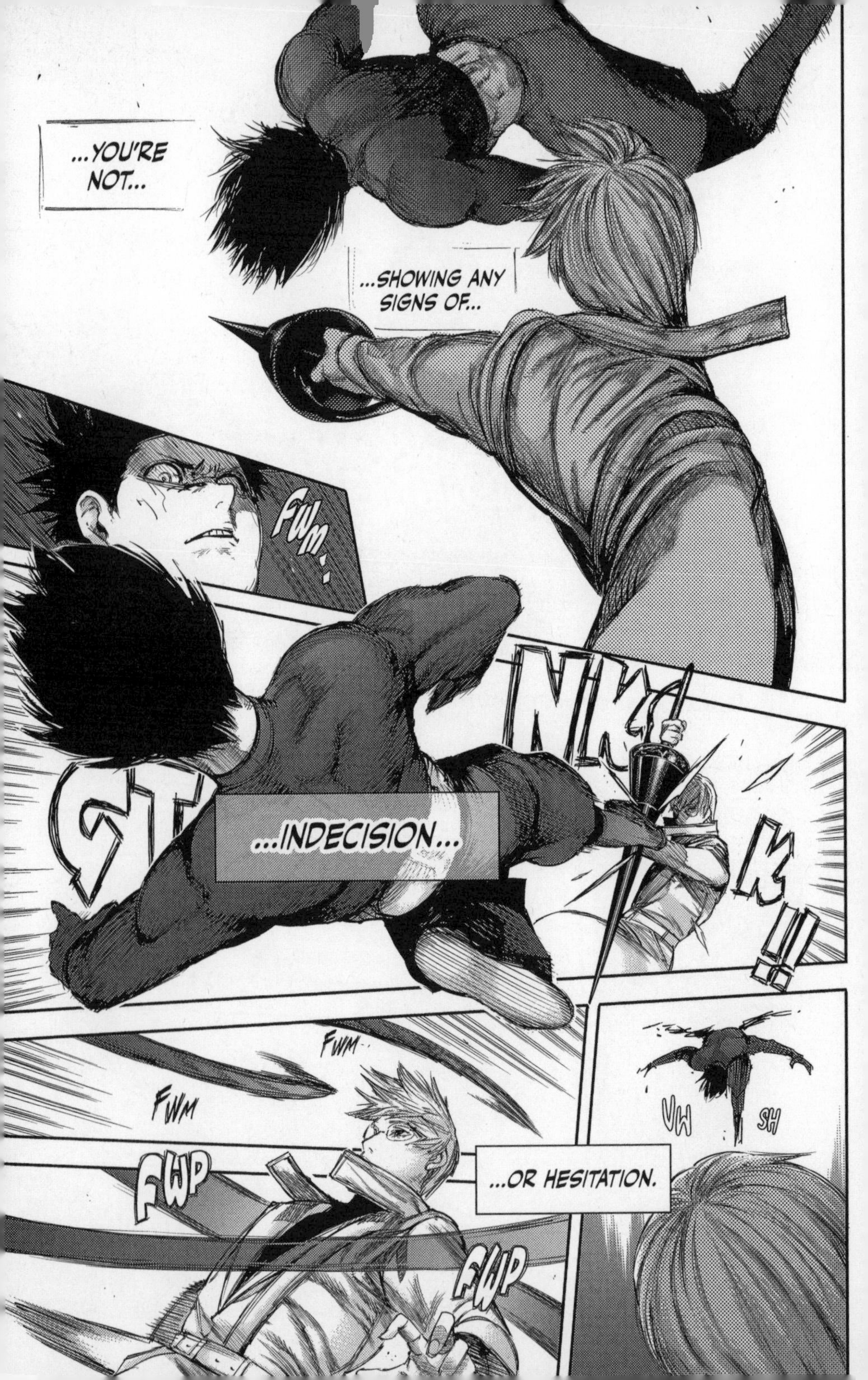
...YOU'RE NOT...
...SHOWING ANY SIGNS OF...
FWM..
NK
K!!
GT
...INDECISION...
VW SH
FWM
FWM
FWP
FWP
...OR HESITATION.

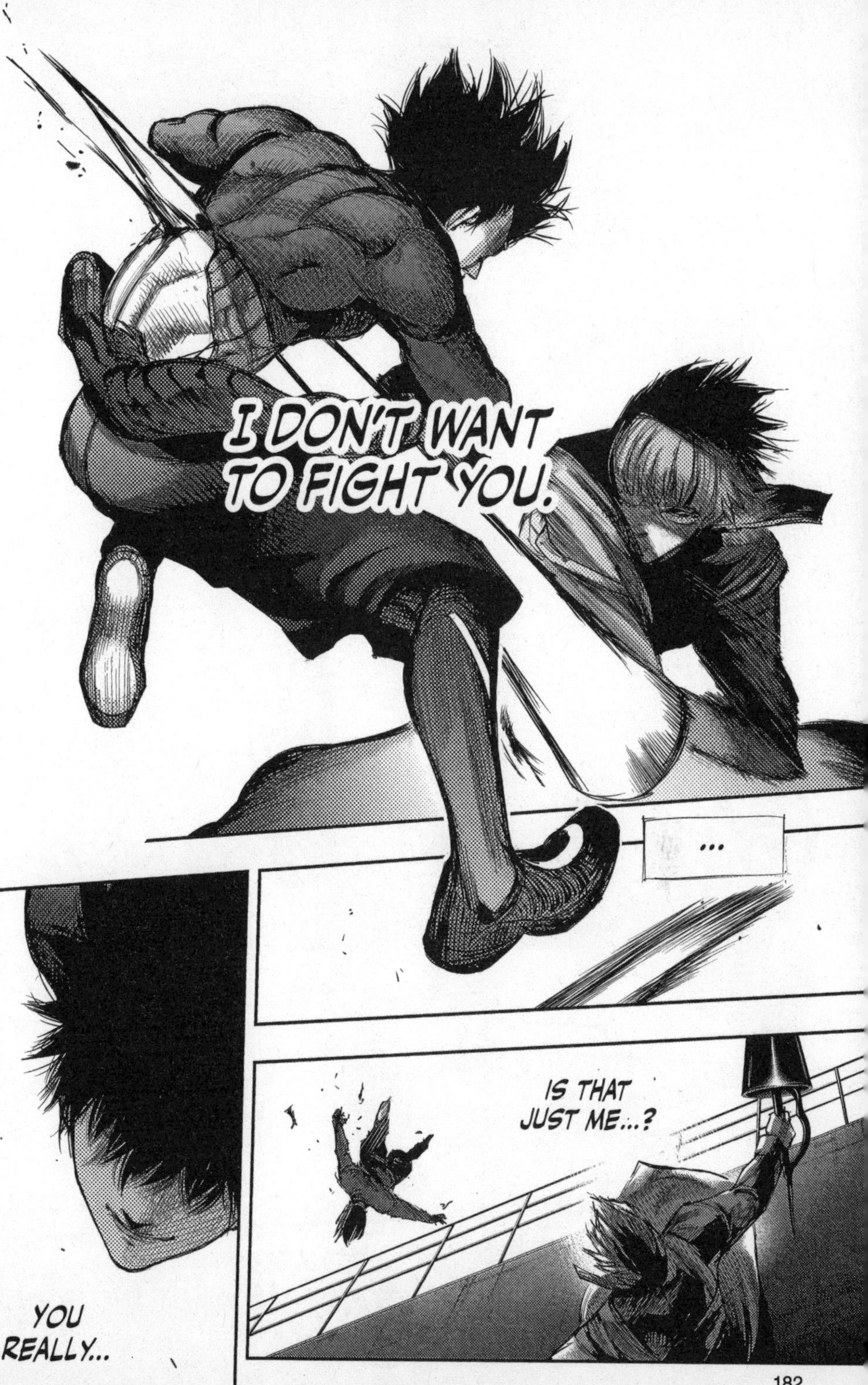
I DON'T WANT TO FIGHT YOU.
...
IS THAT JUST ME...?
YOU REALLY...

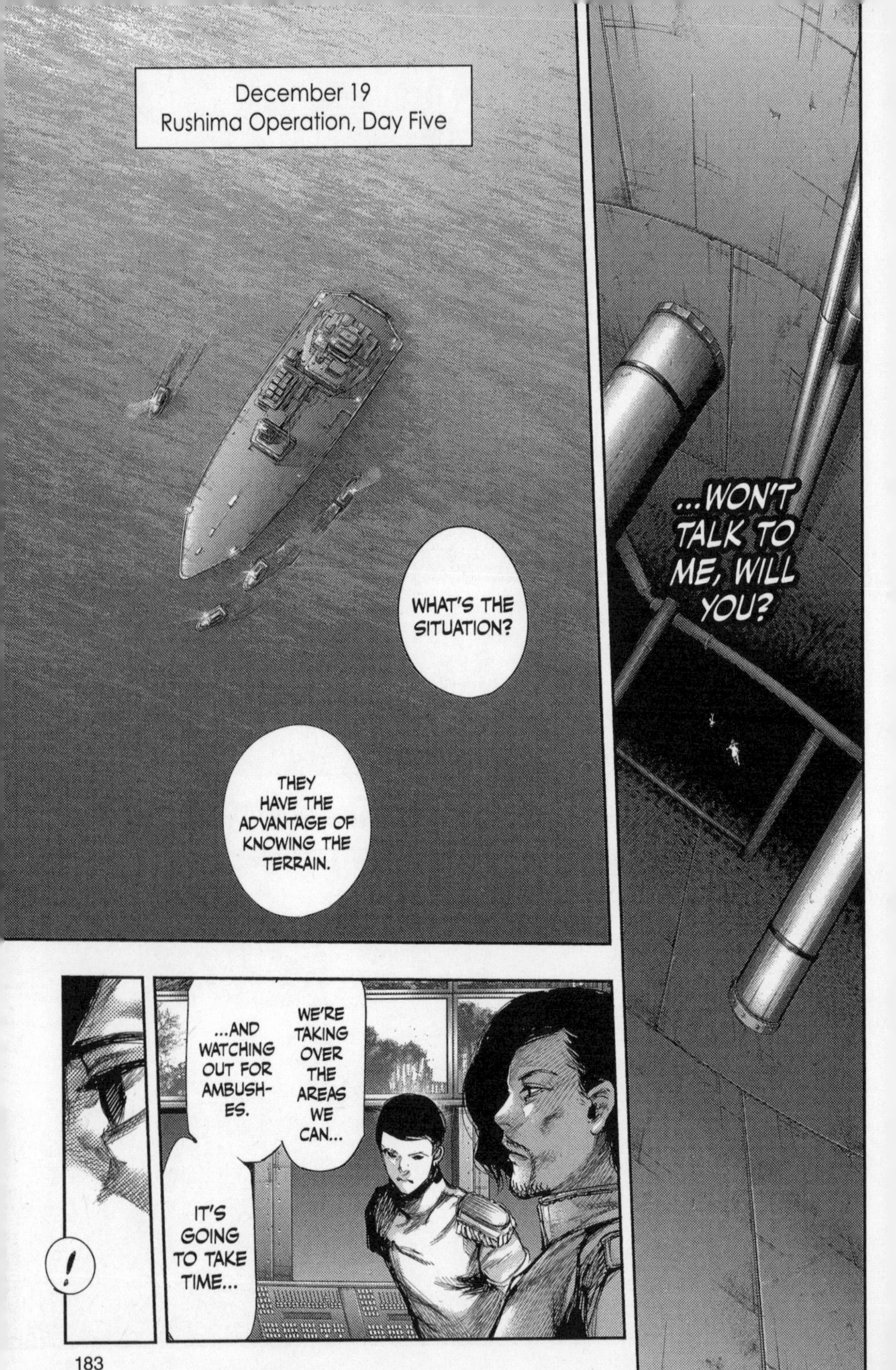
...WON'T TALK TO ME, WILL YOU?
December 19
Rushima Operation, Day Five
WHAT'S THE SITUATION?
THEY HAVE THE ADVANTAGE OF KNOWING THE TERRAIN.
WE'RE TAKING OVER THE AREAS WE CAN...
...AND WATCHING OUT FOR AMBUSH-ES.
IT'S GOING TO TAKE TIME...
!

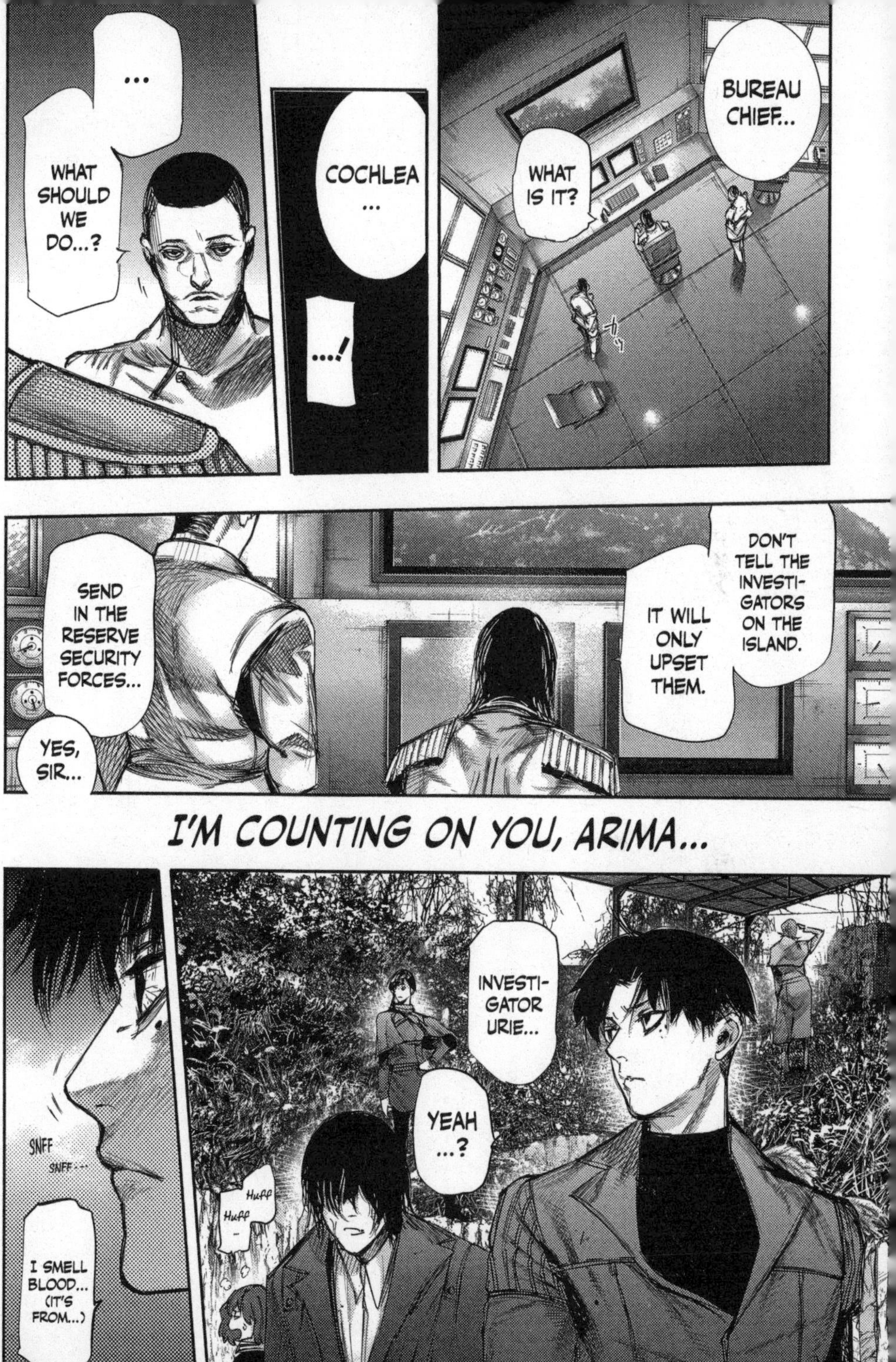
BUREAU CHIEF...
WHAT IS IT?
COCHLEA...
...!
...
WHAT SHOULD WE DO...?
DON'T TELL THE INVESTI-GATORS ON THE ISLAND.
IT WILL ONLY UPSET THEM.
SEND IN THE RESERVE SECURITY FORCES...
YES, SIR...
I'M COUNTING ON YOU, ARIMA...
INVESTI-GATOR URIE...
YEAH ...?
Huff Huff ...
SNFF SNFF...
I SMELL BLOOD... (IT'S FROM...)

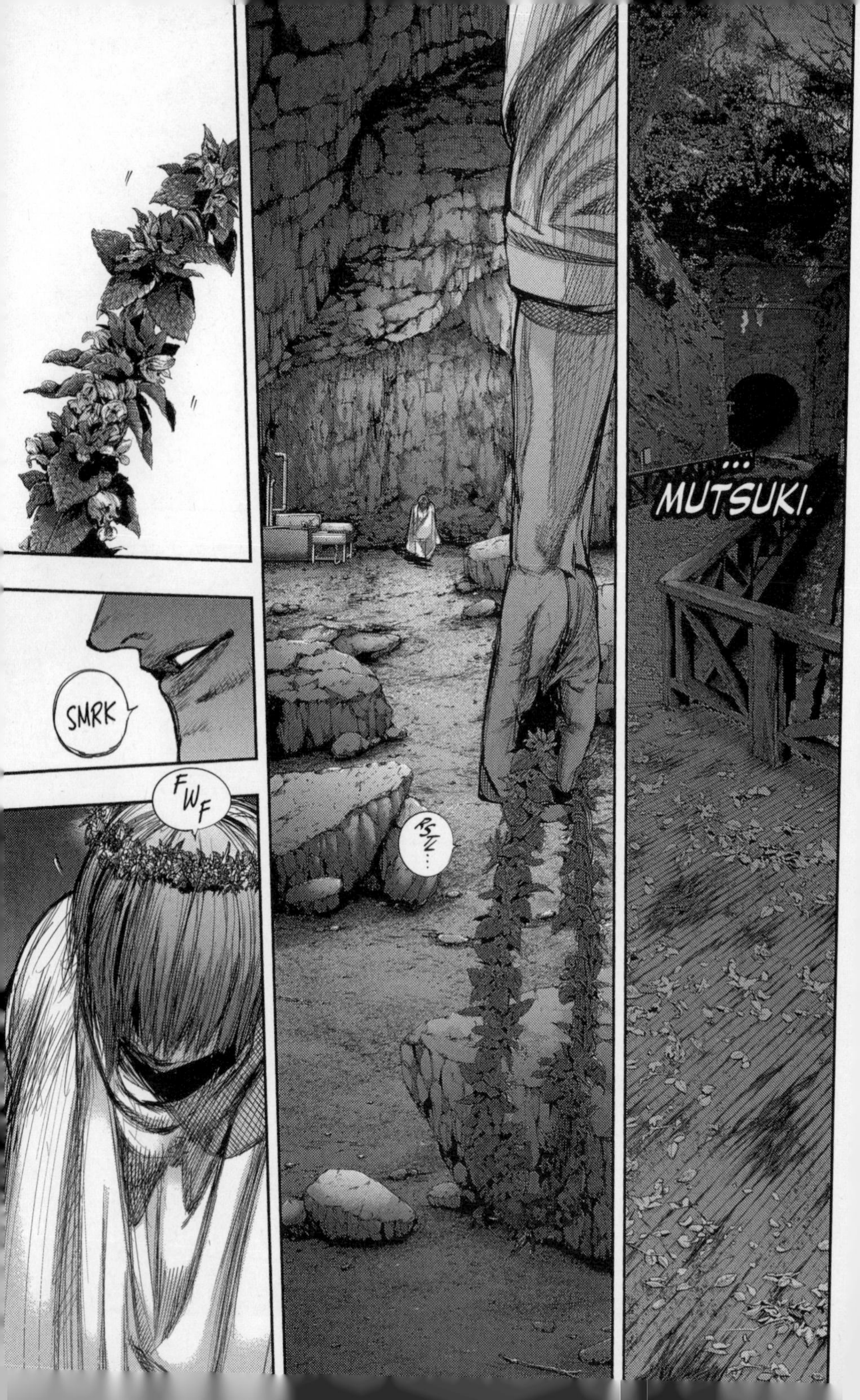
...MUTSUKI.
RSZZ...
SMRK
FWF

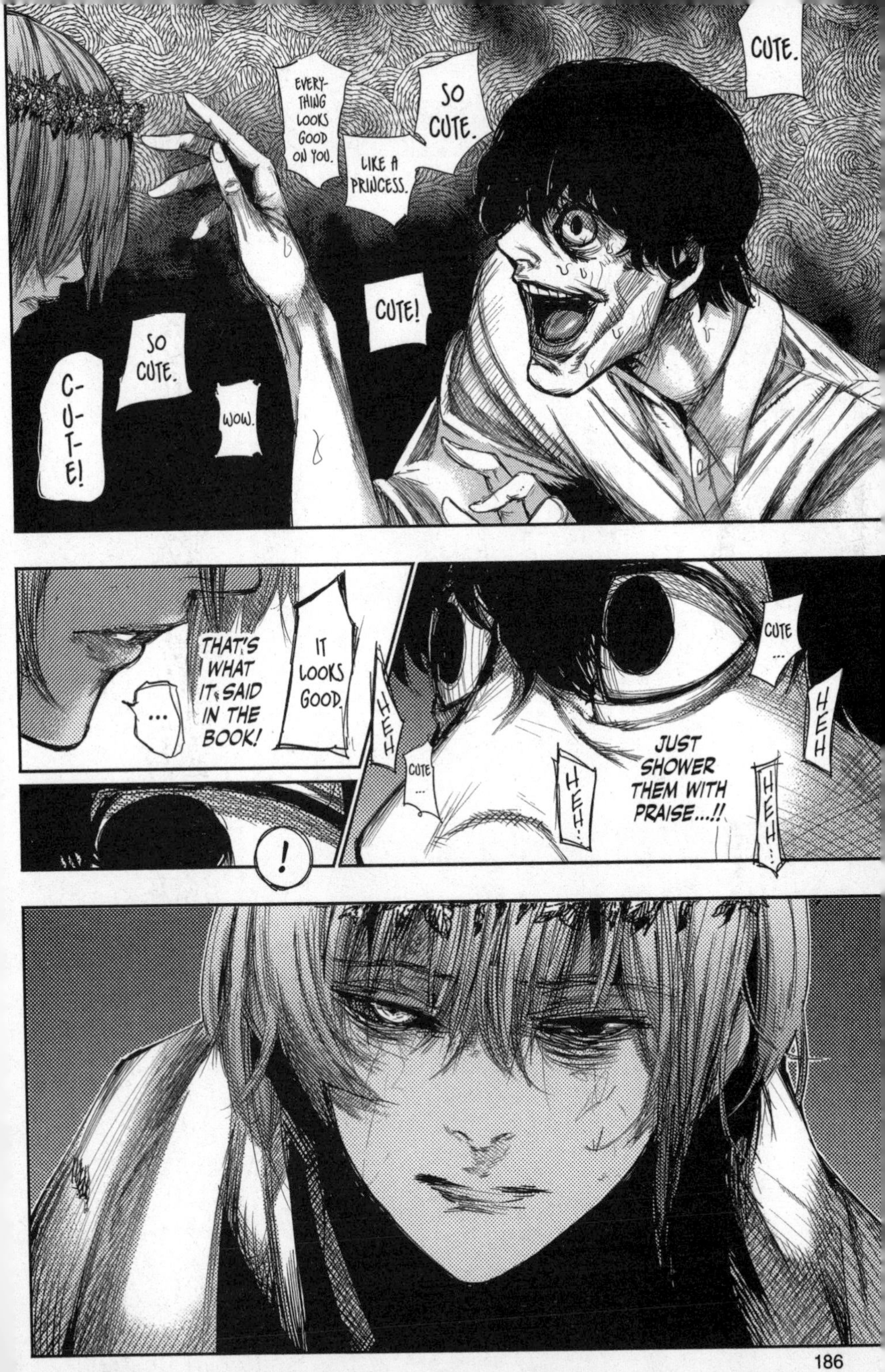
CUTE.
SO CUTE.
EVERYTHING LOOKS GOOD ON YOU.
LIKE A PRINCESS.
CUTE!
SO CUTE.
WOW.
C-U-T-E!
CUTE...
HEH HEH
JUST SHOWER THEM WITH PRAISE...!!
HEH HEH...
HEH HEH...
CUTE...
HEH HEH
IT LOOKS GOOD.
THAT'S WHAT IT SAID IN THE BOOK!
...
!

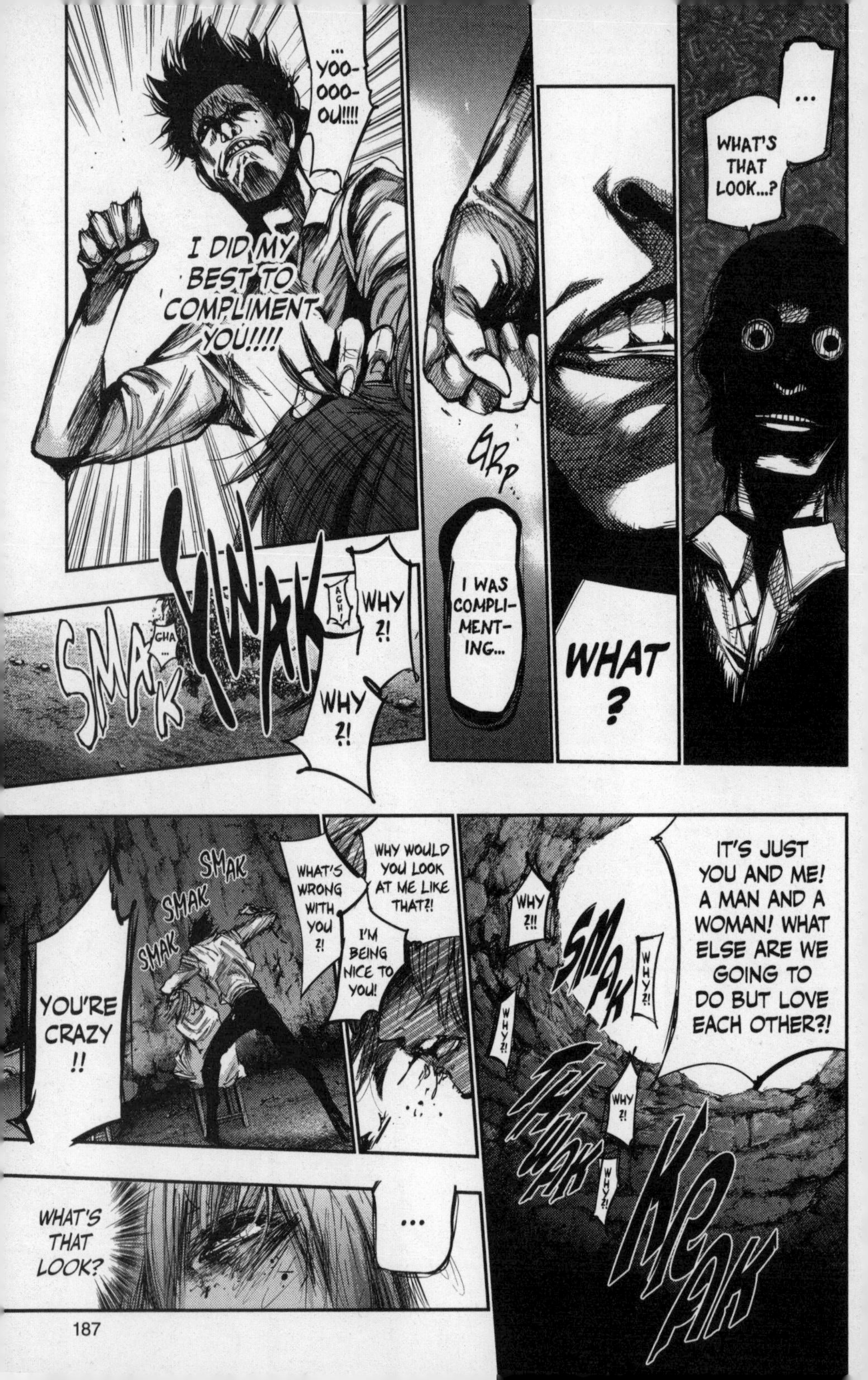
...
WHAT'S THAT LOOK...?
WHAT?
GRP
I WAS COMPLIMENTING...
... YOO-OOO-OU!!!!
I DID MY BEST TO COMPLIMENT YOU!!!!
WHY?!
WHY?!
AGH!
GHA...
SMAK
IT'S JUST YOU AND ME! A MAN AND A WOMAN! WHAT ELSE ARE WE GOING TO DO BUT LOVE EACH OTHER?!
WHY?!!
SMAK
WHY?!
WHY?!
WHY?!
WHY?!
WHY WOULD YOU LOOK AT ME LIKE THAT?!
WHAT'S WRONG WITH YOU?!
I'M BEING NICE TO YOU!
SMAK
SMAK
SMAK
YOU'RE CRAZY!!
...
WHAT'S THAT LOOK?

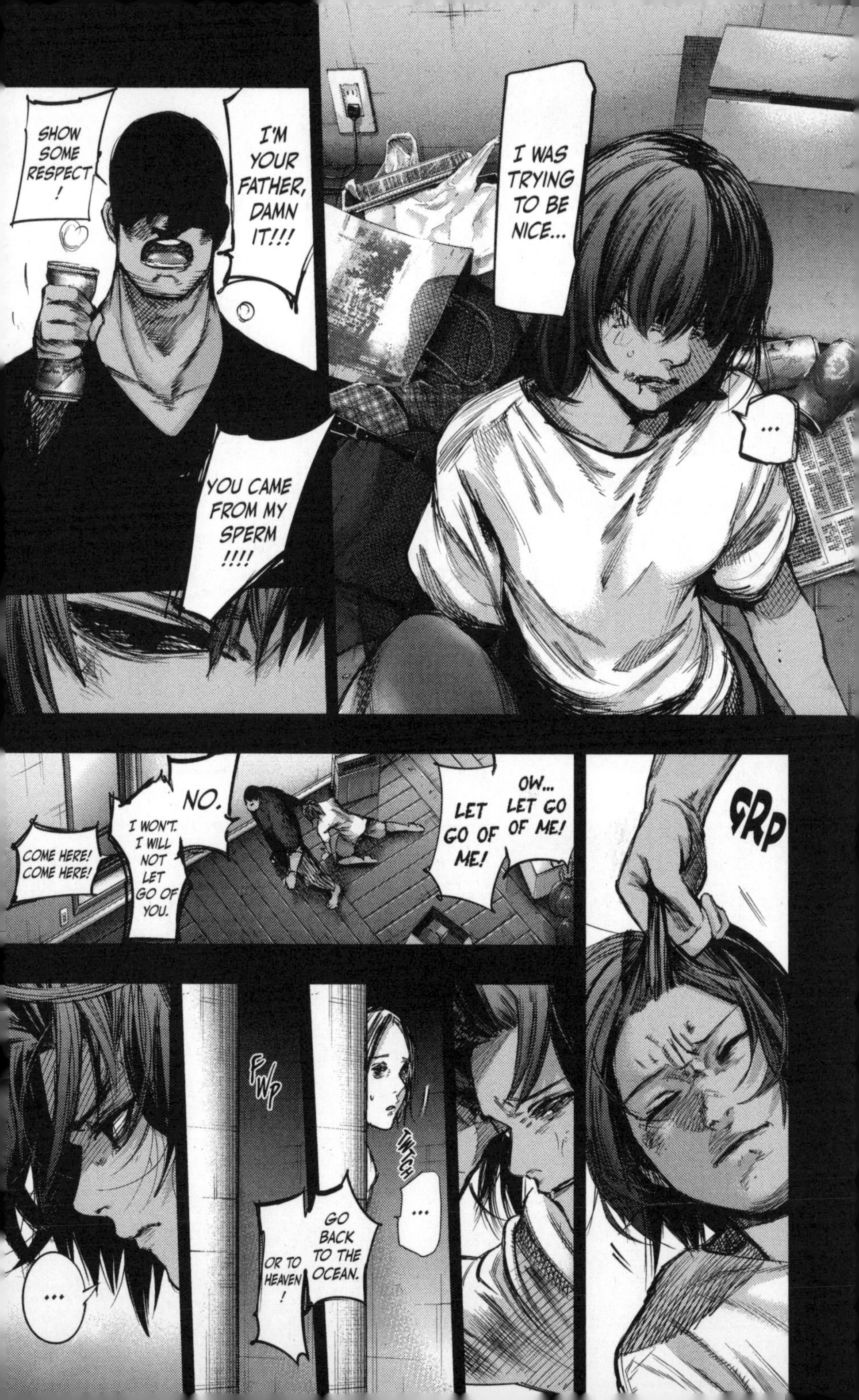
I WAS TRYING TO BE NICE...
...
I'M YOUR FATHER, DAMN IT!!!
SHOW SOME RESPECT!
YOU CAME FROM MY SPERM!!!!
GRP
OW... LET GO OF ME!
LET GO OF ME!
NO.
I WON'T. I WILL NOT LET GO OF YOU.
COME HERE! COME HERE!
TWITCH
...
GO BACK TO THE OCEAN.
OR TO HEAVEN!
FWP
...

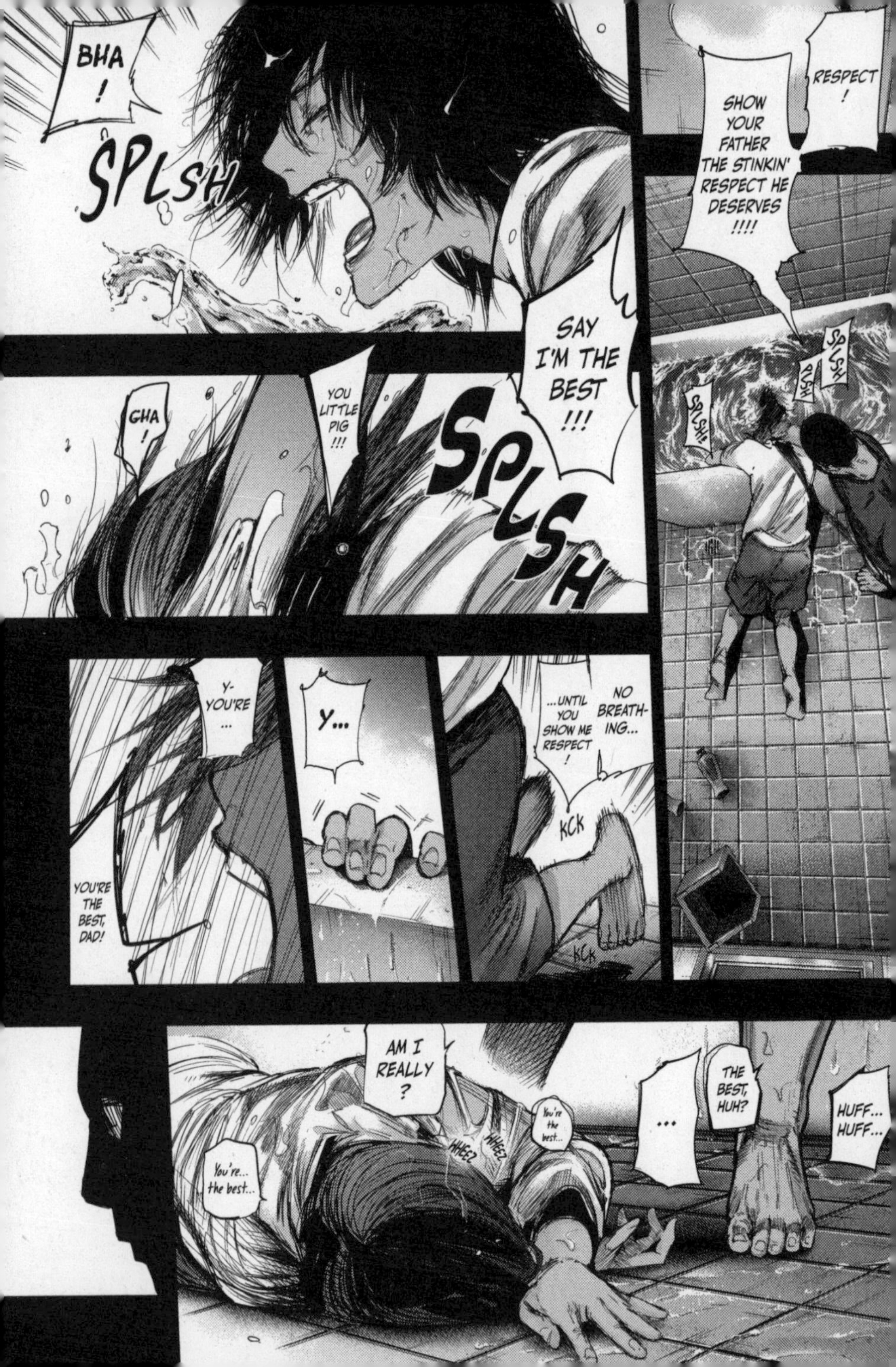
RESPECT!
SHOW YOUR FATHER THE STINKIN' RESPECT HE DESERVES!!!!
SPLSH
SPLSH
SPLSH!!
BHA!
SPLSH
SAY I'M THE BEST!!!
YOU LITTLE PIG!!!
SPLSH
GHA!
NO BREATHING...
...UNTIL YOU SHOW ME RESPECT!
KCK
KCK
Y...
Y-YOU'RE...
YOU'RE THE BEST, DAD!
HUFF... HUFF...
THE BEST, HUH?
...
AM I REALLY?
You're the best...
HHEEZ
HHEEZ
You're... the best...

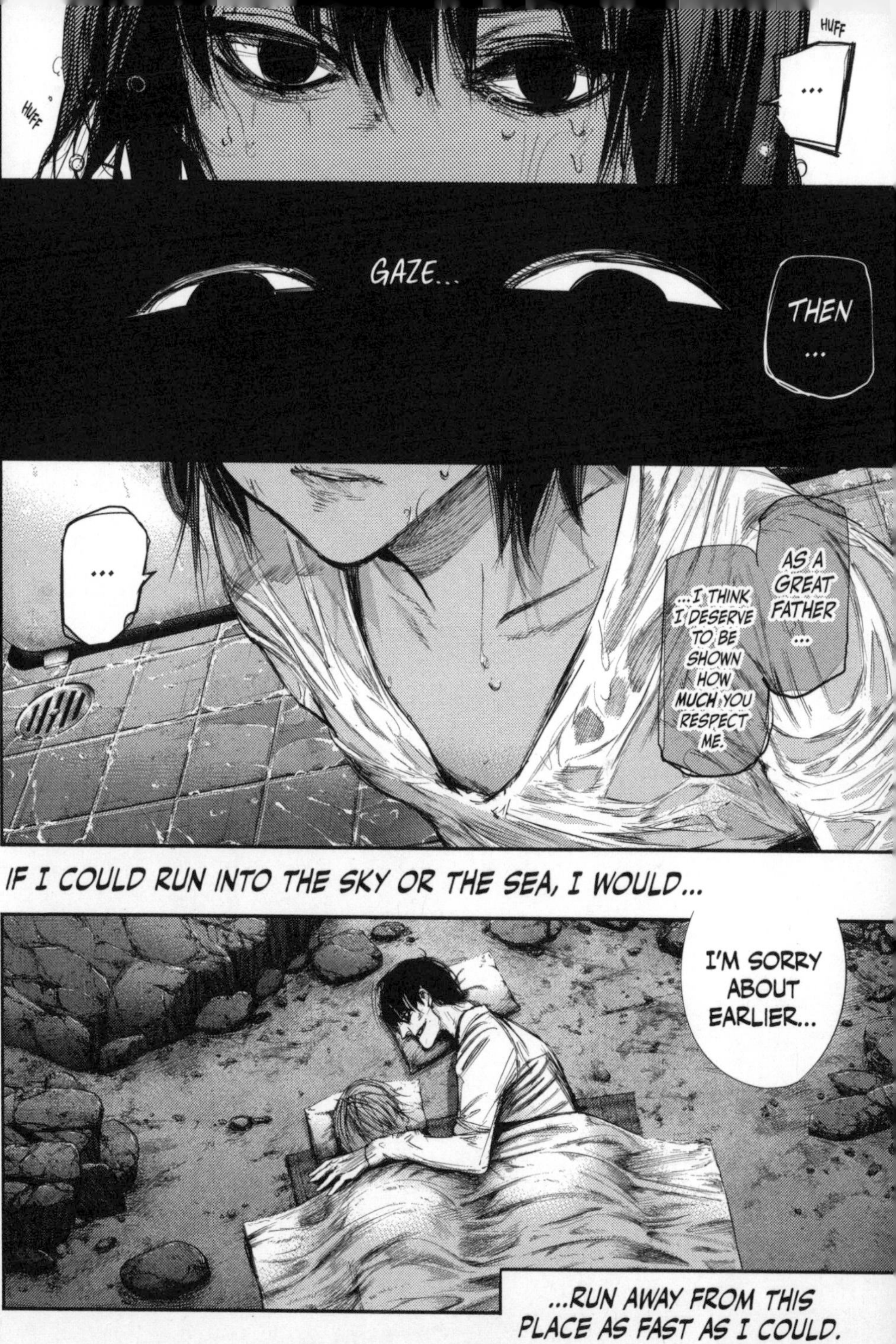
HUFF
...
HUFF
THEN ...
GAZE...
AS A GREAT FATHER ...
...I THINK I DESERVE TO BE SHOWN HOW MUCH YOU RESPECT ME.
...
IF I COULD RUN INTO THE SKY OR THE SEA, I WOULD...
I'M SORRY ABOUT EARLIER...
...RUN AWAY FROM THIS PLACE AS FAST AS I COULD.

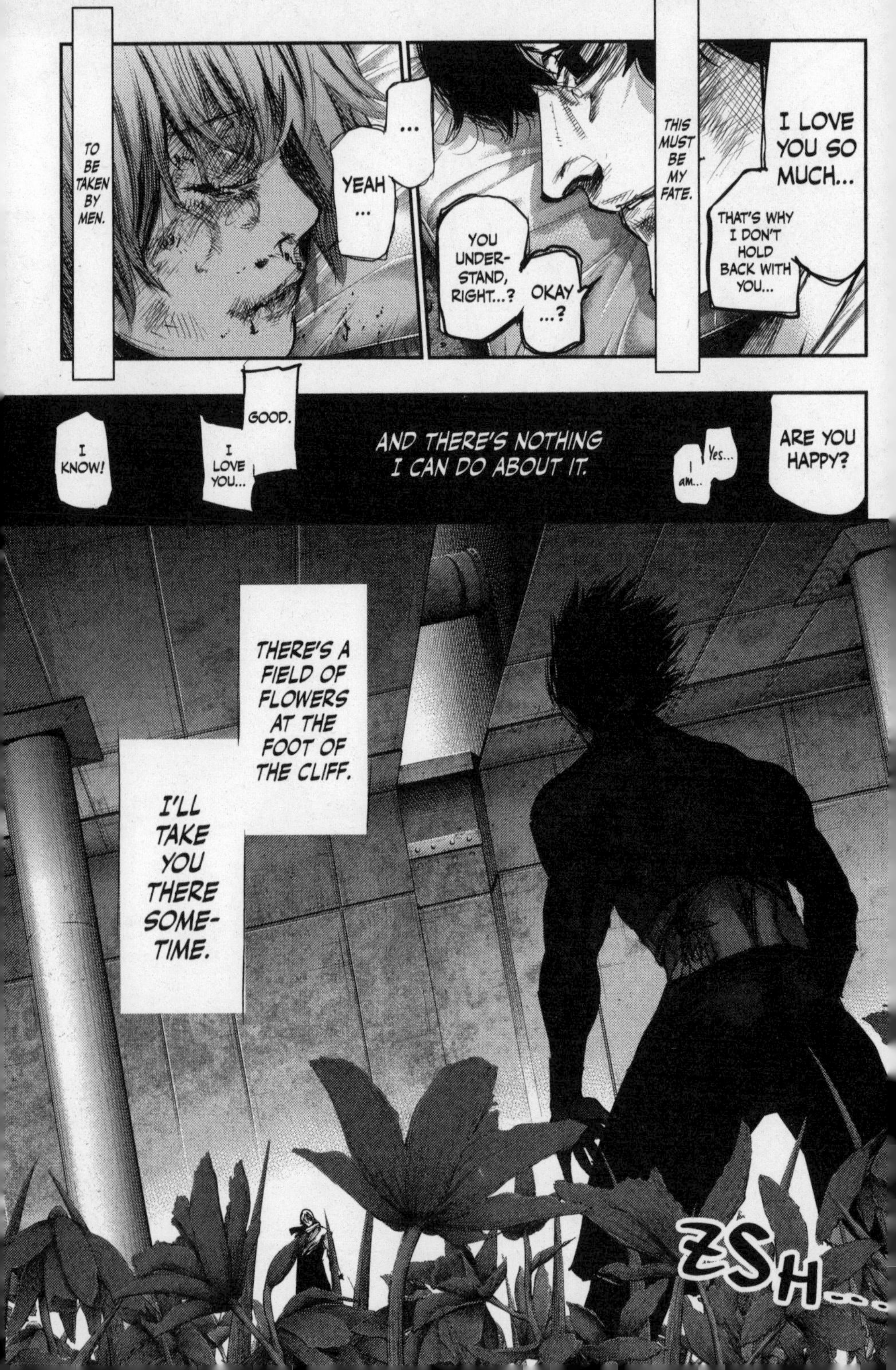

I LOVE YOU SO MUCH...
THAT'S WHY I DON'T HOLD BACK WITH YOU...
THIS MUST BE MY FATE.
YOU UNDER-STAND, RIGHT...?
OKAY...?
...
YEAH...
TO BE TAKEN BY MEN.
ARE YOU HAPPY?
Yes...
I am...
AND THERE'S NOTHING I CAN DO ABOUT IT.
GOOD.
I LOVE YOU...
I KNOW!
THERE'S A FIELD OF FLOWERS AT THE FOOT OF THE CLIFF.
I'LL TAKE YOU THERE SOME-TIME.
ZSH...

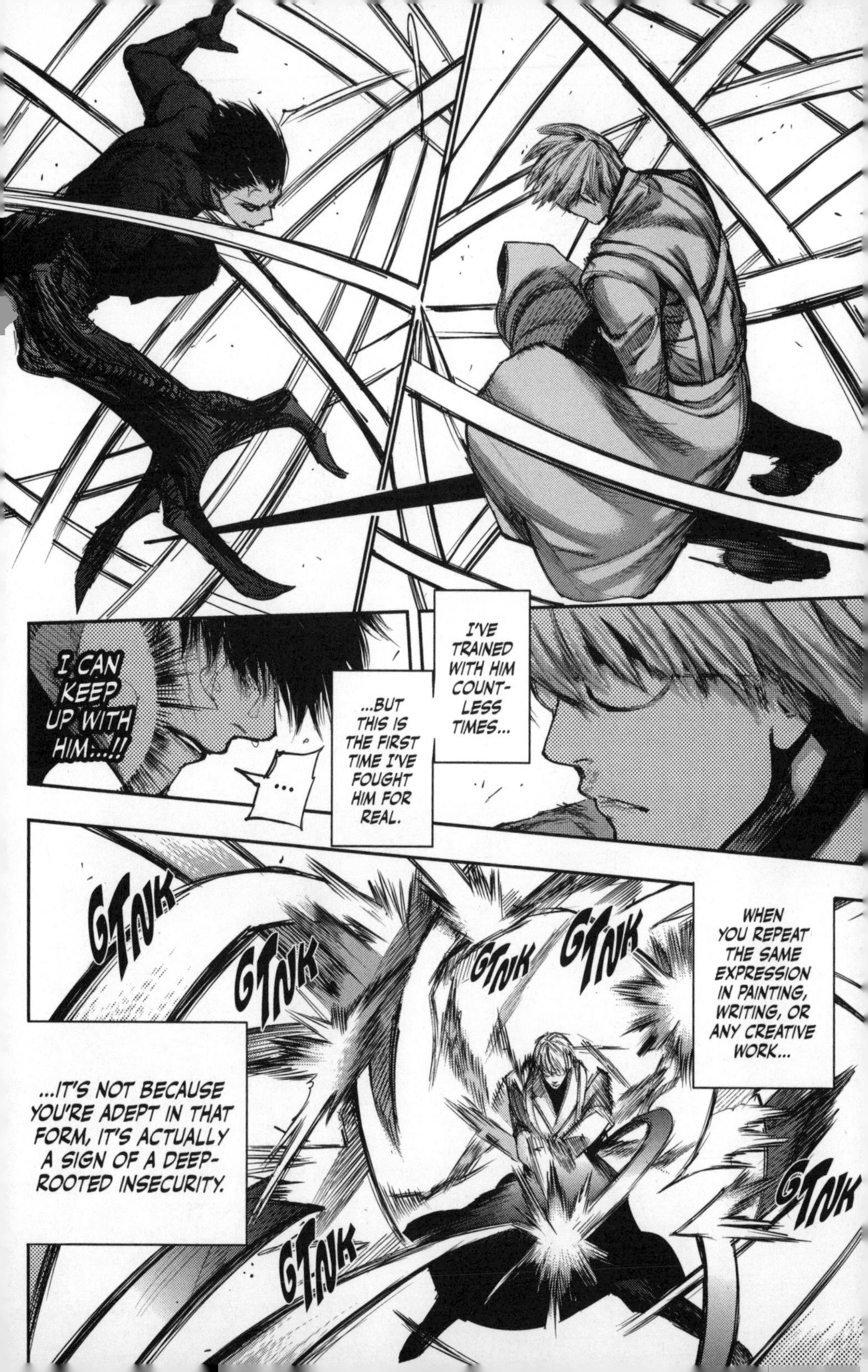

I'VE TRAINED WITH HIM COUNT-LESS TIMES...
...BUT THIS IS THE FIRST TIME I'VE FOUGHT HIM FOR REAL.
I CAN KEEP UP WITH HIM...!!
...
WHEN YOU REPEAT THE SAME EXPRESSION IN PAINTING, WRITING, OR ANY CREATIVE WORK...
GTNK
GTNK
GTNK
GTNK
GTNK
...IT'S NOT BECAUSE YOU'RE ADEPT IN THAT FORM, IT'S ACTUALLY A SIGN OF A DEEP-ROOTED INSECURITY.
GTNK

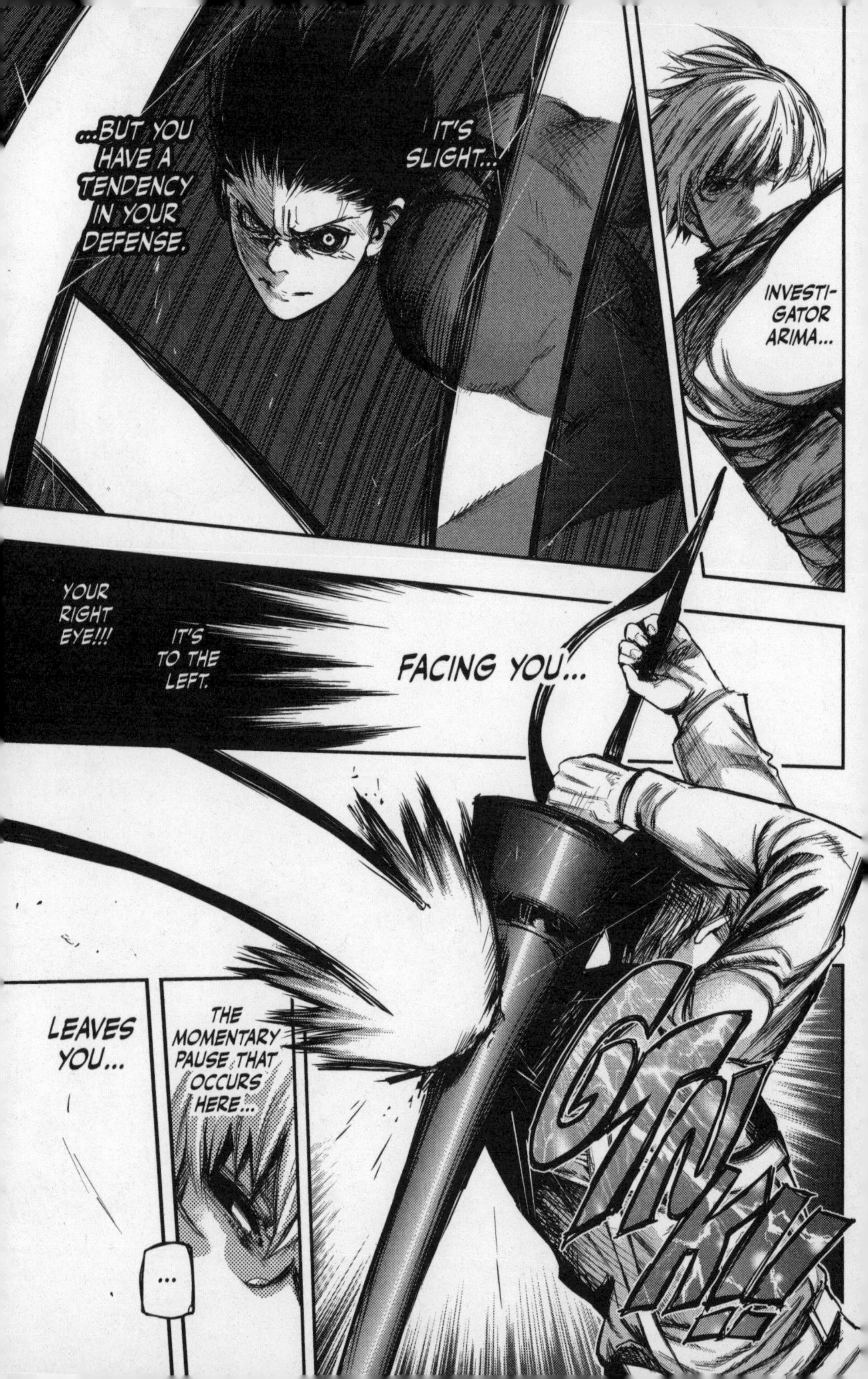
INVESTI-GATOR ARIMA...
IT'S SLIGHT...
...BUT YOU HAVE A TENDENCY IN YOUR DEFENSE.
FACING YOU...
IT'S TO THE LEFT.
YOUR RIGHT EYE!!!
THE MOMENTARY PAUSE THAT OCCURS HERE...
LEAVES YOU...
...

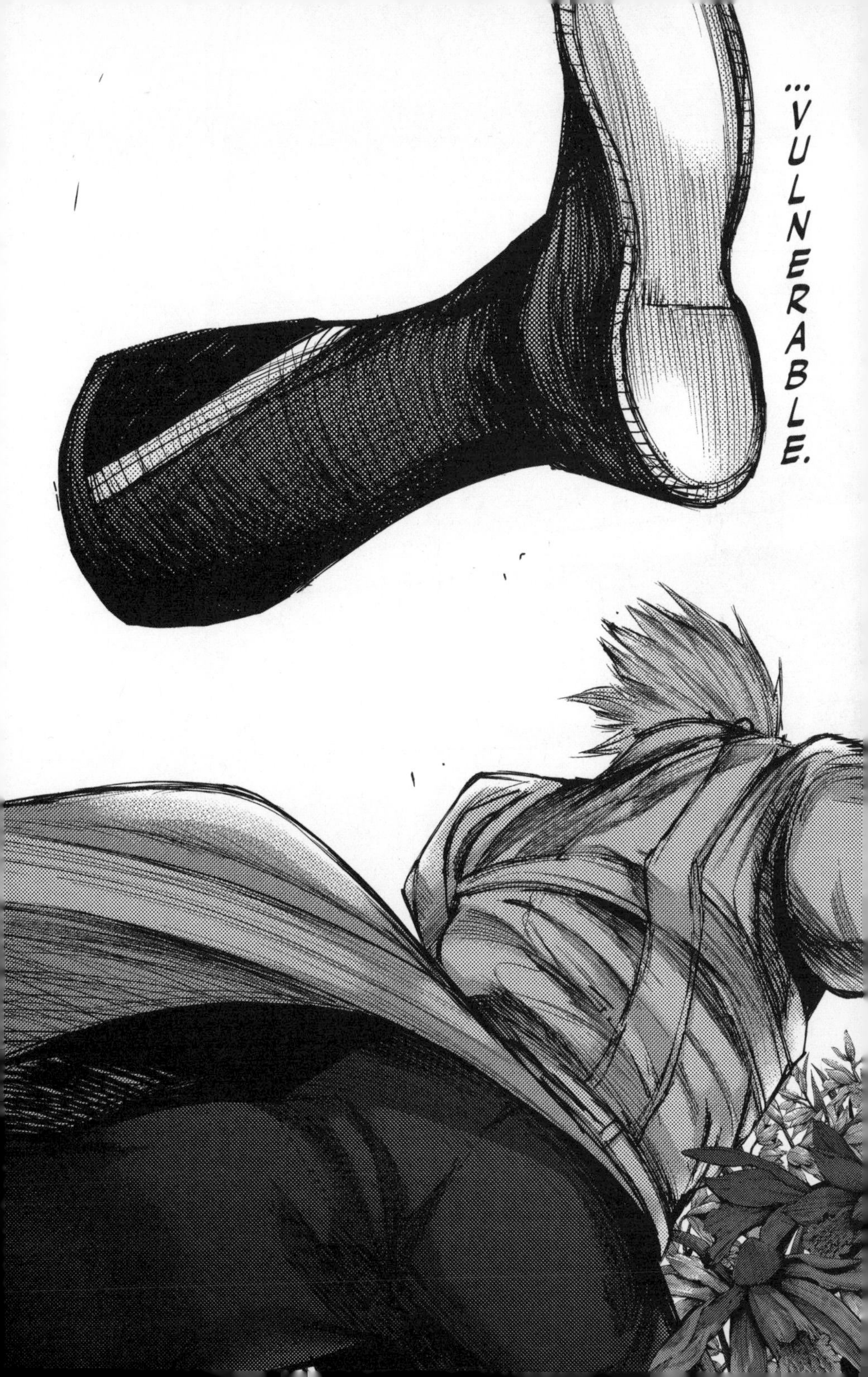
...VULNERABLE.

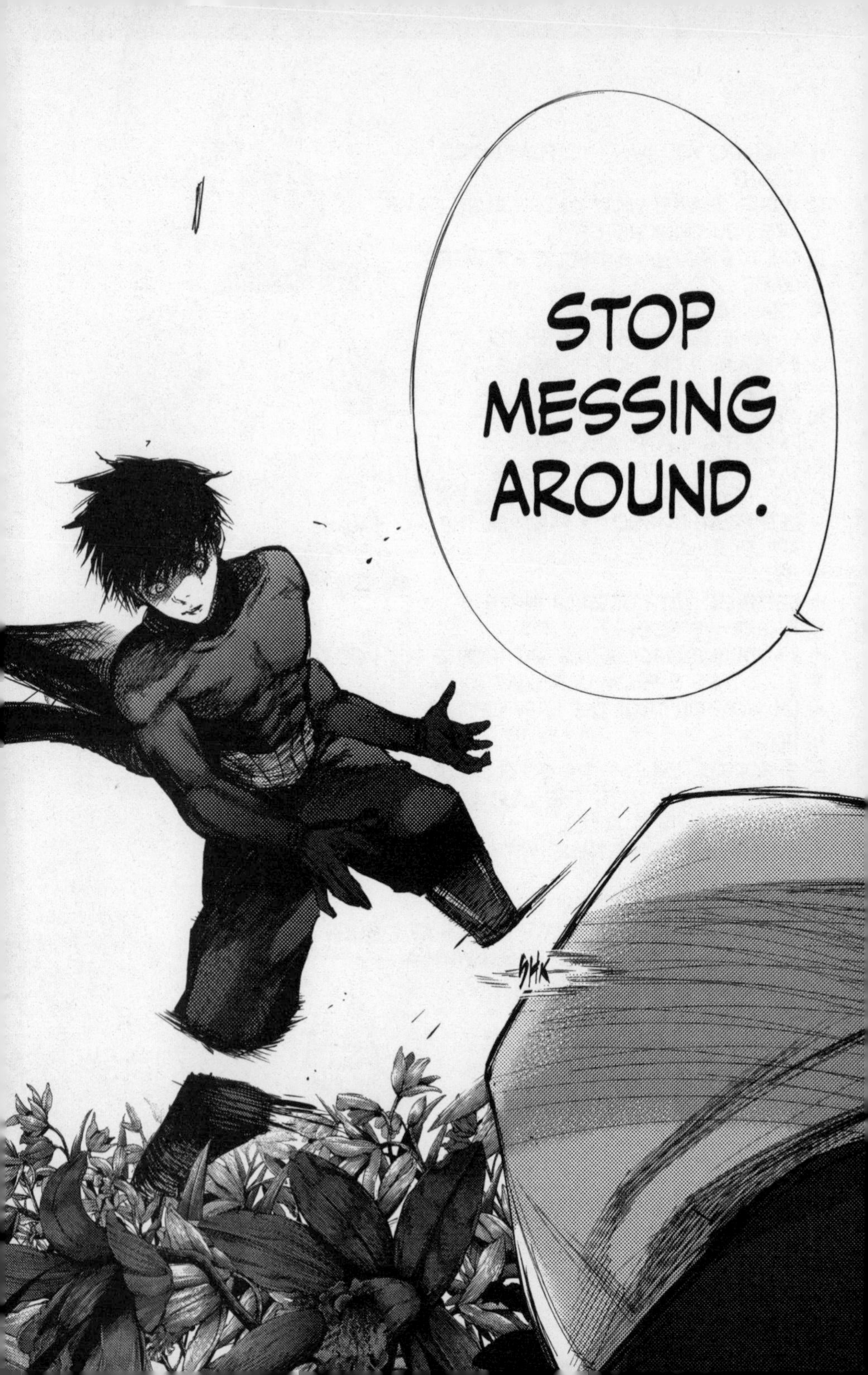
STOP MESSING AROUND.
SHK

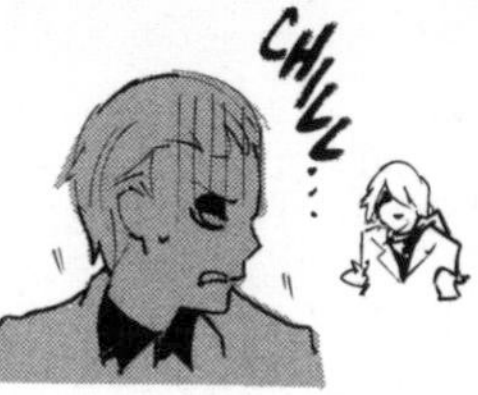
CHILL

H: NAKI, DO YOU WANT TO PLAY WORD CHAIN?
N: WORD CHAIN?! WHAT KINDA CRUEL GAME ARE YOU THINKING OF?!
H: OH, IT'S NOT LIKE THAT. IT'S A WORD GAME...
N: CHAINING OUR WORDS...
H: (THIS IS GONNA BE TOUGH TO EXPLAIN...) UM, FOR EXAMPLE, I'LL SAY APPLE.

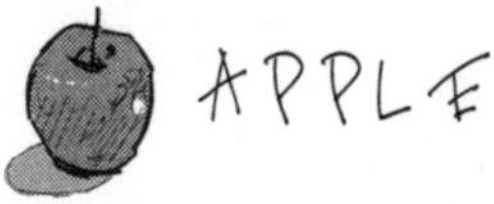
APPLE

N: OKAY.
H: THEN IT'S E FOR YOU.
N: ...? WHERE'S THE E IN APPLE?
H: UH... THE E ISN'T LIKE THE SKIN OR THE FRUIT. IT'S NOT A PART OF THE APPLE...

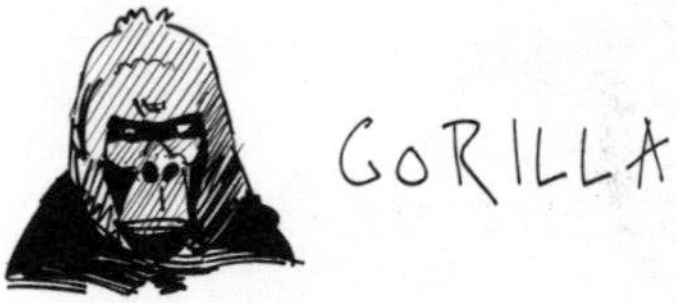
GORILLA

N: ??
H: LET'S GO WITH GORILLA INSTEAD.
N: WHERE WE GOING?
H: I'M TAKING BACK APPLE AND GOING WITH GORILLA.
N: SO I TAKE G FROM GORILLA?
H: UH, NO. YOU TAKE THE LAST LETTER.
N: HUH?!
H: S-SORRY... UM... IF IT'S GORILLA, IT'LL BE A. G-O-R-I-L-L-A. SEE? THE LAST LETTER IS AN A.
N: OH... THE A IN GORILLA.
H: SO YOU SAY SOMETHING WITH AN A.
N: HAY.
H: OH, IT HAS TO START WITH A.
N: HUH? THE START OF WHAT? WHAT'S A? A BUG?
H: NO... THE WORD HAS TO BEGIN WITH A.
N: OH, YOU SHOULDA JUST SAID SO. AGORILLA.
H: ...

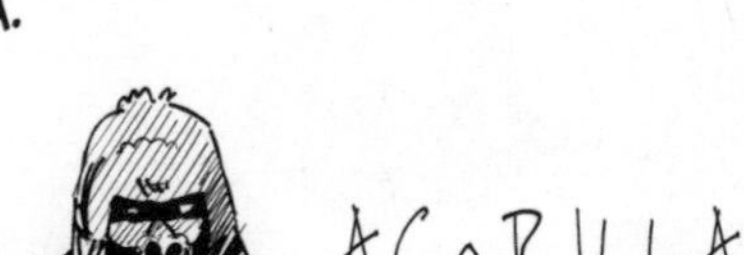
AGORILLA

S: HOHGURO, JUST GIVE IT UP.
H: YEAH...
N: YO, IF IT'S AGORILLA, THERE'S TWO AS?! THERE'S A G TOO! WHAT DO WE DO?!

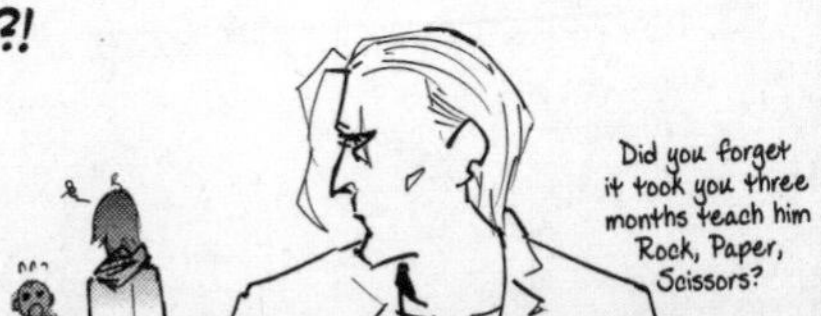
Did you forget it took you three months teach him Rock, Paper, Scissors?
HUMANS

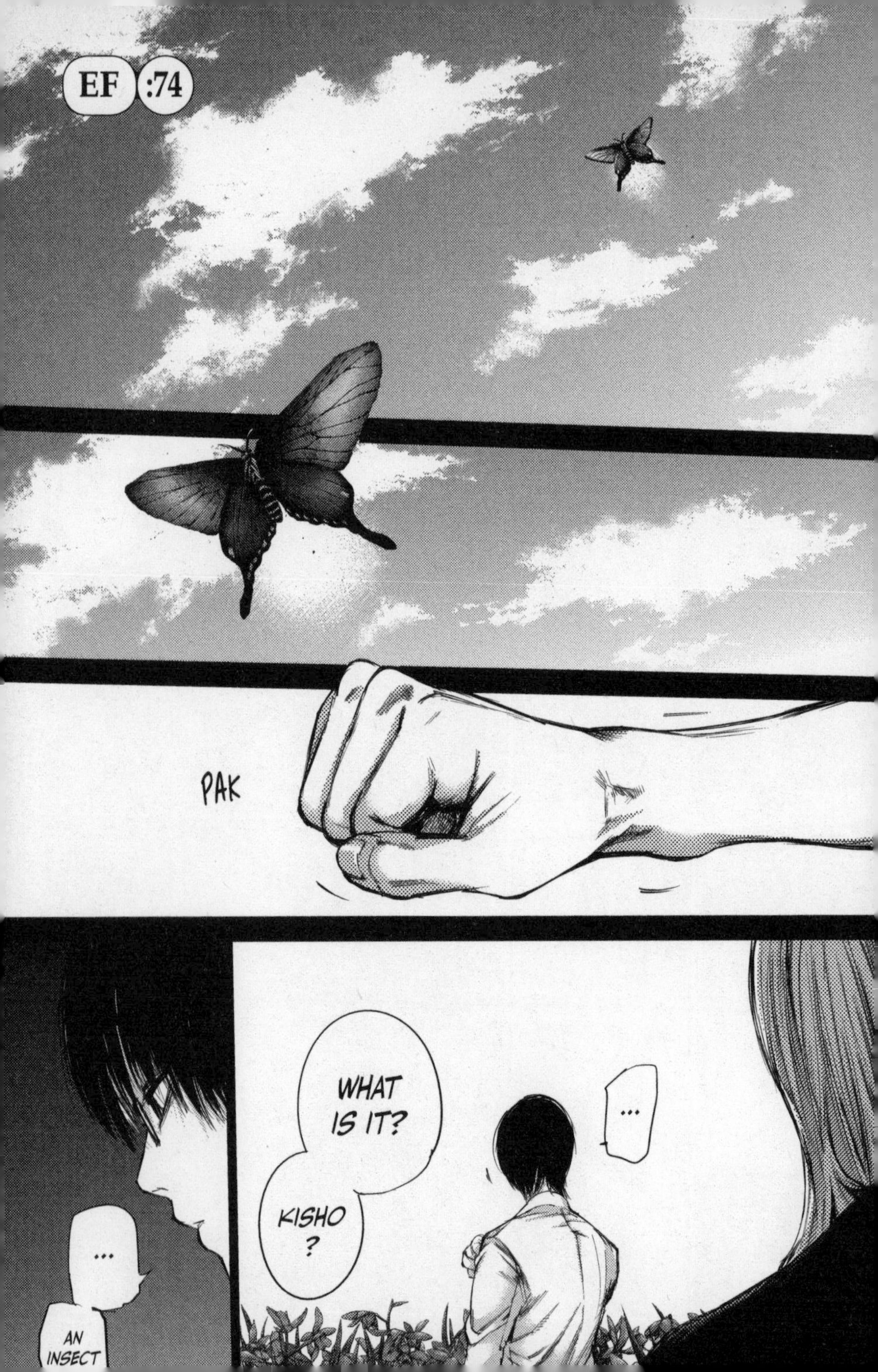
EF :74
PAK
WHAT IS IT?
KISHO?
...
...
AN INSECT

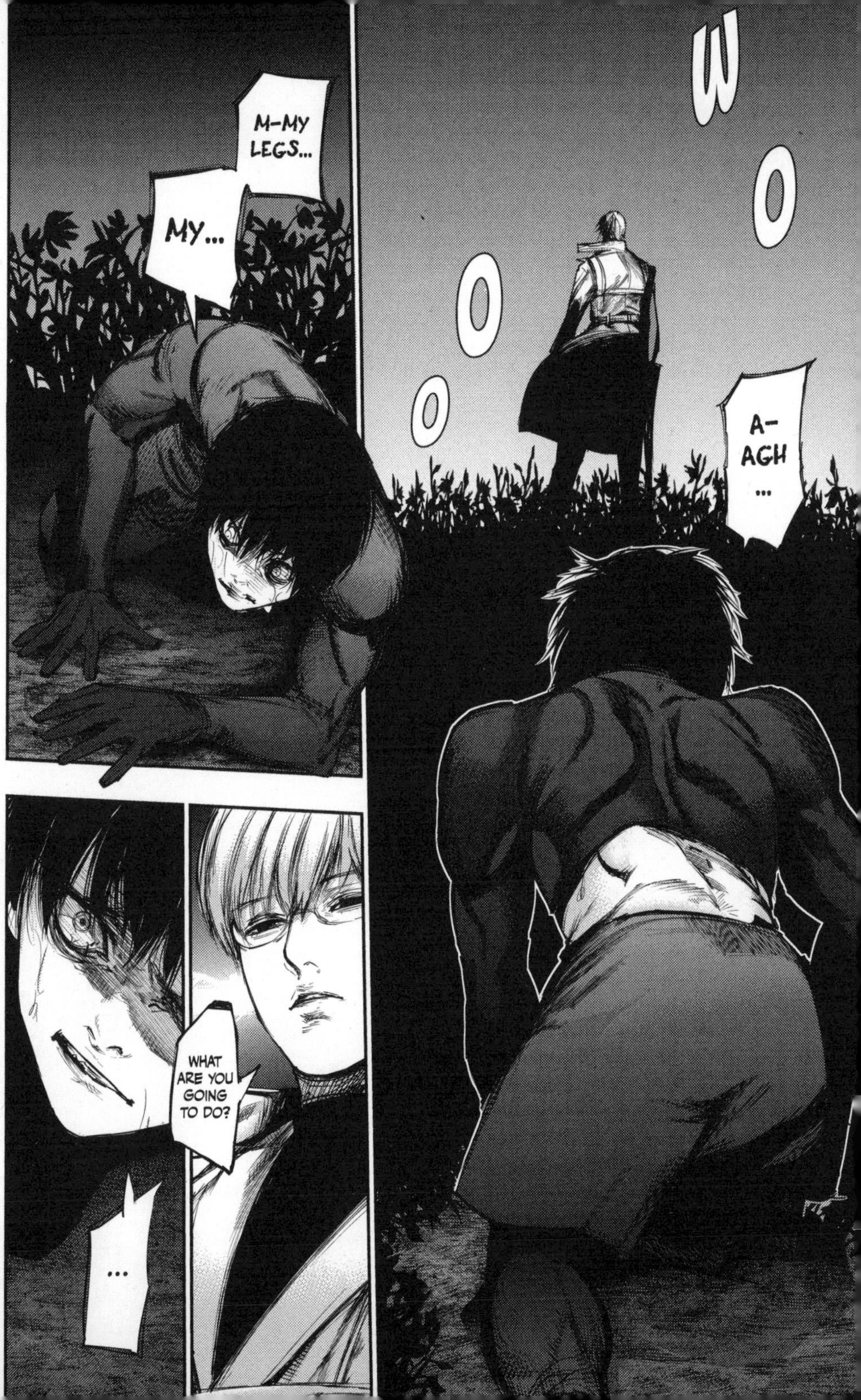
WOOO
A-AGH...
M-MY LEGS...
MY...
WHAT ARE YOU GOING TO DO?
...

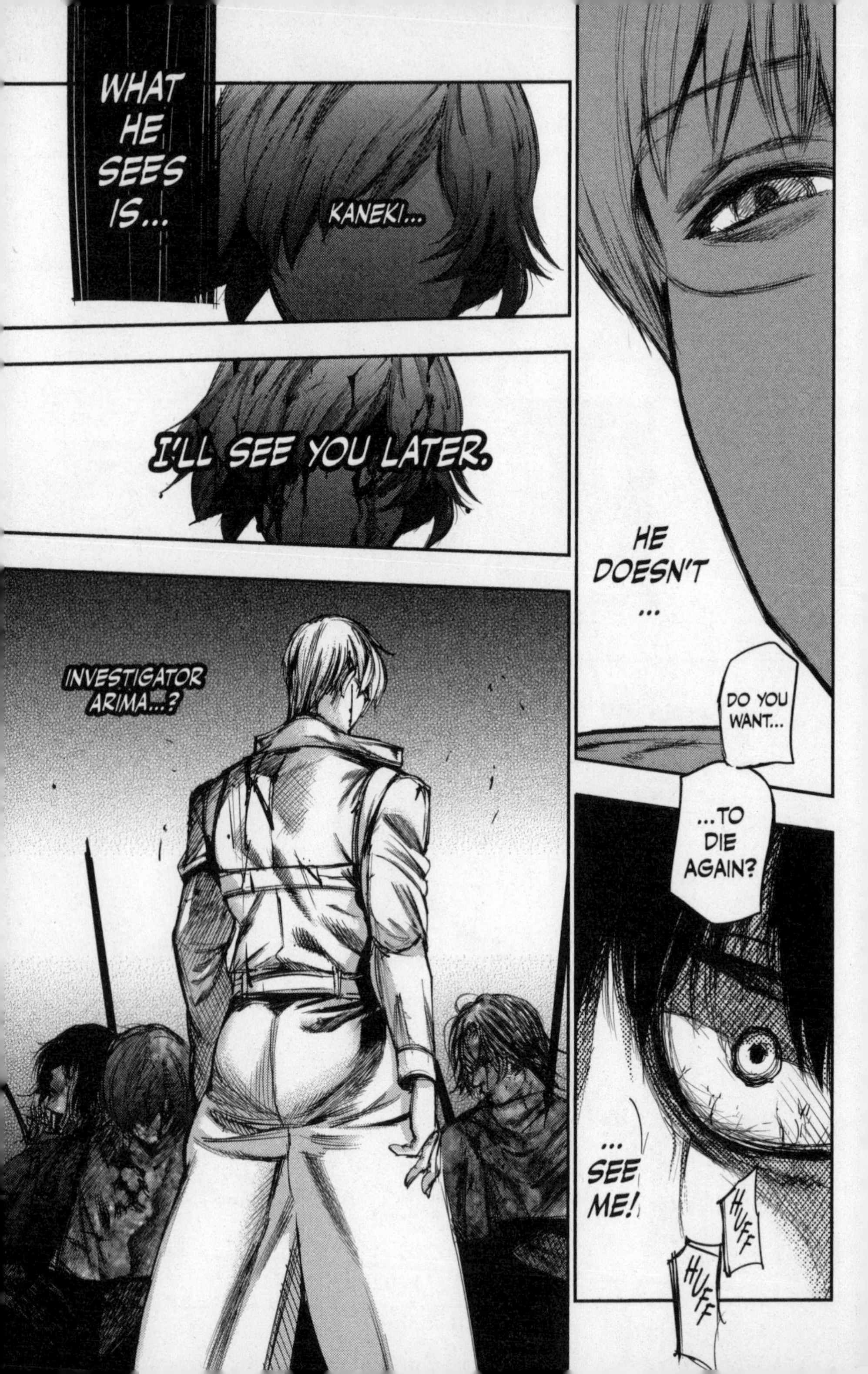
HE DOESN'T ...
DO YOU WANT...
WHAT HE SEES IS...
KANEKI...
I'LL SEE YOU LATER.
INVESTIGATOR ARIMA...?
...TO DIE AGAIN?
... SEE ME!
HUFF
HUFF

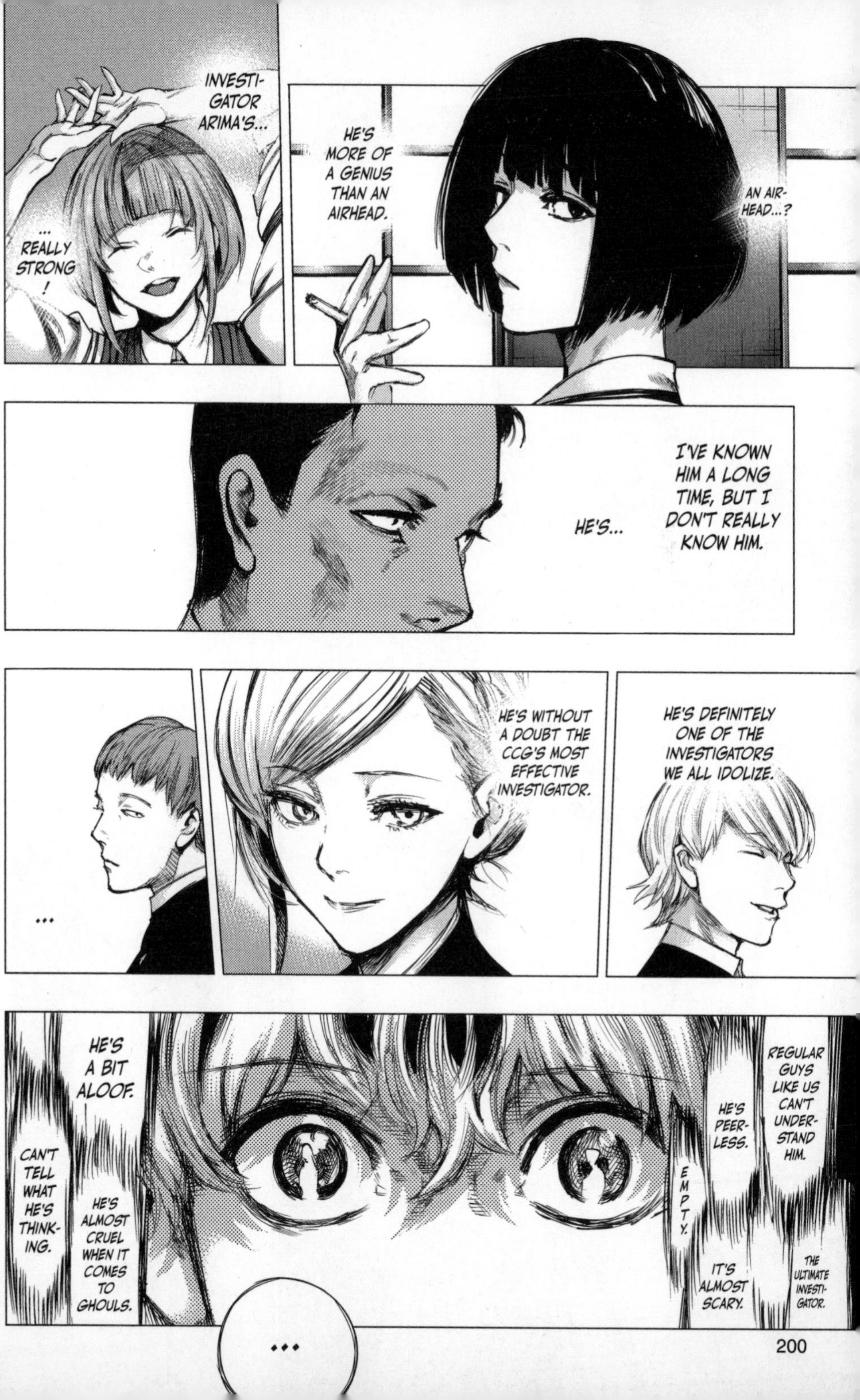
AN AIR-HEAD...?
HE'S MORE OF A GENIUS THAN AN AIRHEAD.
INVESTI-GATOR ARIMA'S...
...REALLY STRONG!
I'VE KNOWN HIM A LONG TIME, BUT I DON'T REALLY KNOW HIM.
HE'S...
HE'S DEFINITELY ONE OF THE INVESTIGATORS WE ALL IDOLIZE.
HE'S WITHOUT A DOUBT THE CCG'S MOST EFFECTIVE INVESTIGATOR.
...
REGULAR GUYS LIKE US CAN'T UNDER-STAND HIM.
HE'S PEER-LESS.
THE ULTIMATE INVESTI-GATOR.
EMPTY.
IT'S ALMOST SCARY.
HE'S A BIT ALOOF.
HE'S ALMOST CRUEL WHEN IT COMES TO GHOULS.
CAN'T TELL WHAT HE'S THINK-ING.
...

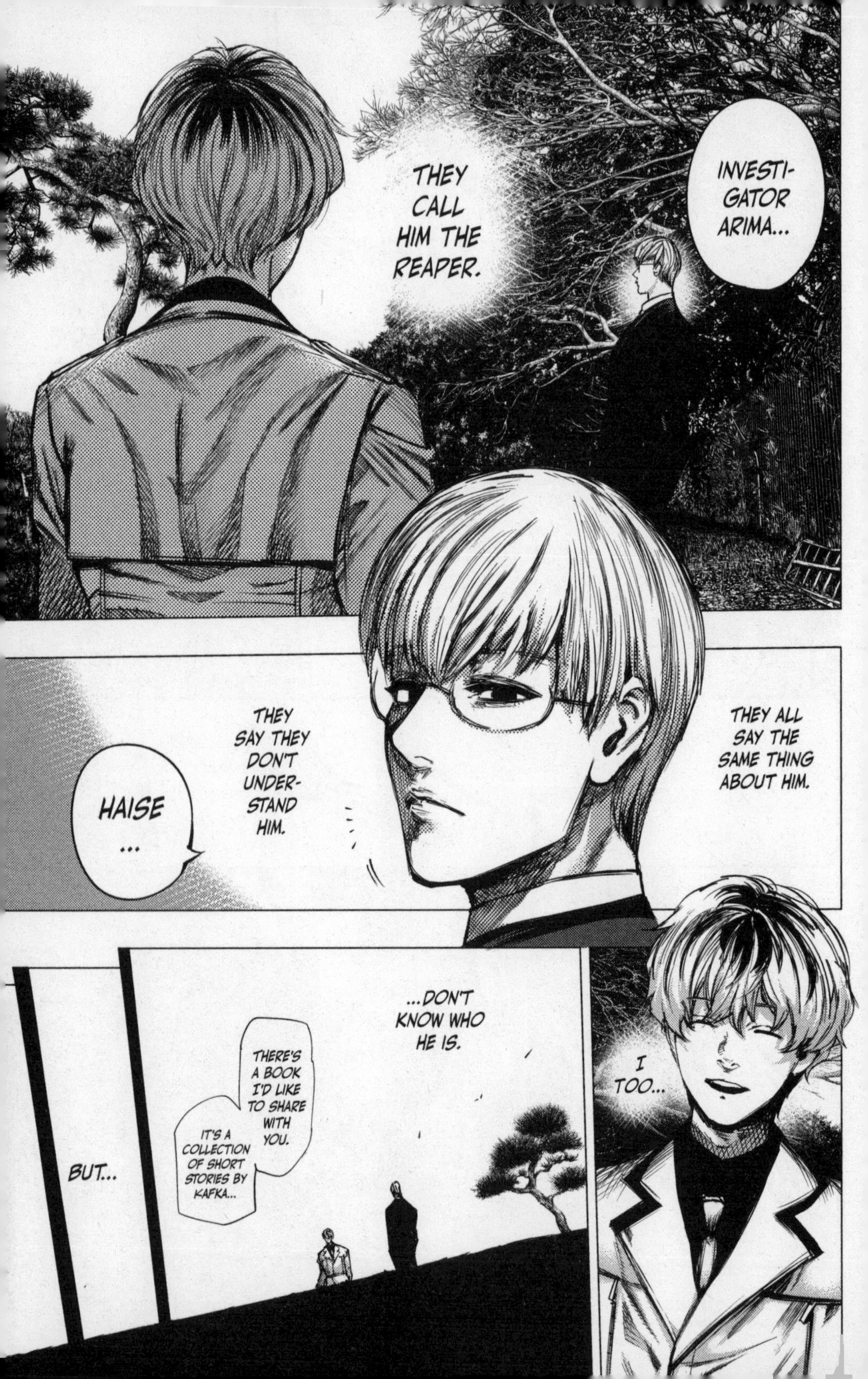
INVESTI-GATOR ARIMA...
THEY CALL HIM THE REAPER.
THEY ALL SAY THE SAME THING ABOUT HIM.
THEY SAY THEY DON'T UNDER-STAND HIM.
HAISE ...
I TOO...
...DON'T KNOW WHO HE IS.
THERE'S A BOOK I'D LIKE TO SHARE WITH YOU.
IT'S A COLLECTION OF SHORT STORIES BY KAFKA...
BUT...

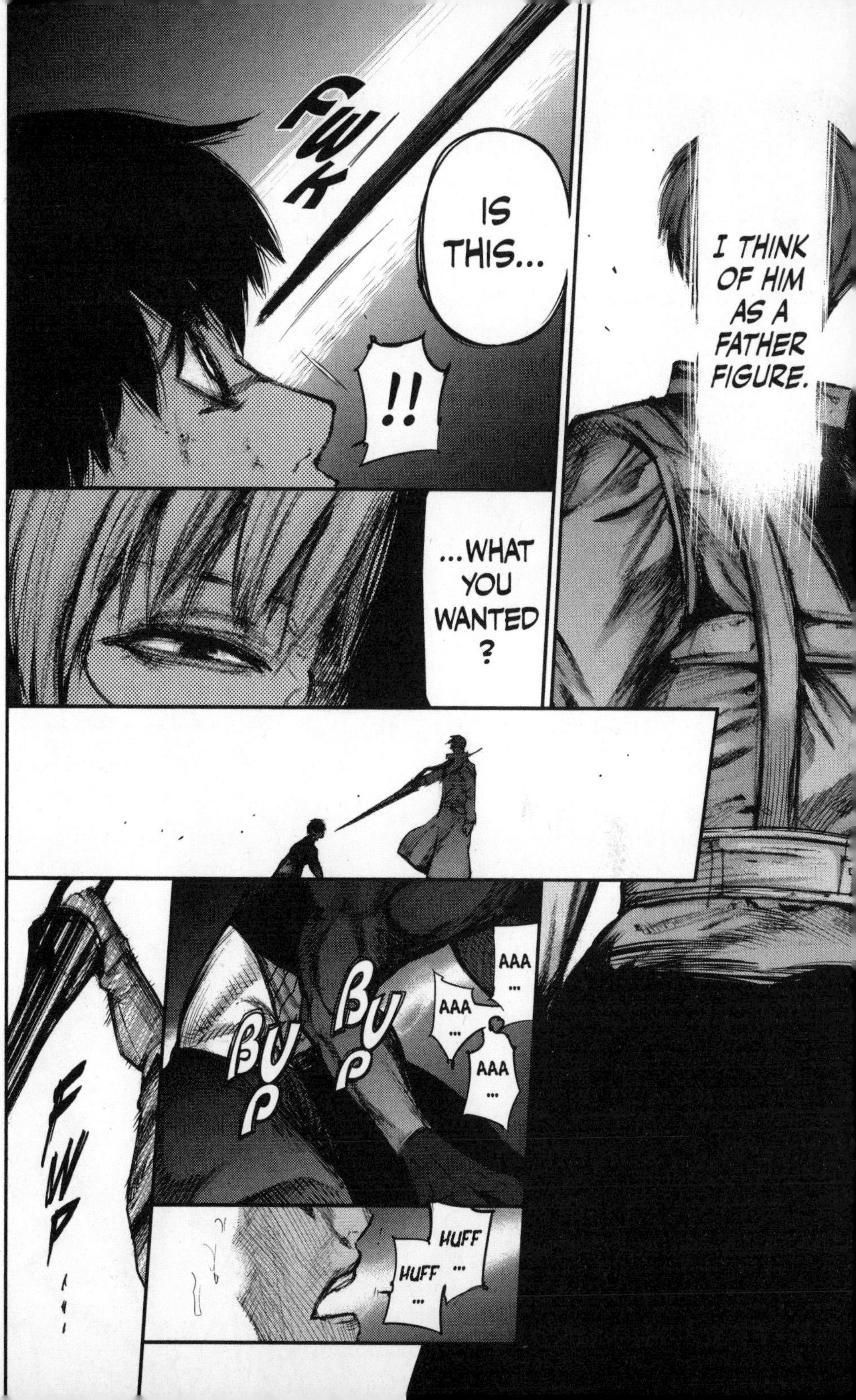
I THINK OF HIM AS A FATHER FIGURE.
FWK
IS THIS...
!!
...WHAT YOU WANTED?
BUP
BUP
AAA...
AAA...
AAA...
FWP...
HUFF...
HUFF...

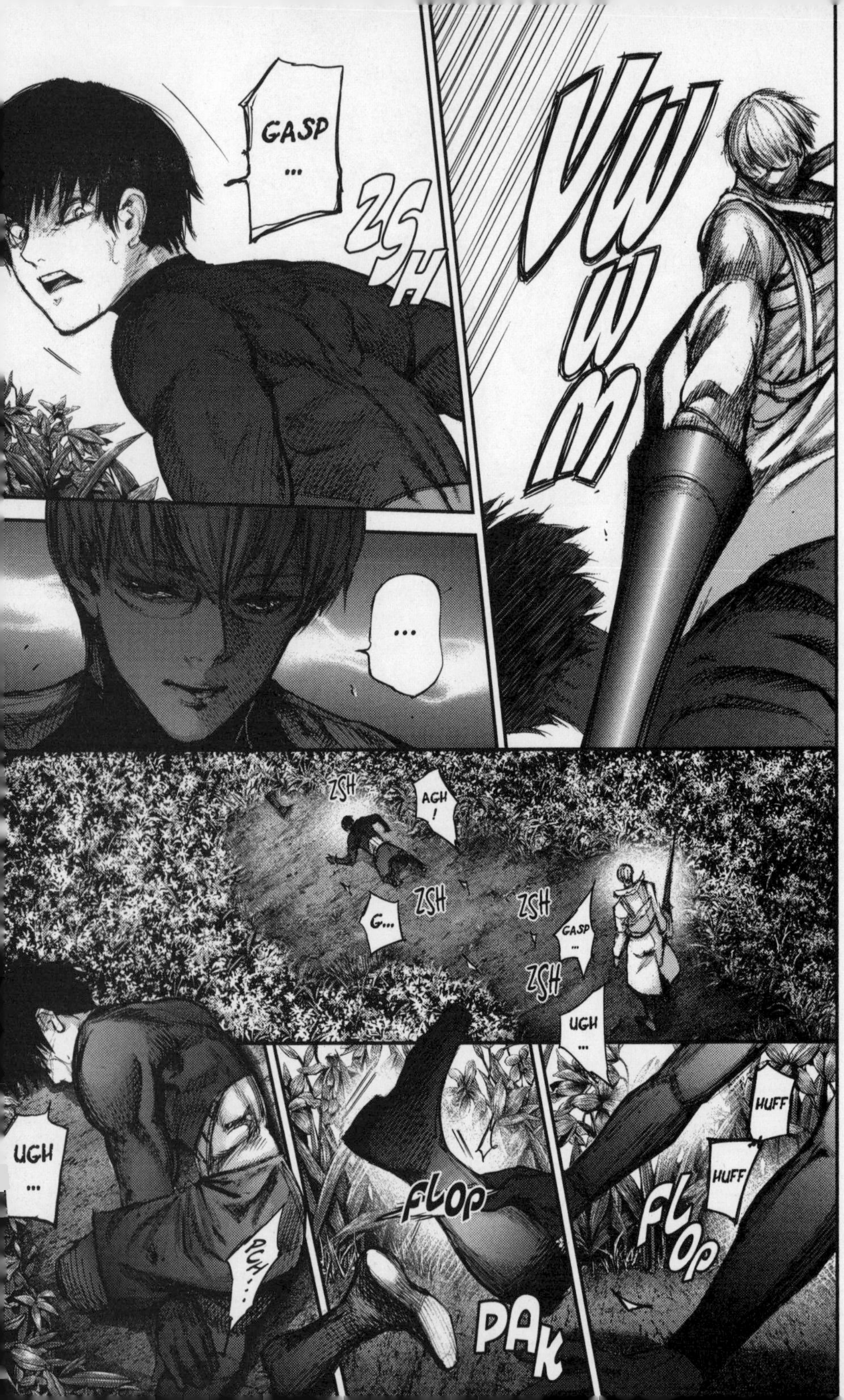
GASP
...
ZSH
...
AGH
!
ZSH
ZSH
GASP
...
ZSH
G...
ZSH
UGH
...
HUFF
HUFF
FLOP
PAK
FLOP
UGH
...
ACH...

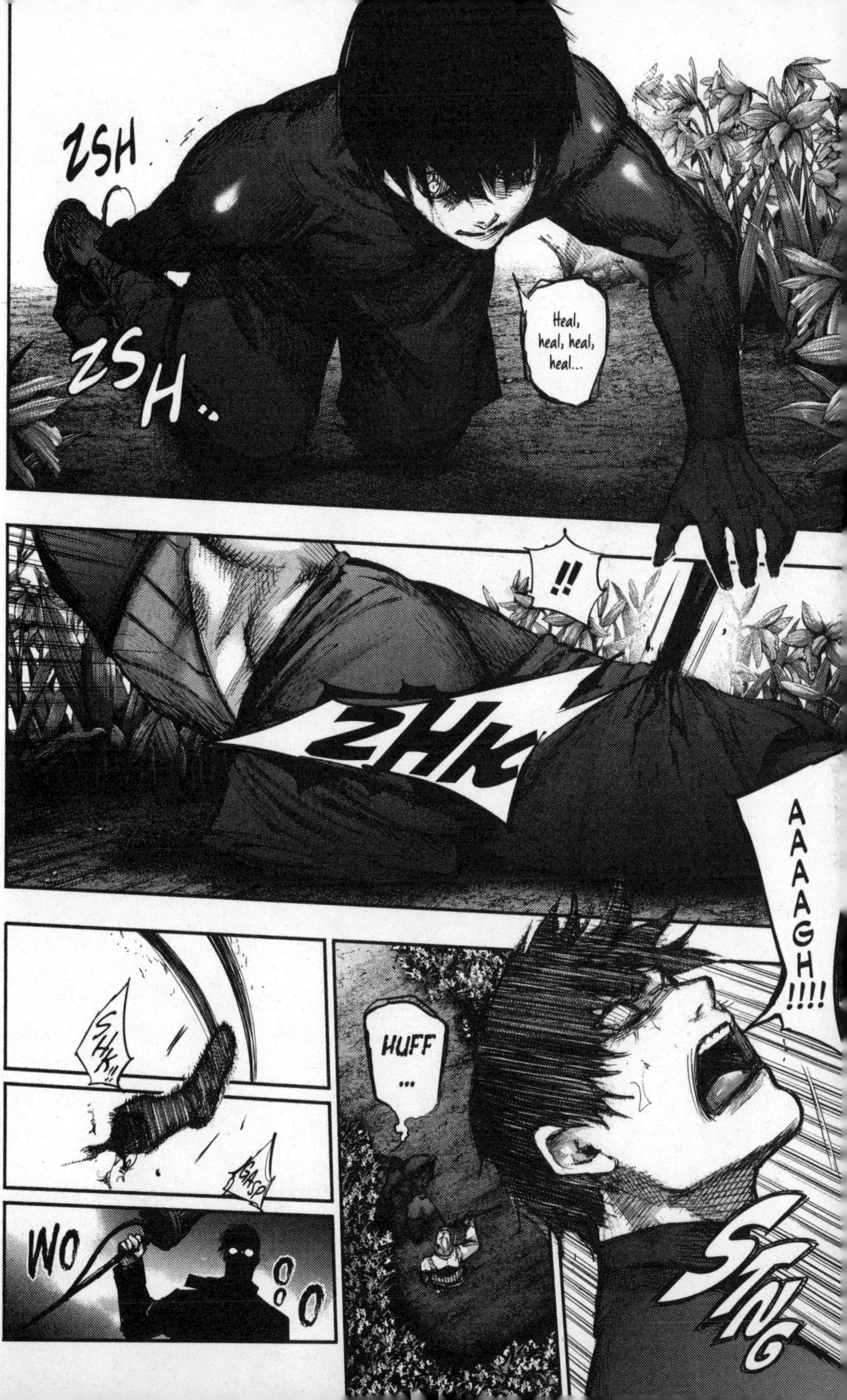
ZSH
Heal, heal, heal, heal...
ZSH..
!!
ZHK
AAAAGH!!!!
HUFF ...
SING
SHK!!
GASP
WO
OO

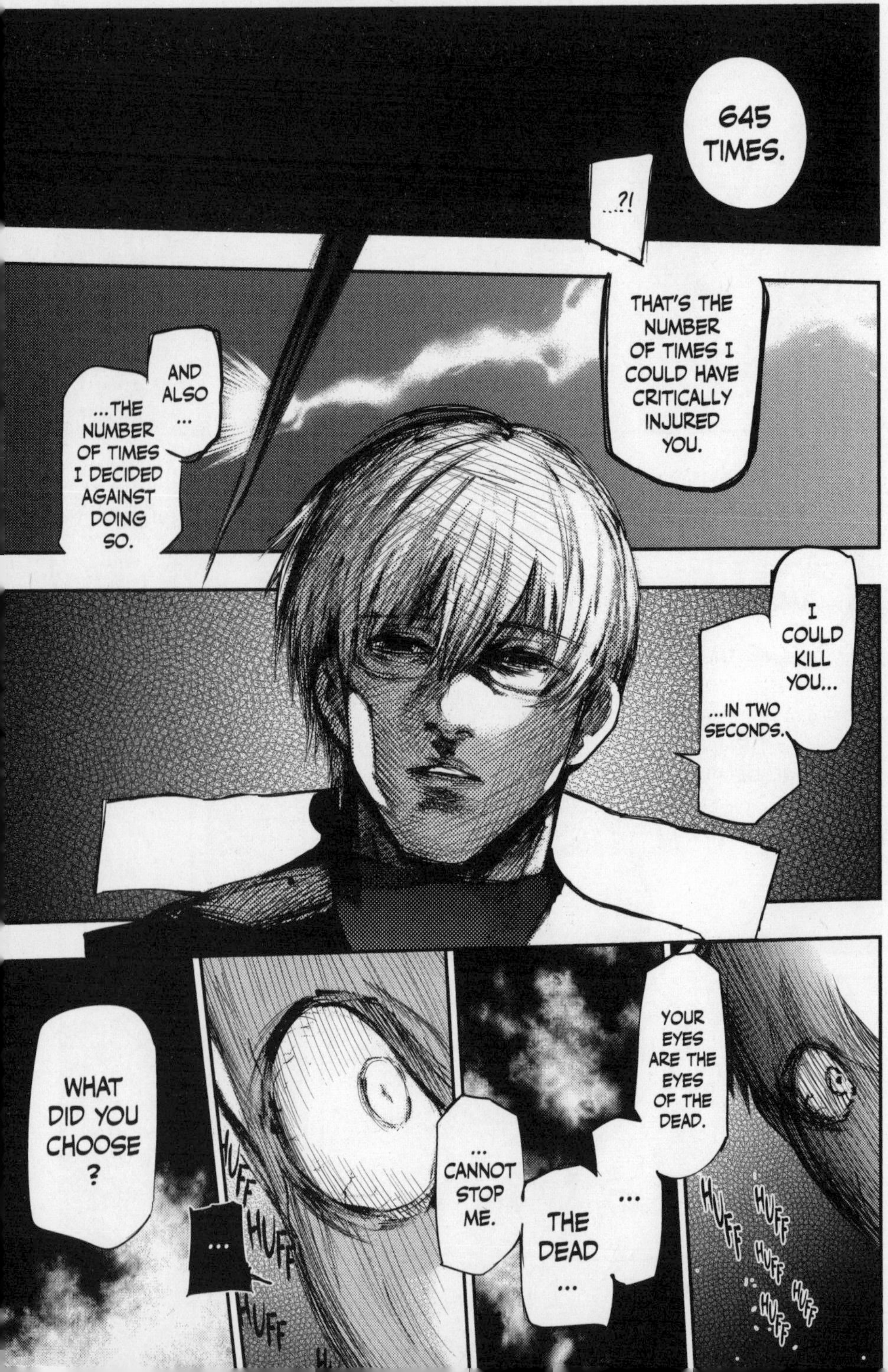
645 TIMES.
...?!
THAT'S THE NUMBER OF TIMES I COULD HAVE CRITICALLY INJURED YOU.
AND ALSO ...
...THE NUMBER OF TIMES I DECIDED AGAINST DOING SO.
I COULD KILL YOU...
...IN TWO SECONDS.
HUFF HUFF HUFF HUFF HUFF HUFF
YOUR EYES ARE THE EYES OF THE DEAD.
...
THE DEAD ...
... CANNOT STOP ME.
HUFF HUFF HUFF
WHAT DID YOU CHOOSE ?
...

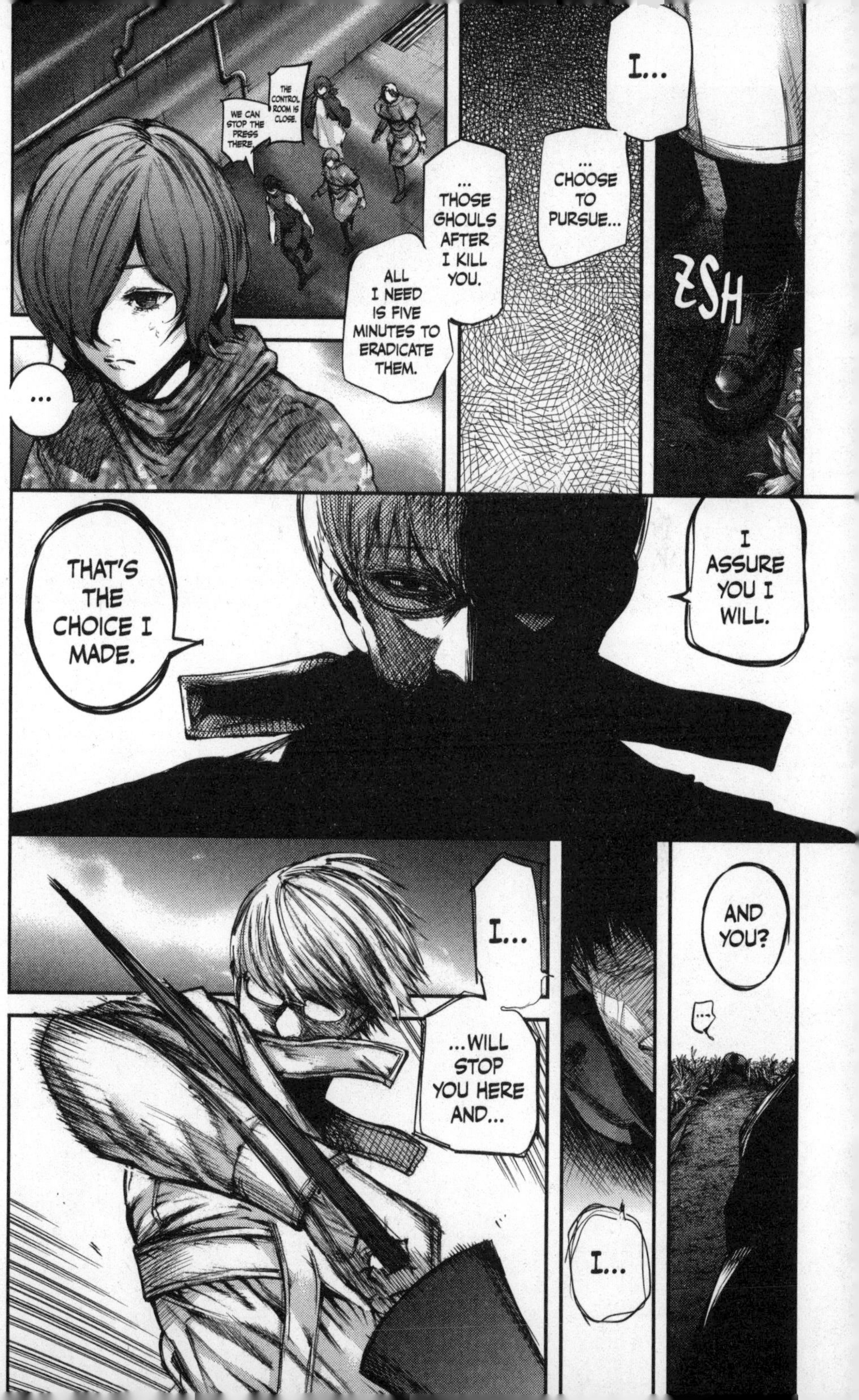
I...
...CHOOSE TO PURSUE...
ZSH
...THOSE GHOULS AFTER I KILL YOU.
ALL I NEED IS FIVE MINUTES TO ERADICATE THEM.
THE CONTROL ROOM IS CLOSE.
WE CAN STOP THE PRESS THERE.
...
I ASSURE YOU I WILL.
THAT'S THE CHOICE I MADE.
AND YOU?
...
I...
I...
...WILL STOP YOU HERE AND...

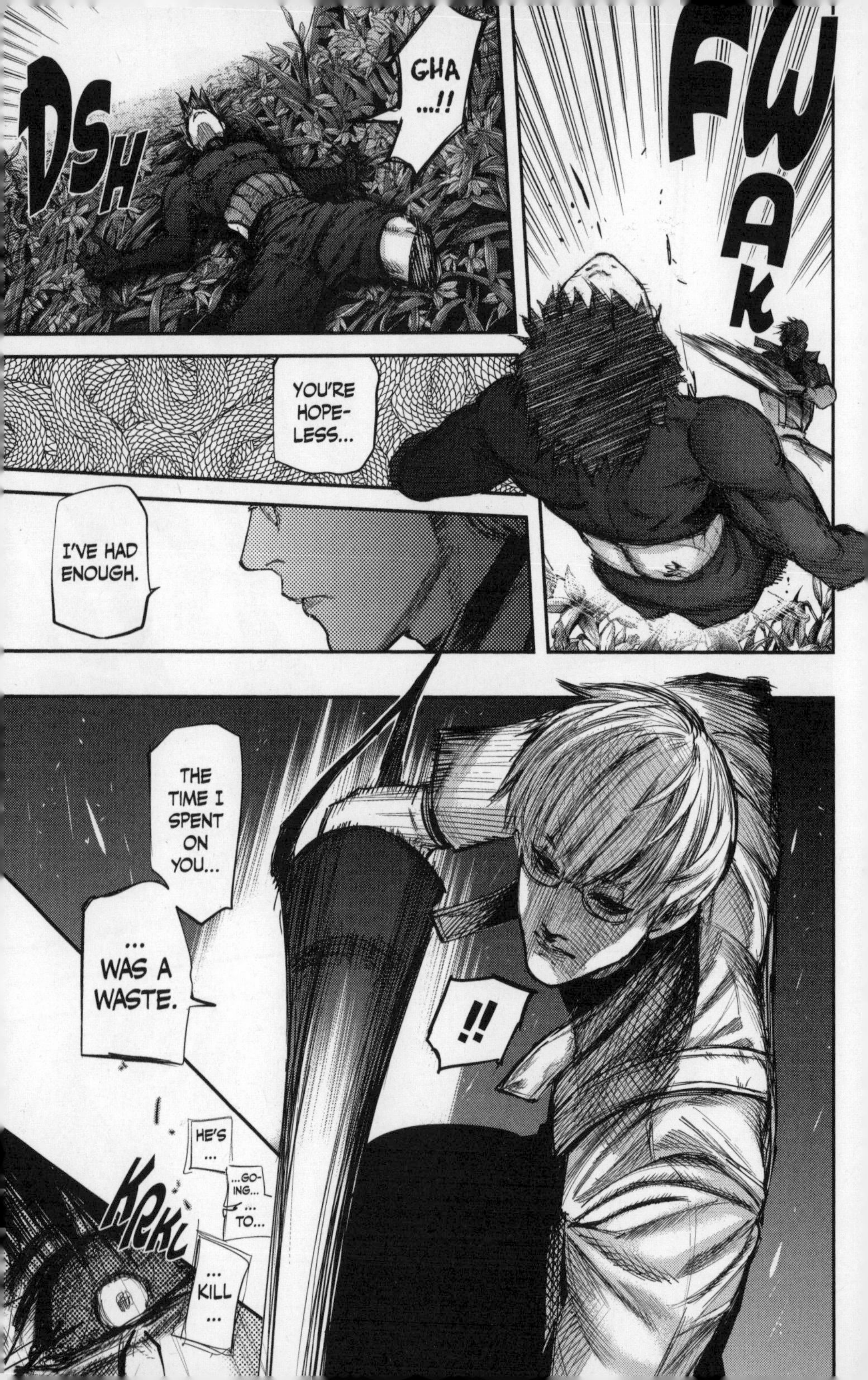
FWAK
DSH
GHA ...!!
YOU'RE HOPE-LESS...
I'VE HAD ENOUGH.
!!
THE TIME I SPENT ON YOU...
... WAS A WASTE.
HE'S ...
...GO-ING... ... TO...
... KILL ...

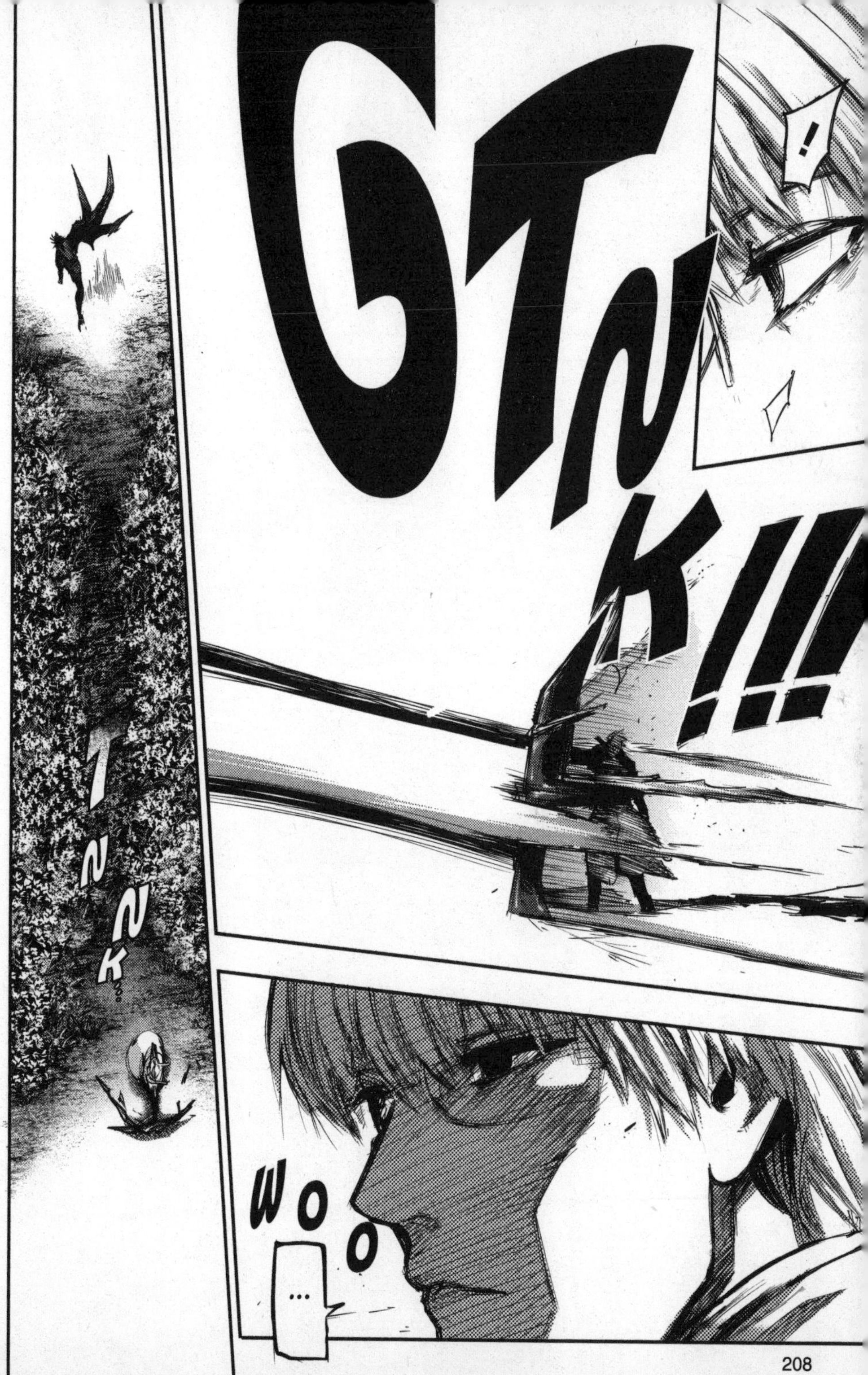
!
GTAK!!!
WOO
...
Tzzk...

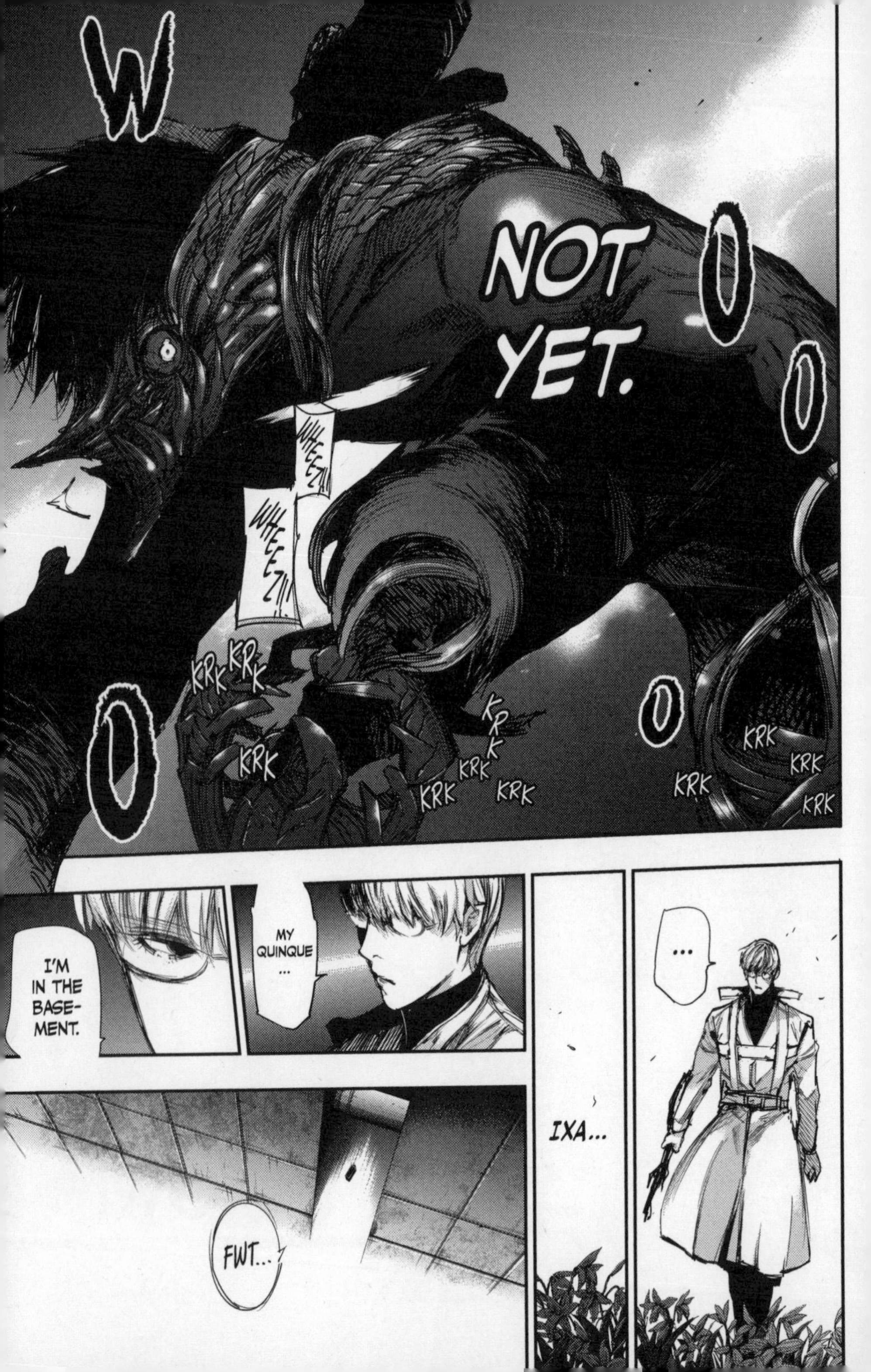
NOT YET.
WOOOO
WHEEZ!!
WHEEZ!!
KRK KRK
KRK
KRK KRK KRK KRK
KRK KRK KRK KRK
...
IXA...
MY QUINQUE ...
I'M IN THE BASE-MENT.
FWT...

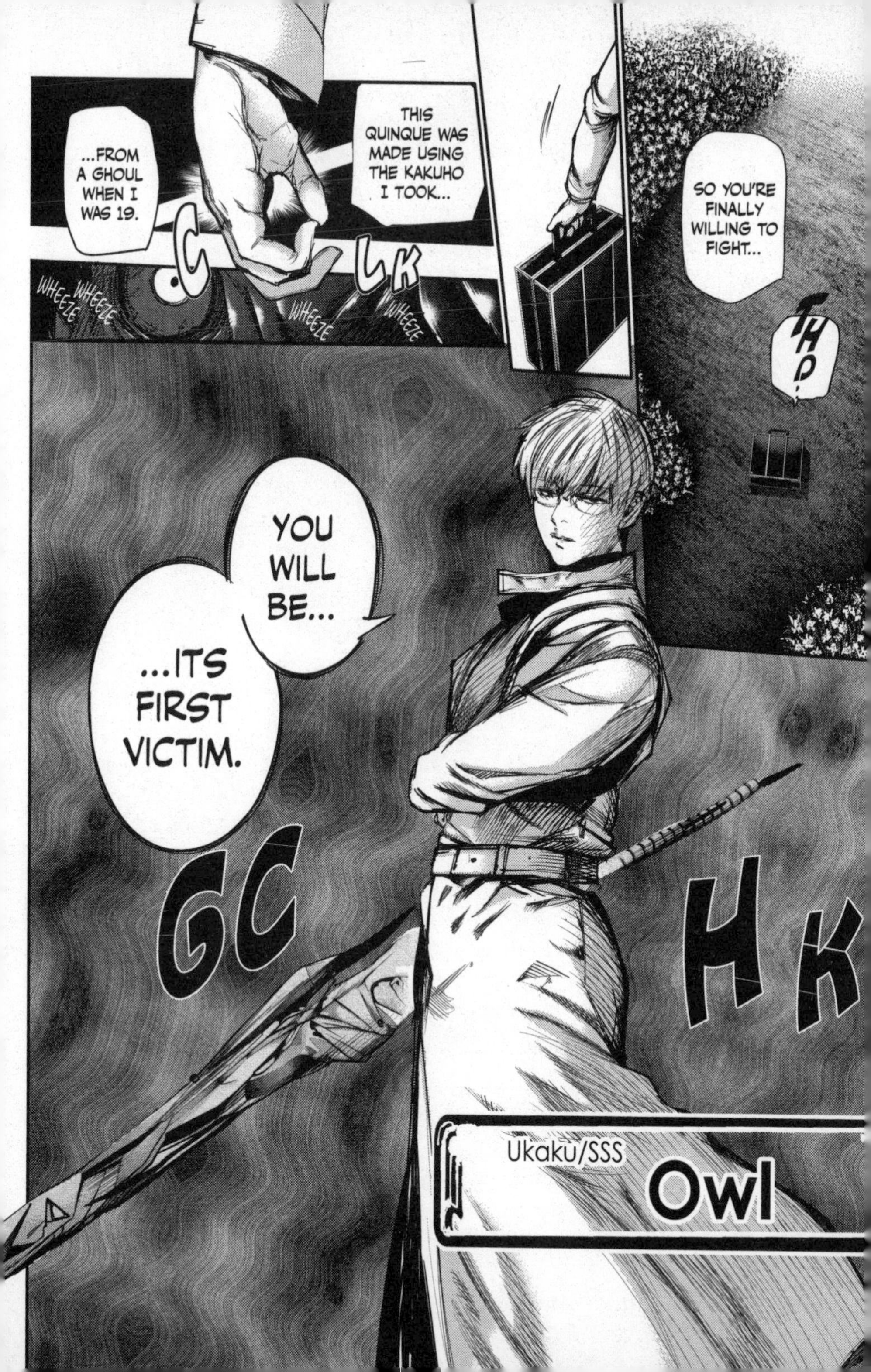
SO YOU'RE FINALLY WILLING TO FIGHT...
THD
THIS QUINQUE WAS MADE USING THE KAKUHO I TOOK...
...FROM A GHOUL WHEN I WAS 19.
CLK
WHEEZE WHEEZE
WHEEZE WHEEZE
YOU WILL BE...
...ITS FIRST VICTIM.
HK
GC
Ukaku/SSS
Owl

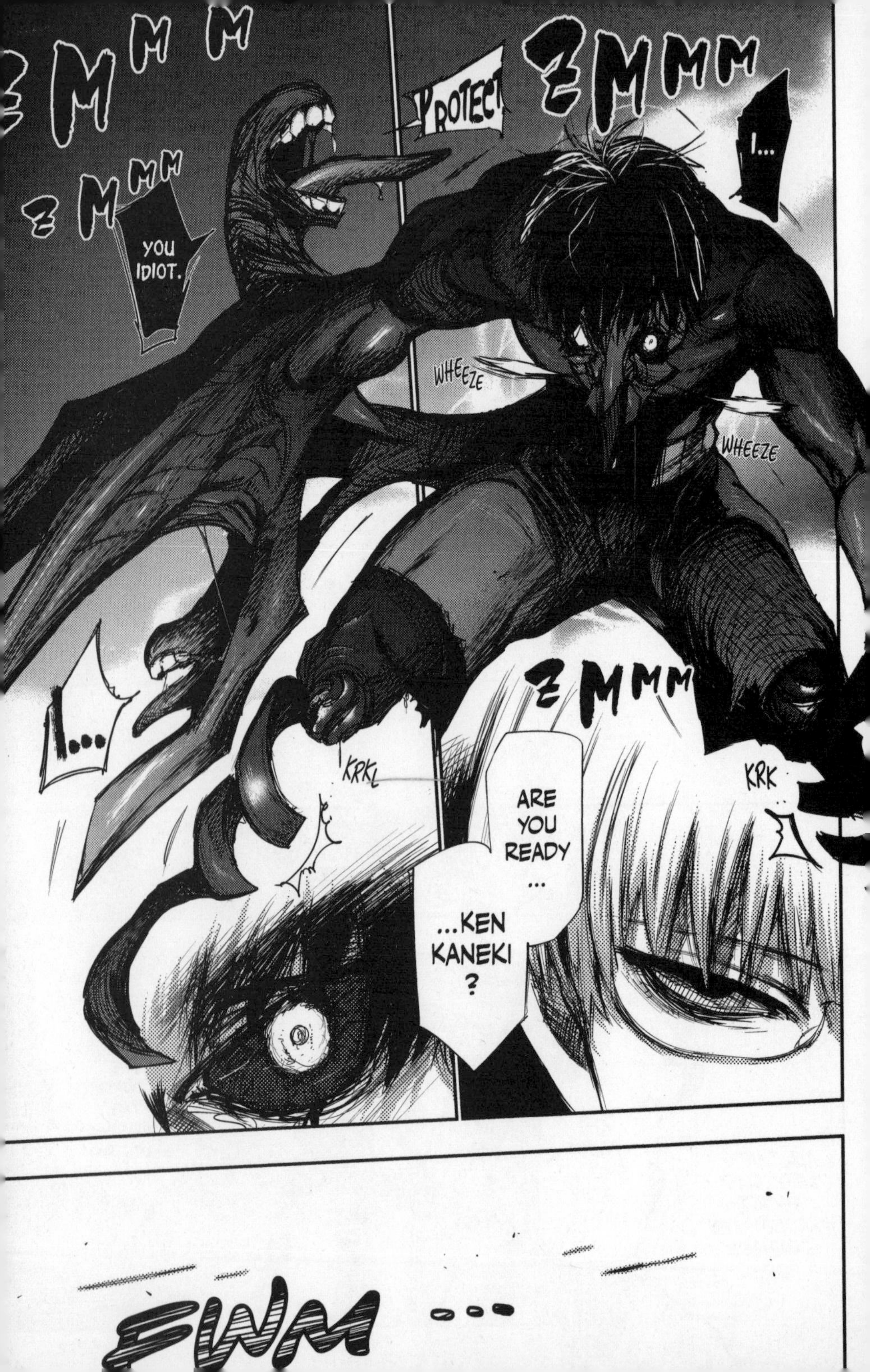
ZMMMM
PROTECT
I...
ZMMM
ZMMM
YOU IDIOT.
WHEEZE
WHEEZE
ZMMM
KRK
ARE YOU READY ...
...KEN KANEKI ?
KRKL
I...
SWM ...

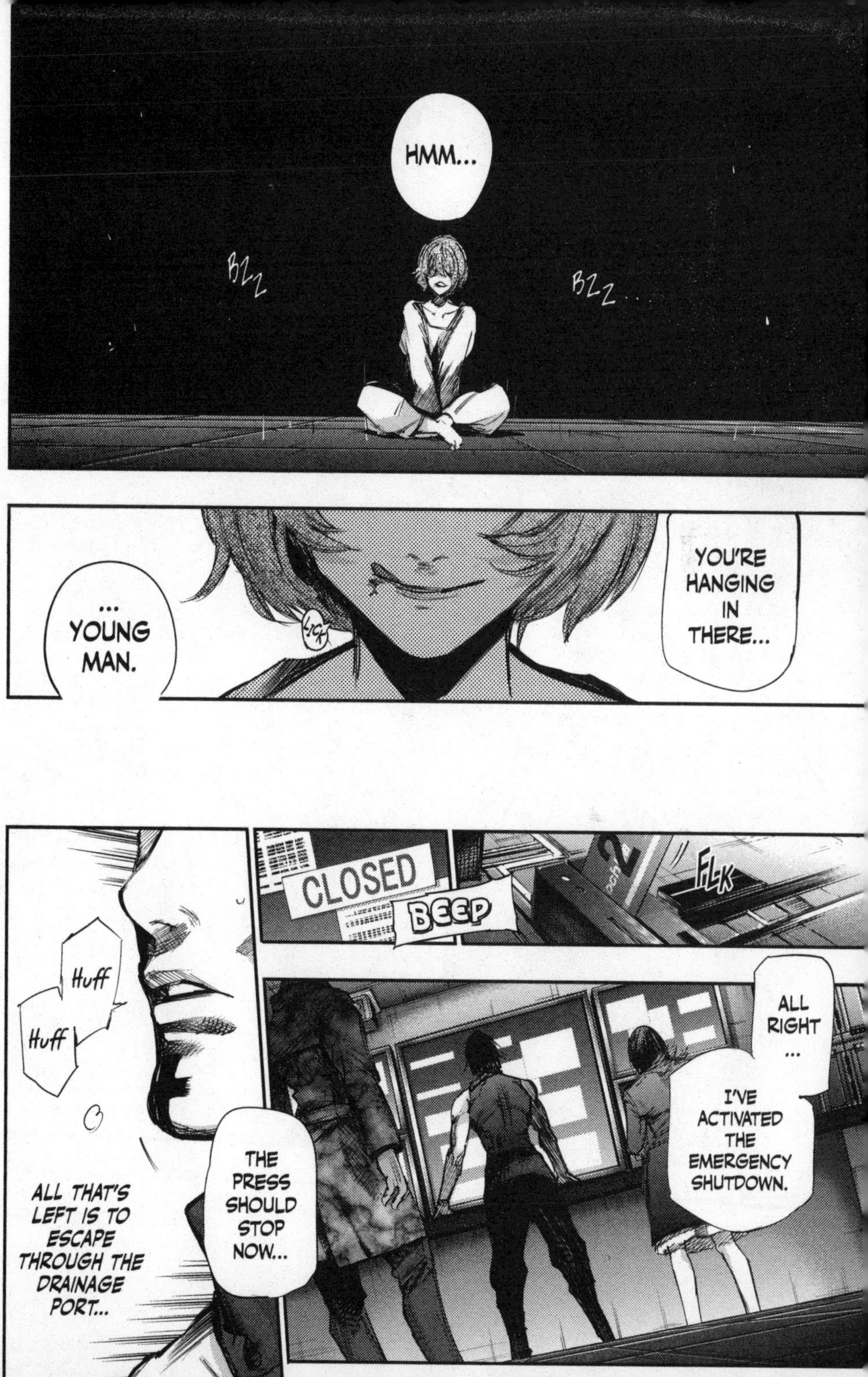
HMM...
BZZ...
BZZ
YOU'RE HANGING IN THERE...
LICK
... YOUNG MAN.
FLK
CLOSED
BEEP
ALL RIGHT ...
I'VE ACTIVATED THE EMERGENCY SHUTDOWN.
THE PRESS SHOULD STOP NOW...
Huff
Huff
ALL THAT'S LEFT IS TO ESCAPE THROUGH THE DRAINAGE PORT...

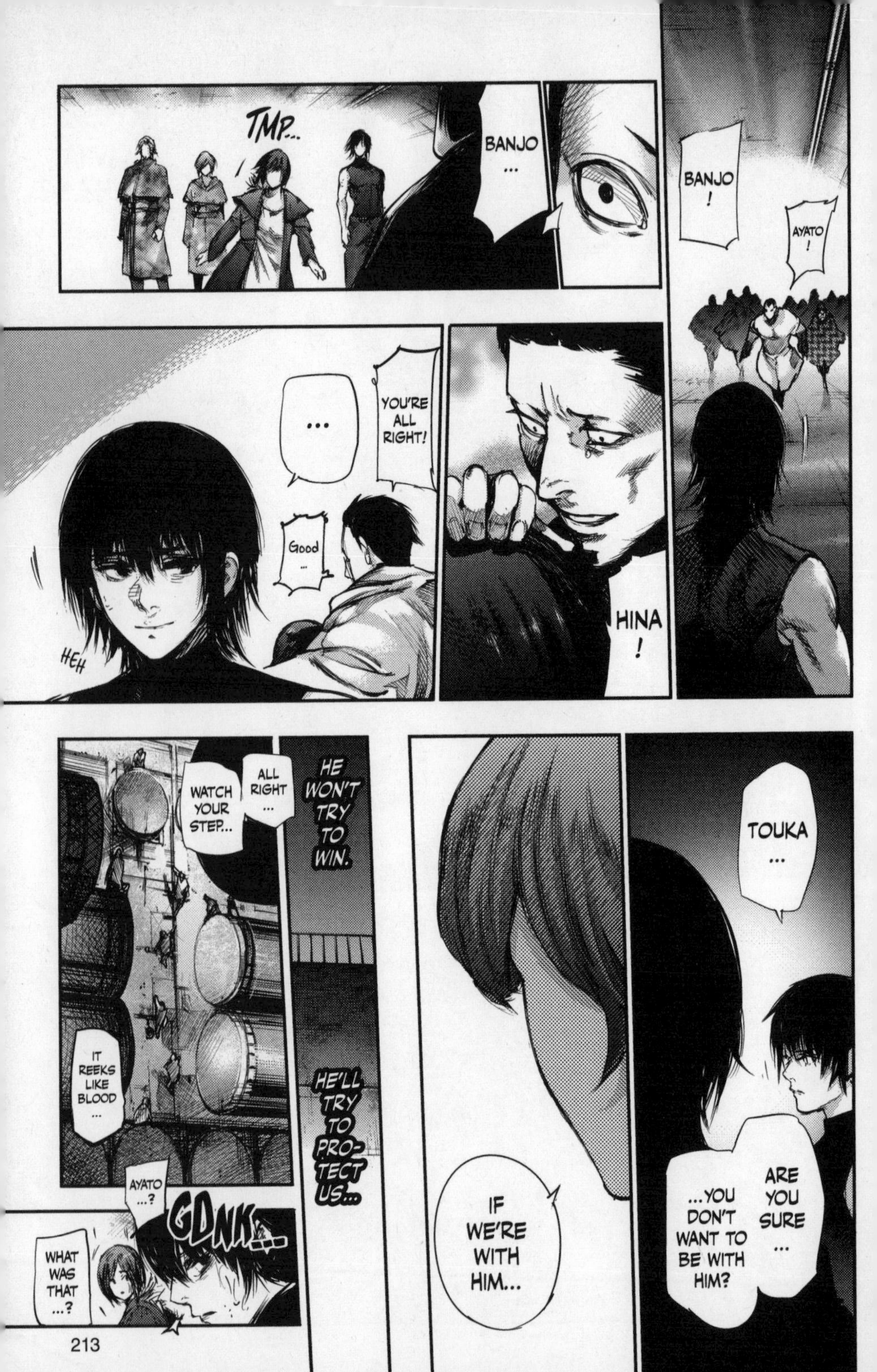
BANJO!
AYATO!
BANJO...
TMP...
HINA!
YOU'RE ALL RIGHT!
...
Good...
HEH
TOUKA...
ARE YOU SURE...
...YOU DON'T WANT TO BE WITH HIM?
IF WE'RE WITH HIM...
HE WON'T TRY TO WIN.
HE'LL TRY TO PRO-TECT US...
ALL RIGHT...
WATCH YOUR STEP...
IT REEKS LIKE BLOOD...
AYATO...?
GDNK...
WHAT WAS THAT...?

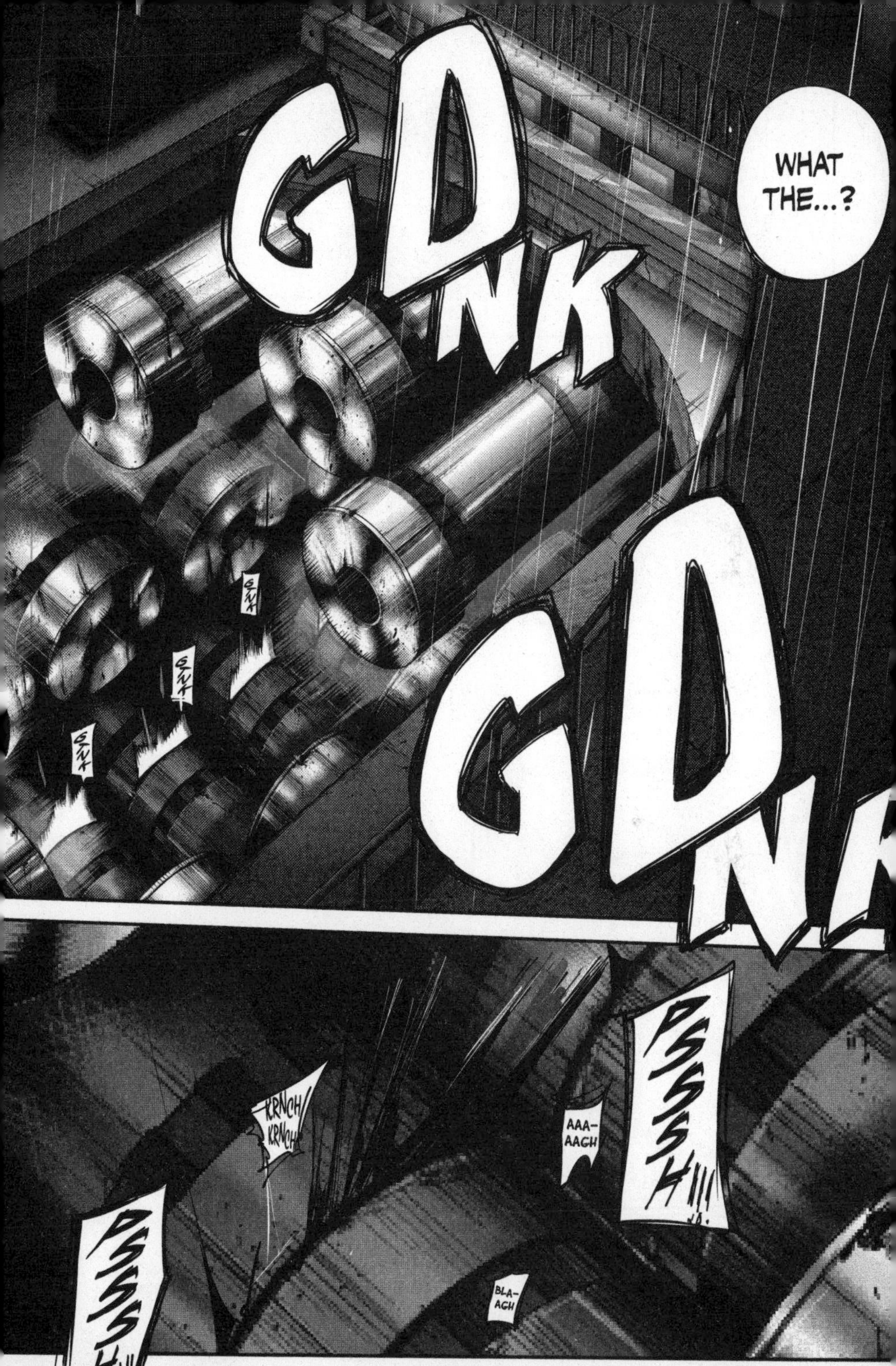
GDNK
WHAT THE...?
GDN
GINK
GINK
GINK
PSSSH!!!
AAA-AAGH
KRNCH KRNCH
BLA-AGH
PSSSH!!

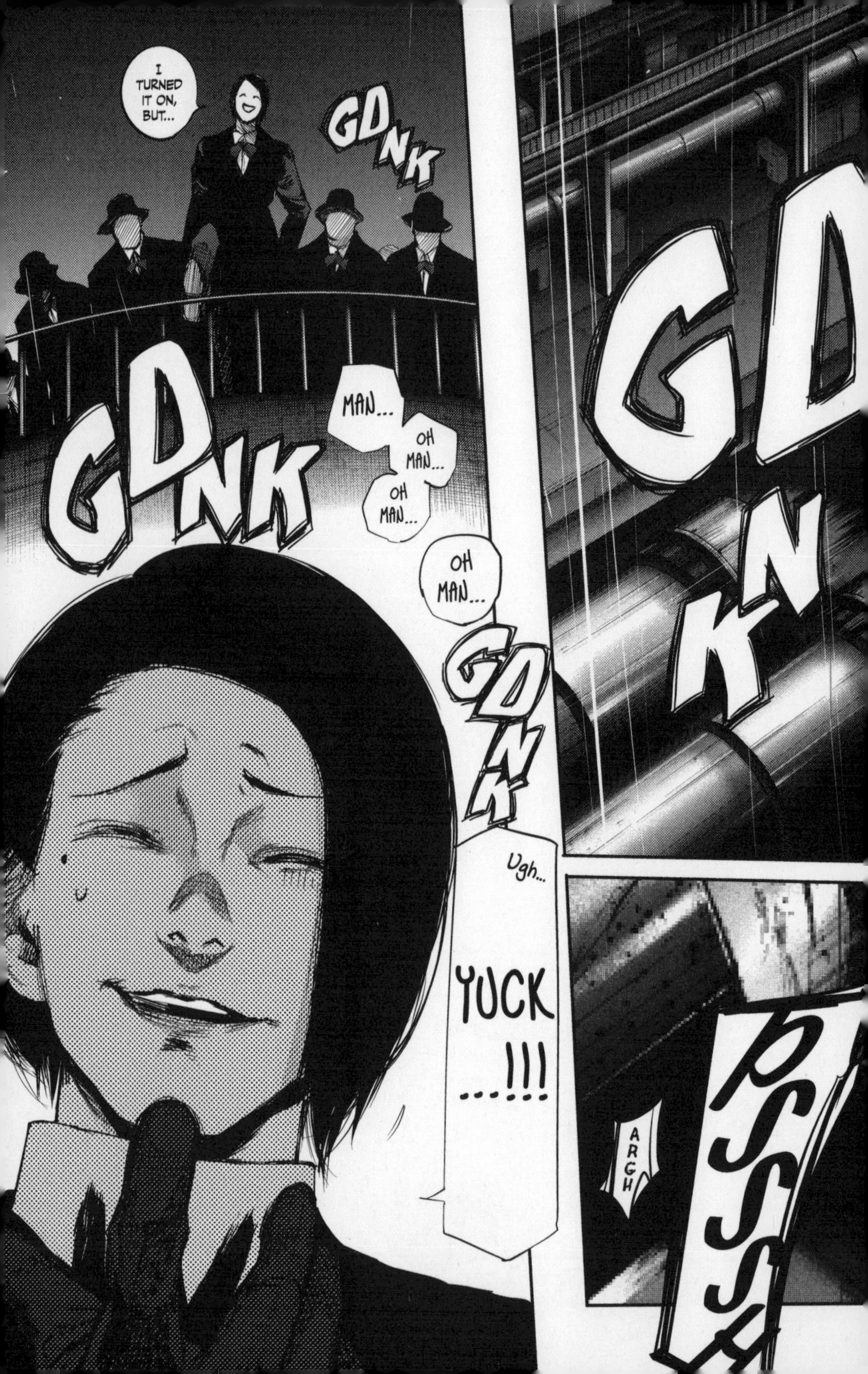
GDNK
ARGH
PSSS
I TURNED IT ON, BUT...
GDNK
GDNK
MAN...
OH MAN...
OH MAN...
OH MAN...
GDNK
Ugh...
YUCK !!!
...!!!

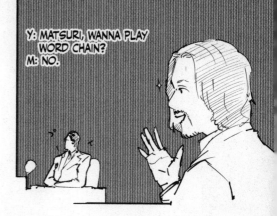

Y: MATSURI, WANNA PLAY WORD CHAIN?
M: NO.

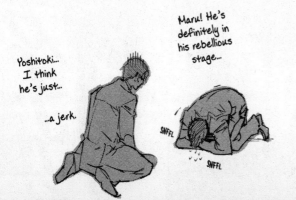

Maru! He's definitely in his rebellious stage...
SNFFL
SNFFL
Yoshitoki... I think he's just...
...a jerk.

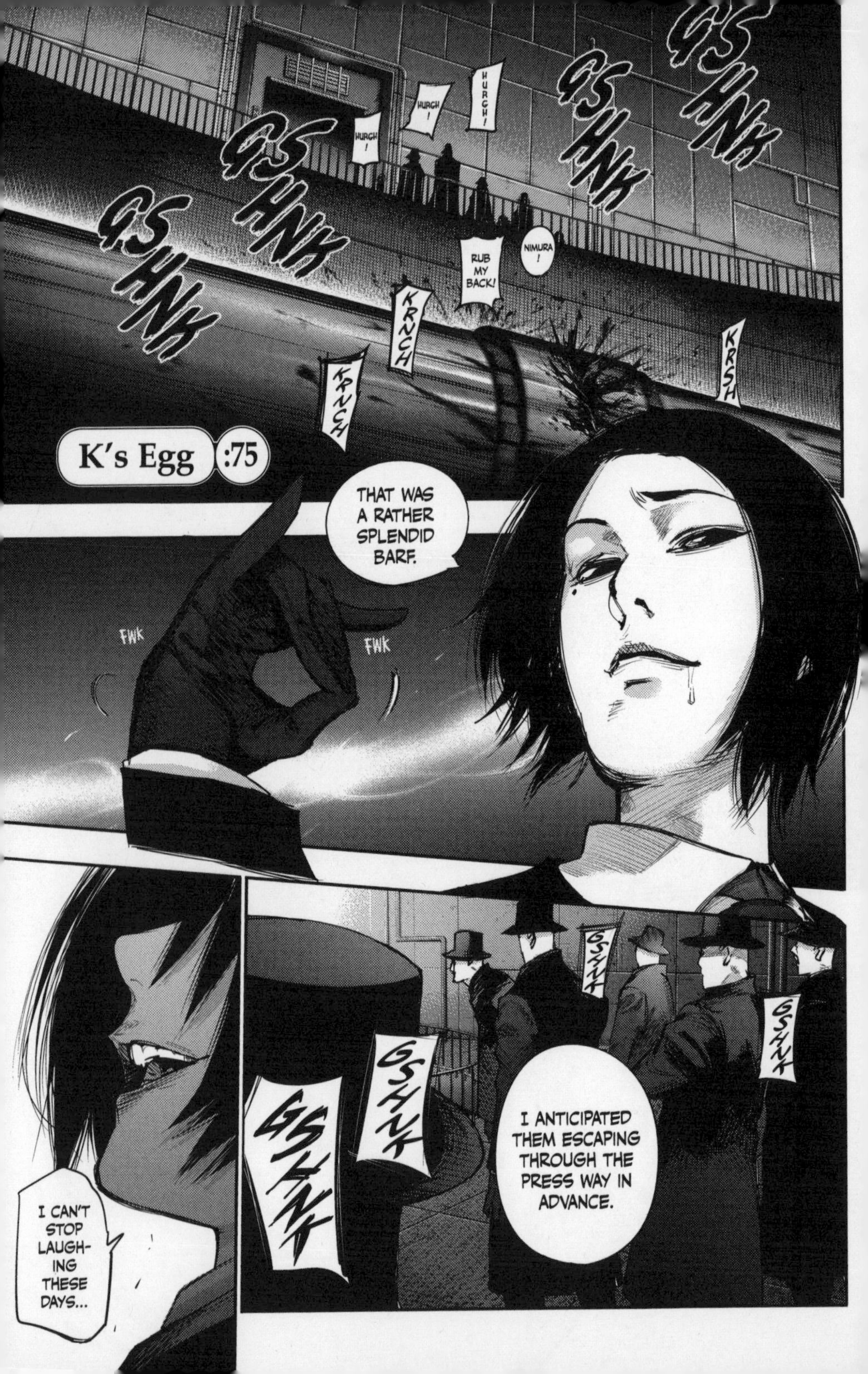
GSHNK
GSHNK
HURGH!
HURGH!
HURGH!
GSHNK
GSHNK
NIMURA!
RUB MY BACK!
KRSH
KRNCH
KRNCH
K's Egg :75
THAT WAS A RATHER SPLENDID BARF.
FWK
FWK
GSHNK
GSHNK
GSHNK
GSHNK
I ANTICIPATED THEM ESCAPING THROUGH THE PRESS WAY IN ADVANCE.
I CAN'T STOP LAUGHING THESE DAYS...

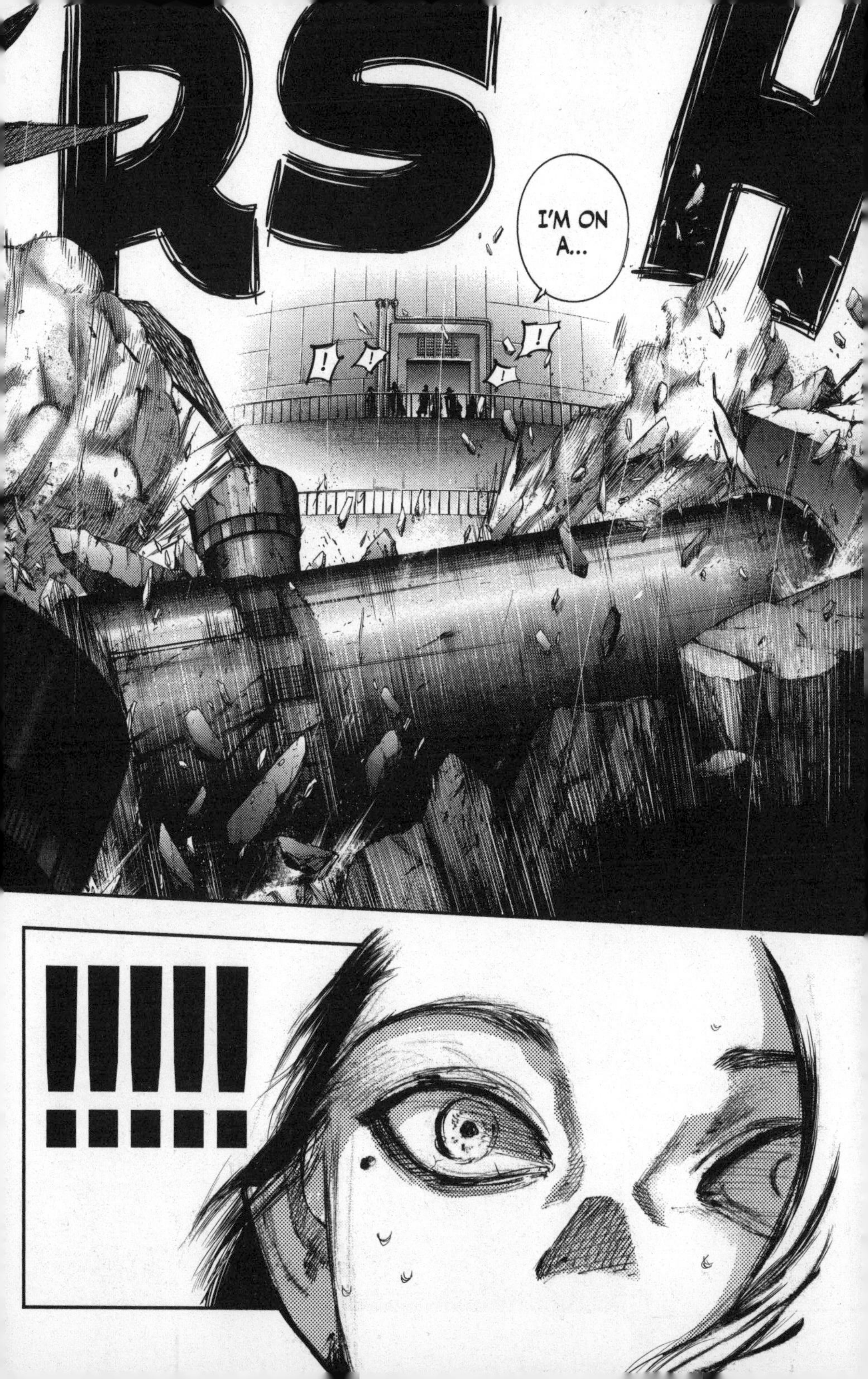
I'M ON A...
!!!!!

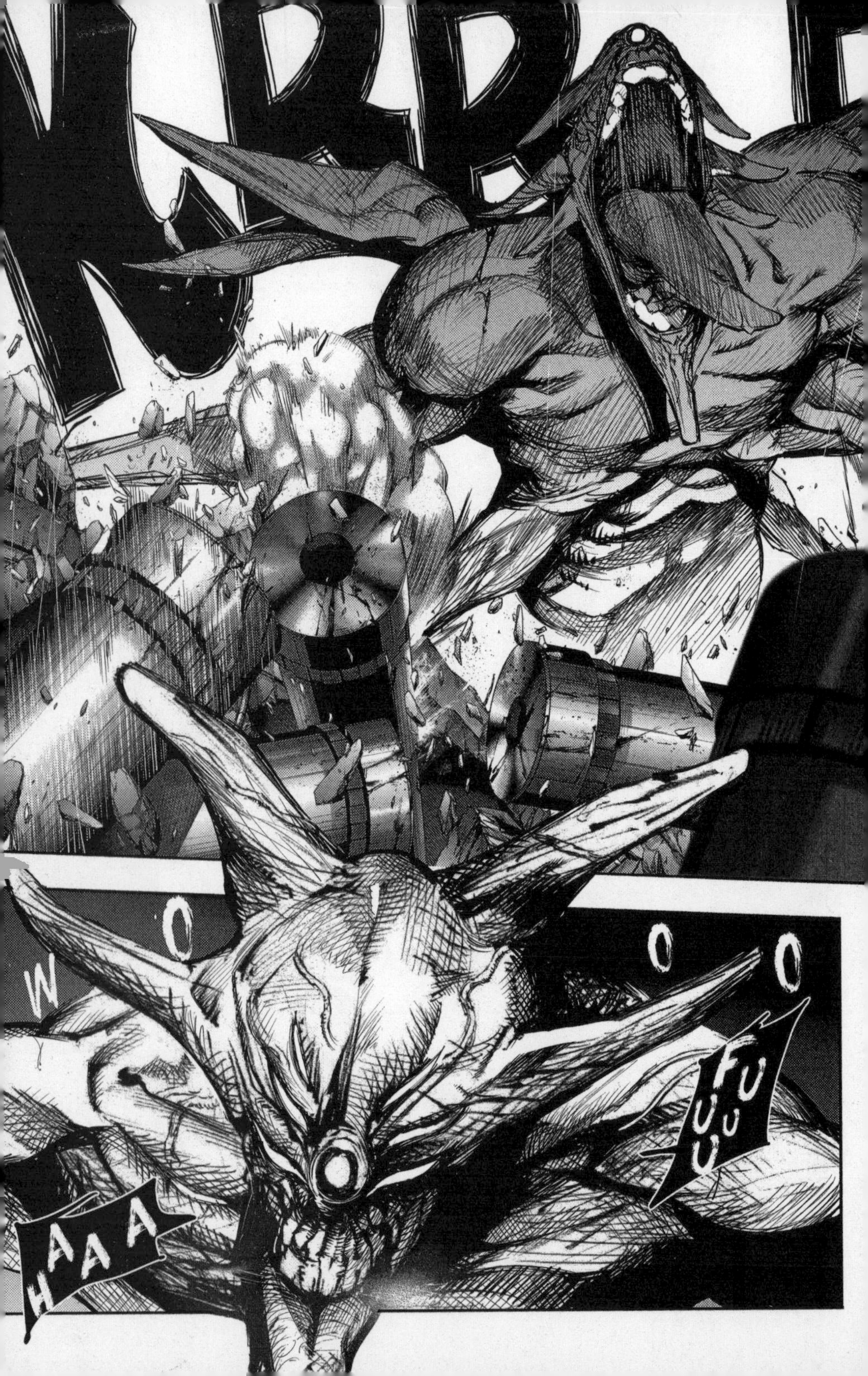
WOOOO
FUUUU
HAAA

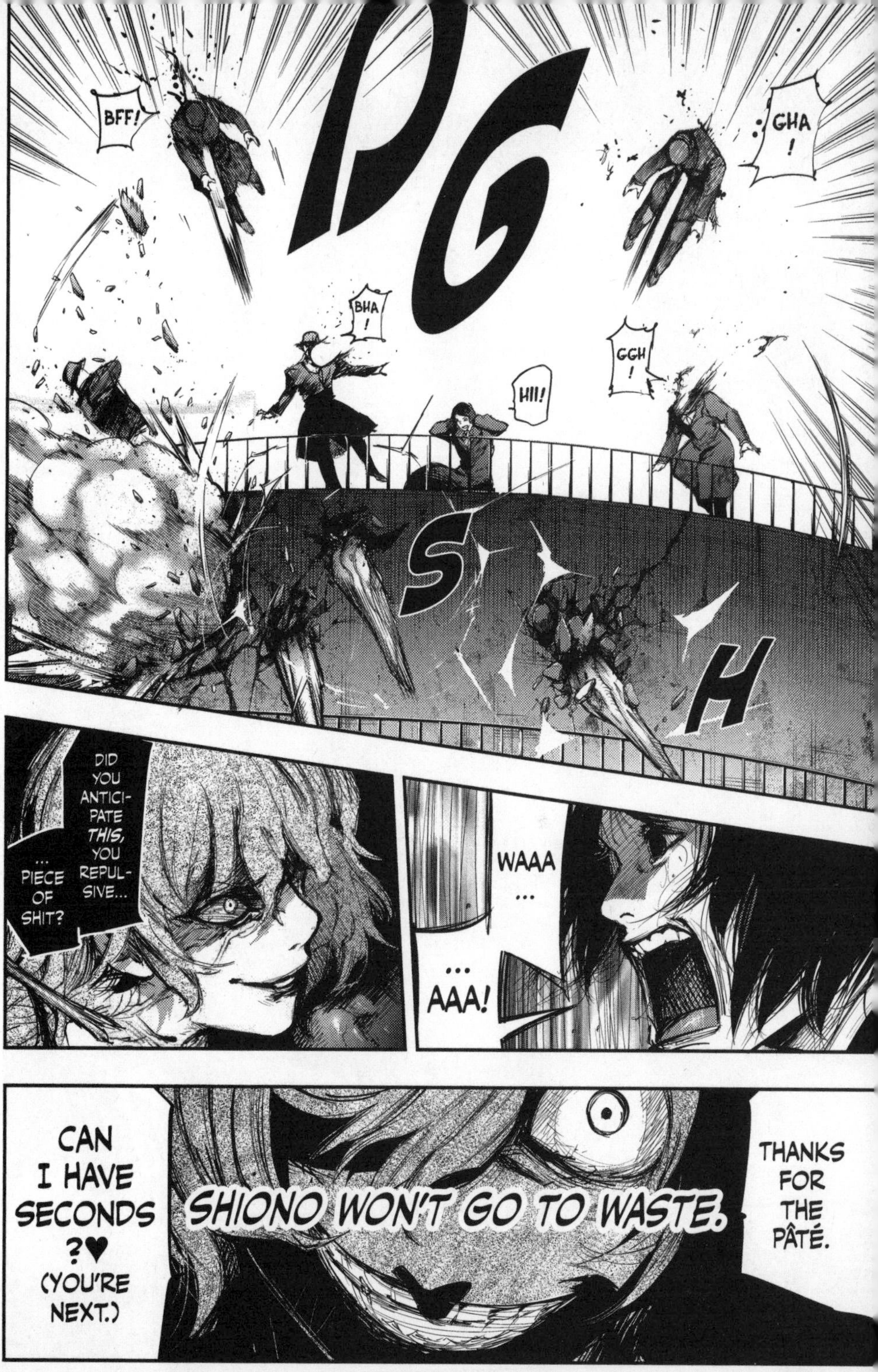
GHA!
DG
BFF!
GGH!
BHA!
HII!
SSH
WAAA...
...AAA!
DID YOU ANTICIPATE THIS, YOU REPULSIVE...
...PIECE OF SHIT?
THANKS FOR THE PÂTÉ.
SHIONO WON'T GO TO WASTE.
CAN I HAVE SECONDS?♥
(YOU'RE NEXT.)

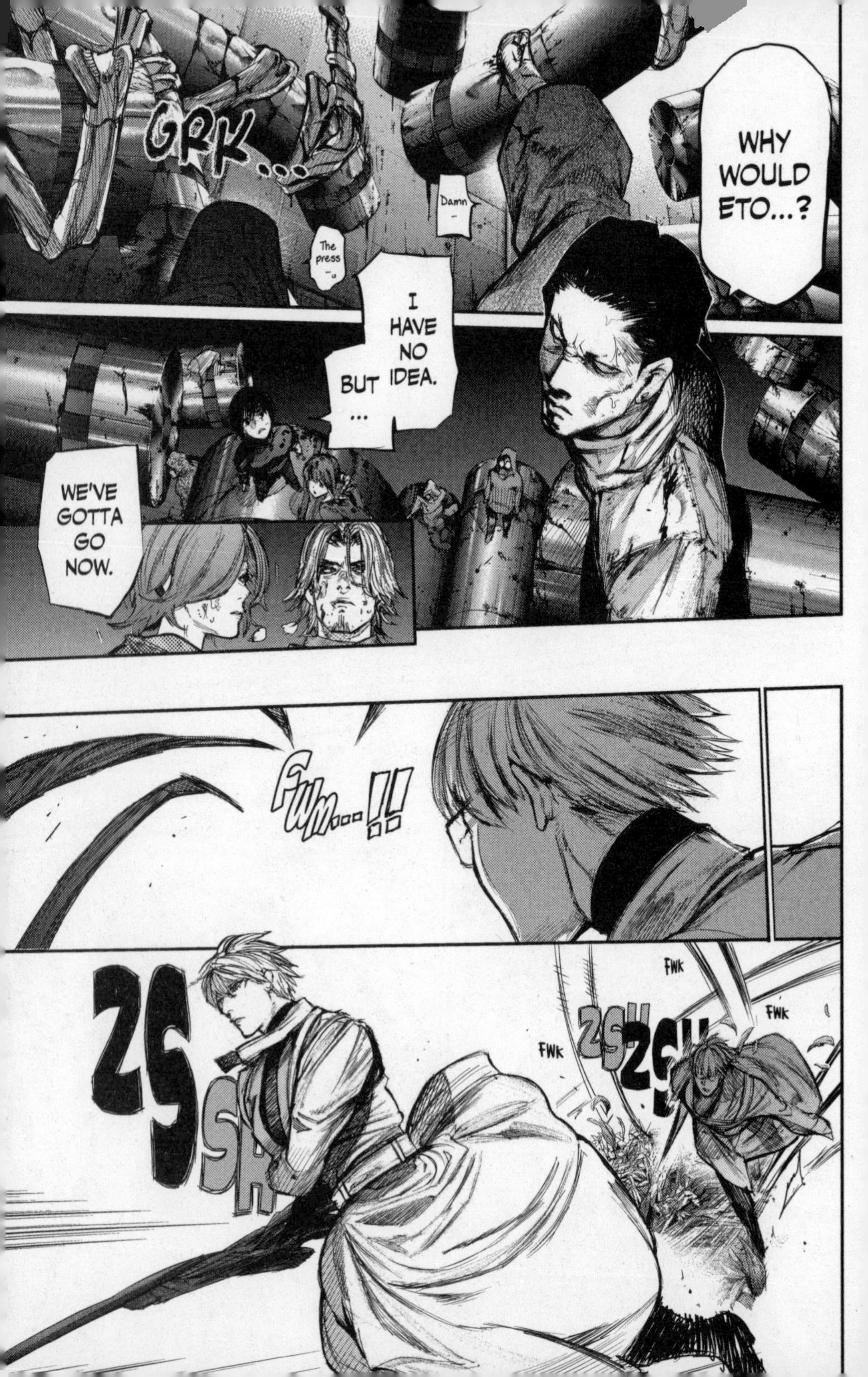
WHY WOULD ETO...?
Damn ...
GRK...
The press ...
I HAVE NO IDEA.
BUT ...
WE'VE GOTTA GO NOW.
FWM...!!
FWK
FWK
ZSH
ZSH
FWK
ZSSH

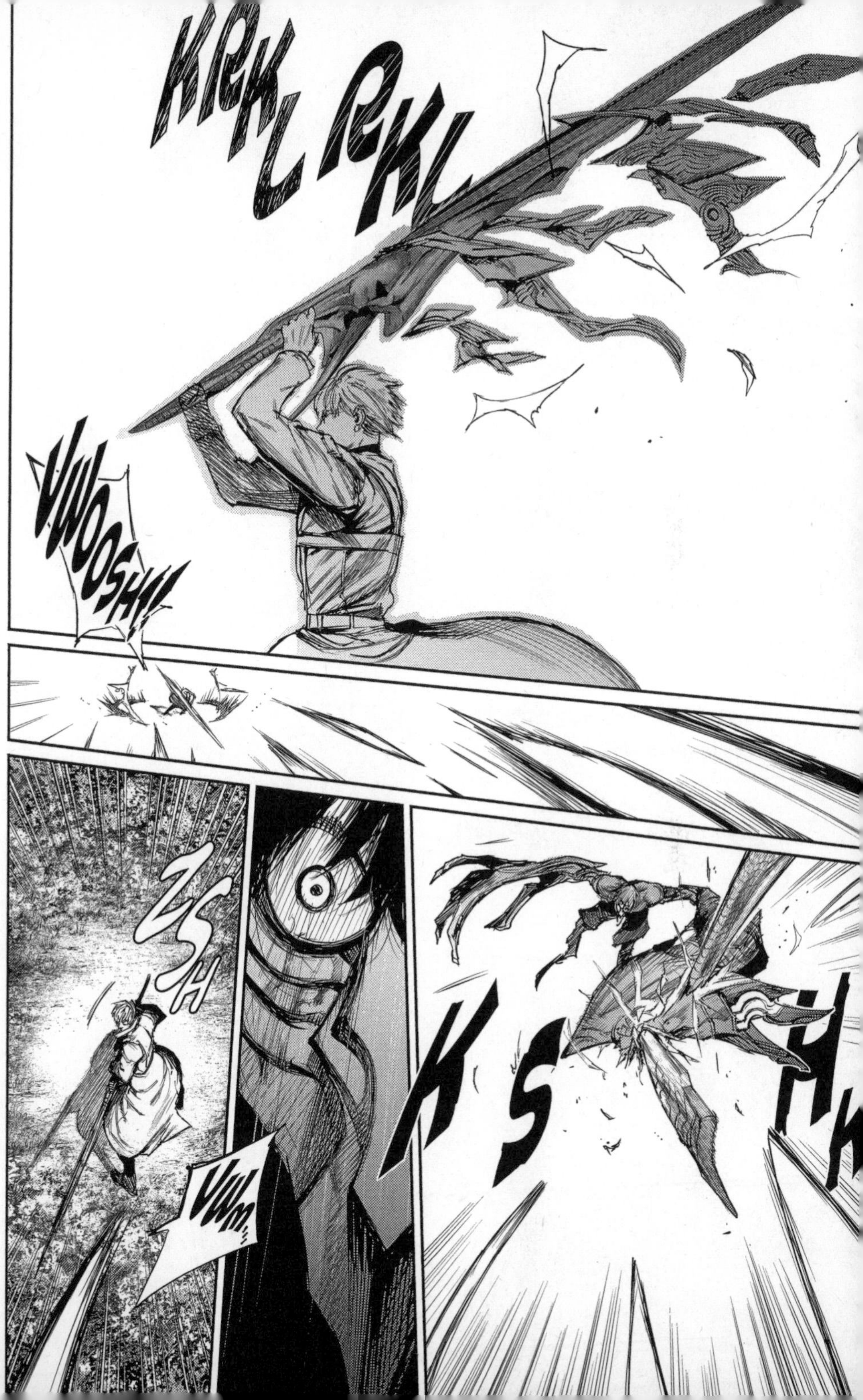
KRKK LRKL
VWOOSH!!
KSHK
ZSH
VUM...

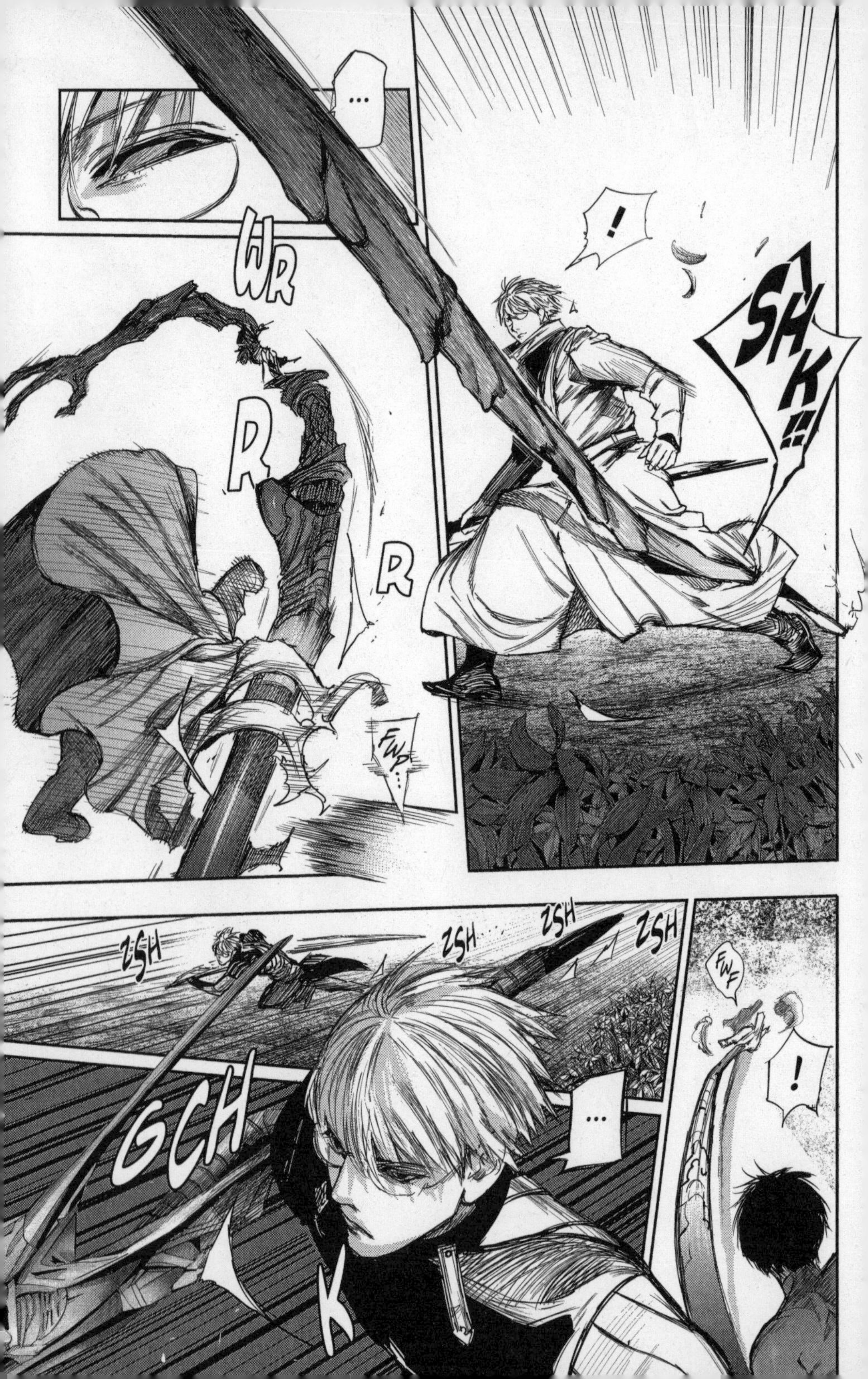
!
SHK!!
...
WRRR
FWP...
FWF
!
ZSH
ZSH...
ZSH
ZSH
...
GCH
K

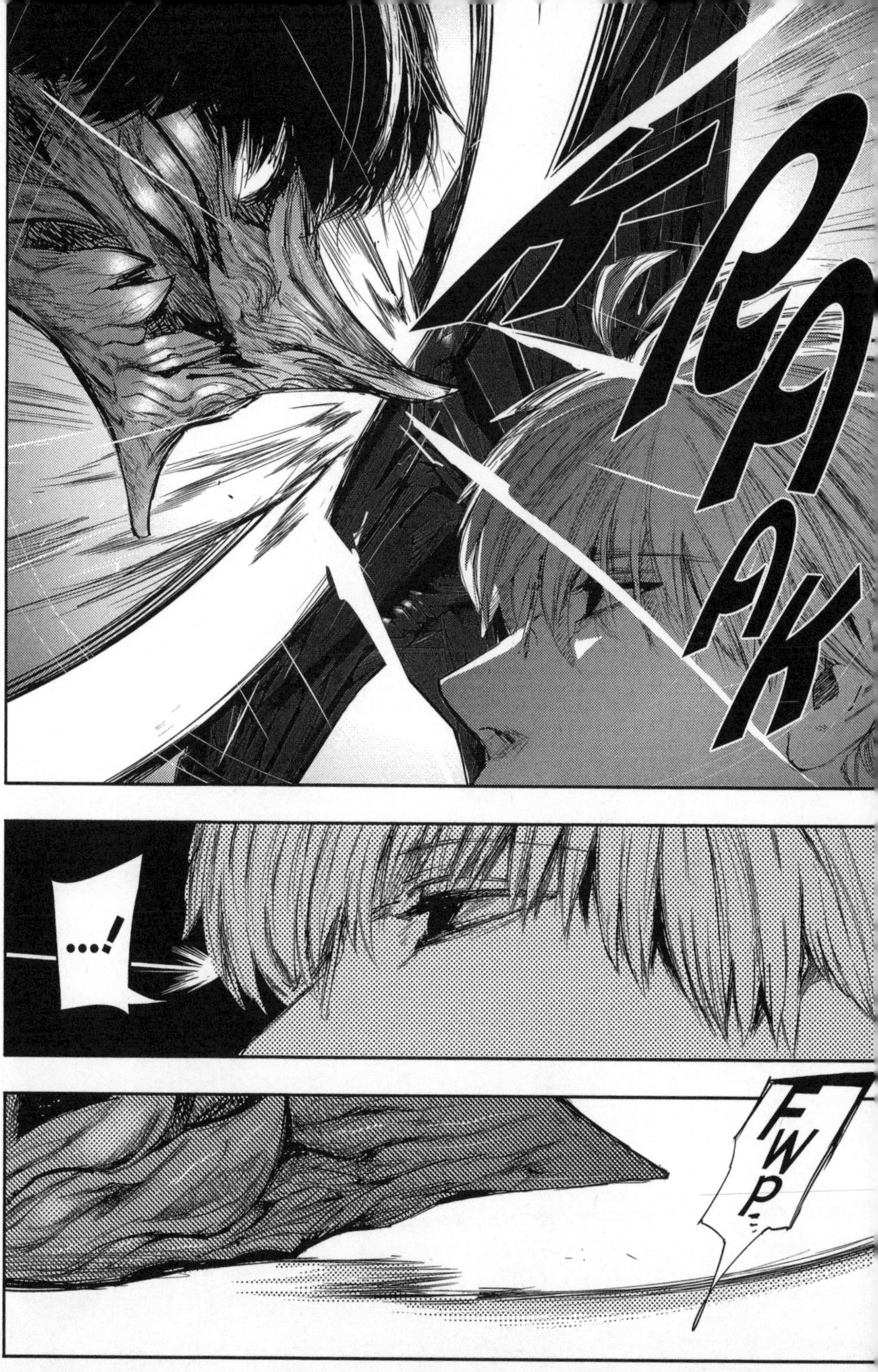
KRAAK
...!
FWP...

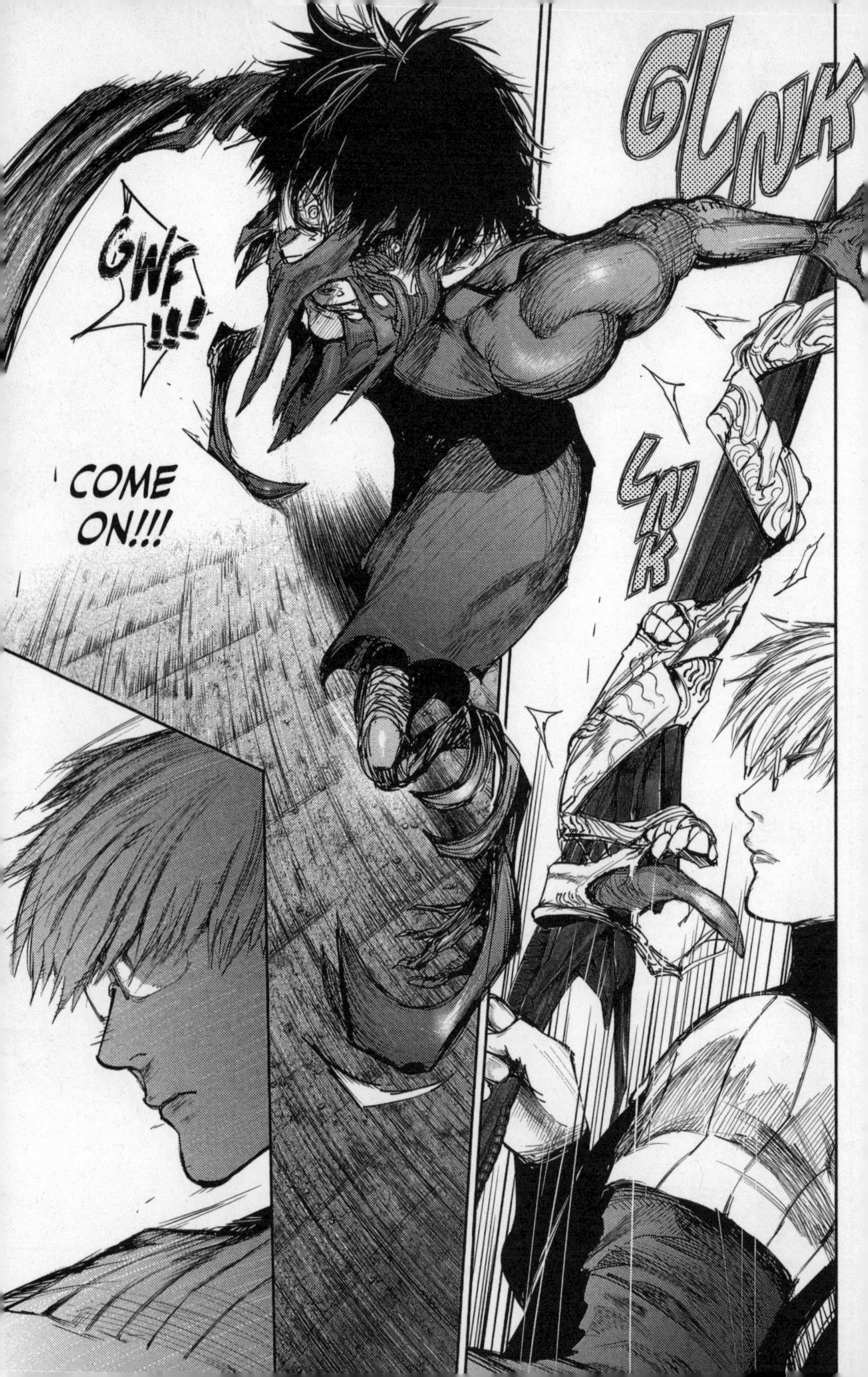
GLNK
LNK
GWF!!!
COME ON!!!

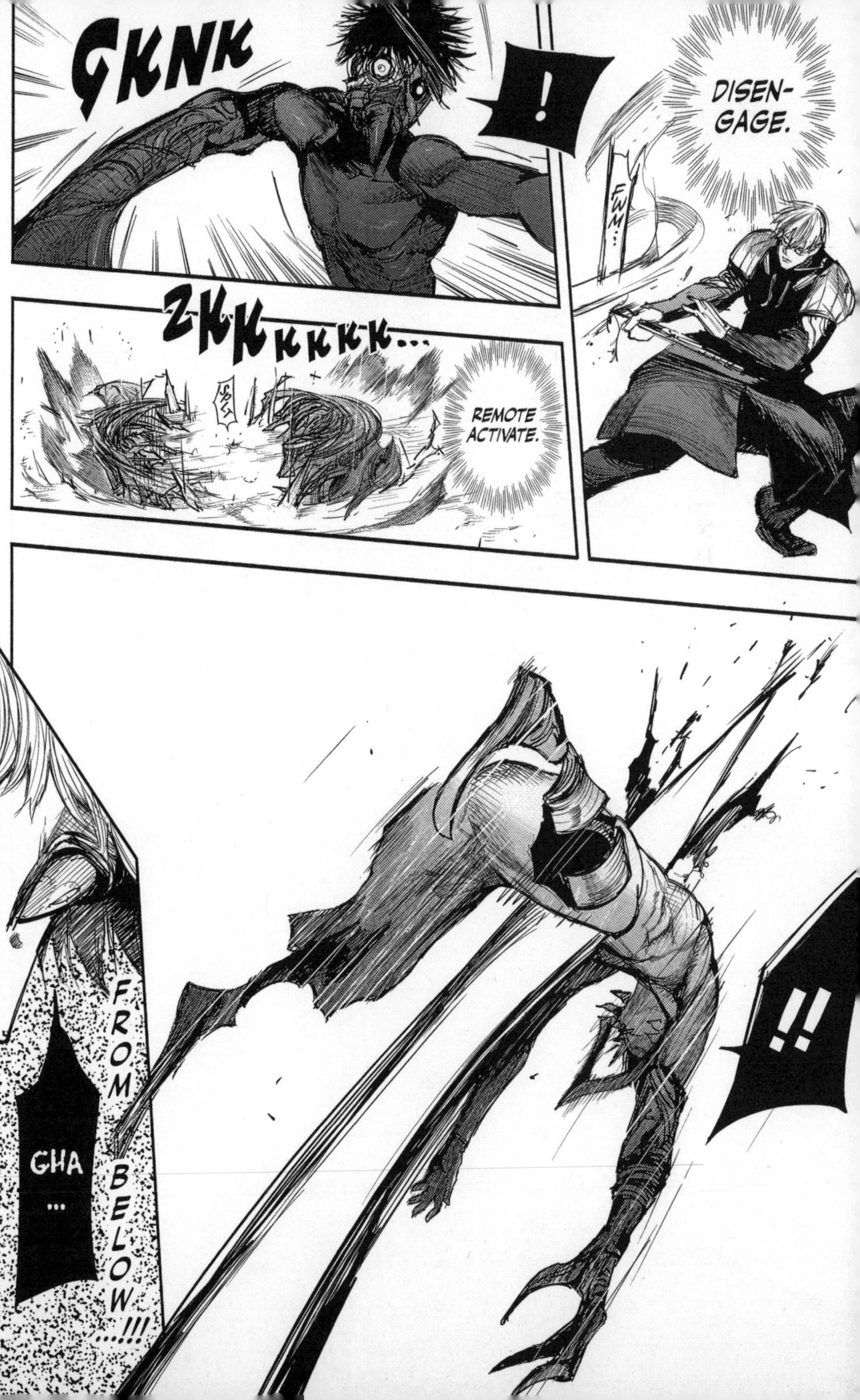
DISEN-
GAGE.
FWM...
!
GKNK
REMOTE ACTIVATE.
ZKKKKKKK...
SPLT
!!
FROM BELOW...!!!
GHA...

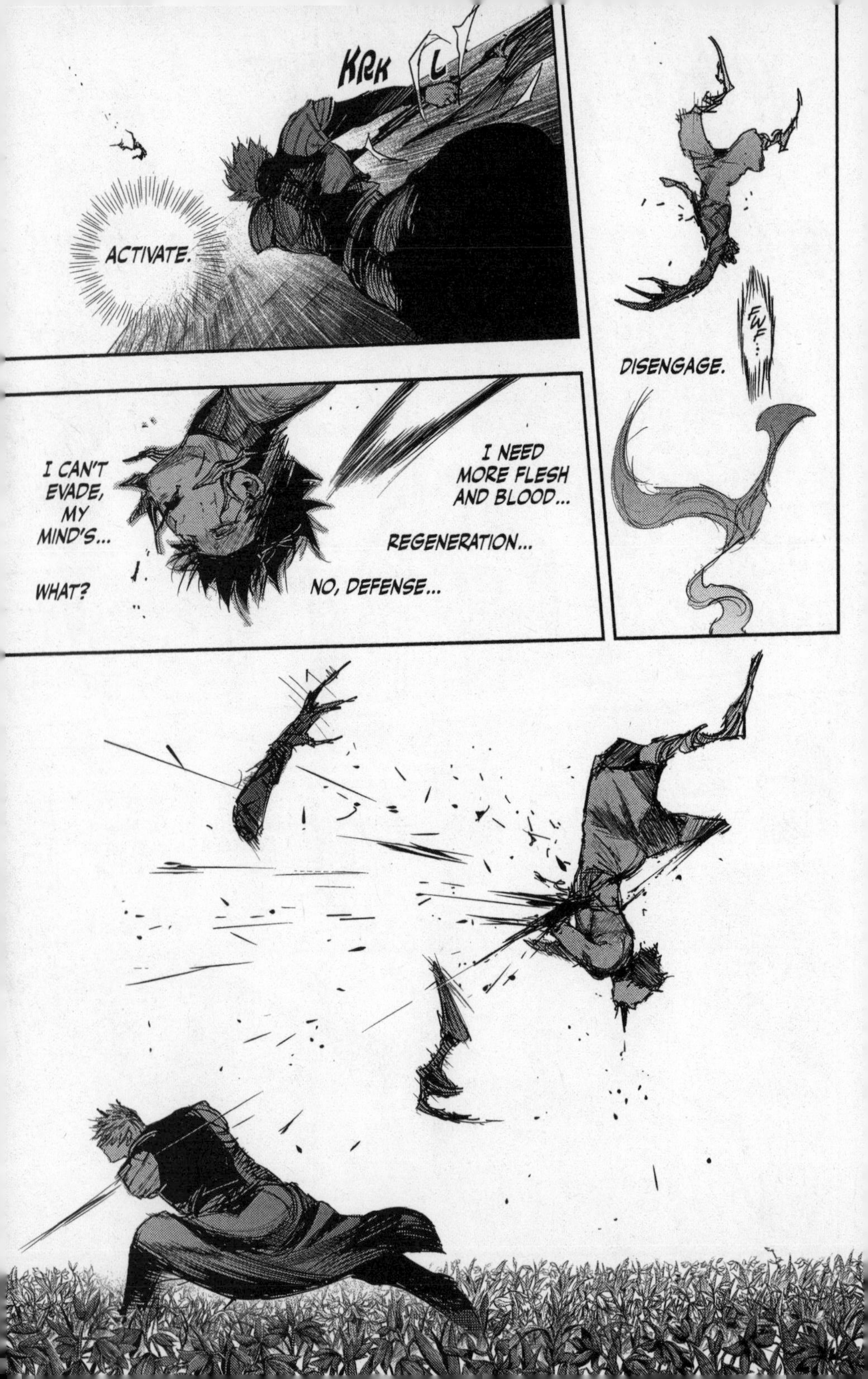
FWF...
DISENGAGE.
KRK
L
ACTIVATE.
I NEED MORE FLESH AND BLOOD...
REGENERATION...
NO, DEFENSE...
I CAN'T EVADE, MY MIND'S...
WHAT?

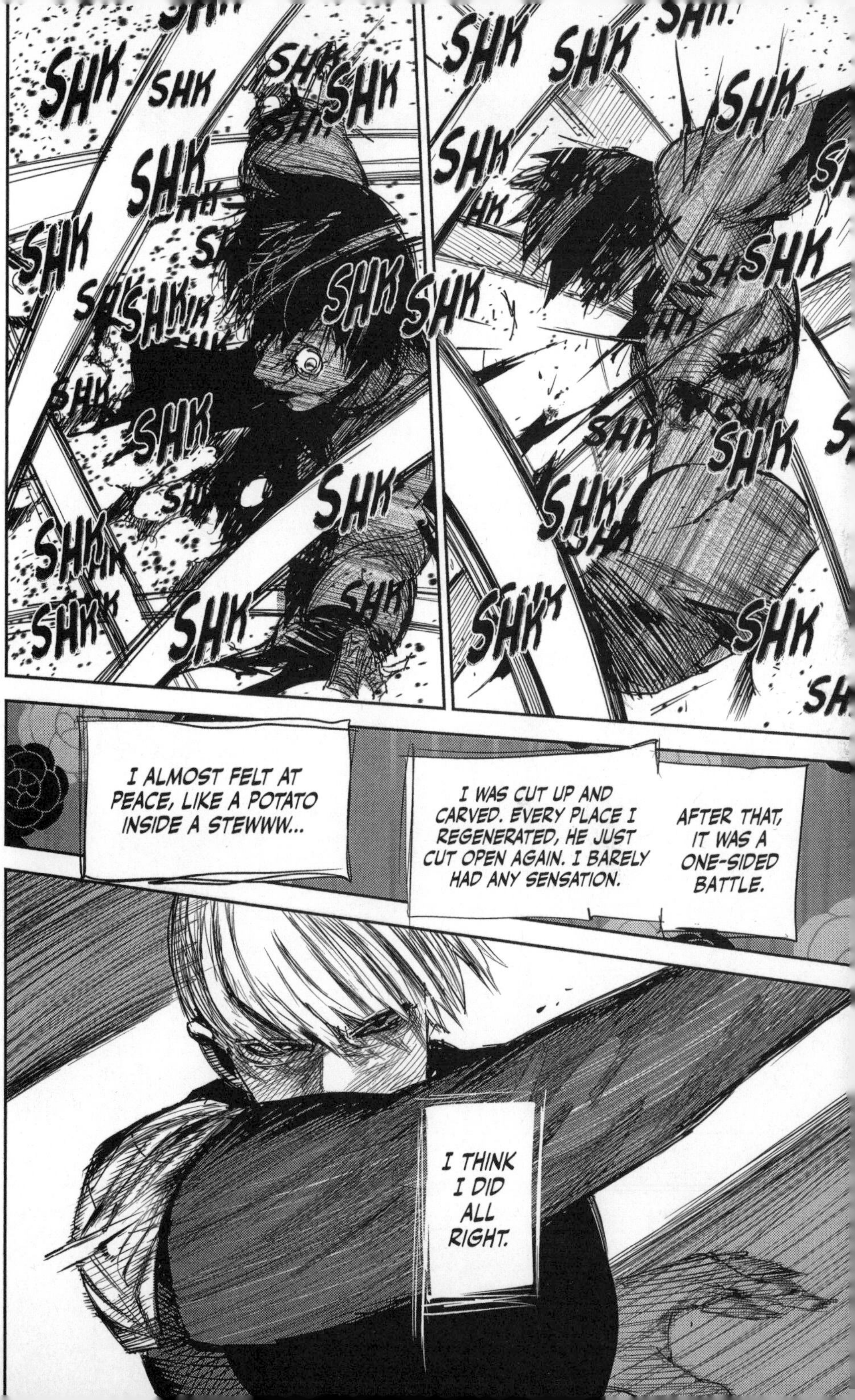
SHK
SHK
SHK
SHK
SHK
SHK
SHK
SHK
SHK
SHK
SHK
SHK
SHK
SHK
SHK
SHK
SHK
SHK
SHK
SHK
AFTER THAT, IT WAS A ONE-SIDED BATTLE.
I WAS CUT UP AND CARVED. EVERY PLACE I REGENERATED, HE JUST CUT OPEN AGAIN. I BARELY HAD ANY SENSATION.
I ALMOST FELT AT PEACE, LIKE A POTATO INSIDE A STEWWW...
I THINK I DID ALL RIGHT.

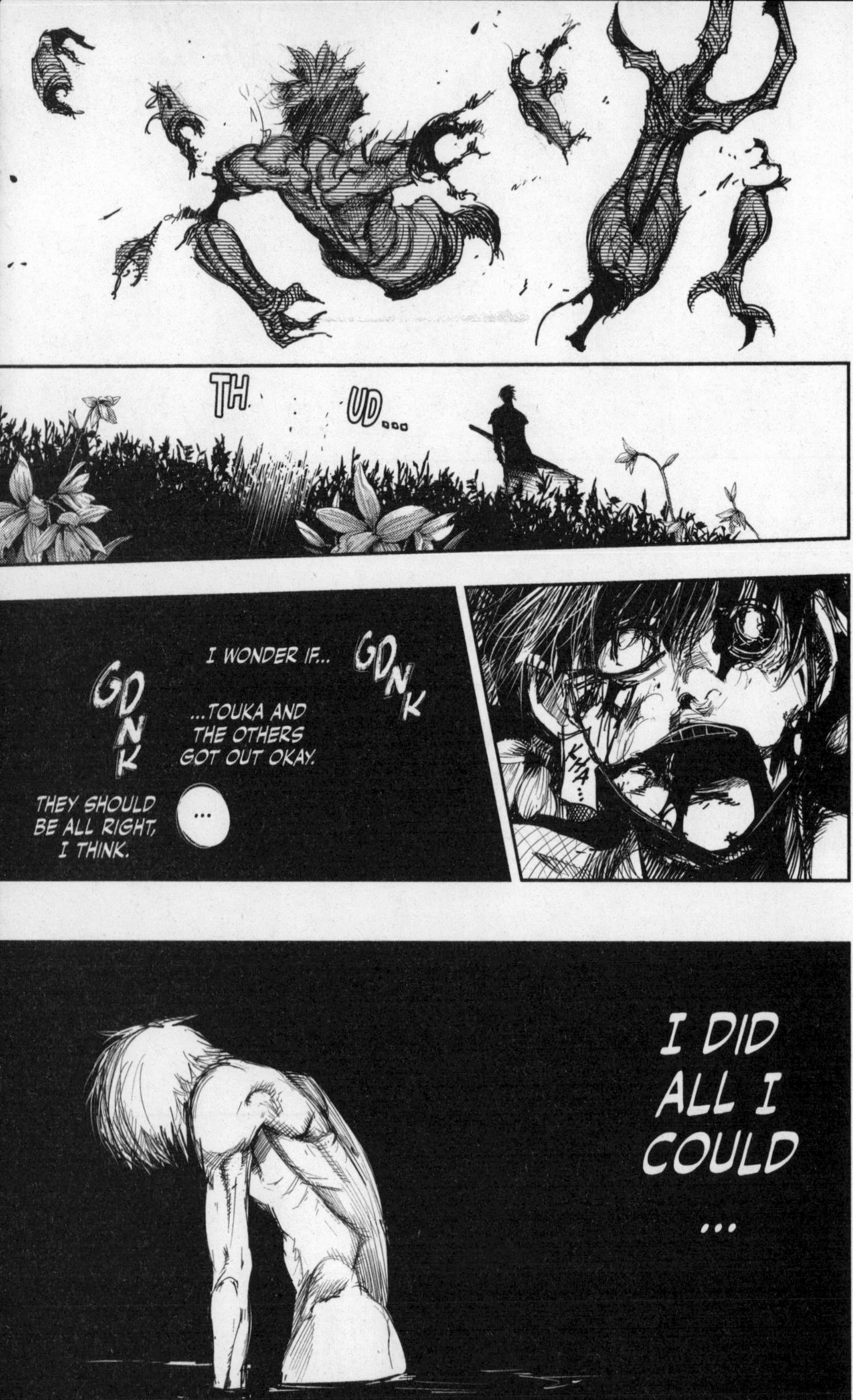
TH UD...
KHA...
I WONDER IF...
GDNK
...TOUKA AND THE OTHERS GOT OUT OKAY.
GDNK
THEY SHOULD BE ALL RIGHT, I THINK.
...
I DID ALL I COULD ...

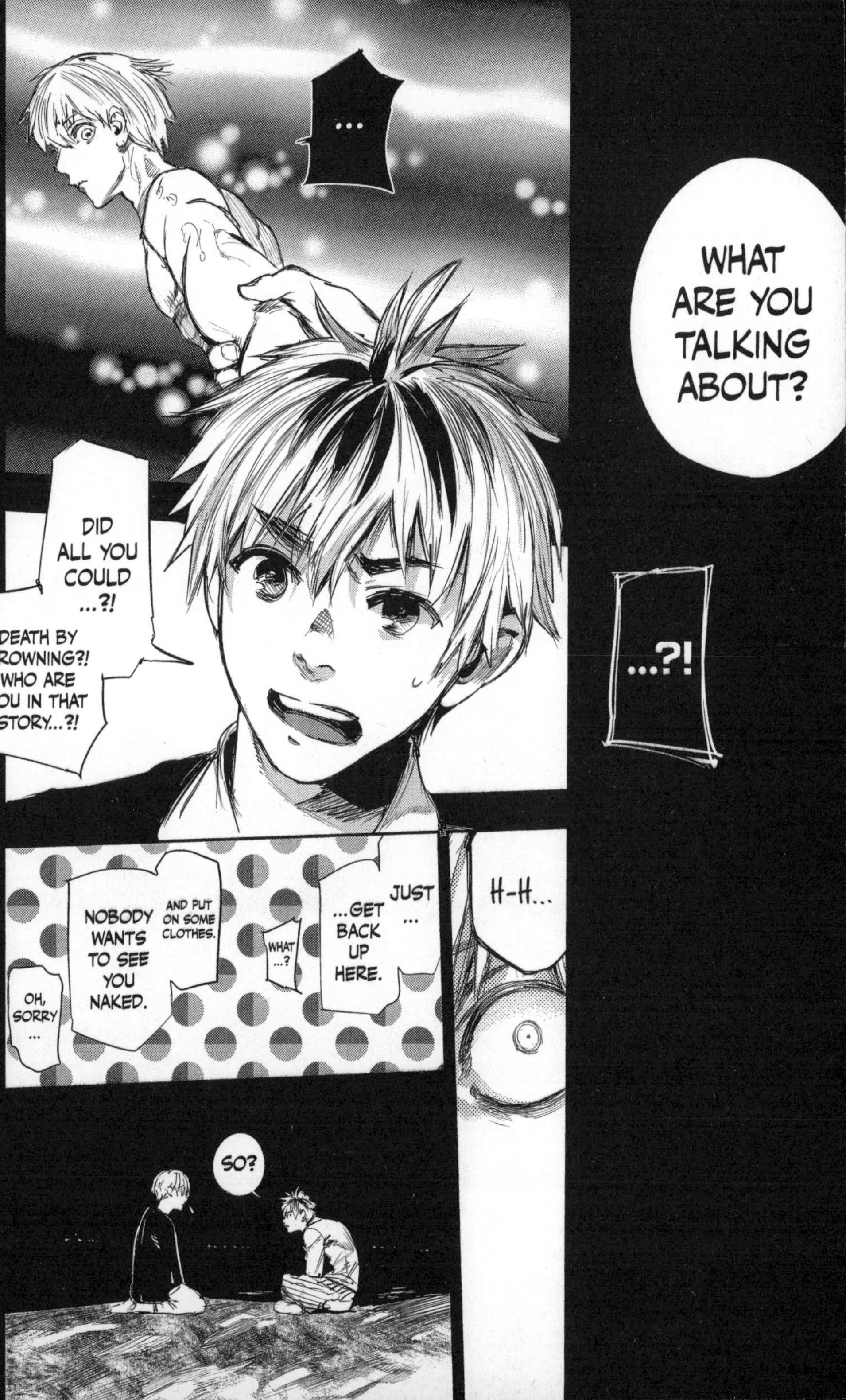
WHAT ARE YOU TALKING ABOUT?
...?!
...
DID ALL YOU COULD ...?!
DEATH BY DROWNING?! WHO ARE YOU IN THAT STORY...?!
H-H...
JUST ...
...GET BACK UP HERE.
WHAT ...?
AND PUT ON SOME CLOTHES.
NOBODY WANTS TO SEE YOU NAKED.
OH, SORRY ...
SO?

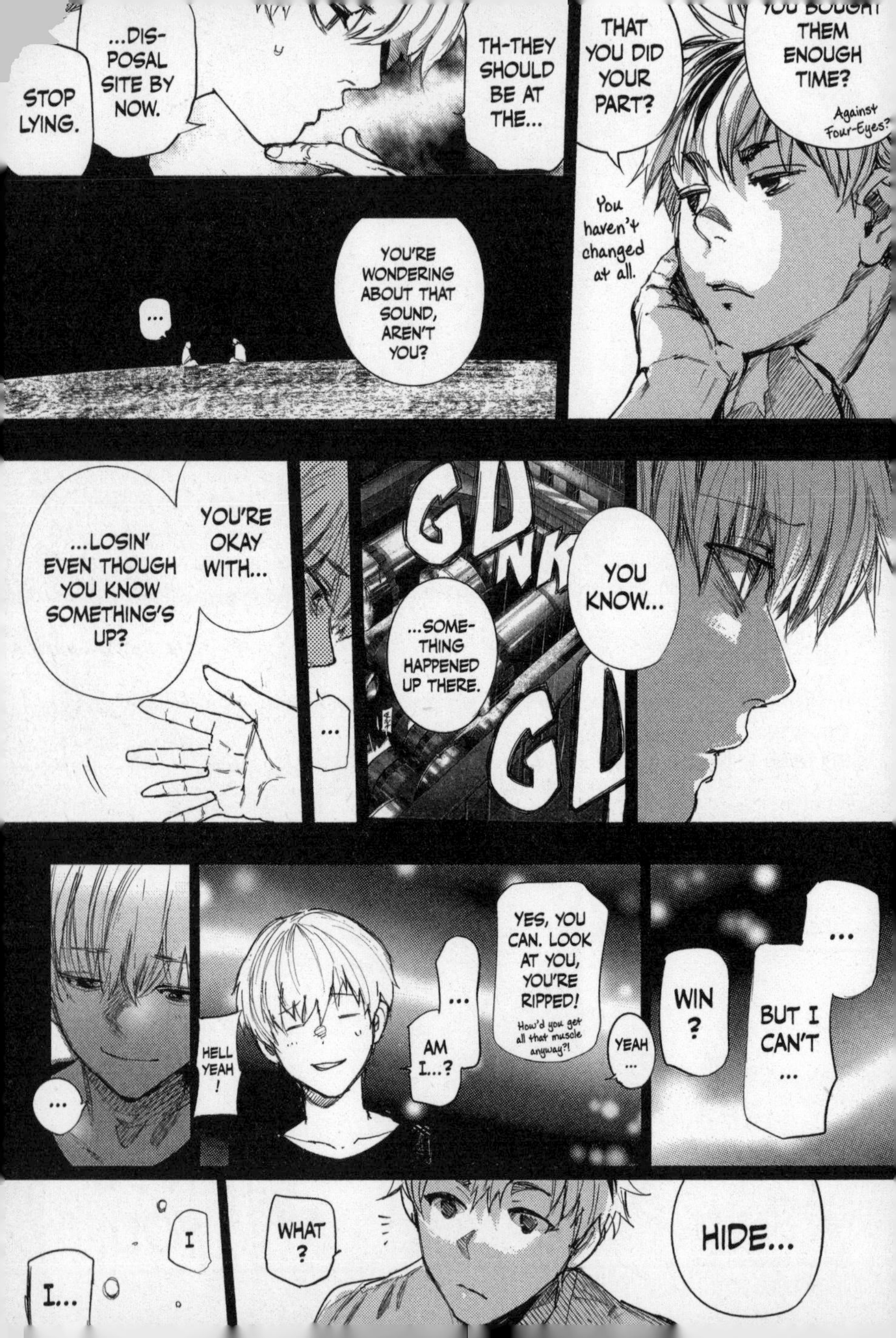
YOU BOUGHT THEM ENOUGH TIME?
Against Four-Eyes?
THAT YOU DID YOUR PART?
You haven't changed at all.
TH-THEY SHOULD BE AT THE...
...DIS-POSAL SITE BY NOW.
STOP LYING.
YOU'RE WONDERING ABOUT THAT SOUND, AREN'T YOU?
...
YOU KNOW...
GD
NK
...SOME-THING HAPPENED UP THERE.
GD
...
YOU'RE OKAY WITH...
...LOSIN' EVEN THOUGH YOU KNOW SOMETHING'S UP?
...
BUT I CAN'T ...
WIN ?
YES, YOU CAN. LOOK AT YOU, YOU'RE RIPPED!
How'd you get all that muscle anyway?!
YEAH ...
...
AM I...?
HELL YEAH !
...
HIDE...
WHAT ?
I
I...

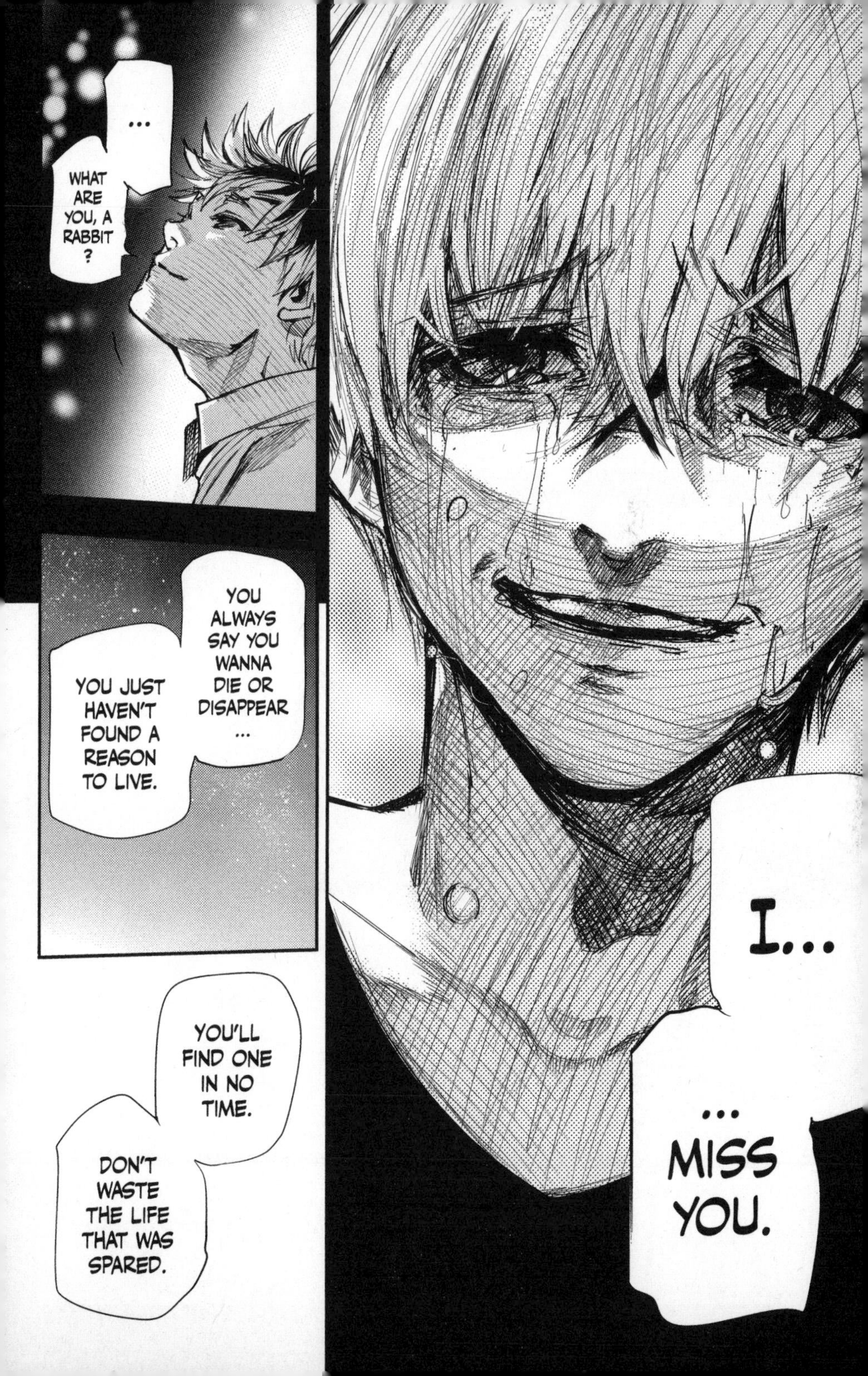
I...
...MISS YOU.
...
WHAT ARE YOU, A RABBIT?
YOU ALWAYS SAY YOU WANNA DIE OR DISAPPEAR...
YOU JUST HAVEN'T FOUND A REASON TO LIVE.
YOU'LL FIND ONE IN NO TIME.
DON'T WASTE THE LIFE THAT WAS SPARED.

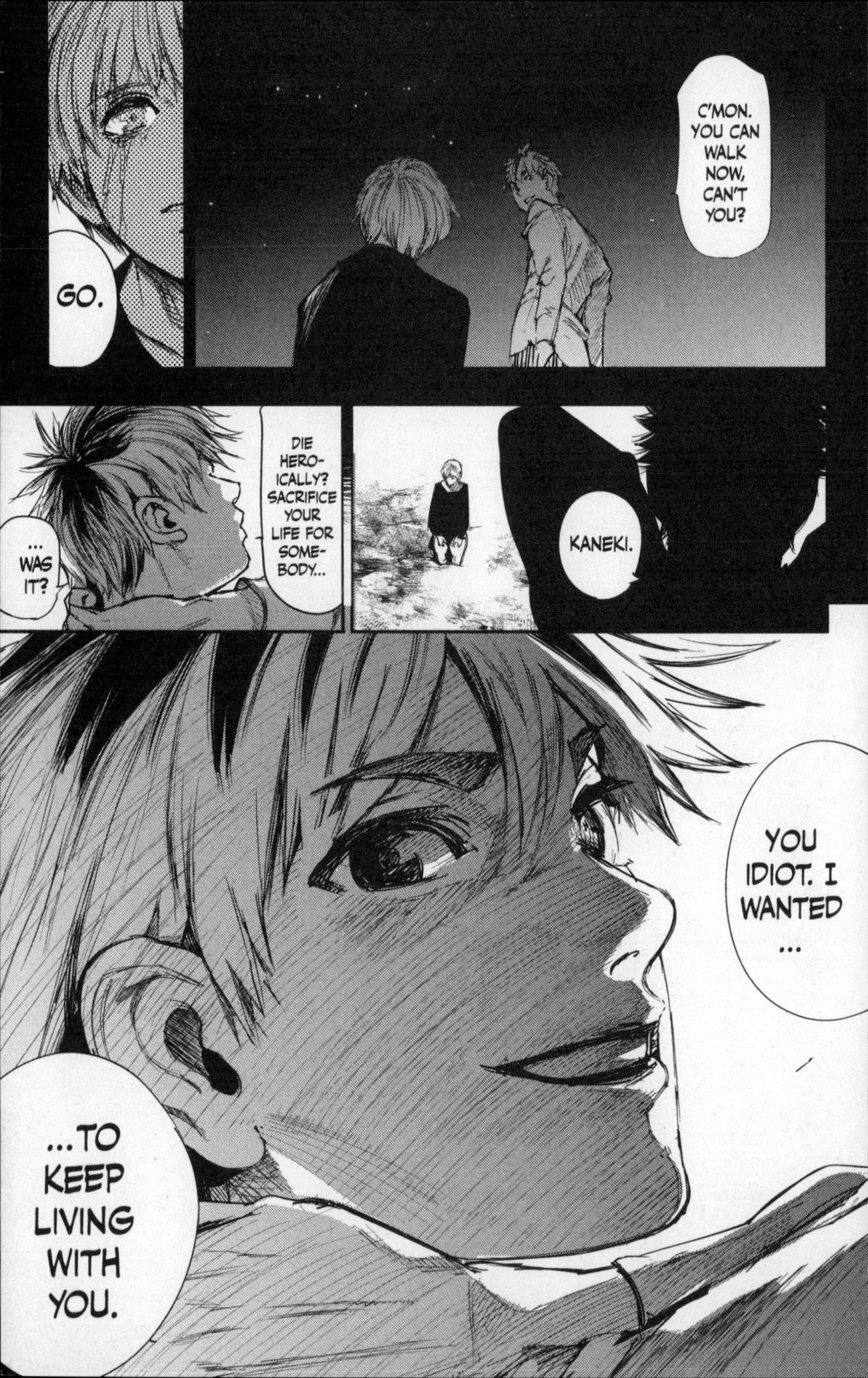
C'MON. YOU CAN WALK NOW, CAN'T YOU?
GO.
KANEKI.
DIE HERO-ICALLY? SACRIFICE YOUR LIFE FOR SOME-BODY...
... WAS IT?
YOU IDIOT. I WANTED ...
...TO KEEP LIVING WITH YOU.

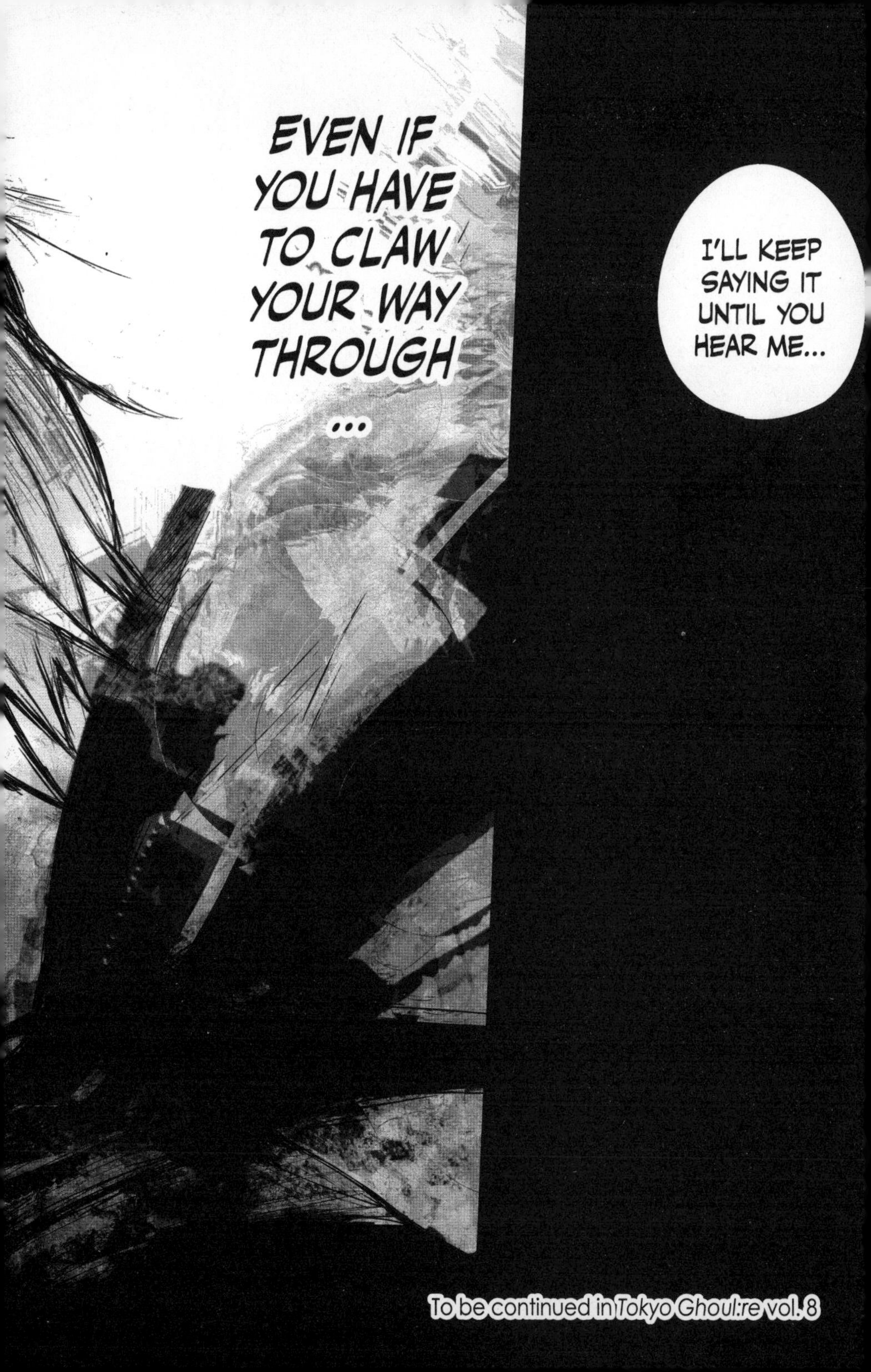
I'LL KEEP SAYING IT UNTIL YOU HEAR ME...
EVEN IF YOU HAVE TO CLAW YOUR WAY THROUGH ...
To be continued in Tokyo Ghoul:re vol. 8

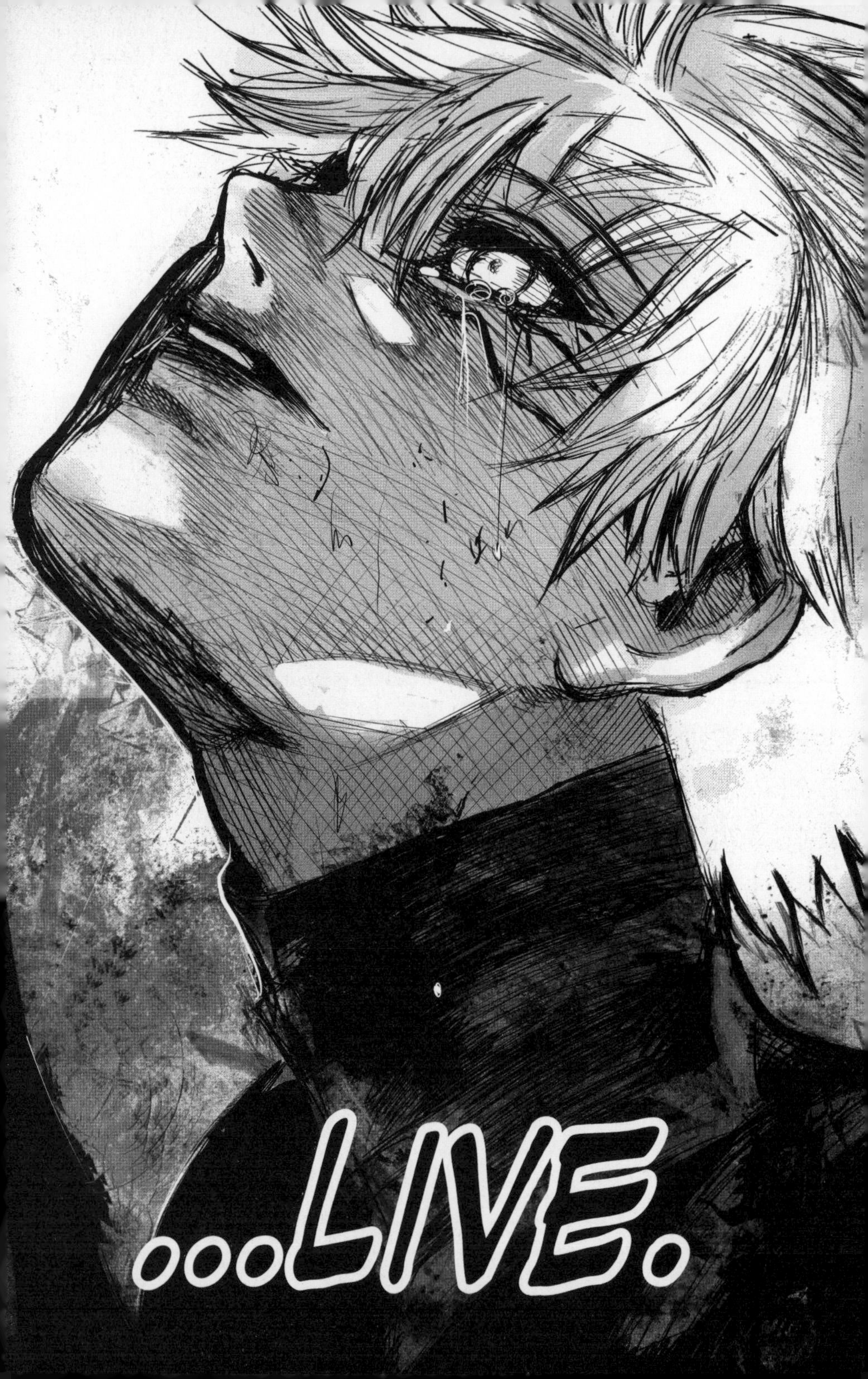
...LIVE.

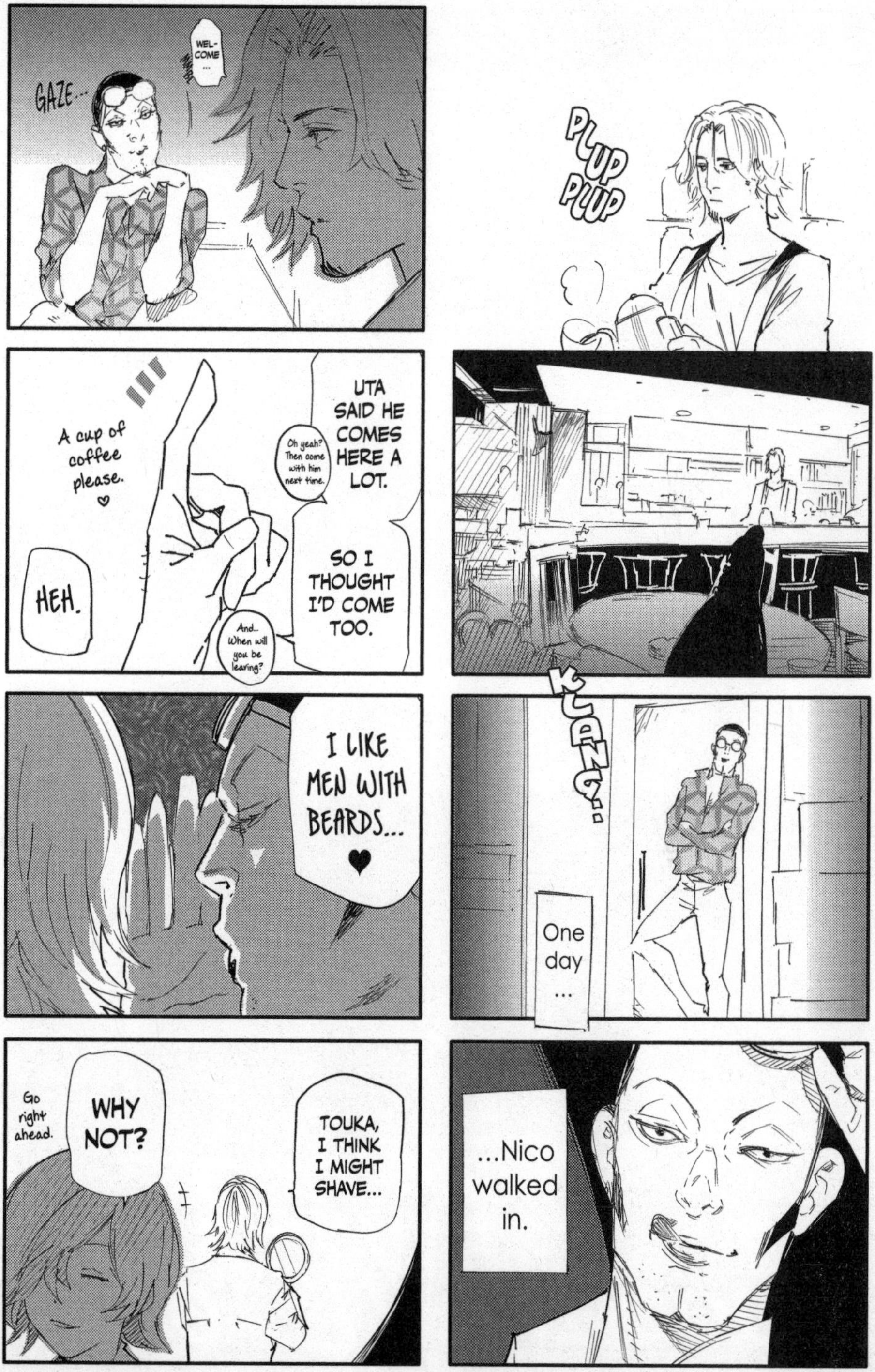
PLUP PLUP
KLANG..
One day ...
...Nico walked in.
GAZE...
WEL- COME ...
UTA SAID HE COMES HERE A LOT.
Oh yeah? Then come with him next time.
A cup of coffee please. ♥
SO I THOUGHT I'D COME TOO.
And... When will you be leaving?
HEH.
I LIKE MEN WITH BEARDS... ♥
TOUKA, I THINK I MIGHT SHAVE...
WHY NOT?
Go right ahead.

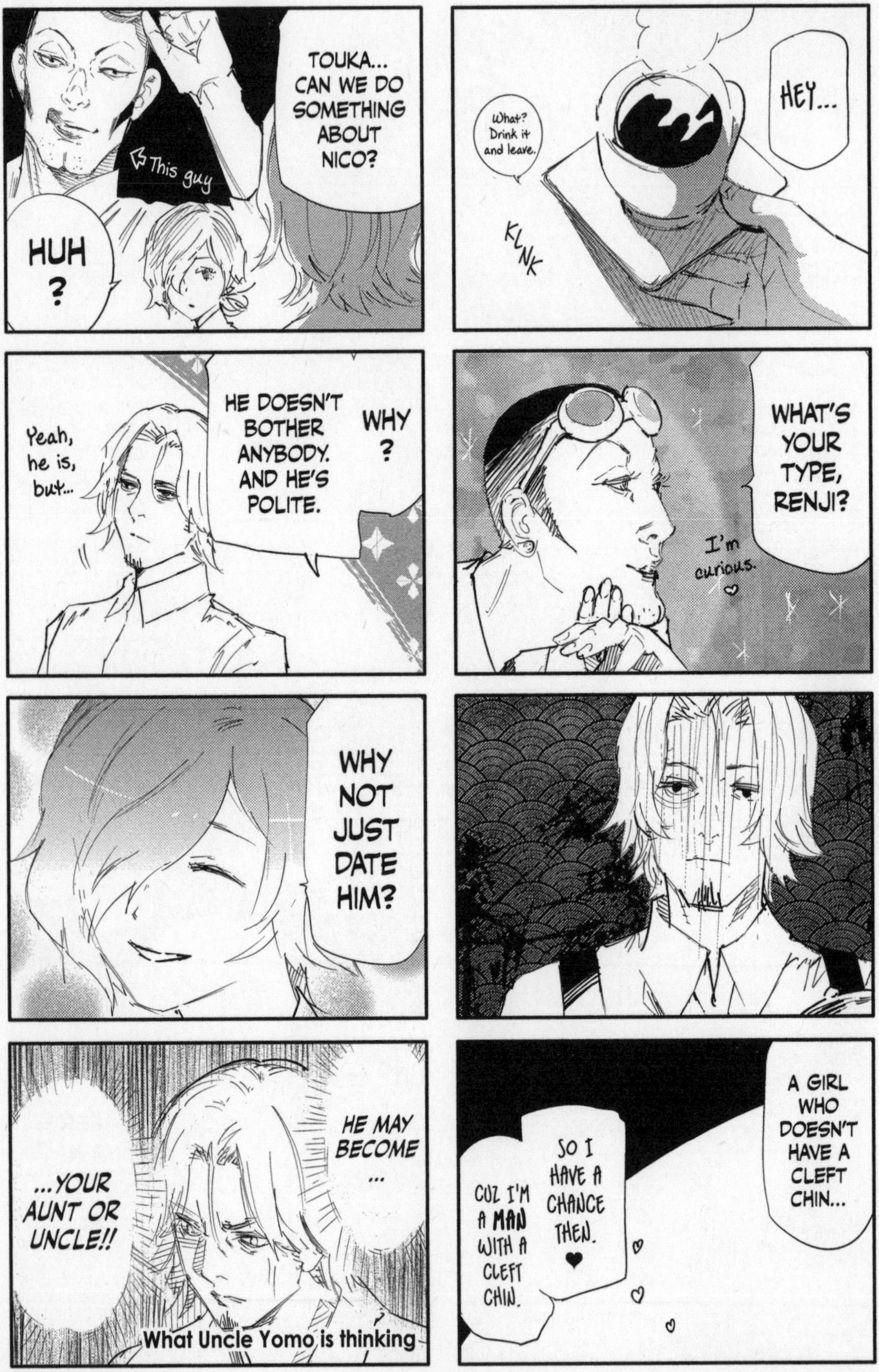

HEY...
What? Drink it and leave.
KLNK
TOUKA... CAN WE DO SOMETHING ABOUT NICO?
This guy
HUH?
WHAT'S YOUR TYPE, RENJI?
I'm curious. ♥
WHY?
HE DOESN'T BOTHER ANYBODY. AND HE'S POLITE.
Yeah, he is, but...
WHY NOT JUST DATE HIM?
A GIRL WHO DOESN'T HAVE A CLEFT CHIN...
SO I HAVE A CHANCE THEN. ♥
CUZ I'M A MAN WITH A CLEFT CHIN.
HE MAY BECOME ...
...YOUR AUNT OR UNCLE!!
What Uncle Yomo is thinking

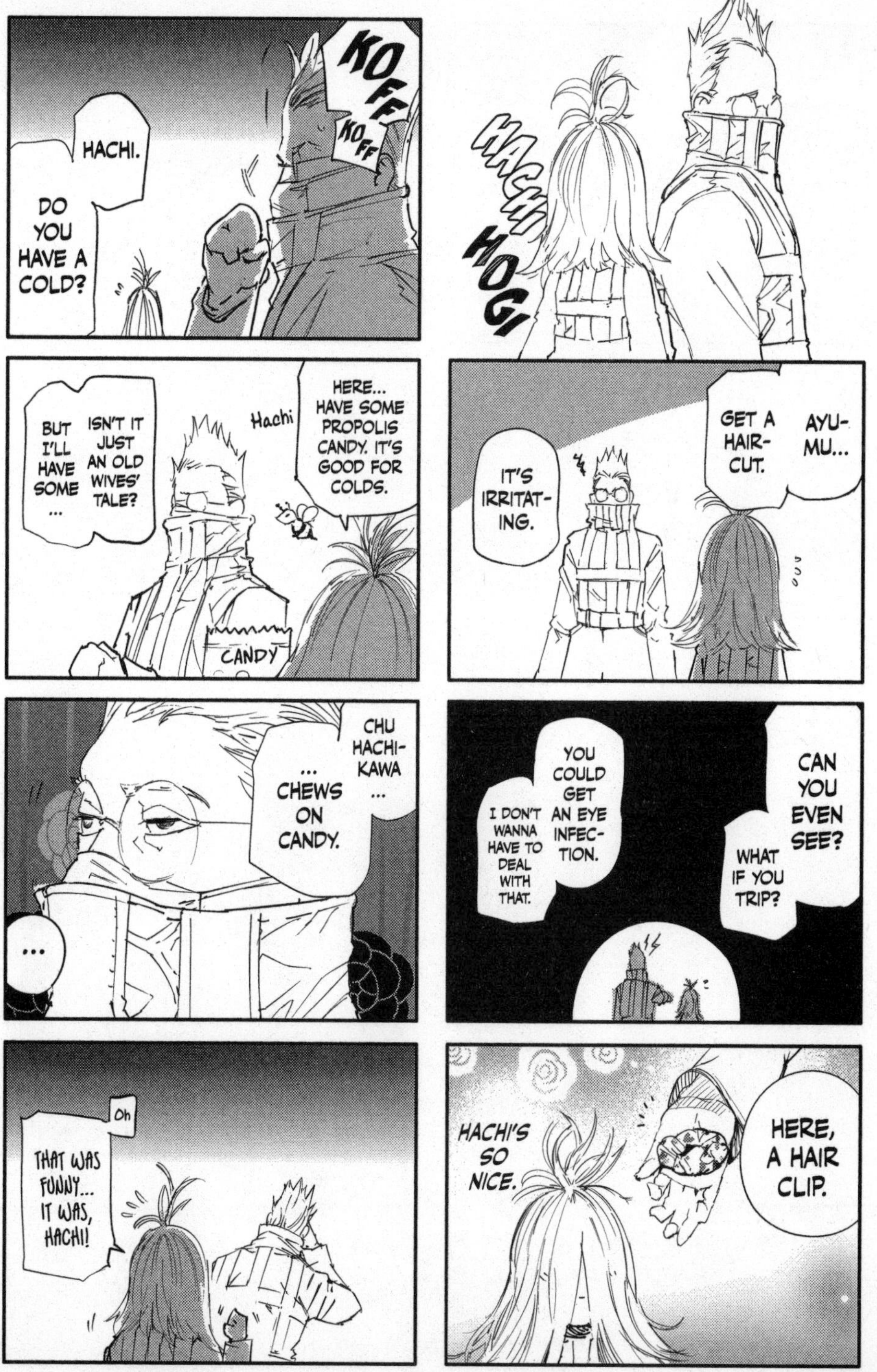
HACHI HOGI
KOFF
KOFF KOFF
HACHI.
DO YOU HAVE A COLD?
AYU-MU...
GET A HAIR-CUT.
IT'S IRRITAT-ING.
HERE... HAVE SOME PROPOLIS CANDY. IT'S GOOD FOR COLDS.
Hachi
ISN'T IT JUST AN OLD WIVES' TALE?
BUT I'LL HAVE SOME ...
CANDY
CAN YOU EVEN SEE?
WHAT IF YOU TRIP?
YOU COULD GET AN EYE INFEC-TION.
I DON'T WANNA HAVE TO DEAL WITH THAT.
CHU HACHI-KAWA ...
... CHEWS ON CANDY.
...
HERE, A HAIR CLIP.
HACHI'S SO NICE.
Oh
THAT WAS FUNNY... IT WAS, HACHI!

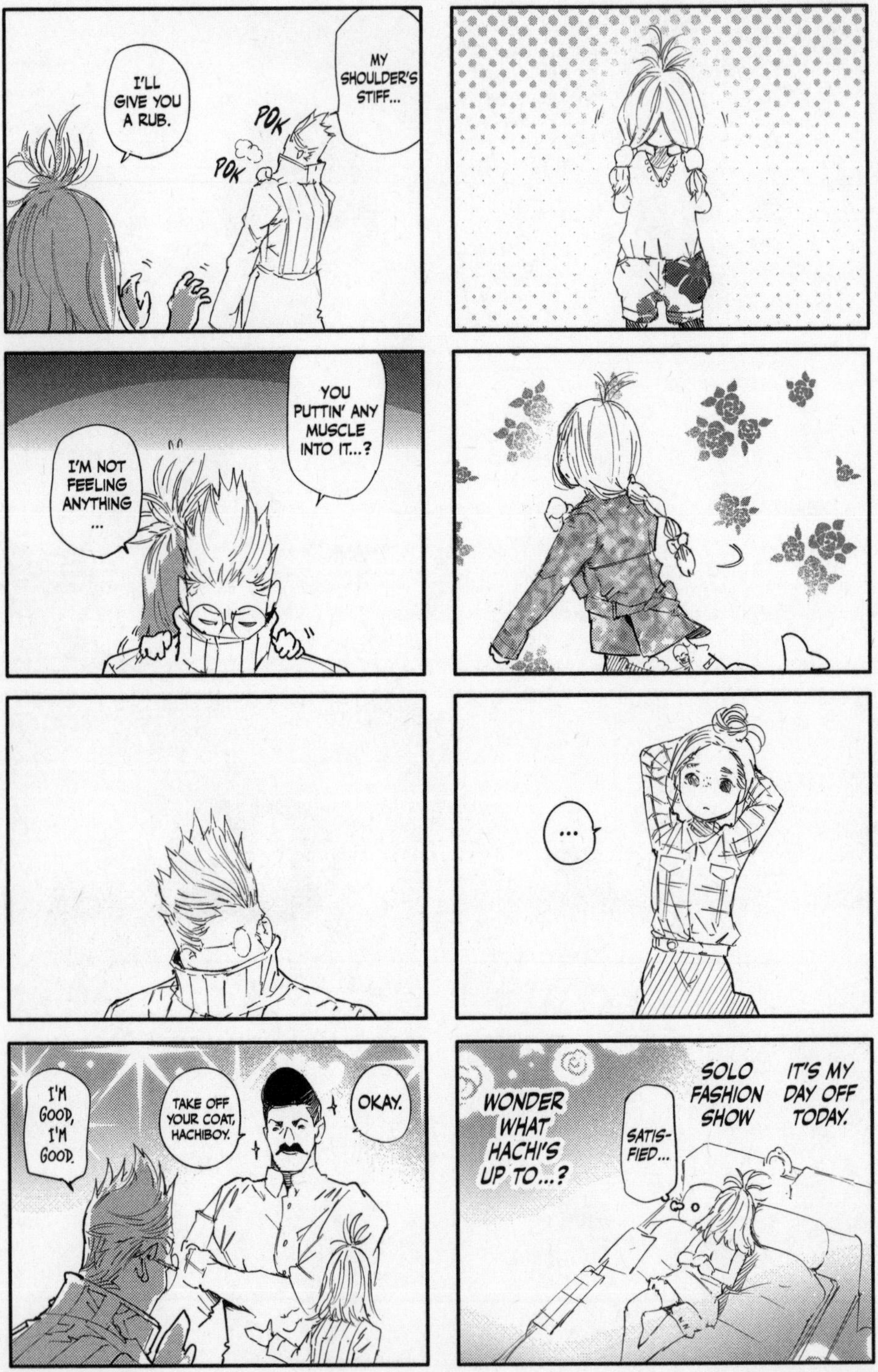
...
IT'S MY DAY OFF TODAY.
SOLO FASHION SHOW
SATIS-FIED...
WONDER WHAT HACHI'S UP TO...?
MY SHOULDER'S STIFF...
POK
POK
I'LL GIVE YOU A RUB.
YOU PUTTIN' ANY MUSCLE INTO IT...?
I'M NOT FEELING ANYTHING ...
OKAY.
TAKE OFF YOUR COAT, HACHIBOY.
I'M GOOD, I'M GOOD.

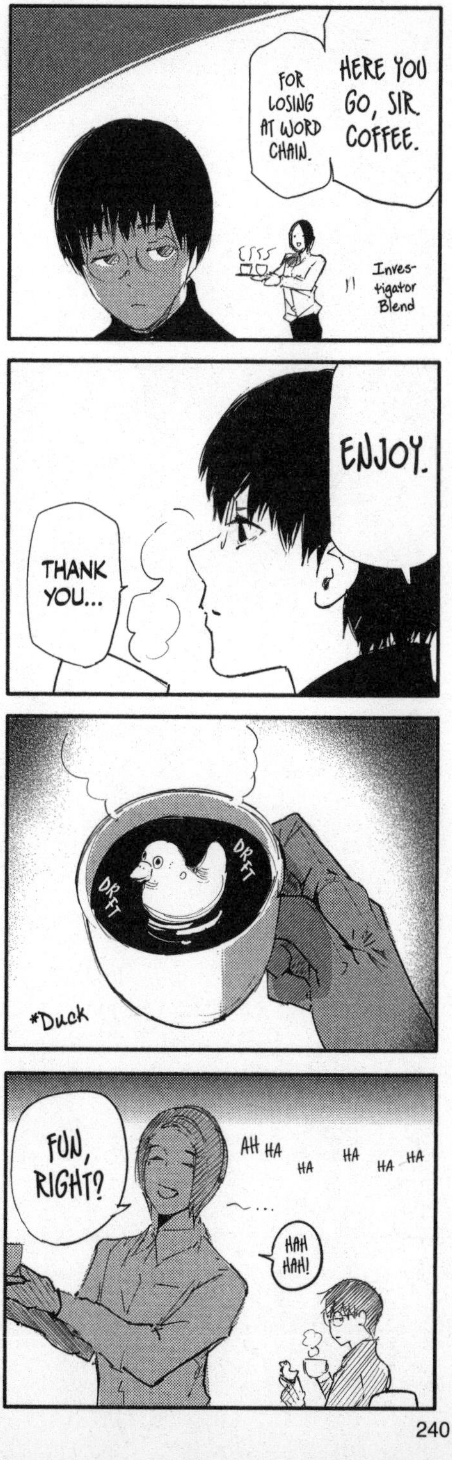
HERE YOU GO, SIR. COFFEE.
FOR LOSING AT WORD CHAIN.
Inves-tigator Blend
ENJOY.
THANK YOU...
*Duck
FUN, RIGHT?
AH HA HA HA HA HA
HAH HAH!
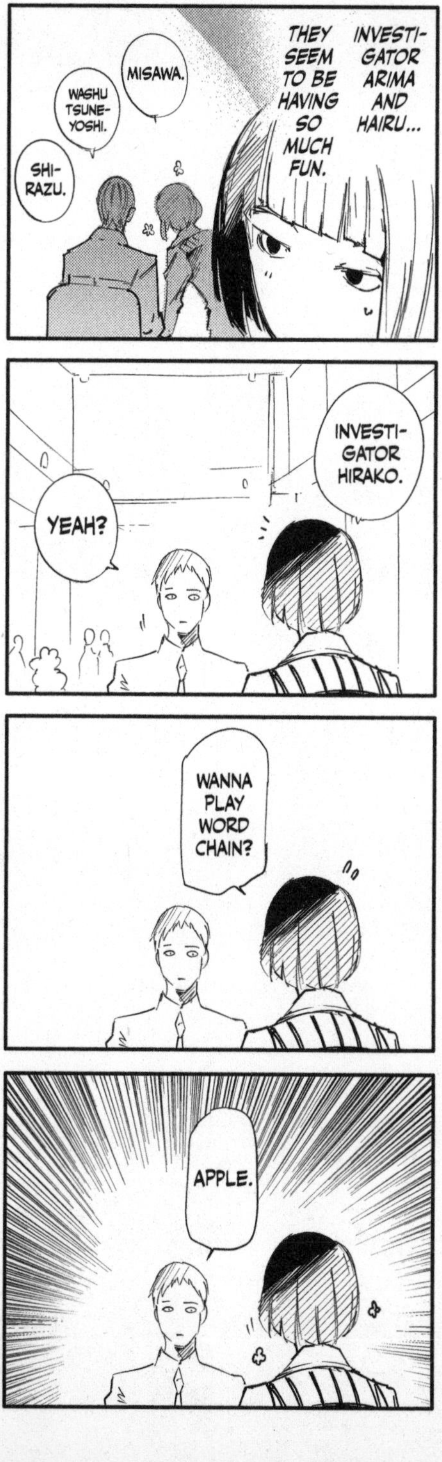
INVESTI-GATOR ARIMA AND HAIRU...
THEY SEEM TO BE HAVING SO MUCH FUN.
MISAWA.
WASHU TSUNE-YOSHI.
SHI-RAZU.
INVESTI-GATOR HIRAKO.
YEAH?
WANNA PLAY WORD CHAIN?
APPLE.

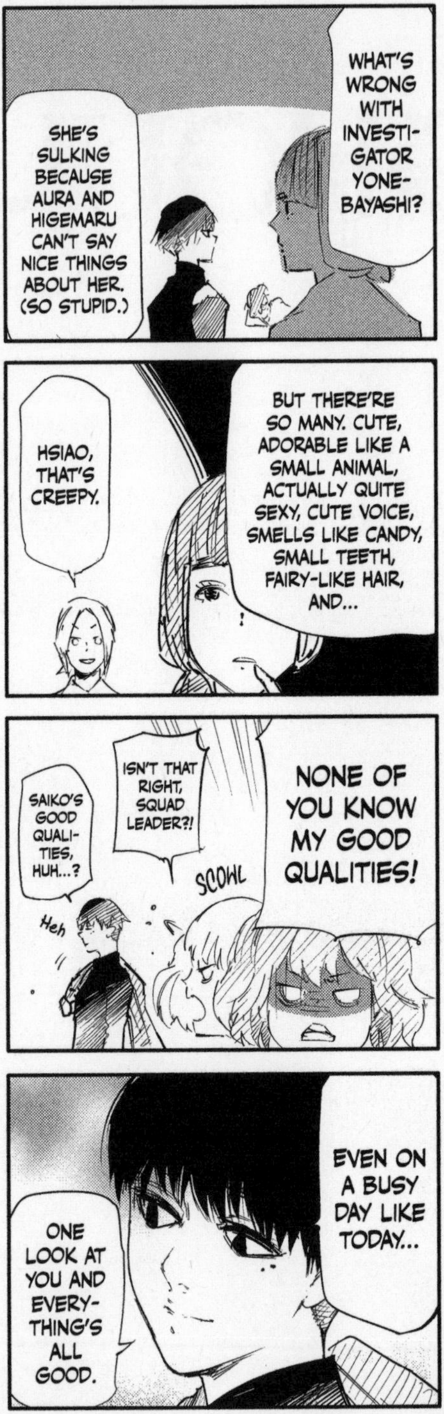
WHAT'S WRONG WITH INVESTIGATOR YONE-BAYASHI?
SHE'S SULKING BECAUSE AURA AND HIGEMARU CAN'T SAY NICE THINGS ABOUT HER. (SO STUPID.)
BUT THERE'RE SO MANY. CUTE, ADORABLE LIKE A SMALL ANIMAL, ACTUALLY QUITE SEXY, CUTE VOICE, SMELLS LIKE CANDY, SMALL TEETH, FAIRY-LIKE HAIR, AND...
HSIAO, THAT'S CREEPY.
NONE OF YOU KNOW MY GOOD QUALITIES!
ISN'T THAT RIGHT, SQUAD LEADER?!
SAIKO'S GOOD QUALI-TIES, HUH...?
SCOWL
Heh
EVEN ON A BUSY DAY LIKE TODAY...
ONE LOOK AT YOU AND EVERY-THING'S ALL GOOD.

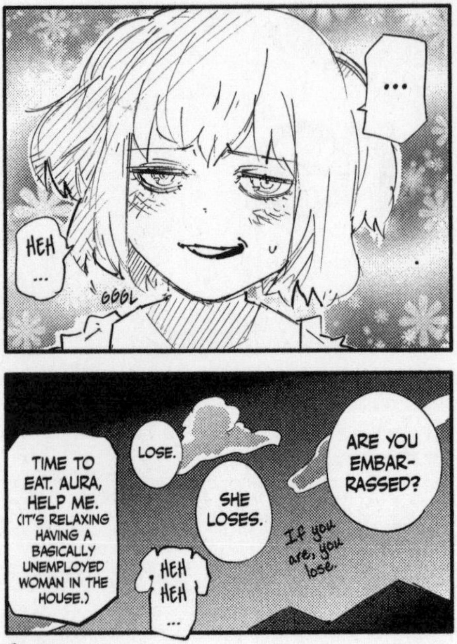
...
HEH ...
GGGL
ARE YOU EMBAR-RASSED?
SHE LOSES.
LOSE.
If you are, you lose.
TIME TO EAT. AURA, HELP ME. (IT'S RELAXING HAVING A BASICALLY UNEMPLOYED WOMAN IN THE HOUSE.)
HEH HEH ...

Staff

Mizuki Ide (~71)
Hashimoto
Kiyotaka Aihara
Rikako Miura
Niina/Nina
Ippo Yaguchi

Comic design
Hideaki Shimada (L.S.D.)

Magazine design
Akie Demachi (POCKET)

Photography
Wataru Tanaka

Editor
Junpei Matsuo

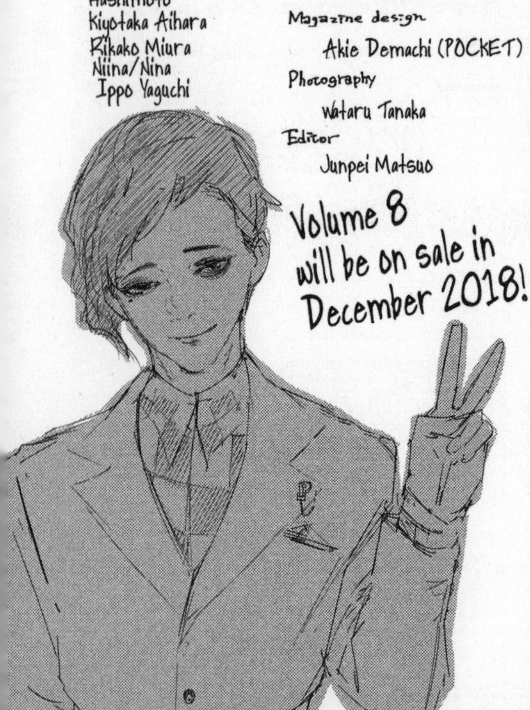

Volume 8 will be on sale in December 2018!

GHOUL:re

HIDEYOSHI NAGACHIKA
(ナガチカ ヒデヨシ)

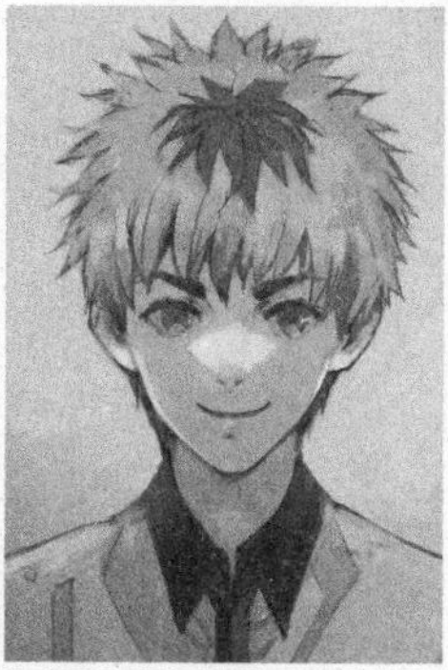

HIDEYOSHI NAGACHIKA

BORN June 10th Gemini

Attended Kamii University

Majored in English in the Department of Foreign Languages

BLOOD-TYPE: O

Height: 171 cm **Weight:** 58 kg FEET 26.5 CM

Likes: Music (foreign), anything fun, **cute girls**, steak

HIDEYOSHI NAGACHIKA

TOKYO

SUI ISHIDA is the author
of the immensely popular
Tokyo Ghoul and several
Tokyo Ghoul one-shots,
including one that won
second place in the *Weekly
Young Jump* 113th Grand
Prix award in 2010. *Tokyo
Ghoul:re* is the sequel to
Tokyo Ghoul.

TOKYO GHOUL:re

Story and art by
SUI ISHIDA

First published in Japan in 2014 by SHUEISHA Inc., Tokyo.
English translation rights arranged by SHUEISHA Inc.

Translation Joe Yamazaki
Touch-Up Art & Lettering Vanessa Satone
Design Shawn Carrico
Editor Pancha Diaz

Printed in the U.S.A.

Published by VIZ Media, LLC
P.O. Box 77010
San Francisco, CA 94107

10 9 8 7 6 5 4 3 2 1
First printing, October 2018

VIZ MEDIA
viz.com

VIZ SIGNATURE
vizsignature.com

ratings.viz.com RATED T+ OLDER TEEN

PARENTAL ADVISORY
TOKYO GHOUL: RE is rated T+ for Older Teen and is recommended for ages 16 and up. This volume contains violence and gore.

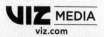

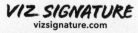